Stormy Passage

STORMY PASSAGE

*A Personal History Through Two Russian
Revolutions to Democracy and Freedom:
1905-1960*

W. S. WOYTINSKY

Introduction by Adolf A. Berle

The Vanguard Press, Inc., New York

Those who are borne in lifeless years
Do not remember their past.
We, children of Russia's fearful times,
Forget nothing.
There is stillness. . . . The clangor of the tocsin
Has sealed our lips forever.
Our hearts, once full of exaltation,
Have been drained lethally.

A. BLOCK

Blessed is he who has walked this world
In its fateful hours. . . .
The gods have summoned him
To share their feast.
He may watch their sublime pageant,
He is admitted to their council,
Still on earth, yet as an Olympian,
He drinks immortality from their cup.

TH. TUTCHEV

Contents

RUSSIA AT THE CROSSROADS: 1906-1907

PRISONS: 1908-1912

YEARS OF WANDERING: 1918-1935

Introduction

by ADOLF A. BERLE

Stormy Passage is the autobiography of my late friend, Wladimir S. Woytinsky. It needs no introduction. Epic in quality, it is a contemporary contribution to heroic literature. This fact is important. In our era heroes have not been wanting. It is high time we knew them.

The American scholarly world and especially the labor movement have known Wladimir Woytinsky and Emma, his wife and colleague, for nearly three decades as quiet, effective, immensely learned scholars of economics and political science. Their works, *World Population and Production* and *World Commerce and Governments*, perhaps their best-known books in English, have been mines of information and ideas for many years. Few American readers realize that Wladimir Woytinsky had lived with and been a part of the Russian social movement since his student days in St. Petersburg; that he had entered the Russian revolution as a student in 1905; that he had been a consistent opponent of the Tsarist government; that he had known Lenin since 1906 and had broken with him in 1917. For a decade he had been in and out of imperial prisons, fortresses, death cells, and Siberian penitentiaries. As the Tsar fell, he preceded Lenin's return to Petrograd in 1917. He had been editor of *Izvestia* and part of the Petrograd Soviet when the moderate socialists were overcome by the rising and ruthless Bolshevist power. While exiled by the Tsarist government to Irkutsk he had met Emma, daughter of a Siberian building contractor, married her, and spent his honeymoon on the Mongolian border even as Russia disintegrated in defeat in World War I and loosed the forces of revolution throughout the world.

The passionate explosion in Petrograd, as Lenin overthrew Kerensky and hunted the moderates out of Russia, found Woytinsky on the Socialist instead of the Communist side. Once more he became a fortress prisoner. Facing a mob trial for his life (it was not the first occasion of the sort), he escaped the Red Guards. In the ensuing confusion, he and Emma made their way to Tiflis in the Caucasus. Thence he came once more to Europe, via Constantinople, as a representative of the then independent Republic of Georgia. When that country was wiped out by the Soviet Union in 1922, Woytinsky was in Italy, and in renewed tragedy as he watched Mussolini ride the tide of anarchy to Fascist dictatorship.

He then settled in the Weimar Republic of Germany. In his new exile he wrote in German and Russian his famous encyclopedic work (in seven volumes), *The World in Figures*. It was an instant European success. This established him as one of the foremost modern economists, and he joined forces with the German labor movement. He drafted a plan for the recovery of Germany as the depression of 1929-32 deepened. Revolutionary at the time, its doctrines are standard American thinking today. When, on March 5, 1933, Hitler swept the board in Germany, the two Woytinskys took up anew the weary road of exile, fleeing to Switzerland. Blocked there by Communist influence from getting a job in the International Labor Office at Geneva, Woytinsky and his wife came to the United States to "discover" America.

The odyssey was over, and high drama ended for them here.

But not their usefulness. Through a joint project of the Rockefeller Foundation and, I am proud to say, of the Twentieth Century Fund, he established himself once more at his work of economic analysis. He remade a superb academic reputation in America (as he had twice made it in Europe) and last year died in peace.

Homeric quality does not come from academic achievement, however great. Woytinsky fought as well as he wrote. He had great ideas, great hopes, great values, and, above all, intense humanity. This quality, indeed, led him to break early with the coldly inhuman Lenin. Repeatedly he backed his ideas, his values, his humane loyalties at risk of his life. He commanded the respect not only of colleagues and crowds but (it saved his life) of common criminals on their way with him to Siberian jails. He resisted the brute cruelty of doctrinaires in Moscow, in Rome, and in Berlin. Woytinsky was a scholar. He was more: he was a warrior for his values.

This autobiography will be a first source of history because of its author's contact with vast events. I think it will be even more important as record of a life-long affirmation of sensitive human courage, as living proof that men can transcend even catastrophic forces.

That is why I have—rightly, I believe—called the book heroic—and its quality epic.

ADOLF A. BERLE

Washington, D.C.
July 1, 1961

Preface

by W. S. WOYTINSKY

The distinction between an autobiography and memoirs is somewhat vague. Webster defines "autobiography" as "memoirs of one's life written by oneself" and "memoirs" as "a history or narrative composed from personal experience or memory; often, esp., an account of one's life or episodes in it, written by oneself." The difference between the two definitions may seem almost imperceptible, yet I wish to stress that this book has been planned and written as memoirs, not as autobiography. I believe an account of my life, dramatic and rich though it has been to me, will be of interest to the reader only insofar as it reflects the experience of my generation and the impact of historical and political events I observed as an eyewitness or in which I took part.

Though early youth forms fundamental moral convictions, the years must, of necessity, change the perspective of the observer. I was not the same person during the first revolutionary storm over Russia in 1905 as I was during the second revolution of 1917; my ideas in the 1950's, when I was touring Asia and Latin America lecturing on world economics and the United States, were not the same as were those in the 1930's, when I was working with labor unions in Germany. Nor can a narrator obliterate entirely events of great import in his personal life. Thus, with my marriage in 1916, comes a new set of personal pronouns: the *I*, *me*, and *mine* become we, us, and ours. And along with the political events—which, all in all, make a rather sad story for my generation—must come some of the mighty, strange, and magnificent wonders of our natural world. Without these, our life would not have been so rich as it was.

The events I describe—covering more than fifty years—are in no sense an attempt to record history. They are, rather, the events I observed, and especially those in which I participated. I have recorded them because I feel that a deeper understanding of Russia's two revolutions—those of 1905 and 1917—may help readers to understand more clearly today's central and most critical problem: the Soviet Union.

To cope with the conflict between West and East, between democracy and totalitarianism, the West needs a far better understanding of the character, origins, and historical background of the Soviet system than it now possesses. Its knowledge of the U.S.S.R. and Communism, based on records that are faked and censored by the Kremlin, is not sufficient. We must turn the spotlight on those years between 1905 and 1917, in which latter year the totalitarian police state, as we now know it, was born. Surely it may be said that Communism has had many forerunners, beginning with the Oriental despotisms of antiquity. But in its present form it came out of Russia, and it has never cut the umbilical cord uniting it to that country.

Communism has surrounded itself with myths. The Communists are credited with the overthrow of Tsarism, the liberation of Russia, and its transformation from a country of illiterate muzhiks into a great industrial power. The common idea is that economic and cultural progress in Russia was ushered in by the Communist revolution. Accordingly, everything that Russia possesses of value is credited to the efforts of the men in the Kremlin.

Actually, Russia looks back at centuries of economic and cultural growth.

The November revolution represents a brief interruption of, rather than the beginning of, the country's cultural progress. Russia's industrialization and westernization were inaugurated in the first half of the eighteenth century by the reforms of Peter the Great. Subsequently her economic development paralleled that of Western European countries, lagging behind the most advanced of them but leaving many others in the rear. The contention of the Soviet leaders that Russia has been built under the Communist regime is sheer nonsense. What they can claim to their credit is the acceleration of progress along certain lines, an achievement that must be weighed against retardation of progress or setbacks in other directions.

On the eve of the revolution of 1917, Russia was a country of striking contrasts. It was primarily an agricultural country, richly endowed with almost all natural resources—coal, petroleum, iron ore, light metals, gold, silver, and platinum. But it was unevenly and only partially developed. It had the largest and most efficient cotton mills in Europe, and its textiles competed successfully with those of the British in Asia. It had modern steel mills that turned out bridges unequaled in the Eastern Hemisphere. Its shipyards not only met the needs of extensive river transportation but could also launch battleships and submarines. Its heavy locomotives, cannons, and rifles were considered among the best in Europe. Moreover, its industrial and mineral output was expanding steadily, though not rapidly enough to meet the needs of the growing population and the military requirements of the Empire.

True, the Russian educational system was inadequate. Some rural areas were poorly provided with elementary schools, but illiteracy was decreasing. The "illiterate muzhik" was disappearing. Though the network of high schools and universities was insufficient, the institutions that did exist were on a reasonably high academic level, providing students with an education comparable with that supplied by similar schools in advanced Western European countries. Moreover, there were close ties between Russian and Western European science. It was common for Russian youths graduating from a university to complete their education abroad—in Germany, Belgium, Switzerland.

In the world of science, literature, and the arts, Russia was undeniably a Great Power. Its intelligentsia was outstanding not only for the quality of its education but also for its political idealism. In familiarity with foreign languages, foreign literature, and the arts, and in the extent of its travel abroad, the Russian intelligentsia was the most international in Europe—indeed, too international, too different from the common people of its own country in language, tastes, way of life, attire. The weakness of the intelligentsia lay in the lack of cohesion and mutual understanding between the "educated" and "non-educated" classes of the nation.

Part of the priceless cultural heritage that had fallen into the hands of the Communists was destroyed or dissipated in the terrible years of civil war, but gradually the new rulers of the nation learned to appreciate the "experts" and made full use of them in building the new economy.

Another myth that prevents a clear understanding of the nature of Communism is the legend that the Communists—and their predecessors, the Bolsheviks—played a decisive role in overthrowing Tsarism in Russia.

True, the political system in old Russia was obsolete and incompatible with the level of its cultural and economic development and the demands of its further progress. The country was run by an incompetent and corrupt bureaucracy, ready to side with landlords against peasants and with employers against workers. The "national" character of the regime was manifest in the oriental pageantry of Palace and Church and in the oppression of national and religious minorities, especially the Jews. But the repugnant features of this regime were offset to some extent by its weakness. The intellectuals traditionally opposed the government, and great Russian literature, with a few conspicuous exceptions such as Dostoevsky, was essentially liberal. The universities were hotbeds of liberalism. Most of the newspapers were liberal—they had to be, since their readers expected them to be critical of the government. Liberal and radical ideas were spreading more and more widely among the workers and the middle classes.

Reaction had held a firm grip over the nation under Alexander III, a rough and cruel despot. But the regime began to crack under his successor, Nicholas II, a timid and feeble-minded weakling who trusted nobody, surrounded himself with charlatans and adventurers, and brought the dynasty to an ignominious end. Thus Russia found itself involved in a war with Japan, a contest for which it was utterly unprepared politically and technically. The chain of humiliating defeats it had suffered on land and sea opened the gate to the revolution of 1905, a broad national upheaval that was unanimous in the cities, though somewhat spotty in the villages. Although this revolution was crushed by force of arms, it left a deep impact on Russian life. Despite the regime of terror under Stolypin (first, Minister of the Interior and then Prime Minister), semblances of parliamentarism and vestiges of freedom persisted. Because the Tsarist government was weak and had no faith in itself between 1905 and 1917, the opposition was regaining ground.

The Bolsheviks played, in those years, a significant role but not a decisive one. I would hesitate to describe them as either the radical or orthodox Marxist wing of the Social Democratic party. Their distinctive characteristic, rather, was loyalty to their leader, Lenin—especially where questions of organization and tactics were concerned. Moreover, this group did not differ greatly from the rest of the Social Democratic party during the revolution of 1905, either in the famous general strike in October or in the armed revolt in Moscow in December of that year. Indeed, between 1905 and 1917, the Bolshevist group had almost completely disappeared from the scene, and in the overthrow of the Tsarist regime in March, 1917 (perhaps because of Lenin's absence), they took practically no part. The Tsarist regime was overthrown by a popular explosion, broader and more nearly unanimous than that of 1905. No one party can claim the credit or bear the responsibility for it. It was a spontaneous expression of the wrath of the people, brought to despair by the disgrace of continuous defeats and the tragic farce of Rasputin's rule over the country.

The Bolsheviks appeared on the scene much later. Their revolution —that of the "ten days that shook the world"—was directed against the political regime that had been established in Russia by the March revolution—that is, against the democratic Provisional Government. It was a riot of the army—more specifically, a riot of rear garrisons passively supported by the front regiments—and it was carried out against the wishes of the great majority of the people. Actually, in the election of the Constituent Assembly, held after the seizure of power by the Communists and under strong pressure by the new government, the Communist party got no more than one fourth of the popular vote. But the party did control the armed forces, and could dissolve the Constituent Assembly as easily as the Tsarist government had dissolved the refractory Duma. This sequence of events gives the lie to the widely publicized myth that the Communists liberated Russia from Tsarism.

Communist propaganda has succeeded in persuading many persons in the West that the Russian people have never enjoyed liberty or yearned for individual freedom, so that the regime the Soviets imposed upon them is in accord with their historical tradition and national character. The truth is that the liberation movement in Russia looks back at a long and dramatic history and has produced more thinkers and martyrs than have such movements in any other country. The movement had its ups and downs, but the Tsarist regime never succeeded in strangling the aspiration of Russia's people for freedom. Even after the Communist coup and the dispersion of the Constituent Assembly, they continued freedom's desperate struggle.

Only the future will show whether the ruthless extermination of opponents, the systematic indoctrination of new generations, and the terroristic methods of dictatorship have made the people forget their yearning for freedom and the relative liberty that existed in old Russia. Even if the Communists accomplish their objective, however, the contention that freedom is not valued by the Russian people, and that these people are preconditioned to serfdom by all their history, rests on insufficient knowledge of the country and its history.

The origin of the Soviet regime in Russia casts light on the place of Communism in the spectrum of liberal ideas. Certainly it cannot be considered the extreme, most uncompromising, expression of liberal philosophy. Its agreement with some liberal slogans is purely accidental and is determined by expediency. Fundamentally, its moral and philosophical premises and those of liberalism are mutually exclusive.

Let us picture a kind of graph of various political philosophies, the classifications to be based on the attitude of each toward the rights of the individual and its respect for human dignity and freedom. It will be on a one-dimensional scale, going from the extreme to moderate left and then from the moderate to the extreme right. At the extreme left would come the ideologies defending the absolute supremacy of the individual against the state or any other collective organization claiming to limit his rights. Next would come ideological systems protecting the rights and freedoms of the individual, but paying increased attention to the possibility of a conflict between his rights and the rights of other individuals and the community. Further, closer to the center, would be ranged ideologies preoccupied with a proper balance between the interests and rights of the community and those of individuals. These would be followed by theories dominated by the idea of the community, with the individual in a subordinate role, dependent on the collective. At the end of the array would come ideologies of a totalitarian state—the extreme expression of Fascism and Communism.

The Communists' deification of the state in the person of its head, their belief in the complete domination of the community over the individual, their contempt for personal freedom, their glorification of obedience as the highest civic virtue, their denial of democratic procedures and their reign through terror—all these are alien to the philosophy of liberalism but characterize other totalitarian systems, such as Fascism and Nazism. Philosophically, Communism, Nazism, and Fascism are not three political systems but one philosophy of government operating under different circumstances. The differences among them are quantitative rather than qualitative. They differ in the proportions in which the same elements are included and in the extent of ruthlessness. Mussolini was the most moderate of the three dictators; Hitler exceeded the two others in nationalistic frenzy; Stalin was unequaled in cruelty, self-deification, and in the degree to which he imposed thought control.

Criticism of Communism must not imply glorification of the old regime overthrown by the March revolution of 1917. The memory of Tsarism remains associated with the pogroms, the Ochrana, the massacre of January 9 in the streets of St. Petersburg, the Beilis affair, the torture chambers in Riga, Stolypin's gallows, the Rasputin scandal. The totalitarian police state of the Soviets did not come as the alternative to that regime but was built, rather, on the ruins of a democracy that had no chance to grow strong and mature during its brief life.

There is one fundamental difference between the Tsarist regime and the rule of the Soviets. The U.S.S.R. is a monolith ruled from the center, uniform politically, economically, and ideologically; old Russia, in contrast, was full of contradictions, with a weak central government and an ineffective local bureaucracy. The official orthodox-monarchistic ideology did not penetrate deeply into the conscience of the people, and its influence was undermined by the scandals in the last years of the Empire.

Moreover, the government, because of its ideological weakness, could not count on absolute submission of its officials to instructions. Among these officials were decent and intelligent persons who followed the voice of conscience rather than the orders of superiors. "Good men in bad places," as the Russian writer Korolenko described them, could be found on almost all levels of the bureaucratic ladder except its very summit, and this made life under the Tsarist rule easier for those who found themselves in open conflict with the regime.

But the Soviet state would treat such men as traitors and prosecute as saboteurs those failing to denounce them. Without total terror and indoctrination of the servants of the state, the Tsarist government was unable to inspire in the people the paralyzing fear or fanatical obedience characteristic of the psychological climate of the Stalin era in the U.S.S.R. In old Russia, not infrequently even an orgy of brutality was marked by sparks of humanity. The Tsarist regime was a loose, weak despotism, full of loopholes and contradictions. The regime of the Soviets is a despotism as cold and rigid as a set of mathematical theorems.

The Tsarist regime also lacked two important attributes of totalitarian despotism: the Iron Curtain and thought control. Even in the days of the blackest reaction in Tsarist Russia thought control was unknown. Censorship was traditionally stupid and unable to stop the propagation of "subversive" ideas in the nation. Between pre-Communist Russia and the outside world there was a continuous coming and going, a continuous exchange of newspapers, books, and correspondence. The subjects of the Tsar, although harassed by gendarmes, at least had freedom of thought, and even some of those who served the brutal and decaying regime were able to preserve their personal integrity and decency.

During a gloomy stretch of my imprisonment in the Castle of Ekaterinoslav, then one of the most terrible dungeons in the Empire, the prison fell into the hands of a sadistic gang of guards. Mistreatment of prisoners became routine. Hundreds were killed. With the aid of my friends, I wrote a detailed report on conditions in the prison and managed to smuggle it out. It was printed in newspapers abroad and submitted to the Duma. The government ordered an investigation that resulted in ending the mistreatment of prisoners. Everyone who worked on the report knew he would be killed if the guards discovered what kind of information he was gathering. But everyone also knew that outside the prison there were newspapers, the Duma, public opinion. One took a chance.

Can one imagine a group of Soviet citizens gathering information in the hope of exposing the misdeeds of government officials? They would not trust one another, and each would realize the futility of any appeal to public opinion in a land that has no place for independent opinion or an independent press.

In my years of imprisonment and banishment, I met persons of decency and integrity on all levels of bureaucracy. I saw a little old man, a chief guard in a prison, quieting a brawl among the convicts by stretching out his hand and showing an ugly scar on it—the mark of a saber blow he had taken in protecting a convict. I met the Governor General of eastern Siberia, Kniazev, who held it the highest duty of his office to protect the rights of individuals and defend the law against encroachments and abuses by the gendarmes and minor officials.

Why is it impossible to imagine a man of moral integrity in a position near the top of the Soviet bureaucracy? Not only because a man of independence and honor could never reach a high position in the Soviet despotism and would hardly survive all the purges, but also because the rigid scale of values of the Soviet regime excludes and weeds out such qualities as decency, dignity, and independence in those who serve the Moloch of the totalitarian state. The iron grip of the Kremlin leaves no place for simple human feelings and sympathy.

In my years of wandering in foreign countries, after the defeat of democracy in Russia, I have realized the deep and tragic impact of the Communist coup—the glorified "ten days"—on world affairs. In Italy, France, Germany, and Austria my wife and I saw Communist parties engaged in a bitter struggle against liberal forces—especially the moderate Socialists—trying to undermine people's devotion to democratic institutions, to kindle nationalistic passions, occasionally even joining with the forces of darkest reaction in order to weaken the existing system supported by the majority. Everywhere in Europe local Communist parties operated as battering rams directed by an invisible force from the Kremlin against the strongholds of freedom and democracy. Communism has been a force of reaction, disorder, and war in Europe.

Time and again I have asked myself what the course of events in the world would have been after World War I if Russia had not emerged from it as a totalitarian dictatorship. Neither Mussolini in Italy nor Hitler in Germany would have come to power if the local Communists, supported and directed by Moscow, had not paved their way to victory. Without Hitler, there would have been no Molotov-Ribbentrop treaty to usher in World War II.

Going further back, one may answer that Lenin's coup would have been impossible in Russia if the second Russian revolution had not exploded in the midst of war, if the country had entered the road of constitutional reforms a decade earlier, after the first revolution.

Historical events are interwoven in a fantastic pattern. Contemporaries find it hard to discern its intricate designs, and the impact of the Russian Drama is one of the greatest mysteries of our time. I do not pretend to have solved this mystery, but perhaps this book will make the reader realize that the time and events described have more than a casual relation to, and bearing on, the dire problems the world is facing now.

w. s. w.

Washington, D.C.
April, 1960

The First Storm Over Russia
1905

PROLOGUE

I T W A S on December 4, 1905, that I first realized I must write down my experiences, without delay, before my recollections faded.[1] The place was St. Petersburg's central prison, the Crosses. I was a lad of twenty, arrested with members of the Council of St. Petersburg workers. The story I had to record was about the first Russian revolution.

. . . After hours of waiting within a ring of soldiers, the prisoners had been loaded into big police vans. The ride seemed endless. Our van stopped in front of a huge, grim building consisting of four wings spreading like spikes from the circular central tower. Again hours of waiting, in the dim light of the prison's reception hall. All of us seemed to be in a stupor, too depressed to talk, too tired to think.

Shortly before dawn, a guard took me to my cell. As in a dream, I saw the long corridor, many stories high, and endless overhanging galleries with rows of doors along them. "Get in!" The heavy lock clicked behind me. I fell on the cot and was asleep before my head hit the hard cushion.

A loud knock on the door awoke me. A guard shoved a piece of black bread and a mug with hot brown liquid through the square window in the door. "Your breakfast and tea," he explained, adding sharply, "Using the cot during the daytime is not permitted."

I began to pace the cell—four steps from the door to the opposite wall with a small window under the ceiling, three steps between two other walls. At the third turn I became dizzy. The next thing I realized was the guard's shout through the door: "Get up! Using the cot . . ." But I felt too weak and only fingered the bloodstained bandage around my head. The guard changed his tone and said, "The assistant surgeon will see you."

A young man in white hospital uniform was bending over my cot. He removed the bandage. "When were you hurt?" he asked. "Some two weeks ago," I answered. "A simple cut." But the doctor was not sure. "One never knows," he murmured, then asked casually, "What is the date today?" "December 4," I answered, "and the skull is not affected. . . . Only a slight dizziness!" "Do you wish to be transferred to the ward?" "No." "Then you may lie on the cot whenever you like." He dressed the wound and left.

[1] In this and the three following parts, all dates are given in accordance with the old Russian calendar: January 1 corresponds to January 14 in the Western calendar.

I lay there daydreaming. Scenes of the past days unrolled before me. A crowd clamored at my feet, all the faces beaming with faith and joy. And, both in the crowd and standing on the platform high above it, I saw myself. I recognized my reddish hair and glinting glasses. A moment later the same face appeared at another place in the crowd. Then I saw an ocean of heads and faces, tossing about like waves in a storm. My glasses emerged here and there in the whirlpool.

I saw the University hall, the broad staircase, the crowd flowing like a stream, jubilant, confident, united. Again I saw myself in the crowd, vaguely recognizable by the hair and glasses, without any other individual features—just a drop in the stream.

The walls of the University spread wider and disappeared. I saw a street but could not identify it—it was so wide that buildings along the sidewalks were in a haze. In the street seethed a joyous, singing crowd, a seemingly irresistible human torrent carried along by the same enthusiasm and faith. Here and there the torrent was blocked by some invisible obstacle. A foaming whirlpool of human bodies developed, then the torrent resumed its flow. Then there was no longer a street, but a borderless plain, and all around were faces. Among them I recognized myself and persons I had met during the past three months without knowing their names, those who had applauded me and those who had ambushed me at a small railroad station, threatening to kill me, ready to gouge out my eyes.

And suddenly I realized that what I was seeing as I lay on the cot, dizzy and detached, was the revolution: the transfiguration of persons brought together by a power immeasurably stronger than human will. I felt I must describe what I saw, but I did not know how to begin. Perhaps I could just recall, step by step, what I had lived through. . . .

When I asked the guard for paper and pencil, he went away and soon returned with a bottle of ink, a pen, and a form for application to the superintendent. I explained to him that I wanted paper to write something for myself. He closed the window in the door and soon reappeared with an answer. "Until the investigation is completed, the prisoner may write only to the investigating authorities and the superintendent."

Again I lay on the cot, overwhelmed by my vision. Perhaps I could write without paper?

As a boy, I had usually scribbled brief notes each night on what I had read during the day: the title of the book, the name of the author, the number of pages, what I thought of the book and had learned from it. Sometimes, however, it was late when I stopped reading, and I went to bed without completing my daily record.

Then I composed my notes orally, sentence by sentence, word by word. I could memorize such notes as if they were written. Now, when I had no paper but had to write, I could go back to the old technique. Moreover, it would fill the long days of solitary confinement.

I made an outline of the story. Then I tried to select the events that belonged to each part and began to tell the story to myself.

Days flew by. The solitary cell did not depress me. My wound healed and the spells of dizziness disappeared, but I kept the right to lie on the cot, daydreaming, sunk in my visions. . . .

Nearly two decades later when a publisher asked me for my memoirs of two revolutions in Russia, I discovered that the events of 1905 were as fresh in my mind as if they had happened only a few months before. The story was deeply engraved in my memory; in 1923 I saw it as I had told it to myself in 1905. . . .

Now more than another three decades have elapsed. In the light of recent events, the first Russian revolution has acquired a new significance. When I think of it now, I realize how close Russia was then to joining the community of free nations.

It is pointless to speculate what the further course of Russian history would have been if absolutism had been abolished by the Manifesto of October 17. This is certain, however: If democratic forces had triumphed at that time, a new balance of political power would have developed in Europe and the rest of the world. Under a constitutional regime in Russia there would have been no place for Rasputin, no place for a second revolution in the spring of 1917, no place for the seizure of power by Lenin and his acolytes before the end of the same year. Seen through the prism of later events, the first Russian revolution acquires a new meaning. It had no revolutionary tribunals, no guillotine. It had only martyrs. They believed they were fighting for the freedom of their own country, but actually more was at stake. Much that the world has suffered in the intervening decades was born of their defeat.

THE APPROACHING STORM

My personal recollections go as far back as the death of Alexander III in 1894 and the accession of Nicholas II to the throne. I remember the endless royal funeral procession, with scores of military bands and a rigid pattern of foot soldiers and cavalry regiments as, with my parents, I watched from a rented window. I recall the change in the portraits of the Tsar in public buildings, schools, and shops; the disaster at the coronation of Nicholas II, when hundreds of people were stampeded to death on Khodynka Field in Moscow. I was a youngster of ten at that time, but I remember angry talk blaming the new Tsar for the catastrophe.

The tide of opposition was rising. A deputation of moderately liberal gentry respectfully asked Nicholas that the voice of the people be heard henceforth by the throne, only to be rudely rebuked for such "senseless dreams." "Let everyone know that I shall defend the principle of absolutism as strictly as did my beloved father," the young Tsar declared.

The liberal voices became louder. Rumors circulated about strikes, political demonstrations, underground organizations, but I did not know about these organizations. Later I learned that groups of radical intellectuals, mainly college students, had established contacts with workers and helped them to organize strikes by providing slogans and leaflets. There were two centers of opposition at that time: moderately liberal opposition in the *zemstvos*—local governmental bodies dominated by the gentry—and the radical opposition, leaning toward socialism, among young people, chiefly in the universities.

Before the turn of the century, two revolutionary parties emerged: the Marxist Social Democratic party (S-D), shaped on the German pattern, and the Socialist Revolutionary party (S-R), which called for union of workers, peasants, and intellectuals, and promised to resume the terroristic battle against the enemies of the people. Both were small underground organizations but had sympathizers in the broad circles of workers and intellectuals.

At that time, the difference between the liberals and revolutionaries seemed to me to be one of degree, and persons more mature than I shared in this concept. The radicals appeared to be hardboiled liberals, while the liberals were half-baked radicals.

My political recollections of the next few years—my last years in high school—are more precise. There was great excitement after the first terrorist acts of the Socialist Revolutionary party. Early in 1901, the Minister of Public Instruction was killed by a terrorist for having threatened to conscript rioting students into military service. Next, the Minister of the Interior was assassinated for persecuting national minorities and mistreating peasants and political prisoners. Both assassinations were openly applauded by the public, especially in university circles. Postcards with the pictures of the terrorists hung in students' rooms along with those of Leo Tolstoy and Maxim Gorky.

On the night of February 5, 1904, Japanese submarines and torpedo boats attacked Russian men-of-war in the harbor of Port

Arthur. The beginning of the war with Japan opened a new page in the history of Russia.

There were rumors that the seizure of forests in the Yalu Valley by the Tsar's favorites, against the stern protests of Tokyo, was more than a foolish adventure; that the government had deliberately provoked the war with Japan in the hope that a quick victory could raise its prestige and help crush the revolutionary movement. This hope seemed to be satisfied in the first weeks of the war. Patriotic demonstrations, with the tricolor banners and the Tsar's portrait, took place in St. Petersburg, Moscow, and other cities. Students of St. Petersburg University knelt in the snow in front of the Winter Palace.

Very soon, however, the situation changed. Russia proved utterly unprepared for the war. It had only a single-track railroad over which to move troops to the Far East and supply them with food and munitions. The Russian army was routed on the Yalu, at Liao Yang, and finally at Mukden. The Russian fleets at Vladivostok and Port Arthur were annihilated. The defeats were particularly humiliating because of the boasting and contempt with which official Russian propaganda had branded the enemy as "macacos"—monkeys.

The people's wrath turned against the generals, the government, the Tsar. The war became more and more unpopular. Rumors circulated about treason in the High Command, and the poison of suspicion seeped into the army. The government felt the ground burning under its feet. Its domestic policy became increasingly erratic. Pogroms were followed by liberal gestures, liberal words by new acts of wanton violence.

The war was actually lost in 1904. The country wanted peace at any price. Official communiqués on the successful "readjustment" of the front line and the orderly "disengagement" of the army from contact with the enemy met with scornful derision. News of the enemy's gains was discussed in the streets with an undertone of relief. The worse the Russian military position in the Far East, the nearer the end of the war appeared. Nicholas II became the butt of bitter contempt. Revolt was rising out of the deep national humiliation.

The curtain raiser of the revolt came on Bloody Sunday—January 9, 1905—a day that became a watershed in Russia's history. I took no part in the events of that day, but it changed the whole course of my life. To explain its effect on me, a youth of nineteen, I must go back a bit.

A PRECOCIOUS BOOKWORM

I was born and grew up in a middle-class family. My father was a professor of mathematics at a polytechnic college, a brilliant teacher with moderately liberal leanings but without any serious interest in politics. He conducted summer courses to prepare high-school graduates for competitive examinations to enter specialized colleges. Because of his exceptional success as a teacher, he always had a great many students and was fairly well-to-do.

I was the second of four children. We received our primary education from private tutors at home, and I entered high school at fourteen. Our father was very proud of this system of private education. Perhaps it was as good for us as a public school would have been. If it did not teach us how to mix with other people, it favored a rapid accumulation of knowledge in our early years.

My first passion was for mathematics. When I was twelve, my father introduced me into the mysteries of calculus. Although I preferred various branches of geometry, at fourteen I was also fairly familiar with advanced algebra. Then I suddenly lost all interest in mathematics and turned to the social sciences. Not far from our home was a private library founded by a well-known educator. It held an excellent collection of books on economics, statistics, and history, and I became its most devoted patron. There was nobody to guide my reading—my father's influence ended with my desertion of mathematics—so I read books on economics at random, jumping from one author to another. At that time, however, I had an almost photographic memory and could readily memorize anything I had read—poetry, prose, arguments, names, and statistics. Thus it did not matter much in which order I devoured the library books.

High school had nothing to offer me. I stood highest in my class and was a kind of freak exhibit for the teachers. After a few weeks I was permitted to bring my library books to the classroom, and I read them without caring what went on around me. In return for this privilege I was always on hand when the director or a distinguished guest visited the classroom. Then I would show off for our teacher—in religion as readily as in Latin or mathematics—by answering the guest's questions.

In summer, I lectured in my father's school. I looked older than I was, had inherited some of my father's speaking ability, and was rather successful in this role. But I was not very popular with my classmates and had few friends among them. Actually, I developed into a bookworm continuously preoccupied with accumulation of new ideas. My ration was at least two hundred pages a day, three books a week, and I made notes on each book I read.

By this time my chief interests were economic theory and history. I devoured the British classics, books of the German historical and Austrian psychological schools, Marxian literature, works of French Socialists and Syndicalists—all pell-mell, without any system, relying only on my memory. When I noticed that facts were getting mixed up in my head, I decided I myself would write a book on economic theory, starting with a general theory of value and using the mathematical method. I worked on this project during my last two years in high school. When I reread the manuscript—about a thousand pages—I felt more confused than ever. Then I decided to send it to Tugan-Baranovsky, an internationally famous Russian economist who had been ousted from St. Petersburg University because of his liberal ideas and who lived on his estate in the south of Russia.

The first words of his reply made my heart jump. He addressed me as "Dear Colleague," commented warmly on my manuscript, and suggested publishing it in a somewhat condensed form. He also asked about my background. Was I one of the younger professors who had appeared on the scene after he had left the University? Where was I teaching? What books and articles had I written?

I replied that I had just graduated from high school and had learned economics from books, among which his own had been particularly helpful. With his return letter, he sent me an introduction to his publisher. The latter accepted the book, and it appeared early in 1906, under the title *Market and Prices*, with an introduction by Tugan-Baranovsky, but by this time I was as little interested in economic theory as in mathematics. I turned its pages as if it had been written by a complete stranger. Three decades later I reread the book and found it immature as far as methodology is concerned but with a freshness and boldness characteristic of very young authors. Tugan-Baranovsky was too generous in judging it, but it contained, in embryonic form, some ideas that became widely accepted a quarter of a century later on the relationship between price fluctuations and consumption patterns, elasticity of demand, and so on.

In the autumn of 1904, enrolling in St. Petersburg University, I registered with the law department because it offered courses on economics and statistics, though I had no illusion about the quality of these courses. I attended one lecture of each teacher in these two sciences and found them equally dull. The faculty, however, had brilliant scholars in other chairs. Professor L. Petrazhitsky, who taught philosophy of law, made a lasting impression on me. For him, right was a psychological and moral phenomenon; law was a pattern of behavior accepted by the community as a just and obligatory standard. According to this theory, the state rests on the prevalence of certain concepts of what is good and evil, and a change in these concepts necessarily leads to changes in a political regime. Ultimately, political progress depends on progress in moral values. This philosophy was in harmony with my own feelings, and I very soon became a humble disciple in Petrazhitsky's intimate circle.

I felt very differently in the economics seminar led by an ambitious assistant professor who was particularly popular among radical students. At first I was impressed by the students' boldness in speaking, but, after listening for an hour, I discovered they all referred continuously to Karl Marx and a few others as infallible authorities. After some hesitation I asked to speak and began by remarking that history had vindicated certain assertions of Marx but had also revealed his errors. The listeners laughed, but at the same time were impressed by the volley of quotations I could hurl against my opponents.

Before the chairman adjourned the meeting, he asked me whether I would like to present a paper sometime during the year. I replied that I could offer a paper on psychological and historic premises of economic theory at the next meeting. Actually, I was very nervous, but I was determined not to appear frightened. And though my first paper firmly established my reputation at the University, I remained as lonely there as I had been in high school. In the seminar, the radical students disliked my disrespectful attitude toward Karl Marx. In Petrazhitsky's circle, I was a stranger because of my interest in economics, and especially in social problems.

In time my reading became more systematic. In the National Public Library I had access to the alcoves of books barred from general circulation by the censor. I remained an introvert bookworm, but I was shifting more and more from pure theory to books with a definite political orientation. After finishing a book, I asked myself what the author's practical conclusions and recommendations were, and was disappointed if he had none. Probably I was approaching a new intellectual crisis, like the one that had made me desert mathematics five years earlier. Moreover, I was tired of stocking my memory with other people's printed thoughts. Perhaps, without realizing it, I yearned for active association with living human beings. And at that time participation in the revolution seemed to be the simplest, most direct, and most dramatic form of such an association.

Russia was in turmoil. The revolutionary spirit prevailed in the University. In the entrance hall of the students' mess, the Social Democrats and Socialist Revolutionaries had desks for the collection of money and distribution of illegal literature printed abroad. There was also a desk of the "liberal" non-Socialist party, but Socialist groups predominated among the students.

I did not ask myself then what had brought the masses of students to socialism. Now, after having observed many national revolutions in various parts of the world, I believe that some tinge of social maximalism is inherent in every broad popular movement. Whatever its immediate goal, a revolution must hold out a bright picture of the future before the eyes of the masses. It must give them hope of liberation from oppression of any kind. In this sense, socialism is not an economic program but rather a dream, a moral postulate for the future. This is likewise true of "freedom" and other slogans of broad national upheavals, such as the first Russian revolution was in its early phase, before internal stresses and contradictions developed. The people rose as in response to a sudden call of the tocsin. I heard its call in a strange setting. And perhaps because the call reached me from far away, it sounded particularly urgent and was tinged with bitterness and reproach.

THE TOCSIN: BLOODY SUNDAY

Before Christmas, 1904, my father took me abroad for a vacation. We visited his favorite spots in southern Germany, and he remained in Munich while I went on to Italy alone. The lovely Arno Valley, the quaint towns, timeless cathedrals, and gorgeous palaces enchanted me. Pictures from history books suddenly became real. I found myself in a new world in which I felt completely alien, lonely, and lost; but, seen from here, Russia and her political turmoil seemed even less real than the Florence of the sixteenth and seventeenth centuries.

Suddenly Russia captured the front pages of local newspapers. She had suffered a new blow in the war with Japan. Port Arthur fell, to the great satisfaction of Italian liberals, who considered Tsarist Russia the stronghold of reaction and sympathized with Japan. A few days later the newspapers carried the headline: STRIKE IN MUNITIONS FACTORIES IN ST. PETERSBURG. The workers of the Putilov mills, the largest munitions factory in Russia, had walked out, and the newspapers speculated that this event would help Japan by slowing down the Baltic fleet, which was steaming toward the Far East.

The next day the papers reported the beginning of a general strike in St. Petersburg. Strikers from the Putilov mills were calling on all workers to join them. Stories in the press declared that the Putilov management had fired four workers; the factory priest, Father Gaponi, tried to intervene on their behalf and, when his plea was rejected, called on the workers to strike. The newspapers described him as the leader of a powerful union that covered all workers in the Russian capital, but this sounded very strange to me. I had never heard of either the holy father with the Italian name[2] or his union.

On January 6, the papers got out an extra: The general strike is spreading in St. Petersburg; strikers clash with the police; troops are being sent to the industrial precincts. Events seemed to be following the classical revolutionary pattern with which I was familiar from books. I was bewildered. The strike itself did not surprise me; I had read in illegal publications that a revolt of Russian workers was imminent. What was surprising was the outbreak of a revolution without apparent participation of the revolutionary parties and under the leadership of a fantastic priest with an Italian name.

The next reports indicated that the strike was spreading and that Father Gaponi had decided on a new step. On January 9, all workers in the capital were to march to the Winter Palace, and Father Gaponi was to kneel before the Tsar and hand him a petition for the eight-hour day for workers, an immediate end of the war, and the convocation of a Constituent Assembly.

The evening editions reported increasing tension in St. Petersburg. The police had warned the public that crowds would not be admitted to the Winter Palace. Father Gaponi replied that no force could put itself between him and the Tsar.

I had an uneasy feeling of having deserted my real world while I wandered in a strange land in bygone centuries. I left Florence on the first morning train. At Munich I had to wait several hours. Newsboys were selling fresh extras in front of the railroad stations: BLOODSHED IN ST. PETERSBURG . . . REVOLUTION IN RUSSIA. . . .

Sitting on the station steps, I read the latest bulletins. On the morning of January 9, tremendous crowds of workers assembled in industrial precincts of the capital and processions started toward the Winter Palace. Some carried national banners; others, icons and the portrait of the Tsar. Father Gapon—the German newspapers omitted the Italian "i" at the end—headed the largest procession, marching from the Putilov district. Troops barred all routes to the center of the city.

In the general confusion, the crowds did not hear the order to stop, if any was given. Nor did they understand the meaning of the trumpet preceding the order to fire. Hundreds fell dead under the

---

[2] Actually, the priest's name was Gapon, a Ukrainian name. Italian newspapers had Italianized it.

bullets and thousands were wounded, with many fatalities among bystanders, both grownups and children.

I returned to Russia with a strange feeling of frustration and guilt. Frustration, because I had discovered how little I knew about my own country; guilt, because I had been so far from it on Bloody Sunday.

Back in the capital, I found that the events of January 9 had profoundly shocked and outraged the public. All blame was laid on the Tsar, who had fled to one of his suburban residences but let his standard fly over the Winter Palace. "Down with the Tsar!" became the slogan in even moderately liberal circles. Gapon was the national hero. In the students' mess, all parties displayed his portraits —full face and profile, sitting and standing in a plain cassock, with a cross on his chest.[3]

A general meeting of students had been called to take a stand on the massacre of January 9. It was held in the main hall of the University, which could accommodate three thousand persons standing and was packed to capacity. A young man opened the meeting in the name of the coalition committee of revolutionary organizations of the University and invited the audience to elect a chairman. When he himself was elected unanimously, he announced the agenda.

All the speakers urged the students to strike as the only effective protest against the infamous crime of the government. This course had been determined in advance, after consultation among revolutionary groups. They called for strikes in all Russian universities, institutes, and colleges, without a time limit. Their arguments were moral and political: We cannot study when the soil under our feet is soaked with blood. We cannot accept education from the hands

[3] There is no longer any mystery about Father Gapon. He was a police agent, assigned to the church at the Putilov mills to counteract leftist propaganda. He founded a monarchistic union of workers to whom he preached obedience to the Tsar, loving father, ever ready to help and protect the workers. When the strike in the mills broke out, he decided to use it to kindle monarchistic feelings and raise his own prestige in the eyes of his police superiors. The latter drafted the original petition to the Tsar and told Gapon to circulate it in the factories, but at that point the wires got crossed. Some workers suggested changes in the petition and Gapon accepted them. The style of the petition remained monarchistic, but its content became openly revolutionary. When it reached the police, the chief ordered the priest to stop the whole nonsense immediately. By this time, however, Gapon feared the terrorists even more than his superiors. His only salvation seemed to be to bring his plan to a successful climax. He was at the head of the procession the police stopped at the Gate of Narva and escaped the bullets by throwing himself flat on the snow. Members of the Socialist Revolutionary party spirited him away to a hiding place, and he was smuggled abroad in disguise. In 1905, he returned to Russia and again offered his services to the secret police but was unmasked by the revolutionaries, tried by a secret workers' tribunal, and hung.

of a government of murderers. We must show the workers and peasants that the students are on their side.

The response was unanimous: to close the University indefinitely and call on all other students in Russia to do the same. This was by no means the first strike of Russian students, but it was the first universal and purely political strike. Such a political strike of college students would be downright nonsense in a democratic country, but in Tsarist Russia, where people had no legal way to express their wishes, the students felt that they, as the young generation of intellectuals, were spokesmen for the nation and its spearhead in the struggle for freedom. Students' riots were therefore a natural form of national protest, and a universal strike of universities and colleges, without a time limit, was the strongest form of such protest.

The meeting ended in solemn silence, interrupted by a loud call from the rear of the crowd: "Do not break up, comrades!"

Behind the speaker's desk hung a full-length portrait of the Tsar in the red uniform of the hussars. A pole rose to the top of the painting and tore the canvas in two. "Away with the Tsar!" roared the crowd. Bystanders rushed to the portrait and tore off pieces of the canvas. I did my part and emerged with a piece at least two square feet.

The crowd, in high spirits, was moving toward the door when a young man addressed me in broken Russian. "Pardon, but could I see your piece? Oh, it looks fine. . . . Must be from a sleeve or the trousers. I have two pieces but they are not worth much—just drapery. They won't show anything in reproduction. . . . Would you kindly give me yours? This is for a New York paper." My piece of canvas, part of the Tsar's uniform, was my first contribution to the American press.

NEOPHYTE OF THE SOCIALIST PARTY

The University remained closed, but the library and the students' mess were open and full of activity and rumors.

The news from the East became worse. The Russian army in Manchuria was licked. The Baltic fleet sent to rescue Port Arthur met its end at Tsushima. Political strikes and agrarian unrest were spreading throughout Russia. Railroad workers walked out, declaring their solidarity with the factory workers slaughtered in St. Petersburg. Riots broke out in army barracks.

The government was panicky and vacillated more then ever between brutal reprisals and concessions. On August 6, the Tsar issued a manifesto announcing his intention to ask the people to elect representatives to a Duma, which would assist him in legislative matters. So vague a promise did not satisfy even moderately liberal groups. The promised consultative Duma was given the epithet of the Bulygin Duma from the name of the minister who allegedly invented it. The call to boycott it, launched by the radical underground, became so popular that the government did not try to hold the elections.

A decree was published conferring autonomy and self-government on the universities. The faculties were invited to take full control, and students were assured that the police would not intrude into academic life.

But the liberal gestures of the Tsar could not appease public opinion, and the humiliating peace treaty with Japan brought a new outburst of public indignation. All Russia seemed ablaze.

About that time I decided to join the revolution.

I had not been converted by any particular book or propagandist, and I was not obsessed by blind hatred of the Tsarist regime. What brought me to the revolution was the revolution itself. I believed that a violent clash between the people and the government was approaching, and I felt the urge, if not the moral obligation, to be with the people in the decisive hour, and thought that only by joining a revolutionary group would I be able to play my part. Since the Social Democratic party seemed to be closest to the workers, the martyrs of Bloody Sunday, I decided to join it.

I knew this step would be a blow to my father who, though a moderate liberal, was strongly opposed to politics at universities. To avoid any quarrel with him, I bluntly told him I intended to leave home. "I am going to join an underground organization," I said. "I know you won't like this, and sooner or later we may quarrel. If I leave our house, we will remain on good terms." My father did not try to dissuade me.

Financially I was fairly independent. Since the age of sixteen, I had earned more at my father's summer school than I needed. I tutored in geometry and physics and received the same pay as teachers thirty years older than I. As a lecturer, I was second only to my father; I carried a full load of teaching, and felt my salary was well earned. Thus I had saved enough to cover a modest student budget for many months ahead.

While I was packing my books and other belongings, my mother asked me if I had made definite arrangements for moving. I told her that I would look for a furnished room.

"If you leave," she said, "we shall have no use for your room and will probably rent it. Perhaps to a student and—who knows?—also a member of your party, whatever it is. We could just as well rent the room to you, without asking you about politics." She burst into tears and said that as long as I came home at night she would know at least that nothing had happened to me. So I remained with the family, officially as a "lodger."

In the University mess the next day I met a student whom I knew as a Marxist and told him I would like to get in touch with someone connected with the party. He seemed surprised but took me to another student, very short, very dark, with an unusually long beard and bright eyes. The gnome did not waste words but bluntly asked me, "You want to join the RSDWP?" These letters meant nothing to me, but he explained that they stood for Russian Social Democratic Workers' party. When I said yes, he asked whether I was a Bolshevik or Menshevik. I confessed my ignorance about the difference between the two factions. "That is simple," he replied. "The Bolsheviks are for the revolution, while the Mensheviks seek a compromise with Tsarism and are ready to betray the workers." Obviously the gnome was a Bolshevik. Since I had no intention of betraying the workers, I told him that, according to his definition, I was a Bolshevik.

"Are you familiar with our organizational and tactical problems?" he continued. "Have you read Lenin's recent writings?" And he gave me two thin booklets: *What's To Be Done* and *One Step Forward, Two Steps Backward.*

The first pamphlet was directed against opportunism in the early labor movement in Russia and impressed me as completely irrelevant to the current situation. From the second, I learned that the split between the majority (Bolsheviks) and minority (Mensheviks) in the party went back to the vote at the party convention in 1903. The controversial issue was whether one could be a party member without belonging to a particular local cell. After reading these pamphlets, I had some doubts as to whether I was entering the party through the right door. I wished to be with the people, with the workers in their forthcoming assault against Tsarism, and was not in the least interested in the dispute between the two factions. Nor did I like Lenin's plan for a strictly centralized party controlled from the top. Then it occurred to me that Lenin had developed this plan years earlier and could not take it seriously now, in the changed situation. A hurricane was sweeping over Russia. I saw and heard, almost physically, the roaring tides of national revolt around us. Who could direct and control them?

At my next meeting with the gnome, I told him that I found Lenin's pamphlets interesting as samples of prerevolutionary thinking in the party but could not see how his ideas could be applied to current conditions. The gnome seemed shocked but after some meditation asked me to join the University group.

A few days later I was invited to the meeting of the committee of this group and was told that I had been elected a member of the committee and assigned to represent the party in the forthcoming students' meetings. The committee brushed aside my objection that I was unfamiliar with the party's views. Obviously I was picked up as a figurehead because of my reputation among students who did not belong to any organization. When I asked whether I was to represent the entire party or only its Bolshevik faction, I was told, "We have a common line—to open the University in the interest of the revolution and to keep it under control. You will represent both factions. The fight is between us and the Socialist Revolutionaries."

The Social Democratic party wanted to call off the academic strike throughout Russia and mobilize the students as the revolutionary element in the cities, whereas the Socialist Revolutionaries recommended continuing the strike and sending students into the villages for revolutionary work among the peasants. St. Petersburg University would be the first to vote on continuation or termination of the strike, and its decision might establish the pattern for other academic institutions.

The S-D strategy appealed to me. I visualized coming events as a revolt of urban crowds, in the style of the French Revolution and the Paris Commune of 1870, and liked the idea of the students staying in the city as auxiliary troops ready for action. I began to outline my future speech at once, completely forgetting that I had only four listeners and haranguing them as if I were addressing the general meeting. They had doubts about minor points, finding some of my arguments too conservative and others too idealistic, but they all agreed my speech would appeal to the bulk of the students. Thus the committee decided that, after making the keynote speech in the name of the party, I should also move its resolution and, if necessary, answer opponents. In short, the committee turned over the whole meeting to me.

FORUM OF THE REVOLUTION

In the crowded main hall of the University, black suits of the polytechnic schools mingled with gray University jackets. A conspicuous brown curtain hung behind the speaker's pulpit,[4] over the huge frame of the Tsar's portrait, destroyed in January.

[4] In the main hall of St. Petersburg University the chairman and speakers occupied a small elevated platform, like that of a preacher in Catholic and Protestant churches.

As I spoke, I had a strange feeling I was repeating each sentence and I found my address colorless in comparison with that of the representative of the Social Revolutionaries who had spoken before me. Just as I was finishing, the chairman passed me a note from the crowd: "Worker Peter wants to address the meeting." The chairman was not sure whether he should let an outsider speak in a student meeting, but I promptly dispelled his doubts. "An outsider cannot vote but may greet the meeting as a guest."

"Worker Peter," a handsome young man in high boots, with a strong, high-pitched voice, delivered a passionate appeal for a brotherly union of students and workers. His speech strongly supported the S-D position, and the S-R had no time to get a bearded peasant to support theirs! The dispute continued, with odds in favor of S-D. When I moved the resolution, it was accepted by an overwhelming majority. The strike was declared ended and the University reopened, in the interest of the revolution.

In the new autonomous status of the University, the students were called on to take a stand on such matters as program requirements, examinations, coeducation, self-government, new courses in social and political sciences. A Council of Students was elected, and the party nominated me as its official representative in the Council.

Suddenly, and to our surprise, the University became the center of workers' gatherings. News of the ending of the academic strike in the interests of the revolution had penetrated into factory precincts. Throngs of workers found their way to the University to see and hear what was going on. They were disappointed to find students discussing academic problems, and to satisfy them it was decided to hold meetings in the University twice a day: in the morning, on academic issues; in the evening, on political questions. As the representative of the party, I was to organize the evening meetings.

My plan to arrange systematic lectures on the history of the labor movement proved unworkable because of the shortage of competent lecturers. The first evening, when the main hall was packed by workers, we had neither agenda nor speakers. I began with a few words of welcome, suggested that we discuss the current political situation, and turned the meeting over to the floor. The ensuing discussion was utterly chaotic. Some of the volunteer speakers were wholly inarticulate. The next day we arranged to have a dozen speakers from various leftist organizations on whom we called intermittently with the volunteers from the floor.

Within a few days the main hall could not hold the crowd. We opened all the large classrooms for supplementary gatherings and rotated the speakers. I had to speak five or six times each evening. Very soon I noticed that what brought workers to the University was less their thirst for knowledge than their desire to get confirmation of their own faith. The crowds made little response to appeals to armed revolt but never tired of listening to speakers who talked soberly about the situation in Russia, the aspirations of the people, and the inevitable showdown of force between the people and the government.

Gradually the character of the meetings changed. Students disappeared completely from the evening gatherings. The leftist parties asked them to stay away from the overcrowded classrooms in the evening to leave room for the workers and thus contribute to the political, revolutionary education of the masses. A routine developed. Until four or five o'clock, the University was the scene of academic work and academic meetings; in the evening, it belonged to revolutionary crowds that converged from all parts of the city.

The academic administration did not oppose this arrangement. The newly elected president of the University knew that, in the event of a conflict, we would not hesitate to resume the academic strike and close the University.

I somehow became the link between the daytime and evening activities in the University. I got to the University at nine o'clock in the morning. There were academic questions to discuss, memoranda to write, conflicts to settle. Probably the students did not really need the representatives of the leftist parties to handle their academic affairs, but, as long as we did our academic job properly in the morning, we were sure of our grip over the masses of the students and could keep our hands on the University's facilities after dusk.

Almost every evening I also spoke at meetings in other colleges. These were of the same type as at the University, but smaller. Then I went back to the University and seldom left it before one or two o'clock in the morning, after the last meeting ended. I had no time for regular meals and seldom saw my parents, but each night I found on a table near my bed a glass of milk and a large piece of cake—the supper my mother prepared for me.

THE POLITICAL PARTIES

To control the campaign, the Bolsheviks organized a group of thirty or forty "meeting speakers," some with considerable experience and high position in the party hierarchy. These self-styled "generals" proved to be mediocre speakers, however, and some had to withdraw after their first performance. The party put me in charge of the group of regular speakers at University meetings. The core of the group consisted of two University students—Krylenko and me—and an underground agitator, Nikolai. The party was officially represented by an obscure Bolshevist organizer, Anton, as stupid and arrogant when he was drunk as on the rare occasions when he was sober. Without contesting his authority as the link between the group and the party, I did my best to keep him from appearing on the platform. When the speakers' group was recognized as a cell of the party, Anton explained to us that as members of an underground organization we should all use assumed names. I chose the most inconspicuous name I could think of, a name as common in Russia as Smith or Jones in this country, and thus became Sergei Petrov for many years.

The Mensheviks had a group of their own. Speakers of both factions appeared together at the meetings, and there was no visible difference in their political programs. Both pretended to represent the working class, while the S-R considered themselves representatives of the tillers of the soil.

In the public eye, the Bolsheviks represented the left wing of the S-D party and the Mensheviks, the right wing. I am not sure that this was the difference. I think the difference at that time was psychological, rather than theoretical or philosophical. The Mensheviks were more pedantic, the Bolsheviks more active. Temperamentally, I was closer to the latter; intellectually, I remained closer to Petrazhitsky than to either faction of the S-D party.

A MEETING AT NIGHT

Many times the workers who attended the meetings in the University said to me, "Too bad all our people can't come here!" "Why can't they?" I asked. The answer was always the same: "Too far from our plant!" In fact, some of our guests had to walk two or three hours to get to the University. Some returned home at three or four o'clock in the morning and had barely two hours of sleep before they left for work.

It was very hard to take the meeting closer to the factories. The factory precincts were heavily patrolled by mounted police. Platoons of Cossacks were kept in readiness at strategic points. An illegal meeting in the open air could end in bloodshed. It seemed possible to hold flying meetings here and there, with the crowd ready to disperse at the approach of the Cossacks, but the psychological effectiveness of such meetings would be doubtful.

Unexpectedly, I was called to an outdoor meeting in the heart of a factory precinct. That evening, the agrarian program was to be discussed in the students' mess. All our meeting speakers were present, when Anton told us that one of the precincts had organized an open-air meeting for that night and wanted a speaker. There was just time enough to get in touch with the headquarters of the local organization and reach the place. Nobody wanted to go on such short notice. Anton asked me if I would go. I replied that I had never spoken in an open-air meeting and did not know what I was expected to say. He waved aside these objections. "It doesn't matter what you say. Just say something about 'away with the Tsar!' and stress the fact that the Bolsheviks are the only ones who defend the interests of the people!" And he handed me written directions for finding the local headquarters.

I was to take the double-deck streetcar in front of the Admiralty and to sit on the upper deck to avoid spies, who allegedly checked only the lower deck. Next, I had to change to a horse-drawn trolley, again taking a seat on the top deck; then alight at the Alexandrovsk village in front of the church, walk back two blocks, turn left, cross a small bridge, go right to the end of the sidewalk, and stop at the third house on the left. I was to knock three times at the door and tell the woman who opened it that Ivan had sent me. "Memorize the address and destroy the note," Anton warned.

The night was cold and windy. I shivered in my light overcoat on top of the streetcar and thought about my speech, but could not find an opening sentence. Then I forgot about the speech completely. For the first time in my life, I was in a factory district. I knew, of course, that St. Petersburg was encircled by locomotive shops, shipbuilding yards, and munitions factories. Some of these plants were among the largest and most modern in Europe and had expanded during the Russo-Japanese War. I knew there were a dozen plants with more than ten thousand workers each in the southern precincts alone, but I had never seen any of them or the workers' settlements around them.

Now I saw endless rows of small shabby houses punctuated by huge brick buildings, some dark, others with lights blazing from numberless windows. The streets were empty. Tongues of flame licked from high chimneys. The air was full of roaring clangor and whistles, but no human beings were in sight. This was the realm of iron, fire, and invisible Cyclopes. By the time the trolley stopped in front of a modest church in Alexandrovsk village, I was overwhelmed by my new impressions and still had not thought out a single sentence of my speech.

At the headquarters I found a bespectacled woman, whom I immediately identified as a trained nurse, and a young worker in high boots. The worker, Pavel, explained that he was a member of the factory cell and the woman was the organizer of the local S-D organ-ization. I looked at my watch and saw that it was nearly eleven o'clock.

"When should we go?" I asked Pavel.

"We still have an hour," he answered. "At midnight we shall get two crews at the point."

"What should I talk about?" The woman threw up her hands.

"How do you like that?" she complained, "we kill ourselves get-ting ready for a meeting, and they send us a speaker who asks what he should say!"

Pavel said meditatively, "Few of our people have been to the city meetings, so whatever you say will be new to them. But you must impress them. . . . Tell them something about the revolution. . . . And about socialism, of course. . . . People are also interested in the eight-hour day. . . . Say something about labor unions and the party. . . . The French Revolution might fit, too. Surely, explain about the Constituent Assembly. Our workers are ignorant, prac-tically muzhiks. . . . Tell them also about the land reform . . ."

"Halt, comrade," I interrupted. "How much time shall I have?"

"Who can tell? You can stay as long as people will stay or until the police arrive. . . ."

"This helps me a lot," I remarked.

We sat together in an awkward silence, I thinking of my speech, Pavel watching the clock. At last he said, "Let's go." He looked at my hat and said disapprovingly, "No good. . . . We have a better one, in case of Cossacks. . . ." And he handed me a big fur hat that covered my head like a helmet.

We went through deserted streets, along fences, crossing empty lots, and sloshing in mud. I thought of my speech. If only I knew how to start! Pavel stopped. Two wooden fences met at an obtuse angle at our right. In the darkness, the field around seemed endless. Dim lights marked streets far away.

Pavel whistled lightly. A cautious cough answered from the dark-ness. Three shadows separated themselves from the fence and came nearer.

"Pavel?"

"With the speaker. What about your end?"

"Everything is all right. Ivan has jammed the lock at the new gate. Everyone will come this way."

"Where's Stepka?"

"With the gang."

"And the patrols?"

"The Old Man is in front of the police station. All posts manned."

Pavel took over the command, alert, confident of himself, sure of his men.

"The first thing to do is to bar the way. I shall be at the corner, with the speaker. You take places one step from each other. Dmitry, you are the last in the chain, the anchor man. Stepka's gang will fall into the line. When I give the command, link arms and stand firm!"

Men began to emerge from the darkness. The first groups of two or three—mostly young boys—came running. A few remained at the corner, others moved a few steps away. A human chain was taking shape, its far end disappearing in the dark.

More and more persons kept coming, all from the same direction. Suddenly Pavel barked the command, "Stop!"

In a moment a barricade of human bodies formed itself across the field. The first rows stopped by our boys added weight to the dam. An angry voice shouted from the rear, "Go on, you riffraff!"

Another voice roared, "What are you starting?"

"Be quiet, comrades," shouted Pavel. "The speaker will tell us. . . ."

"To hell with you and your speaker! You chose a nice place, a nice time."

"This won't be long," Pavel pleaded.

The boys in the chain began to shout, "Quiet! Quiet! Listen!"

I stepped forward, felt my feet sink into a puddle, and started to speak. "You are right, comrades," I said. "This is no place and no time for a meeting. And, of course, it is not fair to stop people by force and make them listen to a speaker whom they cannot see. But do you think it is fun for me to speak here in the darkness, standing in icy water?"

"That is true!" remarked a voice from the crowd.

Now it was easy to shift to freedom of speech, the right of workers to organize, their stake in the revolution.

My speech was interrupted by a shrill whistle. At the cry, "Cossacks!" the crowd dashed to safety. "There are no Cossacks!" Pavel shouted.

People reassembled, and I went on. I spoke of the fear the Tsarist government inspired in the workers and the workers inspired in the government. The revolution, I said, is the victory of men over fear. I did not have to search for words; my only effort was to talk loud enough. I stopped when I felt that I was losing my voice.

A tall oldish man who was standing close to me put his heavy hand on my shoulder and said, "All this is true! Thanks, comrade!"

"All is true!" resounded around me.

There was no applause, but I felt the speech had brought comfort and hope to the persons around me whom I could not see in the dark-ness. I stood in the crowd, moved and weary, when I heard Pavel's voice. "This is all for tonight. Go home, comrades. No bad feeling against us for having stopped you here at night?"

And cheerful, brisk voices answered, "Next time make it in the factory yard, in worktime."

AMERICAN GUESTS

The University students' mess became popular with newspaper re-porters. Once a middle-aged gentleman came to me, produced a cor-respondent's card of the London *Times*, and asked me, "What is the attitude of the leftist parties to the government's foreign debt? How will they stand on the new loan that is being negotiated with foreign bankers?"

This question made me prick up my ears. Rumors were circulating that, after having concluded peace negotiations with Japan, Sergei Witte, then the president of the Council of Tsar's Ministers, had started negotiations for a loan to help the government liquidate the aftermath of the disastrous war and suppress the revolution. The newspapers had reported that a group of American bankers had come to St. Petersburg to put the final touches to the deal.

Although I knew nothing about the views of the leftist parties in this matter, I told the correspondent that victorious revolution would never recognize loans that the moribund regime had made to sup-press it. The Britisher was visibly shocked.

"Do you mean that the new government would repudiate the financial obligations of the old?" he asked me. "Don't you realize that such dishonesty would ruin your credit?"

I replied that the credit of the new government would depend on its ability to meet its own obligations rather than on its willingness to honor the commitments of the bankrupt old regime. Then the correspondent asked me whether I would be willing to come to his place the next morning at ten o'clock. "A friend of mine," he ex-plained, "would be delighted to meet you. He is a very important per-son in his country."

I accepted his invitation. The correspondent—I think his name was Mr. Thompson—occupied a huge, luxuriously furnished room in a private apartment on the Nevsky Prospect. At ten, on the dot, an overdressed young man with blond hair and blue eyes rushed into the room. Mr. Thompson introduced me to him without revealing his name. Obviously, his friend preferred to remain incognito.

The young man started by expressing his views. "Mr. Thompson tells me that if the leftists ever come into power, they will not pay the debts of the present government. I cannot believe this. . . . Moreover, I do not believe they will ever get power."

He expected Mr. Thompson to translate his words, but I replied in English, "Wait and and see."

"The press," the young man continued, "makes much of your meetings. But I have been assured by high—yes, very high—authorities that all you have there is a handful of Anarchists and students. The people—the peasants and the workers—are firmly behind the throne."

"Come to our meeting," I replied, "and check this information."

"How can I? Won't the Anarchists kill me?"

"I guarantee your complete safety," I assured him.

"Where and when is the next gathering?"

"Come to the University tonight. I will keep a place for you."

He looked at Mr. Thompson, who nodded. Then, like a man taking a plunge, he said, "I accept your offer for myself, my three colleagues, and Mr. Thompson."

"Eight o'clock sharp," I told him. "Send me a note from the entrance hall. I shall be in the chair in the main hall."

I was angry at the arrogant young man and decided to show him our meetings in their true light.

At eight o'clock I was in the speaker's pulpit in the main hall when a note signed by Mr. Thompson was handed to me. I hurried to the entrance hall and found the correspondent and four gentlemen, wearing large overcoats and bright gloves, surrounded by a curious and not too friendly crowd. Apparently they were not amused by the loud jokes of the bystanders at their expense, which Mr. Thompson was translating.

The five gentlemen shook hands with me with such profusion of cordiality that the crowd must have felt they were my very, very dear friends. I took them in tow and conducted them, not by the shortest and easiest way, to the main hall. It was packed to standing capacity, but, in the narrow place behind the pulpit kept free for the speakers, chairs had been placed for our guests. The chairman called on me to speak.

I talked about current events, the aspirations of the Russian people, and the imminent victory of the revolution. Nikolai spoke next. His speech was addressed to the Tsar, whom he called the "Anointed Butcher." He looked at the empty frame of the Tsar's portrait as he talked, and his lashing words aroused frantic applause. Krylenko followed. His subject was the interference of foreign capitalists in Russian affairs.

"The emissaries of foreign banks are here, in St. Petersburg," he screamed. "Do they believe that their dollars will change the course of the revolution and give the despots a new lease on life? Comrades, will you let these vultures make money by ganging up with the enemies of the Russian people?"

"Never, never!" roared the audience.

I sat with my guests, helping Mr. Thompson translate the speech and the outcries of the crowd. The guests were alarmed.

"We should not have come here," said one of them.

I tried to comfort them. "You are in no danger. Nobody knows who you are. I apologize for the abusive language of Mr. Krylenko."

"The revolution will triumph over its enemies," Krylenko continued. "The foreign capitalistic sharks will come to us with their claims, showing the note signed—in blood—by the Tsar. What answer will you give them, comrades?"

Blasting replies came from the audience. At last, one of the guests said, "We have heard enough. Please help us get away from here before it is too late."

Mr. Thompson asked me, "Could you take us to the exit? Or would it be better to wait till the meeting ends?"

"Your friends are my personal guests," I replied, "and they may leave whenever they wish."

Once more I took them in tow and ushered them through the crowd to the exit. I went with them to the quay of the Neva. Mr. Thompson was pleased; he thought the meeting very interesting. His friends were almost speechless and kept saying, "Dreadful, dreadful!"

From outside, the venerable red building of the University looked terrifying. Its ground floor was dark, but all the windows on the second and third floors seemed ablaze. Agitated shadows moved across the windows, many open despite the cold autumn night. Clouds of steam shooting up from them looked like tongues of flame, and the whole building seemed to tremble.

"So this is what is going on here," said one of the visitors.

"It is the same in all the colleges," I replied.

"Dreadful," said the blond young man again. "One can't keep far enough away from this mess. We are deeply obliged to you."

We shook hands and I returned to the University.

ACADEMIC AFFAIRS

The authorities in the capital did not interfere with revolutionary meetings. Some provincial officials, however, tried to counteract revolutionary propaganda by pogroms. In some cities, meetings and demonstrations of students and workers were assailed by armed bands that were incited and directed by plain-clothes police agents. In Tomsk, in Siberia, the city theater in which local intellectuals were holding a meeting was surrounded by a mob and set on fire. More than three hundred persons were burned alive or clubbed to death when they tried to escape from the flaming building. But in St. Petersburg the government did nothing. Later the rightist press described the situation as the time "when the government was away." The Tsar and his advisers—military and civilian—were paralyzed by fear of a general mutiny in the army, not yet demobilized after the war. They did not dare use troops against the people and knew no other way to handle the situation. A threat to our control of the University came from another quarter.

The autonomy of the University gave rise to many academic questions that required the joint action of students and faculty members. Faculty leadership passed into the hands of progressive professors, organized in the Academic Union. They were ready to close their eyes to what was going on in the University building after class hours, but regarded with concern our encroachment on academic questions that belonged, according to their conviction, to the jurisdiction of the faculty.

We had organized a Students' Council with somewhat vague responsibilities. It was elected on the basis of proportional representation of political groups, and the S-D list obtained an absolute majority. Then the general meeting voted an academic charter and asked the faculty to reinstate immediately a dozen progressive professors who had been ousted by the reactionary administration. It also decided to apply an "active boycott" against ten professors considered to be reactionaries. I happened to preside at the meeting that voted on the "proscribed list" of unwanted professors. Accordingly I read the list and reported the charges made against each of the candidates. When I came to the name of Professor Georgievsky, a very unpopular teacher of economics, I reported, "Charged of having denounced his colleagues to secret police thirteen times."

With a roar of indignation the meeting voted for his proscription.

A few days later, the president of the University asked the Students' Council to appoint three delegates to meet with a committee of professors. The Council appointed Engel, the favorite chairman of the general meetings, me, and the gnome who had accepted me a few weeks earlier into the S-D party.

We were pleasantly surprised by the composition of the professors' committee, which included Professor Pokrovsky, a brilliant and popular teacher of law, and two equally popular members of the history department. But a surprise of another kind waited for us when Pokrovsky asked us to read the list of professors we wanted to have reinstated or invited to the University and then remarked:

"You are, of course, sure that these gentlemen will appreciate your gesture. Did you get in touch with them and ascertain their views?"

We had to admit that we had had no time to contact our candidates.

"Then let me tell you what most of your candidates would have told you. The dignity of professorship requires that each new faculty member be elected by old members of the faculty on the basis of his scientific qualifications, without any external pressure. Pressure by a meeting of students is as unacceptable to us as an order by the police."

He cooled down when I explained that the academic qualifications of our candidates were beyond question and that our resolution simply meant we wished to have these distinguished scholars among our teachers.

"Now, gentlemen," said Pokrovsky, "let us hear the proscribed list."

"You know it from the newspapers," I said.

"Yes, we know it," he replied, "and we consider it a disgrace to the University. What you have done, gentlemen, is a trial by the mob, a moral lynching. You have condemned people without giving them an opportunity to defend themselves."

And, turning to me, he said, "Please, Mr. Woytinsky, answer me frankly, in accordance with your own convictions: Did these persons get a fair trial?"

To the utter dismay of the gnome I answered, "I must admit that they did not."

"That settles the formal side of the problem," said Pokrovsky. "You will recognize, of course, that a decision made without a fair trial is void. But we would like to single out the case of Professor Georgievsky. He is accused of having denounced his colleagues to the Ochrana thirteen times. How easy it is to cheat you, gentlemen! The man who gave you this information is either a liar or an agent of the police. Unless he has access to the secret files of the police, he could not have known how many times an informer denounced members of the faculty."

The accuser of Professor Georgievsky was the radical assistant professor of economics, Dr. N. He had given this information to me personally, insisting that Georgievsky's name should head the list. Suddenly his game became clear to me, and I said:

"The accuser of Professor Georgievsky will have to prove his accusations or be exposed as a slanderer."

Pokrovsky looked at me with unexpected warmth. "I think we

can accept your promise and drop this case for a time. But I must tell you our decision on your proscribed list as a whole. An active boycott is a threat of violence, and the Board of Professors will reply to the first attempt of violence against any professor by closing the University. This decision is irrevocable."

Next day I went to Dr. N. and asked him for the evidence against Professor Georgievsky. He seemed embarrassed and refused to testify before the students' meeting. "Do not ruin me," he implored. "There are serious reasons why I cannot appear."

Beside myself with anger, I replied, "I understand your reasons and shall not call you as a witness. I shall simply announce in the general meeting that your charge against Georgievsky proved to be slander."

I reported the results of my visit to the Students' Council. The effect was as if a hand grenade had exploded on the Council's round table. Dr. N. was one of the minor leaders of the left wing of the Academic Union. Unmasking him would be a severe blow for his group. The "moderate" members of the Council implored me not to reveal the source of the charges against Georgievsky. Finally, I promised that I would not name Dr. N. if I could persuade the meeting to withdraw Georgievsky's name from the proscribed list.

Engel presided at the general meeting. My report about the reaction of the professors to our requests for the invitation of new professors did not cause much excitement. When I told of our agreement to abstain from an active boycott of reactionary professors until the accusation against each one of them was proved individually, the audience answered with loud catcalls.

"I know how you will hiss when I tell you the reason for our surrender," I shouted. "We surrendered because we realized that the decision of the general meeting was unjust. The condemned did not get a fair trial. . . ." And I pleaded for the revocation of the entire proscribed list, including Georgievsky, on the basis of procedural errors and lack of evidence. The meeting ended with a unanimous vote of confidence in the Council. An investigating committee was appointed and the whole affair was shelved.

The professors were satisfied with our regard for their interpretation of academic freedom. But they also realized we would be conciliatory in academic questions only as long as we could use the University for revolutionary purposes but that we would become adamant if the Board of Professors interfered with our political activities. Thus the compromise was confirmed: science in the morning, revolution after dusk. The University remained in the hands of revolutionary students until the showdown that marked the climax and turning point in the revolution.

THE GENERAL STRIKE BEGINS

The showdown came in the shape of the general strike in October,
1905. No political party had foreseen it or planned it, and none led
it. It broke out suddenly, as fire starts in a forest after a long drought.
A spark strikes a dry leaf and from it the wind carries millions of
sparks to start new fires. It matters little how the first spark originated—from a hunter's smoldering campfire, the butt of a hiker's
cigarette, smoke from a speeding locomotive, or lightning. The
actual precursor of the blaze is the drought.

The advance scouts of the general strike were walkouts in Moscow. A large printing office opened the round in September. Other
printing establishments joined it. Next, bakeries and some factories
on the outskirts of the city followed suit. Here and there strikers
clashed with the police. Workers in the repair shops of a railroad
walked out, protesting against an assault by the Cossacks.

Meanwhile, the meetings in St. Petersburg gave an outlet for
the revolutionary energy of the people, replacing other forms of protest. Not until October 2 did the St. Petersburg printers declare a
strike in support of their Moscow comrades. This, however, was a
minor episode in the political life of St. Petersburg.

Another minor event was the convention of representatives of railroad employees, called by the Department of Transportation to discuss an old-age pension plan. The convention was humdrum at the
start, but workers from the repair shops soon replaced the high brass
on the platform. Political slogans appeared in the speeches. The convention began to attract the attention of the press, and the authorities threatened to dissolve it. Before any steps were taken, however,
rumors that its members had been arrested spread in Moscow, and
workers on the Moscow-Kazan railroad walked out in protest. The
government promptly denied making any arrests, but nobody believed the denial. On October 7, the whole railroad center of Moscow was paralyzed. St. Petersburg workers who wished to know what
was happening in Moscow stormed the evening gatherings at the
University. That night, the crowd was so large that we had to hold a
meeting in the courtyard. On this and on the next day, telegrams
from Moscow and other cities were read from the chair, reports were
made from the precincts, separate gatherings of professional groups
were arranged. On October 8, I was called to a workers' meeting at
the Military Medical Academy, where the question of a general strike
was to be discussed. One after another, spokesmen of revolutionary
parties rose to speak. Every one of them passionately opposed a
general strike. Such a step was pointless, they argued, since it could

not force the government to capitulate. It would be limited to only a few plants and would weaken the workers by diverting their attention from their real goal—assembling forces for the final armed revolt.

The same arguments prevailed during the next two days when workers in Kharkov, Moscow, Reval, and many other cities had already laid down their tools. On October 11, some thirty thousand workers came to the University. The main hall was assigned to railroad employees. After the report of the convention's delegates about their negotiations with Witte, the Prime Minister, the meeting unanimously decided to join the all-Russian railroad strike. This was the affair of the railroaders, however, and did not affect the agitation in other meetings against a general strike.

I was strolling from one meeting to another in the University when a medical student came running up to me. I was asked to come to the Military Medical Academy. The crowd in its large amphitheater was surprisingly homogeneous—all workers from the next precinct. They asked me whether they should join the general strike. Since I did not know the answer, I sent a messenger to party headquarters for instructions and meanwhile called on representatives of the plants to report on the local situation.

My messenger returned with a note: "The Committee is in session. Instructions will follow in half an hour."

Meanwhile the local people were making their reports: "Our workers have made up their minds. Whatever the parties decide, they will strike. . . ." "Everyone will surely join. . . ." And so it went on and on.

Seated at the chairman's table, in the pit of the amphitheater, I watched the faces turned toward it. No doubt, no hesitation—the same expression of firm decision and exaltation on all.

It was close to midnight. The audience waited for words that would summarize its feelings. "Your turn, Comrade Petrov," called the chairman. I no longer needed a directive. "What can I add, comrades? The decision has been made. The general strike is on. This is the hour!"

As I spoke, a young man rushed to the chair and handed a note to the chairman. He read it, reached out to pass it to me, then put it aside. No resolution was voted after my speech. The crowd applauded. The chairman closed the meeting and handed me the note. I read:

"Committee of the RSDWP, Bolshevist Faction. Instruction to speakers: Discuss the pros and cons of the general strike."

The strike was proclaimed in St. Petersburg on October 12 and almost at once became complete.

BEFORE THE SHOWDOWN

If the government had been away, now it returned. On October 12, the Tsar invested General Trepov, the Military Governor of St. Petersburg, with dictatorial powers and ordered him to crush the strike. Trepov began to draw in the reliable military units stationed around the city—battalions, companies, even selected platoons. He did not try to use the railroads; all troops were ordered to proceed under their own power. On October 14, he issued an order to the troops: "Spare no cartridges and fire to kill!" At the same time he announced that no further political gatherings were to be held in educational institutions. Academic authorities were made responsible for enforcing this order and were instructed to close the institutions if they could not do so.

The president of the University called the students together. His voice trembling with emotion, he implored them to agree to a temporary closing of the University. The Students' Council designated me to speak in its name. I began by saying that I fully appreciated the concern of the president for the safety of the University. I agreed with him that we were facing danger but added that all revolutions demand sacrifices. The struggle for freedom had cost the Russian people countless victims. We did not demand further sacrifices. Each should answer for himself. Our only request to the president was not to interfere with those who were ready to face danger. And I moved the resolution: "The University, opened in the interest of the revolution, will stay open whatever may come."

The resolution was adopted almost unanimously. I tried to say something comforting to the president, who stood behind the speakers' pulpit looking like a tragic mask of despair, but he covered his eyes with a trembling hand and rushed away.

Later I was called to an industrial precinct. On the way I stopped at home and changed my clothes, putting on high boots, a Russian shirt, an overcoat, and a worker's cap—an outfit I had acquired soon after my first outdoor meeting. In this disguise, accompanied by local workers, I plodded from factory to factory, addressing crowds in courtyards and workshops. I told them again and again what I believed to be true: that all Russia was already on strike and that the Tsarist regime was bound to collapse.

It was past nine when I returned to the University. The main hall and classrooms were packed as never before. A mass meeting was being held in the courtyard. A student came to tell me that the members of the Academic Union, assembled in a classroom to decide its attitude to the general strike, asked the Students' Council to present its point of view. I went to the meeting. The classroom was full. Young instructors predominated, but there were also some elderly professors. When I took my place at the chairman's table and began to speak, a voice from the audience interrupted me. "We have invited a spokesman of the students, but we don't need to be harangued by a revolutionary worker." Only then did I realize that I was in my proletarian disguise, with trousers stuffed into high muddy boots. The chairman explained the misunderstanding, I apologized for my attire, and continued my speech.

The Academic Union was in a most difficult position. All the liberal professors had decided to join the general strike. However, a strike of professors would have amounted to closing the academic institutions, and this was exactly what radical parties were trying to prevent. Referring to the morning meeting of the students, I said that, because of the particular role played by the University and colleges, the only way the professors could support the general strike was by fulfilling their usual academic functions.

A young instructor asked me, "Does the speaker believe the University will protect the workers from being mown down by machine guns?"

I answered, "I do. In the past four weeks not a drop of blood has been shed within these walls, but I am not sure we would have been able to hold our meetings elsewhere without heavy losses."

"Are you sure the floors and walls of the University will not be stained with blood tomorrow?" insisted my opponent.

"I am not," I replied. "We are taking a chance."

A senior member of the Academic Union remarked, "I am not convinced that the strategy of the revolutionary parties is wise. However, we cannot change it. It leaves us no choice."

And the Union joined in the resolution of the students' meeting. We gained a twenty-four-hour delay.

THE LAST UNIVERSITY MEETING

On the morning of October 15, General Trepov notified the president of the University that he would use military force that day to end the revolutionary gatherings. A flying meeting was held in the half-empty main hall. Not more than some six to eight hundred students had come, but the spirit of those who came was high. A fire-eater from the Caucasus offered a plan to defend the University building: to block all doors except the main entrance, gather material to barricade that last exit, and man the barricade with armed students. I objected and pointed out that this proposal was childish since the University building—narrow and a quarter of a mile long, its whole façade consisting of windows overlooking broad University Avenue—was utterly unfit to serve as a fort.

"Does the S-D party intend to cancel the night meeting?" shouted the Caucasian.

I offered the first idea that came to me: "We shall not cancel the meeting but we will minimize the danger of bloodshed. We will prevent panic and disband if necessary."

Before I could elaborate this plan, a bearded student unknown to me introduced himself as a former officer, a veteran of the Russo-Japanese War, and explained that my plan envisaged, in military terms, preparations for an orderly retreat. In view of the peculiarities of the terrain, we must prepare as many emergency exits as possible and be ready to direct comparatively small groups to these exits and disperse them through the streets at the rear of the University. With due preparation, he said, we could evacuate some twenty thousand in less than fifteen minutes, and we could get that time through negotiations at the main entrance even after an assault on the University had been ordered.

Nikolsky, the bearded student, sounded like a man who knew his business and was used to giving orders. My proposal that he be charged with the defense of the University building was accepted, and he immediately announced enrollment of volunteers in an Academic Legion. He gave the organization a military appearance by setting up headquarters, liaison officers, dispatch carriers, and so on, but actually it was a harmless organization of ushers with armbands of different colors and without weapons.

At eight o'clock a crowd began to assemble. Members of the Council warned people as they entered, "This meeting may end in a clash with the troops. Wouldn't you rather stay away?"

The workers took the warning in good humor. "You are talking about Trepov's order not to spare cartridges? He won't have enough cartridges for all of us."

The crowd—perhaps fifteen thousand—was not quite so large as usual, but its spirit was excellent. I spoke at least ten times. The topics varied according to the desires of the audience, but my effort was concentrated on one purpose—to strengthen self-confidence and discipline in the crowd.

After ten o'clock, troops began to appear before the University. Cossacks, foot soldiers, and cavalry detachments formed a broad semicircle in front of the building. Outside this semicircle there was continuous movement of considerable forces. Following it on a large map, Nikolsky said to me, "They are assembling their forces."

Cossacks galloped in front of the building; a detachment of artillery crossed the Neva Bridge; a company of foot soldiers marched under the windows. "Demonstrations!" said Nikolsky. "Just a bluff."

The meetings continued. I stood in the pulpit in the main hall, beside the chairman, ready to dissolve it. From my vantage point, I could watch the movement of the troops. Mounted Cossacks were forming a tight chain in front of the University.

Suddenly orders were barked, and the chain regrouped in several dark masses. The Cossacks dismounted, horses were taken away. Foot soldiers filled in the spaces between the groups of dismounted horsemen. In the darkness behind the first line of troops I discerned moving masses of men.

A student messenger handed me a note from Nikolsky: "The patrols report that cannon have been set in position. The attack may begin without warning." I sent back word: "I shall begin to disband the meeting as soon as your men take their places."

Then I interrupted the speaker to make an urgent communication. "Comrades! An hour ago I warned you against the provocation planned by Trepov. It has come sooner than I expected. Troops are massed before this building and are ready for an attack. Cannon are aimed at these windows." At this announcement there was a roar of indignation, but not a man moved toward the entrance. From the pulpit I saw two score students with white armbands squeezing themselves into the crowd and forming a chain across the hall.

"We are unarmed, comrades," I continued, "but we are not quitting the fight! We shall abandon this place, but we will reconquer it. . . . Those in the rear, behind the line of the Academic Legion, are asked to leave the hall and follow the ushers to the exits. The others are not to move! I repeat, the fight is not over. We will come back."

The persons in the rear of the hall began to leave through four doors. Suddenly a loud voice asked, "When shall we come back?"

Without thinking, I threw out a reply. "Tomorrow! Armed, ready to fight!"

"Set the hour!"

"Three o'clock!"

"We will come back," roared the crowd.

Leonid, a Bolshevist agitator who stood next to me, grabbed my hand. "What are you doing?" he whispered. "Did the party authorize an armed demonstration?"

But I could not stop. "Those in the rear, behind the line, please leave the hall. Come back tomorrow, ready to fight!"

My voice broke. I nodded to Leonid to replace me. "All back tomorrow, at three o'clock!" he shouted. "Armed! Ready to die!"

We remained in the pulpit until the last man left the hall. Nikolsky met me at the door. "Do you know who ordered the armed demonstration for tomorrow?" he asked.

"Perhaps I did," I confessed.

"You gave the order in this hall," he replied, "but the same instruction was given in all the meetings. This seems to have been a planned action."

Military orders resounded in front of the University. Soldiers, in groups no larger than a platoon, were crossing the street and taking positions between the windows of the building, ready to break in. Then a group of officers approached the main entrance. One of them knocked on the door with the butt of his revolver and shouted, "Open!"

We swung the door wide open. The officers were surprised to see a group of students at the foot of the empty stairway.

"We are the Students' Council of the University," explained our chairman. "And who are you?"

"I am the commanding officer of the forces ordered to disperse the revolutionary meeting in the University," was the answer.

"There is no meeting here. Only the Council." The officer did not seem unhappy at finding no strangers in the building.

The councilmen remained at the University until dawn. I slept soundly on a table in the president's office. On the morning of October 16, the University was in the hands of the Military Governor of St. Petersburg, but St. Petersburg itself was in the hands of striking workers and their Soviet.

THE SOVIET OF WORKERS

To explain the origin of the Soviet (Council) of Workers, which played an important role in subsequent events and gave its name to a new kind of totalitarian regime after the revolution of November, 1917, I must go back a few days.

Memoirs and histories of the first Russian revolution have devoted a great deal of attention to this body but, because of their spirit of partisanship and self-interest, most of these accounts give a distorted picture of its true character. Actually, the St. Petersburg Soviet was nothing but an oversized strike committee. It neither organized nor directed the general strike of October, 1905, and it came to life only after the strike was in full swing. But its importance rose with the mounting tide of the strike, and it acquired a tremendous prestige after its end.

The strike had been spreading through St. Petersburg since the morning of October 12. Crowds of strikers roamed the city, persuading other workers to join them. There was no violence, no damage to factory property. Strikers would enter places where work was still going on. A bench, a boiler, a heap of rails, or shoulders of a comrade formed the rostrum. The speeches were short: "All Russia is on strike. . . . Should you be the last to join?"

And after such exhortations, the crowd, swollen by new recruits, rolled on.

Newspapers appeared as usual. News about the progress of the strike in all parts of Russia added to the workers' confidence and increased panic within the government. On October 12, the Municipal Council of St. Petersburg, a thoroughly conservative body, passed a resolution demanding that the government accede to the economic and political aspirations of the people.

On October 13, the workers in the electric power stations walked out. By nightfall, St. Petersburg was plunged into darkness, and agitated crowds filled the streets in the center of the city.

That evening a handful of delegates from factories and mills of the Neva district met in a classroom of the Polytechnic School and adopted a resolution calling on all striking workers to send their representatives to a Workers' Committee—one delegate for each five hundred workers. On October 14, elections were carried out here and there, and when the Workers' Committee convened it included delegates from two score plants. The group was dominated by Mensheviks, who had conducted elections earlier. An obscure labor attorney, Khrustalev, was elected chairman. He proved to be a resourceful chairman with administrative abilities. On assembling, the Committee did not know what to do, but it finally decided to ask the Municipal Council to provide food for striking workers and assign places for meetings. When a delegation went to the Municipal Council with this request, the Council merely sent it away.

The next day, October 15, 226 delegates, representing nearly a hundred plants, attended the meeting of the Committee. Except for the reports from the plants, the discussion was chaotic and no important decision was reached. The Committee found its role two days later when it realized that it was the mouthpiece of the strikers.

Trepov's order—to spare no cartridges and fire to kill—merely provoked the workers to contemptuous wrath. Several times I heard a grim joke: "We thought they were sparing us, but a three-kopek cartridge is worth more to them than human life."

The self-confidence of the striking workers was supported by the almost universal sympathy of the public. Except for a few staunch reactionaries, the entire population sided with the strikers. The government felt itself isolated, betrayed by its customary supporters, and unsure of its troops.

THE CLIMAX

On October 16, throngs of striking workers invaded the center of St. Petersburg. Small groups moved in from the suburbs and merged gradually into large crowds. People converged to the place where they expected something important to happen.

It was Sunday. All the shops were closed. The trolleys ran in the morning but stopped before noon. The police had been removed from the streets. Droshkies disappeared; there was a rumor that strikers would cut the harnesses of hacks that disregarded the strike.

I found the University surrounded by soldiers, but the officer had been ordered to let students and professors go in. I tried to get in touch with the party organization, but all the wires were mixed up. Finally I learned that the speakers' group was to convene at the Free Economic Society, some two miles away.

In the absence of streetcars and droshkies, I walked there through streets full of workers milling about aimlessly in small groups. Files of Cossacks cut their way through the crowd. A company of foot soldiers beat time with their heavy boots. Another company stood motionless in front of a building. The crowd did not provoke the troops, and the troops did not molest the crowd. It looked as if Trepov was testing his forces.

Not far from the Free Economic Society, a group of workers recognized me. In a moment I was surrounded.

"It has come! Should we build a barricade?"

The street had been torn up for repair; plenty of tools and materials lay around. It would not be hard to barricade the street, but what good would it do and who would defend it?

I admonished the people around me, "Leave the stones alone. . . . Wait for the signal. . . . Do not fall into the trap. . . ."

In the library of the Free Economic Society some fifteen members of our group were sitting on bundles of books, windowsills, tables. Mikhail, a six-foot-six Bolshevist agitator, jumped toward me and grabbed my hand. "Have you seen?" he shouted. "Do you realize what is going on?" His face was livid.

"Shut up or speak sensibly," I replied angrily.

"There, on the street," he continued. "Have you seen?"

"I saw a lot of people . . . troops. . . . Nothing to get hysterical about."

A woman, half-lying on the table, began to wail, "About nothing, he says, about nothing! Blood will flow, by night thousands will be dead. We called them, we brought them into the streets."

"We are the murderers!" screamed Mikhail from the height of his six-feet-six. "Dear me, dear me!" voiced a thin soprano from the corner of the room.

I was so angry I could have slapped someone but, keeping control of my voice, I managed to say, "Ladies and gentlemen, excuse me for intruding. I did not know that a meeting of lunatics was being held here." I turned to the door, but Mikhail barred my way, screaming, "Who is a lunatic? What about the armed demonstrations you ordered for three o'clock?"

"What demonstration? Who ordered it?" resounded from different sides.

"Sergei Petrov ordered it," shouted Mikhail. "At the University."

My self-assurance collapsed. Those whom I had called "lunatics" looked at me with horror. In my confusion I did not notice the arrival of the youngest member of our group, Eugene Litkens. Although only a year younger than I, he looked like a mere boy and was very good at brief emotional harangues of crowds. He liked to go to meetings with me, and we often appeared as a team.

Now Eugene came to my rescue. "Nobody ordered an armed demonstration," he shouted. "But last night, while disbanding the University meetings, all the speakers invited workers to come back today with arms. We had to give the people something to make them leave the University in an orderly way, and this seemed the best thing we could think of."

"We are murderers," cried Mikhail.

"We are murderers," seconded the thin soprano.

Then I said, "I see that there will be no meeting of this group today. I am going back to the University. If things go wrong, nobody will reproach us for having brought the people into the streets while we ourselves remain in safety. Who will come with me?"

Eugene and Nikolai joined me. We hurried through side streets and were lucky in getting a droshky that took us to the quay not far from the University. The situation there was the same as in the center of the city—crowds of workers moving in both directions, detachments of soldiers beating time, files of riding Cossacks.

Almost at once, workers recognized me. "Why so late? People get tired of waiting! Time to begin!"

"We shall begin nothing today!" I declared firmly.

"But we were told last night . . ."

"The order has been repealed by the party. We are not ready."

"Why not? We did not come with empty hands," shouted a youth.

"Show me what you have."

The boys exhibited a couple of knives with fixed blades, short crowbars, an old pocket pistol. We inspected their arsenal and I declared, "Not enough! The order stands. We start nothing today!"

"What shall we do? Our people are here waiting for the signal."

"Tell them to go home. Do not fall into the trap of *provocateurs!*"

For two hours or more we walked back and forth on the quay, urging workers to go home, arguing with the obstinate, comforting those who seemed shocked by the manifestation of the party's weakness. We were happy to see that the crowd was becoming less dense.

Meanwhile the general strike had made further progress in St. Petersburg and in the province. On October 17, Trepov had sent troops to reopen the electric power stations and gas works, but the workers mixed up the switches and by night the capital was again plunged into darkness. To ease the situation, Trepov ordered bonfires at the crossings of main streets. These, however, gave little light, and the city looked as if a torch had been put to it at a hundred points. Then a powerful projector was placed on top of the Admiralty tower at the end of Nevsky Prospect, and a bright beam shot up in the sky. The streets became still darker by contrast, and the crowds greeted Trepov's comet with derision. The panic in conservative circles was increasing from hour to hour. Many people felt that the government had lost all control over the troops, and that power was falling into the hands of a bloodthirsty mob.

But the prevailing feeling in revolutionary circles was that the strike had been lost. The Workers' Committee—which by then had assumed the new name of the Workers' Soviet—tried to meet twice that day, but the first meeting place was surrounded by troops and at the second place police dispersed the delegates. Not until late at night did four score delegates get together in a women's college that, by some oversight, had not been taken over by the military. The mood of the delegates is reflected in their resolution:

Whereas the present strike is not local but all-Russian;

Whereas the struggle of the proletariat of Russia with Tsarism has reached the stage at which the general strike may bring the decisive blow to the shattered despotism; and

Whereas in many cities the tide of the worker movement is rising and the end of the strike in St. Petersburg might harm the all-Russian movement, the Soviet has decided to continue the strike.

A very weak resolution indeed! It implied that, as far as St. Petersburg was concerned, there was no point in continuing the strike, but local workers had to go on out of consideration for other cities.

I did not attend this meeting. Our group of speakers had assembled that night for a conference with representatives of the St.

Petersburg and Central Committees of both factions. The meeting was in a classroom of the Conservatory of Music. The representative of the Central Committee who came to bring us its decision was visibly embarrassed and meekly invited us to ask questions. Someone said, "We have only one question. For a month, following your instructions, we have called people to armed revolt. Where are our arms?"

"We have given you all we have," the committeeman replied.

"Thirty Brownings for self-defense? You are making fools of us. Where are the arms?"

"We have none. We hoped to get some, but the shipment was intercepted."

"Can we get weapons through the military organizations?"

"No. All the units with which we have connections have been disarmed."

"What about munitions shops?"

"The police have confiscated all their supply."

We had no further questions. One of us expressed the feelings of the group: "You have incited us and led us to incite others. You are responsible for a monstrous crime."

After a long silence, the committeeman said quietly, "The Central Committee realizes that the strike is lost. Mass arrests will probably begin tomorrow. Persons who spoke openly in the meetings will be taken first. The Central Committee has therefore decided to regroup all party workers, shifting everyone who has worked in St. Petersburg to the provinces. You are asked to alter your identity papers and, if possible, your appearance, and not to appear at any more public meetings."

Then all hell broke loose. I summarized the feelings of our group. "Give the Central Committee our answer. We consider your proposal cowardly and cynical, and a disgrace to the party. None of us will desert. We will keep on with our work. Is this unanimous, comrades?"

It was unanimous, indeed. The committeeman shrank like a deflated balloon.

"I shall transmit your decision," he mumbled. "The Central Committee does not insist. . . . Actually, this was just a tentative suggestion. . . . Since you feel this way . . ."

We left the dark and empty Conservatory after midnight. The broad plaza in front of the building was deserted. Vague voices came from the distance. The clouds reflected invisible bonfires. The night was chilly. . . . Comrades in battle and defeat, we shook hands and went our separate ways. No arrangement was made to meet again. It seemed to me then that nothing short of death could atone for our guilt of preaching an armed revolt when we had no weapons.

I tell this story not because the feelings of a handful of inexperienced youngsters deserve to be remembered fifty years later but because this was the night of October 17 to 18—the night the general strike had been won. The Tsar had capitulated.

THE MANIFESTO OF OCTOBER 17

I expected to be arrested that night but the police did not come. In the morning I went to the University to get in touch with the party. To avoid unpleasant encounters, I took a droshky. Overnight the streets had changed. All the shops were open. Small groups of people gathered at the street corners. Newsboys ran by, shouting, "Ukase of the Tsar!" I called a newsboy and got a copy of the Manifesto. It was vague in parts, and its end obviously contradicted its beginning, as if it had been written by two different persons. It announced that the Tsar, disturbed by the disorders among his beloved subjects, had decided to establish a constitutional regime. A State Duma would be elected by all the people, and in the future no law would be passed and the government would make no expenditure without its approval. The end of the autocratic regime in Russia, however, was announced in the old autocratic language as an expression of the supreme will of the Tsar, and his autocratic title was explicitly restated.

The Manifesto did not promise any immediate change in the government or say whether the Cabinet would be responsible to the Duma. The power of the latter was not clear. The pledge that no law would be passed without the Duma's approval did not necessarily mean that the Tsar and his ministers would respect the laws voted by the people's representatives. Furthermore, the promise of elections to the Duma by all the people could mean anything from an electoral law with equal rights for all to a system that would leave all the power in the hands of a privileged minority. In brief, the Manifesto, an outgrowth of panic in the ruling circles and a result of a compromise between the different groups around the throne, could be interpreted in many ways according to one's trust in the Tsar and his entourage.

Before the droshky reached the Neva quay, my mind was made up: the Manifesto was a fraud. Our job was to unmask it and carry on the offensive.

Students packed the entrance hall of the University mess. A lib-

eral professor stood on the staircase reading the Manifesto and com-
menting on it, point by point. Its vagueness did not discourage him.
This is how all great constitutions are born, he argued. The era of
despotism and revolutions is over, the nation has entered the stage
of constitutional development.

As soon as he finished, I took his place and asked the audience
whether they shared the speaker's confidence in the sincerity, honesty, and liberal intentions of the Tsar and his gang. Only those
who share such illusions, I said, could accept the professor's conclusions.

The great majority of the students were on my side. Somebody
shouted, "To the Plaza of Kazan!"

This was the name of a huge semicircle off the Nevsky Prospect,
the traditional setting for anti-governmental demonstrations. I immediately cut my speech short. "Yes, all who distrust the Tsar,
forward, to the Plaza of Kazan!"

The crowd moved toward Nevsky Prospect. More and more people
joined the procession. The streets were decorated with the white,
blue, and red national flag. People tore the white and blue stripes
from them, leaving only the red stripes fluttering in the air. Red flags
with revolutionary slogans appeared from nowhere over the crowd.
Turning toward Nevsky Prospect, we met another procession carrying tricolor flags and singing, "God save the Tsar!" Strangely
enough, the monarchists greeted us with a friendly "Hurrah!"

Kazan Plaza was crowded, but the crowd was not united. People
were coming and going. Three or four speakers were speaking at the
same time in different parts of the semicircle. The listeners were
confused and did not care much who spoke or what he said. Several
times a panic broke out. Somebody would shout, "The Cossacks!"
and the people would begin to run. I had the impression that the
panics were provoked deliberately.

A large crowd assembled on University Avenue. Speakers addressed it from the balcony of the University. All of them spoke
against the Manifesto. I ended my speech by tearing up the newspaper and throwing the pieces to the wind. The meeting was improvised in the University's main hall with the usual speakers in the
pulpit. There was no time to get in touch with the party centers and
each spoke for himself, but everyone denounced the government,
the Manifesto, and liberals who were ready to take it at face value.

The city was full of rumors of assaults by troops on demonstrations in industrial precincts. Several Putilov workers were killed. Not
far from the Polytechnic School a mounted patrol attacked the
passers-by, and Professor E. V. Tarle, the popular historian, among
others, was injured.

A crowd gathered in front of the Women's College, where the Executive Committee of the Soviet was in session, and demanded that it lead the procession to the prisons to liberate the political prisoners—an idea inspired by recollections of the storming of the Bastille in the French Revolution. But the Committee hesitated, fearing that the demonstration would end in bloodshed. Unable to dissuade the crowd, it appointed three men to head it. The trio, which included Trotsky, led the procession toward quiet streets far from the prisons and, after endless marching, dismissed the crowd with a warning not to fall into the trap of *provocateurs.*

In the evening, the Soviet convened in a schoolroom of the Women's College. This time some 250 deputies from 111 plants were present. Reports from the precincts were brief: Inspired by success, workers were ready to fight to a complete victory! The question was how to transform this enthusiasm into revolutionary action. The only weapon at the workers' disposal was the strike, and the Soviet was not certain how to use it. After long deliberation, it decided to continue the strike, which amounted to rejection of the Manifesto. The resolution, proposed by the Executive Committee and accepted unanimously without discussion, declared that the workers would not lay down their arms until a democratic republic, the first step toward socialism, was established. It ended with a pledge: "The strike will continue until circumstances call for a change in tactics." It was understood that the change could come in one of two ways—by resumption of work if the demands of the strikers were met, or by armed revolt if they were not.

AFTER THE MANIFESTO

The Soviet was at the zenith of its glory. The public credited it and the revolutionary parties with having organized and directed the strike that crushed the despotic regime.

The Soviet's meeting on October 19 opened with reports from the precincts. The workers were ready to strike until a democratic republic was established, Trepov removed, the Constituent Assembly convened, and hell froze. But the reports from other cities showed that the all-Russian general strike was losing strength. It was hard for the Soviet to call the workers back in view of the resolution it had passed only the day before. It therefore tried to explain the retreat by the argument that "the victorious workers must arm themselves for the final struggle for the democratically elected Constituent Assembly." The reference to arms slipped into the resolution in the same way as the call to an armed demonstration had slipped from my tongue when I urged the crowd to leave the University building.

On October 21, the day the workers went back to their jobs, the government announced a broad political amnesty. This added a note of triumph to the end of the strike. Thus we did not notice that the revolutionary wave had begun to recede at the hour of our victory—after the promulgation of the Manifesto.

In ordering the end of the strike, the Soviet instructed the deputies to organize factory meetings, and several hundred such meetings were held in the capital on October 20. In view of the shortage of speakers, some meetings were held in the morning, others in early afternoon or after five o'clock. On the morning of the twenty-first, before work was resumed, meetings were again called for pep talks. The following day was Saturday, and many plants asked popular speakers to address a factory gathering. Next came Sunday—an excellent occasion to let the liberated political prisoners appear in the industrial precincts.

During this long weekend, factory meetings took hold in St. Petersburg. The political climate of the city changed. During the period of University meetings, the workers and their favorite speakers had been in the limelight. Now political life in St. Petersburg split visibly. Radical slogans dominated the industrial precincts around the rim of the city, while the moderates took over the center, under the spotlight of the press.

This change coincided with a deep cleavage in political forces. The Manifesto of October 17 satisfied the conservatives who had joined the opposition toward the end of the Russo-Japanese War. It did not, however, equally satisfy the moderate liberals—a broad and heterogeneous group that traditionally included a large part of the intellectuals. They continued to distrust the government, but some of them distrusted the revolutionary parties even more. Some would have accepted the goal of a freely and democratically elected Constituent Assembly if it had not been associated with the ideas of armed revolt and a future struggle for socialism. All in all, the moderate liberals still represented a progressive force, but they no longer formed a united front with labor. Thus, very soon after the October strike, a vacuum began to develop around the Soviet.

At that time the factory meetings were my main interest. The crowd was more homogeneous in factories than at the University, and there was more order and decorum. Every plant had a permanent chairman, and some of these men were very able.

In the big mills, the meeting place was fixed by an agreement between the workers' delegates and the management. It usually had a high platform wrapped in red, with the factory's red banners, some of them very elaborate, with gilded fringes and tassels. There were no microphones, of course, and each speaker had to rely on his vocal cords. But I could reach the rear ranks of crowds of ten or even twenty thousand and did not complain of the acoustics. Best of all, I liked the meetings in workshops: long rows of lathes, a cobweb of transmission belts in the air, piles of iron sheets all around.

In some factories, meetings were held in the local church, amid icons, gilded crosses, banners with religious emblems, candles and hanging lamps that flickered along the walls. The speaker addressed the crowd from the elevation in front of the altar designed for the priest. The audience stood motionless, as if in prayer, catching every word. Many women workers considered the meeting in the church as a kind of public prayer, the only difference being that people were praying not for the Tsar, but against him. After one such meeting, a number of women workers surrounded me, and an old woman, in tears, assured me that I had performed the service as well as Father Alexander.

THE BOLSHEVIKS ATTACK THE SOVIET

The rise of the Soviet had come as rather an unpleasant surprise to the Bolsheviks in St. Petersburg. They were accustomed to think of two principal types of labor organization—political parties and trade unions. The latter were supposed to take care of the economic interests of workers while the party assumed political leadership. The Bolsheviks believed that they alone, in the long run, were entitled to represent labor in the political arena, but that now—because of infiltration of intellectuals and peasants into the labor movement— they were compelled temporarily to share this role with other groups, such as the Mensheviks and the S-R. Yet what right had the Soviet to speak in the name of St. Petersburg workers? Perhaps it could have a say in economic matters as a loose big union, but it was not qualified to make political decisions, issue political declarations, and, least of all, act as the mouthpiece of the revolution!

Furthermore, the Bolsheviks could not forget that the Soviet had been founded by the Mensheviks, who had succeeded in packing its Executive Board with their people. However, in the last days of the strike, our High Command reversed its policy. It recognized the Soviet, sent its official representatives to its Executive Board, and instructed its cells in the factories to campaign for the election of "reliable" candidates to the Soviet. At the same time, our group of meeting speakers was invited to attend the sessions of the Soviet and support its activities. We virtually became a part of the Soviet. Very soon a Bolshevist group was formed within the Soviet as its left wing, in opposition to the "opportunistic" majority in the Executive Board led by the Mensheviks. But this group was rather tame and showed no desire to follow blindly the directives of the Bolshevist High Command. Thus our "generals" remained somewhat suspicious not only of the Soviet but also of its Bolshevist faction and the Bolshevist meeting speakers who manifested more loyalty to the Soviet than to the mysterious Bolshevist Center.

Soon after the end of the strike, the Bolshevist party launched an attack against the Soviet. The issue was how the Soviet should pay homage to the Putilov workers whom Trepov's troops had killed on October 18. Originally the Soviet planned mass demonstrations on October 25, but Trepov issued an order forbidding street gatherings, threatening to suppress them by military force. The Bolsheviks considered these threats a bluff and insisted on the original plan, but moderate members of the Municipal Council persuaded the Soviet that Trepov was bent on bloodshed. With tears, almost genuflexions, they implored that the capital be spared, and the Soviet reluctantly agreed to substitute meetings at plants for processions through the streets.

On the morning of October 23, however, Trepov issued a new order. He would allow funeral processions on condition that they follow an agreed route. It was too late to revise the plans again, but the Bolshevist Center ordered its speakers at that day's meetings to move a resolution censuring the Soviet for its timid tactics. The workers applauded the criticism of the Soviet's decision but rejected the resolution of censure.

After this clash, the Bolshevist organization decided on a new strategy: First, to make the Soviet vote to follow the leadership of the S-D party, without raising the question of factions; next, to ask the Soviet to decide that, being a local St. Petersburg organization, it must accept political guidance from the St. Petersburg organization of the party; finally, to make it clear that the Social Democratic party was officially represented in St. Petersburg by the Bolshevist Committee.

This plan provoked violent opposition within the Soviet. The delegates accused the Bolshevist leaders of an attempt to blow up the organization. The official spokesman of the party, who happened to be a highly intelligent fellow, had to use all his diplomatic skill to mollify the delegates. Thereafter the relations between the majority of the Soviet and the Bolshevist faction remained strained, but this did not affect the group of meeting speakers. Most of the group felt that the Soviet was closer to the masses of workers, and therefore closer to the revolution, than to the party.

THE ORGANIZATION DRIVE

A drive toward labor-union organization of a European, mainly German, type had begun long before the general strike. The Mensheviks were particularly active and succeeded in organizing small groups in various plants and occupations. The movement gained a new momentum after the Manifesto. Now the organizers could work in the open; meetings could be called legally by the distribution of handbills; employers could not fire workers for such activities; rather, the president of a local union was recognized as the workers' spokesman not only by the management but also by the police. Some three or four score unions were organized in St. Petersburg after the general strike, and a Central Bureau was established to foster their further development.

I realized the importance of this drive but was too busy with factory meetings and general political propaganda to give it much time, though I went to unionization meetings, large and small, whenever I was called. Two episodes of this phase of my work remain fresh in my memory. In one case I was fairly successful; in the other, I failed completely.

One Sunday I was asked to speak at the inaugural meeting of the union of commercial employees, held in a theater. The audience was less responsive than in the factories, but I was impressed by the opening remarks of the chairman, a young store clerk. He had an insignificant appearance but sounded like a born orator. I had about an hour to speak on the aims of labor unions but proposed to talk for some twenty minutes and then turn the meeting over to him to present the grievances and aspirations of his colleagues.

The plan worked, and the chairman made a fine speech. The meeting ended with the election of a temporary board, with him as president. Then he asked that I be made a member of the board, as educational director and editor of the union's publications. His proposal was accepted with applause, and both of us were sent to the Central Bureau as representatives of the budding union. The union had only four or five thousand members at that time, but there were some two hundred thousand commercial employees in St. Petersburg, so potentially it represented a very large group. For the next two years, as long as I stayed in the capital, I remained in touch with this union.

My role in establishing the union of commercial employees unexpectedly brought me repute as a successful organizer, and I was not surprised when Anton, with a mysterious air, asked me to go with Nikolai to an organization meeting of police officers—a responsible and perhaps dangerous venture, he explained. Our contact man—a very small fellow, soft-spoken and beaming—met us at a municipal power station. He explained that the meeting was just beginning and that only the most progressively minded members of the police force would be there, not more than fifty in all. Then he led us to a wine cellar.

"Where are the police?" he asked the barman. The latter pointed across the street. We entered a suspicious-looking place, a combination of a tavern, rooming house, and I do not know what else. It seemed deserted. A waiter—or perhaps a bouncer—led us through endless shabby corridors and stairways. At last he stopped at a door and whispered, "This is the place!"

We entered a large room with a double bed and a long table covered with a white cloth. Around the table sat a score of men in police uniform, all with side arms, all with tense, immobile faces. Our guide introduced us: the comrades from the St. Petersburg Committee of the S-D party, Bolshevist faction.

The man at the head of the table said, "Take off your coats, gentlemen, and be seated."

After a minute of silence, a heavy police officer with a red face said to us, "Excuse us, gentlemen-strangers. My name is Safronov, senior inspector, Kolomna second precinct. Will you kindly give us your names and addresses?"

The man at the head of the table seemed annoyed. "This is sheer nonsense," he remarked. "We are not interested in the names of our guests." But Nikolai and I wrote our names and addresses on the back of a wine card and passed it around. The faces became more friendly, but the conversation dragged until Safronov said resolutely, "A business of such importance must begin with a drink!"

The suggestion was approved enthusiastically. A waiter was summoned, and Safronov again became the spokesman of the group. "Serve the best you have!" he ordered. "Tell the bar it is for the police! They will know!"

Four huge trays appeared on the table, one with bottles, another with glasses and plates, and two with platters of snacks. The meeting warmed up. The police officers proved worthy of their reputation as drinkers. Nikolai was second to none. My teetotalism was not noticed. When the animation reached its peak, the man at the head of the table, who drank with the others but remained perfectly sober, said, "This is enough. Now let us start. Report, please, Lissevich!"

A middle-aged officer with a narrow horse face adorned by a reddish mustache cleared his throat and began. The main complaint of the police officers, he said, was their low salaries, incompatible with their dignity. They were compelled to accept gratuities, which discredited their profession in the eyes of a public that was not always able to distinguish between gratuities and bribes.

"The best brains in the service," Lissevich reported, "have decided that something must be done to raise our salaries. But we do not know how to begin. Should we organize a union or elect a Soviet or present a petition to the general? This is why we called this meeting. Now, gentlemen-strangers, we want your advice."

I replied that police officers, like any other group of private or public employees, had a right to organize. "Unions of police officers exist in Europe. Why not set up one in St. Petersburg?"

The meeting drank to my health, and Lissevich continued. The police officers had other grievances, too. They wanted changes in their uniform (to make it like that of army officers), promotion according to seniority, election of superior officers by all respectable members of the force, and so on. I wrote down their demands and offered to draft an appeal to all members of the police force to join the union.

The man at the head of the table got up, approached me, and whispered in my ear, "Go ahead. They are smarter than they look. Add a preamble about the role of the police in a democratic state." His eyes were twinkling, and it was obvious that he was a white crow in the police department.

I followed his advice and offered still another plank for the platform—that the police of the capital should be controlled by the democratically elected Municipal Council and freed of political functions, such as search, seizure, and arrests.

The resolution was accepted unanimously as the platform of the new union and the basis for a petition to the general—that is, to Trepov, whose name, out of respect for him, was never mentioned. The occasion called for a celebration. At a wink from Safronov, the empty bottles were replaced by a new array, and the meeting ended in a most friendly spirit. In fact, except for the presiding officer and me, the group was so drunk that, just to please us, they would have signed anything.

With Nikolai in tow, I left the founders of the new union to discuss their problems among themselves and went to the University. When I got home after midnight my mother met me with alarm. "Two police officers have been asking for you." "Order of arrest?" "No, but they looked frightened when they could not find you and waited for you for some time. Then they went away, leaving a note for you."

I opened the envelope. The message was written on a form for collecting fees for dog tags. It said: "Mr. Stranger. For the Lord's sake, do not tell anybody or write in the newspapers about what happened among us. Otherwise we shall all be lost. Respectfully yours, Safronov, Lissevich."

EIGHT HOURS A DAY!

The October strike was followed in St. Petersburg by the outbreak of a spontaneous campaign for the eight-hour working day. Without presenting a formal demand for a shorter workday, workers in some factories voted to work only eight hours instead of the customary ten. The men would report as usual in the morning, recess at noon, resume work with the factory whistle, and, after working eight hours in all, lay down the tools and leave the plant. This arrangement was described as a revolutionary introduction of the eight-hour working day. Technically, however, each working day ended in a walkout. The management countered this move by paying piece workers at the old rates and crediting time workers with four-fifths of their daily wage.

Thus the workers faced the choice of taking a twenty per cent cut in earnings or fighting for higher wage rates. At the factory meetings they asked the party speakers for advice. The only advice we could give was to refer the question to the Soviet. The latter, however, was not ready to handle the situation. A strike committee, elected by factory meetings and itself imbued with the spirit of these meetings, it could not explain to the workers that a temporary suspension of the political strike did not offer a proper opportunity to launch an economic offensive. At the beginning, many delegates in the Soviet doubted whether hours of work could be reduced by the one-sided decision of a factory meeting, but they soon fell under the spell of the general revolutionary psychology.

When the Soviet met on October 29, its agenda did not include the length of the work day. The meeting was called because of rumors that General Trepov was cooking up another pogrom. As usual, the meeting opened with reports. One after another, delegates reported on their progress in reducing hours of work. Some plants were lagging but complete victory was near! In this mood, the Soviet voted a resolution praising factories that had cut their work hours and ordering all workers in the capital to join the movement and to ask for higher wage rates.

There were no dissenting votes, but after the chairman had announced the unanimous decision, a distressed voice spoke from the rear of the hall. "What have we done, comrades? The struggle with Tsarism is not yet won, and we are starting the fight against capitalism!" I, too, felt uneasy but forgot my doubts when the Soviet passed on to the main item on the agenda: the threat of a pogrom in St. Petersburg.

THE AVERTED POGROM

At that time a wave of pogroms was rolling through Russia. In contrast to the anti-Jewish pogroms of Pleve, these were directed mainly against the intellectuals. Though monarchistic traditions had generally faded during the latter part of the Russo-Japanese War, they survived in some groups of the population and gained new strength after the Manifesto. Middle-class persons were afraid of the revolution and tired of strikes. The police fostered the organization of underworld characters into "The Black Hundreds" as a spearhead of a "patriotic movement," and provided them with knives, torches, and plain-clothes agents as leaders.

The wave of violence had not reached St. Petersburg, but in the second half of October rumors spread that Trepov was about to stage a bloody pogrom in the capital. Lists of persons reputedly earmarked for assassination were circulated. Some of them contained names of well-known liberal professors, journalists, and lawyers, while others included the leaders of the Soviet and leftist groups. One list featured the meeting speakers.

The Municipal Council, alarmed by insistent rumors that a pogrom was set for Sunday, October 30, sent a deputation to the Military Governor. General Trepov did not deny the rumors but declared bluntly that true Russians, faithful to religion, motherland, and the Tsar, exasperated by the behavior of students, Jews, and Socialists, were entitled to express their feelings. The members of the delegation reported Trepov's words to the Executive Board of the Soviet as confirmation of rumors of an imminent pogrom. The Board sent notices to all mills and factories and called a meeting of the Soviet for the evening of the twenty-ninth.

Before the Soviet met, however, the precincts took the matter into their own hands. A call went out to marshal defense commandos. Since firearms were lacking, the workers were to carry knives, crossbars, bludgeons, and pikes. The Neva precinct became the arsenal of democracy. Carloads of these weapons were sent to other parts of the city, armed commandos were posted at strategic points, and liaison service was established. By the evening of October 29, some twelve thousand armed workers were ready to meet Trepov's gangs. Only a few hundred had pistols and hunting guns, but all workers had been alerted to go into the streets at the signal. Samples of bludgeons, daggers, and knives were displayed at the session of the Soviet and each factory reported on its enrollment. It was clear that, unless Trepov sent regular troops to assault the city openly, as some provincial satraps had, the workers would stamp out any attack by the police and their Black Hundreds.

No pogrom was attempted on the day set for it. Later, the government denied that it had planned one. Any doubt, however, was dispelled at the trial of the members of the Soviet, after the revolution failed. Since the Soviet was accused of having armed workers, the defense asked to have officers of the St. Petersburg police and Municipal Council called as witnesses to prove that the workers, with their makeshift arms, had frustrated the planned pogrom. By rejecting this request, the government confessed its guilt.

Prevention of the pogrom added to the prestige of the Soviet, which was sagging under the hopeless campaign for the eight-hour day, but just at that time most serious trouble broke out at the gate of the capital, in Kronstadt, a naval fortress on the island of Kotlin.

REVOLT IN KRONSTADT

Unrest had been fermenting among Kronstadt sailors since the summer of 1905. It was rooted in the inhuman treatment of the sailors, their distrust of their officers, the destruction of the Baltic fleet at Tsushima, and rumors about the freedom the Tsar had accorded the people. The discontent came into the open on October 23, when a crowd of sailors assembled in Yakor Plaza, the central square of the city, and decided to present a petition to the Tsar. The petition was put together in a most primitive way. Somebody would jump on the improvised stand and shout, "Make them pay us more!" Another would support him. "Six rubles a month." The crowd would roar approval, and both proposals would be included in the petition. Thus a list of demands was concocted, complete with a plank on unrestricted sale of liquor in the barracks. As the meeting warmed up, political demands were added—freedom for all and government by the people.

So far this was just another meeting, and the military authorities did not pay much attention to it. But, three days later, a marine battalion refused to eat wormy pork. By evening, some of the marines had been arrested and sent to the military prison. A crowd of soldiers and sailors stopped the vans, overpowered the guards, and liberated the prisoners. This incident became the signal for revolt of the entire garrison. Military policemen were disarmed and officers were put under arrest. The rebels, however, did not think of communicating with the St. Petersburg Soviet or of getting ready to defend themselves.

Then the government launched a counteroffensive. Early in the morning, bands of local underworld characters led by plain-clothes policemen broke into liquor stores in different parts of Kronstadt. Barrels of vodka were rolled out into the streets. Attracted by the free treat, sailors joined the crowds in a drunken debauch. The city was in a state of anarchy when Trepov's crack troops landed on Kotlin. The sailors put up no resistance, and by night the city and the fortress were again under the government's control. Several hundred alleged ringleaders were brought before courts-martial. Rumors reached St. Petersburg that the death penalty awaited them all.

The liberal press viewed these events with fastidious disgust, but the workers' reaction was different. They sympathized with the sailors of Kronstadt.

"A foolish thing, this petition to the Tsar! But were we much wiser on January 9?"

"A disgrace to drink free vodka in the streets! But those who offered it are worse than those who drank."

Ready to forget the brawl-and-pogrom aspect of the affair and to consider it as a political revolt, St. Petersburg workers were shocked by the rumors that the sailors might face the firing squad. Before the revolutionary parties could grasp the meaning of the events, the workers made up their minds: by defending the sailors of Kronstadt, they would show all men in the armed forces that the workers were their brothers.

On October 30 and 31, scores of factory meetings adopted resolutions demanding release of their Kronstadt comrades and threatening to strike in support of this demand. A call would come to our group of meeting speakers: "Such and such mills are holding meetings. Send speakers." We would distribute our forces so as to permit the more efficient speakers to cover three or four factories not far apart. There was no time to discuss what we would say or to prepare resolutions.

The factory meetings those days were particularly solemn. Standards and emblems of the defense commandos were added to the customary factory banners. The factory chairman would show the speaker the draft of the resolution and say, "This is how the people here feel." And we would explain the resolution to the crowd and put it to a vote.

On November 1, the Soviet met to discuss the situation. The report on the events in Kronstadt was presented by an undersized youth in a sailor's uniform, with a pale face, blinking eyes, and a flat voice. He did not try to embellish the picture or defend his comrades; he simply asked the workers to help them. He ended his story: "This is what happened. Now they will shoot us. You alone can help."

The speeches were brief, and the Soviet passed a resolution declaring a general strike as an expression of the solidarity of St. Petersburg workers with the sailors of Kronstadt. The strike was to begin the next day and was expected to develop into a new general strike throughout Russia. Along with support of the Kronstadt sailors, it was to express the protest of the workers against the introduction of martial law in Poland. Actually, the St. Petersburg workers were striking for Kronstadt as an issue close to them, but the reference to Poland served to stress the broad, national character of the movement.

THE SECOND GENERAL STRIKE

The strike started briskly. I spent the morning of November 2 at the Putilov mills. Their delegates had asked me to attend the meeting, explain the decision of the Soviet to the workers, and help to stop work in a shop that had not joined the general strike in October—a huge boilershop manned by husky unskilled laborers from remote villages. Traditionally, each foreman in that shop recruited men for his team in the village where he had been born. Relations in the shop were paternalistic, and the bearded boilermakers did not mix with other workers.

After the general meeting, the factory committee met to discuss the situation in the boilershop. Some of its members were critical of the delegates who had asked me to handle the dissenting shop. "What will you say to these ruffians? When one addresses them as 'comrades,' they answer, 'The wolf is your comrade.' They threaten to throw the first speaker who comes to their shop into the furnace. We ought to send them our boys with bolts and nuts." And the committee assigned a commando armed with pistols and bolts to accompany me to the entrance of the shop as a precautionary measure.

Work in the boilershop was in full swing. The air was full of the deafening noise of hundreds of hammers. Nobody answered my greeting. Trying to look as self-confident as possible, I walked the whole length of the shop. Near the wall opposite the entrance was a flat, fairly high boiler. I climbed on it, using smaller pieces around it as a ladder, and stood there in full sight of the commando behind the entrance door. A few bearded men approached my stand, and one of them asked me menacingly:

"What is your business here, mister? Who sent you?"

"That is precisely what I want to explain to you, my friend," I replied.

"We don't need your explanations, mister. Get out before something happens to you."

The group in front of the boiler was increasing and the noise of hammers became louder and louder.

"You, hammerers!" I shouted. "Keep quiet for a moment. People here are asking questions and can't hear what I tell them."

The noise gradually subsided. Now all the men turned toward my stand, and I felt their open hostility. An elderly worker said, "We don't want to listen to your nonsense, but since you come here alone you may speak your piece. Whatever you say, we will not strike."

"That is up to you," I answered. "I shall tell you what I came for and then you will do as you please."

When I finished, a youth jumped on a lathe not far from my boiler and shouted, "The other time they did not tell us about the strike. All they did was to curse, although we are no more Black Hundreds than those wise guys with their bolts and nuts."

I reminded the boilermakers of their threat to throw the Soviet speaker into a furnace. Some laughed, others seemed embarrassed. A man with a bushy black beard remarked that the men on the factory committee had no business telling a stranger about such silly threats. Indeed, nobody intended to do me any harm.

The meeting ended in a unanimous decision to join the strike as a demonstration of the unity of boilermakers with other workers of St. Petersburg.

On the evening of November 2, the Soviet convened to receive reports. The strike seemed to be a complete success.

On November 3, the Soviet met again, this time in the gilded hall of the Free Economic Society. All the reports told of the high spirit among the workers. The chairman read the appeal wired by Sergei Y. Witte, president of the Council of Ministers, to each striking factory:

"Brother workers! Go back to work, cease to make trouble, have pity on your wives and children, do not listen to bad advice. . . ."

At that time many people credited Witte with the reforms announced in the Manifesto. For the workers, however, he was just another minister of the hated Tsar. His appeal to "brother workers" introduced a note of hilarity into the situation. Replying to him, the Soviet began with an expression of surprise at the arrogance of the Tsar's favorite who dared to address the workers as his "brothers," although he knew well enough they were not his relatives. Witte's message was read in factory meetings on November 4, and some of these added spicy words to the Soviet's reply. Workers of a plant that had not walked out on November 2 announced their decision to join the strike by a resolution that said: "We have read Witte's appeal and decided to strike." This exchange brightened the day and made the workers forget their increasing difficulties for a time.

The strike did not spread beyond St. Petersburg. This would not have been alarming if the walkout had been handled as a local affair from the beginning, but, since it had been presented by the Soviet as the curtain raiser for a new national strike, its success had to be measured by the response in other cities, and that was nil.

In some cities, the workers had not recovered economically since the October strike; in others, they had been terrorized by the Black Hundreds. Newspapers that had supported the first general strike were violently opposed to the second. The issue at stake was not made clear to the public, and many people did not know whether workers were demonstrating against the trial of the sailors or intended to continue the strike until the prisoners were released. In St. Petersburg itself, the strike was practically general in industrial precincts but did not extend to the railroads, post office, public utilities, and professions. There was no indication of response in the army barracks.

On November 4, the moderate leaders of the Soviet advised handling the whole affair as a demonstration of protest and calling the workers back, but the majority in the Soviet rejected this proposal.

I spent the next day in the Narva precinct, which included the Putilov mills. Factory gates, fences, and the walls of private houses were plastered with fresh announcements. Knots of men stood in front of them. The management of the Putilov mills and several other establishments announced that all workers who did not return to work immediately would be fired. A dozen plants announced that, in view of the continuing labor unrest, they had decided to shut down. At the same time, the government explained to the public that the Kronstadt sailors were to be tried only for disorderly conduct and were not threatened with the death penalty. It was clear, however, that the pressure of the strike had forced the government to abandon its original plan for bloody retribution. If the death penalty had not been considered, the government would have used this argument at the beginning of the strike. Newspapers, however, tried to persuade the public that the Soviet had engineered the strike under false pretenses.

On November 5, the Soviet decided to end the strike at noon on November 7. To avoid a depressing effect of this decision on the morale of the workers, the resolution called on them to increase revolutionary propaganda in the army and to start at once to prepare for an armed revolt, the decisive battle against moribund despotism.

Again I went from factory to factory, explaining the resolution, urging workers to go back to their jobs, trying to bolster their courage. For the first time, I was speaking out of loyalty to the Soviet and the party rather than from personal conviction. I was exhausted from the endless speeches, and it seemed to me the crowds that shouted approval were equally tired and disillusioned.

The moderate and conservative newspapers were right in holding that the November strike was a defeat of the workers and a victory for the government, but they were wrong in blaming the Soviet and revolutionary parties for having instigated the walkout. They were also unfair in reproaching them for their attempt to involve the armed forces in politics. The army had been in the midst of the conflict since October; indeed, the political struggle had long since developed into a contest for control over the army. The anti-labor slant in the press during and after the November strike caused bitter resentment among the workers. They felt more isolated than ever.

THE STALEMATE

The iron and steel mills, shipyards, and munitions factories owned or operated by the government remained shut after the strike. Many private plants also were closed because of cancellation of military orders when the war with Japan ended. The police and military patrols reappeared in industrial precincts. Employers were ordered to put an end to factory meetings.

On November 9, without consulting the Soviet, the workers of a leading plant in the Neva precinct issued an appeal to all St. Petersburg workers to declare a general strike against the lockouts. I went to the factory, talked to the leaders and rank-and-file workers, and learned that this was an act of despair and collective hysteria.

The Soviet convened on November 12. The main items on the agenda were lockouts, rising unemployment, and the continuing campaign for the eight-hour day and higher wage rates. A woman worker from a cotton mill kindled enthusiasm in the audience by appealing passionately to the men to fight to full victory or death. "All of you," she explained, "are accustomed to a soft life! You are afraid of the hardships of struggle and the threat of a lockout. But we women are tired of our present life and prefer death to slavery!" Yet the reports of the delegates were discouraging. The workers were at an impasse, losing confidence in themselves and in the So-

viet. After a long discussion, the Soviet decided to give up the struggle for the eight-hour workday. This was an unambiguous recognition of defeat.

The sober resolution moved by the Executive Committee was free
from the customary revolutionary phraseology. It declared that re-
duction of hours of work was a national problem and could not be
solved by the St. Petersburg workers alone against the united forces
of employers and government, and it urged the workers to abstain
from offhand actions. Where working hours had been reduced, the
gain should be maintained. Individual plants that had not been able
to obtain concessions from the employer could continue the campaign at their own risk. A general offensive had to be postponed.

The lockout spread. Each day brought new layoffs. Shops that
were at the forefront in the October and November strikes closed
first. Factory meetings became rare. Instead, endless conferences
were held in search of an answer to the question: How could the
workers compel an employer to resume operations or rehire the
laid-off employees?

The Soviet convened again on November 13. Some delegates
demanded a new strike. The great majority were against it. It was
decided to issue an appeal to the public—a tactic of the liberals that
the leftist parties had frequently ridiculed! The Soviet was losing
ground. The activity of the Executive Committee was reduced to
the distribution of relief. Small amounts were handed out to individual workers on the recommendation of factory delegates. Endless
files of applicants besieged the headquarters.

Yet the revolution had not been crushed. On November 13, a
revolt of sailors broke out in Sebastopol on the Black Sea. Lieutenant Peter P. Shmidt, an idealist with moderate rather than revolutionary leanings, was proclaimed High Commander of the Black Sea
fleet. If this revolt had come two weeks earlier, during the November strike in St. Petersburg, it might have been supported by masses
of people all over Russia and have ended in the final victory of the
revolution. But it came too late, when the movement in St. Petersburg was at its low ebb, and workers in Moscow and other large
cities were smarting from the humiliation of having been unable to
support St. Petersburg and Kronstadt. The Sebastopol revolt was
put down promptly, and Lieutenant Shmidt, who had used all his
temporary authority to prevent bloodshed in the fleet and had saved
the lives of hundreds of naval officers, was seized and executed.

The Executive Committee of the Soviet tried desperately to establish contacts with Moscow, the unions of railroad and post and
telegraph employees, and, most of all, with the peasant unions that
were emerging in different parts of Russia. It was too late, however.

The St. Petersburg Soviet itself had ceased to be the center of attraction for progressive forces of the nation.

THE GREAT ENIGMA

Thinking about the forces that opposed one another in the revolution, we came again and again to the great enigma of Russian life—the peasants.

Many people in America and Europe believe that the peasants in prerevolutionary Russia were a submissive, illiterate mass, half-serf, half-savage. This is how they have been described by Communist propagandists and the official historians of the U.S.S.R. Russia's great literature, from Pushkin to Nekrasov, Turgenev, Tolstoy, and Dostoevsky, gives a completely different picture, with some tendency to idealize the moral integrity, spirit of unity, common sense, and dignity of hard-working tillers of the soil, the breadwinners and defenders of the nation.

Living conditions in Russian villages were primitive and the people were poor, but this was not the poverty of farmers in India and the Near East or of peons in Latin America. Even a poor peasant usually had a two-room log cottage (*izba*) with a barn, stable, and other outdoor facilities, a horse or two, and a cow. Not all of them could read and write, but rural education was improving and in some regions nearly every village child received four years of schooling. Sanitary conditions and health services were unsatisfactory, but certainly much better than they are in many underdeveloped areas of the world today. The *izbas* were reasonably clean, and city people did not hesitate to spend a night there, if necessary on the floor, or to drink water from the village well or share a peasant's meal.

There was also a tradition of communal life and self-government in the villages. All in all, the Russian muzhik of 1905 had more of a feeling of independence and was, in many respects, more of a citizen of his country than the inhabitants of the Soviet realm are now. Yet the political attitude of the majority of villagers was an enigma to us at that time.

Agrarian unrest was spreading in the Volga region. The peasants in a village would come together and declare that privately owned land, with the livestock, implements, and stores, belonged to those who worked it. If peasants farmed the land—the predominant use of private land in Russia at that time—a delegation was sent to the landowners. Those who agreed to sign deeds transferring their land to the community were permitted to stay in their mansions; those who did not were ordered to leave. If they disobeyed, their mansions were set on fire. Large estates operated with hired labor were divided among the peasants—not only the land, but also the live-stock, machinery, and other property. Office buildings were burned down.

The movement was spontaneous. The peasants realized, of course, that they were acting against the law, but they considered the laws protecting the landowners unjust and believed that they could get away with breaking them. The "Red Rooster," as they called the burning of landlords' mansions, was flying over the country.

It looked as if all rural Russia was in revolt. But cruel reprisals followed the Red Rooster. Villages guilty of riots were surrounded by troops and the peasants were flogged or shot in front of the vil-lage church. No village resisted. In many places, the peasants met troops on their knees at the entrance of the village, the headman offering a tray of bread and salt to the commanding officer. But un-rest put down in one place broke out in another a few days later.

An all-Russian peasant convention met in Moscow. It was domi-nated by the S-R, but the public was not sure whether the conven-tion represented a cross-section of Russian villages or only a thin layer of rural intellectuals—schoolteachers, agronomists, statisticians of local governments (zemstvos). The workers in St. Petersburg, most of them sons of peasants, firmly believed that the muzhiks would rise against the Tsar. I shared this faith, but I could not visu-alize the common action of villages and cities in the last and deci-sive phase of the revolution. Would the villagers revolt against the government and repulse the troops sent against them? Would the muzhiks seize the railroads and invade the cities? Or would the peas-ants' joining the revolution result in the disintegration of the Tsar-ist army? The village lived its own life, followed its own road. Where did this road lead?

History has supplied the answer. The Russian village then was a house divided against itself. The majority of the people were proba-bly on the side of the revolution, as they later proved repeatedly by their votes. But small groups were devoted to the existing regime, vehemently opposed to new ideas from the cities, frightened by un-folding revolutionary events. And, since there was no unity in revo-lutionary forces, the minority was going to win. This is hindsight, however. In November, 1905, I felt about the Russian village as I had felt about the labor movement after January 9. I believed the decisive battle of the revolution would be fought in the village, and I wanted to be there at that fateful hour.

AMONG SCHOOLTEACHERS

On November 19, the Soviet met to discuss the all-Russian strike of the post and telegraph employees. More than a hundred thousand employees scattered throughout the country were involved. They demanded higher wages, shorter working hours, change in the order of promotion, and so on, but the walkout also had a political undertone as a strike against the government.

The walkout was well organized but poorly timed. The post and telegraph employees could easily have obtained improvements in their working conditions immediately after the October strike, but their chances became slim after the government had crushed the revolts in Kronstadt and Sebastopol. The leaders of the walkout had not consulted the Soviet in advance and asked for its help only after the strike had begun.

The Soviet was eager to do something. Even a partial success of the strike would be a political gain. But what more could it do than vote a resolution, send a telegram of sympathy to the strikers, and issue an appeal?

This was the last meeting of the Soviet I attended. I remember the beautiful hall of the Free Economic Society, the grim faces of the delegates, the speeches marked by hesitation and doubt. I sat against the wall at the rear of the hall, my eyes closed, painfully feeling the futility of words. Someone took the chair beside me and whispered in my ear:

"It is becoming dull here, isn't it?"

I recognized Eugene Litken's voice and said, "Things may change."

"Not here. Come with me, I have something for you."

In the library, Eugene told me he had met that morning, at party headquarters, a schoolteacher sent to St. Petersburg from a district of the department of Novgorod. The teachers of the district were holding a convention and planning to organize a union and asked the party for help and advice.

"Let us go there together," Eugene proposed.

"When and where is the convention?"

"It will open tomorrow morning—the place is six hours by train, on the St. Petersburg-Moscow line. We can still catch the train."

I sent a note to my mother telling her I would not be home that and the following nights, and two hours later we sat in a railroad coach full of young workers who had lost their jobs in St. Petersburg and were going to a factory not far from Moscow. They were in high spirits, sang revolutionary songs, and seemed to have no worries.

The address the schoolteacher had given to Eugene read: "Station

Borovenka, 212 versts from St. Petersburg, Chorino school, ask for the teacher."

We left the train at Borovenka. A long platform, a few railroad buildings along it, a road flanked by snowdrifts around the station, rolling fields buried under snow and crisscrossed by delicately etched fences. No village in sight. The stationmaster with the traditional red cap, the watchman, and the gendarme who had met the train disappeared as soon as it pulled out. As we looked around, we saw a small country sleigh in front of the station. The driver came toward us, a little man in a yellow sheepskin coat and felt boots, his face hidden behind the icicles hanging from his fur hat and bushy eyebrows.

"I guess you are strangers here?" he asked us. "Maybe from afar? Say, from St. Petersburg?" And before we could answer, he continued, "If you are looking for the Chorino school, you must be the people for whom I am waiting. Lazar is my name."

Lazar helped us into the sleigh, covered us with fresh hay, took the coachman's seat, and continued to talk. "Last night, Thomas, our teacher, told me that people from St. Petersburg were coming. They do not know our place, he said, so will you bring them here from the station? And I said, they must be fine people to travel all the distance from St. Petersburg to our village. And so I froze here all night waiting for you." He laughed happily.

The road ran downhill. Three score small log houses flanked it deep in the valley, forming a tiny hamlet. "Borovenka," Lazar explained. "Funny people, those living here. To look at them, they are muzhiks, but they like long rubles from the railroad better than their fields."

The road began to rise, winding between hills covered with snow, with patches of woodland here and there and clusters of log cabins so small and so neatly traced against the snow that they seemed unreal. The horse was all silver under its red shaft bow; the sleigh floated like a boat in an ocean of blue and white. Not a soul was about except Lazar and the two of us. Lying on fragrant hay, we listened to our driver. Now he was telling us about the teacher: a learned man but not proud, always siding with simple people. On his advice the community had subscribed to a newspaper, a good one, that also sided with the poor.

Chorino was considerably larger than Borovenka. It had a modest church, in front of which was the school building, as large as two peasant *izbas* put together. The teacher's house, across the street, was almost as large.

The teacher met us on the porch—a young man, powerfully built, with a broad smile on his ruddy face. His house consisted of a large living room, a tiny bedroom, and a kitchen. The living room was full: a score of young boys in dark coats over bright Russian shirts, their trousers pushed into shining boots; a half-dozen neatly and modestly dressed girls, in white blouses and dark skirts; a few elderly men. Thomas introduced us to a man with a gray beard, a bald skull, and mild, intelligent eyes—Sokolov, dean of the local schoolteachers and initiator of the convention. The young faces around us were flushed after a long ride in the cold, the young voices too loud for the room. Everybody was speaking and laughing at the same time. More and more sleighs arrived. Thomas clapped his hands and declared the convention open. Sokolov, elected chairman, read the agenda: (1) The objective of the schoolteachers' union; (2) its relation to political parties; (3) the plan of work. Then he turned the meeting over to Eugene and me.

We spoke about the need for unity and the organization drive in St. Petersburg and all over Russia. Next the teachers asked us to tell them more about the first general strike, the St. Petersburg Soviet, the Manifesto, the Kronstadt revolt, and revolutionary prospects. The convention warmed up.

During my speech, Lazar and half a dozen elderly peasants appeared in the room. After conferring with them, Thomas suggested a recess for refreshments. His words were met with loud laughter. "Where are your refreshments, Thomas? Your oven is cold." Thomas laughed with the others.

"My refreshments wouldn't amount to much," he said, "but these friends of mine have just told me that you are all guests of the community. They ask you to their homes to break bread with them." The peasants confirmed the invitation by deep bows.

The village, glittering under the snow and sun, seemed a fairy· land. The peasants in heavy coats led their guests to their homes. Eugene and I followed Lazar. His log house was not big, but it was solidly built and well kept. Some fifteen persons, old and young, sat at the long table. The meal was festive and plentiful: a big cabbage pie, cabbage soup with pieces of meat, a thin cranberry pudding. Lazar and his eldest son, a bearded, broad-shouldered man with sharp eyes, led the conversation. They asked us whether new strikes were in sight and how soon the soldiers would come home from Manchuria. We questioned them about the political views of the peasants. Lazar's answer was vague. "That depends. . . . Each village is different. Some follow the teacher; others, the priest." He sighed deeply. "It would have been better but for the strike." Noticing our surprise, he added mildly, "Sure enough, you meant well in the city. Thomas explained to us: a strike helps simple people. But for us, the muzhiks, not every strike is good. When a factory or post strikes, we do not mind. The railroad is different. A muzhik drives all the night to take his produce to the station—no train. The muzhik asks the gendarme, 'When will the train come?' And the gendarme knows the answer. 'Ask the strikers. They have stopped the trains. Wait till tomorrow!' The muzhik waits the whole day and tomorrow it's the same story." And he concluded, "Much harm came from the strike."

After the recess, the convention continued. The Mensheviks from Novgorod joined the meeting—a big, bearded agronomist, Zaloga, and a young clerk, Alexander. The afternoon session opened with a discussion of the relationship between professional unions and the S-D party. The teachers decided to organize a non-partisan professional union with an S-D cell within it. All the members of the convention would join both the union and the cell. Then came the last point of the agenda: What should the union do? Sokolov expressed the feelings of the meeting: "Our first task is not to seek advantages for ourselves but to promote the freedom and happiness of our motherland, Russia."

It was getting dark. Thomas lit a candle on the chairman's table. It gave a small circle of light, leaving the rest of the room in darkness. Expanses of shining snow could be seen through the windows.

Eugene spoke about the importance of revolutionary work by schoolteachers in the villages. Each teacher must be a crusader, a leader, the head of a village commando in the forthcoming national revolt! At my side a girl teacher whispered to another, "Look, isn't he like Archangel Mikhail on the icon?" After his speech the convention voted a resolution calling on all schoolteachers to start at once to organize revolutionary meetings in villages, and after a few cordial words the chairman declared the convention closed.

Thomas asked us if we were too tired for another meeting. We assured him that we felt wonderful after our day with the teachers. "Then I shall call a meeting in the school," he said. "Nobody has gone to bed in the village, everyone is waiting for something. . . . Lazar, will you tell the people that the teacher is inviting everybody to the school?"

"Everybody?" Lazar asked. "Women too?"

"Men and women!" Thomas confirmed. "Young and old! Even the old people who prefer the church to the school," he added teasingly.

"Don't worry," Lazar laughed. "The old won't lag behind the young." Through the window, we saw him talking with a group of peasants in front of the teacher's house and directing them toward the school.

THE OATH

The classroom was almost completely dark. The candle on the teacher's square desk under the icon gave just enough light to see the men in the front row. They were all in heavy sheepskin coats, open at the neck, their gray beards lost in the grayness of the fur. Bushy eyebrows, knotty hands that looked as if they were covered with bark. Unblinking eyes, neither friendly nor hostile.

I could not see the faces of the younger people sitting and standing in the rear. Women pressed along the walls and in the aisle between the benches. Many teachers had remained for the meeting, to learn from us how to preach revolution to the peasants.

Thomas opened the meeting by introducing us. "These people came from St. Petersburg to help us," he said. "You may trust them."

I spoke about the progress of the revolution, falling unconsciously into the style I had used in the church meetings in St. Petersburg. The audience was silent, the faces of the old men in the front row revealing nothing.

Then Eugene talked about the teachers' convention. The audience seemed uninterested. Eugene shifted somehow to the war and the privations of soldiers in the Far East. Why were they sent so far from their homes? He described the trains with recruits in the early days of the war, the weeping women on the platforms, mothers running after the trains along the rail tracks. . . .

Sobs and laments came from the darkness. The old men in the front rows threw disapproving looks toward the rear. Eugene went on, "How many boys came back crippled for the rest of their lives? How many were buried in foreign soil? Will you ever see the loved ones for whom you are still waiting?" Laments became louder, and the old men no longer tried to stop them. I saw tears on some weathered faces in the front row.

"Did the people start this war?" Eugene asked. "Did anybody ask you, the people of Russia, whether you wanted this war? How many other wars will come if the fate of the nation depends on the whims of a single weak-minded man?" And then he concluded, "To insure peace, the people must be the masters of their destiny."

After a brief silence one of the old men said firmly, "That is true." The ice was broken. Everyone spoke at once. In the flickering light of the candle I scribbled a resolution. Thomas, to whom I showed it, whispered to me, "Make it a decision of the community."

I changed a few words at the beginning and, when the noise began to subside, addressed the meeting. "I see that the community agrees with us. Will you decide this way?"

"We will," resounded from the meeting.

Then I read the draft of the resolution and added, "Those who agree, please raise their hands." The entire meeting came into motion. Old men turned toward one another, their shadows moving on the walls. One of them rose slowly from his seat and took a step forward. He crossed himself three times, turned to face the people, and fell to his knees with his right hand raised high over his head. "I swear!" he said in a loud voice. "So help me God!"

The droning of voices became louder. Lazar and still another man were also on their knees before the teacher's desk, their right hands stretched toward the ceiling, fingers set as for the sign of the cross. All over the room men were kneeling and women crying. Many voices repeated, "I swear! So help me God!"

"What does this mean?" I asked Thomas.

He whispered quickly, "You told them to raise their hands. That is what people do when they take an oath."

"And why are the women crying?"

"They think another war is coming."

"Should I explain to them?"

"Why? If the community wants to take an oath, let it do so."

He turned to the meeting and, holding the text of the resolution over his head, said firmly, "This is what the Chorino community has decided and sworn to keep in good faith. So help us God! Is such your will?"

"Such is our will," came the answer from all sides.

Thomas handed the resolution to me and said, "The meeting is ended."

THE COW DEATH

Quietly, without hurrying, the peasants left the schoolhouse. Some stopped to thank Thomas, some looked at us. I sat at the teacher's desk copying the resolution and was the last to leave. The porch was completely dark, but the snow on the road shimmered in the moonlight. A dark mass separated itself from the doorpost, a man in a short coat barred my way, and a voice whispered:

"For God's sake, mister! I must ask you something. Tell me the truth."

Now I could see him—his face was a foot away from my eyes. I recognized the haggard features, the thin blond beard, the restless,

shifting look. I had seen the man at Thomas' house among the peasants who came to invite the teachers to their homes. I had also noticed him in the school: he had knelt in the blinking light of the
candle, at the end of the first row, with his right hand raised. I said
to him:

"I shall be glad to answer your questions, my friend."

"Tell me the truth," he repeated. "From where comes the cow
death? Who sends it to us—the Tsar or the students?"

"The cow death? What do you mean?"

"Men in uniform were sent into the country to let the cow death
loose. But they had a rule about the cow death: the muzhik's stalls
are open to it, and the landlord's are closed. The men in uniform
ride around and bar the roads. Three crosses make the barrier. Seven
days can death stay in each village, until the men come and take the
crosses away and let death loose, to move to another village. And the
men. . ."

"What men?" I interrupted him. I had an uneasy feeling the man
was insane. But he continued with subdued passion.

"Mister, you must know these men. They say that they do the will
of their master, but they do not tell who their master is. Some say
they are sent by the Tsar to punish the poor people, and others say
they are sent by the strikers to make more trouble. . ."

"I don't understand," I interrupted again. "Let us talk with
Thomas; he must know."

"I have talked with him," the peasant replied. "Either he doesn't
know or he dares not tell the truth. Whom should we trust?"

The door of the teacher's house opened. Thomas appeared in the
quadrangle of light. I shouted to him, "Please come here."

In the darkness Thomas could not see me, but he recognized my
voice. He crossed the street, stepped up to the school porch, looked
closely into the face of the peasant, and said to him kindly, "Are you
still asking about the cow death, Egor?"

"What else would I ask?" replied the peasant.

"I told you the truth," said Thomas. "A dangerous cattle disease
broke out. To stop it, the doctors must know what places are infected. Therefore they try to isolate each village for observation.
They call this quarantine."

"You told me this, Thomas," the peasant agreed cheerlessly. "But
those men in uniform are not doctors. What kind of men are they?"

"Don't you trust me, Egor?" asked the teacher.

"I do, but what is the truth?"

"Let us talk about this matter once more, indoors. Come into the
house."

Despite the late hour, the teacher's house was still full of gay excitement. Some teachers were waiting for their sleighs, others planned to stay overnight in Chorino. All were deeply impressed by the meeting, and many asked us to visit their villages. Two girl teachers from the glass factory in a village not very far from Chorino were most insistent. They told us they had been on very good terms with the peasants but that since October the peasants had been showing increasing hostility toward them and the factory workers. "The workers do not care," they added, "but we feel miserable." They asked us to tell the peasants all about the strike and the Manifesto. Eugene and I promised to help the girls and decided to start touring the country the next morning. The Mensheviks from Novgorod asked to join us.

Thomas, busy with the samovar, forgot Egor, who sat on the edge of a bench at the door, his fur hat between his knees, a puddle of melted snow at his feet, sadness and confusion on his haggard face. I could have gained his complete confidence by saying to him, "Those men in uniform are sent by the Tsar to punish the poor people by killing their cattle." But this would have been contrary to our code of revolutionary ethics, and I had to leave Egor alone with his doubts.

THEY NEED THE TSAR

In the morning we decided to begin our tour in the districts north of Chorino, which the teachers considered the most difficult for political propaganda. The road passed a small glass factory, and we singled it out for the first meeting. Thomas suggested stopping at two hamlets on the way. We left Chorino in two sleighs, Eugene and I with Lazar in one, and the Novgorod Mensheviks with a young Chorino driver in the other.

At the first hamlet, the teacher met us in friendly fashion and immediately asked the headman to call the people to the school for a talk about the Manifesto. He wished to offer us tea, but his wife disappeared through the rear door. "You must excuse her," he said meekly. "She is a priest's daughter."

The walls of the teacher's living room were plastered with colored prints of Biblical scenes, saints, and monasteries. When we asked about the political attitude of the peasants, he replied, "Who knows? I never talk with them about politics and religion." And he added timidly, "Religion is superstition, of course. As an educated man, I know there is no God. But one must watch his step."

The classroom was long and narrow, with the teacher's desk at the entrance. Bearded old men sat awkwardly on pupils' benches and desks, others stood in the passage. Women and youngsters were not admitted. The teacher introduced us without committing himself. "These people wish to talk to you about the Tsar's Manifesto. I don't know what they will say."

I began with the remark that we in St. Petersburg did not know much of what was going on in the villages and assumed that peasants, in turn, did not know much about events in St. Petersburg. We wished to tell the villagers what was happening in the capital and learn what they thought about it. The audience seemed interested, but the story of the struggle of St. Petersburg workers found no response. The faces were becoming grim. An old peasant sitting in the front row interrupted me harshly. "Explain why the railroad stopped?"

"I have told you why the workers—"

"You have told us, and we have listened. But other people have told us that the rich and educated people stopped the railroad to bring serfdom back."

Several men were on their feet now, shouting and gesticulating. It was not clear whether they were shouting at one another or at us. I tried to explain that we were on the side of simple people, but the noise became so deafening I had to give up.

Eugene rose, stretching out both hands. The peasants seemed curious to hear what the lad would say. He began to speak of unrest among peasants and the forthcoming redistribution of land. When he stopped, the old man who had interrupted me said, "That is different. That suits us."

He asked us to explain what the peasants might expect from the Manifesto. My arguments for establishing a government for the people and by the people in Russia met with general approval. All was fine until an old man who looked like the village patriarch came to the crucial question: "And what about the Tsar?"

I answered, "There is no need for a Tsar under a government by the people."

Then hell broke loose. The muzhiks stood up and shouted with anger. The patriarch came close to me and said grimly, "What you have said about the people's government is all right with us. But after what you said about the Tsar, we cannot let you go away. Get a rope, brothers."

Standing on a bench, I shouted to the crowd, "Listen! Most people in the cities and on the railroads think as we do. If you rope us and then dare to appear in the city or on the railroad, our friends will rope you. Is this what you want?"

An elderly man said, "We seek no quarrel with the city people.

But we cannot do without the Tsar and we won't let you talk against him."

This gave me an opening. "All right," I said. "You think you need the Tsar, but we in the cities have no use for him. What shall we do? Take arms, brothers against brothers? Is that what you want?"

"No, we want no killing, but we cannot live without the Tsar."

"That is what your hamlet thinks. But what about other villages? What about the cities?"

Two muzhiks with a rope appeared at the door.

"All Russia is for the Tsar!"

I had regained self-confidence. "If that is how you feel, the dispute can be settled without a quarrel," I said. "Let all the people elect their representatives: from a hundred thousand peasants, one peasant; from a hundred thousand workers, one worker; from a hundred thousand merchants, one merchant. Let the people's representatives come together and establish order. If most people want to keep the Tsar, he will stay; if most are against him, he will go."

"With this we agree," said somebody from the crowd. "Let the people decide."

I continued to develop the idea of representative government. The two muzhiks with the rope stood near me and listened. I was ready to move a resolution demanding a democratically elected Constituent Assembly when the village patriarch interrupted me again. "God knows who you are. We muzhiks don't understand these matters. But we wish no trouble. I say, peasants, let them go."

"Let them go!" agreed the crowd.

"This is the decision of the community, misters!" he announced, turning to us. "Now, damn you, away with you!"

We rode on among high snowdrifts. The failure was unexpected and discouraging. Lazar alone remained serene. For him, this was just a noisy meeting; nobody was hurt and no harm was done. He tried to comfort us.

The road led through rolling country. From the crest of a hill we saw a group of some twenty men on the road. Some were sitting on the snowbanks along the road, others stood in the middle, armed with pitchforks, poles, sticks, axes. A tall man in a sheepskin-lined coat stood in front of the gang with a hunting gun in the crook of his arm. As we approached, he held up his gun.

Eugene and I stepped out of the sleigh and faced the group. Nobody returned our greetings, and the man with the gun asked us, "Where are you going?"

"We are passing through your village," I answered. "The road is free to all, I guess?"

"Not for you. What are you teaching?"

Lazar, who stood behind us, replied, "These are fine people, brothers. What they teach about the land is for our good."

"You yourselves can hear what we are teaching." I added, "Call a meeting in the village, and we shall be glad to talk to your people."

But the man with the gun stood before us like a rock. The others came closer, grim and silent. "About the land," said the man with the gun, "we know all we need to know. And we know all about God and the Tsar. The community has decided not to listen to you."

"That is your business," I replied. "If you do not wish to listen, there is no need for us to stop at your place."

"You won't pass," said the man. "The road is ours. Turn back! Hurry up!"

The muzhiks raised their pitchforks and poles. It was hard to turn the sleighs in the narrow track between the snowdrifts. One sleigh toppled over but no one moved to help us. Finally we took our seats again. The man with the gun asked, "Where will you go now?"

"To the glass factory. People there are not afraid to hear the truth."

"Your truth is dog's feed," he replied angrily. "The factory is just the place for you. Go on."

We made a detour and from a distance saw the men still barricading the road.

A HOUSE DIVIDED

The glass factory stood on the rim of a steep hill—a dozen buildings and sheds of various sizes, and behind them barracks and dwellings of workers and managerial personnel. The village was at the foot of the hill—a small church with a blue bulb-shaped cupola and two lines of log cottages, with sheds and a lacing of fences behind them.

The road branched at the entrance of the village. Lazar took the road uphill to the factory and stopped in front of the long, nicely built schoolhouse. The classroom occupied two-thirds of it, and the rest served as the teacher's living quarters.

It was growing dark. All the houses, except the school and teacher's quarters, were lighted. We knocked at the door. The curtain at the nearest window moved a little, then the door opened, and a girl's voice called, "Come in, comrades! We are so happy you have come."

The two girls—the teachers at the factory school and the village school—had locked themselves in the dark house. They told us what had happened that morning after their return from Chorino. The peasant who brought them back had told everyone about the convention and the meeting in the Chorino school. The headman of the village summoned the schoolteacher to the community house. Interrogated by the priest, the driver testified that an oath was administered to Chorino peasants but he could not tell who the new Tsar was. The teacher admitted that a convention of teachers and a meeting of peasants had been held at Chorino but denied the oath story. The priest ordered the girl to repeat what was said about God and the Christian faith in Chorino, and became very angry when she declared that these topics had not been discussed at all. Then somebody said that strikers threatened to burn churches in villages refusing to take an oath to the new Tsar. The headman ordered the girl to go home and await the community's decision, but she was so frightened that she ran to the factory teacher. Both girls were too proud to seek protection from the factory management or the workers.

The girls sobbed and laughed as they told their story. Now, with our arrival, everything would be straightened out, we would explain to the peasants, they would understand. . . . We decided to call a joint meeting of peasants and factory workers. The factory teacher went to announce the meeting to the workers; Lazar went off to invite, first, the village headman and the priest and then all the peasants, knocking at the door of each house. He returned fully satisfied with the success of his mission. The peasants, he reported, seemed to be interested in the meeting. The headman accepted the invitation. Only the priest declined to come. "Why should I go to the school?" he told Lazar. "Tell them to come to my church to confess their sins."

The schoolteachers gave us tea and sandwiches, and at eight o'clock we all went to the classroom. The entire male population of the village—about a hundred men—was there, with the headman in the front row. The factory workers did not mix with the peasants but formed a separate group in the corner. There were perhaps thirty of them, dressed exactly as workers in St. Petersburg dressed for a solemn occasion, with blue or red shirts under their coats, their trousers stuffed into high boots.

The workers and most of the peasants listened with visible interest to our talk on the Constituent Assembly, the Manifesto, and land, but the faces of the headman and other men in the front row remained grim. When I invited the audience to ask questions, the headman replied, "Why should we ask questions? It is enough that we have listened to how you cheat the people!" He got up, turned to the audience, and said with authority, "Faithful Christians! Should we wait until they force us to take the oath to the new Tsar of theirs?

Let us go home!" He moved to the door, followed by most of the peasants.

Now the classroom was more than half empty—only the workers and a dozen younger peasants remained. The workers seemed neither surprised nor dismayed. "Go on, comrades," one of them said to us. "One can speak better to a wall than to those blockheads. Now we can talk among ourselves."

There was a hard knock against the window shutter. It was followed by blows against other windows. A young worker looked through the shutter, trying to see through the darkness of the night. "They are throwing sticks," he reported. "Better bar the door."

The house was bombarded from all sides. Glass in one window was shattered. Cold air flowed into the room. The lad returned to his observation post at the window. "Not more than a score of them," he announced. "No firearms. They won't hold out against knives."

A war council was held. Factory strategists recommended a sortie. "To knives, comrades!" the lad shouted. He produced a long knife from the edge of his boot. Five other youngsters, with similar knives, joined him. Screaming and shouting, they jumped from the porch of the schoolhouse into the darkness and fanned out right and left. The besieging army, taken by surprise, fled. The workers returned, some jubilant, others a little disappointed that it had not come to blows.

It was impossible to resume the meeting, but we stayed for an hour or more talking about the conditions in the factory and the village. All the factory workers were city people, some from as far as St. Petersburg or Moscow. The local peasants were hostile to the factory. The origin of this hostility was not very clear to us but the cause might be in the monarchistic feelings in the village. There was no point in trying to reach the villagers through the factory workers. And there was also an abyss between the few young peasants who had remained in the classroom and the rest of the village. The workers and the young peasants thanked us warmly for the meeting, and we returned to the teacher's room to consider further plans.

THE AMBUSH

We were eight now: Zaloga and Alexander, Eugene and I, the two girl teachers, Lazar, and the other peasant driver from Chorino. I asked Lazar what he thought of the prospects of our campaign.

"You can do nothing with these people," he said. "Perhaps, sometime later. . . . What can we do but go home?"

The other driver nodded approval. The girls, in tears, pleaded,
"Take us with you. If we stay here, the muzhiks will kill us." We
decided to leave as soon as the horses were ready.

Someone knocked lightly on the door. The factory teacher
opened it halfway and stopped as if petrified by fear. The village
teacher whispered to me, "That is Gerassim, the headman's brother,
chief of the Black Hundred in the village. He was not at the meeting."

The man in the doorway was tall and seemed huge in his long,
fur-lined coat. His face was dark, with sharp, shrewd eyes, bushy
eyebrows, and a broad black beard. He held his fur hat in both
hands and asked meekly, "Would you let me come in, Miss Teacher?"

"Of course, of course," the girl murmured. "Step in."

Gerassim bowed to all of us. After a brief silence, he said to the
factory teacher, "Too bad I could not come to your meeting. It is a
disgrace, I should say. The muzhiks are rough people, without
education. One must have patience with them." Again he bowed
deeply to all of us. Both girl teachers were beaming.

"That is all right, Gerassim," said the factory teacher. "We are
happy that you see the things this way. . . . Will you stay with us
for a cup of tea?"

Gerassim sat down on the edge of the bench, holding the cup
in his hands. When Lazar and the other driver put on their sheepskin coats, he asked them casually, "Are you going back tonight?"

"Yes," Lazar answered. "No time to waste. We are going to cut
trees and distribute firewood in Chorino tomorrow."

"This is the proper time to cut trees," Gerassim agreed. "Did you
come by the upper road? Each year we have the same trouble on
that stretch. The wind blows the snow away on the hill. A hell of
a road for horses."

"Is the lower road better?" Lazar asked.

"You will see the difference," Gerassim replied. He drank
another cup of tea, thanked us once more, and left the room rather
hastily.

The road Gerassim recommended was as bad as that on the crest
of the hill. We had to follow the empty sleighs on foot. When we
passed a barn at the far end of the village, a voice barked from the
darkness, "Stop, you others!"

Men rushed toward us from both sides of the barn and from
the woods across the road. We were attacked from right and left
but there was nobody between us and the sleighs.

I shouted, "Everyone into the sleighs!"

Eugene shouted to the attackers, "Keep off or we shall fire!" And he shot into the air. The teachers reached the sleigh first, the Mensheviks followed them. Eugene and I covered the retreat with our small Brownings.

"Stop, you others, give up your guns!" barked Gerassim's voice in the darkness. "Take them, boys! Only these two have arms." Eugene expected me to fire, but I could not consider shooting at the peasants. I cried to Eugene, "To the sleighs!" We rushed to the nearest sleigh. The peasants were irresolute. They threw sticks, stones, and poles at us but did not dare come close.

When we were out of reach of the pursuers, Eugene asked me, "You did not wish me to fire?"

"No, you could not shoot into the air twice," I replied.

"Would it have been better if they had caught us?" he asked.

"We had to take the risk. How would you feel if we had escaped after killing or wounding somebody?"

After a long silence Eugene said, "You are right. One shot in the air was all we could afford in self-defense."

TRAPPED

We reached Chorino before dawn. Thomas had bad news for us. The rumors that strikers were touring the villages and compelling the peasants to take an oath to the new Tsar had spread throughout the district. Not all the peasants believed the rumors, but some villages were ready to meet the strangers with axes and pitchforks. Thomas knew that Chorino would not fail him, and most of the teachers who had attended the convention felt fairly secure personally, but the situation had become difficult in some places and our visit to these spots would only worsen matters. Thomas therefore advised us to cut our tour short, go back to the next city, and be ready to return on short notice. He invited the girl teachers to stay in Chorino in the meantime.

"You can stay with Lazar or with some other peasant family," he said to them. "Nobody will come to Chorino from your village to molest you."

We decided to follow his advice. It was not easy to find someone to take Zaloga, Alexander, Eugene, and me to the Borovenka station since all the peasants were at work in the communal forest. Finally a sleigh appeared before the teacher's house, driven by a woman in a man's sheepskin coat, felt boots, and fur hat, and we left Chorino.

Again we crossed the fairyland of sun and glittering snow with an exquisite, ever-changing design of trees, fences, and toylike log houses scattered over the silver expanses.

At the outskirts of Borovenka some fifty men were assembled in front of the blacksmith's shop. They let us pass and followed our sleigh silently. Another crowd, mainly women and children, milled in front of the station. They seemed to be waiting for us.

Pretending not to notice the hostile crowd, we went into the station, bought tickets to Novgorod, and went to the large shabby waiting room. I have reason to remember this room well. The wall left of the entrance had two glass doors and two windows overlooking the platform. Under the windows stood a long bench. The wall to the right had four windows, opening on the road leading to the station. The wall facing the entrance had one small door with a sign: "For first-class passengers." Next to this door was a big stove with a clock above it. Left of the entrance, the fourth wall had a low, narrow door with the sign: "Keep out." It was half-open and one could see the telegraph room, narrow as a corridor but as long as the main waiting room, with a glass door leading to the platform.

When we entered the waiting room it was empty. Only a watchman in a shabby railroad uniform sat on a stool near the stove. But a crowd began to pour into the room, forming a wide half-circle around us. We were trapped. The clock showed 2:20, half an hour before our train was due. I told my comrades, "If we are attacked, we will retire into the telegraph office and hold out there until the train comes."

Suddenly the crowd made way, and three men in city fur coats and lambskin hats stepped forward, followed by the station gendarme. They came close to us and one of them, a large man with a trimmed grayish beard, asked us sternly, "What kind of people are you? What is your business? Where do you think you are going now?"

Playing for time, I replied casually, "We will answer your questions. But first tell us who you are to question us."

"We have your number," the man shouted. "You came here to teach people that there is no God in heaven and should be no Tsar on earth. That's your business! Now answer: Who sent you here?"

I turned to the gendarme. "This man is accusing us. Would you take over the interrogation?"

The gendarme replied, "These people are well known here. You are not. Why should I interfere?"

The muttering crowd moved forward and we stepped back toward the telegraph room. The clock showed 2:40 P.M. Still ten minutes, if the train was on time. Eugene and I took our pistols out of our pockets and held them in sight. The man who had questioned us turned to the crowd. "Christians! These fiends are enemies of our holy Church and the Tsar. They stopped the railroad and burned down the church. They want to restore serfdom. Death to them!"

The crowd moved nearer. I raised the revolver and was ready to fire when I realized I was alone at the door of the telegraph room. Eugene had noticed that the door to the platform on the far side of the waiting room was open and dashed toward it, certain that we would follow him. He had almost reached the door when the watchman struck him on the head with a piece of firewood, and at the same moment Zaloga and Alexander threw themselves under the bench. If I fired now I would leave all three comrades in the hands of the mob. So I shifted the guard on my Browning, dropped it into my pocket, and stepped further back into the corner. The man who had questioned us shouted, "Christians! This is the main fiend. Get him!"

Unseen hands pulled me out of the corner. Blows fell on my head. I realized I had lost my glasses and felt blood in my mouth, but I sensed no pain, fear, or anger. Then I blacked out.

When I came to my senses, everything seemed dark about me. I wiped the blood from my eyes and saw some felt boots in front of me in puddles of melted snow. Eugene was lying a few feet from me. Without glasses, I could not see his face clearly, but I did see that he wore only a shirt and underwear, his blond hair was a clot of blood, and there was blood on the floor around his head. With some effort I got up and took a step in his direction, but two men grabbed me. Rough hands tore at my clothing and boots.

Then I heard the train arriving. The crowd waited in silence, but no one entered the room from the platform. The train left. The room again was filled with the roar of the mob. Another blow on my head laid me on the floor again, and I could not get up.

The empty space in front of Eugene and me suddenly widened. A man in a long black coat stood between us and the peasants. I heard him saying, "What are you doing, brothers? Have you forgotten that murder is the greatest, unforgivable sin?"

An angry voice interrupted him. "Mind your own business, Father! Your place is in the church, not here!"

"My place is where I can prevent a sin," the priest pleaded.

"There is no sin in killing these fiends!" replied the angry voice.

But the priest stood between us and the mob, and the muzhiks did not dare push him away. Suddenly somebody shouted, "Brothers! The cause of all evil, the Chorino teacher, is not here."

Through the roar of the mob I could hear the faltering voice:

"Brothers! Don't damn your souls. Remember God's words: Thou shalt not kill."

The voice came from the far end of the room. The priest was trying to keep the peasants from rushing to Chorino.

WHAT TO DO WITH THEM?

Part of the crowd left the room. An elderly man with a face weathered to the color and texture of leather stepped over me. "Each one in his turn, son," he said. "The people will dispose of all of you, one by one. Now think of your sins."

Eugene opened his eyes and, moving his bruised and swollen lips with effort, asked me, "Will they kill us?"

Before I could answer he blacked out again, and his head fell on my lap. The muzhiks discussed in a matter-of-fact way what to do with us. One thought that the ax blade was as good for us as the butt end. Another insisted we must be burned alive for having burned the church. One stepped over me and grabbed my shoulder. "Look here, you wise guy!" he shouted, holding a silver coin two inches from my eyes. "Why is this a ruble? Because it carries the Tsar's picture. Now, put the mug of a muzhik on it, and the ruble will be worth nothing. All my life I have broken my neck to put aside a few rubles, and here you come to ruin me! Drag their bowels out, brothers!"

It appeared that the ringleaders had gone to Chorino with the priest and that those who remained in the station were to guard us until the others returned. Hope flickered for a moment. A man in an officer's uniform entered the waiting room and strode resolutely through the crowd. The gendarme stood at attention. The officer looked at Eugene and me lying on the floor, covered with blood, and began to bellow, "What goes on here? A murder? In a public place! On railroad property! You will all go to Siberia for this! Gendarme! Deliver these men to my sleigh. I am taking them to the city."

Encouraged by this interference, I got up and helped Eugene to the bench. But the muzhiks had little respect for the officer.

"Take to the city those whom you have caught, mister sheriff!" they shouted. "These men have set five churches on fire. The people have caught them, and it is up to the people to decide what to do with them."

The sheriff tried to argue, but the muzhiks shouted louder and louder and began to push him toward the door. The officer grew frightened. To restore his authority, he declared that he would go to

Chorino and stop lawlessness there. He dismissed our situation, shouting to the crowd, "If you go to Siberia for these men, remember that I warned you."

"Nobody will go to Siberia for these two," the muzhiks replied. "The people will dispose of them."

As soon as the sheriff disappeared, they again threw Eugene and me to the floor.

E Y E S

Blood dripping from the cuts on my head blinded me. I wiped it away and again could vaguely see the waiting room and the crowd. Everything seemed remote and impersonal.

A freight train arrived but nobody paid any attention to it. The room was no longer packed, but some fifty or sixty peasants stood about us in a semicircle, guarding us for the trial.

Eugene came to himself and looked at me. I read the question in his disfigured face and nodded. He closed his eyes again. Then I saw a yellow, wrinkled face just before my eyes. An old woman with a heavy homespun kerchief around her head bent over Eugene, lamenting, "Not older than my grandson. . . . Is your mother alive? And grandmother? Both must be alive. . . . Our muzhiks are worse than beasts. . . . What did they do to the boy? . . ." And, turning to the crowd, she said in a voice shaken by tears, "Why do you let him suffer? Kill these two at once!"

A man stepped out of the crowd, leaned forward, looked closely at us and exclaimed, "I know these men! I heard them speak in Chorino. By God, I did." People pressed around him. He stooped over me, small, poorly dressed, with a sparse blond beard, patched felt boots. "I heard every word. Brothers, did they talk! The reddish one talked like a priest, and the blond one also. And both moved their arms, thus and thus." He tried to imitate our gestures.

A stern voice asked him, "What did they say, you clown?" The man said meekly, "How should I know? They are educated people."

I lay on the floor, my head against the leg of the bench, reconciled to the thought that these were the last minutes of my life. I had only one desire—to see to the very last what was going on around me. Without glasses, I had to strain my eyes even to make out the faces of those in front of me. Probably there was something odd in my look, for several times I heard, "This one is still gazing. . . ."

An old man stooped over me. He looked very round in his thick yellow coat girdled by a red kerchief. His beard was snow white, his face red all over. With blinking blue eyes under heavy gray eyebrows, he looked like Old Man Frost, the Russian counterpart of Santa Claus. He stared intently at me and touched my shoulder lightly. "You know, son, why the people have decided to kill you? Because they fear you will harm them. But what harm could you do if we gouge out your eyes? You would just walk like this. . . ."

He closed his eyes and took a few steps, imitating the walk of a blind man. Then he turned to the crowd. "Christians! Let us tear out the eyes of this one. Then he can go where he wants."

Somebody remarked that, blinded or not, the prisoners had to be guarded until the people decided what to do with them. But the old man insisted on his plan. "Give me some splinters, brother," he said to the watchman. The watchman handed him a piece of firewood and an ax. He cut the wood in long splinters, sharpened one of them, tried the end on his palm, and said mildly to me, "Say good-by to God's light, son!"

He stepped behind me, wedged my head between his knees, and leaned forward. He looked at me, I looked at him. He seemed to hesitate. Then he said piously, "God help me!" and struck me in the right eye. Perhaps he did not see clearly what he was doing or his hand trembled. The splinter tore in the eyebrow but missed the eyeball. Then he remarked sheepishly, "A splinter is not good for this job. Does somebody have a knife?"

"I have one!" volunteered a youngster. I saw his dirty jagged knife close to my face. The old man stretched his hand to get it, but the youngster shouted, "Keep off! I shall do it! The knife is mine."

Some people supported the old man, others sided with the youngster. The dispute was interrupted by outcries from the road in front of the station. "Here they come!"

Everyone rushed to the entrance, forgetting Eugene and me.

THE PEOPLE'S TRIAL

The prisoners—Thomas and the two girl teachers—had been placed at the head of the crowd pouring into the hall. After them came the sheriff, followed by a crowd of peasants. Many of them were drunk.

The sheriff stopped in the middle of the waiting room and said to the crowd, "You'll get an award for having helped me to catch these criminals. Now go home. I will deliver them to Novgorod."

His voice was drowned in outcries: "The people caught them! The people will try them!"

"Keep order!" the sheriff bellowed. "This is a public place! Gendarme, clear the station!"

But the drunks pressed toward the sheriff and forced him to retreat with the prisoners to the far corner of the room. Suddenly he opened the door to the room for first-class passengers, pushed his prisoners ahead of him into the room, and locked the door from the inside. The mob started to batter the door with fists and feet. Somebody screamed, "Get them through the windows."

A score of men dashed to the entrance. Blows against the shutters, the clang of broken glass, deafening cries, screams of women. . . . Then the noise subsided. The door of the small waiting room opened. Men with clubs came through it, some stained with blood.

After a brief silence—or perhaps it only seemed to me that there was a moment of silence—a voice said, "In the name of Christ, these two come next."

Everyone turned toward Eugene and me. It seemed to me they were moving very slowly. I was still on the floor, Eugene's head on my lap. Somebody pulled him away. I saw his hair, soaked in blood, swing in the air. At the same moment I was raised from the floor. Blows fell on my head and body. My last sensation was a terrific noise—whether it was the roar of the mob, the approach of a train, or the collapse of the world, I did not know.

THE RESCUE

I saw a row of high leather boots and gray-brown coats before me. A shrill voice barked orders. "All unauthorized persons leave the room! Platoon, clear the station! Archipenko, double the posts at the windows! Put guards around the building!"

The space between us and the leather boots became wider. Two men with white aprons over their coats lifted Eugene from the floor and laid him on a bench. I managed to get up by myself.

I asked a man with an apron about Thomas and the girl teachers.

"The girls are all right," he replied. "The man has a cut across the skull. Heavy bleeding . . . but no danger."

"And he?" I nodded at Eugene.

"We shall know soon."

Eugene regained consciousness only momentarily, then lost consciousness once more. The doctor cut his hair off, examined his wounds, and began to put in stitches. I found my trousers and overcoat in a heap of garments in the corner and put them on. Then, very slowly, holding to the walls, I crossed the waiting room to the door for first-class passengers. Four soldiers stood guard at the broken windows stuffed with rags. The floor was littered with fragments of glass and wood, wet from melted snow and stained with blood. Thomas, his head bandaged, was lying motionless on a sofa, covered to the neck with a white sheet. The girl teachers were huddled in armchairs. They became hysterical at my appearance. With their help I washed my face, but we could not stop the bleeding from the cut above my right eye.

While the doctor and his assistant were examining and dressing my wounds—none of them very deep—the girls told me what had happened in Chorino. They were in the teacher's house when the woman who had driven us to Borovenka returned with the news that we were trapped. Then the crowd of Borovenka peasants surrounded the house. The priest who came with them tried to prevent violence. Soon the sheriff joined him, and they finally made a bargain with the mob. The priest would keep away, the sheriff would go with the party to the station, and no harm would be done to the prisoners on the way. I knew the rest.

Thomas opened his eyes. Apart from the weakness caused by loss of blood, he seemed all right. Zaloga and Alexander were bruised, but their condition was not serious. The doctor regarded only Eugene's injuries as grave. He departed, leaving with us his assistant, who immediately set about getting us food.

Soon a tray with tea and a loaf of white bread appeared on the table in front of the sofa where Thomas was lying. He half-rose on his elbow and manifested an excellent appetite. Eugene vomited each gulp forced into him by the doctor's assistant. I could not eat because my front teeth had been loosened and my jaws were bleeding.

The waiting room was empty except for the soldiers keeping guard at the broken windows. Through the window I could see the road in front of the station. The crowd was larger than before and seemed more excited. The muzhiks shouted at the soldiers, "Who are you to defend the enemies of the Tsar? Will you fire on your brothers?"

I told the sergeant that I wanted to speak with the commanding officer. A young lieutenant in a neat uniform came at once and asked what he could do for us. I asked him what his instructions were.

"To restore order at the station, clear it of violent elements, and insure the safety of persons who, reportedly, were attacked by the mob," he replied.

"And you do not think of delivering us to the mob?" I asked.

"Certainly not! That would be contrary to my instructions, duty, and honor!"

"Then will you watch your men?" The lieutenant flushed, thanked me, and at once took steps to break contacts between his soldiers and the crowd.

After midnight a train arrived with the investigating attorney and half a dozen other officials. The attorney wanted to question Eugene first, but I pointed out that Eugene was in no condition to stand questioning, and he agreed to examine us simultaneously. He began by saying sternly, "Listen! Do you hear?" The mob was roaring behind the broken windows. After a long pause he continued, "Unless you tell me the whole truth, I shall not be able to take you away from here."

We testified that we had attended the convention of school-teachers in Chorino and had spoken to peasants in Chorino and another village, and to peasants and workers at the glass factory. As to the content of our speeches, we suggested he question the people who had heard us. The attorney then asked whether we had set fire to churches in the district. I replied by asking how many churches had burned down in the neighborhood in the past forty-eight hours. He agreed that he had no official reports of any.

After other formalities, the attorney announced that all seven of us were under arrest and ordered the lieutenant to deliver us to the state prison in Novgorod.

A train arrived. The lieutenant ordered the soldiers to form two lines on the platform, from the door of the waiting room to the nearest car, but the muzhiks broke through the lines. Then the officer took his whole company to the platform and opened a wide passage from the station to the train. Soldiers who were not protecting the passage linked arms in a ring around us. In this way they got us through the mob to the train. Six soldiers under the command of a sergeant boarded the train, while the young officer remained at the station with most of his company.

The train began to move. The distance between us and the station was increasing rapidly. I fell asleep.

IN NOVGOROD PRISON

The jail in Novgorod was a large three-story building surrounded by a high brick wall with wooden turrets. A matron took the girls to the women's ward; Zaloga and Alexander were assigned to the pre-trial detention quarters; Eugene, Thomas, and I were taken to the prison hospital, where we received adequate medical care and were treated with all possible consideration. Thomas and I were recovering rapidly, but Eugene's condition worried us; indeed, he never recovered completely.

After eight days, the state's attorney came to the prison, called all seven of us to the superintendent's office, and announced that the charge against Thomas, the girl teachers, Zaloga, and Alexander had been withdrawn and they would be released at once. Eugene and I would be held for trial on the charge of having advocated the overthrow of the existing form of government, under Article 129 of the Penal Code.

"That is a legal error," I said. "The government to which this article refers is the autocratic monarchy. It ceased to exist after the Manifesto of October 17. Since that time the form of our government has been in a state of transition. Everyone is permitted to have his own ideas on desirable changes. You may accuse us of inciting the people to violence, if you can prove the charge, but I don't see how you can refer to Article 129."

The attorney replied, "The preliminary investigation does not indicate that you incited anybody to acts of violence. But the circumstances indicate that you did advocate a change in the government that could not be effected without the use of force. Perhaps you are right about Article 129. . . . I cannot commit myself . . . . Present your opinion in writing, as a legal objection to preventive custody."

I had the paper ready an hour later. It was sent to the attorney at once, and the next day, after a consultation with the president of the court, he ordered our release from the prison.

Eugene was asleep when our train stopped at the station of Borovenka, and I did not waken him. The sight of the stationmaster, gendarme, and watchman aroused no emotion in me. This was just an obscure station, one of hundreds along the line.

At home I was met as one resurrected from the grave. Newspapers had spread exaggerated tales of the riot at the Borovenka station: I had been blinded, mobbed, murdered. I had wired to my mother from the Novgorod prison saying only that I had been arrested through misunderstanding and that I felt fine. The family found me in better shape than they had dared hope, though I was very weak and my head was bandaged and my face swollen. They asked me about my plans and I promised to take things easier the next week or two.

THE LAST DAYS OF THE SOVIET

On the surface, nothing had changed in St. Petersburg. The lock-outs continued, the need among the workers was increasing, the newspapers paid little attention to the Soviet. But there was a vague anticipation in the air of something big about to happen.

Perhaps this anticipation came from the strike of the post and telegraph employees. Because of the interruption in communications, wild rumors spread in the city, and a panic developed on the stock exchange. The collapse of the stock market was headlined in the newspapers and everybody began to talk of the imminent collapse of the ruble.

This crisis gave the revolutionary parties a new idea. The St. Petersburg Soviet issued an appeal to the workers and other poorer classes to withdraw their money from public savings institutions and to ask for specie, preferably gold, in payment of wages and salaries. This effort to foment panic was wholly unrealistic. Workers had practically no deposits in banks, and how could they get their wages in gold from a factory cashier when he had only his usual assortment of notes and small coins to put into the pay envelopes? If they refused to take their wages in notes, on what would they live? The appeal proved a complete fiasco.

The post and telegaph employees were losing their battle, but encouraging news began to come from other quarters. Revolts had broken out in the Far Eastern army. Unrest was reported among troops in Kiev, Kharkov, and a half-dozen other places. Was this a new revolutionary tide?

This time, however, the government was prepared to meet the emergency. On November 26 the shock troops of General Trepov surrounded the headquarters of the St. Petersburg Soviet and seized its president, Khrustalev. The government did not arrest other members of the Soviet and its Executive Board, leaving the next move up to them.

This was a deliberate provocation and the Soviet fell into the trap. It met the same evening and resolved: "The Tsarist government has captured the President of the Soviet of the Workers. The Soviet has elected a new President and will continue its preparations for armed revolt." These were empty words. The Soviet could not *continue* "its preparations for armed revolt" because it had never *started* such preparations except to arm the workers' commandos with daggers, poles, and bludgeons as a defense against a pogrom in St. Petersburg.

On December 2, the Soviet met in the hall of the Free Economic Society. Although I was not fit for any revolutionary work, I went to the meeting, partly out of curiosity, partly to be with friends at a time when everything hung in the balance. The meeting opened with a lengthy report of the Executive Board. I could not follow it word for word, but it impressed me as a piece of daydreaming. The reporter—it may have been Trotsky—intoxicated with his own oratory, elaborated on the plan to force the government to surrender by issuing a manifesto that would bring about its bankruptcy.

This manifesto called on the people of Russia to boycott bank notes and ask for payment in gold and silver in all transactions, to withdraw their deposits from the banks, demanding specie, and to refuse to pay taxes. To this appeal was added a declaration that the Soviet would oppose the repayment of foreign loans raised by the Tsarist government at a time when it was waging war against the people. The signatures of the Central Committee of the Peasants' Union and revolutionary parties did not add much to the strength of the manifesto. What were the depositors to do when the bank had no gold or silver? What would the refusal of workers and peasants to pay taxes mean in a country whose budget was based on excise and indirect taxation, mainly from its monopoly of the sale of vodka?

The Financial Manifesto repeated on a larger scale the Soviet's similar appeal to the workers. Since that had failed, what chance of success did this have?

I attended the Soviet session as a guest and could ask to speak only as a representative of the party. But the party had signed the Manifesto. I sat in the rear of the gilded hall, my head bandaged, half dizzy, helpless, and miserable. I also felt that, even if I were able to prove to the delegates that the Financial Manifesto was pure nonsense, I would have no answer to their question: "And what do you recommend instead?"

I was as empty-handed as the others.

In fact, the Manifesto was a confession by the Soviet and revolutionary parties that they stood disarmed before the enemy.

The next morning, December 3, the Financial Manifesto appeared in all progressive and moderate St. Petersburg newspapers. The moderate newspapers printed it partly because of pressure from the printers, who refused to release the papers unless it was carried on the front page. All papers that published the document were suspended the same day.

In the evening the Soviet was called to a meeting in the hall of the Free Economic Society. On my way I stopped at Eugene's house. He was in bed and, though very weak and absent-minded, seemed relaxed and cheerful. I promised I would return the next morning.

Approaching the hall an hour after the meeting was supposed to have come to order, I noticed that something was wrong: detachments of police on the street corners, military patrols, soldiers massed in the courtyards. No guards, however, were posted at the entrance of the building. As soon as I reached the door, somebody opened it briskly from inside and shouted, "Come in." I was almost dragged into the entrance hall and found myself in the middle of a ring of policemen. An officer ordered, "Go to the main hall!"

The delegates and guests were crowded into the hall, encircled by a double line of soldiers with rifles and fixed bayonets. When I was pushed inside the circle, a man who sat at the chairman's table said flatly, "Order of the Executive Committee: Offer no resistance, answer no question, destroy all personal papers and arms."

Nobody moved. The soldiers along the walls looked as if they had been carved out of solid rock. The silence was broken only by a soft clanking of tools at the chairman's table, where two youths were busy smashing the small arms passed to them from the assembly. How small was the heap of weapons before them in comparison with the fence of rifles and glittering bayonets all around! The hammering stopped—the last tiny revolver had been broken.

The registration of prisoners began after midnight. Nobody told his name. All were registered under sobriquets assigned by the police: "Round Hat," "Blond Whiskers," "Wide Belt." I was registered as "Letters W.W. in Galoshes." Before dawn the prisoners were loaded into police vans, twenty or thirty in each. What was our destination? Jail, or the Fortress of Peter and Paul, or the firing squad? Our van had no windows, but after a long drive over cobblestones the wheels hit a smooth surface. A long bridge! Now we knew, we were crossing the Neva. Our destination was the central prison—the Crosses.

IN THE CROSSES

Time ceased to move. I was alone with my thoughts and dreams. How badly I needed rest! I enjoyed lying on the cot in my cell, composing my memoirs sentence after sentence, remembering step by step what had happened in the past three months. Since I had refused to tell my name, I could neither get letters nor receive visitors. Moreover, I made no effort to establish contact with other prisoners or get news from the outside world. I was simply in a stupor of fatigue.

My solitude was broken by one of the guards, a young soldier repatriated from the Far East. He showed me touching attention. In the morning, instead of handing hot water for tea through the window in the cell door, he would open the door quietly, put the can on the table, cover it with my fur hat, and leave the cell on tiptoe so as not to wake me. When he was on the night shift on my corridor, he would open the window of my cell and talk in a whisper. Usually he told me about his home and service in the army in Manchuria. I felt that he needed someone to whom to tell his story. We both had an urge to think of the past.

Two weeks after the arrest, during the usual half-hour solitary walking in one of the courtyards of the prison, I recognized a member of our group of meeting speakers at a ground-floor window. He told me the news: Moscow is in revolt. The troops are refusing to fire. The city is in the hands of the workers.

I asked my guard about these events. He had heard nothing but promised to bring me a "good" newspaper. Next day he handed me one. Though its title had been torn off, I recognized it as a Menshevist newspaper. From it I learned that the revolt of the workers in Moscow had been drowned in blood.

REVOLT IN MOSCOW

Later I learned many details of the Moscow "armed revolt" from people who had taken part in it, some as political leaders, others as members of workers' commandos, defending the barricades.

The tocsin rang from St. Petersburg, where the workers replied to the arrest of their Soviet by a general strike. The newly elected Soviet proclaimed the walkout as the signal for a general revolt of all freedom-loving citizens. A strike in St. Petersburg and Moscow and on all Russian railroads was set for December 7. But the St. Petersburg workers, emotionally tired and economically exhausted by two preceding walkouts, did not respond. In addition, the conference of railroad workers failed in its attempt to stop rail traffic. The trains continued to run, with soldiers posted on each locomotive and in each passenger car. Attempts at sabotage were frustrated by strong patrols guarding the tracks. Actually, the December strike was limited to Moscow, and the government concentrated all its forces on crushing it.

From the first day, the strike in Moscow was marked by attacks of the police and troops on the workers. On December 8, the second day of the strike, artillery appeared in the streets. A school building where a meeting was held was bombarded and set on fire. Rumors spread that the Cossacks had been ordered to ransack the city, and people began to throw barricades across the streets to defend their neighborhoods. Hundreds of barricades were erected in all parts of the city—some primitive, others elaborate and enforced with stones and bricks. But these preparations were without plan; each city block tried to protect itself, and none had armed men behind the barricades.

The Moscow Soviet could not convene: its Executive Board had been arrested and there was no central party organization to direct the movement. Only weak, sporadic attempts to resist the troops were made at a few points in the suburbs—and these became known as the "armed revolt." After a few days, the government succeeded in "cleaning up" the central part of the city, but barricades still blocked access to the factory precinct of Presnya. Radical groups, hunted in other parts of Moscow, sought refuge in this area. There was some semblance of order in the defense of this precinct, but actually it lay open to attack, with throngs of people ready to die for freedom but with pathetically inadequate organization and practically no arms.

As in St. Petersburg when a pogrom was expected, fighting commandos were organized in Presnya factories—small groups of young workers with pikes and daggers, some few with pistols or hunting guns. In all, they had hardly more than two hundred pistols to defend a line more than ten miles long against the assault of some hundred thousand regulars.

Yet Presnya remained in the hands of the rebels because the military commander of Moscow did not have a single regiment that was wholly reliable. He distrusted his troops and feared that any regiment might join hands with the workers in the event of a direct engagement. To terrorize the defenders and raise the morale of his own troops, he ordered a bombardment of Presnya.

This was the climax of the revolt: all fury of field artillery against a handful of workers with useless pistols. Meanwhile, General Trepov managed to send two crack regiments of the Imperial Guard from St. Petersburg to Moscow. They were told that their assignment was a sign of the Tsar's particular trust in them, and their arrival in Moscow sealed the victory of the government.

The last act of the Russian revolution of 1905 was a massacre in Moscow, as its first act had been a massacre in St. Petersburg. On December 19, the St. Petersburg Soviet announced the end of the abortive strike. Once more the order of retreat was couched in revolutionary terms: the strike was suspended in order to begin the organization of an armed revolt.

Actually this was the end. The hurricane of the revolution had blown over.

BACK TO FREEDOM

All was quiet in the Crosses. Physically I had entirely recovered, but I was confused in my thoughts and feelings. Life was not so simple as it had seemed to me half a year earlier when I told my parents of my decision to join the revolution. I had dreamed of being with the people. But where were "the people"?

I had some doubts whether the road we had followed was right, but I knew I had neither chosen nor determined this road. I had, therefore, no feeling of guilt for the defeat. Simply, I was lost and did not know what I should do next.

The Executive Board of the Soviet sent word to the prisoners to tell their names to investigating authorities. Early in January, 1906, the government decided to limit the case of the St. Petersburg Soviet to two or three score men. All the others arrested on December 3 at the Free Economic Society, some five hundred in all, were released. I was among them.

Droshkies were waiting at the entrance to the Crosses, as in front of a railroad station. I took one and gave the address of my parents. I had not seen them since my arrest but had written to them, and my letters were mailed by the friendly young soldier from the Far East. My mother and sister had brought food, linen, and all the little things that could increase my comfort in solitary confinement. I felt no break with them—the break was in myself. I was like a train stopped suddenly while running at full speed.

But this was not my individual shock. Millions had been stopped this way. Before my eyes was the back of my cabby, round, stooped, immovable. Was he not a man of the people? I asked him:

"How is business these days?"

"Thank God, it is picking up," he replied. "One should not complain, there is order. It was hard under freedom."

"Was freedom so hard on you?"

"Sure! They would not let one drive, would cut his harness. And in our business, whether or not one has a fare, one must pay three rubles a day to the boss for the droshky, horse, hay, and oats."

This was not quite the answer I had anticipated. I had to find out what the true feelings, aspirations, and hopes of the people were . . . if I decided to stay with them after all.

Russia at the Crossroads
1906-1907

T HE revolt in Moscow had been crushed. The government had won the battle. Had it also won the war against the people's discontent?

The Manifesto of October 17 remained in force. Stout defenders of the throne called themselves the party of October 17—the Octobrists. Moderate liberals stood for a constitutional monarchy. Would the establishment of a constitutional monarchy and fulfillment of the promises of the Manifesto amount to at least a partial victory of the revolution?

Russia stood at the crossroads. To realize the promises extorted from the Tsar by the revolution would establish a democratic regime from the border of Germany to the Pacific. To repeal the Manifesto would leave the struggle between the government and the people unsolved.

The fate of Russia remained in suspense until the end of 1907, when, after the dissolution of two Dumas, the political regime in Russia was stabilized as a compromise between absolutism and pseudo-constitutionalism. Under this regime Russia fell prey to the infamy of Rasputin, the ordeal of war, the tragedy of a new revolution, and ultimately the new despotism.

THE FIRST ELECTION CAMPAIGN

I was released from prison at the end of January, 1906, and went the next day to register for the new semester at the University. It had returned to the routine of academic life. I was somewhat embarrassed by questions about my health and my plans for the future. I was in perfect physical condition, as rested as after a long stay in a sanatorium, and I had no plans. My companions, however, expected me to resume activities with the Students' Council, the Union of Commercial Employees, and the party. The Students' Council was preoccupied with the organization of a co-operative canteen. The Union of Commercial Employees reminded me of my promise to help them with their cultural magazine. Within the party, the Bolsheviks and Mensheviks were fighting for power. None of these issues appealed to me.

The labor movement in St. Petersburg had suffered a terrible moral defeat in December when the workers could not block the sending of troops against Moscow. Their main plague, however, was unemployment, largely a consequence of the November lockouts.

All the news from the provinces was bad. Punitive expeditions were roaming through the country, competing with one another in sadistic executions and massacres of prisoners and hostages. But the fire of revolution still glowed under the ashes. The newspapers headlined local terroristic acts, assaults on the police, armed resistance against arrest, holdups in the name of the revolution.

The distribution of political forces had changed. The moderately liberal Constitutional Democratic party (the Cadets) had proclaimed its allegiance to the constitutional monarchy. At the right, new parties emerged, ranking from a small conservative group of Peaceful Reform to the pogrom-minded Union of Russian People.

The Black Hundreds tried to gain support among workers disillusioned with the leftist parties. Patriotic pubs were opened in factory districts, but they were patronized mainly by property owners, police agents, and derelicts. In the Neva precinct, the workers disposed of one such pub: a hand grenade was hurled through a window into the barroom, and fleeing guests were greeted with another hand grenade and a volley of revolver shots. Many were killed or wounded but nobody was arrested, although the assault occurred in plain sight of a crowd.

On February 12, 1906, a manifesto announced the forthcoming election of representatives to the Duma. These representatives of the people were to convene on April 27, in St. Petersburg. The electoral law provided for indirect elections, with separate voting by landowners, peasants, wealthy people in the cities, factory workers, and the rest of the urban population. In each constituency the landowners and urban property owners combined could be sure of a majority, but a split in their vote would give a majority to the parties supported by the other groups of voters.

The leftist parties faced the choice of taking part in the elections or boycotting them. The Bolshevist organization called a conference to discuss the problem—a secret meeting in a fashionable private school. The keynote speaker was Lenin, whom I heard here for the first time. His speech seemed colorless and monotonous; he repeated words and whole sentences again and again and did not argue against his opponents. Rather, after having presented their views in a more or less caricatured form, he would say, "This is ridiculous. They are too smart not to know how ridiculous this is, but they think workers will not notice."

Lenin, however, was an effective speaker. He seemed to hammer his ideas into his listeners' heads not by arguments but by the almost hypnotic power of his will. After having brought home a statement

—for example, that the revolutionary tide was rising—he would draw a conclusion—that the party must have an aggressive plan of action. Then, after repeating this thought several times, he would move to the next conclusion—all with the appearance of absolute certainty that his statements were irrefutable and with derisive contempt for those who thought otherwise. His thesis was that the revolution was on a new upswing and the Duma would be a roadblock in its way. The workers would gain nothing in the new parliament. The party must therefore boycott the elections. Lenin's speech was followed by a lively discussion. All the speakers agreed with him.

The Mensheviks were envisaging another tactic: to take part in the first stage of the elections and boycott the final stage. In comparison, Lenin's tactic had the advantage of simplicity. The Minister of the Interior, Durnovo, an old bureaucrat notorious for his arrogance, added vigor to Lenin's argument by sending out secret instructions to rural police chiefs and ordering them to control elections by "using armed force if necessary" but "without creating bad feelings in the population." After these instructions had leaked to the newspapers, Durnovo explained that he intended to use armed force solely to protect the patriotic majority of the people against the intimidation by a criminal minority. "The government is confident," he announced, "that measures of coercion employed to this effect will be greeted with gratitude by all true Russian men and women." Simultaneously, a new decree was published that penalized advocacy of the boycott with a prison term. Now the Bolsheviks could ask the voters: "Are you for the boycott and against Durnovo or for Durnovo and against the boycott?"

In the students' mess, a few days after the publication of the decree, Anton handed me an invitation to a pre-electoral meeting arranged by the Cadets. The invitation had been addressed to the St. Petersburg Committee of the S-D party, and the latter designated me to speak in its name. I felt unprepared but said I would go.

A galaxy of substantial citizens occupied the front row, and a brilliant panel of liberal leaders adorned the long table on the dais. A police officer sitting at a separate desk added a note of respectability to the scene. The keynote speech was delivered by a venerable, gray-haired professor, Miliukov. After enumerating the government's crimes—abuse of power, ruthless cruelty in suppressing unrest, pogroms and the like—he concluded, "The Duma is called upon to put an end to this disgrace. Vote for the Constitutional Democratic party!" Then he challenged those who disagreed with him to speak up.

I was the first to ask for the floor. I began by saying that I accepted the speaker's appraisal of the existing regime but doubted his conclusion. Then I elaborated the maxim that it is impossible to fight bullets with ballots—a maxim I now hold erroneous but then thought very convincing. My address was interrupted repeatedly by applause. The Cadets had not anticipated an attack from the left. Their arguments against the boycott sounded as if they themselves were not sure of their position. The meeting proved a success for our tactics and set a pattern for the election campaign in St. Petersburg, which centered on the contest between the Cadets and the Bolsheviks.

The law barring the advocacy of boycott proved to be a greater handicap for the moderates than for the leftists. When a police officer interrupted me in another meeting and threatened to dissolve it, I turned to the chairman and said:

"This is a meeting of your party. As a guest, I do not wish to inconvenience you. Furthermore, the strongest argument in support of my thesis has been presented by this gentleman in uniform. I have nothing to add."

The chairman, pointing to the excitedly applauding audience, said to the officer, "You are aiding the leftists. Can't you use your brains?"

The officer, red in the face, replied, "In the force, we are not supposed to use brains. We follow instructions."

When the St. Petersburg Committee asked me to organize the S-D campaign, I found that most of the party propagandists could not cope with open meetings. Finally, I picked four or five more sophisticated than the others and persuaded the organization to forbid volunteers to take the floor in meetings at which our "licensed" speakers were present. My own task was to fence with the Cadet professors and lawyers. By imitating their somewhat pedantic style, I easily gained the reputation of being a "serious" political speaker. Several of my speeches were transcribed and published as pamphlets, bringing me unexpectedly high royalties.

My father attended half a dozen meetings at which I spoke and was impressed. "I would prefer to have you stick to mathematics," he said to me after a meeting, "but politics may also be a career." At home, he and my mother told me that they would reconcile themselves to my obsession with politics if I would persuade my older brother to keep out of this dangerous business. "He is of no use to your party," they pleaded. "You are at least in your element on the stage."

I succeeded in getting my brother to abstain from public speeches. But personally I did not enjoy the campaign. I felt that all we could achieve by advocating a boycott was to shake the people's confidence in the Duma, and I doubted whether this would strengthen the revolution. The results of the election failed to dispel my doubts. The Cadets obtained a great majority in St. Petersburg, but the voting was light. There was no way of telling whether the absentees had boycotted the Duma or stayed home for lack of interest in politics itself.

The peasants remained the greatest enigma of the electoral campaign. They took the nomination of electors to county conventions very seriously, often nominating them after public prayer and giving them detailed instructions. These "mandates" dealt chiefly with local problems: to ask the government to repair a bridge or build a flour mill; to demand the removal of a gendarme sergeant; to cut the rent, to transfer ownership of the forest of an absentee landlord to the community, and the like. The political composition of the peasant electors was not clear. Most of them refused to discuss politics with newspaper reporters, and up to the day when the Duma convened on April 27 nobody knew how the villages had voted.

By the end of the campaign I was thoroughly fed up with it and felt an increasing urge to go back to my books, to learn more about history, public finance, constitutional problems, land reform. I felt I needed years and years to fill the gaps in my knowledge. Then suddenly an insignificant event gave a new direction to my thinking.

BREAD AND WORK!

I was in the students' canteen with a briefcase full of books from the University library when Eugene took the empty chair at my table. "I need your help, Sergei," he said. He told me he was in touch with a group of unemployed workers who had decided to demand bread and work from the Municipal Council, and he asked me to draft a petition for them. My first draft was disappointing. I tried again, with no more success. "To write for other people," I said to Eugene, "I must feel what they feel."

The next morning I went with him to one of the emergency hot-meal stations for the unemployed organized by the Union of Engineers. Despite the early hour, people were idling in the dining room. Most of them were middle-aged or elderly men. I asked Eugene's friends, "What would you say to the Municipal Council if you were called to testify before it?"

They replied briefly, each in his own way. I put further questions. Then we went to other stations. In the evening, writing the petition, I was able to identify myself with the men whose feelings I was trying to express. The next day the delegates from twenty-four stations assembled in one of the dining rooms. Seated around a long unpainted table, they looked more like peasants than factory workers. They spoke with solemnity, probably stemming from their feeling of responsibility toward their families and all the unemployed. The petition was accepted unanimously, and it was decided to organize a Council of the Unemployed.

The following day I made a tour of the St. Petersburg newspapers, vainly trying to interest them in the campaign. I finally succeeded in persuading the manager of a small liberal newspaper that mass unemployment under unsettled political conditions was a seedbed of anarchy and that the situation in St. Petersburg might become very serious if nothing was done for the unemployed workers. We made a deal: the paper would be the organ of the Council of the Unemployed in its campaign for bread and work, and I would do the writing.

Each morning I toured the hot-meal stations and the quarters of the unemployed. Then I wrote articles and notes about their needs and the unrest among them. I discovered how to make news—hot news—out of the issue. The tide of anarchy was mounting in Russia, bombs were exploding, revolutionary holdups were widespread. Could one be sure that the tide would stop at the gates of St. Petersburg?

The Municipal Council was then discussing plans to construct new bridges and install electric tramways to replace the old-fashioned trolleys drawn by horses. Such projects would provide the right jobs for the unemployed, but there were rumors that the Council was negotiating contracts with German firms. The workers believed the Council deliberately planned to place orders abroad in order to starve them, and they held the reactionary councilmen personally responsible for their misery. I faithfully reported their feelings to the newspapers. To maintain a continuous flow of information, I also sent out brief notes about the number and composition of the unemployed in each precinct and progress in the election of the Council of the Unemployed.

The timing of the campaign proved excellent. Because of the approaching elections to the Duma, police pressure had relaxed somewhat and we could act with increasing boldness. Moderate newspapers began to pay attention to the movement. For my new friends, the unemployed, this seemed magical, and they believed my articles would bring them bread and work. I was less optimistic but thought we could get something if only we succeeded in putting enough fear of God into the City Fathers.

The newly elected Council of the Unemployed named me its president. It did not occur to me that I should have consulted the party before calling the new organization to life, and I was somewhat surprised when the St. Petersburg Committee of the S-D party invited me to report on the movement. Accepting the invitation for Eugene and myself, I decided to use this opportunity to ask the Committee to print our petition and leaflets. I discovered, however, that even the Bolshevist members of the Committee were alarmed by my activity, while the Mensheviks looked at me with undisguised hostility. After my report, cross-questioning began.

"Who gave you the authority to start agitation among the unemployed?"

"Don't you know that 'bread and work' is an old anarchistic slogan?"

"Don't you realize that your demand is unacceptable to the Municipal Council?"

I became angry and told the Committee members in a very undiplomatic way that I considered them doctrinaires blind to realities. The Bolsheviks were impressed, but the Mensheviks remained adamant.

Both groups were critical of the final paragraph of the petition the unemployed were planning to present to the Municipal Council. "If you refuse our demand, we shall return to our comrades and tell them so. Next, you will have to deal not with us but with all those who sent us here."

"What does this mean?" asked the leader of the Mensheviks. "Is it a threat?"

"Yes, a deliberate threat. My articles are full of threats. In this one," I tossed the clipping to him, "I have threatened that typhoid may develop in St. Petersburg as a result of hunger and destitution."

The Committee voted—ten to eight—a resolution instructing Eugene and me to change the final paragraph of the petition and to abstain from electing employed workers as factory delegates to our Council. We refused to comply with this resolution and challenged the Committee to take disciplinary measures against us.

After we had left the Committee, I realized that our clash with the party could create serious difficulties for the Council. Moreover, there was still the problem of printing the petition and leaflets. I decided to try my luck with *The Wave*, a daily newspaper slated to appear in a week or two and connected, I had heard, with the Bolshevist Center.

The receptionist stopped us at the entrance. After I gave her my name, a tall, slender man with the head of a Biblical prophet came to the reception room and took us to his study. When I told him about the meeting of the St. Petersburg Committee, he offered to take us to the "Old Man." We walked through a dozen rooms, passed several doors with receptionists' tables, and reached a small cubicle. A little bald-headed man in shirt sleeves sat at a desk with heaps of clippings, galleys, and manuscripts before him. I recognized Lenin.

He asked for details. "How was the voting? Ten to eight? This means that one of our men was trapped by the Mensheviks. It does not take much to straighten out such a thing." Then, in a more serious vein, he said, "The unemployed have been the most active force in many revolutions. How about yours? Could you bring them into the streets?"

"That is not our purpose," I replied. "We are interested in aiding the unemployed."

Lenin's laugh was friendly, almost kind. "Of course, of course. Heading the movement, you have to say this. If, in addition, you *feel* this way, your words must sound the more convincing. How many copies do you need? Only twenty thousand? You could use more."

He marked "100,000" on my scripts and passed them to his assistant, a little bespectacled man, who said to me, "In the students' canteen, at our desk, at this time tomorrow."

I started to leave, but Lenin stopped me. "You are on our list," he said. He showed me the galley of the front page of the newspaper, with my pen name, "Sergei Petrov," in the list of contributors. "Now, write something for the first issue."

Lenin continued to be interested in the Council of the Unemployed. I do not know whether he was in sympathy with the movement or sided with it because the Mensheviks had been against it. But at the time when I was drifting away from the party, my work for the unemployed brought me close to Lenin and therefore close to the Bolshevist organization.

Our Council decided to submit its petition to the Municipal Council at its last meeting before the Easter recess. The deputation consisted of fifteen members—half the Council. In the event of an arrest, the other half would continue the campaign. Four men were chosen as spokesmen. I acted as the coach of the team. We rehearsed each speech, separately and all together, and each speaker memorized his part.

But when we reached the huge two-story reception hall of the Municipal Council, we were told the session had been postponed for lack of a quorum. The arrival of our group aroused curiosity among the councilmen present, one of whom asked who we were. Our oldest spokesman, Nikitin, announced in his booming voice, "We are the delegation of the unemployed."

Immediately we were surrounded by a crowd of councilmen, municipal officials, and reporters. An important-looking gentleman explained to us, "The Council will not convene today. It is difficult to get a quorum on Easter eve. Everyone has personal affairs. . . . You see?"

"We see," replied Nikitin. "Shopping, Easter table, wine for the guests. . . . We can see that such affairs have left the councilmen no time to listen to the voice of the unemployed. But they will hear that voice. You bet they will!"

Reporters took notes. A councilman volunteered to take us to the mayor. We replied, "We have been elected to speak to the Council."

A reporter asked, "Something for the press?"

"Report that the delegation of the unemployed was here but the councilmen were too busy with preparations for the Easter table to talk with them. Report that we will come again."

After we left the Municipal Building, I suggested a stop at a tearoom. We found a cheap one patronized by coachmen and sat there in a dark and noisy basement, with heavy teacups before us. The delegates were disappointed, but I was in high spirits. "We have two weeks for the campaign before the next meeting of the Municipal Council," I said. "We shall use this time to strengthen our organization by elections in the factories." I worked out a plan. When it was time for the shift to change, men fired from a factory would assemble at its gate, stop the workers who came out, and call a flying meeting in support of the unemployed. One of our people would address his working comrades, tell them how we had knocked in vain at the door of the Municipal Council, and ask them to elect delegates to our Council.

Those were busy days. We had eight precinct organizations. I toured four southern precincts one day, four northern ones the next. The Soviet of Unemployed began to take shape. Eugene's health was failing rapidly and I remained the only intellectual in the group. All the others were workers, older than I and more experienced in party work as Mensheviks, Bolsheviks, or Socialist Revolutionaries. There was no time to discuss tactical questions. Somebody had to make decisions, and the group entrusted the command to me.

Now the question of the unemployed was in the headlines. The Union of Engineers asked us to include its representatives in our delegation to the Municipal Council. The Cadet-electors to the Duma made a similar offer. We thanked both groups and suggested they each send separate delegations.

My most vivid recollection of those days is of the endless muddy sidewalks along which I splashed from factory to factory. Each evening we met in one of the hot-meal stations—exhausted, but with a feeling that things were moving. The police did not bother us, but the day the Municipal Council was to meet after the Easter recess, they raided the office of the Union of Engineers, where our delegation had planned to meet. The raiders got there too early, however, and the engineers warned us of the ambush.

We arrived at the Municipal Building half an hour after the time set for the session. The entrance hall and the broad staircase were packed with the usual political crowd—journalists, lawyers, engineers, students. The galleries in the session room were likewise packed to capacity. The Union of Engineers pleaded for the support of hot-meal stations and pledged its co-operation in planning public works. The electors to the Duma reminded the Council of its responsibility for the welfare of the city. Then the chairman invited our delegation to address the assembly.

Nikitin mounted the chair, put on his heavy round glasses, got out our petition, and read it in a stentorian voice. He continued, "We know you gentlemen councilmen. You represent the wealth of the city, we represent the poverty. But most people in this rich city are poor. We speak in their name when we demand bread and work for the unemployed." Our next speaker, Malyshev, a fire-eating Bolshevik with a grim look and golden heart, discussed the origin of unemployment in St. Petersburg. Everything went smoothly and all the speeches were delivered as planned. Only the last speaker, Boroda, a thin-faced youth, added to his prepared remarks, "You have not suffered the pangs of hunger! You have not experienced the humiliation of unemployment! When I was leaving my precinct this afternoon, a crowd of men and women surrounded me, saying, 'Go to those usurers, speak to them. If they don't understand human words, we will all go and take them by their throats.' "

The galleries applauded frantically. The councilmen sat in morose silence.

The Municipal Council decided to appropriate half a million rubles for hot-meal stations and appointed a temporary committee to draw up a plan for public works. Only liberals—a small minority in the Council—were elected to the Committee. Its chairman, a well-known Cadet lawyer whom I had often met in pre-electoral meetings, approached me and said smilingly, "A fine performance. You must be satisfied, Mr. Woytinsky—excuse me, Mr. Petrov."

I replied with the request that a meeting of the new Committee be called immediately. "After that session," I said, "we will tell you whether we are satisfied."

We presented only one demand—that the Committee should instruct our Council to make a census of the unemployed and, without delay, open registration for public works through eight precinct offices. At first the Committee was puzzled by our insistence on having this minor question settled at that late night hour, but the chairman grasped the meaning of our proposal. "This makes sense," he said. "I second the plan. . . . No objections? Accepted. The session is adjourned. Now, gentlemen, you can go ahead without being harassed by the police. Are you satisfied now, Mr. Woytinsky —excuse me, Mr. Petrov?"

Were we satisfied! We had won a sizable loaf of bread for the unemployed and legalized our organization to carry on our campaign for public works!

Two days later the St. Petersburg S-D Conference convened to discuss our clash with the Committee.[1] This was our day. The Conference was unanimous in approving our conduct and condemning the attitude of the Committee. I accepted the reproach of having failed to keep the party informed of our activities and promised that in the future the Committee would hear from us whenever we were going to start something. Peace with the party was restored.

THE DUMA OF WRATH

The people had voted against the government. The rightist groups supporting the government, from the Octobrists to the Black Hundreds, received scarcely one per cent of the popular vote. Moderate liberals may have received five or six per cent. All other votes were cast for the Labor Group and Socialist parties. However, because of the system of indirect voting and unequal distribution of "electors" among the various classes of voters, the distribution of seats in the Duma was very different. The Cadets, together with national minority groups, obtained nearly two hundred seats out of the total four hundred. The reactionary parties to the right of them got eighty seats, and the representatives of the peasants' Labor Group, about a hundred. A score of workers' representatives originally joined the Labor Group but later formed a separate group. Thus the Cadets, who represented a small right-wing minority of the popular vote, became the center in the Duma.

A clash was inevitable between the Duma and the government, then headed by a sullen and reactionary bureaucrat, Goremykin. The government decided to try to weaken the Duma by discrediting it in the eyes of the people and to dissolve it as soon as it got out of hand. The opposition parties in the Duma were deeply split. The avowed goal of the Cadets was to persuade the Tsar to appoint a liberal Cabinet. A government acceptable to the Cadets probably

[1] Within the S-D organization in St. Petersburg, the Committee was the executive body, and the Conference was a broader policy-making body.

would also have satisfied the Laborites, but they did not believe the Cadets could achieve their goal by persuasion. They thought their force was in the people and that only the people could compel the Tsar to yield power.

The inauguration of the Duma was a great day in St. Petersburg. Streets were packed with crowds that warmly greeted the peasant deputies as they reached the Tauride Palace, especially those dressed like simple muzhiks.

The people's representatives were then taken to the Winter Palace. The Tsar read a speech of two paragraphs, one greeting the Duma and the other warning and threatening it by implication. The peasants were shocked by the display of fabulous luxury, the costumes of ladies of the court, the arrogance of the courtiers, and, most of all, by the Tsar himself—his insignificant appearance, barely audible voice, furtive look. This first meeting of the Duma with the Tsar became the favorite subject for speeches of peasant representatives in factory meetings.

Such meetings were very popular in the first two or three weeks after the Duma's inauguration. The workers would tell the management that a member of the Duma was coming to the factory to talk to them about the Duma. The management could not object and the police could not intervene. The deputy would begin with a greeting and then the workers would ask questions: "Have you been in the Palace? Did you see the Tsar? How does he look?"

The deputy would tell the story: ". . . And then the door opened and men in uniforms rushed in. All covered with gold. Enough on one man to feed three villages for a year. And the Tsar was there. By God, you should have seen him—the poor soul, scared as a rabbit. They had probably told him that we were evil men, so he did not dare come near us and kept behind the guards."

The Duma began its work with a reply to the Tsar's address. The draft, prepared by the Cadets, demanded political amnesty, freedom, agrarian reform, respect for civil rights, and change in the government. But these demands were wrapped up in the argument that they were the means of strengthening the power of the Tsar and protecting the throne against revolutionary storms. This language damaged the prestige of the Duma in the eyes of persons with liberal leanings and failed to bring it into favor with the monarch.

Soon after the Duma had voted its reply to the Tsar's address, the Laborites and S-D called a public meeting in the huge hall of the People's House. The spokesmen of the Labor Group called on the citizens to support the Duma in its struggle against the government. "Citizen Karpov" was announced as the next speaker. A small, pale man with a big bald skull and narrow slanted eyes appeared on the stage. His charges that the Cadets were traitors and the Laborites weaklings met with an outburst of applause. He warmed up. "To support the Duma in its desperate attempts to support the throne? Is this a joke, comrades?" he screamed. And he called for mobilization of forces outside the Duma for direct revolutionary action.

This was Lenin's first public speech at a mass meeting in St. Petersburg. The impression was overwhelming. The audience booed down the Cadets who tried to reply to "Citizen Karpov," and his resolution was carried almost unanimously. Even a few well-known Cadets in the audience voted for it!

The popularity of the Duma was at a low ebb. Then came a new blow from the other side. The Tsar declined to see the Duma's Committee and let Prime Minister Goremykin deliver his reply to the people's representatives: "There will be no amnesty and no agrarian reform."

The moderates were at their wits' end. With only eleven dissenting votes, the Duma voted the resolution moved by the Laborites —a demand that the Cabinet resign and be replaced by one enjoying the confidence of the people. The attitude of the masses toward the Duma changed abruptly. There was no longer any doubt that the people would support the Duma in the event of an open break with the government. St. Petersburg was in a turmoil. The police suspended radical newspapers. Political gatherings were forbidden, but meetings were held in factories.

Again I found myself in a political whirlpool. With peasant members of the Duma, I went from factory to factory. My job was to introduce our guest speakers. Most of them were unaccustomed to flying meetings, some were not very articulate, and others were plainly nervous, but these things did not matter.

To check the growing popularity of the Duma, the government mobilized the Black Hundreds. Police rounded up criminals and the scum of the big cities and had them sign telegrams to the Tsar, imploring him to dissolve the Duma. The government published such telegrams with an expression of the Tsar's gratitude. The Duma countered with a campaign of interpellations about acts of lawlessness and brutality by local authorities—executions, torture of prisoners, floggings of peasants. The purpose of the moderates in this campaign was to show the Tsar how bad his ministers were. One of the Cadet leaders expressed this view eloquently:

"The Tsar cannot be wrong. He is not to blame for the evil done in his name. What is the meaning of the demand not to criticize the misdeeds committed allegedly on the order of His Majesty? Should we hold the Tsar responsible for all bloodshed by his ministers? Never!"

Such subtleties, however, deceived nobody. The result was to expose the crimes and evils of Tsarism. The Duma greeted the ministers with catcalls: "Murderers! Hangmen! Butchers! Resign!" This is how the First Duma acquired its historical name, the "Duma of Wrath."

There was a short period when it looked as though the Duma would become the rallying point for progressive forces. But the revolutionaries distrusted the Cadets, and the Cadets wished no alliance with the revolution. The deep split between the Cadets and the Laborites came into the open in the discussion of agrarian reform. The Cadets introduced a bill designed to reduce the scope of tenure and to transfer a large part of the privately owned land to the peasants, with fair recompense to landowners. The Labor Group submitted a bill based on the idea of collective ownership of land and its periodic redistribution within the community.

Reactionary circles met both projects with rage. Perhaps their indignation against the Cadet bill was particularly strong. They denounced it as an attempt to destroy the landowning nobility, the strongest support of the throne.[2]

The decisive clash between the Cadets and the Laborites did not come on the matter of agrarian reform, however, but on the question of tactics. The Labor Group demanded election of agrarian committees to assess land needs and resources in each department, county, and precinct; such committees, it believed, would insure the people's participation in solving the land problem. The Cadets, however, barred discussion of this plan. This was the turning point. From that day on, the Duma began to lose ground.

The Labor Group of the First Duma had no brilliant leaders, but it represented the majority of the Russian people and knew what they were after: more land for the peasants, more education for their children, freedom from greedy landowners and rapacious policemen. The members of the Group knew also that the Tsar and the government sided with the landowners against the peasants and with the rich against the poor. And this was about all they knew of politics.

THE S-D GROUP IN THE DUMA

The emergence of the workers' S-D group in the Duma strengthened its left wing but at the same time provoked violent attacks against the Duma from the right.

[2] The author of the Cadet bill, the brilliant and scholarly banker Herzenstein, was later assassinated by the Black Hundreds.

Early in June, the group was reinforced by the representatives from Georgia. They were more mature politically than other members of the group, and their arrival brought more clarity to the political alignment within the Duma. The most colorful among them was the gray-headed Isidor Ramishvilli, a bright although poorly educated village teacher. One of our precincts invited him to speak at an open-air Sunday meeting in a clearing in the woods, a couple of miles from a through road.

The place could be reached only by trails. Security patrols circulated between the road and the meeting place. A moss-covered rock served as the stand for the speaker. Some five hundred men had gathered when I arrived with Ramishvilli. The old man climbed the rock with youthful agility. Small and frail, with a deeply tanned, wrinkled face, he looked like an eagle perched on the rock, and his arms moved in the air like wings. He spoke broken Russian, with a Caucasian accent.

"Your cause, comrades, is a sacred cause! Sacred for all Russia . . . for all the world. . . . We can be crushed now . . . but we shall win in the end. . . . If we perish, our children will remember and bless us. . . ." Each sentence was a cliché, but his speech sounded like a song. It did not matter what the old man was saying. The crowd was fascinated by his high-pitched, trembling voice, his brown wrinkled face, and his gray hair flying in the breeze.

A patrol came running and reported that soldiers had been seen between the road and the clearing. But Ramishvilli objected to closing the meeting. "Come nearer," he shouted to the patrol. "Come nearer. Let the soldiers come and listen to the people's representative!"

The old man was talking about the work in the Duma when the white summer tunics of small groups of soldiers began to appear between the trees around the clearing.

"Come nearer!" he called. "Come, listen to a people's representative. Why should you carry arms among friends? Put your guns away. . . ." He continued his speech while the soldiers trickled through the crowd and pressed around the rock, piling their rifles at his feet.

After the meeting, the soldiers, joined by a young officer, warmly thanked Ramishvilli for his speech.

The S-D group in the Duma became a new source of discord within the party. The Central Committee, dominated by the Mensheviks, called on the workers to support the group. The Bolsheviks who dominated the St. Petersburg Committee described this policy as support of the Cadets. While the conflict concerning agrarian reform was nearing its climax in the Duma, the two factions in the

S-D organization in St. Petersburg were wholly absorbed in internal struggles.

THE DUMA CAPITULATES

On June 20, the government published a declaration: There will be no compulsory alienation of privately owned lands; the peasants have nothing to expect from the Duma; all their hopes must rest with the Tsar and his government. The Cadets introduced a resolution stating the firm intention of the Duma to enact an agrarian law based on compulsory transfer of privately owned land to the peasants and calling on the people to keep quiet, preserve order, and wait. The Laborites objected to the concluding paragraph of the resolution. In the final vote, the resolution obtained 124 votes against 53, with more than 100 abstentions. Obviously it did not represent the voice of the Duma. The proposal to publish it received only 120 supporting votes with some 160 abstentions.

The Duma of Wrath had reached the end of the road.

AMONG THE UNEMPLOYED

The Council of the Unemployed had an impressive network of hot-meal stations and registration offices in all parts of the city. It included delegates from many large factories. They were supposed to aid the unemployed in finding work, but actually the Council had become an important factor in the economic labor movement. It registered striking workers as unemployed, distributed meals to them and members of their families, and occasionally opened special stations near striking factories.

The employers complained to the Municipal Council, and the chairman of the Municipal Committee summoned me. "Are you distributing meal tickets to the strikers?" he asked.

"Certainly! How can we discriminate against them?"

"But the city appropriated money for the unemployed, not for strikers!"

"What is the difference?" I replied. "Their families must eat. Didn't all our men lose their jobs because of strikes?"

"Don't you see the difference between political and economic strikes?"

"All right," I agreed. "Our stations will put up signs: 'For political strikers only! Those who are hungry because of economic strikes are not admitted. Signed . . .' You will sign the order."

The chairman yielded to this argument.

The welfare operations of the Council were expanding. Its stations were distributing up to forty thousand meals daily. It obtained an appropriation to give the unemployed allowances for rent and interest on pawnshop loans—an unprecedented step in Tsarist Russia, where almsgiving was the usual form of public welfare.

All this, however, did not solve our main problem. We asked for "bread and work" and obtained only bread. The Municipal Committee manifested no interest in public works, and the office of the mayor openly opposed this idea. The unemployed were becoming impatient, and I felt responsible for the delay. Indeed, the people around credited me with having gotten money for the hot-meal stations and believed that I must have some trick in my bag to get them work also. "Why don't you do something about work?" they asked me at our local headquarters and on the street.

The Council of the Unemployed convened to discuss the situation. The meeting was attended by 150 delegates, among them representatives of a score of the largest mills in St. Petersburg. The delegates suggested a new press campaign. I explained that the newspapers would have no interest in our cause during the dramatic clash between the government and the Duma. Any other plan? I had none to offer and had difficulty keeping the meeting in order. In irritation, I remonstrated with a particularly emotional speaker. "What is the point of shouting here where no councilman can hear you?"

Laughter followed this remark, but suddenly I realized that what I had said was not a joke. "Here is a plan," I said. "Let us go to the Municipal Council and tell the councilmen what the workers think of them."

"They will not admit us," Nikitin remarked soberly.

"We will crash the gate!"

"By force?" Nikitin asked.

"Why not? There are not more than twenty guards in the building. We can send a delegation of sixty or eighty men."

"But the councilmen will not listen to us. They will run away as soon as they see us," Nikitin insisted.

"We won't let them run away," I said. "How?" "The session room has two doors and we can crash both of them."

Two delegates, Malyshev and Boroda, supported my plan. If it worked, we would get something for our men; if it did not, the police would arrest us for disorderly conduct but they would not close the hot-meal stations. The meeting adopted the new plan. I told the S-D Committee casually that we were sending a new delegation to the Municipal Council. Nobody asked for details, and I did not have to explain that we intended to invade the Municipal Building by force.

The day was set for June 20. But when the seventy delegates—half of our Council—assembled in the hall of the Union of Engineers, little of the enthusiasm with which they had voted for the plan was left. Most of the delegates were skeptical, some were cynical. Malyshev and the vice-chairman of the Council, Zagoraev, defended the plan. Half a dozen of the delegates from the employed workers wanted to call off the whole affair. I offered to open an emergency session of the Council to reconsider the whole question.

"The decision must be unanimous. Either we all agree to go or we do not go at all."

There were neither chairs nor benches in the room. The furniture consisted of a large unpainted table used for sorting and packing the mail. I conducted the meeting standing on the table. Zagoraev opened the discussion by describing, step by step, how the delegation would proceed, his confidence impressed the delegates, and unanimity was restored. It was decided that Malyshev and I would lead the party that would enter the session room through the rear door, on the side of the offices, while Zagoraev, a six-foot-six giant and excellent speaker, would head the group making its way through the entrance hall. In each party, a "commando" of four husky boys would be in front, to deal with the guards should they try to stop us. Nobody was to carry any arms.

We proceeded to the Municipal Building in small groups and formed the two assault parties. Police posted at the entrance for office personnel paid no attention to the group led by Malyshev and me, probably taking us for the night shift of a repair or maintenance crew. The corridors were deserted, with only two guards at the door to the session room. We pushed them away and rushed along the aisle between the rostrum and the seats of councilmen.

The chairman jumped from his armchair and shouted, "Who are you, gentlemen?"

The delegation roared, "The un- emp- loyed!"

The councilmen left their seats, shouting and screaming. Some tried to hide under the desks.

Suddenly I noticed that we had failed to synchronize the entries of the two parties. Zagoraev and his men were not there. The councilmen also noticed that the front door of the room was free and hurled themselves toward it. We did not try to stop them, but marched at their heels into the hall. There the arrival of Zagoraev and his group, coming from the main entrance, increased the general confusion.

We took up a position in the middle of the hall, under the huge chandelier. The mayor, surrounded by a score of councilmen, approached us and said sternly, "Your behavior is highly unbecoming. What is your business here?"

"That is what we intended to tell you. Why didn't you stay to listen?"

"Because of your disorderly conduct!"

"Our conduct was perfectly orderly," Malyshev replied, "but you must be ashamed of yourselves. You behaved like scared rabbits."

Meanwhile, uniformed police took positions at the windows and doors of the hall. Suddenly a brawl started. A councilman rushing to a washroom had been stopped by a police sergeant. The Council guards came to his rescue and the sergeant was knocked down and dragged to the middle of the hall by the victorious councilman. Holding his glasses high in the air, he shouted, "This brute slapped me in the face! He broke my glasses. He could have killed me!"

We held our position. Some councilmen tried to talk with us and we explained to them that we had come to the Municipal Council to get a decisive answer: Will there or will there not be public works for the unemployed?

Then loud noises came from the courtyard—the trampling of horses, barked orders. I went to the window. The yard was full of Cossacks. We were trapped.

After a caucus, the mayor came toward us. "Misters unemployed," he said, "believe me, I did not call the Cossacks. I am going to ask the Military Governor to remove them."

"That is your business," Malyshev replied. "We did not ask you about the Cossacks. We are asking about public works."

We were tired of standing in the middle of the hall. The chairman of the Municipal Council ordered the waiters to put chairs under the chandelier and invited us to sit down. It was long after midnight. Nobody had left the building. Councilmen were crowded around the bar at the far end of the hall, talking among themselves. A few reporters strolled back and forth. I saw that they got information about our plans. If we were arrested, a new Council of the Unemployed would take over the next day; the unemployed would hold the Municipal Council responsible for whatever happened to us.

The waiters put up a long mahogany table in front of us and brought large trays with tea and sandwiches. We were hungry but not sure whether it would be proper to accept this attention from the councilmen. On the other hand, it was a friendly gesture on their part and we did not want to be rude. While we discussed the problem our tea got cold. Finally we decided to accept the treat but to pay for it—five kopecks for a glass of tea or a sandwich. We put the money on a tray with a polite note.

The mayor returned and shortly afterward the Cossacks withdrew from the courtyard. We sat under the great chandelier while the men dozed in armchairs along the wall. Then the Council chairman approached us with a score of councilmen and offered to escort us to the street—as a protection against the police. We declined the offer. A councilman asked us:

"What are you waiting for? It is time for all of us to go to bed."

The big clock in the hall showed 3:00 A.M. Malyshev announced our decision.

"We will leave *after* the councilmen."

They began to fade out, one after another. We remained in the empty hall. The waiters turned off all the lights along the walls, leaving only the big chandelier over our heads. Then we retired.

The next day the office of the mayor telephoned us that the Municipal Council would convene before the weekend and elect a permanent committee for the supervision of public works. We were invited to send our representatives to give the Municipal Council useful information related to the question on the agenda. Only three spokesmen were admitted to the session, but we obtained a dozen visitors' tickets to the balcony. Malyshev, Zagoraev, and Nikolai Petrov spoke for the organization. All three speeches, prepared in writing and repeatedly rehearsed, were moderate in tone but stressed the danger of an outbreak of anarchistic acts if the Municipal Council did not keep its promise to provide work for the unemployed. I marshaled the silent deputation on the balcony. When the vote came, we stood up, holding onto the railing, and stared at the councilmen. They seemed disturbed, and some of them tried to let us know they had voted for public works.

We had won the campaign and could tell our men that they would soon have work. I met our speakers at the entrance of the session room. Malyshev and Boroda had tears in their eyes. They hugged and kissed me, while the councilmen looked with amazement at this outburst of sentimentality among the "tough guys" whom they called "misters unemployed."

A wave of optimism and goodwill spread among the unemployed. Elated by the successful campaign, I had been giving little thought to the rapidly deteriorating political situation. Suddenly I learned from a newspaper that the Duma had been dissolved.

THE END OF THE FIRST DUMA

When the members of the Duma came to the Tauride Palace on July 9, they found it locked and surrounded by troops. Most of the deputies assembled in Viborg, at that time a Finnish city some two hours by train from St. Petersburg, and issued an appeal to the nation. They urged the people to maintain order and at the same time appealed to them to exercise passive resistance to the government and particularly to refuse to pay taxes or give recruits to the army. It was a weak and confused document. Later the Bolsheviks accused the Cadets of having lured the members of the Duma to Viborg to keep them from getting in touch with the people and organizing resistance to the government. There was some truth in this accusation. When the government prosecuted members of the Duma who had signed the Viborg appeal, many Cadets testified that their purpose had been to prevent the revolutionary upheaval that might have resulted from dissolution of the Duma.

St. Petersburg was calm. No demonstrations, no strikes. Reports about the reaction of the people in the provinces were few and vague. And suddenly, like thunder out of a clear sky, came news: Revolt has broken out in Sveaborg, the naval fortress of Helsinki. . . . It is spreading. . . . The mutinous garrison has seized the city. . . . The workers are joining the revolt. . . . Finland's railroads are paralyzed. . . . The rebels are calling on St. Petersburg workers to help them. . . .

Actually, the unrest in Sveaborg had nothing to do with the Duma's dissolution. As in other military riots in Russia at that time, the immediate cause was trivial. Two soldiers were arrested for a minor breach of discipline. When their comrades protested, they too were taken into custody. As protests increased, the High Command decided to arrest the entire company. Other companies of the same regiment overpowered the military police. Then other regiments joined in the riot, and by evening the fortress was in the hands of the rebels. Next, the railroad workers walked out to block the trains transporting troops from St. Petersburg.

The movement spread no further, however. The naval units in the harbor of Sveaborg and the troops stationed outside the fortress did not side with the garrison. On July 20, the navy began to bombard Helsinki, while the Cossacks and foot troops advanced from the mainland. The revolt was crushed before the S-D organization in St. Petersburg decided whether or not to support it.

Just then revolt broke out in Kronstadt. All communication with the fortress was broken off. The St. Petersburg Committee of the party assembled hurriedly. Somebody asked me whether our Council of the Unemployed had connections with the fortress. I said no, but we had some good men on the waterfront, and I offered to go to Kronstadt. The Committee told me to hurry.

In our registration bureau close to the waterfront, two of our men volunteered to provide a launch for me. An hour later they returned with bad news: nothing could be done before dusk. After sunset we went to the shore. Two youths came with me with tools for cutting chains and starting a motor without a key. Others were combing the beach and the inlets for a boat. This was one of the white nights of a St. Petersburg summer. One could see patrols and sentinels everywhere. We spent all night searching for a gap in the defense but found none. We heard salvos of guns from the gulf. After dawn we returned to the bureau and learned that everything was over in Kronstadt. That very evening the ringleaders had been shot on the ramparts of the fortress and their bodies thrown into the sea.

The day after order was restored in Sveaborg and Kronstadt, a strike started in St. Petersburg. Workers in some factories walked out, but there was no unity in the movement. The Mensheviks called on the workers to support the Duma; the Bolsheviks charged the Duma with treason. The strike collapsed on the third day. Next, a general strike was proclaimed in Moscow, but this, too, ended in failure.

The grim era of Stolypin began. In contrast to his predecessor, Goremykin, Stolypin had brains and was ready to combine ruthless suppression of the revolution with some moderate reforms, provided such reforms did not affect the principle of absolutism. Nevertheless, between the days of Ivan the Terrible and Stalin, his was the worst orgy of political terror. Thousands of "suspects" were jailed, deported, or killed by a firing squad. A new wave of violence swept over Russia. Police officers were ambushed and assassinated. A suicide squad of S-R blew up Stolypin's residence. Stolypin answered by introducing "military field courts," instructed to pass and execute death sentences within twenty-four hours after the suspect was seized.

The S-D party went underground, and its central organs were transferred to Finland. In St. Petersburg, however, some vestiges of freedom remained, among them the Cadet newspapers, a few labor unions, and the Council of the Unemployed.

THE BEGINNING OF PUBLIC WORKS

It was then that the Council of the Unemployed received its first requisition for workers. The new Municipal Committee had intended originally to use our organization only as a hiring office, but later it realized that it needed our co-operation in dealing with the unemployed and asked us to act as a co-operative construction contractor. We would have accepted if we had been sure of enough jobs for all our men. We anticipated, however, that public works would fall short of this goal and feared that, as a contractor, we would be unable to establish a system of rotation to distribute the available jobs among all the unemployed on our waiting list. We therefore suggested that the Municipal Committee itself should be the contractor while we would deliver the labor force and assume responsibility for firing, hiring, and maintaining discipline on the job. The agreement also provided for an eight-hour day and a flat wage for all—one ruble a day, plus ten kopeks for carfare.

These were fair conditions. Our men might have thought them unexpectedly favorable except for the particular character of the work. The jobs assigned to them were mainly in earth-moving projects. The most important single project was to build an earthen dam to protect the Neva harbor against floods. Building steel bridges also entailed a lot of earth moving. Furthermore, in order to put as many men to work as possible, we banned the use of labor-saving machinery and insisted that all earthwork be done with hand shovels, pickaxes, crowbars, and wheelbarrows. The work was hard on our men, most of whom were accustomed to less strenuous jobs at a lathe, and it became particularly so in the winter, when the ground began to freeze. But we succeeded in establishing an ideological halo around our public works: the eight-hour working day and self-government!

In view of its new responsibilities, the Council of the Unemployed tightened its organization. It established eight precinct councils consisting of delegates elected by the unemployed and employed workers. The St. Petersburg Council included all precinct councils, plus representatives from the public works. The executive board consisted of two representatives from each precinct and one from each public works project. The president, elected by direct ballots of the unemployed and employed workers, was charged with general control over the precinct councils and entitled to dissolve them and prescribe new elections if necessary. I was again elected unanimously to this position and became a slave to commitments for which I was unprepared.

I was still a youngster of twenty-one, without administrative experience. My judgment of people was often wrong. I was too credulous, and Malyshev used to tease me for having a soft spot for crooks and cranks. I handled my job by sheer strength of will and the support of half a dozen able and devoted comrades. We worked as a team, but the others pushed me to the head of the organization, crediting me with ability to make decisions and get people to obey them. I think my only advantage over them was that I could write better than they, knew how to talk with the Municipal Council, and remained a trifle aloof from the crowd—not enough to provoke resentment but enough to give orders. All the leaders worked without remuneration, but I had no financial worries. Publishers paid me royalties on my pamphlets, and I continued to lecture on physics in my father's courses during the summers of 1906 and 1907.

Although the Council of the Unemployed became largely a workers' welfare organization, it kept its revolutionary flair, and our registration bureaus were open for use by underground party organizations. Two score soldiers and sailors from Sveaborg and Kronstadt were hiding from the police with identification cards we provided, and some of them were employed on public works. We likewise provided refuge and work for a dozen farm hands who had escaped firing squads in the Baltic provinces. Apart from other considerations, it was good to have these politically mature and reliable men on the works.

I also continued to work in the S-D party, as a member of the St. Petersburg Committee and the Conference. There was nothing exciting in the activity of these organizations and I was not interested in the squabbles between the Bolsheviks and Mensheviks, but I wished to maintain contact between the organization of the unemployed and the party. Among the unemployed I was at home. I liked the people with whom I worked and felt that they loved me. In the party, by contrast, I was a stranger.

LENIN

My position in the party was rather unusual. The Bolsheviks were using me increasingly as a figurehead and spokesman at public meetings but did not trust me in internal factional affairs. I had little respect for the Marxian gospel and still less for the leaders of both factions in the St. Petersburg organization. The leader of the Bolshevist faction, Zinoviev, was almost as obnoxious to me as the Menshevist leader, Dan, and I had no doubt that both reciprocated

my feelings. But I was an asset to the party as president of the
Council of the Unemployed and also as a man with wide personal
contacts with workers who was equally ready to speak before a
crowd in a factory yard or a sophisticated Cadet audience. I did not
speak much in committee meetings, however, partly because they
bored me and partly because I felt hostility around me.

Strangely, the only man in the Bolshevist organization with
whom I was close at that time was Lenin. He did not belong to the
St. Petersburg organization officially but used it as a sounding board
in his fight against the Mensheviks for control over the party. He
knew, of course, that I was a dubious Marxist or no Marxist at all.
But for some reason—Lenin did nothing without calculation—he
became interested in me. After a Bolshevist conference in Kuokkala,
Finland, where he was living in hiding, he asked me casually,
"Would you come to see me tonight? We could chat over a cup of
tea."

It was considered a great honor among the Bolsheviks to be invited to the Old Man's home. Moreover, he was one of the few men
on the political horizon whom I respected. I accepted his invitation.
He was living in a small two-room cottage typical of a Finnish peasant's. It was poorly furnished but neat, and there was a feeling of
simple hospitality in its narrow living room.

I spent the evening with him and his wife, Krupskaya, and later
was often their guest. Our relations never reached the stage of
friendship; Lenin had no real friends around him, only people
whom he wished to meet for some practical reason. I never knew
what he expected of me, but between the middle of 1906 and the
end of 1907 I met him almost every week and was closer to him
than to anybody else in the party. Thus I learned to know not only
the Old Man who was to play such a tragic role in Russian history a
decade later, but also his inner circle, the Bolshevist Center.

The testimony of people who met Lenin at different phases of his
life differs widely, and my personal impressions do not always agree
with those of others. He was a complex personality, given to sudden
changes in mood, manners, and relations with persons around him.
He could be an irresistible charmer with those he wished to win as
followers, but he impressed others as an arrogant snob. Moreover,
the Lenin of 1906-7 whom I describe here was very different from
the Lenin of 1917, of whom I shall speak later, and the Lenin who
ruled all Russia ruthlessly in the 1920's.

He was a fanatic, but there was no fire in his fanaticism. Rather,
it was cold, like a steel blade. He was perhaps the most unemotional
man I have ever met in politics. No hate, no compassion, not even

any irritation against his opponents. His ruthlessness in polemics never stemmed from a personal grudge—each word, even each slanderous innuendo in his writings, was coldly calculated.

He was, above all, a thinker and a logician, and his strength was in his single-mindedness. He knew no doubt, no hesitation. For him, his ideas represented the absolute truth, his program was the road to salvation, and any deviation from this program was an act of folly or treason. When he treated his opponents in the party as fools and traitors, he was not manifesting bad manners or a violent temper but was giving a precise expression of his conviction. If those who disagreed with him were not fools, they *must* be traitors; if they were not traitors, they *must* be fools. He had a strong messianic complex, but it was completely impersonal. His taciturn, unpretentious wife and his followers regarded him as a man of destiny, but he never boasted or even spoke of himself.

Lenin was simple and friendly with the people and would listen with visible interest to even the incoherent talk of a half-illiterate worker, his big bald head slightly cocked, his narrow eyes screwed up, and an understanding smile on his lips. He liked such talks and often got something out of them. He believed that the masses, left to their own resources, would never find their way to socialism. They could gain victory in revolution only by following the lead of a Socialist party, which, in turn, must be led by the revolutionary elite. But at the same time he believed in the revolutionary intuition of the masses. To lead the masses one must understand them, he repeated time and again.

Lenin's thinking in private conversation, as in his pamphlets and articles, was a combination of doctrinairism and pragmatism. He would elaborate some quotation from Marx and draw conclusions in an irritatingly pedantic way, then inject a reference to current conditions that would give unexpected strength to his position. His thinking was strictly departmentalized—rigid and doctrinaire in theory, highly opportunistic in action. His speeches were seldom spontaneous; he did not improvise on the impulse of the moment. He took time before committing himself, and in his inner circle he let others talk while he listened, nodding approval, smiling, and letting the rest guess whether or not he agreed with them.

His companions would ask him before an important decision, "What would you advise, Vladimir Ilyich?"

Lenin's eyes would narrow to thin slits and he would answer with a sly smile, "I do not know. Let the workers decide. They see it better."

I saw him in a conference at which the workers were airing their displeasure and criticizing his leadership. He listened patiently, occasionally nodding approval, and then said, "Surely this was our mistake. The one who makes no error is either a freak or a fool. The wise man is the one who is able to see and correct his mistakes."

It was easy for Lenin to change his mind if he thought that conditions had changed. But when he made a decision, that was the law for his faction and there was no appeal against it. He was a thinker in the sense that he had a fruitful and completely independent mind, but he lacked the intellectual humility that usually goes with the capacity for thinking. His intolerance shocked me the more as I personally was always inclined to a sort of agnosticism and considered all truths as working hypotheses, valid for our current stage of knowledge. What reconciled me with Lenin was his absence of vanity.

Lenin did not like to have yes-men around him and treated them with undisguised contempt. Apart from his technical aides, most people I met at his home in Finland were persons who were devoted to him but remained independent. Some had disagreed with him more than once. He held no grudge against them so long as he could count on them in fundamental matters. And he could rely on them! Once a decision was made, Lenin's authority was supreme in his circle.

Bogdanov, the best economist of the Marxian school in Russia and a member of Lenin's inner circle, once said to me, "I have often disagreed with Ilyich, but he has almost always proved to be right." I was less certain of Lenin's superhuman wisdom. Once I told him I thought I had discovered the clue to his philosophy.

"And that is?"

"A non-Euclidian axiom: The part is more than the whole. Labor is more than the nation, the S-D party is more than the labor movement, Bolshevism is more than the party, and your Center here is more than the Bolshevist faction."

He laughed heartily. "There is something in that. Of course, the part that is the salt of the whole is more than the rest of the whole."

Lenin was an incomparable master at winning proselytes. One of his approaches was to eradicate any moral "prejudices" in the converted. He recognized no morals, no rules of decency in politics, and had nothing but contemptuous mockery for the concept of honor. "Revolution is a dirty job," I heard him say. "You do not make it with white gloves."

I did not like this attitude. I kept faith with Petrazhitsky's theory of the state as a moral phenomenon and regarded the revolution as a clash between the old and new systems of moral values. To Lenin, this was ridiculous idealism.

A fight against moral inhibitions was an important aspect of Lenin's political propaganda. People engaged in revolutionary work often profess a double scale of moral values—one for people in general, another for revolutionaries. The advocates of such a double code of morality justify it by contending that the goal of a revolution is always to replace the scale of values imposed on the people by the oppressors with another scale of values that accords with freedom, justice, and equality. But Lenin's idea was that revolution needs no justification—least of all a moral justification—and is itself the highest criterion of right and wrong. Whatever is expedient for the revolution—according to Lenin, for the Bolshevist party—is right; everything that fails to serve it is valueless or evil. This philosophy of absolute amoralism in politics had a destructive effect on the young workers whom Lenin converted into "professional" officials of the organization.

Most of the persons in Lenin's immediate circle were men of high political and personal integrity. But he believed that a revolutionary party also needs obedient scoundrels, such as Anton for minor errands or Zinoviev for more responsible dirty jobs. They could be drunks, wastrels, gigolos, embezzlers of party funds, notorious liars, or cowards. Lenin kept them in the organization as his personal palace guard. "Ours is a big business," he explained. "We can use all kinds of trash."

His moral indulgence was sometimes grotesque. Anton, for example, was one of his protégés despite the conspicuous blots on his escutcheon. Once the party organization sent him from Russia to Geneva with funds for the local Bolshevist group. He arrived without money but with a cloak-and-dagger story about his narrow escape from the police. Later it was proved that he had squandered the party's money in a drunken spree in a brothel. Lenin came to his defense. "Perhaps he went there to escape spies," he suggested. "And not much money was involved."

I do not know whether Lenin even then was dreaming of personal power. My impression is, rather, that he had some anarchistic leanings and thought of a society without a centralized government. Perhaps Bakunin, with his vision of a revolutionary hurricane that creates new life by destroying the old world, was closer to Lenin than was Marx.

No one who came into personal contact with Lenin could remain indifferent toward him. Some loved him, others hated him; some fell completely under his influence, others followed him to a certain point and later became his implacable enemies.

My attitude toward him was somewhat different from that of the others. Because of my skepticism concerning Marxism, I was not impressed by his erudition in Marxist literature. Moreover, his excursions into the realm of history and philosophy seemed to me naïve and even ridiculous. I liked him for his revolutionary temperament, strong will, and resourcefulness. I knew, however, that, while he kept me in his inner circle, he did not trust my loyalty to his faction.

In 1907 an S-D convention—Bolsheviks and Mensheviks together —was to meet abroad. I do not remember precisely the rules for electing delegates, but the principle was that each faction would have one delegate for each hundred votes cast for its candidates in the local party cells. Although I did not campaign personally, I had more votes than all the other Bolshevist candidates in the St. Petersburg organization together, partly because of the votes of the unemployed. My votes, added to those cast for other Bolshevist candidates, would have given the faction five additional seats in the convention. But in the Bolshevist conference that made the final arrangements, Lenin barred my election, declaring that it would be better for the faction to lose all five places than to have Sergei Petrov sit in the convention. The Committee gave me the choice of going to the convention as head of an independent group or transferring my votes to the faction's list of candidates. I chose the latter.

The next time I saw Lenin he said to me, "You may wonder why we did not confirm your election. I objected to your presence at the convention. I knew you would vote with the Mensheviks if you liked their position better than ours. Worst of all, many delegates to the convention will be on the fence, and if you walked out, they would walk out with you. Was I right?"

"You were," I replied. "I would not accept any mandate with a factional string attached to it. Moreover, I would not have left the unemployed for the party convention."

Lenin was satisfied for the time being with my conditional allegiance to the group. This episode brought us closer together. I had no political ambition, was only moderately interested in party affairs, and did not feel humiliated by Lenin's opposition to me. Rather, I was flattered by his recognition of my independence. After all, he was the boss and wanted to have his group at the convention marching as a troop at the parade, executing his orders. I was not suited to such a performance.

Perhaps I was then under the spell of Lenin's personal charm, but it was neither his nor any other political doctrine that held me in the revolutionary movement. Torn between my scientific interests and everyday drudgery among the unemployed, I asked myself why I could not go back to my books. The urge that I had had in the heyday of the revolution to be with the people had faded away. There was no longer any revolution or any "people" to join. But I felt a strange obligation toward the unemployed. I had joined them on a momentary impulse to help them with their petition. That had seemed easy and not binding on me. But now I had around me people who believed they needed me, and I could not quit. What I did was essentially labor welfare work, but somehow it kept me chained to the revolutionary movement.

I once tried to explain this to Lenin. He seemed interested, amused, and incredulous.

IN THE DEPORTATION PRISON

My work was suddenly interrupted. The prosecuting attorney summoned me to his office and handed me an order of the circuit court to deliver me to the Novgorod Detention House in expectation of trial for having advocated the overthrow of the government in November, 1905.

In the deportation prison I was locked in a dark cell, about two and a half by one and a half yards, with no furniture other than a narrow cot. Light penetrated into the cell through a low, narrow grilled door that opened onto a long corridor. A vague sound of voices came from behind the grille. From a low whisper they gradually became louder and louder, until a barking command interrupted them.

"Silence! Prisoners are not permitted to talk."

After a brief spell of silence, whispers started again, then voices began to rise. I stood at the door listening. A voice quite close to me asked:

"A new arrival? Do you hear me?"

"I do."

The voice came from the cell at my right. The speaker and I were two steps apart but we could not see each other. He asked when I had been sentenced and under what articles of law. When I told him he remarked, "That is strange. You do not belong here. Everyone here has been sentenced to the gallows. Report at the inspection round. They will transfer you." However, when the inspection round passed through the corridor, I did not report to the officer.

That night my neighbor called to me again, "New arrival, who are you?"

I told him about the Council of the Unemployed.

"I am from the Putilov works," he said. "You know the place? Are our folks in the Council?"

He told me his story. His name was Jacob and he was a welder by trade. He did not belong to any party but had walked out with the others in January, and again in October and November, 1905. In January, 1906, he was in a brawl with another worker. They came to blows. Jacob struck the other man, who, in falling, hit the sharp end of a bench. His skull fracture proved fatal and Jacob was arrested for manslaughter. The man with whom he had exchanged blows turned out to have been a member of the local Black Hundreds, and the prosecution changed the charge from manslaughter to a terroristic act. Jacob was sentenced to the gallows but, in consideration of his youth, the death penalty was changed to life imprisonment.

When he finished his story, a voice came from the other side of my closet. "They did not change my sentence. My mother asked them. The general threw her out."

Nobody on the corridor slept that night. Voices boomed, each telling another story. Were the men talking to themselves or was each addressing his invisible neighbor?

In the morning I was taken to the general deportation ward. When I passed the adjoining cell I saw a tall youth with a haggard face and a shaven head at the grille. He said rapidly, "If you see the people at Putilov, give them my greetings. Tell them, from Jacob the welder; they will know."

The deportation ward was a very long, high hall, like a railroad depot. It had long narrow tables with benches in the middle and straw sacks on the floor along all four walls. Two rows of cell buckets flanked the grille. Men in rags, some in civilian clothing, others in prison garb, a few in irons, were milling between the tables and straw sacks. A tall man in fetters approached me. "Political? Come with me. I am the headman here." He led me to a group of men sitting on their sacks on the floor. "One of yours. Make space for him."

Thus I was introduced into the political community of the ward. Most of the prisoners were awaiting deportation to penitentiaries in various parts of Russia. Others were peasants charged with participating in agrarian revolts, prisoners brought to St. Petersburg from provincial jails, and suspicious characters who did not wish to tell who they were.

Next day the warden told me that the Union of Engineers had offered a bond of three thousand rubles for me, and the Council of the Unemployed expected to get me out in a few days. There was also a package from home: a shirt, a towel, a toothbrush, a couple of handkerchiefs, a cake of soap, and some food. I returned from the warden's office to the ward, my hands full and my heart warmed. And I kept this feeling within me while the petition of the Union of Engineers traveled from desk to desk and from office to office. Somebody in the court objected to my release on bail, but his superior ruled in my favor. Then somebody in the Military Governor's office wrote a memorandum pointing out that since I was behind bars where I belonged there was no point in setting me free.

The ward was full of noise, stench, filth. But life was not bad there. For the first time in many months I had no responsibilities and could do as I pleased—sit against the wall with closed eyes and listen to noises around me or look around and listen to nothing. I needed this kind of rest badly. After three or four weeks I was released on bail.

THE SECOND ELECTION CAMPAIGN

The campaign for elections to the Second Duma, in the winter of 1906-7, was in full swing, and again I found myself in it up to the hilt. The electoral law had remained unchanged, but the government was trying to block the election of liberal and radical candidates by arbitrary interpretation of its provisions. The idea was to eliminate opposition candidates, beginning at the lowest step in the election, and sift the electors at each subsequent stage. The peasants would be forbidden to elect a village schoolteacher, clerk, or priest unless the candidate was living in the community in which he was born. Residence requirements for workers were raised. The courts were instructed to start prosecution of prospective candidates suspected of liberal or radical leanings.

The radical parties no longer thought of boycotting the elections, but they had no common electoral strategy. In contrast, the Cadets developed a plan of action on two fronts. They attacked the rightists by denouncing Stolypin's regime of violence and lawlessness; the task of the Duma, they told the voters, was to put an end to this regime. Then they asked how the Duma could ensure law, order, and freedom in Russia. And they answered by severely criticizing the revolutionary parties and their tactics in the First Duma. "You use a violin to play on, not to drive nails," Miliukov explained. "Likewise, you must use the Duma for legislation, not for fomenting strikes and unrest."

At the first electoral meeting, I paid tribute to Miliukov's metaphor. "The point is well taken," I said. "The Duma is neither a violin nor a hammer, but Professor Miliukov is right in stressing the distinction between the Cadets and the left. It is up to the voters to decide whom to send to the Duma—violin players or wreckers who will become builders."

The two arguments became the leitmotiv of the dispute.

I was arrested twice during the campaign. After a speech that contained sharp criticism of the government, a police officer stationed in the auditorium invited me to the entrance hall. There a platoon of policemen surrounded me and the precinct chief shouted:

"March! Go!"

"Where do you think I should go?" I asked.

"To my quarters," he replied.

The man was drunk. I turned to the open door of the meeting hall and shouted with all the strength of my lungs:

"Citizens, I am arrested! I invite all to follow me to the police station, as witnesses."

Then I took my overcoat and said to the police chief, "Now we will go to your quarters."

We were surrounded by an excited crowd. The chief sobered up at once.

"What are you starting here?" he shouted. "I have invited you to my office to ascertain your name and address." I gave him the information and returned to the meeting hall. After the meeting some two hundred citizens escorted me to the border of the precinct.

Another time I described the policy of "interpretation" as "a foul play worthy of swindlers." The chief of the precinct police, who attended the meeting, arrested me and charged me with having insulted His Majesty the Tsar and his ministers in calling them swindlers. After reading the charge sheet, I asked the officer:

"Are you ready to witness under oath that I called the Tsar a swindler? Are you ready to name the ministers whom I described this way?"

He answered grimly, "You did not name them, but everybody understood what you meant."

"You mean that when I spoke of swindlers without naming them, everybody understood that they were the Tsar and the ministers?"

"I did not say that!" he protested.

"You did!" I insisted. "You have insulted the Tsar. I have witnesses. I do not know whether you will ever get a conviction against me, but I guarantee you that you will be kicked out of your uniform."

The police chief reread his charge sheet, looked intently at me and my witnesses, and said, "Don't try to scare me. I'm not such a dumb cop. But you have shown your hand. If that is your defense, the case will never be brought to trial. We can dismiss it now." He tore the charge sheet to pieces, we shook hands, and I went home.

All in all, the campaign in St. Petersburg could not have been called free, but police interference did not do much harm to the opposition parties. It was different in the villages. However, even Stolypin's police could not compel the peasants to vote for the candidates recommended by the government—a practice that became common later under the Kremlin regime.

The S-D party decided to present its official candidates in the workers' elections and to abstain from campaigning among the peasants. It had no clear policy for urban elections and vacillated between the policy of party lists and a coalition with other parties. In St. Petersburg, the Cadets tried to unite all progressive groups. The Laborites and the S-R were ready to enter into a coalition with them if the S-D participated in the plan. The Mensheviks were willing to accept this policy, but the Bolsheviks insisted on a pure party ticket. Amidst the party squabble, I offered a new plan—a coalition of the S-D with the S-R and the Laborites against the Cadets and the rightists. This plan became popular with rank-and-file party members, but met with vehement opposition in the St. Petersburg Committee. Thus, my proposal resulted in the three-corner split in the organization.

Lenin followed the dispute with great interest but did not commit himself. I suspected that he was on the side of the "pure ticket," but when I asked him, he answered with his usual sly smile, "I do not know. . . . It depends. . . ." At the party conference, held in Finland, he threw all his influence in support of the policy of the pure lists, but after a violent clash between the two factions he changed his tactics and recommended the "left bloc" strategy as the best way to isolate the Menshevist faction and annihilate it politically. The rump conference, without the Mensheviks, accepted this plan and I was asked to negotiate with our prospective allies. After the meeting Lenin said to me, "Your plan has saved the day. It is good to have something to fall back on when the need arises."

Our prospective allies accepted all our proposals—a left bloc was their old dream. We met a serious difficulty, however. The law provided for secret balloting in the first stage of the election in urban areas, but the government declared that no pre-printed ballots would be counted unless the blanks had been stamped by the local municipal authorities. It ordered the latter to issue no blanks to parties not registered by the police. As a result of these interpretations, no party left of the Cadets could obtain the blanks.

When we discussed the situation with other leftist parties, a spokesman of the Labor Group proposed a plan. A group of priests with liberal leanings would form an alliance of Christian Love (or something of the kind) and announce its intention of entering the election in St. Petersburg. After obtaining stamped blanks from the Municipal Council, the group would enter into a coalition with the Laborites, pass the blanks on to them, and quietly dissolve. I did not like this plan and told our allies that we should try to get the blanks in a more honest way, by straight counterfeiting.

Through workers in print shops, the party had connections with all the large printing firms. It did not take long to locate the shop in which the official blanks were printed, and we soon had a complete set of ballots identical with those used by the registered groups. Next, a municipal official close to the Council of the Unemployed volunteered to lend us the municipal seal for a night. Electrolytic replicas of the seal were made in no time. Two days later I showed our allies the blanks. They found them wonderful.

After the elections, the Attorney General ordered an investigation. A committee of experts appointed to find out how the left bloc got the ballots came to the conclusion that the blanks conformed to the law.

The elections to the Second Duma revealed a shift to the left among the voters. If the Duma had been elected in a more or less democratic way, it would have had a leftist majority of 75 to 80 per cent, and a minority opposition consisting mainly of moderate Laborites and Cadets. Not a single candidate right of the Cadets would have been elected. However, the distribution of the electors among different classes of voters cut down the strength of the left and enabled the extreme right to drag their representatives into the Duma. The leftists' victory in the popular vote gave them no comfort. The country remained in the iron grip of the government, which maintained order with the aid of field-martial courts that issued from one to two hundred death sentences a month.

THE SECOND DUMA

The new Duma convened on February 20, 1907. Its inauguration gave an opportunity for demonstrations around its meeting place, the Tauride Palace. Crowds cheered peasant and worker delegates, booed down those who looked like substantial citizens. The police permitted factory meetings of workers with the S-D deputies. The speakers were very cautious, however, and left the audiences disappointed and bored.

Almost immediately after the inauguration it became clear that, in contrast to the First Duma, the Second Duma had no working majority. The strength of the Cadets had been reduced to ninety-nine seats as compared with roughly double that number in the First Duma. The Octobrists and Monarchists together had seventy-nine seats. The Social Democrats and Laborites together had 222 seats out of four hundred and could have formed the majority if they had united. Actually, however, some Laborites voted with the Cadets, and some could not make up their minds and abstained from voting. Thus, the Cadets dominated the Duma through a weak and unstable majority formed from their own group, the rightists, and splinter votes of the Labor Group. The policy of the Cadets was expressed by the slogan: Spare the Duma! In practice, this meant abstaining from action that could irritate Stolypin or the Black Hundreds.

Two weeks passed. The government ignored the Duma. The Cadets were using extreme caution and the Laborites were reluctantly following them; the Duma was rapidly losing the sympathy of the public. Suddenly Stolypin announced that he intended to present the Duma with an outline of his program. The name of Stolypin was so closely associated with a regime of gallows that discussion of his program in the Duma was bound to lead to a clash between the left and the government. The Cadets therefore proposed that the Duma refrain from discussing the address of the Prime Minister. The Laborites accepted the proposal; the S-D rejected it.

After Stolypin's speech, businesslike in form but contemptuous of the elected representatives of the people, the spokesman of the S-D group mounted the rostrum. He was a young man, tall and lean, with unusually handsome features, a resonant voice, and a noticeable Caucasian accent. This was the first public appearance of Irakli Tseretelli.

"Many people," he said, "will be surprised by the silence of the grave with which this assembly has met the declaration of the government that dissolved the First Duma and introduced field-martial courts. This silence, however, expresses the depth of your indignation. No outcries, no roars would be adequate to express the feelings of the people toward this government. . . . We do not ask the government to yield to the will of the people. We know it will yield to force alone. We ask the people's representatives to build up the necessary force."

Tseretelli became the most popular speaker in the Duma. Although he belonged to the Menshevist wing of the party, the Bolsheviks recognized him as the party's mouthpiece. Who could have suspected then that, a decade later, the same hall in the Tauride Palace would hear Tseretelli speaking in the first and last session of the Constituent Assembly, challenging Lenin with the same passion, in the name of the same democratic principles?

The Cadets continued their efforts to convince the Tsar that he should hand over power to them. The Black Hundreds argued before the Tsar that the moderate liberals in the Duma were no better than the extreme left.

There was some similarity in the positions of the First and Second Dumas, but the distribution of forces in the nation had changed. Stolypin's government was stronger than Goremykin's, and the people were more nearly unanimous in their opposition to the Tsarist regime. The open clash between the nation and the government was near, but the revolutionary spirit in the people was gone.

Life in the S-D party was wholly dominated by interfactional squabble. The Mensheviks demanded a party trial of Lenin, accusing him of having slandered them in a pamphlet criticizing their tactics in the St. Petersburg elections. The pamphlet was indeed insulting, if not directly slanderous. I moved a resolution in the St. Petersburg Committee not to distribute it in the local organization but was beaten by a narrow margin. When I told Lenin the reason for my motion, he laughed genially. "You are too thin-skinned, Comrade Petrov, and do not know the Mensheviks well enough."

His good humor was genuine. He always enjoyed his opponents' blunders, and the campaign the Menshevist High Command launched against him at this time was the greatest blunder he could have hoped to have them make.

PUBLIC WORKS

My work for the Council of the Unemployed was becoming increasingly tiring. I seldom had more than four or five hours of sleep and rarely saw my parents, sister, and brothers. All day I was surrounded by people, listening and talking, resting only in the trolley on the way from one spot to another. And I had to keep all my appointments, decisions, disputes, requests, and promises in my head, without benefit of secretary and files. The only satisfaction I got from this killing job was that I liked the persons with and for whom I worked.

Our main difficulty was with the slow development of the projects. Engineer Nurberg, in charge of work in the harbor, agreed to place five to six hundred additional men on his project, but his plan was vetoed by Bers, the chief engineer of the Municipal Committee. After long negotiations, the Committee authorized Nurberg to hire two hundred more men. I went to the harbor, called a conference of foremen and worker delegates headed now by Zagoraev, and asked them whether they would be able to handle the situation if, instead of two hundred men as requested, twelve hundred should report for work. They thought they could if the workers came at intervals— some two hundred men each half hour.

We spent the night assembling and organizing the crews. In the morning the operation began. I directed it from the central office; Zagoraev had command in the field. The first two hundred men arrived half an hour before the morning whistle and were sent to a remote section of the works. The second party of two hundred was absorbed similarly. When the third party appeared, Nurberg telephoned, complaining about the violation of the Committee's instructions. I replied that we relied on his ability, administrative skill, and sympathy with the unemployed. He thanked me, but half an hour later he called again—another party of two hundred had just arrived; he must report to the Municipal Committee. I asked him to report that I personally had sent men to the harbor and was sending more.

Then a call came from Bers—he was angry and accused me of blowing up the public works. The president of the Municipal Committee also called to ask me if it was true that I had deliberately violated the established procedure.

"Certainly I did," I answered. "How else could I prove to you that the work *can* be expanded?"

We agreed to meet at the harbor. The people at the project were as busy as beavers; shovels were swinging, wheelbarrows running. The work was going on in perfect order. After a tour of the works, the chairman said, "I cannot approve of your highhanded act, but I promise you the work will be continued on today's scale."

This was one of the few happy days on the public works. Our everyday chores were less gratifying. When we assumed responsibility for order and discipline at work, we did not realize that these included, among other things, an obligation to look after the drunks. Since drunks swinging pickaxes were not only a nuisance but a serious danger to other workers, it was necessary to remove them from the place. The task was particularly difficult on Mondays. I learned that there were different stages of drunkenness and that the opinions of a drunken man and a sober man may differ widely in classifying marginal cases. Our attempt to have a panel of local experts arbitrate the disputes proved unworkable. On Mondays, not all the panel members were entirely reliable!

Then the Anarchists appeared on the scene with a new popular slogan: Freedom to drink! Each individual, they preached, knows best what is good or bad, dangerous or safe for him. Nobody should tell his fellow men when, what, where, and how much he may drink!

I remember one Monday at the harbor in the summer of 1907. Suffocating heat, dust, quarrels all over the place. First I had to arbitrate a dispute about the cause of a minor accident in a ditch. The workers blamed the foreman, he accused the crew. Then a clash broke out between a crew and its delegate. Next I was called to the office where a drunk refused to give up his pickax. He swung it about while talking with the engineers, foremen, and delegates but denied that his gestures were a threat. I put an end to the scene by taking the tool out of his hands and ordering him to go home, with the warning that he would be fired for good if he disobeyed. I left him fuming and went back to the ditches where another dispute was in progress. The whole day passed this way. By evening I was exhausted and angry at myself. What was I doing here? What kind of political activity was this?

Walking toward the trolley after the whistle, I noticed that the drunk was shadowing me. At the edge of the works he overtook me. Standing in front of me, he asked:

"Is this the end of our grounds, Comrade Petrov? May one drink beyond that line?"

"Yes, you may if you want to make a fool of yourself."

"Then here is something for you. . . ."

He put his hand into his pocket. Thinking that he would come out with a stone or a knife, I got ready to meet an assault. But he pressed a flask of vodka into my hand.

"I had enough," he explained, "but you must be dead tired. A good gulp is what you need. I shall cover up. . . . Nobody will see."

"Thanks, comrade," I said to him. "I would like to take a drink with you, but you know those who work in the party are advised against drinking—after a gulp people talk too much."

"Too bad," he sighed. "I was saving vodka for you."

"All right, take it home and drink it to my health!"

The man hugged me. His sentimental mood may have been stimulated by alcohol, but I could not discern any traces of drunkenness in his kindly smiling eyes.

"I did not intend to make trouble," he assured me, "but you said yourself, people talk too much after a gulp. How right you are!"

THE SOLDIERS AND THE SECOND DUMA

The government played with the Duma as a cat plays with a mouse, making it clear that it could stop the talks in the Tauride Palace at any time. Only a small minority of the people—certainly less than in 1905—now backed the throne. The arrogant self-confidence of the government stemmed from the fact that, after the end of the war with Japan and demobilization of the huge wartime army, it had succeeded in regaining complete control over the standing army. This raised the question: Could the Duma win the soldiers over to its side?

Soon after the elections I wrote an article in the Bolshevist monthly paper, *The Proletarian*, suggesting that the Duma initiate legislation to improve the material and moral conditions of men in the armed forces. After this was published, a university student, Sapotnitsky, who represented the military organization in the St. Petersburg Committee, told me that his group was planning to approach the S-D deputies in the Duma and ask for action along the lines I had suggested. He invited me to a conference of his men with the S-D member of the Duma, Gerus.

The meeting took place in a dormitory of a polytechnic school in a remote suburb. Some twenty persons were present—about half in military uniform, neatly dressed, with cleanly shaved faces. Two or three wore glasses. Obviously they were not rank-and-file privates, but regimental pharmacists, staff clerks, musicians. Gerus was a slow-moving, slow-speaking man in his late thirties. Other civilians were mainly students (of both sexes), secretaries of the military organization. The representative of the organization introduced the deputy to the group. Then Gerus invited the soldiers to report their grievances. They spoke with sincerity and restraint. The discussion was interrupted by an alarm that proved to be false. On the way back to the city I talked with Gerus about the plans of the organization. He thought it should first present a petition to the S-D deputies and it was agreed that I would write a draft.

On May 4, I handed the draft to the representative of the organization. It summarized the grievances the soldiers had presented to Gerus and outlined the action they expected from the Duma. The next day I learned that the organization had approved it. All was settled: in the evening the soldiers would go to the S-D group of the Duma.

The same night the police raided the apartment of my parents. This was not the first raid in our home, and we were prepared for it. I did not keep any illegal papers at home, and my mother always had refreshments ready for the night raiders—liqueurs and caviar for the officers, vodka and snacks for the enlisted men. In this way we were sure that the police would leave the apartment, and especially my father's library, in order.

The officers were very polite. Their superior complained:

"These are difficult times. One sleepless night after another. . . . They send us here and there, into such houses as yours. What logical thing can one find in such a fine place?"

"What 'logical' things are you looking for?" I asked him.

"Something one can understand. Say, a notebook with addresses, a cipher code. . . . Or a lab, a bomb. . . ."

They found nothing "logical" but, when the search was over and the bottles were emptied, the officer handed me, with a deep sigh, a warrant to be taken into custody regardless of the result of the search. I was escorted to a precinct detention house, where I found about forty persons who had been arrested the same evening at the headquarters of the S-D group. There were no soldiers among them; the police had raided the headquarters half an hour after the soldiers had left, but we were sure that the raid was connected with the soldiers' visit. The police had not found their petition but knew of its existence. Much later we learned that Sapotnitsky was under secret observation, and that a spy—allegedly also a University student— had been planted in the rooming house where he lived. This spy stole the draft of the petition from Sapotnitsky's desk, copied it, and took the copy to his superiors.

The plan of the police to catch the deputies red-handed with soldiers in their headquarters failed because of an error in the timing of the raid. The Duma protested against the raid. Stolypin answered with an order to search the headquarters and seize the files of the S-D group and its individual members. The Duma protested again, but the government contemptuously rejected the protest.

STOLYPIN'S COUP

The petition of the S-D military organization to the Duma was, of course, an illegal act from the point of view of military discipline, but it involved no responsibility on the part of the Duma or its S-D group. The soldiers' deputation got no farther than the receptionist's table at the entrance of the group's headquarters. Fearing a police trap, the members of the Duma who happened to be there asked the soldiers to leave at once. Other deputies neither saw them nor heard of their arrival. Yet Stolypin used this incident as a pretext for getting rid of the Duma. On June 1, he presented it with an ultimatum: Strip fifty-five members of the S-D group of parliamentary immunity.

The S-D group demanded that the Duma answer the government's attempt to maim it by appealing to the people. But the Cadets still tried to spare the Duma. A parliamentary committee was appointed to check the charges against the fifty-five deputies. The committee decided to reject Stolypin's ultimatum but asked for time to complete its report.

Tseretelli spoke before the Duma in the name of the S-D and

the Labor Group. "If you wish to fulfill your historic mission for which the people sent you to the Duma," he said, "then, on the eve of a coup planned by the government, at the hour when the government has put the bayonet on the agenda, put the fundamental problems of the people's life on your agenda!" His appeal was rejected. The Duma adjourned and never convened again. On June 3, a Sunday, a Manifesto was published dissolving the Duma and radically changing the electoral law. The S-D deputies were arrested. The government was confident of its police force and army. Stolypin had won the gamble.

THE EBB

I spent about two months in the precinct detention house, with two score prisoners taken in the first raid of the S-D group. We were locked in a ward consisting of four big rooms opening on the corridor. The ward was not overcrowded and was reasonably clean, despite the cell buckets. The doors on the corridor remained open day and night. The food was satisfactory. There were a few interesting people among the prisoners, among them old Isidor Ramishvilli and a Menshevist writer, Martynov.

A debate was arranged between Martynov and me, and we exchanged arguments during three long evenings. He was a poor speaker and I had seldom met so weak an adversary. But a strange thing happened to me during that debate: I began to feel that Martynov's position was much stronger than his arguments. The dispute finally boiled down to the question of the relation between the moderate liberals and the radicals in the revolution. Most listeners thought I had demolished my opponent and were surprised by the conciliatory tone of my concluding remarks. Actually, by the end of the debate, I had abandoned my original thesis that the radicals should follow their own course and pay no attention to the moderates.

Since the defeat of the revolution of 1905, I had had increasing doubts about a policy that isolates the labor movement from other groups. While debating with Martynov, I had an opportunity to check my own arguments and realized that the anti-liberal slant in our propaganda had been a grave mistake.

Early in July, the police began to sift the prisoners in our ward. Some were released on bond, others set free. A few were deported to Siberia on administrative order. The trial of the S-D deputies was to be limited to the members of the parliamentary group and half a dozen members of the St. Petersburg S-D military organization. Since the police had no evidence of my connection with the latter, I was set free.

As after my ill-fated trip to the villages in November, 1905, I found that things had changed while I was in prison. The S-D organization in St. Petersburg had been practically liquidated. The Council of the Unemployed was disintegrating. During my arrest, Anarchist gunmen had killed our engineers, Bers and Nurberg. The first was a hard-boiled reactionary with a deep dislike for the workers; the second was a kind man with liberal leanings, sympathetic to our cause. After these murders, the Anarchists launched a campaign among the unemployed, trying to seize control of the Council. Furthermore, some of the old members of our organization were inclined to try a new tactic—to send threatening letters to the reactionary councilmen and murder the most vicious among them. For this purpose a secret terroristic group of "Revengers" had been founded.

When I told Lenin of the "Revengers" and their plans, he asked, "How strong might the group be?"

"Perhaps two or three dozen cutthroats."

"Could they hurl a hand grenade at those municipal scoundrels?"

"They could. This is what makes the situation so grave."

"Perhaps that would be worth trying," he remarked meditatively.

Feeling that my time in the movement of the unemployed was over, I decided to resign from the Council and resume my work at the University. Though I remained president of the Council until my successor was elected, I registered for three examinations and passed them after an evening's preparation for each.

The examination in the philosophy of law brought me face to face with Petrazhitsky, who had been released shortly before from the Crosses after three months' detention for having signed the Viborg Manifesto. He greeted me with unexpected friendliness.

"Happy to meet you here, colleague," he said. "Last time we met in an electoral meeting, on different sides of the fence, and it was a pure accident that we did not meet in the Crosses."

"We spent our summer vacation in different resorts," I remarked.

"This difference is accidental," he went on in his pedantic way. "Do we meet today, too, accidentally or are we both back in academic life?"

When I confessed that I had not made up my mind, Petrazhitsky remarked, "Politics and science do not mix. To be in politics, one must sacrifice a part of his wisdom, and to be in science during certain historical eras one has to renounce other values. But let us perform our official functions. May I ask you some questions? What is Hegel's definition of law? . . . All right. And my definition? And your own?"

To his great satisfaction I answered, "My definition is the one I have learned from you."

My examinations in Roman civil law and international law were equally pleasant. This, however, was only a brief intermission. It was not so easy for me to break away from the unemployed.

I LOSE THE CONFIDENCE OF THE UNEMPLOYED

The hot-meal stations had long been closed. All that was left of the organization were the public works, and some of these were nearing completion. Construction of steel bridges was still in full swing, but layoffs in the harbor were impending, and the Anarchists accused Zagoraev of siding with the management. One morning when I was in our central office he called me to the harbor.

"I am through," he yelled over the phone. "I resign. Pick another fool to replace me!"

At the harbor I found a hostile and excited crowd. A trivial incident had occurred between a foreman and a gang of workers, and Zagoraev, after investigating, exploited the incident. A general meeting was called in the courtyard before the office.

When I mounted the stand, I was met with outcries and abuses. Unable to restore order, I shouted to the crowd, "Before I continue as your chairman, I must know whether I have your confidence. Those who have confidence in me, please raise their hands."

A dozen hands were raised timidly and promptly withdrawn.

"Now I reverse the voting," I continued. "Those who have no confidence in me, please raise their hands." A forest of hands went up.

"The decision is unanimous," I declared. "I am leaving the chair. Moreover, I cannot remain at the head of the Council without the confidence of the crew on its largest work project. Herewith I resign. The meeting is closed."

I left the meeting embittered. Not until I was in the trolley car did I realize that I had been freed of a tiresome and thankless responsibility. I spent the next day at the University. I attended a fine lecture, examined the catalogue, had long theoretical talks with colleagues. I was just finishing lunch in the students' mess when a boy came running to me. "A crowd of the unemployed are asking for Sergei Petrov," he said, "but they mean you."

Some fifty or sixty men from the harbor were in the entrance hall. The leader of the group, one of the worst troublemakers in the harbor, grimly handed me a sheet of paper. I read: "Order. Comrade Petrov is ordered to resume his duties as president of the Council of the Unemployed at once. The undersigned are ordered to take him back to the harbor. By force if necessary."

The "order" was signed by hundreds of men. I gave the paper back to the head of the deputation. "You are plain crazy," I told him. "How can you force me to be your president?"

"We can," he replied. "We looked into the statute. It says nothing about the right of the president to resign. If the people wish you to stay, you'd better stay."

The men were deadly serious. They all spoke at once. "The people are mad. . . . You cannot treat them this way. . . . You must explain. . . ."

I noticed two youths of the "Revenger" group and asked them, "What are you doing here? Are you armed?"

"Sure enough! We must take you back to the harbor."

More amused than angry, I agreed to go to the harbor and talk with the people. In front of the University I took a droshky and asked the head of the deputation to share it with me. The "Revengers" squeezed themselves into the front seat.

The crowd in the courtyard before the office greeted me with cheers. I again mounted the stand. "If you wish," I said, "I shall conduct this meeting, but I would like to know what its purpose is."

The head of the deputation replied, "People are mixed up! You asked whether we have confidence in you. Surely we have none. We trust nobody. You did not ask whether we wished you to resign. You decided for yourself, like a Tsar. People cannot take this from you."

"I see," I replied. "Now you have sent a commando with the order to use force against me. And you expect me to continue as president of this organization?"

"You must," shouted the crowd.

This sounded like a vote of confidence.

"Do you wish to say that I was not a bad president after all?" I asked.

A "Revenger" shouted, "You must have been a good one. The people won't let you go."

I began to think of parliamentary ways of solving the crisis. Per-

haps a vote reversing the non-confidence resolution of yesterday
would do?

"All right," I said, "I shall take a vote. Those who desire me to
remain the president raise their hands. . . . Now, those who are
against. . . . The decision is unanimous. . . ." When the cheers
subsided, I continued, "Should I accept your decision as a vote of
confidence?" There was a silence. Then a high-pitched, almost
hysterical voice cried, "We trust nobody."

"If you do not trust me," I shouted back, "look for another
president. I have had enough of this."

Then bedlam broke out. "You have no right to quit when people
need you!" The meeting became utterly chaotic. Some shouts were
abusive, but as the tumult went on, I again began to feel the ties
between me and these people. I could not quit so long as they
needed me. With great effort I restored order and said, "To hell
with the vote of confidence! I don't care whether you trust me or
not. I trust you and shall stay with you."

THE LAST CAMPAIGN

This meeting—I did not know that it was to be my last meeting in
the harbor—also brought me back to party work. Little was left of
the party organization in St. Petersburg. Workers were deserting
the factory cells. The leaders disappeared behind the Finnish border.
Some had already settled in Paris and Switzerland, traditional havens
of Russian political refugees. The St. Petersburg Committee continued to meet but had nothing to discuss at its meetings.

The main event in party life was the approaching trial of the
S-D deputies. They were to be tried behind closed doors, *in absentia*.
When I raised the question of a protest campaign, the Bolsheviks
in the Committee showed little interest, while the Mensheviks suggested issuing a leaflet. My proposal to organize factory meetings
and call for a general walkout on the day of the trial met with a
storm of objections. "We have no speakers, and if we had, nobody
would listen to them." I felt that the honor of the party required a
demonstration.

"The workers feel the infamy of this trial," I said, "and will respond to our appeal for a protest. If we cannot hold a meeting on
factory premises, I can bring fifty or a hundred unemployed workers to the gate of any factory and stop the crew. . . . We need no
speakers. Every worker can say a few words in a flying meeting."

Since the Mensheviks were against my proposal, the Bolsheviks
came out in support of it. Then the Mensheviks realized that the

campaign would amount to support of their deputies, and my plan was accepted unanimously.

I volunteered to start with a couple of meetings, and it was decided to begin with the cartridge factory on Vassily Island and in the Putilov works.

The first meeting proved to be easy. The factory was not far from the public works in the harbor. I knew the place well—a single police post at the gate, the next post half a mile away, and the nearest police barracks three miles distant. At the hour the shifts changed, I was at the grilled factory gate with a commando of about fifty youths from the harbor. We stood on the far side of the street. As soon as the gate opened, the boys crossed the street, linked arms, and formed a semicircular chain in front of the entrance. I mounted the nearest curbstone, the crowd pressed around me, and those in front shouted to those in the rear, "Come closer. . . . On behalf of our comrades of the Duma. . . ." I had a good half hour for my speech and disbanded the meeting when mounted police appeared in the distance.

It was not so easy to arrange the meeting in the Putilov works. The entire area was guarded. There were strong detachments of police at each gate, foot and horse patrols, reserves on vacant lots. A flying meeting at the gate was out of the question. On the other hand, a meeting in a shop would expose its workers to reprisal. We therefore decided to hold an open-air meeting inside the premises, at the crossing of two roads.

After dusk I went to the house of a mechanic who had promised to take me into the works. He gave me his old work clothes and told me where to hang the badge in the entrance office and where to go from there, following him. I passed the office without difficulty but, without my glasses, very soon lost my guide. At that moment somebody tapped me on the shoulder and whispered, "Follow me."

A bearded man passed me and I went after him. He stopped between two high piles of rails and said, "We can wait here. But your face shows. . . . A bit of oil would help. . . ." He handed me a rag soaked in machine oil.

As in the old days of 1905, the air was full of whistles and clangor. We climbed on a pile some ten to twelve feet high. People appeared in front of the pile—first in small groups, then in strength. The passage was filled with men. Somebody shouted from the darkness, "Stop, comrades! On behalf of our deputies in jail. . . ."

I could not see the people around the pile. Without thinking of my disguise, I took out my glasses and put them on. Now I could discern the faces turned up to me, tired, tense faces soiled with oil and soot. Again, as in 1905, I felt myself a part of the crowd. I be-

gan to speak—not about the Second Duma and its members wait-
ing trial, but about the men around me and what they had lived
through in the past three years. The Bloody Sunday of January 9.
. . . The October strike. . . . The brief elation of victory. . . .
And then the long chain of defeats, humiliation, misery. . . . The
Duma of Wrath and its end. . . . Gallows, firing squads. . . .

"Do you remember Jacob, the welder? I met him in the death
cells. I saw him behind the iron grille, chained for life. He asked me
to bring his greetings to all of you!"

And I continued the story of the past years. The S-D group in
the Second Duma, the champion of freedom, the last hope of the
workers. . . . The Duma is gone, and those who were the people's
spokesmen are now in jail, being tried by the lackeys of the Tsar.
. . . The last, the bitterest humiliation! . . . It is up to the workers
of St. Petersburg to show that they remember them.

I was interrupted by a roar of excited voices: "A strike! On the
day of the trial!"

The crowd moved slowly toward the entrance. I went with the
others, my cap pulled over my eyes, machine oil all over my face,
an iron teakettle in my hand. The office was full of police. I felt
suspicious glances at my face, but nobody recognized me under the
disguise.

ARREST AND ESCAPE

Three days after this meeting the Executive Board of our Council
met in a public works office to map a plan for a new campaign.
About forty persons were present when the building was surrounded
by the police. After a superficial search for arms, we were taken to
the nearest police station. There we declined to give our names,
insisting that the Council was a municipal organization and the
arrest was illegal.

The chief of the precinct police declared that he was ready to discuss the legal questions with the president of the unemployed, Mr.
Petrov, but the trap was obvious and I did not respond. A comrade
gave me his identification papers, and I busily memorized my new
name, date of birth, address, and names of relatives. The registration
routine took several hours. Then we were escorted to the Crosses,
but the superintendent of the prison declined, for some reason, to
let the party in, and finally we were moved to a precinct detention house miles away. We reached it after dawn.

The front section of the building was occupied by the fire department and police offices; the courtyard was littered with piles of

building materials. The wings on both sides of the courtyard were used as barracks for the police force; the rear building served as a detention house—an old, shabby, three-story structure with small barred windows and a narrow grilled door. From the small and dirty entrance hall, a staircase ran to the upper floors. A guard was posted on the platform of each floor, between the grilled doors to the two wings. There were grilles also at the foot and head of each flight of stairs.

Our party was taken to the third floor. The ward left of the platform was occupied by petty offenders—apparently pickpockets, vagabonds, and drunks. The opposite wing was empty. One of its four rooms was under repair; in the others, the walls, floors, and ceilings were covered with fresh patches of mortar and paint. The turnkey showed us to these rooms.

When I awoke after a brief nap, two of my companions were sitting beside my plank bed. "Comrade Petrov," one of them said, "we have discussed the situation. You must get out of this hole." Artem, a member of the Council of the Unemployed and president of the stonecutters' and bricklayers' union, had a plan of escape for me. "Our men work here," he said. "I can get in touch with them."

In the afternoon he called me to the room where three men in soiled aprons were working in the midst of loose bricks, mortar, and boards. One of them was a heavy, broad-shouldered muzhik with penetrating blue eyes; another, a puny man of fifty with a worried look on his thin, unshaven face; the third, an apprentice with a face covered with splashes of clay from eyes to chin.

Artem introduced me to the trio. "This is the man we must get out of here."

Fedor, the heavy man with blue eyes, looked me up and down and said flatly, "It can be done. In a barrel."

"Tonight?" I asked him.

After a little hesitation he answered, "We are six men living together, all from the same village. I must tell them. If they agree, we will go tomorrow."

The next day Fedor did not come to work. When Artem asked the puny man about Fedor, he answered grimly, "He will not come. He is a righteous, God-abiding man. Some others are rabble." He explained that Fedor had told his companions that he intended to free a prisoner. One of the gang objected and threatened to denounce Fedor to the police. A quarrel developed. Fedor spat on the other man, took his gear, and left the quarters.

I proposed a new plan to the puny man. I would disguise myself as a bricklayer. At noon we would take a handbarrow and carry the barrel with mortar and timber waste to the courtyard—he in front, I in the rear, my face splashed with clay and hidden behind the barrel. He agreed to help me.

My companions shaved my beard and mustache to make me look like a bricklayer's apprentice. Artem converted a bed sheet into a bricklayer's apron and showed me how to carry trade tools in its pockets.

Next morning, in full disguise, I went to see our bricklayer. The man was jittery.

"Forgive me, for God's sake," he said. "I have a family and am not as good a man as Fedor. Go alone, and Christ help you!"

"How will I pass the gate alone?"

"Take a pail and just go to fetch some lime for me. With the Lord's help, you will pass. The guards are just fools. . . . When you tell them, 'Let one through for lime,' they let one through."

Artem made a paper cap for me such as bricklayers use at work, emptied a bucket of clay mixed with water over my head and shoulders, and plastered my face, hands, and boots. We waited until noon. When the bell rang for distribution of food to the prisoners, I took the pail and stepped to the grille leading from the ward to the platform. The bricklayer yelled to the guard, "Let one through for lime! Hurry, no time to waste."

The guard opened the grating, let me through, and closed it behind me. He was ready to open the gate leading from the platform to the stairs when a prisoner at the grating of the opposite ward shouted to him, "That guy is a political! Watch, he will escape."

The guard turned toward me, ready to grab my arm. I put the pail down and said to the roaring knave, "Making fools of working people, eh? Do I work for your amusement? Does he carry his keys for your fun?" Then, turning to the guard, I added, "Pay no attention. These riffraff know no better."

He opened the gate and shouted to the guard on the lower platform, "Let one through for lime! Hurry!"

I went down the stairs, grumbling, "Once riffraff, always riffraff."

In the courtyard I went to the lime pit, filled my pail, rearranged and shortened my apron, and went straight under the gate to freedom.

From the police station I walked to the quay of the Neva, took a ferry to the other side, and walked to the nearest public works office. There I changed to less conspicuous work clothes. A few cautious telephone calls turned up an apartment where I could await further events safely.

DECISION

The morning newspapers carried the story of the arrest of the Council of the Unemployed and my escape. This ended my work for the unemployed. I had been the official head of the organization too long to be of any use to it while hiding from the police. Thus my escape from the prison proved futile as far as the Council was concerned. From a purely personal point of view, it would be sensible simply to surrender to the police. What did they have against me? The old Borovenka affair, the Council, the meetings. . . . If I surrendered now, I would probably be subjected to a year in prison and deportation for a year or two. Then I could go back to my books, reading, writing. But I did not like this simple solution.

At the first opportunity, I crossed the border into Finland and settled in Terioki, where many party workers were in hiding. My plans were vague. Before thinking of the future I wanted to write a report on the movement of the unemployed. My friends brought me the files of our Council and other documents. It was wonderful relaxation to live in a little cottage, half buried under snow, and to work on the manuscript from early morning until late at night, with only brief interruptions when somebody knocked at the door.

By the end of November the book was ready, and I was again facing the question of where I should go from there. I felt that my decision would determine the course of my life for many years to come.

Lenin tried to persuade me to go to Switzerland with him and take over one of the party periodicals, promising me full independence in my work. But I knew I would not be independent working with Lenin and I could not commit myself to go the whole way with him. In addition, as time went on I became increasingly reluctant to leave Russia. Pressed by Lenin to explain my reasons, I said, "In the past two years we have been calling on the people to revolt. Many of those who have followed our call have paid with their lives or their freedom. We cannot desert those who are left."

"If all revolutionaries thought this way," Lenin replied, "the cause of the revolution would be lost."

"We have piled up too many bills," I insisted. "Some of us must stay to pay."

Lenin looked at me with an expression of understanding and sympathy. He did not smile. "This is a conflict between feelings and the cold logic of the revolution," he said. "You have decided to follow your feelings. Too bad. But you know what you are doing and why."

Several local organizations had asked the Central Committee to send them someone to direct their work. I was assigned to Ekaterino-slav (now Dniepropetrovsk), the center of the party organizations in South Russia. I accepted the assignment without enthusiasm. After the revolution was crushed, attempts to resume local S-D work were desperate rear-guard actions. I was joining one such action for no better reason than that I did not want to quit.

Prisons
1908-1912

I DID not last long in underground work. Following the advice of party experts in conspiracy, I had dyed my hair black but I failed to retouch it often enough and it soon became reddish at the roots. Any spy could see at a glance that something was wrong. Things would not have been better, however, if I had been a first-rate conspirator. The secret police had their agent in the heart of the Ekaterinoslav organization.

In the city the Mensheviks predominated among the workers on the railroad and in the flour mills and among Jewish craftsmen; the Bolsheviks had a well-equipped printing shop and good contacts among the intellectuals. I managed to persuade both groups that the party was too weak to afford the luxury of factional squabbles. When all the remaining S-D cells had been merged, we decided to launch a four-page monthly tabloid, *The South Russian Worker*. Later on we would send our men to other southern cities and organize a regional conference.

The S-D workers of Ekaterinoslav were delighted to see the intellectuals ready to work together. I remember a meeting of the S-D cell in the railroad repair shop. A middle-aged, sedate, baldheaded man was particularly enthusiastic. Beaming all over, he repeated, "This is wonderful. Now we can organize our organization."

The secretary whispered to me, "One of our best men. Not too bright, but reliable as gold. He has not missed a single meeting."

This golden man was the agent of the secret police.

An editorial committee was appointed, the topics for the first issue of the newspaper were parceled out among contributors—half of them Mensheviks, half Bolsheviks—but since none of them could write, I had to fill all four pages except for a piece of poetry and local news.

The secretary, Alexandrova, told me that Misha, the boy who ran our secret printing shop, wished to see me. The next day I met him at Alexandrova's home. He was a skinny boy with a pale, almost transparent face and big sad eyes. He handed me the galleys of my articles. Without wasting time, I took a pencil and started to correct them.

"Are there any errors?" the boy asked timidly.

"Of course," I replied. "Galleys are supposed to have errors."

"That is because of the poor light," he said. "I did not recheck them." His beautiful eyes filled with tears. He looked like a hurt child.

"For first proofs, this is an excellent job!" I said promptly. "No commercial printing shop could do better!"

The boy was happy. After he had gone, I learned from our secretary that Misha had worked for the Jewish worker organization (the Bund) since 1905 and later had volunteered to operate the printing press for the S-D party. He claimed to be eighteen years old but was probably under seventeen—a very nice lad but ill, with advanced tuberculosis and serious heart trouble. I protested against employing a sick child in an underground printing shop, but Misha insisted on his right to work for the party and it was not easy to replace him. Then I declared that I could not write for a paper printed in a shop that exploited child labor. A physician, member of our organization, intervened. After he had confirmed Misha's serious illness, it was decided to close the printing shop after the first issue of the newspaper and to let Misha have leave for rest and medical treatment.

Two days later the police raided our printing shop and Misha was arrested. The police seized the type set for the newspaper, together with manuscripts and corrected galleys. The organization stuck to its guns and immediately issued a flyer announcing that the seizure of the press would not stop the publication of *The South Russian Worker*. The leaflet was set by S-D printers in commercial printing shops, but they could not print it without attracting attention. I printed it myself in the home of a flour-mill worker, Isaac, using a rudimentary device that could hardly be called a "hand press."

The next step was to restore the printing shop. The party called on its sympathizers among the printers, and in no time they brought us more type than we could use. Meanwhile, party mechanics built a new printing press. A man was found to run it—a shy, unemployed printer, Chilkovich. He had a wife and a baby. The young mother volunteered to be shut up in the shop with the husband.

Again I wrote articles for the newspaper, received and corrected the galleys. On the eve of the newspaper's appearance I was aroused from sleep by the ringing of the doorbell. The house was surrounded by police. After my room was searched minutely, I was escorted to the prison. That same night Chilkovich and his wife were arrested at our new printing shop. The police also seized our secretary and a student who kept the party's files at his home.

The Ekaterinoslav S-D organization went out of existence.

IN THE CASTLE OF EKATERINOSLAV

The prison of Ekaterinoslav, known officially as the Castle, was a huge three-story building with a heavy round tower at each corner and a high brick wall around the vast courtyard. On top of the wall were a walk and turrets for the guards. A belfry topped the entrance office.

The Castle was designed to hold four or five hundred prisoners, but during the two and a half years I spent there the number ranged between one and two thousand. Some had been sentenced, others were in pre-trial custody or were held on administrative order. The prisoners were almost evenly divided: those held or convicted for political crimes, common criminals, and "criminal-politicals," a motley group consisting of peasants arrested for agrarian unrest, soldiers and sailors accused of mutiny, and persons charged with holdups committed for political reasons.

I was taken to Room 12, a political pre-trial ward. Most of its four score inmates were in pre-trial custody, charged with participating in the S-D and S-R organizations; others were Anarchists. The latter were very different from the hysterical and confused characters whom I had met in the harbor of St. Petersburg. My place on the plank bench happened to be next to Chardash, the leader and theoretician of the group. He was a tall man in his early thirties with a hard, unsmiling face. From him I learned that his companions, arrested in different parts of south Russia, had been brought to Ekaterinoslav for a mass trial. Some were in Room 12, the rest dispersed in different wards all over the prison.

Chardash himself was a man of considerable erudition: he had recently returned to Russia from Heidelberg, Germany, where he had studied philosophy and history. He firmly believed that society was rotten in Europe as well as in Russia. Half measures such as political freedom and parliamentarianism could not help. Salvation lay in the destruction of all existing institutions. I recognized an echo of Bakunin in his words, but something new had been added to the old ideas of the father of Russian and European anarchism. Chardash believed in what he called "motiveless violence." As he explained: "If you must annihilate your enemies in order to free the world, you should kill them as lightning does, not like a hangman." A few acts of motiveless violence were committed in south Russia in 1906-7. Bombs were hurled into a café patronized by the rich in Odessa and into two or three luxurious hotels. Each time, innocent people were killed and wounded. It seemed almost unbelievable that one could consider such acts as a way toward freeing mankind.

Another remarkable Anarchist was Pavel Abramchuck, a young man with a curly beard and the mild brown eyes of a dreamer. He had a soft, musical voice and liked to talk about books. His favorite authors were Tolstoy, Kropotkin, and Stirner. Once he saw me reading a book on geology and asked about it. I showed him a few of its maps and pictures. He was spellbound when he saw a picture of the earth as a ball floating in space. "How strange!" he said. "I am approaching my end; they will hang me. But I never have thought about the earth under my feet. I have thought only of what is good or evil." Pavel was charged with murder; resisting arrest, he had shot and killed a police officer.

Many criminal-political prisoners were close to the Anarchists in their hatred of society. Some were hard-boiled gunmen; others, confused youths who did not know how and when they had entered the road that had brought them to the foot of the gallows. They were completely fearless. Their contempt for death came largely from lack of attachment to life. Later, when executions became an everyday routine in the Ekaterinoslav Castle, one could occasionally hear a clear, almost cheerful, boyish voice shouting in the corridor:

"So long, comrades! I'm on the way to be hanged!"

Personal contact with these men showed me how false it had been to interpret the acts of violence in 1907-8 as guerrilla warfare. Those were acts of individual despair, after the collective revolutionary struggle had been crushed.

TYPHUS

Apart from the stench, filth, and noise in the overcrowded ward, conditions in the Castle were bearable. The prisoners had a daily half-hour walk in the courtyard during which one could exchange words with comrades in other wings of the prison. For a small bribe to the guard, one could also exchange uncensored letters with friends or relatives in the city. The food was bad, but the ration of half-baked rye bread was sufficient.

Suddenly typhus broke out. It started in the particularly filthy criminal wings and began to spread to other parts of the Castle. The prison hospital was packed to capacity. Stretchers with corpses began to appear in the courtyard. Our room asked the superintendent, Fetisov, to transfer the sick to the municipal typhus barracks. Our headman, himself a medical student, tried to explain to the superintendent that the infected prison could set off epidemics in the entire city. Fetisov replied, "That is above my head!"

The inmates of Room 12 tried to think of ways of attracting public attention to the typhus in the Castle. The Socialists proposed a hunger strike. The Anarchists advocated a demonstration to begin with shouting followed by smashing and burning the furniture. Since I was new and on good terms with both groups, each tried to win me to its side. Finally I took the side of the Anarchists. I thought that hardly more than two hundred of the approximately one thousand inmates in the Castle would go on a hunger strike and that some of these would quit before the public learned about the unrest in the prison; perhaps two score would continue, but neither the public nor the authorities would pay much attention to them. On the other hand, the entire prison, the political and common criminals alike, would take part in the demonstration, and there was a good chance that it would attract public attention in the early—shouting—phase. Finally all groups agreed on this plan.

On my insistence, a modest slogan was selected—a demand the administration could meet readily: "Court Attorney to the Castle!" I expected the attorney would come before the assault on the furniture began. The headman of our ward presented an ultimatum to the superintendent: "The prisoners demand that the Court Attorney come to the Castle by noon today." Fetisov replied that he could not accept so insolent a demand.

Precisely at noon, with the ringing of the bell on the belfry, the demonstration started. All the inmates, massed at the open windows, yelled in chorus, "Court At—tor—ney to the Castle!" The shouts carried beyond the walls of the prison. Prisoners on the upper floors could see a crowd about the Castle. The inmates continued to shout in relays. At 5:00 P.M. the Court Attorney arrived. After briefly questioning our headman and the prison physician, he ordered the superintendent to transfer the sick to the municipal barracks and to disinfect the wards in which there had been typhus.

AN ATTEMPT TO ESCAPE

The prison relaxed. The epidemic continued, but the new cases were promptly isolated, the plank beds disinfected, and the straw sacks burned. Prisoners who returned from the municipal barracks were full of praise for the doctors. But what had impressed them most was that there were only two guards on duty and two in reserve in the whole building and no bars in the windows! Their talk gave me the idea of escaping from the prison by simulating typhus. This was a crazy notion. In each attempt to escape, a prisoner gambles his life, and the sentence I was facing for participation in the party did not justify the risk. Later I realized that my plan was the almost physical reaction of an active youth against the lock on the door, the bars in the windows, the turreted wall around the courtyard.

I consulted a roommate, military nurse Duvin. An old hand at simulating illness, he told me some tricks of his trade. A big dose of bromine causes a rash similar to that characteristic of typhus; a mixture of cocaine and ipecacuanha provokes a high temperature; inhaling smoke from a cigarette made of tea is good to complete the clinical picture. Next, Duvin taught me how to get the proper pulse beat and "adjust" the temperature reading. The trouble, however, was that all the drugs dilated the pupil of the eye. Duvin therefore advised me to keep my eyes closed during the medical inspection and warned, "If something goes wrong, don't blame me. Medicine is a dark science!"

Duvin obtained the required medicine from a friendly doctor in the city through a guard, and we set the day for the experiment. On its eve, I told Pavel of my plan. "I hope you will succeed," he said mildly. "I shall look for some other way." He had thought of a similar plan. Since escape was a matter of life or death for him, I offered him my drugs but he refused them. Finally we agreed that I would wait for him in the barracks.

Before midnight Duvin gave me a spoonful of bromine and half a glass of the cocaine and ipecacuanha mixture. I waited on my straw sack for the medicine to take effect, but nothing happened— my pulse was strong and even. Duvin seemed embarrassed. "Medicine," he repeated, "is a dark science. Whatever dose the doctor prescribes, it is safe to take three times as much."

He gave me two spoonfuls of the mixture. Pacing the chamber, I felt increasingly dizzy but my pulse showed no change. "Give me some more!" I demanded. He handed me the flask.

Again I paced the room. My teeth chattered, my feet became so heavy that I could not move them. Duvin pressed a tea cigarette between my lips. Its taste was abominable—I still remember it, and that is why I have never taken up smoking. Duvin helped me to my plank bed. My toes were freezing, as if they had been plunged into ice water. The cold rose to my knees and thighs. My whole body was paralyzed. I had a strange impersonal feeling that the end was approaching. Then I fainted.

In the morning Duvin took me to the prison hospital with a temperature of 107°. The assistant surgeon, Pushkin, recognized typhus at once. That afternoon the prison physician confirmed his diagnosis, adding, "If the temperature does not fall, prepare the sheet for my signature." The next day the sheet was signed. The corridor cleaners carried me to the prison gate on a stretcher; two convoy soldiers lifted me into a droshky and took their places on the front seat.

Spring was in the air. The trees were covered with a green mist of buds. Although I was fully conscious, I let the soldiers carry me to the barracks. There an assistant surgeon in an immaculate white uniform ordered them to take me to Ward No. 1, designed for critical cases.

The ward was a large room, full of light, with four beds on each side. Mine was the last to the right of the door. All the others were occupied. Some patients were moaning under their blankets. One in the bed in front of mine called to me gently, "The new one! Take it easy. They will mend you."

Later the chief doctor arrived, an old man with snow-white hair and beard. He examined me very carefully and asked softly how and when the sickness had begun. Then he lifted my glasses, raised an eyelid, examined the pupil, and put the glasses back. He bent over me and looked at me with understanding and gentle eyes. Then he said to the nurse, "Write 'Typhus, undetermined.'"

Turning again to me he said, "Good luck to you!"

Duvin's medicine had not fooled the old doctor, but he did not betray me.

The nurse brought me a soft-boiled egg and a glass of milk, a very small glass. I was hungry and wondered why they used such small glasses in the barracks. When she came to take the glass and plate away I said, pointing at the next bed, "This one also asked for an egg."

The nurse was incredulous. "How could he? He is unconscious!"

"He seemed to be conscious when he said, 'Give me an egg for Christ's sake.'"

The nurse brought another soft-boiled egg and put it on the table between our beds. When she left, I ate the egg. The following day I repeated this trick. "Adjusting" the thermometer, I made my temperature chart show 104° in the morning, 106° in the afternoon. The patients in the ward of critical cases were not supposed to eat much, but I had to keep up my strength. Another patient said to me, "Hungry? Take my ration."

"And you?"

"I am quitting." For two days he asked the nurse for more food and let me have it. Then he died in the night.

Each night somebody in the ward died. In the morning the assistant surgeon examined the beds and marked with chalk those from which the patients were to be removed. Then two orderlies appeared with a long pole and three towels. They stretched the towels on the floor in the middle of the room, two feet apart from one another, put the corpse on the towels and the pole on the corpse. Then they tied the towels in knots over the pole, raised it to their shoulders, and carried the bundle away.

It became more and more difficult to pretend to be ill. I waited for Pavel. Escape from the barracks seemed easy, but I was rapidly losing strength. I could not sleep at night, was half dizzy in the daytime, and wondered whether I had caught typhus after all. A week went by. At last a guard came to Ward No. 1 and called me. "Can you stand up? A pal of yours has come to see you."

With a great effort I reached the window on the corridor. Isaac, a member of our organization from the flour mill, stood outside. He told me that the comrades in the Castle asked me to wait. I replied that I could not wait much longer. If Pavel did not join me in two days, I would report for transfer back to the prison. The next day was almost unbearable. In late afternoon the guard touched my shoulder. "Your pal is here again. Can you crawl?"

Isaac was under the window with a small bag in his hands, a cigarette between his lips. He handed the bag to the guard for inspection and asked him if prisoners were permitted to smoke. "The doctor does not like the smell but they may smoke at the window," the guard replied. Isaac handed him a package of cigarettes and passed me the one held between his lips, explaining, "This one is lighted."

Back in my bed, I unrolled the cigarette. The message was in the mouthpiece: "Nobody will come. Go alone. Will wait for you at the corner, Sunday and Monday after 10:00 P.M."

Sunday was Easter, so the guards, like many other people in the city, would be drunk. The timing was good!

There were two routes: through the window, if both guards were on the corridor; through the door, if the corridor guard left his post. Now I must choose the right moment and the right direction.

But I was very weak. First I had to get a little food and some rest. That night colored Easter eggs were distributed to the patients, even those who were unconscious. I had plenty of food but I could not sleep.

On Sunday people were coming and going. In the afternoon all four guards established themselves in the corridor just in front of the ward, with a generous supply of vodka. They drank and treated the nurses and the assistant surgeon. One guard played the balalaika, the other sang and danced. Then a quarrel broke out, all shouted at the same time, the women screamed.

Finally the noise subsided. The two guards who were not on duty left. One of the other two returned to his beat under the window. I saw the glow of his cigarette as he paced back and forth in the darkness. The fourth guard put a bench across the entrance door in the corridor and sat with his head sunk on his knees. I went up to him. He was asleep, the passage to freedom was clear, but I could not open the door without awakening him. Clinging to the wall, I moved carefully along the corridor toward another entrance.

The corridor was deserted, but the assistant surgeon was sitting on a chair in front of the other entrance door, his head hanging, asleep. As I passed him and had the doorknob in my hand, he suddenly jumped up. Too drunk to recognize me, he hugged me and began to explain that he never slept when on duty. He could have been silenced by simply pushing him away, but I did not have strength to raise my hand. Then, without any visible reason, he became excited and began to shout, a chair fell, and before I could break away from him the guard stood before me, a pistol in his hand. Clinging to the wall, I retreated to my bed. The guard seemed bewildered. Then he suddenly realized what had happened and rushed into the ward with his pistol ready, bellowing.

"Shut up!" I shouted, "or tomorrow I'll report that you were drunk and almost let a prisoner escape." The guard was frightened and meekly begged me not to ruin him and his family.

The next morning I was taken back to the Castle and assigned to the hospital. I was not penalized for my attempt to escape. The assistant surgeon who had stopped me reported that I had walked in the night during delirium—a rather common occurrence in the typhus barracks.

A PLAN THAT FAILED

Pavel obtained permission to see me in the hospital and told me what had happened in the prison during my absence. He had tried to simulate typhus but gave up Duvin's medicine. Next Chardash tried, with the same result. Then the plan was dropped. Pavel felt that I had missed my chance by waiting for him. As if paying his debt to me, he invited me to join in another bold plan. The Anarchists were planning a mass breakout through a breach in the wall. They were gathering their forces in the city. Pavel had been slated to escape through the barracks in order to run operations outside the prison.

"A wagon with dynamite will be thrown against the wall," Pavel whispered in my ear. "Our men with hand grenades will cover the approaches to the Castle. We shall have enough dynamite to blow up the locks, enough pistols to overpower the guards, to open all the cells. . . ." The pipeline to deliver dynamite and pistols into the prison was established. For a hundred rubles per package, the assistant surgeon, Pushkin, was to smuggle in munitions. Would I act as middleman between him and the Anarchists?

When Pavel left I considered his plan. It might work. Recently a prison in south Russia had been blown up similarly and the prisoners had been freed. It would be sheer madness, of course, for me to take part in this adventure, but I could help men fighting for their lives without joining in the break.

The next morning Pushkin, a young man with a dark face, tiny mustache, and hard, arrogant eyes, entered the ward. He inspected two or three patients, then sat down on my cot while testing the heart and lungs of the patient on the next one. Without turning his head he whispered to me, "Right-hand pocket." The turnkey stood at the door, looking in the other direction. I put my hand into the pocket of Pushkin's white uniform, felt a hard, heavy object, slipped it under my straw pillow, pulled the blanket over my head, and lay motionless, as if asleep.

This became a routine. Each day Pushkin would deliver a package. Half an hour later one of the Anarchists would pick it up. One morning, however, I got the package but nobody came to take it. The guards were searching the hospital, room by room. I thought of throwing the dynamite into the cell bucket. . . .

An old peasant, Nesterenko, whose cot was at the far end of the ward, came to me. Gray, unshaven, very taciturn, with sly narrow eyes, he made a laughingstock of himself in the ward by kneeling each night for a long prayer. Now he whispered, "Hot stuff in the pillow? Let's switch. They are too smart to suspect an old fool like me."

The search party came to our room. The guards went directly to my bed. They opened the pillow and my straw sack and examined them with the utmost care. Nesterenko sat on his cot, with all his belongings displayed for inspection—an old hat, a pair of puttees, an empty tobacco pouch, with tobacco spread over the pillow. The chief guard, Belokos, threw a contemptuous look at this display, touched the tobacco on the pillow, and proceeded to the next bed. When the guards left Nesterenko returned my pillow with the dynamite, grinning. "I told you how smart they are."

Before long Pavel came to tell me that the plan had to be given up. It conflicted with a project conceived by the criminal-politicals in Room 10. There were twenty-two of them, all threatened with the death sentence, and their cases were slated for the next session of the military court. They had planned to escape by blowing up the prison wall from inside and had obtained a small quantity of dynamite when they learned of the Anarchists' plans. The latter needed two weeks more to complete their preparations outside the prison when Room 10 was notified that the session of the military court would begin in three days. It was impossible to reconcile the two plans. Room 10 had to strike at once, not later than April 29, and the Anarchists could not be ready before May 10. The men in Room 10 sent an ultimatum to the Anarchists: "We shall make a try on April 29. We have nothing to lose. A bullet is better than a noose. After us, you will have no chance. Better give us your stuff. Perhaps we will have enough to do the job."

I asked Pavel what I should do with the last package I had received for his friends. He answered indifferently, "Pass it on to Room 10. Perhaps it will help them."

The same day a Black Sea sailor, Leonid Ivanov, came to the ward. He was a short, powerfully built man with a coarse, tanned face and small blue eyes. I had met him in Room 12 before he was transferred to the criminal-politicals. "Pavel told you all," he said to me. "I am in Room 10 now. I do not care whether it is a bullet or a noose. Others do. We go tomorrow. You can pass your stuff to us by air telephone." Room 10 was just above us. Sometimes a package of tobacco could be sent from one room to another on a string, the air telephone, in full view of the guards. That evening a pouch with a protruding pack of cigarettes was lowered to the window of our ward and returned to Room 10 with a parcel of dynamite.

THE EXPLOSION

On April 29 I stood from early morning at the barred window looking at the courtyard. The prisoners were walking in two enclosures of barbed wire along the side walls between the prison building and the entrance office. Four guards were assigned to each walking party. Two guards were pacing the middle of the courtyard.

Shortly before noon the politicals of Room 12 appeared in the enclosure at the right. A quarter of an hour later prisoners of Room 10 appeared in the left enclosure carrying their straw sacks. This was nothing unusual; after the typhus demonstration, inmates had been permitted to air their beds and blankets. They shook their straw sacks and piled them up near the wall at the far end of the enclosure. Then they continued to walk at the other end while Leonid Ivanov, with a teakettle in his hands, stopped in front of the pile of sacks. He laid the kettle on it and stooped over it as if lighting a cigarette. Then he ran to the others.

In a second or two there was a thunderous explosion. The air was full of smoke, fire, burning straw. The strength of the explosion blew out windowpanes. Doors on the prison corridors were torn from their hinges. But when the smoke rolled away one could see that the prison wall, although blackened by flame and smoke, remained intact. A cry of anguish and despair came from the courtyard.

The guards had disappeared. The left enclosure was empty; the inmates of Room 10 scattered and hid themselves. Inmates of Room 12 lay on the ground. In the middle of the courtyard stood a lonely old tree. A man crouched behind it, facing the entrance, and I recognized the broad shoulders and big head of Leonid.

A volley of shots came from the office building. The guards were firing through the prison windows at the men of Room 12 in the courtyard. Shots resounded inside the Castle, too, where the guards in the corridors fired through grilled doors into the cells. Then the entrance gate in the office building opened and guards armed with rifles rushed into the courtyard. Leonid fired twice in their direction. The guards withdrew behind the gate. Gunfire became more intensive. Leonid fell, then rose and leaned against the tree. The entrance gate opened. Leonid shot at the guards and they rushed back. Then he fell again, rose to one knee, still aiming at the gate, and rolled over.

Guards were running toward the prison building. Some of them stopped at the right enclosure. The headman of the political prisoners rose from the ground and shouted, "Nobody has attempted to escape here. The enclosure is closed. Count us."

The chief guard shrieked, "Shoot this Jew for me!"

The headman fell. The guards rushed into the prison. More shooting resounded under the vaults. I lay on my cot. The thunder of shots was mixed with shouts, curses, screams of fear and anguish. I do not know how long this lasted.

Shrill orders were heard from the courtyard. I rose from the cot and went to the window. Soldiers with fixed bayonets were entering through the gate. Two companies, with officers. They were posted in right formation on both sides of the gate. An officer barked, "Arms!" Then he turned to the prison, surrounded by smoke, and shouted at the top of his lungs to the guards, "At—ten—tion! Cease fire!"

Firing under the prison vaults stopped.

CARNAGE

That day twenty-seven prisoners were killed and forty-four wounded, some of them fatally. One guard was hurt by glass splinters. Two pistols were found, one in Leonid's hand, the other on the ground in the left enclosure.

In the evening the soldiers were withdrawn from the prison. Later a guard told me, "Our gang was plain mad. If it hadn't been for the troops, they would have killed the last man here."

After dusk all the guards except those on corridor duty were assembled in the office to celebrate the victory. Stolypin had sent a telegram to the superintendent: "Well done. Expect faithful service from all. His Majesty expresses gratitude to your men." The Governor of the province added a ruble per man for vodka. The guards shouted hurrahs, sang the national anthem. The celebration went on all night—clapping hands, stamping feet, the shrill tunes of an accordion, the tinkle of a balalaika.

The prison doctor and Pushkin were dressing wounds in the hospital corridor. Two or three wounded prisoners were brought into my ward and put on the floor. I asked if somebody would help me put one of them on my cot, but nobody responded. One of the wounded was a boy from Room 12. He recognized me but soon became delirious and died before dawn.

The prison was given over to massacre. Belokos became the absolute ruler. Before the explosion he had been a mean man who made life miserable for the common criminals but was cautious with the politicals. Now he revealed himself as a sadist on the verge of insanity. Among three score guards he picked half a dozen brutes who shared his delight in beating defenseless men. With them he went from wing to wing. He would pace the line of prisoners, looking at their faces, and order his commando, "Take this one!" The victim was dragged to the corridor, thrown on the floor, kicked and beaten to unconsciousness, then dragged to the dark dungeon to recover or die from internal injuries.

Back in Room 12 I found striking changes. Eight men had been killed on the day of the explosion. A few had died of injuries and a few had been transferred to the death row—the section of the prison for persons sentenced to the gallows. Those who remained spoke in whispers. Almost every day Belokos and his commando picked out someone for a beating in the corridor.

My turn came a week after I had come back from the hospital. During the morning inspection Belokos stopped in front of me and shouted, "You, orator! Give me your glasses!" He put my glasses into his wallet and ordered, "Take him!"

Like the others, I was dragged into the corridor and thrown on the floor. There was no feeling of humiliation—as there is no humiliation in being kicked by a horse, bitten by a dog, or mauled by a savage brute. I felt the blows, but I am sure that my tormentors did not hear me moan. They dragged me downstairs and threw me, dizzy and half conscious, into the dungeon.

IN THE DARKNESS

I found myself in complete darkness, mud and water under my knees and hands. A hoarse voice called, "You, newcomer, step up. Follow the wall. It is dry here."

"Not very dry . . ." said another voice.

I heard clanking chains. An invisible hand touched my shoulder and led me to a comparatively dry spot.

There were seven of us in the round room under one of the towers. We sat for a time in darkness and silence. Then a quiet voice asked, "Newcomer, are you a political? You must be an educated man. Tell us something."

"What should I tell you?" I said. "I am no taleteller."

"I did not mean a tale," replied the voice. "Tell us something about books. We are all simple people. Tell us what is in the books that educated people read."

I searched my memory for some long story that would appeal to the imagination of my invisible listeners and decided on the history of the earth. Along with mathematics, astronomy and geology were hobbies of mine, and I started a popular lecture—or, rather, a series of lectures. From time to time the listeners interrupted me with questions.

Time ceases to exist in complete darkness. At irregular intervals, always unexpectedly, the door to the corridor opened and Belokos entered with two guards to count the prisoners. One guard usually carried a lantern. The air in the dungeon was heavy, it was difficult to breathe, and the guards did not stay longer than was necessary to count us. Once the flame of the lantern went out for lack of oxygen. Belokos and his commando rushed to the corridor and stood at the open door. "If they suffocate here, I shall be held responsible," he said to the guards. "Let the stinkers get air."

I spent six days or more, perhaps ten, in the darkness. Then I was transferred to a room in the tower.

THE TOWER

The towers of the Castle were originally designed for the most dangerous prisoners, and each room was connected with the hall by a narrow passage intended for special guards. In my time, however, the passage had been made part of the circular space. There were two bunks with straw sacks in the passage and four plank cots in the tower proper. When the tower was overcrowded, from two to four additional straw sacks were put on the flagstone floor.

In the tower I met a few comrades from Room 12. Misha was among them, and I was shocked when I saw his emaciated face. The tower was isolated from the rest of the prison, but we could exchange scribbled notes with other prisoners with the aid of the corridor cleaners—usually petty felons.

Mistreatment and beating went on in the wards for common criminals and criminal-political prisoners and especially in the row of those sentenced to death. Each morning the corridors echoed with curses, blows, and screams. In addition, the prison was plagued by hunger and lice. For a month all prisoners had been deprived of any food except bread and water—a pound of bread per day and a dipper of dirty tepid water. In June, soup was added to the ration—a stinking, turbid liquid with nondescript rubbish swimming in it. I tasted it on the first day but threw up, and during the following two months I, like many others, had nothing but half-baked bread and abominable water.

Lice and other bugs multiplied with unbelievable rapidity. The planks of the cots, the cracks in the walls and floor, and the frames of the windows were full of bugs, while lice appeared in waves from nowhere after dusk. We spent most of our time fighting the vermin. Some common criminals collected bugs and lice in bottles and matchboxes. Contests were arranged to see who could catch the most in a week. We tried to clear our tower by exterminating the vermin systematically, inch after inch. But some cracks in the walls were beyond our reach, and new waves of lice descended on us again and again.

By now the investigation of my case was completed. Together with Misha, Chilkovich and his wife, Alexandrova, and the student who had kept the party files, I was charged with participating in the S-D organization and the case was referred to the military court.

Two other tower inmates were awaiting trial under similar charges. Others faced more serious accusations.

Nikolai Komarov, a likable, cheerful youth, a member of the S-R party, faced a death penalty for a holdup of which he knew nothing. The holdup took place at dusk, the witnesses had not noticed the faces of the two gunmen, but an elderly lady gave a vivid description of the checkered cap worn by one of them, and Nikolai's cap happened to fit the description.

Leo Rappoport, an unsmiling lad arrested in December, 1905, was charged with the murder of the Governor of Ekaterinoslav province, General Gelichevsky. The charge rested allegedly on his confession. The day of the assassination, the boy, then fourteen years old, quarreled with his mother, who had refused to let him go out with his girl friend. Enraged, he wrote a note to his mother: "You are treating me like a baby but I am a grownup and have joined a revolutionary party that entrusts me with most responsible acts. Today, for example, I shot General Gelichevsky. . . ." Somehow this letter fell into the hands of the police. It was presented to the military court as a confession!

Yegerev, six and a half feet tall, had to stand trial as the ringleader of an armed revolt in November, 1905. He had just returned from Manchuria, still in uniform, with a service medal. Not very bright and a timid soul by nature, he had learned only one thing in the service: to obey orders. When a demonstration was called in his village and he was told to take his place in the front row, he obeyed; when, as the tallest man in the crowd, he was told to carry the banner, he took the pole. Now the demonstration was described as an armed revolt and he, as the leader, was facing the noose.

The most serious case was that of Karpov, a mining engineer. Tall, of aristocratic appearance, he was the director of a large coal mine. As a sympathizer with the S-R party, he harbored members of underground organizations in his house and occasionally supplied the party with dynamite. Through an *agent provocateur* planted at the very top of the party, the secret police had traced the origin of explosives used in a terroristic attempt and Karpov was arrested. Interrogated, he answered with quixotic straightforwardness. His chance to escape the gallows was slim.

These were the permanent inmates of the tower.

AN ASSIGNMENT

The routine of life in the tower was broken from time to time by the arrival of new prisoners, political and criminal, recently arrested or transferred from other prisons or other wards of the Castle. For some reason the tower was used for deportation and reallocation cases. I questioned the newcomers about what was happening outside our tower, in other prisons and in the free world. I liked to memorize their answers, as if I were writing them down in a notebook. This gave me the illusion of being on a journalistic assignment Just so, I thought, I might sit at a campfire in the wilderness and interview haggard and ragged strangers emerging from nowhere in the basin of the Upper Amazon River, in Tibet, or in the Altai Mountains. On such an assignment also I would be exposed to hunger, stench, lice, danger of sudden death, and I would listen to the yarns of strangers, trying to disentangle truth from fancy. In fact, I might have accepted a journalistic assignment to a prison. I might have come to this place voluntarily, to live among these men and share their privations. Surely I would have had enough strength to carry out my mission!

I do not remember how I hit on this theory of "assignment." Perhaps it was originally a joke, but it became a wonderful philosophy in a place like the Castle of Ekaterinoslav. It protected me against self-pity and kept me fit and active.

The mistreatment of the prisoners in the Castle ranged from simple beating, like the roughing up in police stations all over the world, to deliberate torture. What had started as the guards' revenge for a moment of fear became a routine. Many prisoners were beaten to death without the slightest provocation on their part, though their death certificates specified pneumonia. If I were a journalist assigned to report on the prison, obviously it would be my job to expose these facts. . . .

I asked a lawyer who was in touch with political prisoners whether he and his friends in the city could get publicity for a factual account of the prison. He promised that every effort would be made to distribute the report as widely as possible, but added that he considered it too dangerous to draw up such a report within the prison and did not recommend such a venture. I decided to disregard his warning.

My campaign plan envisaged three steps: first, to establish a network of trustworthy "correspondents," at least two men in each ward; next, to assemble facts, checking and rechecking each bit of testimony; then, to write the report.

The cracks in the walls—the hiding place of the bugs—provided an excellent cache for my files. The tower was strategically located for contacts with other wards. The guards in the hall of our wing were not very mean, the hall cleaners were ready to carry mail from ward to ward for a pinch of tobacco per letter. In a month I had assembled about a hundred cases of unwarranted beatings, some of them fatal. These were hard facts—with names, dates, precise details attested by scores of witnesses. Writing with a sharp pencil, I could put twenty-five lines of forty letters each—the content of half a regular typewritten page—on a sheet of cigarette paper of the usual size, 2¼ by 1¾ inches. My report comprised about a hundred such sheets. We passed them to our friends outside the prison in the seams of dirty shirts and underwear sent out for laundering.

Two or three weeks later a lawyer who came to the prison to see his clients brought us big news: the report had been published in a Russian émigré newspaper in Switzerland and excerpts from it had appeared in French and German newspapers under such titles as "The Torture Chambers in Ekaterinoslav" and "The Infamy of Tsarist Prisons." The S-D group in the Third Duma introduced an interpellation, and its spokesman read the whole report into the Duma's record and asked for an investigation.

A few days passed. Through the prison grapevine I knew that some of the criminal-political prisoners mentioned in my report had been called to the superintendent's office and questioned. Nobody from the prison administration was present at the interrogation. The investigator who cross-examined the witnesses tried to catch them in contradictions but did not intimidate them and treated some of them to cigarettes. One of my "correspondents," a common criminal lifer, was questioned for several hours. At the end the officer released him, saying, "That will do. Everything tallies with the report. Thank you."

Two more days passed. Just after the evening inspection an unusual commotion began in the hall. Belokos was shouting orders, guards were running, hall cleaners were sweeping the floor, others were carrying out the stinking barrels. The prison was getting ready for an inspection by high officials.

I saw them cross the courtyard—a man in a general's uniform followed by a dozen civil officials, then Fetisov and his assistants. The procession toured the ground floor, then the second floor. We heard Belokos barking, "Attention!" And another voice commanding, "At ease!" Then silence. Clanking of padlocks. Again the same command in another room.

At last the procession came to our wing and entered the large ward adjoining the tower. Pressed against the door, we could hear a husky voice speaking to the prisoners. "We had no knowledge. . . . The law admits no corporal punishment in prisons. . . . I shall hold the superintendent responsible. . . ." The procession did not enter our tower.

There was no more beating or mistreatment in the prison, though the regime was severe. Belokos remained chief of the guards. Food was abominable but a trifle less loathsome than before.

A lawyer who defended our group came to the prison to see me. He told me that the date of the trial had not yet been fixed and added casually, "You know, Woytinsky, I would advise you to ask for transfer to another prison. . . . It seems that the administration suspects that you are the author. . . . Of course I denied this rumor, but something might happen. . . ."

I interrupted him. "Please tell Fetisov that the stuff came from me, and everybody in Ekaterinoslav and St. Petersburg knows that. Then I will be perfectly safe. They will be afraid of me."

However, I was not entirely sure of my position. Very soon I had a chance to test it. After the explosion, the prisoners had been forbidden to go near the windows and the guards in the courtyard were instructed to shoot at anyone they could see behind the bars. The window in the tower was so low that it was hard to move about the room without coming into view of the guards. One day Misha carelessly approached it. The guard noticed him and reported to Belokos, who rushed into our chamber. "To the dungeon!" he shouted. "Who stood at the window?"

I answered, "I did."

Belokos opened his mouth but stopped short. "You did not," he said after a brief silence.

"I did," I insisted. "Ask the guard."

He looked at me with suspicion. Then he said firmly, "Why should I? I know your tricks." And he slammed the door behind him furiously.

I was immune. Belokos avoided our tower. The guards in the courtyard no longer harassed us.

FACING THE GALLOWS

Along with gathering material on the mistreatment of prisoners, I kept up a correspondence with inmates about their cases and wrote their applications to the courts and other legal papers. Most of my clients were facing the gallows, some for revolutionary activity in 1905 and armed resistance at the time of their arrest; others, like Nikolai and Yegerev, under false accusations. The sentence depended less on the evidence presented by the prosecuting attorney than on the president of the military court. Justice was reduced to a sordid gamble. A few knew in advance that they would be hanged and were not interested in the pre-trial procedure; others tried to defend themselves but were lost in the jungle of legal terms and references to the paragraphs of the Penal Code.

Legal murder—execution of innocent people—had become a common practice under Stolypin and impressed nobody. A military judge or prosecutor did not attract public attention by the number of death sentences he imposed in a single session. Only carefully staged mass trials hit the headlines.

I remember two such cases well—the case of the armed revolt in Gorlovka in 1905, and the case of the 103 Anarchists. Although very different in origin and outcome, these cases were characteristic of the state of Tsarist justice at the time when I had the rare opportunity to observe and study its operation from inside one of the grimmest prisons of the Empire.

THE CASE OF THE ARMED REVOLT IN GORLOVKA

The Ekaterinoslav courts served as a central slaughterhouse of south Russia and tried cases arising from numberless local riots. That of the armed upheaval in Gorlovka included the strike on railroads and in coal mines in the Donetz Basin, local riots, the disarming of railroad-station gendarmes, and the erection of barricades in some villages.

The charges were focused on events in a small mining town, Gorlovka, where the miners had held a meeting and decided to resist the approaching troops. Defense commandos were formed, some of them armed with crossbars and pistols. Their clash with the troops did not materialize, however, since the officer in command of the troops sent against the town stopped his train a few miles from Gorlovka, unloaded his men, and presented an ultimatum to the miners. The crowd dispersed and the station was cleared without a shot. A few ringleaders were arrested and the affair seemed to be forgotten. Later, however, as the grip of reaction tightened, more people were arrested in and around Gorlovka and all revolutionary events hundreds of miles away from this town were pulled together into a mass trial with 132 defendants. In 1909 the prosecution demanded death sentences for all of them, and the president of the court told a defense attorney, "Half these scoundrels will hang!"

Most of the defendants had been carried along by the storm of 1905, as were millions of workers, peasants, and intellectuals. Their lawyers suggested an appeal to the Tsar for mercy in advance of the trial. The majority accepted this advice; one third rejected it. The administration segregated the "patriots" from the "rebels" in the prison and on the benches in the courtroom. Then, following the superintendent's advice, the "patriots" organized a church chorus. On December 6, 1909, the Tsar's birthday, they sent a telegram to the Tsar with best wishes for his happiness and a plea for mercy. The same day the Gorlovka chorus made its first appearance in the prison church.

The trial went on. The political prisoners said that the "patriots" were traitors. The leaders of the "patriots" replied in a collective letter. "There are different kinds of people among us," they wrote, "but none of us ever had any tie with revolutionary parties. If fear of death means cowardice, we are cowards. But we have betrayed nothing, denounced nobody. We have made a poll among ourselves. Out of eighty-eight of us, seventy-three have children, more than two hundred children in all. You must understand and forgive us. Our only guilt is that we are weak and frightened."

This letter provoked heated controversy among the political prisoners. Most of them considered it a piece of despicable hypocrisy. The leader of the "rebels," a big coal miner, Tkachenko, wrote a message that was also circulated in the prison. "In our case," he wrote, "revolutionaries have been mingled with persons who have no allegiance to the revolution. The latter are entitled to fight for their lives according to their own standards. If, by refusing to join them, we have exposed ourselves, we have done this of our free decision."

Shortly before Christmas the court announced the sentence: thirty-two men were sentenced to death, sixty-one to prison for ten years or more, and forty-one were set free. All those sentenced to the gallows were transferred to Death Row in chains and handcuffs. The group consisted of fourteen "patriots" and eighteen "rebels," but the next day the "patriots" were brought back to the common ward and freed of their irons. The "rebels" remained in the death cells. I saw them during their walk in the courtyard. Month after month they waited for execution, and for some of them the strain proved unbearable. Two, and later six others, signed a petition prepared by their lawyers. Their sentences were commuted. But ten Gorlovka men refused to yield. They were hung in the summer of 1910.

THE CASE OF THE 103 ANARCHISTS

The Anarchists' case was another *cause célèbre* in Ekaterinoslav. Between 1905 and 1907 many holdups and other acts of violence were committed in south Russia. The police recorded all of them as "anarchy," but few culprits were caught. On the other hand, the prisons were full of persons suspected of being Anarchists. An ambitious investigating attorney, Shpiganovsky, conceived the idea of allocating the unsolved cases of anarchy among the suspects. He extorted confessions from two or three prisoners and enrolled two others as supporting court's witnesses to confirm the police records.

Shpiganovsky worked patiently to weave his web. The charges, however, did not hold together—the sixty odd crimes for which there were "witnesses" had no relation to one another, and there was no evidence of conspiracy among the defendants. The arrest of Chardash gave Shpiganovsky the idea of "organizing" a conference of Anarchists. Chardash would incite the others to crimes, while the rank-and-file members of the convention would report their plans and misdeeds and intentions to Chardash.

Among the suspects held in our tower for two or three months was a fugitive sailor, Galkovsky, an epileptic but a quiet and humble man in the intervals between his attacks. Because of his frequent fits, he only vaguely remembered what had happened a few days earlier. One could persuade him, for instance, that the ward had received loaves of white bread the preceding week, instead of the usual black bread. At first he would say, "I do not know." After some persuasion he would agree that he had seen and eaten the white bread.

Shpiganovsky began to work on him and made him sign a statement describing a convention of Anarchists in his home. It alleged that some sixty persons had been present at the opening of the meeting and fifteen more had arrived before its end. Chardash presided. His keynote speech took four pages—Shpiganovsky concocted it by piecing together excerpts from Anarchist leaflets and pamphlets. Among those present were . . . here followed a long list, each with particulars, like this: Pavlov, Ivan, son of Simon, twenty-six years old, born in Volkovo of Kalish precinct, Kuznetsk county, Novorossiisk department, welder in the repair shop of Ekaterinoslav railroad, wanted by police for harboring an unknown suspect of a holdup in Briansk in 1906. His aliases are Long Brother and Lightning. . . .

Galkovsky seemed to have known everything about each of his guests, and his information agreed with the police files in every detail. On the basis of this testimony, Galkovsky and 102 other prisoners were charged collectively with conspiracy and numerous other crimes. The prosecutor demanded the death penalty for all of them. When Galkovsky showed me the list of charges and asked my advice, I said, "You are a damned liar and a double-damned fool! How could you sign this nonsense?"

"I do not know," he replied. "I thought I was signing a deposition that I knew nothing."

"But how could you know the name, age, and place of birth of all these men?"

"I could not. The judge ordered me to sign that I knew nothing."

Then I said to Galkovsky, "If you want me to help you, tell me everything about your house. How large it is? How many windows are there in the living room? Where are the doors? What furniture do you have? A bed, a table, two chairs? . . . How large is the table? Now, think hard. How many people can be packed into your living room? Four? But if they are pressed together like sardines in a can? Six? And if somebody stands in the door? Seven? Is that all? Think hard—your life depends on it. You say seven is the limit. Not eight?"

Then I wrote a petition to the president of the court, in the name of Galkovsky. It began with the statement that the defendant was a very sick person, an epileptic, and did not remember what he had signed at the request of an investigating judge. However, he did remember his one-room house in Old Market Street. When he and his wife sat at the table, just enough room was left for two more persons. The list of charges declared, however, that there had been a convention of some seventy-five persons in his shack. He must have been out of his mind if he had said that to the judge. The complaint concluded with a request for an examination of his hut.

His request was sustained. The president of the court ruled the whole investigation void. Shpiganovsky was fired and the case was closed. Most of the defendants were set free. Others, including Chardash, had to stand trial on individual charges independent of the affair of the 103.

AFTER THE SENTENCE

Our case was tried by a military court in the summer of 1909, a year and a half after our arrest. The case was trivial. The existence of a party organization was proved by our two presses and proofs of *The South Russian Worker*, with corrections in my handwriting. Two of the defendants were acquitted, all others sentenced to four years of forced labor and deportation to Siberia for life. For Misha, as a minor, the sentence was commuted to three years of prison.

My mother had come from St. Petersburg to see me before the trial. There was little comfort for either of us in the reunion: I did not wish to tell her of conditions in the prison, and the news she brought me from home seemed far away. I loved her and wished to comfort her, but I could not conceal my impatience when she begged me to take care of my health. "Watch what you eat," she urged. "If you do not feel well, call the doctor. I am told he is a competent and fine man." Actually, the prison doctor was one of the basest characters in the administration.

After the sentence my mother was allowed to see me only once.

I told her that the sentence was not bad; four years was the least I had anticipated. She again urged me to take care of my health, reminding me that we had tuberculosis in the family.

All convicts sentenced to forced labor had to be examined medically by a special commission before they were shackled for the first third of their term. With others, I was called to the office. The commissioners sat behind a long table: a stout, kindly-looking bespectacled man in the middle; an official of the Justice Department; a middle-aged officer with a bored expression on his face; the prison doctor and the superintendent. The doctor examined those who complained of some serious illness. Prisoners in very poor shape could be excused from wearing fetters.

When Fetisov called my name, the chairman turned to him and said in a half whisper, "A writer, from a good family, well known in St. Petersburg." Then he turned to the prison doctor and said, "Rheumatic fever, I presume?"

"Yes, Your Excellency," nodded the doctor. "The prisoner has been under my observation. Rheumatic fever."

I interrupted him. "That is not true. I have never been under your observation and do not have rheumatic fever or any other disease."

The doctor replied with irritation, "I keep a record of each cell, and I am supposed to be able to recognize rheumatic fever when I see it."

The chairman looked at me intently and waived my objection: "All right, all right, have it your way, you have no rheumatic fever. But the commission must rely on the official report of the physician, rather than trust the prisoner's word." And he ordered the superintendent to write: "Fit for labor but without shackles." Later I learned that the chairman was a new inspector of penal institutions in Ekaterinoslav and had conducted the investigation of the mistreatment of prisoners. He knew I had written the report and was paying me a literary honor.

ILLNESS

Actually, I was not as healthy as I pretended to be. My physical condition had deteriorated as a result of undernourishment and lack of fresh air. Boils broke out on my legs and arms, but others in the tower were in worse shape, Misha alarmingly so. He was coughing blood, but when I persuaded him to report to the pharmacy the prison doctor threw him out as a chiseler. I took his bloodstained handkerchiefs, went to the doctor, and reported Misha's symptoms as my own. The doctor obligingly prescribed the hospital ration for me—a glass of milk for breakfast and a slice of white bread for the noon meal. In addition, he gave me some drops and told his assistant to give me an extra blanket. A few days later I similarly obtained aspirin and ointment against rheumatism for Misha. The doctor was all sweetness toward me, though he must have seen that I was a phony patient.

Much later I learned that he was taking money from my mother. After my trial, she had called on him in his private office and complained of a sore throat. The doctor gave her a twenty-kopek prescription and was ready to pocket the usual one-ruble fee when my mother timidly pressed a twenty-five-ruble note into his hand. He thanked her and asked whether she had any relatives in the city, perhaps in the prison. She told him that her son was in the Castle, and she was worried about his health.

"Don't worry," said the good doctor. "I happen to be the prison physician and can keep an eye on him."

"I do not know whether I should impose on you," she said hesitatingly.

"No trouble at all—twenty-five rubles a month."

Knowing nothing of this arrangement, I loathed the doctor but went to the pharmacy each week to get medicine, a tube of tooth-paste, or a cake of soap for tower inmates. Meanwhile my own condition did not improve and boils covered my entire body. I had spells of dizziness and would lie for hours on the cot with strange optical hallucinations—the tower turning around me, the walls changing shape and forming unexpected corners. These spells were accompanied by spasms of dread.

My companions did not notice the change. For them I remained the strong man without nerves. Misha was first to realize I was seriously ill and urged me to go to the doctor, but I refused fiercely to ask the rogue for favors for myself.

One morning when I lay on the cot, Yegerev sat down at my bedside and began to ask me how I felt. Fever? Headache? Sweat? Did I have any trouble in breathing or swallowing? The poor soldier was earnestly worrying about me. In the afternoon he re-ported to the guard that he was ill and wished to see the doctor at once. This sounded like typhus to the guard, and he took the prisoner to the hospital. Yegerev proudly returned from the doctor with a vial of some potion and a box of pills . . . for me! He had complained to the doctor of weakness and dizziness, describing my symptoms. From this day on he acted as my nurse and so, not to disappoint him, I swallowed his drugs. Next, he obtained a glass of milk for me for breakfast.

Now the tower was getting two glasses of milk each morning—one glass was for Misha, and Yegerev insisted that I have the second. After two days of this treatment, I told him that I felt much better, thanks to his medicine and milk. To prove my point, I let him feel my muscles. He agreed that I was out of danger. Then we started rotating our ration of milk among the eight of us. Misha had his glass every morning, and the others got half a glass every fourth day.

The fall of 1909 was unusually cold in Ekaterinoslav. The round wall of the tower was covered with a film of ice and finger-thick icicles formed on the window frame. The tower had no heat, but in the passage, between the circular ward and the hall, was a stove originally designed to keep the guard warm. Firewood was given to the inmates only on days when the temperature sank below freezing. The day's ration was four logs, each eighteen inches long and as thick as a man's arm, two matches, and a spoonful of kerosene. Because of the draft in the chimney, the stove could not raise the temperature of the air in the tower, but we could get heat that radiated from the mouth of the stove. We arranged the logs inside like a campfire and warmed our hands and feet before we went to sleep. Thus we were warm for at least half an hour each night.

This was a miserable existence—hunger, filth, and cold. I was tired of my self-imposed role of a strong man able to take anything without flinching. Realizing that I had to do something to keep my mind busy, I invented a task for myself to test whether I had retained any mental ability.

The only books we had in the tower were two bulletins of the Prussian Statistical Office that my mother had brought me. The guards let us keep them because of the big crowned eagles on the cover. These bulletins contained wage statistics of Prussia. I read and reread the tables until I had nearly memorized them. Then I decided to try to analyze correlations between the different series and find out whether they permitted any theoretical generalization. Thus I found myself engaged in a study of the theory of wages. During the day I thought of the figures, and at night, after having warmed my hands at the stove, I made calculations and wrote as long as I could hold the pencil between frostbitten, swollen fingers.

Later my book on wages was published in St. Petersburg. Tugan-Baranovsky, with his usual kindness toward me, referred to it in his course as a new theory of wages. Actually my ideas were very close to those that John Bates Clark had developed some two decades earlier. Neither Tugan nor I, however, had ever come across the works of the American economist, and the bargaining theory was new to us.

THE TRIP TO NOVGOROD

In November, 1909, I was summoned to appear before the court in Novgorod for trial on the four-year-old Borovenka affair. The order had been sent to Ekaterinoslav by mistake. In Russia, a person sentenced by several courts had to serve only the longest term, so that the Borovenka case had been absorbed by the sentence of the military court at Ekaterinoslav. The summons to Novgorod was therefore a free ticket for a junket.

The trip began rather uncomfortably, in a prison coach packed with common criminals. Except for a handful of political prisoners, about half the party consisted of harmless tramps and the other half of recidivists—"regulars." Although I was in the ragged garb of a convict serving a forced labor sentence, my glasses made them suspect me of being a political, and the regulars treated me with unconcealed enmity. The bosses, "Ivans" in prison slang, were particularly hostile.

The first halt was in Kursk. The party was herded to the prison on the outskirts of the city and locked up in the deportation barracks. Here other parties were added to the Ekaterinoslav crowd, and we all were taken to a barnlike ward. The criminals, recidivists and tramps alike, rushed through the gates, fighting for the better places on the floor. I was tossed aside, and when I passed the gate the only place left was a stinking straw sack beside the cell buckets. I preferred to spend the night sitting on the bench rather than lie down in loathsome filth.

The common criminals noticed my predicament. Somebody shouted, "You, political, you don't like to be treated like us others." I did not answer. A man in chains and manacles, an important "Ivan" to judge by his manner, came to me and asked, "What is your name?" When I gave it, he said loudly, so that everyone in the room could hear him, "Are you, mister, the one who exposed the brutes of Ekaterinoslav? We know that you made no distinction between your pals and our men. We appreciate it when anyone is fair to our people."

He took my bag and led me to the row under the window where I was offered the best sack of straw. For the rest of the trip I did not have to carry my bag, rush for a better place in the ward, or wait in line for hot water. The "Ivans" did their best to make my journey as comfortable as possible. They even extended the same favors to other politicals in the party.

In Novgorod I was locked up in the deportation ward with nondescript petty offenders, the overflow of the scum of St. Petersburg.

I noticed in the courtyard a group of political prisoners in civilian clothes and asked the chief guard to be transferred to the political ward. The chief, an undersized old man with a long gray mustache and a row of medals on his breast, seemed puzzled. I still had my glasses, but my rags did not fit into his concept of politicals. "If you are a political," he said, "I shall transfer you to those of your kind. But if you are a thief or a crook, you must be pleased with your present company." He went at once to check my papers. Half an hour later I was in the political ward, washed, in clean linen under a fresh prison uniform.

The Novgorod prison seemed cozy after Ekaterinoslav Castle. Its politicals were all serving comparatively short terms—two or three years—for minor offenses such as dissemination of subversive leaflets or disrespectful remarks about the Tsar. Since I had been brought to Novgorod as a defendant in the Borovenka case, I was treated like other politicals except that I was not permitted to wear civilian clothes.

I asked the chief guard whether Eugene Litkens was among the prisoners. He remembered that a young man of that name had been brought to the prison a couple of years earlier and then transferred somewhere. I understood that he had been freed on bond.

The old chief guard ran the prison as though it were his private household. His word was law for guards and prisoners alike. I saw him quieting a brawl among the common criminals in the court-yard. He rushed into the excited crowd and shouted, "You see this?"

He lifted his left hand high over his head. The hand was de-formed by the scar of a blow that had almost chopped off the thumb. The riot immediately subsided and a voice replied, "Surely we see, uncle."

"Then listen!" shouted the chief. "Attention! Turn around! March to the ward!"

The crowd obeyed meekly. My companions explained the old man's gesture. Long ago, a fellow brought to the prison by a convoy had tried to escape. The undersized guard and the soldiers ran after him. The guard first caught up with the prisoner and grabbed him by the arm. A soldier overtook them and raised his sword to strike the prisoner. The guard barked, "Keep off! I am in command here!"

The soldier shouted back, "You are in command in the enclosure but here I do as I please."

He struck at the prisoner's head, but the guard intervened and took the blow on his bare hand. Thereafter he became a hero among the common criminals. By showing his deformed hand, he was saying to them, "You know me? Did I save one of yours? Now, what I say goes."

He was impeccably honest and required the same of the guards he sent to the market to buy food for the prisoners. I heard him instructing a recruit, "Each prisoner's kopek must be accounted for. Who steals from a free man is a thief. So what? But if you steal from a prisoner, you are mean and despicable, the meanest man in the world."

A week before the trial I was called to the office and shown my files. There was nothing new except a record from the city hospital. The prisoner Litkens, transferred for observation to the ward for mental patients, had died of tuberculosis. With him died my revolutionary youth.

My sister Nadya came to visit me. I had not seen her for three years but could not see any change in her. She was young, attractive, full of artistic interests, and as fond of me as before. However, all her kindness could not pierce the wall between us. She remained in Novgorod for the trial and asked me to conduct my defense in the grand style. I explained to her that this would be pointless: the new sentence would be absorbed by the term I was serving. But Nadya worried over my lack of interest in the matter, thought such passivity was not in my character, and hoped that a public appearance—even in the docket of defendants—would raise my morale. I promised her I would make a political speech if it came to a trial.

The trial, however, was a disappointment to her. At the opening, the judge asked me to identify myself by name and status. I answered, "Woytinsky, Wladimir, sentenced to four years of forced labor and deportation to Siberia for life." The prosecuting attorney asked the court whether this sentence had been certified officially, and, after the clerk confirmed that it was in the file, the trial was adjourned and the Borovenka affair was closed.

I returned to the ward. My roommates had often asked me about Ekaterinoslav, but I was reluctant to talk about the Castle of Death. The night after the trial, when I was ready to go back to Ekaterinoslav, they asked me again. This time I was in a talkative mood. I began to tell them about the massacre of April 29, the reign of terror, the death sentences, the execution of innocent people. We recessed late in the night, and I concluded the story the next evening. My companions urged me to write down what I had told them. This seemed like a good idea, but the whole story was too long, and I wrote down only the part about the death sentences and executions.

Novgorod had a small group of intellectuals who sympathized with leftist parties. They called themselves the Political Red Cross and tried to help political prisoners. My companions smuggled my manuscript out to them, asking them to try to publish it. Later the story appeared in one of the leading Russian magazines, *Vestnik Evropy*, and was reprinted in book form in several languages. It was signed by the letter "S," which remained my pen name for many years. Although the article was not very well written, it attracted public attention.

The local assistant court attorney, himself a member of the Political Red Cross, was among the first to read the manuscript. He suggested to Nadya that he spare me the return to Ekaterinoslav by keeping me indefinitely in the Novgorod prison. Nadya liked the idea but doubted whether I would accept it. The president of the Red Cross, a gentle elderly lady, came to see me. All I had to do, she said, was to ask the superintendent to postpone my transfer to Ekaterinoslav for health reasons. The superintendent would send the petition to the court attorney. The latter would ask for my papers for examination. The papers would be sent to his assistant, who usually handled such questions, and he would simply pigeon-hole them. In the absence of the reply to my petition, I would serve the rest of my four years of forced labor in this peaceful, quiet place, with books and an opportunity to write.

This friendly proposal called for at least a polite reply, but it sounded to me like an invitation to desert my companions in the Ekaterinoslav Castle. Taking my hands into her frail ones, the old lady asked timidly, "You will write to the superintendent?" I assured her I would. The same day I wrote to the superintendent that the affair for which I had been brought to Novgorod was terminated and asked for my return to Ekaterinoslav.

The journey back was uneventful. In the Moscow deportation prison, the assistant superintendent noticed that, contrary to regulation, I had no chains. "Where are your irons?" he asked. I answered that I did not know. Suspecting I had rid myself of chains by some trick, he ordered that I be shackled hand and foot.

The party passed through Orel. The city had two prisons: the State Prison and the Central Penitentiary. The latter was one of the two darkest spots in Russia's prison network (the other being the Ekaterinoslav Castle). Its inmates were subjected to merciless beating and mistreatment. Many had been beaten to death, and several—Sapotnitsky, among others—had committed suicide.

When the train was approaching Orel, the convoy began to check the lists of prisoners, singling out those who were to be transferred from the railroad station directly to the penitentiary. One of the men in my compartment, a young man with dark hair and a pale face, was to be delivered to that grim place. A soldier stepped into our compartment, measured him with his eyes, and asked, "To the penitentiary? A bad place for Jews! You are one, eh?"

The young man did not answer. The soldier unbuttoned the collar of the prisoner's shirt. "What did I say? No cross on his neck!"

The soldier had been speaking harshly, but suddenly he unbuttoned his own uniform, took off the silver cross he wore next to his skin, and put it about the prisoner's neck. "My mother gave it to me," he whispered. "It is a sin to give a mother's blessing away, but God will forgive me." And he rushed from the compartment.

I LEARN CARPENTRY

I returned to Ekaterinoslav after five months' absence and was taken directly to the tower. It was like coming home after a journey, but all the news was grim. There had been many executions during the winter; Pavel had been hanged; Chardash had died of tuberculosis; many had died of typhus.

During the morning inspection Belokos entered our tower. He stood in front of me, waiting for me to ask to be unchained. Then he asked:

"Complaints?"

"None."

This game continued for three weeks. To his consternation I had no complaint. In the meantime, I had learned how to wear the chains with a minimum of discomfort and was reluctant to assert my right to be freed of them. Then one day Belokos came running to the tower. "Woytinsky, to the smithshop!" He rushed me to the basement and ordered the smith to unfetter me. "We have twelve hundred men in the prison," he grumbled. "I cannot remember who is to be shackled and who not. Each prisoner must report for himself." The inspector of prisons was to make the tour of the Castle that afternoon.

It was early spring. The only tree in the courtyard—the one under which Leonid had died—was covered with fresh leaves. The yard was full of activity—axes swinging and saws singing among piles of logs and boards. Each day during the half-hour walk I looked with envy at the working prisoners. The noise of hammers, saws, and axes sounded like sweet music, the fragrance of fresh chips was delicious, the drops of resin on the boards and slabs sparkled like diamonds.

I was not sure whether carpentry was a form of forced labor to which I was sentenced or a privilege, but I told my companions in the tower that I would like to enroll as a carpenter. They thought this a good idea but doubted whether I had the strength to handle a heavy ax. Only Karpov decided to go along with me.

When we reported to Fetisov to apply for work as carpenters, he inquired if we had experience in this trade. I answered that prisoners sentenced to forced labor need not necessarily be experts in the jobs assigned to them. He agreed and assigned us to the carpentry commando engaged in building market stands. The work was divided between two gangs, thirty men in each. Both foremen wanted to have us. I chose the slow-moving, quiet Ukrainian, Ostapenko, a peasant serving a ten-year sentence for agrarian riots.

Proud of the preference I had shown for him, Ostapenko at first gave me the easiest jobs, pretending that they required education. For example, he had me nail boards to the frame of the stand, explaining that without education one could not properly count the nails and keep them in a straight line. But I asked him to let me hew the poles, the most important job. The prison bought round-wood, and the prisoners had to square the logs into four-by-four or six-by-six poles with axes. Some logs were green and crooked, others knotty; the axes were not very sharp. Ostapenko chose the easiest logs for me, sharpened my ax himself, patiently taught me how to hold it and how to strike. Indeed, under pretense of giving me instruction, he tried to do the work for me.

The prison had a contract for two types of stands: square, low stands for meat and vegetables, and high, octagonal, turret-like constructions for newspapers and soft drinks. The square stands used more boards than poles, while the turrets required long, smoothly hewn poles and were crowned with a pyramidal roof. My ambition was to hew the long poles, but it was not easy to make the grade and I never did get so far as to build the octagonal roofs. With this limitation, I acquired some experience in carpentry and can still handle the tools of this venerable trade fairly well.

Karpov was then busy in the joiner shop drawing blueprints for pieces of furniture. Since we both had access to tools, the administration decided to transfer us from the tower to a building at the rear of the Castle, isolated from the rest of the prison. The rear building consisted of a single row of double cells. It was a quiet place, but its memory evokes a gruesome picture.

The building was separated from the Castle by a narrow strip of courtyard. Our windows were some four feet above the ground, and just in front of them, on the ground level, were the windows of the cells in which prisoners sentenced to death were awaiting execution. We saw them milling about in their cages or lying on the floor in fetters and manacles, often with hands chained behind them. We recognized some of them through the bars and could occasionally exchange a few words. And we saw the guards, headed by Belokos, beat them, and the armed convoy take them, one after another, to the gallows.

The death row was the last thing I saw before I was transferred to the Central Penitentiary of Alexandrovsk, one of the largest Siberian forced labor prisons.

THE LONG ROAD

The transfer to Siberia found me indifferent. It did not matter much to me where I served the rest of my term. I left Ekaterinoslav in chains, but my papers indicated permission to wear glasses.

It took us six or seven weeks to get from Ekaterinoslav to Irkutsk. The party included common criminals and politicals, all chained, all in the same ragged garb. Most of the time I traveled with Rogovsky, a likable fellow who could discuss books and politics, recite poetry, and hum prisoner songs. We pooled our meager resources. My friends had succeeded in smuggling two five-ruble gold pieces into the Eka- terinoslav prison for me, and I kept them hidden in lumps of sugar. Rogovsky had a few small coins in the cloth buttons of his clothes. With five kopeks a day to add to the prison ration, we were not hungry.

The guards were not unkind. Only on one long leg of the journey did we get a convoy hostile to the prisoners, because of trouble with the preceding party. In revenge, the soldiers emptied the bucket of drinking water in the prisoners' coach. The day was hot and the walls and roof of the car were sizzling. This was the nearest to torture I had ever suffered or witnessed. Personally I could stand thirst and heat fairly well, but some prisoners fainted and others became delirious. The guards were obviously trying to provoke a riot. But the "Ivans" saw through their game and kept the party under control.

As the party proceeded eastward, its composition began to change. The crowd of chained prisoners was joined by bearded muzhiks de- ported without trial for agrarian unrest. After the Urals, strange char- acters joined the convoy—vagabonds and convicts who had been set- tled in Siberia, had escaped from the settlement, and been caught and shipped back. When caught, most of them refused to give their names and pretended to have forgotten everything. The practice was to resettle such nameless tramps as "Ivans without Memory." When they escaped for the second time, they proudly carried their last pa- pers in which they were registered under this nickname. Most of them were good-humored, talkative people. They knew every prison in Siberia and east Russia; the more experienced among them knew every guard by name. An old man with a long snow-white beard boasted that he had made the round trip from Yakutsk to Moscow and back more than ten times, each journey taking from a year to a year and a half.

We traveled several days with the old man and were locked together in the deportation ward in Krasnoyarsk. The barracks had three huge rooms with wide arches between them. Each room had plank beds in the middle. My place was between Rogovsky and the old hobo. I carried the lumps of sugar with the money knotted in a handkerchief tied to my belt. In the morning, I discovered that the kerchief was gone.

Rogovsky was certain someone had stolen the money and thought we could do nothing about it. But I wanted to make a try. Standing on the plank bed, I clapped my hands to attract attention and said, "During the night I lost a kerchief with some money in it. If anybody has found it, please return it to me! I am going to the penitentiary, and that money is all I have."

My speech was greeted with loud jeers. "Why do you tell this yarn? Lost, found!" the old tramp said. "Sheer nonsense! Somebody has stolen your money, so better look for the thief!"

"There are many thieves here," I answered, "but no decent thief would steal money from a prisoner, especially one on his way to the penitentiary."

He laughed sadly. "How foolish can a learned man be! I am telling you—look for the thief."

Three hours passed. The tramp came to me again and asked, "Have you found the thief?"

"I am not looking for a thief," I replied.

"Oh yes, you are waiting until that honorable gentleman who found your money returns it to you. You will wait a long time! Where do you think you are? Nonsense!"

In the evening he asked me again: "Still waiting for the thief?"

"There was no theft!" I replied.

The old man sighed and said regretfully, "There was none. Here is your money. Keep it. You lost the kerchief and I picked it up. I made up my mind. If you, mister, say this was a theft, the money is mine. But it looks as though you really believe no decent thief would steal money from a prisoner. All right with me. Keep your money." He seemed both angry and sorry things turned out that way.

The last lap of the long journey was forty miles on foot from Irkutsk to Alexandrovsk, in two days. The road ran from hill to hill, through forests and fields, with villages in the valleys. Never had I seen the sky so blue, the trees so green, the clouds so white. Never had I noticed that clouds were like domes with rings of angels above them. I had not seen the world in this way in my younger years, and I had a strange feeling I had learned to see it so in prison. In fact, my dreams at night in Ekaterinoslav Castle were full of mountains, rivers, forests, and meadows covered with flowers. On the trip from Irkutsk to Alexandrovsk those dreams were becoming real. The party crossed the Angara River on a ferry. And this again was the river of my dreams, with water so clear, the ferry seemed to float in the air.

I was dead-tired at the end of the first day and walked with excruciating pain during the second. My feet were covered with blisters, my puttees soaked with blood, but this trip remains one of the few radiant spots in my memories of those years.

ALEXANDROVSK PENITENTIARY

The party passed through a village surrounded by fields and forested hills. A strange village: men in prison garb—gray shirts, pants, and caps—were coming and going, apparently unguarded and mingling with local peasants. We were in Alexandrovsk. It was located at the mouth of a narrow valley perhaps a mile long. At the end of the valley was the penitentiary, a large compound encircled by a high red brick wall with wooden watchtowers.

Roll call was taken in a broad corridor, divided into small enclosures by iron grills. After the party had been locked in a large hall with plank beds along the walls, the turnkey called me to the door. A man in neat prison garb shook my hand and asked, "How many politicals do you have in the party?"

"There must be a score."

"Please make a list. And make a note of those who could direct courses or give lectures." Noticing my surprise, he explained, "I am the headman of the political Collective, Zhdanov."

I had heard the name. Zhdanov was a well-known political defense lawyer, close to the S-D party, serving a forced-labor sentence. He told me that the political prisoners in the penitentiary were segregated in special wards, had some self-government, and were allowed to pick out those in arriving parties whom they wished to accept into their community, the "Collective."

This organization owed its existence to Zhdanov and Saur, an S-R journalist sentenced to forced labor for life for a military mutiny in 1905. They had persuaded the superintendent that a sort of honor system would give him a guarantee that political prisoners would make no attempt to escape. The superintendent, a former officer who had quit military service in mysterious circumstances, was a good-hearted man and despised himself for being a jailer, especially a jailer

of politicals, whom he respected as educated people. And since he believed his main responsibility was to prevent the escape of the prisoners, he made a pact with the politicals.

Saur became the official spokesman of the Collective. Zhdanov
took charge of newly arrived parties and the prison library. But the
soul of the organization was Eugene Timofeev, the politicals' headman for internal affairs. Nobody could match him for patience and
tact. His life and death are characteristic of the thorny path of Russian revolutionaries of his generation. Liberated by the revolution of
1917 after eleven years in prison, he was again arrested by the Soviets
for defending the Constituent Assembly and sentenced to death. The
verdict was suspended; he was kept in prison for several years as a hos-
tage and then exiled to Siberia. Time and again he was arrested, released, and rearrested. In 1936 or 1937 he disappeared. It is not
known whether he met death in a torture chamber or was shot.

In my time, the political Collective consisted of some two hundred
men. Probably a hundred more used services of the organization without being members. The main privilege of the politicals was that,
thanks to segregation, they could keep their wards clean and could organize their life according to a self-imposed timetable—"Constitution." The morning hours were used for cleaning the ward; next came
two hours of silence for the benefit of those who wished to read or
study; an hour after lunch was free of restrictions; then again two
hours of silence, and so on. In the ward to which I was assigned, the
evenings were devoted to lectures and "organized" entertainment.

The Collective enjoyed two other privileges: the politicals were allowed to keep samovars—Russian-type teakettles—and make tea after
the evening inspection, and they also had control over the prison library, which consisted of books donated by their relatives and friends.
These books were classified under a dozen headings, and those dealing
with economic and social problems were catalogued separately and
marked with an asterisk on the back.

The gendarmes got wind of the existence of the samovars in the political wards and of the "asterisk section" in the library. They questioned the superintendent, who denied everything. Not satisfied, the
gendarmes complained to the prison inspector in Irkutsk, and a curious feud developed between the prison inspector, backed by the gendarmes, and the superintendent, supported by the Governor General,
Kniazev. The prison inspector was bent on seizing our samovars and
the marked books. He used to try to catch us by surprise, but his office was in Irkutsk, and to reach Alexandrovsk he had to cross the Angara River by ferry. The ferry was manned by former convicts, and the
superintendent instructed them to telephone his office when the
enemy was approaching. This warning gave the penitentiary guards

time to remove the samovars and asterisked books. After a guided tour through the prison, the superintendent would invite the inspector to the administration club. A chorus of balalaika players—common criminals—would be summoned to the evening party, and in the midst of the celebration the superintendent would find time to phone the chief guard. "Return the samovars to the politicals!"

Prison food was insufficient but we were permitted to supplement the ration by purchasing foodstuffs in the prison canteen. In our room the prisoners pooled all the money they received from home so that we had a budget of some ninety rubles a month, a ruble and a half (seventy-five cents) per person. Laundry, soap, tooth paste, postage, needles and thread took more than half the budget. The rest—fifteen kopeks per week per person—was spent for tea, sugar, and improvement of food on Wednesdays and Fridays. Our ward was proud of this system of budgeting—a "complete commune."

Along with complete or partial community of budget, all the political wards had an arrangement for distributing work among the inmates. Each person had definite responsibilities: sweeping, washing dishes, cutting bread. My responsibility was lecturing—a lecture each Saturday on any subject I chose. Actually, many lectures stretched over two or three evenings, and some weeks I lectured nearly every day—mainly on economic theory. The acoustics in the ward were bad and I had to force my voice to be heard by everyone, including the guards who pressed against the grille, but I always found before me a mug of hot sweetened tea to ease my throat. Sugar was rationed in the commune—one lump no larger than a joint of one's little finger per person per day—but usually one of the listeners would drop his ration into my mug.

Several times our ward arranged debates on controversial issues. I recall a long discussion on the problem of national minorities in Russia in which I was completely eclipsed by a shy Jewish boy. He told the story of the Jewish labor movement in a small town in one of the western provinces, the ghetto of Tsarist Russia. His name was Khanin, and later I met him in New York as one of the leaders of Jewish American labor.

Again, as in the tower, I felt an urge for theoretical work. The work on my lectures led me to examine the origin of basic concepts of political economy and their interpretation by different schools. I prepared a series of talks on this subject and wrote them down in book form.[1]

One of my most vivid memories of the Alexandrovsk penitentiary

[1] I sent the manuscript, of some one hundred sixty pages, to a St. Petersburg publisher, who gave it for review to an expert in Marxist theory. The latter lost the manuscript.

is its courtyard, some fifty acres, with a well in the center. From this point the walls around the field looked like a hedge. High above them ran the skyline of forested hills. In summer all the trees looked alike, and it was difficult to distinguish differences in the shades of green. As fall approached, the colors began to change. Some patches of the green velvet became lighter, others darker. Then brown and red spots appeared overnight and turned into flashes of gold. Next, the golden sparks began to grow and expand until they merged into a conflagration. Strolling in the courtyard, I felt as near to the taiga as if I were wandering among the cedars and larches.

IN THE WORK GANG

The Russian penal system was full of contradictions. It included the grim Ekaterinoslav Castle and the cozy Novgorod prison, the torture chambers of Orel, and the samovars in Alexandrovsk. Siberian penitentiaries belonged to the brighter side of the picture. From the beginning of the nineteenth century they played an important role in the colonization of Siberia. Convicts, after serving one third of their term, were usually transferred to work gangs and housed in barracks outside the stockade. Most of them were employed in the fields and workshops of the prison or in mines. After thus serving the second third of their term, they could be settled in a village and might acquire land and become farmers. After the turn of the century, the prison population had outgrown the penitentiaries' demand for labor. Siberian prisons still had work gangs, but most of the prisoners sentenced to forced labor were kept in confinement and idleness, exactly as in European Russia.

In Alexandrovsk the work gangs were employed mainly in the fields around the prison, for woodcutting, repair and maintenance jobs, and the like. They also included gardeners, stable hands, coachmen, clerks, and—last but not least—musicians, singers, and dancers to entertain the administration. Though prisoners in the work gang wore prison garb and slept in the barracks, they could go to the village with oral permission from the chief guard.

During an inspection visit to Alexandrovsk, the Governor General, Kniazev, noticed that only the common criminals were working outdoors and asked the superintendent the reason for this discrimination against the politicals. When the superintendent answered that he knew of no legal ground for this practice, Kniazev instructed his counsel, Batarevich, to look into the question. The latter reported that the law made no distinction between the political convicts and others, and Kniazev ordered the superintendent to apply the law to all prisoners. The gendarmes objected, pointing out that the politicals might exert a demoralizing influence on the local population, but Kniazev refused to rescind his order.

About that time my sister Nadya came to Alexandrovsk to visit me—twelve days in a train for a few hours of reunion with the prodigal son of the family. The friends my sister found in Irkutsk advised her to ask Kniazev for my transfer to a work gang. In the palace of the Governor General she was received by Batarevich, who proved to be familiar with my articles in the *Vestnik Evropy* and other St. Petersburg magazines. He introduced Nadya to the Governor General. Kniazev was not sure whether I was eligible for the work gang, but Batarevich dispelled his doubts. Then Nadya mentioned a law that authorized prisoners to build their own huts on prison grounds, and Batarevich confirmed that this law had never been repealed. The Governor General remarked he liked this idea and thanked Nadya for having brought the law to his attention.

In December, 1910, the first five political prisoners were transferred to the work gang: two former members of the Second Duma; Zhdanov, a long-term S-R, and I. All five of us were listed officially as aid pharmacists and were billeted in the back room of the prison pharmacy. The pharmacist did not object to us, but someone in the administration alleged that the pharmacy, with its traditional (strictly unofficial) operations in alcohol, was no place to billet politicals. The superintendent called Zhdanov and told him we had better look for other quarters and jobs.

To justify our status in the work gang, each of us had to find a suitable occupation. One of the Duma members, a physician by profession, decided to practice in the village; another, a former schoolteacher, offered to give private lessons to the children of the guards. Our S-R companion was assigned to work in the prison's art shop. Zhdanov appointed himself cook for our small community. I was ready to work as a carpenter with other prisoners, but the chief guard rejected my services. The superintendent asked me whether I could do something more in line with my professional skills, and I said, "I am a writer. I shall write." He did not object. Informally, I spent much time on the self-imposed duty of postmaster general for the Collective, supplying it with newspaper clippings and maintaining an exchange of uncensored letters between the prisoners and their relatives and friends.

We had been sheltered temporarily in a tiny cottage on a hill overlooking the prison grounds, just on the border of virgin taiga. The valley was blanketed with glittering snow. The roofs of the prison and other buildings were pure silver, but the wind had kept the trees free of snow, and the naked birches and larches made an exquisite tracery on the green velvet of pines and firs. When the inspector ordered the superintendent to eject us from the tiny cottage and use the latter to store empty barrels, all five of us moved into my own *izba*, a log cabin Nadya had bought for me in the village for 125 rubles (approximately sixty dollars). It was built in Siberian style, of large logs twenty by twenty-four inches thick and had two rooms, with a stove in the smaller one, and a covered porch. A team of prisoners took the *izba* apart in the village, numbered the logs and boards, carried them to the prison grounds, and reassembled them.

The cabin was an excellent place for writing, but one day the chief guard came to tell me that he had received a list of occupations in the working gang, and writing was not among them. He understood, however, that "writer" was just another word for "clerk" and was willing to employ me as a clerk in his office. I did not like that plan for, as an office clerk, I would be caught in the middle of the petty frictions between the common criminals and the administration. I volunteered to work, rather, as a hammerer in the smithshop. The chief guard was surprised by my choice but gave me the job. I was just beginning to learn the trade when he assigned me to another— "a more intelligent" job, as he called it—that of a stock clerk in the prison warehouse. Later I gave lessons to the ten-year-old son of a prison official, and each Saturday the boy brought me an apple or blackberry pie baked by his mother.

In the spring the superintendent asked me to measure the flow of water in the stream running between my cabin and the barracks and to draw up plans for a water wheel and a sawmill. After a careful survey, I reported there was not enough water in the stream but that I thought it worthwhile to explore other streams in the forests around the prison as potential sources of power. The superintendent asked me to do so. This was just the job for me! I could stroll in the track-less forests, exploring hills and ravines, measuring the flow of brooklets and springs. The taiga was full of water, but the streams were too small and too far apart to use for a power station. After two months' research I presented a report recommending abandonment of the project. But meanwhile I had discovered charming clearings and meadows in the thicket. And what an abundance and variety of wild flowers! Siberia has a long frosty winter and a sultry summer, with a short growing period, and flowers do not last long and have no fragrance, but their colors are as bright and rich as in the tropics.

In 1911, two score political prisoners were in the work gang. Some few were permitted to live with their families in the village. Our colony in Alexandrovsk was steadily increasing. In the summer new recruits were added to the political work gang. To get hay for its sixty or more horses, the prison rented many thousands of acres of meadow, some of them twenty or thirty miles distant, but haying was a problem. Labor was short at this season, and often more than half the hay was lost. Saur proposed to the superintendent that he let the politicals harvest the hay. The Collective would guarantee that all workers would return to the prison. The superintendent accepted the offer.

The departure was a great event in Alexandrovsk. Four guards were assigned to convoy the party of four score prisoners, who, all together, had some seven hundred years of forced labor to serve. I volunteered to join the party. We walked the whole day along winding rural roads, from hamlet to hamlet, an unusual procession of cheerful, exuberant men in prison garb, with two guards at the head and two others escorting the train of three carts with scythes, kettles, and provisions. Peasants greeted us with cheers.

We reached the first meadow at dusk and at once started to build huts. Young birches were felled and thrust into the ground, one and a half to two feet apart, to form the outer circumference of the hut, except for a three-foot space left for the entrance. Then, after the perimeter was secured, the tops of the trees were turned down toward the center and branches interwoven to form the ceiling and reinforce the walls. Freshly mown grass served for beds. A field kitchen was built in the middle of the camp. The huts were completed by the light of campfires. Supper was ready. I strolled from fire to fire, talking to friends I had left behind bars when I transferred to the work gang.

In the morning we started mowing in the traditional Russian way—one of the most taxing and, at the same time, most exhilarating jobs imaginable. Each group of eight or ten mowers has a section of the meadow; the headman of the group starts mowing; the next man goes three steps to the right and two steps behind him; the third man comes at the same distance from the second, and so forth. The whole group follows the rhythm set by the headman and moves along the front, twenty-four to thirty steps wide, as a unit; another group covers the next section of the meadow.

The work went on until sunset. Suddenly pitch-black darkness enveloped the meadow, and before supper was ready a torrential rain and storm broke out. Our campfires were drowned, our huts flooded, and we sat under the downpour fascinated by flashes of lightning, each revealing new cloud formations. Then the storm whirled away, the stars reappeared, and the silence was interrupted only by the gurgling of invisible brooklets. We could not sleep, not because there was no dry spot but because the night, every moment of it, was too beautiful.

Next day we resumed work. A dozen prisoners stayed in the huts, however, too tired to move. But the four guards—all local peasants—

asked to be admitted to the work gang. They would show us how Siberians brandish the scythe!

Toward evening, horsemen appeared on the border of the meadow, converging on our party from all sides. We were surrounded by mounted guards and soldiers. The assistant of the superintendent dismounted and handed our guards an order: Take all prisoners back to the prison. The gendarmes had sent a telegram to St. Petersburg stating that preparations for a mass escape of political prisoners were being made under cover of haymaking. The Department of Justice ordered the Irkutsk authorities to take immediate measures to prevent the escape. Surrounded by a strong convoy, the party returned to Alexandrovsk.

I entered the prison building with the other prisoners, but the chief guard turned me back. "Each one," he explained, "returns to his ward. You, Mr. Woytinsky, go to your cabin."

Despite frequent changes in my official status in the work gang, my main occupation remained the same. I wrote about life in prisons for the *Russkoe Bogatstvo* (*Wealth of Russia*), the favorite organ of the progressive intelligentsia, and on political issues in short-lived, more radical periodicals. I signed my articles "S," but this pen name was no longer a secret. The superintendent was proud of having a writer in his work gang. Three magazines, among them an issue of the *Russkoe Bogatstvo*, were confiscated because of my essays, but no charge was raised against me. The only trouble I had with the administration at that time came from my activity as the "postmaster" of the Collective and from my literary contributions to the S-D newspaper in Irkutsk.

The guards searched my cabin nearly every week but the search was usually superficial. Whenever a thorough inspection was ordered from Irkutsk, the chief guard warned me, "Keep the barracks clean, guests are coming. . . ." Once, however, I was caught off guard. In the afternoon I had gotten a large bunch of clippings ready for the Collective, but the man who served as the mail pigeon did not appear. Waiting for him, I had my mail on the table when the searching party arrived. The superintendent reproached me bitterly. "I did not expect that you would abstain completely from corresponding with the prison," he said. "But how could you, a writer, an educated man, let my stupid guards catch you red-handed?" I was punished by being forbidden to leave the prison grounds for three months.

The case of the Irkutsk newspaper threatened to become more serious. The paper—a weekly of tabloid format—was founded by Professor Rozhkov, my companion of old times in the St. Petersburg Committee, and he persuaded me to contribute satirical sketches on current political events in a style then popular in Russia. The gendarmes complained to the inspector of prisons that the subversive sketches signed "S" came from the work gang in Alexandrovsk. The inspector forwarded the complaint to the superintendent, and the latter called me to his office, showed me the clippings, and asked whether I recognized the signature.

"I shall not deceive you," I replied. "These are my articles. But I would like to see how the gendarmes will prove that charge. You know how stupid they are." This remark was balm to the superintendent. He began to tell stories about the stupidity of the gendarmes and his own shrewdness. At the end of the conversation, however, I promised him to stop working for Rozhkov's newspaper.

ON THE THRESHOLD OF FREEDOM

In December, 1912, I was released from Alexandrovsk and became a deportee in Siberia, a status in many respects similar to that of paroled convicts in the United States.

As freedom approached, I tried to evaluate my experience in the past years. More than seven years had elapsed since I had joined the revolutionary movement—two years of political activity, five years of prison. I had seen terrible things during that time and had lived through grim hours. But what I had suffered personally had not been much in comparison with privations of others around me. Indeed, I was leaving the prison with a feeling of guilt for the comfortable conditions in the rear building of the Ekaterinoslav Castle, in the political ward of Novgorod, in the work gang of Alexandrovsk.

I counted those who would not return. The chance of survival in Ekaterinoslav had not been more than one in a hundred. How did it happen that I was still alive? Perhaps I had more physical resistance or was luckier than others. Or was it the consequence of the talisman that protected me against humiliation and self-pity—my theory of "assignment"?

The seven-odd years of political activity and prison had created an abyss between the intellectually arrogant youth I had been on entering the University and my new self. I realized that the scientific career I had started so promisingly with my first precocious book was ruined. St. Petersburg, the University, and my family seemed far away. With so many friends gone, I felt lonelier than ever. And I felt no impulse to find new friends, to associate with other people, or belong to a community. Looking forward, I saw only emptiness— no plans, no desires, no strong ties to anything.

At the same time, however, I felt that prison experience had enriched me. The dungeons had taught me to see the trees and flowers, the sky and clouds, and to understand men as they are, independent of their education and political leanings. I had learned to accept people with all they have of good and evil, strength and weakness. This was very different from the feeling of unity with the crowd that had so elated me in 1905. To be united with the crowd, one does not need to understand individual man. With understanding comes, rather, some remoteness and aloofness. . . .

Much later I realized my experience was similar to that acquired through a long sickness or exposure to danger in the trenches. Nearness to death and helplessness in the face of it are always the same.

Some thirty-five years later, in the United States, I met a man recently liberated from a Japanese prisoner-of-war camp, Alfred Oliver, Jr., a colonel and chaplain in the United States army. He was a tall, heavy man, an athlete, with short gray hair, piercing gentle eyes, and a steel collar about his neck. His vertebrae had been broken and he could not turn or bend his head. We sat on a bench in the garden of a small country boardinghouse. I asked him about the campaign in the Philippines, the death march, the prison camp. He talked about his missionary work in China, the death march, and people who were with him, some two thousand men in prison camp, but said very little about himself. Then I asked him about his steel collar. He answered slowly, choosing the words:

"You see, I was the senior officer in the group. They wished to humiliate me in order to break the morale of my men. They tried to humiliate me by beatings."

I remarked, "All jailers think they can humiliate a prisoner by mistreatment. They do not know that it is much worse for a man to see mistreatment of those who depend on him and not to be able to intervene."

The chaplain asked gently, "Where did you learn that? You were not there."

"I have been in other prisons," I answered.

A strange closeness developed between the gallant soldier-priest and me, a closeness that lasted to his death. Very different roads brought us to captivity, but our experience in an important section of our lives had been the same, and in captivity each of us had learned the same things.

Siberia
1913-1916

T HE word "Siberia" was associated in Russia with clanging fetters, marching gangs of convicts with half-shaven heads, exiles languishing in hamlets buried under snow, vagabonds in the mysterious taiga. In contrast, the Siberians considered their land a treasure chest of untapped resources, a land where nature was stern and life austere but full of opportunity and promise.

Siberia is half again as large as the continental United States and comprises half the U.S.S.R. Its northern expanse is practically uninhabitable, but its southern part includes fertile plains in the west and heavily forested plateaus in the center and east.

Fugitives and hunters from Moscovia penetrated into Siberia in the sixteenth century. A century later Russian scouts appeared on the Pacific. Forts were built in the wilderness as defenses against the native nomadic tribes of Mongolian origin, and settlements grew up along the rivers. Then came gangs of convicts, involuntary settlers of the frontier. Many old Siberian families cherished the memory of forefathers who had come to Siberia in fetters and later gave their names to gold mines in the Vitim Mountains or to ships plying the Yenisei and Lena. In the nineteenth century the Cossacks settled along Siberia's southern borders. They were followed by new trains of convicts and peasant settlers. Those who succeeded in the struggle for survival developed a type of farm life rare in European Russia: a large family, frequently including from four to six workers; a farmhouse built of round larch logs twenty inches thick; a courtyard encircled by a fence reminiscent of a stockade; eighty to a hundred acres under the plow and many hundreds more in forests, with fields in the clearings.

In contrast to European Russia, Siberia knew neither seignorial landowners nor serfs—only convicts and free settlers. Intermarriage of peasant settlers and former convicts with natives gave rise to a new race, free from traditions, strong and shrewd, reserved toward strangers. The native tribes of Mongolian origin did not merge entirely with the Russian settlers. Villages of the Buryats remained in the south, and pockets with a Yakut population in central Siberia, while the Tungus roamed the forests farther northwest and Samoyeds camped in the Arctic region.

Siberia has had a colorful political history. Beginning with the seventeenth century, it was ruled by magistrates who combined the features of oriental satraps with those of Roman proconsuls. They were allowed to rob the native population but could not take their loot back to Moscow. When a governor was recalled by the Tsar, his train would be stopped and searched at the Urals and a large part of his gold and precious furs taken for the Tsar's treasury.

In my time, Siberia had a dozen cities of fifty thousand or more inhabitants, with a municipal water supply, electricity, paved streets, high schools, and a municipal theater—in short, everything to be found in provincial cities of European Russia. But northern Siberia remained untouched, with small villages and hamlets far apart from one another, surrounded by intractable forests.

Hundreds of inhabited points were marked on Siberia's maps. Official records showed either the population of these villages in 1897, the year of the first nationwide census, or the number of chimneys. Towns were reported with two to three chimneys, and others with one chimney or no chimney at all—camps of igloos in the Arctic region, abandoned post stations, and villages that had been planned in the eighteenth century but never built.

The revolution of 1905 had brought a new wave of settlers to Siberia—political exiles. They were distinctly different from the outlaws and political rebels taken to Siberia in the nineteenth century.

Before 1905 almost all the political prisoners deported to Siberia were intellectuals—the flow of convicts discharged by the prisons of European Russia included only a few "politicals," and they were easily absorbed by the local communities as village clerks or accountants of commercial firms. Later they moved to cities where they could work as teachers, lawyers, physicians, journalists, bank officials, and the like. They formed the nucleus of the Siberian intelligentsia.

In contrast, the new political exiles, participants in the mass rebellion in 1905, included former sailors and soldiers, workers and peasants, and semi-intellectuals. They were brought by the carload and scattered among remote hamlets, and most of them had neither money nor skill that could be used in the new environment. A few became farmhands, but others lacked the physical strength and endurance for manual work.

The Siberian peasants looked on them with grim contempt. They respected the politicals who were useful to the community, but a man had to wait a long time for an opportunity to prove his usefulness to a Siberian hamlet. In large villages and towns an exile had some chance to find work, but in the wilderness he was practically doomed. Furthermore, many found the transition from the prison routine to half-freedom in a new grim and austere environment difficult and painful. Tragic casualties, accidents and suicides, a few weeks after release from prison were not rare.

The dream of the political exiles was to be settled somewhere along the Trans-Siberian Railroad, and the most coveted place was Irkutsk, the capital of eastern Siberia.

JILKINO

I was assigned for settlement to the village of Jilkino, located on the high shore of the Angara River, across from Irkutsk. Two rows of solidly built log houses flanked a broad and straight road. They had high fences with strong gates that were always closed. Every window had voile curtains and flowerpots. On one side of the road, snow-covered fields stretched behind the row of houses to the horizon; on the other flowed the river, as blue as the cloudless sky, between snow-covered shores.

After a long search I found a room with board (for twelve rubles— six dollars—a month) in a peasant house. My landlady, Stepanida, warned me not to trust malicious rumors about the village. "Those who say that we sow and reap not in the fields but on vodka barrels are liars," she said. "To listen to them, all the thieves of Irkutsk hide here. Nonsense! There are other dens than ours around here!"

I took her word for this and thus preserved my memory of Jilkino in all its fairy-tale sweetness. The Angara, in its winter attire, was as striking as when I had seen it from the ferry on the way from Irkutsk to Alexandrovsk. In the morning it was hidden under a dense cloud. The air was perfectly clear on the shore, but a white curtain hung over the river. As the sun rose, the curtain began to thin. First the forested hills on the far shore emerged on the horizon, then the river appeared in its snow bed, a blue ribbon on glittering silver brocade. A couple of miles upstream the dark wall of the forest behind the river was broken by a cluster of white and red buildings and the palace of the Governor General, an imposing structure with lofty columns and three rows of glittering windows.

At the other end of the village was the monastery of St. Innokenty, one of the most revered shrines in Siberia, with a large but somewhat incongruous dome surrounded by two score whitewashed houses —dormitories of monks, workshops, barns, storehouses, and a large guesthouse, all encircled by a beautiful old park. Each morning pilgrims thronged to the monastery for prayer and miraculous cure, but the influx of visitors was particularly large on Saturday evening, after the night service in the church. Then sledges with amorous couples from Irkutsk stopped in front of the monastery guesthouse, where liquors were sold at any hour. An old monk waited at its door. He looked tired and bored and when I asked him about his work, he sighed.

"We are all sinners, son. Before the war, with the aid of St. Innokenty, we could make ends meet, but since the yellow pagan opened his damned shop, we cannot live on miracles. The Lord sees everything and will forgive our sins."

The yellow pagan to whom he referred was a Chinese lama—a tall, very lean man with an emaciated, deeply tanned face and sparse gray hair around his bald head. He practiced medicine in an office close to Stepanida's house, so that I could observe his technique.

His aides, all in long yellow robes, would line up the visitors in the waiting room. Then the lama, dressed in a shining golden gown, would emerge from behind the partition with a long iron arrow in his hand. Facing a patient, he would ask:

"What ails you?"

The patient would point to his head, back, or stomach. The lama, humming an incantation, would touch the sore spot with the arrow and proceed to the next patient.

Pilgrims who swarmed to the sepulcher of St. Innokenty used to stop at the office of the lama as well and divided their donations between the monastery and the "yellow pagan." The monastery's efforts to remove the competition were futile. The lama had influential supporters in Irkutsk, including the wife of the Governor, and the Jilkino police were instructed not to interfere with the activities of the "Chinese doctor." In justice, it must be pointed out that neither did it interfere with the monastery's sale of liquors to nocturnal guests.

ON THIN ICE

The first Sunday after my arrival at Jilkino, I went to Irkutsk. A marvelous two-mile walk along the bank of the Angara, a fascinating ferry crossing, and I was in the city. I had the address of an S-D lawyer, and he and his wife received me with great friendliness. Half an hour later Rozhkov arrived, as buoyant as ever, bristling with journalistic plans. After dusk I returned to Jilkino with a bundle of books and magazines. I spent my days reading and hiking along the Angara.

My next trip to Irkutsk fell on Christmas Eve. The crossing was rough. Pieces of ice were floating in the river, knocking against the ferry. This time I met more people—political exiles and local intellectuals. The lawyer and his wife did not let me return to Jilkino that night, and I slept on the sofa in their living room.

Next morning I went to the ferry landing. The river was wrapped in fog. Two policemen posted at the pier stopped me. "No crossing today!" I returned to the lawyer's and spent another day meeting people and talking politics. By evening I was tired of this pastime and yearned to go back to Jilkino.

Early the next morning I was at the landing. There was no fog over the river; its surface was steel gray. The guards at the pier had been replaced by a large signboard: "Danger! Keep off!" I stepped on the ice. It seemed solid enough. I took a few steps—the ice did not crack. Without hesitation I started toward the far pier. The surface stretched like a sheet of glass from shore to shore, but beneath it pieces of ice moved with unbelievable speed. More than once the ice under my feet seemed to bend, but this might have been an optical illusion.

I had passed the middle of the river when I noticed a change: the ice no longer looked like a sheet of glass but was uneven and opaque, like a pile of fleece. Suddenly it broke under my feet. I had time to stretch out both arms. The ice was at my armpits, its thin crust holding my weight. I began to test the ice blocks within reach of my hands. The nearest were either too small or too slippery to provide a hold. Then I found a fairly large block, seized it with both hands, and began to inch my way in its direction. I do not know how long it took until I was lying on the solid ice. I was completely exhausted, but the thought that my soaked overcoat would freeze to the ice made me stand up. Since the Jilkino shore was nearer than Irkutsk, it seemed sensible to continue the crossing.

The ice again became smooth and transparent and I reached the shore without accident. It was good to feel the soft snow under my feet! Unfortunately, there was no dwelling on the shore between the pier and Jilkino. To keep myself warm I began to run. When Stepanida saw me, out of breath, in a soaked and frozen overcoat, she threw up her arms and asked, "Were you sober or drunk when you fell through?"

"Sober," I managed to answer through chattering teeth.

"Too bad," she replied. "Ice water is all right for a drunk, but bad when one is sober."

She poured a glass of awful vodka into me, followed by a glass of strong hot tea with the same vodka. Then she ordered me into bed and covered me with all the blankets she could find in the house. I awoke after dusk. I felt as tired as after a day's hard work and at first could not remember what had happened. Yet, thanks to Stepanida's treatment, I did not catch even the slightest cold.

When I told my Irkutsk friends of my adventure on the thin ice, they persuaded me to apply to the Governor General for transfer to the city, a place where I could find a job so as not to risk my life crossing the Angara.

THE GOVERNOR GENERAL

Before being admitted to the Governor General, all petitioners were interrogated by his counsel, Batarevich, who helped them formulate their requests. He looked at my petition and said warmly, "Jilkino is no place for you. People should not be settled where there is no work for them." He made a note on my petition and took me to the office of the Governor General.

Kniazev—a tall man with a dignified appearance and a mild voice —met us at the door of his huge study. He read my petition silently and asked Batarevich, "You know the request? Do we have precedents to rest on?"

"Oh, yes! A fully justified request!"

"I am glad you think so," replied Kniazev. He wrote his decision on my petition and passed it on to Batarevich for action. I was ready to leave, but he stopped me and said, "Now we can chat a little."

After a casual remark about the Siberian climate, Kniazev remarked, "I know that you and your friends have definite political convictions and I respect those who do what they consider right. But I have often observed that persons who have served their term for belonging to an illegal party believe this term legalizes their status as S-D, S-R, or Anarchist for the rest of their lives. The government does not share this idea, and I have no power to change this situation. May I ask you to do me a favor: whatever you do, watch your step. Do not talk much with people whom you do not know. Do not keep at home documents and notes that can be turned against you. Use caution in your correspondence. Do not let the gendarmes catch you."

I promised the Governor General to pass his words on to other political exiles. He walked with me to the door of his office. I thanked him and he, in turn, thanked me.

The official reply to my petition came in two or three days. The inspector of prisons informed me that, by order of the Governor General, I was permitted to live in Irkutsk until further notice.

RETURN TO POLITICAL LIFE

In Irkutsk I met many people who knew me either from St. Petersburg or from my writings in different magazines. I found myself in the center of local politics, which consisted mainly of endless talks about what was going on in the country and what was going to happen. But political life all over Russia was much the same.

Irkutsk was a significant administrative and cultural center. It had two daily newspapers, two banks, a fine regional museum, and an excellent theater. Former political exiles played an important role in its intellectual life.

By tradition, the local administration was liberal; there was no reactionary gentry in the region, and officials who came to Irkutsk from European Russia found the local soil unfit for Black Hundred ideas. Then there was Governor General Kniazev, with his high standards of dignity, justice, and fairness. The Governor of Irkutsk was a comparatively liberal gentleman who saw no reason to quarrel with Kniazev. The latter, however, had enemies in Irkutsk. The local archbishop denounced him as a Red Judo-Mason, and the gendarmes accused him of associating with the revolutionaries.

The political climate of the city reflected the confusion prevailing all over Russia. Tsarism had triumphed in the war against the people. Order had been restored, but not the Tsar's prestige. Anarchy was spreading downward from the top. Russia's political life was dominated by three forces—the conservative (Octobrist) Duma; the government, for which the Duma was not reactionary enough; and the circle about the Tsar—Rasputin and the Black Hundreds—for which the government was not tough enough.

The new electoral law had abandoned all pretext of letting the "best men elected by all the people" participate in legislation. The electors were redistributed in such a way that the big landowners had an absolute majority in almost all constituencies. Thus, most of the seats in the Duma were turned over to the decaying nobility. Only a dozen seats were kept for workers' representatives in the large cities, and another dozen for peasants, while a few more were left to the luck of the ballot.[1]

The Duma obediently went through the motions of legislation, grinding out the bills submitted by the government. Yet certain parliamentary features had trickled through into political life, and the hand-picked Duma became a public forum in which the numerically weak opposition could air its grievances. It could do this largely because the rightist majority was not indifferent to the voice of the press, and most Russian newspapers had liberal leanings.

The government was not strong enough to impose thought control and muzzle the people, and journalists with courage were able to speak their minds despite the oppressive laws and police regulations. Their

[1] Of the 440 deputies in the Third Duma, 144 belonged to the Black Hundreds and openly called themselves "Monarchists"; 148 were Octobrists; and 26 represented the national minorities of similar political leanings—in all, 318 deputies were reactionaries of various shadings. The rest of the Duma included the Progressives, Cadets, Laborites, and S-D. From 1908 through 1914, there was little change in these figures. The Fourth Duma, elected in 1912, was an exact replica of the Third.

sharpest criticism was directed against the scandals in the high places associated with the name of Rasputin, the closest friend, spiritual father, and political adviser of the Tsar. Stolypin, who up to the end opposed the rising power of the "Mad Monk," was shot to death by a revolutionary terrorist, and there were insistent rumors that police had been informed of the plot and had not taken any steps to prevent it. The Tsar seemed to be glad of having rid himself of his Prime Minister, the last strong and more or less independent man in his entourage.

Hating the Duma, the press, and the intelligentsia, haunted by the feeling of insecurity and his own inadequacy, suspicious of the advisers who might influence his decisions, distrusting his own ministers, the Tsar found counsel, support, and comfort only in Rasputin, an illiterate adventurer who posed as a true Russian muzhik and holy man, preaching unrestricted debauchery as a way to repentance and salvation. Rasputin was a shrewd, calculating faker, the most resourceful among the many charlatans who surrounded the throne. Using the technique of primitive hypnotism of a Siberian medicine man to comfort the sick Tsarevich, he had ingratiated himself with the Tsar and the hysterical Tsarina. At the same time he enjoyed the support of the Black Hundreds by serving as its mouthpiece in the palace. Rasputin had appeared at the court in 1909, but only after the death of Stolypin did he advance to the position of unofficial ruler of the Empire in religious and political affairs as the Tsar's "dear friend." Now, in 1913, towering above the traditional pageantry of the court, eclipsing the Tsar, stood the striking figure of a village conjurer, with long pitch-black hair, the piercing eyes of a madman, an unkempt beard covering his breast, the long powerful arms of a gorilla, dressed in strange operatic attire—the black cassock of a monk, the knee boots of a muzhik, and the cross of a priest glittering through the beard.

Public opinion resented, most of all, Rasputin's interference in church affairs. The "monk" had installed himself as the head of the Orthodox Church, making and breaking bishops and archbishops. His ambition in this field was limited only by the fact that he did not know all the bishoprics. As a native of Siberia, however, he knew all Siberian dioceses by name and he wished to keep them all under his control through his appointees. Kniazev made no secret of his sympathy with the ousted Siberian church dignitaries. His influential friends in St. Petersburg kept him informed about the career of the "monk" at court, and the news promptly leaked from his palace to the local society.

The predominating political mood of the people in Siberia was decidedly against the government and especially against Rasputin, the Tsar, and the Tsarina. But the political parties of the left had few followers outside the circle of political exiles. The S-R party was deeply disorganized by the revelation of provocation at its top: one of its leaders had been unmasked as the agent of the secret police. The S-D party was reduced to a shambles by the struggle between the Mensheviks and Bolsheviks. There were some S-D "generals" abroad who pretended to represent Marxist groups dispersed all over Russia, but at best these were splinters of the old organization, without any contact with the masses. In January, 1912, a Bolshevist conference allegedly attended by representatives of "more than twenty" S-D organizations met in Prague, proclaimed itself an All-Russian Party Conference, excluded Mensheviks and their sympathizers from the party, and elected a Central Committee of its own.

The Social Democrats in Siberia learned this news with mixed feelings. A few Bolsheviks accepted it as the rebirth of the party, but the great majority considered the whole affair a bluff and the new Central Committee a fraud. Rozhkov and I shared this attitude. We had not been very close to each other when we worked in the St. Petersburg Bolshevist organization in 1906-7. In my eyes he was a doctrinaire Marxist with ready answers to all questions, while he disliked my critical attitude toward Marxian orthodoxy. Time had not ironed out the difference in our views and temperaments, but we found ourselves in agreement in political and tactical questions and he persuaded me we should work as a team. I accepted his offer, and thus began my literary adventures in Siberia.

A CAUTIOUS S-D

Rozhkov was a rotund fellow, with a protruding paunch, pink cheeks, and a red nose; he was always smiling, his eyes squinting, his glasses jumping. He hated pomposity, big words, and sentimentality. Talking with him, one would hardly believe he was an outstanding scholar, a ranking professor of Moscow University, and the author of several excellent books on Russian history. He was an extrovert with an urge for public activity. As soon as he arrived in Irkutsk—when I was still in Alexandrovsk—he launched an S-D weekly, *Irkutskoe Slovo* (*The Irkutsk Word*). The paper was not very good, partly because Rozhkov himself was a mediocre journalist, but he succeeded in kindling public interest in it by a continuous series of "campaigns." One of these became famous. *The Irkutsk Word* was the only newspaper in Siberia that disclosed the intolerable conditions in the Lena gold fields long before the outbreak of the strike that ended in a massacre of workers and ushered in a wave of labor unrest in Siberia and European Russia.

The gendarmes demanded that the Governor shut down the paper and banish Rozhkov to some remote village. Unable to find direct of-

fenses against the law, they pointed out some trivial violations of administrative regulations. The Governor then imposed a fine of two
hundred rubles—the minimum prescribed by the regulations. The
fine was paid by the friends of *The Irkutsk Word*. The next week the
gendarmes extorted another fine, Rozhkov gave up, and the paper went
out of existence.

A few months later, however, when we first met in Irkutsk, he told
me of his plans for a daily newspaper, *Novaya Sibir'* (*New Siberia*).
He insisted that it was easier to run a daily than a weekly. Only the
first year might prove somewhat difficult, financially speaking. This
time he intended to be particularly cautious, so that the gendarmes
would find no pretext for interference. Sure of success, he had made
a contract with a not very respectable small printing shop that specialized in printing handbills and obscene verses for brothels. The shop's
charge was reasonable: a hundred rubles for each issue, including
paper, printing, and office space in a narrow passage behind a row of
cabinets.

Since October, 1905, there had been no preliminary censorship of
newspapers in Russia, but no printing shop could issue a paper without
the signature of a licensed "responsible publisher." Rozhkov had
solved that problem, too. An old woman who operated a soft-drinks
bar in the basement of the printing shop agreed to sign the newspaper as its responsible publisher. The editorial staff consisted of
Rozhkov, Chuzhak, who handled the literary and arts department,
and me. Chuzhak was a gloomy, taciturn man with an acute dislike for
his fellow men in general and his newspaper colleagues in particular.
An adamant Leninist himself, he despised us as renegades from Bolshevism and despised himself for working with us—which he did without any pay, as a public service, just as did the rest of us. He was a born
journalist, with a biting, brilliant style.

We agreed that Rozhkov would take care of the business side and
we two would have equal responsibilities as editors, but actually Chuzhak let me determine the policy of the newspaper, within the framework of police regulations.

There was not much to determine. We reprinted whatever news
about the labor movement in Russia and abroad we could pick up
from St. Petersburg and Moscow papers; we gave publicity—and occasionally headlines—to statements of the Black Hundreds, presenting them as the expression of government policy; commented ironi-
cally on the parliamentary antics—or so we regarded them—of the
Cadets; printed information on the life of political exiles. This was
about as far as a legal S-D newspaper could go.

Working conditions on the *New Siberia* were miserable. Cramped in the narrow space behind the cabinets, each of us had to write two or three articles every day, at the same time checking the proofs, answering telephone calls, and talking with visitors. Our articles were probably a notch or two above the level of other provincial newspapers, but I found little satisfaction in this work.

The newspaper was continuously in financial trouble. The circulation did not rise fast enough. Advertisements could be obtained only at "special rates." Twice New Siberia was fined for articles about local strikes, but otherwise we could not complain of administrative persecution. Our newspaper perished because of an inexcusable mistake on our part.

Our deficit was increasing from month to month, and our "angels" could not meet it indefinitely. We were at the end of our wits when Rozhkov conceived the idea of asking the local theater to stage a benefit performance for our paper—a practice not uncommon in Russia. An organization would pay the theater a lump sum and try to collect much more by selling the tickets to its sympathizers. The theater agreed to put on the local première of a current hit in St. Petersburg. The terms were very generous: we were to pay only the cost of heating and lighting the building. With luck we could net up to two thousand rubles and meet a two-month deficit! The tickets sold quickly, mainly among workers and commercial employees.

The theater management, in its turn, advertised the première in the usual way, without mentioning that the tickets were being distributed by political exiles. To conform with police regulations, the cashier of the theater demanded only that we deposit in the booking office all the money we were collecting for the tickets. After the performance the receipts would be checked against the stubs of tickets sold, we would receive the money, and pay the agreed sum to the theater.

The audience was rather unusual. I sat with Rozhkov in the second row, among our printers, and we were both touched at seeing our timid, poorly dressed girl mailers in armchairs—five rubles apiece—in the first row. I do not remember the title of the play or what went on on the stage. No sooner had the curtain gone up than an usher came to us and whispered, "The gendarmes are in the box office."

Rozhkov went to talk with them. The officer asked him, "Are you the Mr. Rozhkov who has rented the theater for this evening? Since when are you in the entertainment business?" Rozhkov answered that the purpose of the performance was to raise funds for the New Siberia.

"A worthy purpose," admitted the officer. "Your license, please?"

"What license?" Rozhkov asked in surprise.

"Whatever your purpose, you must have a license to run a public show and sell tickets. Sign here, please."

All our receipts were confiscated. The police had a clear case against us. Rozhkov was ordered to leave Irkutsk for Chita, a smaller city east of Baikal. That was the end of *New Siberia*.

On the eve of Rozhkov's departure, we came together for the last time at the house of one of our angels. Rozhkov was buoyant as ever, but a little ashamed of himself. "How did we let them catch us with this nonsense?" he wondered. "I thought I knew all the regulations by heart!"

BOLDER LITERARY VENTURES

After Rozhkov's departure I had to step into his shoes and carry on S-D journalistic ventures in Irkutsk. I lacked his exuberant energy and his ability in public relations and fund raising, but was probably more of a journalist. The idea of another daily paper as cautious as *New Siberia* did not appeal to me. Instead I thought of publishing a magazine, with a much bolder assault against the government, restrained in form but radical in its approach to current events.

Practically, this would be a weekly or monthly magazine that would meet legal requirements but ignore censorship regulations. Each issue would be a salvo against the government, and after each issue we would be ready to see our headquarters raided by the gendarmes, the license for our publication revoked, and all of us, including the responsible publisher, arrested.

These ideas found sympathy among local Social Democrats. Some of them were not sure whether my plan would work, but all agreed it was worth trying. However, the new type of publication required a new type of "responsible publisher." The responsibility of such a publisher for minor violations of police or censorship regulations was comparatively light—a fine or, in an extreme case, from one to three months' detention. For his tame newspaper Rozhkov had been able to use the services of obscure individuals who agreed to take a chance for the fixed fee of five rubles per signature. Bolder publications exposed the responsible publisher to the risk of a year behind bars, and we had to find volunteers among the local sympathizers who would sign the newspaper, accepting my warning that the issue was "hot." Several persons offered their services, and I warned each applicant of his or her responsibility.

Early in the summer of 1913, all formalities were completed. I had at my disposal licenses for *Sibirskoe Slovo* (Siberian Word) and *Novoe Sibirskoe Slovo* (New Siberian Word); enough funds for five or six issues, and a formal agreement with a printing shop. The second license was obtained in case the first was revoked. It remained to round up a group of contributors, prepare the copy, and send it to the printer.

Meanwhile the political climate was changing. Under the impact of scandals connected with Rasputin, the monarchy was beginning to cave in. The new Minister of Justice, one of Rasputin's appointees, decided that the best way to rally the good people of Russia around the throne was to expose the diabolic designs of the Jews. Since people were not impressed by the usual Jew-baiting in the Black Hundreds papers, he decided to charge the Jews with kidnaping and murdering Christian children. Such accusations had been made before against some non-existent Jewish sects. This time the task was to prove that the Bible and the Talmud directed all Jews to kill Christian children and use their blood. The "Bloody Slander" was to be the prologue to a new wave of pogroms and renewed administrative persecution of Jews throughout Russia.

To herald this new policy, the government arrested a poor Jewish tailor, Beilis, on the outskirts of Kiev and arranged to have him tried before a carefully selected jury of half-illiterate peasants and small merchants.

The affair started in a house well know to police in Kiev as an underworld den. Thieves brought their loot there to pass on to dealers. The woman Cheberiak, who ran the place, also carried on illicit traffic in vodka and was active, together with other underworld characters, in local patriotic organizations. Suddenly her name appeared in the headlines all over Russia. In the woods behind her courtyard, the body of a slain boy was found. His throat had been slashed and his body bore signs of beating and torture.

The neighbors recognized the boy as the nine-year-old son of a couple that owned the house next to the headquarters of the thieves. The mother of the slain boy testified that several days before his disappearance the lad, playing, entered the backyard of the Cheberiak house. The woman Cheberiak caught him, accused him of spying, ordered him to tell exactly what he had seen, and threatened to teach him a lesson. Taken to the police station, she testified that she had seen an old Jew with a butcher knife drag the boy into the woods. She identified him as Beilis, the tailor from the next block. She also remembered the date of the crime, the eve of Passover. . . . Then the police experts discovered that the boy's throat was slashed in accordance with the prescriptions of the Talmud.

The case became the focus of public life in Russia, like the Dreyfus case in France in the 1890's. The public felt that thousands of human lives were at stake. Scores of lawyers—in fact, the elite of the profession, Christians and Jews alike—volunteered to defend the humble tailor. The liberal and moderate press considered the Beilis affair a national disgrace. Such was the situation in the autumn of 1913, when we were planning a new S-D publication in Irkutsk.

I was going over copy for the first issue of the *Siberian Word*, trying to inject more punch into it, when one of our contributors came to me excitedly. He had heard the new archbishop, Serafim, preach on the Beilis affair in the cathedral and brought me an almost verbatim report of his sermon. It was dynamite. I asked him to check his text with some others who had attended the church service. In the evening he returned with a corrected script. The transcript seemed reliable but out of keeping with conventional ecclesiastic language, which was usually embellished with Slavic and archaic words used by churchmen in Russia. So I obliged the Very Reverend Serafim by rewriting his sermon in a style appropriate to his high office.

The sermon began with the statement that the trial of Beilis had solved the mystery of the disappearance of Christian children each year on the eve of the Jewish Passover. It had proved that these innocent children were kidnaped and murdered by the Jews for their diabolic rites. The Archbishop also declared that the use of Christian blood was not the sole misdeed of the Jews and enumerated their other crimes: thievery, forgery, revolution. The sermon ended by extolling the virtuous Russian people and the Holy Orthodox Church in contrast with the Jewish people and their unholy synagogue damned by the Lord.

I added a brief introduction and a concluding note to this oration. In the first, I said that the Archbishop had wisely chosen the subject for his sermon: no other question agitated all decent people in the nation more than did the Bloody Slander. "Here is the authentic voice of the Church, and we regret that the cathedral was not large enough to house all the people who should have heard the sermon. The *Siberian Word* therefore presents this gem of ecclesiastic piety and wisdom to its readers." In the concluding note I pointed out that there was only one weakness in the sermon: Since the court had not yet convicted Beilis and there was no evidence that he had abducted and murdered the Christian child, the Archbishop might have violated the Lord's commandment: "Thou shalt not bear false witness against thy neighbor."

The issue of the *Siberian Word*, with the sermon on the front page, had the effect of a bomb explosion. All copies were sold out by noon, and by evening single copies were being resold for five or ten rubles apiece. The Archbishop rushed to the Governor to demand reprisals against the newspaper. The Governor asked whether the sermon was reproduced correctly. "Yes," the Archbishop admitted. "The scoundrels planted their spies in my cathedral."

The Governor took the newspaper to Kniazev. "The sermon *is* sacrilegious," the Governor General remarked sadly. "But how can we prosecute a newspaper for a *faithful* reproduction of the Archbishop's sermon delivered publicly in the cathedral?"

The Archbishop, however, found support among the gendarmes, and the Irkutsk court ordered an investigation. Our responsible publisher was charged with contempt of the Holy Church and inciting disrespect of the Archbishop. But the witnesses confirmed that our report was exact in every detail, including my imitation of church lingo. The defense contended that the Archbishop himself was guilty of contempt of the Church when he used it to spread the Bloody Slander. Finally the publisher was sentenced to three months of prison, but our lawyers appealed the sentence. The appeal was sustained by the high court, and the case went up to the Supreme Court (which was called Senate) in St. Petersburg. Meanwhile the trial of Beilis had ended in his acquittal—evidence that the Archbishop had borne false witness! The Supreme Court did not decide the case until 1915, when the publisher was found guilty of disseminating information that, though true, was damaging to the prestige of the Archbishop.

After this first successful issue of the *Siberian Word*, we went on, ready to see our paper suspended after each issue. We had a continuous flow of articles from outside, some of them really good, but public interest began to subside. The gendarmes were on their toes. They did not harass me personally, but in the fourth or fifth issue they discovered an article on a local affair that allegedly violated police regulations. Yielding to the pressure by the gendarmes, the Governor ordered suspension of the *Siberian Word*.

EXPLORING SIBERIA

Reading about the unexplored expanses of Siberia, I fell under the romantic spell of the wilderness, perhaps as a belated reaction to years of confinement. I had no experience in outdoor life and did not know whether I was physically fit for it, but I decided to explore the remote and little-known range of Dzhugzhur at the Sea of Okhotsk.

I chose this particular area by pure accident. In the regional museum I had seen a water color by an unknown artist—a quiet river with strange trees and shrubs along its shores. The river was wrapped in fog, but the rays of the rising sun flooded the treetops. The title read "A Summer Morning on the Maya." I liked the name of the river and looked it up on the map of Siberia: a long winding river that flows from the Dzhugzhur range at the Okhotsk Sea into the Aldan, one of the northern tributaries of the Lena. Little had been written on this area. The local museum had only a report of an expedition to the

Okhotsk Sea via the Lena-Aldan-Maya rivers in the middle of the nineteenth century, a few articles on the native tribes, and cursory references to the Aldan basin in general descriptions of Siberia. It seemed an ideal place to explore. I asked Kniazev for permission to make a trip to the Dzhugzhur Mountains. He was pleased with my interest in Siberian geography and gave me a certificate authorizing me to travel for exploration purposes in all eastern Siberia—the area under his jurisdiction.

Then I offered the largest newspaper in Moscow, *Russkoe Slovo* (*The Russian Word*), a series of essays on the land I intended to visit. The newspaper sent me an advance payment for my travel expenses. An S-R exile settled in a village not far from Irkutsk, Mikhail Vedenyapin, volunteered to go with me. He was a few years older than I, not very tall but broad-shouldered, and had long black hair, a long beard, a deeply tanned face, and wonderful blue eyes. He was much better prepared than I for an adventurous expedition. Born on the Volga, he had worked as a lumberjack in his youth, had built and operated rafts on the river, and was, in addition, an expert hunter.

We went by cart from Irkutsk to Kachuga on the Lena, changing horses in each village; the peasants refused to go further than the first station from their home. We reached the Lena at the beginning of the navigation season. The river was swarming with rowboats taking prospectors and miners downstream to the gold fields. They were a noisy, cheerful crowd. Alongside beardless youths in bright Russian shirts one saw patriarchs in strange attire, with broad belts and vests studded with silver buttons. Old prospectors wore such buttons as decorations to prove their wealth and success in life; each button was worth half a ruble and would be accepted at that value in any pub on the Lena. I counted more than two hundred buttons on the vest of one gray-bearded giant. People came to the river—some in carts, others on foot—from the nearest railroad station, a hundred and fifty miles away. Kachuga was the terminal point of their land journey. Here each party would buy a flat-bottomed boat for the farther trip down the Lena to the mouth of the Vitim, the gateway to the mysterious land of gold fields—the Russian Wild West.

Life in Kachuga was concentrated on the waterfront, the high bank of the Lena. Most of the boats displayed there for sale had from three to five pairs of oars and could accommodate from twelve to twenty men with their goods and chattels. They sold like hotcakes, but we were looking for a smaller boat for the two of us. A peasant, with three score boats for sale, said to us:

"What you are asking for, brothers, is a fisherman's skiff. You need a boat to go to the gold fields."

"There are just two of us," replied Mikhail. "A skiff with a pair of oars is all we need."

The peasant shook his head. "If you are only two, better stay where you are. People do not move by twos in these places."

"Is the river bad?" I asked.

"The river is good, but the people are bad at this season. Look at those fellows! Who knows where they come from and where they are going? To slash the throat of a man for his shoes and belt is as easy for them as that. . . ."

"Nobody will slash our throats," said Mikhail, and he showed the man a small Browning he carried in his hip pocket.

The peasant looked at him intently and decided, "Maybe you can go in a skiff. I have one at the landing place, not new but still good. Ten rubles is a fair price."

The skiff was patched and almost black from weather, but, after a careful inspection, Mikhail found it seaworthy. We bought it and went to the village to get our luggage.

The sun was low when we finished loading. Mikhail took the oars and let me operate the rudder. The current was unexpectedly strong; in no time Kachuga had disappeared behind the river bend and we were on a winding stream, with the virgin forest all around us. There was no trace of human habitation on the shores, but the river was full of life, with hundreds of boats moving downstream. The air resounded with songs, the thumping of balalaikas, and the trills of accordions.

A boat with some fifteen men on board overtook us. Passing close to our skiff and almost touching it, the steersman, a dashing prospector, his vest all covered with silver buttons, asked derisively, "Only two in your party? How far do you expect to go?"

"We shall meet you at the gold fields, brother!" answered Mikhail.

"Good luck, and look around!" shouted the steersman.

Suddenly it became dark and cold on the river. We put on our overcoats. The banks rose higher, the stars became brighter. The water was pitch black.

"We could go on all night," Mikhail suggested. "You can sleep at the stern and later we can change places."

The water was gurgling beneath us, behind the boat, and under the oars, and I fell asleep. I woke up when Mikhail called my name. He was sitting still, his oars out of the water, listening intently.

"What has happened?" I asked him.

"A boat is following us."

"I hear nothing."

"They stopped when I stopped rowing. Listen now. . . ."

He began to row, and we immediately heard the oars splashing behind us in the darkness. He stopped, and after two or three strokes the other boat stopped also. No sound came from the darkness.

"They have two or three pairs of oars," remarked Mikhail. "A fairly large boat. . . ."

"Should we land?"

"No, we are better off on the river. Even if they have evil intentions, they would have slim advantage over us on water."

"Let them pass us?"

"They would have passed us hours ago if they had wanted to. They are keeping their distance."

Mikhail was rowing with all his strength. We heard the other boat following us but could not see it. The moon was high in front of us. Perhaps those in the strange boat could see the silhouette of our skiff.

Suddenly Mikhail whispered to me, "Turn the rudder to the right. There is a light on the shore, steer right above it."

We could see clearly the outline of a bark and shadows of people around a campfire at the edge of the forest. The boat that had followed us stopped in the middle of the river, then turned abruptly, steering toward the campfire and cutting across our course. With three pairs of oars and six oarsmen, she made better speed than our skiff. She was between us and the campfire when we noticed lights high on the other bank—a village! Now we were completely safe.

"Put your rudder left," whispered Mikhail. "They may sleep at the campfire if they wish. The river is ours now."

When we were back in the main current, Mikhail turned the oars over to me and took his place at the stern for a brief nap.

In the morning we landed on a low bank, lit a fire, and made tea. The map showed we had made less progress than I had expected.

"There is no point in wasting time for meals," said Mikhail. "Next time we shall make tea on the river." He put a piece of sod about four feet square on the bottom of the skiff and arranged strong green sticks on both sides of it to support a kettle or pan. Meanwhile I collected dry brushwood for our little kitchen.

Henceforth we stopped only at rare villages to replenish our provisions. Only once did we sleep in the forest at a splendid campfire, because it was too cold on the river. We kept in the middle of the stream, in the strongest current, but it took us four days to reach Ust Kut, some three hundred miles from Kachuga.

It was clear that, at this speed, it would take too long to get to the mouth of the Aldan. We therefore decided to trade the delightful discomfort of our skiff for the steamer. We boarded the vessel roped to the pier, and I gave the captain a letter from his company that assured us of free passage on all its craft. By steamer, overtaking the prospectors' rowboats, we reached Yakutsk in eight days.

The scenery varied from forested hills to abrupt ravines with clearly visible outcrops of coal—the Lena coal fields, known in the eighteenth century and rediscovered by the Soviets in the 1930's. Many stretches along the Lena are dangerous for navigation because of rapids, shifting shoals, and treacherous turns. Such places were marked by huge black-and-white wooden shields on the shores. The helmsman followed the route indicated by a pair of shields until a new pair showed a change of direction.

When the steamer approached a particularly dangerous spot, boats with local pilots surrounded her, but our captain had no use for their services. After thirty years on the Lena, he trusted himself and his self-made map. It consisted of some two hundred sheets, each twelve by thirty inches long, glued together so that they formed a huge roll. The river was shown in the middle of the strip, without regard for points of the compass. Both banks of the river, its coves, islands, and branches were marked with local landmarks, such as unusual trees, rock formations, villages. The map had no distance scale but was divided into sections by the hours of a trip downstream. The captain had sketched this log during his first trip, so as to avoid paying tribute to the local pilots, and improved it each successive year.

We spent a few days in Yakutsk, waiting for the steamer to the Aldan and Maya. Yakutsk had a large colony of political exiles—perhaps a hundred or more in the town and as many in villages around it. Despite continuous denunciations by gendarmes, the local administration considered them the intellectual elite, and most of them had some professional or clerical job—in the power station (built by a political exile), regional museum, official newspaper and printing shop, schools, public library, and the like. The colony was avid for news and gave us a most cordial reception, but the city was depressing. The capital of a region four times as large as Germany and France combined, it had fewer than two thousand inhabitants and consisted of one-story log houses, set far apart, with endless fences flanking the wide dusty streets. The place looked dead—almost no traffic in the streets, few people on the wooden sidewalks, few trees and shrubs behind the fences. This was the season of northern white nights; it was as light at night as in the shade in daytime. But the suffocating heat of the day was followed by frost after sunset.

After Yakutsk, where the Lena is more than ten miles wide, the scenery became monotonous, with endless expanses of stormy gray water and endless taiga on the shores. The steamer halted at the mouth of the Aldan. There was a settlement somewhere not far from the landing—a Siberian "town" with three or four chimneys—but no building was visible from the river. Steamers visited this place four times a year—twice on the way from Yakutsk to Nelkan on the Maya and twice on return trips. Our steamer was the first since the preceding autumn, and her arrival was a major event. A crowd assembled at the landing to greet her and watch the unloading of crates, barrels, and bags.

I went ashore in a canoe. The landing was surrounded by the virgin forest. There was only a small opening, too narrow for a cart, in the wall of trees interwoven with lianas. Nearby lay the contraption the natives used for transportation—two young flexible birches tied together, with a rope attached to the trunk ends and the tops spread on the ground. A horse was harnessed to this vehicle. The crates and barrels were put on the tops and dragged. Some young men were hiding behind the trees. Then a few women and children joined them. All were fascinated by the sight of the steamer and the pile of goods at the landing. They exchanged remarks and jokes among themselves but did not approach the landing. Then three men boarded the steamer—two grim Siberian peasants and a native, a slim youth with a bronzed face, bright smile, and sparkling white teeth.

As we moved on, the steamer would drop anchor from time to time and emit a long, shrill whistle. After a minute of silence, a shot would answer from the depth of the taiga. Then a boat from the steamer would take a few bundles and bales ashore and return after unloading them. Again a long whistle, the anchor would be hoisted, and the ship would continue upstream.

The unloading was supervised by a sedate middle-aged man who shared the stateroom with us. I asked him about his business. "This is Tungus country," he explained. "The natives live here and there. They do nothing but hunt. I bring them powder, brick tea, butter, flour, cartridges, lead—everything they need."

"And how do they pay?"

"With furs in the winter. The year's bag brings them twenty rubles, forty rubles, sometimes even a hundred rubles. But they don't need money. They get everything from me."

"Do you leave a separate package for each customer on the bank?"

"Why? That would complicate things. Everybody takes what belongs to him from the pile. No trouble. There are no white people around here."

IN THE WILDERNESS

At Nelkan we were at the last outpost of civilization. The village consisted of a dozen log houses. Two of these were substantial cottages occupied by local merchants; two, smaller buildings—one for the school, the other for the priest—if one came. The only other structures were primitive log cabins and barns. The village also had a cemetery with a tiny chapel.

Nelkan was the terminal point of navigation on the Maya and the beginning of a winter trail across the Dzhugzhur, to the port of Ayan on the Okhotsk Sea. The main traffic was in Japanese tea, delivered from Okhotsk on reindeer in the winter and floated in boats and on rafts to Yakutsk in the spring. Transportation over the mountains was in the hands of nomadic Tungus. Each fall, with the first snow, they went down to Ayan with their reindeer and sledges, took the freight to Nelkan, returned for a new cargo, and thus traveled back and forth until the spring thawed the snow. There were three passes over the mountains, each used for eight or ten years and then abandoned for fifteen or twenty.

It was raining in Nelkan, and while we waited for the weather to clear we got ready for the journey. Filipov, the bigger of the two Nelkan merchants, gave us a barn for quarters and offered to help us plan the expedition. He had crossed the range several times, always in winter. With his aid, I made a rough map of the route, somewhat similar to the log of the Lena captain. I tried to mark the trail with the ravines, marshes, and rivers it crossed, and to sketch signs that would help us recognize different points—peaks on the horizon, unusual boulders, occasionally a cross beside the trail, traces of an old camp, and the like. It seemed to be about 175 miles from Nelkan to the Okhotsk Sea and the trip might take about fourteen days. Meanwhile Mikhail bought a pack horse and replenished our provisions. The problem of provisions seemed very important, because local people could not tell us whether we could rely on hunting and fishing at this season.

We spent the last evening at Filipov's house. He had been in Irkutsk several times and knew the Lena like the palm of his hand. His house was furnished with stuffed armchairs, woolen curtains, and bearskins. The living room featured a phonograph with a huge pink and green horn ornamented with yellow roses.

We were treated to a tasty fish pie. The merchant's wife, a six-foot Amazon with huge hands and feet, seemed unhappy until she could make us take a third helping.

"Did you see movies?" she asked us. "I was in the theater in Yakutsk once, with my sister, but could not stay until the end. Believe it or not, there might have been a hundred people in the room, by God! The chairs were set right close to one another, and then suddenly the lights went out! I closed my eyes and prayed. If somebody hits you on the head in the darkness, you may see him again in the other world."

Filipov, somewhat embarrassed, interrupted his wife. "Don't think she is a coward. . . ."

But she kept on. "Have you ever seen a railroad? Even traveled on one? Weren't you afraid? Just when we were leaving the theater with my sister, there came a train on the trestle. Real people in the cars, and they laughed as if they did not worry a bit! You know they teach the actors to ride in a train, to jump into fire, and what else. I would never, never learn such tricks."

Filipov interrupted again. "This comes from living in the wilderness. Last winter I left for Ayan and she was alone in the house when a bear tried to get the frozen meat on the porch. She just picked up the gun, opened the door, and shot him on the threshold. There's his pelt."

He pointed to a huge bear rug on the floor. The lady of the house dropped her eyes modestly and mumbled, "Who speaks of bears? What could a bear do to me?"

I measured the rug and the lady with my eyes and decided that the bear had had no chance against her.

Next morning we crossed the shallow Maya in a birch-bark canoe, leading our horse by the bridle. It took time to pack our equipment and provisions. The sun was high and the air full of mosquitoes when we started on the trail. The route, no more than a footpath in many places, ran from one hill to another, with marshes and streams in the valleys and barren rocks on the crests. My map proved reasonably accurate, but I improved it here and there, making clearer the direction of each valley and introducing new landmarks. Thus I marked the double peak of Kivagi left of the trail on the third day of our journey.

That day we noticed a tiny box on an old tree leaning over the trail. I climbed up and examined the object—two boards about six by nine inches bound together by a strip of leather, and between them three pieces of black, bloodstained hide. A Tungus is a fearless hunter and does not hesitate to attack a bear with an ax or a knife if he has no gun at hand, but he believes that the angry spirit of a slain bear may dog him the rest of his life, scaring game away or calling on other bears to avenge it. The hunter therefore leaves the nose and paws of the animal he kills in the forest, to mollify his spirit.

The next day we noticed that grass on the trail was crushed, as if somebody had been there before us. A little further, in the mud of the bank of a creek, we found the imprint of a heavy, broad paw. A bear! The animal had halted at the creek, milled around, and resumed his march eastward. The traces were confused under an old larch, as if the bear had been going in circles. The bark showed deep scars where the bear had tried to get fresh sap from the trees. The scars were seven feet above the ground: our bear was a fairly large beast. After this discovery we went beating the teakettle like a drum. But the bear seemed to keep the same distance ahead of us. Before sunset we halted on a high bank of a river and decided to keep two campfires burning through the night. We felled a score of young pines and arranged them in two heaps, the thick ends put together and the tops in opposite directions. In the morning we lost the tracks of the bear; it must have turned into the thicket.

The trail was becoming more difficult, the taiga more dense, the scenery more forbidding, but our progress was uneventful. On the ninth day the heat was suffocating. We waded across several small streams and crossed a fairly wide river, the Aimcha, but cool water did not refresh us. In the afternoon the heat became unbearable. There was no breeze, the air was heavy and sticky. Unable to keep pace with the horse, I asked Mikhail to go ahead with it and I tried to follow them as best I could. Once I stumbled and fell and lay there—perhaps five minutes, perhaps half an hour—before I could get up. The forest had ended. The trail was crossing a broad meadow. Behind it, not very far away, was a new slope. The next creek must be at the foot of that hill, quite close. But where was Mikhail? He could not have crossed the creek. . . .

Suddenly he took my arm. "Take it easy!" he said. "After a rest you will be all right." He had put up the tent on the shore of the river. The fire was blazing in front of it, water was bubbling in the kettle, and a soft bed was waiting for me—heaps of moss covered with a deer hide that we had carried from Ayan as a tarpaulin for our baggage. I fell asleep before my head touched the bed.

THE CHELYASIN

We were awakened by deafening thunder. Then a torrential downpour began. All our luggage was soaked. We had to wait until it dried before we could load it. The march was particularly strenuous that day or seemed so because we had not had enough rest. Late in the afternoon we reached a long, smooth slope in the valley of the Chelyasin, the last river before the foothills of the Dzhugzhur. It was a winding stream in a very broad, partly dry riverbed. The stream itself was not very wide but it was too strong to cross where the trail hit it. We forded it two hundred steps upstream, where the current was broken by a string of shoals. On the far bank we found a clearing in the woods. While Mikhail was hobbling the horse and building a camp-fire, I put up the tent. After a solid meal of canned ham and peas, we sat at the fire.

In the morning Mikhail aroused me. His voice was anxious. "Bad news, Wladimir. The horse is gone!"

We rushed after the fugitive. Tracks led from the clearing to the river. The horse had been jumping, with its forelegs hobbled. The tracks disappeared on the pebbles, but it seemed unlikely that the horse would have jumped into the stream at this point. Which way could it have gone? Mikhail ran to the right down the stream, and I to the left. Soon pebbles gave way to smooth sand. There were no hoof marks. Obviously our Rosinante had taken the other direction. I heard a distant pistol shot. Thinking Mikhail was signaling that he had found the horse, I headed back toward our camp. Then came two shots, one after another—a signal of alarm. I began to run, lost my way, and had to retrace my steps. Finally I saw Mikhail clumping heavily along the river.

He had found the horse—more exactly, its body—on a shoal in the middle of the stream. His first thought was that it might be alive and he ran toward the shoal, but the current swept him off his feet and carried him toward a tree trunk lying across the river. He seized a branch but could not find a foothold. Then he drew his pistol and fired to attract my attention. When I did not answer, he began to inch along the branch. Then he fired twice, and again there was no response. So he continued to pull himself along the branch, trying to extricate his legs from under the tree. Finally he found a kneehold and crawled on the trunk.

We went to the place where the dead horse lay. All we could salvage was the rope. Back at our camp we breakfasted in silence. Then Mikhail began to check the provisions while I studied the map. The situation looked gloomy. We were about as far from Nelkan as from Ayan, but the trip ahead might prove more difficult than the way back. Furthermore, we could not carry our tent and other equipment and provisions. We seemed to have no choice but to abandon everything except food and weapons and head back toward Nelkan.

I did not want to give up. I went to the river. The map failed to show the course of the Chelyasin below the point where we had crossed it, but obviously it belonged to the basin of the Maya. It made no difference whether it discharged into the Aimcha or directly into the Maya. In either case it would carry us to Nelkan. I asked Mikhail, "Can't we build a raft?"

"Surely we can," he replied. "But you cannot ride a raft on a mountain stream. This stretch is not too bad, but who knows what is further downstream?" But finally he agreed that we could try.

Along the river were many dead trees, bleached by the sun. We went upstream, selecting straight trunks of the proper thickness. Then we cut the logs down to twenty feet with the ax and floated them to a place where we could assemble them to make the raft. By noon we had five logs ten inches thick and two of fourteen inches. We cleared a space along the riverbank so as to have a shallow, well-protected basin, keeping each log in its floating position. The next task was to hew the logs so that they would fit one another. They held together tightly enough, the thicker ones at the outer edges. Then we cut two crossbeams, hewed deep grooves at the ends of the long logs, and fitted the crossbeams to them.

Working knee deep in the water in our basin, we noticed that the river abounded in fish. Mikhail found a piece of wire in our luggage and bent it to make a hook. This he attached to a rod with a piece of string, and before dusk he had caught a couple of fairly large fish. We were so excited by the catch and so tired that we decided to postpone assembling the raft and indulged in a luxurious feast: fish soup, quantity unlimited, with rye biscuits.

We were back at work before sunrise. I held the logs together while Mikhail lashed them to the crossbeams with the rope. Next we tightened the raft, wedging pieces of wood between the logs. In the middle we built a platform for the luggage. Then we cut half a dozen long poles of green wood to guide our craft. By evening the raft was ready. We tested it, hurling it against the boulders. The crossbars did not move.

Next morning we loaded our belongings on the platform, covered them with the deer hide, secured with sticks, took our positions at both ends of the raft, and pushed it off into the middle of the stream. The current seized the raft and threw it forward. It moved as smoothly as if we were flying in the air. Before I knew it we had passed the shoal with the corpse of our horse. The trees along the riverbanks flashed by as though seen through the window of a train. The raft did not roll—it pitched, its beam rising and falling.

The sun was bright, the air clear and fresh and full of tunes. The river wound now eastward, then westward, and I wondered how much northerly progress we had made. The mountains east of us closed in and looked grim, almost black, in striking contrast to the radiant vegetation on the left shore. We were flying along without knowing where. My knees were stiff and I could not move my legs without acute pain, but I felt that this was the most delightful journey I could imagine.

Before dusk we noticed a change in the river. It was widening, and we could not find its main current. We poled the raft to the left bank. This was an inviting place to camp for the night—level ground covered with lush grass, with huge trees widely separated from one another, straight as columns in a cathedral. We tied the raft to a tree and climbed up the bank to reconnoiter. The river had become a wide lake. The tempestuous Chelyasin was far away at the right. To the left was a wall of dead trunks piled one on top of another. In some places the wall was as high as the living trees on the shore. The ends of the dam were hidden by rising fog.

We unloaded our luggage and made a big fire. The night was beautiful. The foliage, illuminated by the fire, formed a green vault over our heads. The air was fragrant, and the murmur of leaves and water sounded like mysterious music.

LOST IN THE TAIGA

In the morning we went to explore the river. It was blocked from shore to shore by a log jam of trees brought down from the mountains by floods. Here and there living trees had grown through the Cyclopic pile. We pulled the raft along the edge of the barrier and climbed on top of the dam. On one side we saw the lake and, far away, the river; on the other, a maze of tree trunks. We tried to cross the dam by climbing and jumping from tree to tree but progress was slow. Several times we fell from slippery trunks, or a rotten log gave way under our feet. Late in the evening we returned to our camp, bruised and exhausted, and stretched ourselves beside the fire.

The next day Mikhail went along the left edge of the dam while I explored its right flank. Neither of us could reach the open river beyond the barrier, but we learned that the woods left of the dam were full of streams running in all directions while the opposite shore was dry and rising. After sunset we transferred our camp to the high bank. In the morning we continued our exploration and late in the afternoon came to a clearing overlooking a river. This could not be the mainstream of the Chelyasin, but it might be one of its branches. We decided to move our tent to this river and build a new raft there. Our provisions were running out, and Mikhail suggested that we ration the food.

Back at camp, we dismantled our raft. The ropes that had held it together seemed to be in fair condition. Then we carried our luggage to the new camp site in two installments. The distance was hardly more than four or five miles, but it seemed like a very long operation.

We put up our tent on a narrow level strip of land along the river and spent our fifth day building the new raft. We intended to make it somewhat smaller than the first—only six logs, not more than fourteen feet long. All the trees we found were half green. Our ax grew blunt and it took much effort to sharpen it. While Mikhail was hewing the logs, I used the hunting knife and a stone to fit them to one another. My hands were bleeding and I felt I was losing strength. Before dusk we tightened the ropes as firmly as we could and tested the raft by hurling it against the bank. A couple of logs loosened. The new raft was not seaworthy.

During the night a torrential rain fell. The river rose, flooding the strip of land on which our tent stood. In complete darkness we dragged our luggage uphill. We were soaked, and even if we had had strength enough to put up the tent once more it would not have helped us. So we just sat in the mud under the rain, waiting for the sunrise.

In the morning the sky was blue again, the sun bright. We checked our goods—nothing was lost. But the river had risen several feet and we could not work on the raft. Mikhail, waist deep in water, checked the raft, examined the river, and returned grim and dejected. "This raft will not hold us," he reported, "and the place is not good. Let's look around."

We climbed to the top of the hill above our camp. From this point we could see the dam and streams in the forest above and below it. The stream on which we had built our second raft disappeared half a mile from the site of our camp, under the piles of dead wood, but a quarter of a mile from it there was a strip of open water in a wide sandy bed. This was obviously the continuation of the Chelyasin. We moved the luggage to the new site, put up the tent, made a campfire, and spread out all our belongings to dry. The river, the taiga, and the sky seemed unreal to me. I was half delirious. Mikhail made me lie down beside the campfire and put a towel with cold water around my head. Later I crawled to the river and kept my head in the water. This was only a brief spell of weakness, however. By noon I had recovered enough to help Mikhail select logs for the new raft. He was some two hundred feet away from me when I heard him shouting, "The gun, Wladimir, the gun!"

I ran to the tent and brought him the rifle. He disappeared into the thicket. A shot, and he emerged from behind the trees holding a big bird over his head. His eyes were shining. He awoke me when dinner was ready—and what a dinner! A bucket of turkey stew and slices of roast turkey with toasted biscuits! Mikhail seemed completely confident, but later that night he said to me, "We are out of danger now, but wouldn't it be a good idea to write a few lines and leave the note here in a sealed can?"

"Nobody will find it," I replied. "And what would you write?"

"That we were here, that we were perfectly happy and that we left this place confident we would find our way home."

I signed this note with him. Here, in the wilderness, we indeed felt perfectly happy although we were not sure what awaited us. I still had a long road ahead. Mikhail's life was to end earlier—in one of Stalin's dungeons.

We started the next day with a substantial breakfast—more hot turkey stew, more roast turkey, hot cocoa, biscuit crumbs.

Mikhail picked out a tree sixteen or eighteen inches thick for the raft, and we cut it into two logs fifteen feet long. The tree seemed dry enough, but when we tried to drag the logs to the river we found them unusually heavy. We realized how much strength we had lost. We rolled the logs to the water and floated them downstream to the campsite. Then we added two smaller logs to the thick ones to keep them apart and adjusted the crossbars. We found it hard to tighten the ropes, but otherwise the work went well. Before sunset, when the raft was ready and I was resting on hot pebbles, with the back of my head in the cold water, Mikhail went into the thicket and returned with a couple of partridges. We went to sleep with full stomachs, even more confident and happy than we had been the night before.

In the morning we packed and loaded our luggage and pushed the raft into the current. It slipped to the middle of the river and slowly went to the bottom. The logs were green, and, after having absorbed more water during the night, they would not float. We salvaged the luggage and brought it to the shore, leaving the raft in the river.

I lay on warm pebbles looking at the skyline above the far shore of the river. If only we knew where we were! Suddenly I noticed a brown-gray spot above the waving line of the green. I examined it through the field glasses. It was a rocky peak, a lofty point on the right, and a terrace below it on the left. I got out my map. Kiwagi! Only I was seeing it now from the side opposite the one I had sketched from the trail. I looked at the compass. The peak was some fifteen degrees right of north. I called to Mikhail, "That is Kiwagi! If we go straight north we shall pass at its foot and hit the trail three days' march from Nelkan."

We left our tent and, taking only the most essential equipment, crossed the river, and went into the virgin taiga by compass. Our further journey took us across gently rolling land with evergreen forests, with a stream or spring in every hollow, and provided us with plenty of dry wood for campfires on the slopes. The best hunting was along the streams early in the morning. Mikhail did not miss a single shot. After three days' march we hit the Nelkan-Ayan trail. Three

days later we stood on the shore of the Maya, shouting for the boat-
man to take us across the river.

THE BEGINNING OF THE WAR

Soon after our return to Nelkan a steamer arrived from the Lena, the
last of the season. We boarded her. The captain invited us to share
his meals in the stateroom. One day he casually mentioned at the
table that he had heard in Yakutsk that recruits were being con-
scripted, though he did not know why.

There was no telephone or telegraph connection between Nelkan
and Yakutsk, and radio was unknown in Siberia; news traveled slowly.
We did not learn about the beginning of the World War until we
reached Yakutsk. Even now, after decades of research, historians have
found it difficult to retrace the chain of events leading to the conflagration of 1914, but to people in the Siberian wilderness the events
of the summer had a nightmarish quality. Newspapers took several
weeks to reach Yakutsk and rarely got to the remote villages. All that
we knew came from rumors.

In the middle of August, as our steamer passed villages along the
Lena, we could observe the people's reactions to the war. Landing
places were crowded with men who had been called up. There was a
spirit of sullen resignation among them and in the watching crowd
as they were loaded onto barges.

The newspapers were full of vituperation against Germany, predicted her immediate defeat, glorified the gallant Allies, and called on
the Russian people to rally around the throne. But this propaganda,
reminiscent of the days of the Russo-Japanese War, was not very
successful. The first month of war proved disastrous for Russia. Two
armies were wiped out in the abortive offensive against East Prussia,
and among the troops lost in this operation were the best-trained
divisions, the Tsar's guard. Those who survived the debacle of Tan-
nenberg believed that their regiments had been led to destruction by
treacherous officers—some of them scions of aristocratic families with
German names.

The sudden shift from the solitude of the taiga to the turmoil of
political events, rumors, and passions was overwhelming. I felt as if
our trip to the Dzhugzhur had been an attempt to flee from political
realities—another unsuccessful attempt at escape.

The political picture had changed drastically in the nearly five
months since I had left Irkutsk. The country was facing new problems;
political forces had regrouped. The liberals had joined forces with the

reactionaries, offering to support the government in the interest of national defense. They made no secret, however, of their hope that the manifestation of their loyalty would persuade the Tsar to change his domestic policy and take persons with progressive leanings into the Cabinet. This policy undermined the prestige of the liberals in the eyes of the people, and its failure was to become one of the major causes of the growing anti-monarchist feelings in previously moderate circles. At the same time a split had developed within the left. Some of the S-D and S-R leaders called for national unity and support of the war effort; others denounced Russia's participation in the war as an adventure of the disintegrating Tsarist regime and declared that the masses of the Russian people had no stake in the clash between German and British imperialism.

The "patriotic" movement was particularly strong in radical circles in the early phase of the war, when many intellectuals volunteered for military service, but it did not last very long. At the beginning of the winter of 1914-15, a wave of defeatism began to rise rapidly. Since the Tsar and his generals had brought Russia into the war, its outcome was their responsibility. Each defeat of the Russian armies was therefore a blow for the Tsarist regime. Victory over Germany would bring no advantage to the Russian people and would result only in strengthening reaction. Such thinking implied that the Russian people would gain nothing from Germany's defeat but might gain their freedom as a result of Germany's victory.

ANTI-MILITARIST CAMPAIGN

Before I had time to formulate my own attitude to the conflicting political currents, I was confronted with a practical task. The local Social Democratic circles expected me to resume journalistic work and launch a magazine that would help crystallize public opinion among the exiles on the war, and perhaps within a much broader group of intellectuals in Siberia. I was not ready for this task and had no clear idea of the platform for the new magazine. Certainly it would take a stand against both the slogan of national unity, which amounted to the support of the Tsar, and that of defeatism, which amounted to the support of German imperialism. But many unresolved questions lay between these two extremes.

Most of my S-D friends were spending that summer in Ussolye, a village on the Angara some twenty miles from Irkutsk by train, and I went there to discuss the situation with them. Politically, the local S-D colony was under the strong influence of Tseretelli. He was a Menshevik without attachment to any particular faction and up to

that time had not manifested great interest in the journalistic ventures of the exiles. But he followed political events closely and was one
of the first among the moderate S-D who tried to outline a policy
against the war while, at the same time, rejecting defeatism. He
believed such a policy was possible for a Socialist party if it approached the war as an international problem. The ultimate aim, he
reasoned, must be not the victory of either coalition but a durable
peace based on justice. Neither blind support of the national government nor crippling opposition to the war effort would serve that purpose. By undermining the military policy of the Tsarist government,
Russian Socialists might become the tools of German militarism.
Similarly, the German Socialists, by challenging the Kaiser, might
ultimately lend support to the forces of absolutism in Russia. The
solution should be a co-ordinated movement on both sides for a
negotiated peace, without victors and vanquished, without annexa-
tions and indemnities.

This plan sounded logical. *If* the Socialist parties of Germany,
Austria, France, Italy, Great Britain, and Russia succeeded in mobilizing the masses of the people behind the slogan of just peace; *if*
they were able to co-ordinate their efforts so as not to help the imperialist forces of either coalition; *if* they could gain confidence and support of other political parties—then the World War could be ended
and a durable and just peace established. But the success of the plan
depended on several *if*'s, and this was the source of its weakness. Indeed, the state of affairs within the European Socialist movement
should not have fostered any illusions in this respect.

Since 1889, the European Socialist parties had been loosely united
in an International Federation, dominated ideologically by the German and Austrian Marxists. Under the strain of the war, a deep split
had developed in their ranks; in each country the majority of the
Socialist party joined the National Unity front, while the minority
shifted toward revolutionary defeatism. The Socialist majorities were
represented in most of the war cabinets and accused the minorities
of treason to the national cause. In turn, the minorities accused the
majorities of betraying the ideal of international socialism and believed that only common action of radical minorities against the
Socialist majorities and the government would achieve a just peace.
The plan of common action of Socialist parties developed by Tseretelli ran in the same general direction and, in retrospect, appears to
be the Russian—or more precisely, the Siberian—version of ideas
that had found their expression at the Socialist conference in Zim-
merwald. The difference from the West European Zimmerwaldism
was that Tseretelli thought of common action of the Socialist minorities and majorities.

I spent several days in Ussolye talking with Tseretelli and was impressed by his arguments, but his program did not satisfy me. It called for long patient work within the split Socialist parties but left little opportunity for immediate action in each country. I saw the immediate evil in the chauvinist propaganda, and thought that it must be met by an educational campaign. Should not such a campaign start with an analysis of the war as a hopeless attempt to solve by force of arms problems that could be solved only by negotiation? In the course of the talks at Ussolye I decided that before publishing a new magazine I had another task to accomplish.

Back at Irkutsk, I plunged into work on a pamphlet entitled *A World Conflagration*. I worked feverishly and completed a booklet of some 160 pages in less than two weeks. Not certain how good it was, I read the manuscript to a group of two dozen S-D exiles. They were enthusiastic. Actually, it was not badly written but, along with a sound analysis of facts, it harbored some false notions. It overemphasized the idea of a stalemate and failed to recognize the possibility of the appearance of new forces on the military scene and the probability of scattered revolutions that would tip the scales in the military contest and lead to a chain of unconditional surrenders rather than a negotiated peace.

In Ussolye opinion concerning my essay was divided. Tseretelli was most critical and reproached me for lack of international spirit in handling an essentially international problem. Indeed, I had given little weight to Tseretelli's central idea—international action by the Socialist parties. After making some minor changes, I mailed the manuscript to St. Petersburg. The publisher to whom I offered it wired that he was sending it to the printer. A month later he sent me some sixty galleys, each with a large stamp: "Forbidden by the Censor of the First Military District." [2]

Discussing my essay with friends in Ussolye, I evolved the idea of publishing a magazine that would present our views on the war in a systematic series of articles in the first issue, leaving to chance whether a second issue would follow. Tseretelli agreed to join the editorial board and present his views in his own words. I would elaborate my ideas, as would other contributors, within our common conception, decidedly rejecting both national unity and defeatism.

---

[2] Later I met the censor who had banned the booklet. In 1917, under the Provisional Government, I was appointed Commissar of the Northern Front and charged with restoring the morale of the troops. One high officer with whom I worked was the commander of the 45th Corps, General Boldyrev. Once, when we were inspecting the troops together, he told me that the only sensible book on the war he had ever read was submitted to him for censorship and he had to forbid it. He remembered the title: *A World Conflagration*, but did not recall the name of the author.

Rozhkov, who was then visiting Ussolye, promised to contribute articles on internal affairs. I took over the responsibility of finding other contributors and publishing and distributing the issue.

I still had a license for a weekly, Sibirsky Zhurnal (Siberian Journal), signed by a middle-aged lady, a sympathizer of the S-D party. I called on her and told of our plans.

"There will probably be only one issue. All the copies will be taken away from the printing shop before the first copy reaches the police department. Your sentence will probably be one year."

She replied quietly, "Make it worth that sentence."

The first issue of the Siberian Journal appeared on December 23, 1914—sixteen pages in tabloid format. In addition to Tseretelli's keynote article on the policy of the Socialist parties during the war and four or five articles of mine, it contained a survey of the internal political situation in Russia by Rozhkov, a survey of war literature by Chuzhak, and half a dozen other features. None of the articles could be construed as inciting to criminal action, but from the first line to the last the magazine represented a severe criticism of the official war policy and a call for a negotiated peace. The issue became widely known in European Russia and in Socialist circles abroad. This was a political rather than a journalistic success—in all justice, Tseretelli's success.

The journal was closed, of course, and the responsible publisher was arrested. But meanwhile I received a new license. A former schoolteacher came to me, a faded woman stricken by polio. She wanted to serve as the next responsible publisher. I felt embarrassed and said, carefully choosing my words, "We cannot accept your sacrifice. Prison will be too hard on you."

She interrupted me. "You mean these braces? To me the difference between freedom and prison is less than to others. And the sacrifice is smaller, too."

She took a license for Sibirskoe Obozrenie (Siberian Survey). Its first issue appeared in January, 1915. Although as good journalistically as the Siberian Journal, it received less acclaim. Actually, it could not do much more than reaffirm the ideas outlined in our preceding publication. The new magazine was closed after the first issue, and the brave woman with braces disappeared behind bars.

I began to prepare a third publication. In order to make it distinctly different from the first two, I planned to build it around the problems of war economics, especially the wartime controls in Germany. However, it was difficult to obtain the necessary information, the police had warned the local printing shops to take no orders from the S-D exiles, and the plan did not materialize.

Early in 1915, a large magazine, Sovremennik (The Contemporary), appeared in Petrograd.[3] Its program was not very clear, but the list of contributors read like a Who's Who in radical journalism. The editors asked me to contribute, and I sent a long political article, which was barred by military censorship, and several essays on Siberia, which were printed.

Meanwhile Rozhkov launched a weekly in Chita. He returned to his old idea: a publication only a shade more liberal than other local papers, but with more attention to labor. He urged me insistently to write for his paper, and I gave him weekly *Pis'ma o Voyne* (*Letters on War*) and the story of my trip with Mikhail, which *The Russian Word* could not publish because of wartime conditions.

BACK TO PRISON

Early in the spring of 1915, I was arrested on order of the local chief of gendarmes. After a month of solitary confinement in the Irkutsk prison, without books and writing materials, I was interrogated. The young gendarme officer had laid out on his desk the reprints of my articles, our Irkutsk publications, and other material and galleys taken in my room.

"Did you write all this?"

"Yes, all that is signed with my name, my pen name Sergei Petrov, or the respective initials."

"And this also?" He showed me the galleys with the stamps of the military censor in Petrograd.

"This book would have appeared under my full name if it had not been forbidden by the censor."

"Glad to hear that," said the gendarme affably. "You will get four years of forced labor for this. You know the law."

"I know, but you do not," I replied. "This must be your first literary case."

The young officer became livid. "This is treacherous, subversive writing," he shouted. "Article 129, deportation for a free man, four years of forced labor for a deportee!"

"The crime of subversive writing is committed in the place in which the piece is published or distributed," I replied. "This book was intended for publication and was set in Petrograd. It is no business of yours unless you have an order from the Petrograd authorities to investigate the case."

From the legal standpoint my reasoning was foolproof. The gendarmes' mistake was that they combined my Petrograd articles and

[3] Early in World War I the German name of the Russian capital "St. Petersburg" was changed to Russified "Petrograd."

those I had written for local publications. They could have broken down my defense if they had limited the charge to the latter, but they wished to bring the whole bill of particulars against me. The officer who questioned me became angry and threatened to get me. Confident of my legal position, I told him that any attorney to whom his superiors would direct my case for trial would tell them they were ignoramuses and were trying to handle matters that were above their heads. "You will soon learn whether or not we are ignoramuses!" he fumed.

A month later I was set free. For some reason, this time I found a comparatively brief spell of solitary confinement rather depressing. I felt tired and sought rest in a trip to the steppes and mountains at the Mongolian border. Completely relaxed, I returned to Ussolye, planning to spend the end of the summer there. But at Ussolye I found that the village sheriff had an order to deliver me to the Irkutsk jail. The warrant was written on a crumpled sheet torn from a notebook and the reference to the law was illegible, but the situation was clear: the gendarmes had reopened my case.

Again I was confined to a solitary cell. Six weeks passed. The assistant inspector of prisons came to inspect the jail. When he came to my cell and asked if I had complaints, I answered, "I would like to know the legal reason for my detention."

"You are serving your two-year term," he replied.

"What term? I have not been tried."

"Your case—criminal propaganda against war—was tried in a police court *in absentia*. . . . The police have the right to try deportees in this way for minor violations. You know—a simplified procedure, no lawyers admitted, presence of the defendant not mandatory."

I knew about this simplified police-court procedure in handling minor offenses committed by criminal deportees, such as disorderly conduct and petty theft, but it had never been applied to political cases. I wrote a complaint to the Governor General immediately, accusing the local gendarmes and police of having arbitrarily assumed jurisdiction in a case that could be tried only in the courts in Petrograd, the place where the alleged crimes had been committed. I also pointed out that a body ignorant of the limits of its own jurisdiction should not be permitted to pass sentence on books and articles even if the writer happened to live in the territory where this body might have jurisdiction over such offenses as a drunken brawl.

I sent the complaint to the prison office. Half an hour later the assistant superintendent came to return my petition. "You will have to rewrite your complaint," he instructed me. "It contains disrespectful remarks against the authorities."

"I shall not change a single word," I said. "The moment the paper left my cell it became a part of the mail of the person to whom it is addressed. Do you think that the Governor General will recognize your right to check his mail?"

Two days passed. I was sleeping soundly when the door of my cell opened. The assistant superintendent said sweetly, "How do you do, Mr. Woytinsky? Sorry to disturb you at night, but you must go home."

The prison was some three miles from the city, on a road that was passable only in dry weather and in autumn was knee-deep in mud. I was not eager to wade through it in the middle of the night and said that I would rather leave in the morning. The officer left but soon came back.

"Very, very sorry, Mr. Woytinsky, but the order is not to detain you a minute longer. You must leave right away." As a privilege, I was permitted to wait till dawn in the hall for visitors.

When I went to thank the Governor General for intervening, he said with a smile, "As a judge, I have seldom come across a case as clear as this—a criminal conspiracy originated by the gendarmes. They persuaded the prison inspector and police that they could get you without a regular judicial procedure. Then the three officials sat together as a police court—which they were not—and wrote the sentence." He added, "The gendarmes brought your pamphlet and other articles here. I would not say that I agreed with you but, as long as I am Governor General, there will be no twisting of the law here, either because of a personal grudge or for any other considerations."

Such were the contradictions of the administrative and judiciary systems in Tsarist Russia! These included manifestations of barbarism and lawlessness but, in contrast to the system that developed later, left even political exiles in Siberia some freedom and civil rights.

THE WAR COMES TO SIBERIA

The war that had seemed so remote from Siberia was coming closer. Russian armies were falling back with tremendous losses. It became more and more obvious that Tsarist Russia was unable to wage a major war. The Ministry of War was headed by an incompetent and frustrated courtier; the High Command over all the armed forces was in the hands of the uncle of the Tsar, Grand Duke Nicholas, an arrogant disciplinarian who was abysmally ignorant of military affairs and had no interest in the lives and welfare of the soldiers. The army, held in obedience by a regime of iron discipline, was beginning to crack under the strain. Its weakest point was the enlisted men's distrust of their officers. The reverses had made the soldiers particularly suspicious, and the officers felt themselves surrounded by hostility.

Before the end of the first year, economic difficulties developed. Sugar and meat became scarce. The railroads were deteriorating. The fiscal system, based largely on the monopoly of the sale of vodka, was on the verge of collapse as a result of wartime prohibition. Prices were rising. The workers asked for higher wages, and employers had to meet their demands. The government was aware that things were getting out of control and reluctantly accepted the offer of the Cadets in the Duma to enlist municipal and regional government bodies in an effort to improve medical services in the army, speed up munitions production, distribute and ration scarce foodstuffs, and care for refugees from the occupied western provinces. The Union of the Cities and Townships and War Industry Committees that emerged from this plan helped temporarily, but politically their existence was in itself evidence of the government's failure. Moreover, they were filled with persons of liberal leanings.

A chapter of the Union of the Cities was formed in Irkutsk. One of its first steps was to launch a study of the effect of the war on the local labor market, and I was appointed director of the project.

Waves of refugees from the western provinces were beginning to reach Irkutsk. Most of them came from villages the Cossacks had burned down in compliance with the "scorched earth" policy of Grand Duke Nicholas. A local committee made a survey of the availability of the refugees for local industries. The questionnaire began with the query: "Name of your village? What happened to it?" The answers showed the feelings of the refugees. All that these uprooted and bewildered men and women knew about the war was that they and their families had been loaded into trains and deported while their houses had been burned down and all their property destroyed by order of some general. The High Command could not have invented anything more stupid than the "scorched earth" policy. It left the Germans the fields they needed for the next year's planting and relieved them of the civilian population, which they might have found a liability and a source of trouble. Naturally this policy gave substance to the rumors of treason by the heads of the army and in the Winter Palace.

There were no riots in military barracks, no street demonstrations. All was quiet on the surface, but Russia was approaching a crisis similar to that of 1905 and caused largely by the same factor—a government that commanded no respect of the people and was too weak to wage a war.

But the approaching crisis was deeper than the one twelve years earlier. With a half-insane Emperor who had turned his power over to the false monk whom he and the Empress called "Our Dear

Friend"; with the subservient, incompetent government; with the disintegrating army—its enlisted men distrusting their officers and both soldiers and officers distrusting the High Command; with the Church taken over by Rasputin's appointees; with the masses of the people despising the Tsar, his ministers, and his generals and distrusting the hand-picked Duma, Tsarist Russia was a crumbling tower.

MY MARRIAGE AND HONEYMOON

It was then that I met the girl who was to become my wife and lifelong companion. A friend invited me to greet the New Year with him and his wife. They had bought a box in the theater for the occasion. In the box I found myself beside a strikingly beautiful girl with enormous black eyes. We spent the intermissions chatting about nothing. After the theater my friend asked me, "How do you like her?"

I answered evasively, "So-so."

"If you think she is just so-so, you are a fool," he replied pointedly.

For the next three months she disappeared from my sight, but I often thought of her, the girl with the enormous black eyes and gentle voice. Then suddenly I met her by pure accident, again at the theater. This time I feared letting her vanish from my life. I saw her and her younger brother home from the theater and was very much disappointed that she did not invite me in. But as I was leaving, she called me back casually to say that she would be glad to see me again if I should have a free evening.

Next day I persuaded myself that this evening would be free. I telephoned the girl and spent several delightful hours with her. We knew very little about each other, but we talked as if we were old friends and had met after a long separation. This feeling of closeness to another person was unusual for me. On leaving, I forgot my briefcase (not unintentionally) and had an excellent pretext to see her again the next evening. This time I did not pretend to forget anything but left the briefcase in the entrance hall and said to Emma, "I shall pick it up tomorrow, at the same time."

All this was out of character for me. In addition, I realized how little I could offer the girl. I was a deportee engaged in political activities that promised me nothing but new troubles. Also, I looked older than my thirty years, and she was twenty-two but looked like a college girl of eighteen. Moreover, I suspected that I would not be the choice of Emma's mother. Nevertheless, a few days later I suggested to her that we try a game—a contest in earnestness—to look straight into each other's eyes and see who would lose by laughing first. She accepted the challenge and did not laugh, but it took her some time to realize that the "game" was a pretext for me to look more closely and longer into her lovely eyes.

The next Sunday we went for a walk along the bank of the Angara. She wore a black silk hat with a broad white brim. She told me later that, noticing for the first time the expression of admiration on my face, she attributed it to the hat. This was the decisive day in our growing closeness. We exchanged reminiscences. She asked me about my childhood and what had brought me to Siberia and told her own story—high school in a provincial town in western Russia, a women's college in St. Petersburg, teaching after graduation in an elementary public school in North Caucasus for a year, then the trip to Siberia where her father was a contractor in the construction of military barracks. After his death she remained there with her mother and brothers and sisters. Although she had majored in history and economics, she was most interested in educational problems and child psychology. What impressed me most in her, perhaps even more than her appearance, was her sincerity, independence of judgment, and the complete absence of clichés in her speech. She was not a rebel and showed little interest in politics and the revolutionary movement. But I felt in her more real freedom of mind and spirit than in most of the people I met in revolutionary circles.

What surprised me most was that the girl seemed to like me. A week later I asked Emma to go with me to Ussolye to meet my political friends. The pleasure of the trip was marred for me at the beginning. Strolling along a country road, we passed a farm. Three urchins were sitting on the fence. They measured us with their eyes and the oldest said loudly, "Gosh, is she pretty!" And another replied as firmly, "And he is not pretty at all!" I had never been particular about my appearance, but in the special circumstances of that day I considered the remark very ill-mannered.

During that walk we decided to get married. For our honeymoon we went to Arshan, a mountain resort at the Mongolian border, and then took a long trip in a rowboat down the Angara. The road across the steppes and Arshan had a beauty I had not noticed during my trip a year earlier.

In Arshan we rented a cabin, not much larger than a solitary cell and as poorly furnished. Yet it was wonderful, with long splits in the walls and holes in the roof through which stars glittered and the moon shone. The cabin overlooked a turbulent mountain stream. A trail along it led into a deep canyon, skirting waterfalls and rapids. The stream had cut terraces in the rocks, revealing snow-white marble inside the mountain. The water fell in cascades down a gigantic stairway, whirling in deep basins, white, turquoise blue, and green. The climbing was steep and difficult. Few visitors went further than to the first terrace above the cluster of cabins. To penetrate into the canyon one had to wade through the river and make frequent detours through the woods, but Emma was tireless and fearless. It was fun for both of us to stroll in the virgin forest, finding the path by the sound of the waterfalls. In the evenings we read together, and I discovered that she read poetry beautifully. We had a small book of poems of Rabindranath Tagore in a Russian translation, and I shall always associate these poems with the blackness of the Arshan log cabin, a solitary candle on an unpainted wooden table, and stars glittering through the holes in the walls and the ceiling.

On the Baikal we bought a fisherman's boat with a flat bottom and two pairs of oars—a luxuriously spacious vessel for two. I built a canopy of green birch branches at the stern for Emma and a hearth in the middle of the boat. We also fixed a sort of Frigidaire at the bow— a bucket covered with towels soaked in the ice-cold river water. In this boat we leisurely traveled downstream for about twenty days, stopping in villages for a night's rest and to replenish our provisions and stretch our legs.

The Angara is perhaps the most beautiful of the great Siberian rivers. It has the most limpid water and its bottom is covered with variegated pebbles. On its shores dark virgin forests alternate with verdant fields. On some of its islands woods have been cleared to yield space to meadows. Its villages are larger and wealthier than those on the Lena and face a road, with back yards of the houses and truck gardens descending to the river. Our trip included an element of exploration. Before leaving Irkutsk, I had arranged with a Petrograd newspaper to write half a dozen articles about the impact of war on the Siberian village. We talked with the peasants, visited fields abandoned by soldiers' wives, occasionally observed the distribution of meager allowances to soldiers' families. People were bitter about the war and the government.

We would halt at a village after dusk, drag the boat up and secure it on the shore, climb up to the road and knock at the windows of one of the more substantial houses. At some there was no answer for fear of vagabonds, but once we were let in we were treated like welcome guests. Beds would be prepared for us or hay sacks laid on the floor in the living room, a samovar would appear on the table and, despite the late hour, we would be offered a hot meal. In the morning we got breakfast and provisions for the day: fresh buns, hard-boiled eggs, butter, milk, cottage cheese, and occasionally a pie with fish caught that very night. On leaving, we gave a silver ruble (half a dollar) to our hosts, and they thanked us, bowing, for such generosity.

One Sunday the sun was high when we were leaving the village.

Many villagers stood at the landing to watch us. After I had arranged the luggage and the shelter at the stern, I took the oars and said to Emma, "Here we go! Make yourself comfortable." Several people laughed as if I had said something funny. An old woman remarked, "City women have it better than we here. I thought that he would make her row, but look, she is resting and he's at the oars!" A young woman added defiantly, "One can see. City people have more brains than our muzhiks!"

Our last halt on the river was at Bratsky Ostrog, a large village above the impassable rapids of the Angara. In the sixteenth century, when this place marked the eastern limit of Russian penetration, a wooden fort had been built as an advance post of the Empire. Weathered and black, it still stood on the shore. It could hardly have housed more than ten men, but its garrison had a brass cannon and could lord it over the native tribes for several hundred miles around.

The village had a flour mill and several tiny shops, and offered some opportunities for work. When we got there it held more than forty political exiles. The colony wanted to celebrate our visit and to hear political news. A meeting was called at night, in a large *izba* on the outskirts. We talked behind closed shutters, and patrols were posted outside. A candle flickered on the table. In the darkness I could not see how many people were in the room, but I had the feeling of speaking to a huge crowd, as in 1905. Emma sat in the first row, quite close to the candle. I could see her face, even her eyes, and was speaking mostly to her.

We gave our boat to the oldest member of the political colony, who had become a fisherman and whose greatest ambition was to own a boat with two pairs of oars. On the next lap of the journey, by cart, from the Angara to the railroad, we had bad luck with the weather— 250 miles of mud, under pouring rain—but that did not darken our honeymoon in the least.

Back at Irkutsk we settled in two furnished rooms rented from a middle-class family. We had much to learn about living together. I discovered how lonely I had been all the past years, probably since my early youth. My conscious life appeared to me as a succession of periods of feverish activity and lethargy. Actually, I had never been strongly attached to life, was not aware of its value, and had no clear plans for the future. Now all this was going to change.

In contrast, Emma knew exactly what she expected from life and marriage: she would accept marriage only as a complete union of two lives and personalities. The process of mutual adjustment of two persons as different as we required time. It was not completed until much later, and has been more nearly perfect on her side than on mine.

In the beginning Emma had little interest in politics but did not object to my activities. Yet marriage may have weakened my ties with local S-D circles. I had my home now, and Emma had no urge to establish new acquaintances. Moreover, the political climate in Irkutsk was changing rapidly. The new conditions were not favorable for publishing a new magazine or for any other collective action, but they offered possibilities for individual action, such as speeches in public and semi-public meetings. In this way I carried on the campaign of the *Siberian Journal* against official flag-waving patriotism—instead I defended the idea of a just negotiated peace. Of course, I had to choose my words when speaking publicly, just as I had in meetings before the election of the Duma in Petrograd, but this was not a serious obstacle. I could express my views clearly enough. In general I continued my political activity openly, as if I were sure of my rights, to the dismay of the gendarmes, who were reluctant to take drastic measures against me after the scandal over the sentence they had tried to impose upon me through the police court.

I mailed Emma's picture to my mother and was surprised by her answer. She expressed a hope that everything would turn out all right, but I could read between lines that she was worried. I sent her another photograph, showing Emma and me together. Then she wrote that she no longer was worried about my future and confessed that she had been rather scared by the first picture. In her broad black and white hat, Emma had seemed to her too glamorous a girl for her son in Siberia. A few weeks later my father came to Irkutsk to visit me and meet his new daughter-in-law. He looked much older than when I had last seen him, and I was quite surprised to hear him say I had not changed greatly in the intervening decade. It seemed that more than ten years separated me from the time I had left the capital.

PORTENTS OF THE REVOLUTION

This was the autumn of 1916, a time of confusion and growing tension. The air was full of rumors. The government tried to minimize the significance of continuing defeats and retreats of the Russian armies. The war bulletins spoke of successful regroupments of troops, readjustments of defense lines, evacuation of overexposed and strategically worthless positions. But in every home was a map of the theater of military operations and people realized that the armies of the Tsar were losing every engagement on the front from the Baltic to the Black Sea. The fact that the Tsar had removed his uncle from the Supreme Command of all armed forces and assumed personal control of military operations did not improve the army's morale. The Tsar commanded no more respect than did the generals suspected of treason.

At that time I was working as an economist and statistician with the military expedition purchasing meat for the armed forces in Siberia and Mongolia, a half-military and half-civilian organization. In general, it used veterinary inspectors as purchasing agents, and a learned veterinarian headed its central office in Irkutsk. My task was to sift and analyze the reports of local agents and prepare surveys of the expedition's operations for the War Ministry and the Duma. Some local reports were almost illiterate, others fairly good, and a few excellent. Supplementing them with information from other sources, I could turn out surveys to the complete satisfaction of the high brass in Petrograd, which had no inkling that a political exile was working in the main office. When Very Important Persons from the Ministry of War were expected to visit our office, its head advised me, "The office will be quite crowded during the next week. You might be more comfortable working at home. If you need anything, just call us up." After the departure of the guests I would get a carload of fresh news, rumors, and gossip from the capital.

News from Petrograd also leaked via the palace of the Governor General and the office of the Governor. Thus the politically interested public in Irkutsk was fairly well informed about the developments on the front, erratic changes within the government, the rise to power of obscure individuals picked up by Rasputin, the rumors of treason and a forthcoming palace revolution, the break between the moderates and rightists in the Duma, and so forth. Most reports were related to Rasputin in one way or another. Between the orgies in expensive night spots and talks on church affairs that were his main pastime, he was giving increasing attention to military operations and foreign policy. The rumors pictured him as the head of a pro-German party at the court, preaching separate peace with the Kaiser as the means of saving the throne. Even now I do not know whether these stories were true, but the role the "mad monk" played in the tragic end of the dynasty has been largely determined by the legend woven around him, the Tsar, and the Tsarina—that the reverses of our armies were due only partly to the ineptitude of the generals but mainly to treason, to Rasputin's conspiring with the Tsarina and perhaps the Tsar himself to make a separate peace with a victorious Germany. No revolutionary propaganda could have done more to undermine the throne than this legend.

Public opinion was deeply impressed by the speech of Miliukov, head of the liberals, in the Duma in which he enumerated the blunders of the government and after each charge asked, "Was this stupidity or treason?" The implication was that there was a consistency in these blunders that could not be explained by stupidity of the members of the ruling clique but revealed its intention to bring Russia to defeat and help Germany to victory. A careful investigation failed to confirm Miliukov's grim suspicion. In the course of the monarchy's disintegration, power had slipped into the hands of stupid, completely irresponsible, and frivolous individuals, but they were not traitors to their country, as the legend had portrayed them.

In January, 1917, Rasputin was killed. Three men were involved in the conspiracy—a member of the Tsar's family, a young aristocrat, and a leader of the Black Hundreds. They gave the public a full account of the murder. The "Dear Friend" of the Tsar was invited to a princely palace. His host treated him to arsenic in a tart downed with champagne, but the poison had no effect on the drunken man. Then the Black Hundreds man killed him with a pistol shot. The police officer posted in front of the palace rushed to the door, but the host sent him away, explaining, "A mad dog has been shot!" The body was put on a sledge, taken to the Neva, and pushed through a hole in the ice.

The newspapers were forbidden to report or comment on this event, but a detailed mimeographed account, allegedly coming from the Governor General's office, circulated in Irkutsk and a large cartoon appeared in one of the leading newspapers of Petrograd: The Neva covered with ice and snow, against the silhouette of the Fortress of Peter and Paul in the background; a large hole in the ice in the foreground, with tracks of a sledge and footsteps around it; and the legend "Farewell, Dear Friend!"

The loathsome details of the murder did not lessen the public's applause. The government did not dare to prosecute those who boasted of having shot the mad dog. The Tsar had had no power to protect his dear friend and had no power to avenge him.

THE VOICE FROM THE ARMY

More rumors were reaching Irkutsk. I was not impressed by the gossip about the imminent palace revolution. This possibility seemed remote, and I doubted whether it could change the course of events. But I was becoming increasingly absorbed in wondering how the disintegration of the Tsarist regime at the top would affect the armed forces at the front.

A young soldier stopped me on one of the main streets. I recognized Sechkin, a local worker, a Social Democrat, who had been called into military service a year earlier and was home on leave. After brief training he had been sent to the front and had often been under fire. I asked him, "How are things at the front?"

"If they do not make peace soon, there will be a revolution." He spoke loudly, paying no attention to the people around us.

I said quietly, "Let's go somewhere else. Too many people here. . . ."

"You mean the police?" he interrupted. "We spit on them in the trenches. A soldier at the front does not give a damn for the officers either. What can they do? Whoever tries to gag the men will get the first bullet."

This defiance was alien to Sechkin's character, and for a moment I thought he was drunk. I took him to a quieter street where we could talk freely. He was sober but excited, eager to talk about what he had gone through. Senseless death under fire, aimless movements of troops, foolish orders, and—treason, treason everywhere! I asked myself how many other soldiers believed they had been sent to their death by traitors. Obviously the whole army could not be in Sechkin's state of mind, but it was also clear that in some sectors of the front, disintegration had reached a stage at which the army had ceased to be an obedient tool. If this spirit spread further, it would end the regime of absolutism.

The tide was mounting and a new storm was approaching. A decade earlier the revolution had been crushed by the armed forces because there was no unity in its camp. Now the people had another chance. Now the oppressors were losing control over the armed forces. What would the new revolution bring to the people?

The Rise and Fall of
Democracy in Russia
1917

AFTER New Year's Day, 1917, Irkutsk was filled with rumors of unrest in Petrograd: strikes, street riots, clashes between the Duma and the government. Suddenly the government decided to get tough with the opposition and arrested workers' representatives in the War Industries Committees—an insane step in view of the role these committees played in expediting the output of munitions and strengthening the morale of the troops. In February the newspapers reported a food shortage and mounting tension in the capital.

In Siberia all was quiet. The political exiles, however, had their troubles. Kniazev had resigned and was succeeded by a reactionary bureaucrat, Pilz, who had been instructed to restore order in Siberia, allegedly endangered by the leniency of the former Governor General. Pilz ordered a cleanup of the exiled intellectuals in Irkutsk. Many of these, however, had more or less essential jobs in the Municipal Council, the banks, city theater, newspapers, and commercial establishments. Yielding to the protests of their employers, Pilz canceled, one after another, all his deportation orders except the one to expel me . . . to the village Jilkino, just across the river, a measure intended to satisfy the gendarmes without interfering with my work for General Koslov's expedition.

Emma had left Irkutsk to visit my mother and sister. I was in bed with the flu when, on March 13, a police officer brought me the order to leave Irkutsk at once. He was satisfied with my reply that I would go as soon as I had recovered. That evening Pilz invited half a dozen prominent local citizens to his office and suggested that they form a committee to deal with any unrest that might develop in Irkutsk. When the citizens replied that they did not anticipate disorder, he said that there was trouble in Petrograd and it might spread. They asked for details, but he replied grimly he had told them all he knew.

On March 14 a telegram reached Irkutsk through the railroad wire system appealing to railroad workers to remain at their posts. It was signed by an organization that called itself the Temporary Committee of the Duma and made no reference to the government. This seemed to indicate that there was no longer a government in Petrograd. Pilz therefore ordered his office to start a file under the heading: *The Change of Power in Petrograd*. That was his last official act.

THE NEW ORDER

That same evening the Irkutsk newspapers received by telegraph the first message of another new organization, the Petrograd Soviet of

Workers and Soldiers, signed by Chkheidze, the head of the S-D group in the Duma.[1]

March 15 was a day of universal jubilation in Irkutsk. Meetings were held on street corners. Crowds with red flags marched in the streets to the tunes of revolutionary hymns. The police disappeared. The citizens themselves maintained order. During that day a score of labor unions were founded, and all political parties formed local chapters to elect representatives to the Citizens' Committee. In the evening the Committee convened in the Municipal Hall. Tseretelli was elected its chairman. Telegrams from Petrograd, mutual congratulations . . . delegations claiming seats in the Committee. . . . The delegation of the Orthodox Church was particularly impressive. Speaking for twenty-four parishes, it asked for forty-eight seats in the Committee but was satisfied when the chair recognized the clergy as a professional group and assigned them one seat, along with one seat to the lawyers, one to the physicians, and one to the teachers. After midnight the regiments located around Irkutsk converged on the Municipal Building to express their devotion to the revolution and their loyalty to the Citizens' Committee.

The next morning we received a telegram from the new Minister of Justice, announcing amnesty for all political prisoners. The telegram was signed by Kerensky, chairman of the Labor Group in the last Duma.

I spent the day at the local jail, supervising the release of political prisoners. Shelter was to be provided for them. Some twenty Anarchists asked to be housed together, and the Citizens' Committee assigned a vacant school building to them. They at once hung out a red flag proclaiming: "Away with the war!" A rumor spread that the school building housed German spies. Soldiers from nearby barracks suggested shooting them, and others wanted to burn the school. Someone called up the Citizens' Committee. Just back from the jail, I rushed to the spot, explained to the excited crowd that the Anarchists were cranks rather than traitors, and persuaded the Anarchists to take the flag down.

That day I heard many soldiers say, "Now the power is ours!" They sounded, however, as if they were not quite sure of themselves. On March 17 a group of soldiers came to the Citizens' Committee. A young lieutenant presented their grievances. Their main demand was to demote the officers whom they did not trust and replace them by officers elected from the ranks. Facing Tseretelli, the young man

[1] I am using the Western (new style) calendar, which antedates the Russian (old style) calendar by thirteen days. The early days of March, according to the new calendar, fell at the end of February in the old-style calendar. Therefore Russian writers often describe the revolution in March (new style) as the "February Revolution."

shouted, "The soldiers will not stand for abuses any longer. They are in power now!"

Tseretelli replied firmly, "Yes, you, the armed forces of our country, have power so long as you serve your country. But if you try to put your own desires above the will of the people, you will become a handful of rebels. Therefore do not talk about your power when you are presenting your complaints to the civil authorities." Tseretelli's words greatly impressed the soldiers, and they assured him of their loyalty. "There are always some complaints in the barracks," they said, "but to the soldiers the Citizens' Committee is like God in Heaven."

The same day a dozen officers came to the Committee to report the enlisted men's growing distrust of the commanders. They recommended that a military parade be held on Cathedral Plaza. The district commander approved the plan and the parade was called for March 19. The day was sunny and frosty. The troops were received by the district commander surrounded by his staff, all on horseback. The Committee's presiding board stood some ten steps away. The soldiers stood at attention while Tseretelli harangued them.

"It has been reported to the Citizens' Committee that the soldiers of the Irkutsk garrison do not trust their officers. The army cannot exist if enlisted men distrust their superiors and officers distrust their men. In the future only officers who enjoy the confidence of the revolutionary government will serve in the army. The district commander will continue in command as long as we trust him. But as long as he holds his post, we demand that you, the soldiers, execute all his orders."

The soldiers answered with the customary "Hurrah!" Then the regiments passed in ceremonial review before the commander. Custom required that the colonel commanding each regiment present his outfit to the reviewing general and join the latter's staff, while the regiment proceeded to the barracks under the command of a subordinate officer. The colonel who headed the first regiment stopped briskly in front of the district commander, saluted him with his saber, then turned around, saluted the presiding board of the Citizens' Committee, and resolutely strode over to us. Other colonels followed his example. By the end of the review we were surrounded by officers. The district commander seemed to have been forgotten.

That evening a large delegation of officers came to our quarters and explained that, so far as the officers were concerned, the demonstration was premeditated. The garrison distrusted the district commander as a "political" general. The delegation begged the Committee to have him replaced by a colonel, a hero of the Russo-Japanese War who had been repeatedly decorated for his valor and was senior to the present district commander in years of service. The next day the

Committee ordered the district commander to turn over his command to the colonel and wired the Provisional Government in Petrograd to ask confirmation.

Meanwhile soldiers elected their regimental committees and a Soviet of Workers was formed in the city. Since there were no large factories in Irkutsk, the Soviet did not arouse much public interest. Soldiers' regimental committees gravitated to the Citizens' Committee. Moreover, the Soviet itself recognized the Committee as the highest local authority and asked only for representation in it. The composition of the Committee had changed. The members of the old Municipal Council and representatives of liberal professions were now in the minority, while the representatives of workers and soldiers formed the majority. Politically, the organization was dominated by moderate Socialists, with Tseretelli as their leader.

On March 20, in view of alarming rumors, the Committee decided to put the local high officials of the old regime under house arrest. When the Committee's representative went to Pilz's mansion to announce this decision, the deposed Governor General thanked him for protection and requested as a favor that the number of guards assigned to him be doubled.

The Provisional Government asked all the old officials to continue their work, but most of them did not know how to handle the new situation. The District Attorney wanted to know in whose name the courts should announce their decisions. The Bishop, surrounded by church dignitaries, asked what to substitute for the prayer for the Tsar in church service. He offered a new version: "Lord bless the rightful rulers of the country." We approved it.

Developments in Irkutsk in these days were typical of the Russian provinces. Everywhere the people accepted the change in power whole-heartedly. Everywhere the troops declared allegiance to the new order, and the elected representatives of various groups took over the local government. After the overthrow of the Tsarist government in Petrograd, local authorities surrendered without the slightest attempt to resist. Violence and vengeance were rare. The old regime had collapsed like a tower of playing cards. Everywhere the victory of the new order was celebrated joyously. In two respects, however, the situation in Irkutsk differed from that in other provincial cities. First, the Citizens' Committee represented a very broad coalition; second, it was led by political exiles, involuntary guests of Siberia who were more interested in national and international political problems than in local issues.

Very soon we confronted the problem of war and peace. The soldiers and officers asked us whether their regiments should send to the front the "marching companies" that had completed the requisite training. The railroad workers asked whether they should stop the trains with munitions arriving from Vladivostok or expedite their progress westward.

Without hesitation, we embraced the policy of national defense, stressing that the revolution had fundamentally changed the character of the war. The free people of Russia were no longer bound by the designs of the Tsarist government but had their own stake in the war. A victorious Germany would eventually restore the Tsar's power. The aim of free Russia was a just peace, but to achieve it the nation had to be strong and ready for sacrifices. We realized, of course, that this policy required elaboration and must include measures to promote a just peace, but in Irkutsk we had no opportunity to work out such measures. The political platform of the moderate Socialists who controlled the Citizens' Committee was formulated by Tseretelli and became known far beyond Siberia as a further development of the ideas of the Siberian Zimmerwaldist group.

RETURN TO PETROGRAD

Emma learned of the revolution en route from Irkutsk to Petrograd. She wanted to return, but the rails had been cut behind the train and she had to go westward. At the stations she saw jubilant crowds, people bewildered by the whirlwind of rumors and conflicting news. She found Petrograd in the same state of jubilation and confusion.

I left Irkutsk on March 24 with two score other political exiles. Our train was known officially as "the Train of the Deputies of the Second Duma," and its locomotive carried red banners with appropriate legends, but actually it was an ordinary train with two special cars for the exiles. The Citizens' Committee had made Tseretelli and me its emissaries to the Provisional Government.

The journey took ten days. We saw red flags and huge crowds at each station—peasants, soldiers, workers. The air was full of jubilation without a single discordant note. The people seemed united in devotion to the revolution. I had a vague feeling of uneasiness and apprehension, however, and asked myself how deep this enthusiasm was and how long it would last.

It took the newspapers eight or nine days to get from Petrograd or Moscow to Irkutsk. In Siberia we had only glimpses of current events from telegrams and learned details from the newspapers days later, when the news seemed old stuff. Now, traveling westward, we could absorb two days' information each day. Gradually the early days of the revolution began to emerge from the fog.

THE FIRST DAYS OF THE REVOLUTION
IN PETROGRAD

The revolt had come almost as unexpectedly to the political parties, the Duma, and the government in Petrograd as to us in Irkutsk. The murder of Rasputin—December 17, 1916—had been a mortal blow for the Romanov dynasty. Many conservatives believed that a palace revolution was the only way to prevent the overthrow of the monarchy by a popular uprising that would bring radical elements to power. But then it was too late.

On March 8 riots broke out in Petrograd with a street demonstration of seventy to eighty thousand striking workers in the outskirts of the city. At its start crowds of workers milled about in the streets, while queues of women lined the sidewalks before the grocery shops and bakeries. Neither queues nor demonstrations were an unusual sight in Petrograd, but on that day the women joined the demonstrations and the angry crowds began to snowball. Slogans demanding "Bread! Higher wages!" appeared from nowhere over the crowds. Some bakeries were raided. Thousands of workers went into the streets to manifest their sympathy with the strikers. Before evening, new slogans floated in the air: "Away with the police! Away with Tsarism! Away with the war!" But unrest was still limited to the industrial outskirts of the capital, and the newspapers described it as a local, non-political affair.

On March 9 disorder continued on a large scale and spread to other parts of the city. Striking workers demanded higher wages to compensate for the rise in the price of bread. Crowds of strikers invaded the center of the city, where they were joined by the students. More bakeries were raided, and revolutionary slogans and outcries were seen and heard everywhere. But the government was slow to realize the seriousness of the situation and made no attempt to quell or localize the unrest. Nor was any step taken to negotiate with the strikers.

On March 10 the strike became general. Though its purpose was to protest against low wages and high prices, many banners bore the slogan "Away with war!" Police posts were withdrawn and the angry crowds rolled through the capital unopposed. They stopped in front of police stations, broke in, manhandled the officers, took their arms, and moved on.

Cossacks were sent to clear the streets in the center of the city. In several places they refused to obey the order to charge. Some left their outfits and joined the workers. By evening the Cossacks had become the people's heroes. Events had gotten out of the hands of civil and military authorities, and the Minister of the Interior sent a telegram asking instructions from Nicholas, who was then at army headquarters at Mogilev. The Tsar replied: First, dissolve the Duma, the main source of trouble; second, suppress the riots at any cost, with full use of military force.

Rumors circulated that the Duma refused to adjourn, but actually it decided to obey the Tsar's order although its members remained in Petrograd for "private conferences." The committee of these conferences later became known as the Temporary Committee of the Duma.

To execute the Tsar's second order, the Military Governor of Petrograd summoned several regiments of the Imperial Guard to Nevsky Prospect. The troops were ordered to fire and the crowds were mowed down and scattered, but this was a Pyrrhic victory for the government.

Rumors of the massacre spread throughout the city, arousing public wrath. During the night groups of workers went from barracks to barracks urging the soldiers to join the people. The soldiers promised to turn their guns against the officers should these order them to fire against the people. Excitement grew among the troops. That night was decisive. Between sunset of March 11 and dawn of March 12, the Petrograd garrison joined the revolt. Then and there local disorders became a revolution.

On March 12 the Military Governor had no time to think of dispersing the crowds in the streets. His most urgent task was to prevent an open uprising in the garrison. A hand-picked task force was sent to the barracks to arrest the ringleaders. The force departed in good order but never reached its destination. Men began to drop out of the ranks to plunge into the crowds on the sidewalks. The few who remained in formation warned the officer that they would not fire and were ordered back to their quarters.

Before noon, soldiers of several regiments broke into the arsenals, took arms, and assembled on the parade grounds, ready to march. They did not know where to go but they wanted to join the people. Two regiments—Volynsky and Litovsky—started almost simultaneously to march toward the Tauride Palace. Policemen were shot down in the streets. Armed crowds broke into the Crosses and other jails and liberated political prisoners and many common criminals as well. The courthouse and the headquarters of the political police (Ochrana) were set on fire. There was strong suspicion that the burning of the latter building with all its archives was instigated by agents of the old regime.

The government disintegrated. Some cabinet members thought of resisting from the Winter Palace but abandoned this plan and went into hiding. The entire city was in the hands of mutinous soldiers. Throngs of them, some with fixed bayonets covered with the blood of their officers, converged on the Tauride Palace, which attracted them as the seat of the Duma and still more as the headquarters of the newly formed Soviet of Workers. Under the white colonnade of the Palace the regiments were met by Rodzianko, the stout reactionary president of the Duma, and Chkheidze, chairman of the Soviet. One regiment after another passed in front of the Palace and asked Chkheidze to admit their representatives to the Soviet, which at once became the Soviet of Workers *and Soldiers.*

Neither the Tsar nor the members of the Duma realized the meaning of these events. The Tsar believed he could save his throne by sending troops from Mogilev to reconquer Petrograd. The Duma believed it could save the monarchy by persuading Nicholas to abdicate in favor of another member of his family. Actually the Duma had as little control over events as the Tsar.

On March 14, Kronstadt revolted. The sailors massacred their officers. The Moscow garrison came into the streets to proclaim its devotion to the revolution. The Tsar left Mogilev for Tsarskoe Selo, but his train was stopped by railroad workers at a small station, Dno (Bottom), and later moved to a siding in Pskov. Actually a prisoner in his own train, Nicholas summoned Rodzianko to an audience, considering making him the head of the new Cabinet, but Rodzianko could not reach Pskov: the railroad workers refused to provide a train for him without a safe-conduct and an order from the Soviet.

On March 15, Rodzianko obtained the Soviet's permission to go to see the Tsar, but it was too late for them to discuss the appointment of a new Cabinet. In the evening the Tsar received the Duma representatives in his stranded train and agreed to abdicate in favor of his brother, Grand Duke Mikhail. The Duma circles were confident that they would stop the revolution by enthroning a new Tsar.

This plan, however, provoked outbursts of indignation among Petrograd workers and soldiers. A group of officers appeared in the Tauride Palace and told the Duma Committee that any attempt to restore the monarchy would cause violence in the garrison and endanger the lives of the officers. Even if a new Tsar were enthroned, his overthrow would be only a matter of hours. The abdication by Mikhail the next day was a pure formality that did not change the course of events an iota. The reign of the Romanovs was ended not by the abdications of Nicholas and Mikhail but by a national revolution spearheaded by the workers and soldiers in Petrograd. The deposed Tsar was brought to Tsarskoe Selo and imprisoned in a suite of rooms in his palace.

Out of these events emerged the Provisional Government and the

Soviet of Workers and Soldiers—the two bodies destined to play the leading roles in the developing drama.

THE PROVISIONAL GOVERNMENT

As early as 1916, when there were rumors of an imminent palace revolution, some journalists used to speculate on what kind of government setup the public would accept. Several lists of hypothetical cabinets, under Nicholas' successor, circulated in political circles. Most of them included the names of a few moderate and liberal members of the Duma and a few old-school bureaucrats who had not been directly associated with Rasputin and were therefore considered liberals.

In the hectic days of the revolution, the Temporary Duma Committee fell back on one such list. In view of the changed situation, the old bureaucrats were dropped and Cabinet posts were offered to Chkheidze and Kerensky. Chkheidze rejected the offer in order to remain at the head of the Soviet; Kerensky accepted despite his party's objections.

The list of members of the Cabinet had been drawn up before the Soviet informed the Temporary Duma Committee that it wished to discuss the conditions under which it would support the new government. At the joint session on the evening of March 14, the Soviet delegates, headed by Chkheidze, presented a platform of eight points and the Duma Committee accepted it with only minor verbal changes. Thus was the program of the Provisional Government established: 1. Full amnesty for all political, religious, and military prisoners; 2. Freedom of speech and the press, freedom to unionize and to strike, with extension of political rights to men in the armed forces; 3. Abolition of all class, religious, and national discriminations; 4. Immediate preparation for democratic elections to the Constituent Assembly; 5. Creation of a people's militia to replace the police; 6. Democratic elections of local governments; 7. A pledge not to disarm or remove from Petrograd troops that had participated in the revolution; 8. All rights enjoyed by other citizens to be accorded to soldiers not on active duty.

Two features were striking in the negotiations between the Duma Committee and the Petrograd Soviet. First, the new government had no program of its own but merely underwrote the platform of the Soviet; second, the Soviet's platform was a makeshift job, concocted in a hurry. It omitted any reference to such fundamental problems as war and peace, industrial relations and labor conditions, the distribution of land among the peasants, and other economic measures. Indeed, it was not a statement of national policy but, rather, an agreement on certain points of immediate concern to both parties. Strangely enough, this lopsided document became the only declaration of the intentions of the Provisional Government.

The Soviet published an appeal to the soldiers and the people (agreed upon in advance with the government) stressing the democratic character of the government's program and promising to support the Cabinet "so far as it executes its commitments and fights against the old regime." A government so formed could not pretend to be legitimate in any sense of the word. Its only basis was the agreement between the Duma Committee and the Soviet.

PUZZLES OF SOVIET POLICY

The Petrograd Soviet was the center of the revolutionary storm. It had invested the Provisional Government with power and determined its platform. However, its own position on the question of power—the cardinal question of any revolution—was as puzzling as its own political program. After its abortive attempt to saddle the country with a new Tsar, the Duma Committee was thoroughly discredited in the eyes of the overwhelming majority of the people. All strength lay in the hands of the groups gravitating to the Soviet. But the Soviet's leaders were reluctant to accept even partial responsibility for the government, and preferred to establish a Cabinet consisting of elements foreign to them and even hostile to the revolution, reserving for themselves the role of vigilant watchdogs.

In retrospect, I think they chose the wrong road. A strong and stable government could have been formed after the March revolution only on the basis of co-operation between the revolutionary, democratic forces represented by the Soviet and the progressive elements of the Duma—that is, on the basis of a political coalition of the left. Did the leaders of the Soviet fear that, once in the government, they would be under overwhelming pressure of the masses and compelled to go further than the circumstances—primarily the war inherited from the old regime—would permit? Or was their decision determined by psychological factors? The second seems more likely. Most of the Soviet leaders had come up in underground work against the Tsarist regime and were accustomed to look upon government, courts, coercion, police, and other attributes of authority as evils. They had no will to power and found it difficult to visualize themselves in the role of ministers.

I did not realize then how grave a mistake the Soviet leaders had made, but as we journeyed toward Petrograd I felt very keenly that the Soviet was drifting rudderless in the storm. Its paper, *Izvestia*, presented a chaotic agglomeration of appeals, resolutions, and articles, without any leading idea except glorification of the revolution. On the same page it called on the people to maintain order and demanded that the Provisional Government permit any citizen to kill any counterrevolutionary general on sight. Patriotic and even chauvinist resolutions passed by individual factories and military units appeared alongside demands for immediate peace at any price. It was impossible to delineate the policy of the Soviet in this chorus of divergent claims. All this was disturbing, and by the end of the trip I felt more confused than elated. I observed a similar mood in other returning exiles.

We reached Petrograd on the rainy morning of April 2. The Soviet had planned a reception for the members of the Second Duma, with flags, bands, and speeches, but the train was seventeen hours late and only Emma and my mother were waiting for it on the nearly empty platform of the shabby and dirty station. We went to my parents' apartment. The family reunion fell short of my anticipations. All of us had changed. We had much to tell and to ask one another after the ten years I had spent in prison and exile, but events had stunned us, and we could not at once pick up the threads of old times. I felt as if I did not belong to myself, and my parents took it for granted that I would not have much time for them. Emma's impressions of Petrograd were as discouraging as those I had from reading newspapers and *Izvestia*. She also was full of concern about what was going on. After a brief exchange of thoughts with her I went to the Tauride Palace.

THE TAURIDE PALACE

The Palace had been built by Prince Potemkin, the famous favorite of Katherine the Great, to celebrate the conquest of the Crimea (Tauride). Katherine Hall, its immense ballroom—designed to accommodate twenty thousand dancers, according to legend—looked like a combination of a crowded marketplace and a military camp. Thousands of persons sat and lay on the floor along the walls— peasants, sailors, soldiers with their rifles in piles. Here and there people pressed around a speaker. Processions were coming and going with flags and bands. The air was full of smoke, steam, and deafening noise.

I met Chkheidze in his office. A small elderly man, with gray hair and beard, he sat quietly at the huge desk, wearing a heavy overcoat with a fur collar. Sick and dead-tired, he listened patiently to what Soviet officials reported to him but did not talk much. When he did speak, it was mostly, "We shall look into the matter," or "Thank you," or "This can wait." He asked me to join the Executive Committee of the Soviet as the editor of *Izvestia.* "The paper is a disgrace," he said. "Maybe you can clean up the mess."

I spent the afternoon wandering in noisy Katherine Hall and strolling from office to office. In many I saw old companions of the first revolution, but new faces predominated. Politically, I felt somewhat a stranger. Remembering 1905, the leaders of the left wing of the Soviet expected me to join them and were eager to take me around and unburden themselves of political gossip. They were shocked when they discovered that I considered national defense, strengthening of the army, and self-restraint of workers essential to the consolidation of democracy in Russia. The revolution had erased former distinctions between the parties. There were "former Bolsheviks" who felt the demand of the present hour just as I felt it, and "former Mensheviks" who were intoxicated by revolutionary phraseology and talked a language repulsive to me.

That evening the workers' section of the Soviet convened in the former session room of the Duma. At first the discussion was disappointingly dull; the delegates sat silent, as if bored. Then Chkheidze announced that the members of the Second Duma had returned from Siberia. The meeting gave them a standing ovation. Tseretelli mounted the rostrum. Calling for unity of all progressive forces of the nation, he stressed the danger of isolation of the revolutionary advance guard. A large part of his address elaborated the tasks of foreign policy. The speech was a tremendous success. A few hours after his return from exile, Tseretelli was again the recognized national spokesman of democracy.

The Soviet was a loose and shapeless organization. I do not know whether it had any bylaws, except for the basis of representation of workers and soldiers. It consisted of a workers' section and a soldiers' section. The joint session was supposed to amount to a revolutionary parliament. Actually, it was a mass meeting reflecting the predominant moods of the masses but unable to work out political decisions. Policy-making was in the hands of the Executive Committee, a body of some fifty or sixty members, almost as shapeless as the Soviet. Sometimes it was in session from ten o'clock in the morning till late at night. No agenda were prepared in advance. Discussion of political problems was interrupted continually by the arrival of delegations and emergency telephone calls. Decisions were often voted without a clear understanding of their implications.

In the first days of the revolution the Soviet was dominated by left-wing journalists who did not identify themselves with the Bolsheviks but leaned strongly toward them. The majority of the Soviet, while applauding their oratory, did not share their radicalism. Chkheidze was probably the best exponent of the more moderate views, but he was a poor speaker and, as the chairman of the organization, he was reluctant to express himself on controversial issues and to enforce any particular policy. Tseretelli, who was politically very close to him but could formulate and defend his views with greater vigor, became the leader of the majority in the Soviet. His strength was not only in his exceptional oratorical ability—he was the best speaker in the Russian revolution in 1917—but also in clear and forceful political thinking and personal integrity that commanded respect even from his political enemies. But he was more a bard of the revolution than an organizer of victory and, like most Russian intellectuals, he was better in defending the principles he cherished than in fitting them to the cruel realities of life.

Under the influence of Tseretelli, a realignment began in the Soviet and the Executive Committee. The cleavage between the right and left wings became deeper and clearer. At the beginning, the right wing seemed firmly united while the left wing had no leadership and no unity of purpose. The situation changed a month later, after the arrival of Lenin.

CONFLICT OF POWERS

Russia was in poor shape when Tsarism collapsed. A sizable part of its territory was occupied by the Germans; the army was disorganized; the people were yearning for peace; peasants were demanding immediate redistribution of land; economic life was out of balance. To solve these and other problems, the country needed a strong government that inspired the people's confidence. Unfortunately, the Provisional Government could not meet this requirement. The masses of the people had confidence only in the Soviets and committees they had elected. Each city and each village had its own Soviet. In contrast to the organizations thus named under the Communist dictatorship later, these were freely elected councils close to the people. In the absence of other public authorities, some provincial Soviets acted as local governments, issuing regulations, appointing police officers, and so forth. Even when they did not share in such functions, the Soviets had tremendous moral and political power.

On the other hand, the Provisional Government was too closely associated with the Tsarist Duma and the old regime to command the people's respect. Workers, soldiers, and peasants simply could not understand why they should obey this group of individuals. Facing an order emanating from the new government, they would ask their Soviet whether they should execute it. Once they had obtained assurance that the order was all right, they complied because of their confidence in their elected representatives. After pledging its support to the Provisional Government, the Petrograd Soviet tried to endorse governmental orders in advance by saying to the people, "As long as the Soviet supports the government, you must execute its orders as if they came from us." Such a blanket endorsement often proved insufficient, however, so that the Soviet had to reiterate the general rule time and again with regard to specific governmental orders. Thus masses of the people became more and more convinced that the authority of the Provisional Government depended wholly on Soviet support, which was partly true although the government tried to forget this hard reality.

Moreover, in the turmoil of the first days of the revolution, when there was no public authority in the country, the Soviet had issued proclamations and orders that should have come from the government, and these orders could not be repealed without provoking serious trouble and possible outbursts of violence. The most significant of these were the "Order Number 1" to the Petrograd garrison and the "Message to All Peoples of the World."

"Order Number 1" was issued on March 14 in an effort to restore discipline in the Petrograd garrison. Its chief purpose was to remind the soldiers that they had to obey the orders of the civil authorities. As such an authority, the Soviet ordered the soldiers to elect regimental and company committees, send representatives to the Tauride Palace, and follow the instructions of the Soviet and their elected committees in all political actions. It further prescribed execution of service orders of the Duma Committee (unless contradictory to the Soviet's orders) and instructed the elected committees to keep control over the arms of their respective military units. It demanded, further, observance of strict military discipline in service while stating at the same time that soldiers out of service were entitled to all civil rights. This order was issued before the Provisional Government was formed and therefore could not be described as a case of diarchy. But without power to repeal it, the government, military High Command, and conservative circles continued to regard Order No. 1 as a thorn in the flesh.

The other act branded as diarchy by the rightist groups was an appeal to the people of the world issued by the Soviet on March 27:

Conscious of its revolutionary power, Russian democracy declares that it will oppose the aggressive policy of the ruling classes by all means at its disposal and calls on the peoples of Europe to joint action in favor of peace. . . . We address ourselves to our brothers, workers of the German-Austrian coalition. . . . We shall firmly defend our freedom against any reactionary assault from within and without. The Russian Revolution will not retreat in the face of bayonets and will not yield to foreign military power. But we call [on the peoples of Austria and Germany] to break the yoke of their half-despotic governments, as the people of Russia have broken the yoke of Tsarism. Refuse to serve as a tool of conquest and oppression in the hands of your kings, landowners and bankers, and together we will put an end to the war, that terrible carnage, the disgrace of mankind, that darkens the bright days of the birth of freedom in Russia.

The foreign policy proclaimed in this message was unacceptable to the Provisional Government. However, the Petrograd Soviet, like any other organization, was entitled to proclaim its view on the war without interfering with the affairs of the government.

In general, diarchy consisted not in this or that act of the Soviet but in the fact that it had more prestige and more power than the government. The conservative press stressed the fundamental difference between the government and the Soviet. The first represented the nation as a whole, while the latter was a "private organization." Yet this "private organization" was elected by many hundred thousands of workers and soldiers and commanded their loyalty, while the government's power rested on the agreement between the Duma Committee and this private organization. It could not remain in power without the latter's active support.

This was one of the most serious problems confronting the Petrograd Soviet and its Executive Committee. We could not compel the masses of workers and soldiers to trust such members of the Provisional Government as the Minister of Foreign Affairs, Miliukov, or the War Minister, Guchkov. We could only assure the people that we supported the government on the basis of the agreed program and would support it so long as the government honored its commitments. But the conservatives were not satisfied with this conditional support. Their aim was to eliminate the elected councils (Soviets) from public life, and they were confident that the people, deprived of the advice of their representatives, would sooner or later turn to them and learn to consider them as rulers of the country.

The irony of the situation was that the democratic forces represented in the Soviets were fully responsible for the weakness of the Provisional Government. They had weakened it not by interfering with its activities but by declining to participate in it in the early days of the revolution. They might have corrected this mistake by taking the initiative in reorganizing the government on the basis of a coalition and accelerating the convocation of the Constituent Assembly. A workable electoral law could have been drafted in a few weeks. Preparations for an election could have been completed in two months. Thus a Constituent Assembly could have convened in June. It is interesting to speculate what would have been the course of events in Russia and abroad if a strong Provisional Government with a vigorous participation of democratic groups had taken over the helm after the March revolution; and if this government had succeeded in convoking the Constituent Assembly and transferring power to a regular government in, say, four or five months.

THE POLITICAL PARTIES

The lack of consistency in the policy of the Soviets was due partly to the split in the political parties of the left. Formally, there were two leftist parties on the scene—the Socialist Revolutionary party, which had absorbed the bulk of the former Laborites, and the Social Democratic party. The latter had definitely split between the Mensheviks and the Bolsheviks. The Bolsheviks represented the extreme left in the Soviets, while the S-R and Mensheviks formed the center and right wing. This block, however, was split among half a dozen or more loosely defined groups. Tseretelli, with his desire to ensure democratic peace and his opposition to the annexationist policy of the Cadets, was not patriotic enough for the moderate Laborites, now representing the right wing of the S-R party, while the left elements of the same party considered his policy too nationalistic and contrary to international socialism. Actually the moderate socialist majority in the Petrograd Soviet was a loose agglomeration of members of several groups.

My own position in this political spectrum was close to the center—or perhaps somewhat right of center—of the majority of the Executive Committee. However, during my first two or three weeks in Petrograd I remained in touch with dissident Bolsheviks whom I tried to win to the policy of national defense. Later I shared with the Menshevist leader Dan the responsibility of editing *Izvestia*, writing resolutions and appeals for the Soviet, and interpreting its decisions in editorials. Dan wrote articles and declarations explaining our policy in terms of the party program. I tried to reach a broader audience of workers and soldiers. Although we generally agreed on political matters, we were too different temperamentally to find pleasure in our close association.

MEETINGS AND SPEECHES

As it had been a decade earlier, political life in Petrograd was marked by meetings and speeches. Along with other tasks, my duty was to present the views of the Executive Committee to crowds in concert halls and theaters, military barracks and factories.

The meetings in the theaters and concert halls were usually organized by the Cadets, largely for anti-Soviet progaganda. However, the prestige of the Petrograd Soviet was so strong that the audience would be disappointed if no Soviet speaker appeared on the scene. Here politics was mixed with entertainment. It seemed absurd to me to be sandwiched into a program between a tenor in a dinner jacket and a glamorous soprano, but that was the style of the time. The star of the concert-hall meetings was Kerensky. Occasionally the front row showered him with flowers; he would pick up red roses, press them to his heart, and throw them back to the public. This also was part of the style of the time.

The meetings in barracks were restrained and sometimes outwardly dull, but they had a tragic undertone for me. Their purpose was political education. The soldiers—sometimes three thousand men or more—seemed friendly, even sentimental, but I often felt a wall between them and myself. The first words of the speaker, usually greeting the listeners in the name of the Executive Committee of the Soviet, invariably got noisy applause. But the questions of the audience after the speaker's address often revealed the hidden discontent among the troops: "When will the war end?" "Why should we reinforce the front now that the Soviet has offered peace to all peoples?" "Why do the officers who opposed the revolution remain in command?" "Why should we carry on drill training?"

Order and discipline among the troops were maintained by regimental committees elected during the first days of the revolution and manned by those who first grasped the situation and could explain it to their comrades. Often these were intellectuals—army clerks, pharmacists, and volunteers who had joined the army for patriotic reasons, most of them excellent people with a sense of responsibility for the morale and fighting spirit of the army. They were the bulwark of order in the new army, and I was surprised to discover that officers looked upon them with suspicion and poorly hidden hostility.

The factory meetings were different. The Soviet representatives usually shared the platform with spokesmen of the leftist opposition. The latter did not attack the Soviet directly. Rather, they "deplored" the hesitation and weakness of its majority. We had the whip hand in these meetings, but very soon our influence began to weaken.

In the first days of the revolution the Soviet had decreed the eight-hour workday. A few weeks later the new arrangement was formalized by an agreement between the Soviet representatives and the association of manufacturers. Factory councils were established and employers, scared by the revolution, were ready to make any concessions to the workers. But prices outran wage increases, there was a shortage of almost all goods, and the living conditions of a working family in May or June were no better than in March, when angry crowds had milled about in the streets of Petrograd demanding bread and higher wages. The Bolsheviks exploited this situation and succeeded in inciting strikes, mostly in public services and transport.

Suddenly frictions developed between the workers and soldiers at the front. The reactionary press had opened a campaign aimed to turn the army against the Petrograd workers. It spread the story that the March strikes had been instigated and financed by Germany. The officers at the front told the soldiers that the workers in the capital were loafing and sabotaging defense. Delegates of regiments at the front came to Petrograd to check these charges. They met with a cold and sometimes hostile reception and went back with resentment against the workers. Angry resolutions from the front poured into the Tauride Palace.

Workers in the munitions factories visited by such delegations asked the Executive Committee to do something against the counter-revolutionary propaganda at the front. The first measure was naturally to have a representative of the Executive Committee at the meetings of workers and delegates from the front. A crowd of soldiers would invade a munitions factory at night to check on the work of the night shift. The workers would telephone to the Tauride Palace, the operator would transfer the call to Chkheidze, and the latter would call me with apologies, explaining that there was no reason, of course, for my going to that particular meeting, but, if I were not too tired, my presence there would be a great help. I would drive to the factory, usually at about three o'clock in the morning. All work would have been suspended; the workers would be assembled in the court, nervous and angry, facing grim, suspicious, and often arrogant soldiers. There was no way to find out what kind of delegates they were. They looked like men from the trenches, but usually they had no credentials. My function was not to investigate the charges but to reconcile the two parties, explaining to the workers the source of the soldiers' suspicions of them and making it clear to the soldiers that slanderous rumors about the workers were spread by reactionaries for political purposes.

I felt that the tired, embittered, and angry soldiers were victims of demagogic propaganda. They might curse the workers for having an easier life than they had in the trenches and repeat the nonsense about German money as the cause of the March upheaval, but by no stretch of imagination could I visualize them siding with Guchkov or Miliukov and helping the reactionaries destroy the new order.

The Soldiers' Section decided on a large-scale goodwill campaign at the front. Delegations from large mills and factories in Petrograd were sent to the front with gifts from workers to the men in the trenches, as an expression of solidarity between the two groups. The delegations were instructed to distribute the gifts personally to each company. The campaign went on for several weeks and reached the most remote sections of the front. Friction between the soldiers in the trenches and workers was not completely eliminated, but angry soldier delegations disappeared from the Petrograd scene. By this time, however, night meetings in factories and military barracks had become routine in Petrograd, and I had more than my fair share of emergency calls after midnight.

THE CAMPAIGN FOR PEACE AND NATIONAL DEFENSE

The response to the message the Petrograd Soviet had addressed to workers and Socialist parties abroad was disappointing. Within Russia the reaction was mixed. The great majority of the public understood the message as a demand that the Provisional Government renounce the aims for which the Tsarist government had waged the war, such as the acquisition of the Dardanelles and Constantinople, the old dream of Russian nationalists. The masses of the people—peasants, workers, soldiers—instinctively approved scrapping all Russia's territorial aspirations. On the other hand, the conservatives were enraged by the desire of the Soviet to dictate foreign policy to the government.

There was no evidence that German and Austrian workers took the message of the Soviet seriously. In contrast, the German High Command answered it with a promise that its troops would not fire at Russian positions so long as the Russians did not attack. The purpose of this offer was clear: a *de facto* truce on the eastern front would facilitate Germany's operations in the West.

The French and British governments considered the Soviet's appeal a threat to their plans. After the heavy reverses in 1915 and 1916, both countries had planned to prosecute the war with increasing vigor, counting on the eventual entry of the United States into the conflict. A possible withdrawal of Russia from the Alliance would have been a serious blow to their strategy, and they saw no reason to change their diplomacy and revise treaties to appease the revolutionaries in Petrograd. Their policy toward Russia was rather to keep her in the war as long as possible and obtain her maximum military support. With this purpose in view the Allied governments, in addition to working through the usual diplomatic channels, entered into direct contact with the Soviet through the representatives of the Socialist parties in the war cabinets.

The Socialists in the European Allied and neutral nations were split. The "majorities" supported the war efforts of their governments, the "minorities" opposed the war, and their extreme left-wing groups followed a defeatist policy. When the Soviet called on the Socialist parties of the Allied nations for joint action to achieve a just peace, it had in view chiefly the right-wing Socialists represented in those governments. But the latter would not side with the Petrograd Soviet without the consent of their governments, and these would not act against the desires of the Provisional Government in Russia. Thus the success of the campaign launched by the Soviet depended, from the very beginning, on the position taken by the Provisional Government.

On the initiative of Tseretelli, the Executive Committee of the Soviet therefore asked the government to renounce officially, in the name of Russia, the imperialist aims of the war and to request the Allies to do the same. This demand met with violent opposition from Miliukov, who believed that the overthrow of the Tsar ought not to affect Russia's foreign policy. But the President of the Government, Prince Lvov, agreed with Tseretelli, and on April 10 the Provisional Government published a declaration of foreign policy in which it stated that the aim of free Russia was not domination over other nations or acquisition of new territory but a durable peace based on the right of all nations to self-determination.

From the point of view of the Soviet, this vague statement could be interpreted as a step toward a peace policy. The problem had another aspect, however. Russia could exert influence on the policy of other belligerent nations only so long as she herself remained belligerent. Disintegration of her armies would force her to sign a separate peace or truce with Germany (which reputedly had been Rasputin's plan), and that would end her participation in the Concert of European Great Powers. Thus the policy of a just democratic peace demanded a vigorous policy of national defense.

This aspect of a peace policy was brought to the attention of the leaders of the Petrograd Soviet at the All-Russian Convention of Soviets that opened in the Tauride Palace on the day the Provisional Government issued its foreign policy declaration. The convention was poorly prepared and politically confused. Its only outstanding feature was the reports of the army representatives. Conditions at the front were alarming, they told the convention. The morale of the troops had been very low even before the fall of the Tsar. Then the revolution created a vacuum in the psychology of the soldiers, whose military indoctrination was based on allegiance to the Tsar. After the Tsar was deposed, only new ideas could hold the army together. A new peace policy could be the answer. The task was to make it clear to the soldiers that the revolution had changed the war objectives radically. The campaign for the army's revival was to be merged with the peace campaign.

Tseretelli was the keynote speaker on national defense. I had to draft the resolution stressing the role of a strong army in the defense of the revolution. "As long as the war lasts," I wrote, "weakening the army's capacity for active operations would be a blow to freedom and vital interests of the nation. For the purpose of effective defense of revolutionary Russia against aggression, the people of Russia must mobilize all their force to strengthen the front and rear."

This draft, violently assailed from the left as militaristic drum-beating, found warm support among the representatives of the front organizations and the resolution was carried by an overwhelming majority. Of eighty delegates who called themselves Bolsheviks, thirty voted for the resolution. Its significance lay in the fact that it committed the Petrograd Soviet to a definite policy not only toward the front army but also toward the rear garrisons, and especially the Petrograd garrison.

Most of the regiments in the capital were "reserve" regiments, designed for training recruits and providing reinforcements to the front—usually entire companies with equipment and officers. This practice was interrupted by the March revolution. Since that time, in view of the revolutionary reputation of the Petrograd garrison, commanders at the front had not been eager to get reinforcements from the capital. However, the majority in the Executive Committee believed that the Petrograd garrison should not be exempted from the defense effort demanded of the whole nation. After the convention, the Soldiers' Section passed a resolution instructing the Petrograd regiments to resume sending marching companies to the front as demanded by the War Ministry.

The Bolsheviks seized the occasion to incite the soldiers to disobey the order. "The imperialistic war waged by the Provisional Government," they said, "serves only the wealthy classes. Let them fight the war! The revolutionary regiments must remain in the capital to defend the revolution!"

These arguments appealed strongly to the enlisted men. Dispatch of marching companies became increasingly difficult. Regimental committees that insisted on executing the order were losing their hold over the men. The Executive Committee had to "push" each company assigned to the front. First, a regimental meeting was called and a resolution was passed stating the readiness of the soldiers to defend their free motherland. Then special talks were held with the men of the marching company. All marching companies departed according to schedule, with music and red flags, but we were paying a high price for each dispatch. The Bolsheviks were not strong enough to stop the marching companies, but their influence in the garrison was rapidly increasing. They were becoming the party of the dodgers in the regiments.

As the trouble-shooter of the Soviet, I stood closer to the campaign of dispatching the marching companies than any other member of the Executive Committee. In retrospect, I think our effort to make the Petrograd garrison share in the defense of the country was the main cause of the soldiers' shift from us to the Bolsheviks, who demanded no sacrifice from men in reserve regiments and promised them the safe and serene life of janizaries of the revolution.

LENIN ARRIVES

Lenin's return to Petrograd on April 15 changed the balance of power in the Russian revolution. His aim was to regroup the forces represented in the Soviet—by uniting the radical elements, strengthening their activity, and weakening and isolating the moderates. Characteristically, he disregarded completely the conservative and reactionary forces.

The revolution had found Lenin in Switzerland. As the leader of the extreme left wing of the international Socialist movement, he defended a defeatist position for Russian Socialists during the war. Since this policy led him, perhaps unintentionally, to support the cause of Germany and the Central Powers, Britain and France listed him as an enemy while the Germans considered him a potential ally. Lenin therefore refused to return through France and asked the Germans for a *laisser-passer* for himself and his party. The German Military Command permitted him to cross Germany in a sealed railway car. The conservative papers in Russia used Lenin's association with the Germans to denounce him as a German spy. The moderates in the Executive Committee deplored his return across Germany, but refused to join the chorus of those who charged him with espionage. After some discussion the Executive Committee decided to give him the customary welcome. Chkheidze went to the station to greet him.

THE AUTHOR AS A STUDENT AT THE UNIVERSITY OF ST. PETERSBURG, 1904

Woytinsky, already a precocious scholar, enrolled in the law department. Here he strengthened his belief that political progress depends upon progress in moral values.

INTELLECTUALS AND STUDENTS IN THE 1905 REVOLUTION

Here, holding red banners high, they demonstrate their sympathy with the workers.

(Photo from "An Illustrated History of Russia," by Joel Carmichael: Reynal and Company, N.Y.)

BLOODY SUNDAY, JANUARY 9, 1905

The day the author calls a watershed in Russia's history brought him back from Italy to join his fellow students in protesting the government's infamous crime.

(Photo from "An Illustrated History of Russia," by Joel Carmichael: Reynal and Company, N.Y.)

STRIKE AT THE PUTILOV MILLS, 1905

*(Photo from "An Illustrated History of Russia,"
by Joel Carmichael: Reynal and Company, N.Y.)*

*Workers at the Putilov Mills in St. Petersburg—Russia's largest steel mills
—strike in protest against Bloody Sunday.*

MEETING IN THE TAURIDE PALACE, 1917

*Katherine Hall of the Tauride Palace—a ballroom built to accommodate
20,000 dancers beneath its glittering chandeliers—takes on a different
aspect as thousands of peasants, sailors, and soldiers jam its parquet floor
in the dense confusion following the fall of Tsarism.*

*(Photo from "An Illustrated History of Russia,"
by Joel Carmichael: Reynal and Company, N.Y.)*

(Photo from Bettmann Archive)

VLADIMIR I. LENIN

"Perhaps the most unemotional man I have ever met in politics." Despite the author's closeness to Lenin during the first revolution, he knew that Lenin "did not trust my loyalty to his faction."

IRAKLI G. TSERETELLI

An orator of exceptional ability, who in 1905 fought passionately for democracy against the Tsar and in 1917—as the true leader of all democratic forces—against the Communists.

ALEXANDROVSK PENITENTIARY IN SIBERIA

Where the author was imprisoned from 1910 through 1912 by the Tsar.

CONVICTS ARRIVING IN SIBERIA

From Russia to Siberia came the convicts—common criminals and politicals, bearded muzhiks and good-humored vagabonds—those who came for the first time and those who knew every prison guard by name.

THE AUTHOR IN EXILE

Even as a political exile in Siberia in 1915, the author continued to write for the Russian press and to direct a municipal study on the effect of the war on the local labor market in Irkutsk.

THE FUTURE MRS. WOYTINSKY

In Siberia the author found not only exile but love and marriage. His mother, who first saw her future daughter-in-law in this picture, expressed fear that a girl in such a hat might be too glamorous for her son. On seeing a later photograph of the young couple together (left), she felt sure her son would be happy.

SIBERIA: LAND OF UNTAPPED RESOURCES

Siberia, land of the Lena—a river as wide as the sea—and of the taiga, the forest primeval; a land of majestic beauty and untapped resources, where nature was stern and life austere but full of opportunity and promise.

(Photo courtesy of Ullstein Verlag, West Berlin)

(Photo from Bettmann Archive)

STREET SCENE, JULY 3, 1917

Violence and death come to hundreds of victims as Kronstadt sailors demonstrate for the Bolsheviks and against the Provisional Government.

(Photo from Bettmann Archive)

THE DEPUTIES TO THE MARCH, 1917, PETROGRAD SOVIET MEET IN THE TAURIDE PALACE

"The Soviet was a loose and shapeless organization . . . consisting of a workers' section and a soldiers' section. The joint session was supposed to amount to a revolutionary parliament. Actually, it was a mass meeting reflecting the predominant moods of the masses but unable to work out political decisions."

(Photo from "An Illustrated History of Russia,"
by Joel Carmichael: Reynal and Company, N.Y.)

THE TSAR'S SOLDIERS JOIN WITH THE PEOPLE

Young and old, large and small, the debonair and the not-so-debonair join
forces in the first days of the 1917 Revolution.

FORTRESS OF PETER AND PAUL

The author was imprisoned here by the Communists after they had defeated the armed resistance organized by him in November, 1917. Because of lynchings of political prisoners by Communist mobs, Emma Woytinsky brought her husband a tiny package of cyanide for the ultimate emergency.

SOLDIERS OF THE REVOLUTION

Traveling on the running board and fenders of an automobile, a Russian soldier of 1917 holds aloft the red flag affixed to his bayonet.

**THE WOYTINSKYS CLIMBING
THE TYROLEAN ALPS**

*The free, clear, windswept world of
the mountain-climber—after years
of prison, war, and confining scholarly labors—became the Woytinskys' passion in their middle years.*

**MAP SHOWING THE MANY TRIPS MADE BY THE WOYTINSKYS
IN THE UNITED STATES**

*"We had an insatiable desire to see the new country and crossed it fourteen
times from coast to coast and eight times from the Canadian border to the
Gulf of Mexico. There is an indescribable magic in the American scene."*

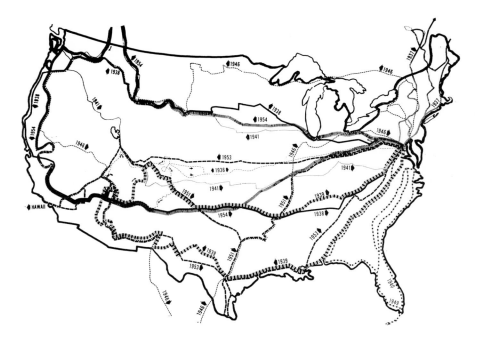

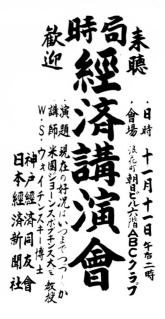

POSTER ANNOUNCING A LECTURE BY MR. WOYTINSKY IN A JAPANESE UNIVERSITY

Such lectures, given throughout the Far East during 1955 and 1956, gave the Woytinskys an opportunity to exchange ideas with peoples of different cultures and to search for mutual understanding. Because the Japanese language uses syllables, the letters "W.S." were used (third column from left), which enabled the author to identify the poster.

PRESS CONFERENCE IN SÃO PAULO, BRAZIL

Their last trip abroad, under the auspices of the U.S. State Department, was to Latin America. In São Paulo, as in the cities and remote areas of fifteen other republics, the Woytinskys told about the United States—not only about its economic and social system but about its spirit, the patterns of its thinking, its attitude toward other peoples.

The Bolsheviks added a military note to the occasion by bringing up a couple of regiments and an armored division.

Lenin had not changed in appearance since I had last seen him. The same brisk movements, the same twinkling eyes and sly smile. He recognized me in the group of members of the Executive Committee on the platform, embraced me, and asked, "Again with us, Comrade Petrov?"

"I do not know where you stand," I replied.

"We shall talk it over," he laughed, rushing to the exit. In the parade reception room of the station Chkheidze greeted him, but he did not listen. He stepped briskly to the plaza and looked intently at the crowd—the ocean of red flags, tanks, ranks of soldiers. Then he climbed on top of a car and began to speak in his old way, self-confident and contemptuous of those who disagreed with him. He denounced the Provisional Government as a bunch of counterrevolutionary imperialists, denounced the majority in the Soviet and its Executive Committee as fools and cowards, called on the workers and soldiers to take over power and transform the imperialist slaughter into a world revolution. The crowd did not register much enthusiasm.

On Lenin's invitation, I rode in his car from the station to Bolshevist headquarters. He did not say a word the entire way. Bolshevist headquarters occupied the palatial mansion of a prima ballerina, Kshessinskaya, who was regarded in Petrograd as a close friend of Nicholas. Early in the revolution a regiment had used the building as a club. Then it was turned over to the local Bolshevist organization, and the latter transferred it to the Central Committee. Bolshevist party workers and delegates to the All-Russian Convention of the Soviets were assembled in the main ballroom. I recognized among them several army representatives who had voted with the majority of the Executive Committee. There were also a dozen or more guests. All waited patiently while Lenin huddled with his Petrograd lieutenants. He emerged from the caucus after midnight.

A strange meeting followed. The exquisitely luxurious room, with golden garlands carved on white Corinthian columns. Three hundred men and women on folding chairs, all listening intently to the diatribe that would become the Sermon on the Mount of a new church. The crux of Lenin's program was a merciless fight against the Socialists, who had betrayed the revolution by supporting the Provisional Government and the war. In his first appearance before those who were to become the core of his army, Lenin deliberately hurled the most abusive language against his opponents. He seemed to sift his listeners, saying to them, "Either you follow me or join the traitors, the fools, the lackeys of the bourgeoisie!"

In this speech, Lenin mingled Marxian terminology and old clichés with strange new slogans. Why should we wait for a peace concluded by governments? Make peace with your German brothers, regiment by regiment, company by company, through fraternization! Why should we wait for the Constituent Assembly? Seize power at once through the Soviets and write your own laws. The agrarian question? Let the landless peasants and farmhands take land wherever they find it. Financial problems? There is money enough in the vaults of the banks! Economic troubles? There will be none if the Soviets control production and distribute the product! Then he turned to organization problems. The Socialist parties have failed miserably. Even the term "Socialist" and "Social Democrat" sound infamous. Let us declare openly that we are not Socialists but Communists— the name of the truly revolutionary vanguard of the labor movement in Marx's time!

Lenin talked on like a man obsessed by a vision. When he finished, before dawn, he asked if there were any objections or questions. For a minute nobody responded. When his eyes met mine, I stood up and said that his program was utterly unrealistic. He was not familiar with conditions in Russia and had not given thought to the implications of the war. He had not presented facts to support his ideas. His peroration was a list of arbitrary catchwords.

Part of the audience applauded, but the majority was not on my side. Lenin listened with a smile, as if to show that he had anticipated precisely these objections. "Comrade Petrov," he replied, "is mistaken when he says I am not familiar with conditions in Russia. On the way from Finland to Petrograd I shared a compartment with a soldier from the front. He told me all I need to know about the war, and I will not trade his words for the lies of reactionary newspapers that Comrade Petrov considers such wells of wisdom." These words provoked a thunderous ovation. Nobody asked for the floor. The meeting was closed.

The next day a joint meeting of Bolsheviks and Mensheviks was called in the session room of the Tauride Palace to discuss the possibility of a united front in the war-and-peace policy. An hour before the meeting the Bolsheviks held a caucus. I attended it as a guest. Lenin was there, with his usual sly smile. Someone asked him about the possibility of an agreement with the Mensheviks. First he declined to open the discussion, then he took the floor, warmed up, and repeated, with minor variations, his speech of the preceding night.

Then everyone went to the session room. The unity meeting had been widely publicized, the galleries were packed, and reporters from all the major newspapers were there. Chkheidze, as the chairman, recognized Lenin as the first speaker. Lenin started with a blank statement: "There can be no pact between revolutionary and counterrevolutionary forces. We are at war: the Mensheviks are supporting imperialism, the Bolsheviks are fighting against it; we are for the world revolution, the Mensheviks are against it." Once more he repeated the whole litany, for the third time in twenty-four hours. Now the emphasis was on the fight for control over the Soviet, the fight to the end between the Bolsheviks and the moderates.

The discussion that followed was rather tame. Tseretelli reminded Lenin of Engel's warning that the greatest danger of the revolutionary class is to seize political power prematurely, before the objective, economic conditions for liberation have developed. He stressed, however, that Lenin proposed to take over power without acts of violence, just gaining the majority of the Soviets for his policy. Concluding his speech, Tseretelli expressed the conviction that Lenin would be forced to recognize that he could not win in an ideological struggle for the souls of workers and peasants. Of other speakers, only Goldenberg, a lawyer close to the Bolsheviks, was alarmed by Lenin's pronouncements. "Not everyone who has heard this speech realizes its impact," he said. "The flag of civil war has been raised from this tribune. Lenin has announced his candidacy for the vacant throne of Bakunin, the apostle of world anarchy!"

During the discussion Lenin quietly left the meeting. Some thirty men followed him. Those who remained voted to rally the S-D party around the program of democratic peace and national defense. This group included some twenty former Bolsheviks. It was clear that in the future there would no longer be "Bolsheviks" and "Mensheviks" as two currents within the S-D party. Two forces opposed each other, no longer as political adversaries but as enemies. That was precisely what Lenin wanted. He had gained his first tactical victory—an irreconcilable split within the Soviet forces.

THE COMMUNISTS GAIN GROUND

The Bolsheviks—or Communists, as they began to call themselves— started the campaign under the new command. They selected the regiments of the Petrograd garrison as their first target, concentrating their attack on our most vulnerable point—the marching companies. They used the departure of each company to show the soldiers that their party alone defended them. This was a well-planned campaign, a *mélange* of lofty slogans with the appeal to the self-interest of men called to the front. Sometimes Communist agitators posed as front soldiers and told the Petrograd regiments that the front needed no reinforcements; all it needed was peace, and the only purpose in rushing reinforcements to the front was to prolong the war. At the same time, the Communists urged the workers to keep their brothers, the soldiers of the Petrograd garrison, from being sent to the trenches by the government and the Executive Committee. Some factories took the bait and passed resolutions demanding the immediate end of the war, resignation of the Provisional Government, transfer of all power to the Soviets, publication of the Tsar's secret treaties, and the organization of a proletarian Red Guard. Other resolutions protested against moving revolutionary troops from the capital.

By the end of April a dozen factories and one regiment (First Machine Gunners) had openly aligned themselves with the Communist party.

To increase the efficiency of the Executive Committee, Tseretelli suggested the appointment of a bureau consisting of Committee members who supported the policy of the majority. This plan, however, provoked heated opposition from the left-wing Mensheviks, who found it undemocratic. After long discussion a bureau was elected, but with representation from all factions, including the Communists. The new bureau was as divided against itself as the Committee. Tseretelli's plan was defeated.

A REGIONAL CONVENTION

The political situation in the provinces was better than in Petrograd. I got some insight into conditions in Finland at the regional convention of the Soviets in Helsinki. The convention was limited to Russian workers and troops in Finland. Some 125 to 130 delegates were almost evenly divided among sailors, soldiers, and workers. The sailors declared themselves almost unanimously for national defense. They had strong sympathy for the S-R as a peasant party, but expressed themselves in their own colorful and forceful way, stressing their responsibility for the security of the capital, and seemed deeply worried about the inroads of Communist propaganda in Kronstadt and the Baltic fleet.

The soldiers were less articulate, and most of them followed the leadership of the sailors. The workers' delegates were divided on almost every question. About half supported the left wing of the Petrograd Soviet but without the Bolshevists' vehemence. Their arguments sounded sincere and occasionally aroused a response in the ranks of sailors and soldiers.

The discussion went on in a friendly way. I tried to explain to the convention why we could not base national defense on the idea of world revolution. All delegates agreed that the Executive Committee might be right after all.

The convention began on the afternoon of April 29 and lasted until long after midnight. At the end I had almost lost my voice and thought that everybody was equally tired, but the delegates wished to talk on. Side issues were raised—about the Constituent Assembly, the agrarian question, secret treaties.

The convention unanimously—with only two abstentions—voted support of the Provisional Government, but it attached important reservations in the form of "so far as" clauses—so far as the Provisional Government did this and continued to do that. The resolution on war and national defense, reiterating the decision of the All-Russian Convention but with more emphasis on the need to strengthen the army and navy, was adopted by 113 votes to 4, with 5 abstentions.

The convention closed with an ovation to the Executive Committee. I went back to Petrograd rested and happy.

THE CLASH ON FOREIGN POLICY

The revolution went on—endless conferences, deputations, enthusiastic resolutions, vehement lamentations in newspapers, meetings and speeches; cheerless days, sleepless nights. The Soviet was at the peak of its glory. The government was doing its everyday job, evading controversial issues, postponing decisions on crucial questions, waiting until the revolutionary storm blew over while loudly proclaiming devotion to the new revolutionary order.

The first open clash between the Petrograd Soviet and the government broke out on the question of foreign policy. The government's declaration of April 10 seemed to have established mutual understanding between the Cabinet and the Soviet about the general orientation of foreign policy. But on April 27 the government announced in the press that it had no intention of approaching the Allies about a joint discussion of war aims or peace terms. The Bolsheviks used this declaration as evidence that the agreement between the Executive Committee and the government was a fraud.

Then the Executive Committee asked the government to hand over the text of its declaration of April 10 to the Allied and neutral governments as the official program of Russia's new foreign policy. The majority of the Cabinet agreed. Instructed to prepare an appropriate note, Miliukov dispatched the government's declaration abroad with a memorandum explaining that the purpose of this action was to put an end to the rumors of Russia's intentions to conclude a separate peace with the enemies, and that the Provisional Government's declaration was in conformity with war aims announced by the Allies and Russia's treaties with other nations. The memorandum ended with an expression of confidence in the final victory of the Allies and a peace "with all necessary sanctions and guarantees."

The majority of the Executive Committee felt that Miliukov's note was a fatal blow to its policy of co-operation with the government and to national defense. It was impossible to call on soldiers to defend old treaties signed by the Tsar! Moreover, Miliukov's contention that the government's declaration had changed nothing in Russia's foreign policy was contrary to the assurances the government had given the Executive Committee. The left wing of the Executive Committee demanded an immediate break with the government, and this demand found some supporters in the ranks of the moderates.

Long after midnight the session of the Executive Committee was adjourned. I spent the rest of the night on a sofa in the Tauride Palace. Early in the morning the session resumed. The leftist members felt that they had an excellent opportunity to kill the policy of co-operation with the government. The moderates were losing ground. At this point we learned that a solution of the crisis had slipped from our hands. Workers and soldiers were gathering in the streets to protest the "provocation" of the Minister of Foreign Affairs. Telephone calls began to pour into the Palace. Work had stopped in many mills. The workers planned to go in force to the Marinsky Palace, the seat of the Provisional Government, and demand Miliukov's resignation. Unrest also developed in the barracks; the soldiers were arming themselves. . . .

With two other members of the Committee, I was asked to take measures to keep the soldiers in the barracks and the workers in the factory districts. We rounded up members of the Soviet and the delegates from the provinces and the front who were in Petrograd and assembled all the cars at the disposal of the Soviet. Then some ten of us sat at a battery of telephones, calling mills and barracks. "The Executive Committee is in session. It has not called for street demonstrations. Any offhand action will be contrary to its wishes." Our men rushed in all directions hammering the message: "Keep quiet! Wait!" Perhaps we were overcautious, but we feared that the first regiment that appeared in front of the Marinsky Palace with a demand for Miliukov's resignation might force its way into the building and destroy the precarious balance of power in Petrograd and in Russia.

Our efforts were only partially successful. We did keep workers in the southern factory precincts from marching to the center of the city, but the S-D leaders in the northern districts refused to obey. News from the Viborg district seemed particularly alarming. Crowds of workers were merging, and armed groups were appearing at the head of the procession moving toward the center of the city. When we got the report that some fifty thousand workers were crossing the Neva bridges on the way to the Marian Palace, the session of the Executive Committee was adjourned and Chkheidze drove with me to meet the crowd. We overtook it in the Marsovo Pole (Mars Field). The column was marching twenty men abreast, with armed men in front. Chkheidze ordered the chauffeur to stop in front of the procession. The column halted, and he asked the leaders the purpose of the demonstration.

"We are defending the revolution!" was the reply.

"Why do you carry arms?"

"Against the enemies!"

Chkheidze addressed the workers, thanked them for their loyalty to the revolution, and urged them to return to their homes. Then I spoke from the top of the car. The people around us were morose. A former member of the Council of the Unemployed stood near the car. He said to me reproachfully, "Instead of being in front of us, Comrade Petrov, you are sending us back to our homes."

On the order of its leaders, the column made a detour around our car and went on, but it stopped at the edge of Mars Field. A meeting was held, a resolution passed expressing bitter disappointment in the policy of the Executive Committee, and the crowd was disbanded.

While we were busy at Mars Field, an infantry regiment appeared in front of the Marinsky Palace in march formation, with arms but without officers, under the command of a private. At his order the soldiers encircled the building. The leader entered the palace with a handful of soldiers, asked for the Chief of Government Affairs, and handed him a resolution demanding Miliukov's resignation. The people in the palace considered that the government was under arrest, but the leader of the demonstration returned to his regiment, formed it into a column, and marched it back to the barracks. After all, this was a *peaceful* demonstration although it had a threatening undertone.

The members of the government were sure this threat had come from the Tauride Palace. Actually, the demonstration was organized by the chairman of the regimental committee, Linde, on his own initiative. He was a mathematician and astronomer by training and profession, deeply devoted to the idea of national defense. When he learned of Miliukov's memorandum, his first thought was that it would undermine all our work in the army. Only the immediate resignation of Miliukov, he thought, could save the situation. Convinced that the Executive Committee would react similarly, Linde called on the men to march to the Marinsky Palace but forgot to notify the Tauride Palace of his plan.

In the evening the Soviet met in the *aula maxima* of the Naval

School, one of the largest halls in Petrograd. The building was surrounded by a huge crowd of workers and soldiers. After fruitless discussion, the Soviet passed a resolution demanding a joint meeting of the government and the Executive Committee. The meeting was called at once, in the Marinsky Palace. A group in front of the buildings—perhaps two or three hundred in all—greeted the arriving members of the government with cheers and the leaders of the Soviet with boos. This was a counterdemonstration that the Cadets had hurriedly organized in support of Miliukov.

The meeting opened at 10:00 P.M. and was even more chaotic than the sessions in the Tauride Palace and Naval School. The ministers complained bitterly about the worsening situation in Petrograd and accused the regimental committees of undermining the authority of the command, and the Soviet of having staged hostile demonstrations to terrorize the government. The Soviet spokesmen stressed the spontaneous character of the demonstrations and denounced Miliukov's note as undermining the authority of both the government and the Soviet. Tseretelli demanded that the government issue an official unambiguous declaration on its foreign policy. The government finally yielded to this demand.

After midnight I returned to the Tauride Palace and took stock of the day's events. Some hundred thousand workers, in organized columns, a few of them armed, and five or six regiments carrying arms had participated in the demonstrations in the center of the city. We had kept at least five times that number of workers and soldiers out of the streets. All of the demonstrations were directed against Miliukov, rather than the Provisional Government as a whole, and expressed loyalty to the Soviet. The movement had not fallen into the hands of the Communists, although some groups with Bolshevist leanings took part in the demonstrations.

I spent the rest of the night in the palace at the telephone. Excitement in the barracks was mounting. Many regiments were holding meetings. Groups of soldiers went from barracks to barracks, "just to keep in touch with the others." In most barracks the men had taken guns and ammunition from the arsenal and refused to return them. Armored divisions were readying their tanks.

The regimental committees implored us, "Order some action, or the men will act on their own."

The Tauride Palace called back, "The government has agreed to publish a rebuttal of Miliukov's note. The crisis is almost over. Any precipitous act would be harmful."

At the same time, the Cadets were busy calling their sympathizers to Nevsky Prospect for an all-day demonstration in support of Miliukov. Their demonstration started at noon, but despite the challenge we held firmly to our stand: no processions of workers or soldiers in the center of the city!

Suddenly a report came in that an artillery regiment was moving toward the Marinsky Palace. We called the barracks and learned that the regiment had been ordered there by General Kornilov, Commander of the Petrograd Military District. The telephone rang again. The regiment had been stationed in front of the Marinsky Palace as a demonstration of the government's strength, its guns trained on the streets converging at the Plaza around the palace. The regimental committees reported that the soldiers had left their barracks in answer to a service call, without knowing they would be used for a political demonstration against the Soviet. If they learned the purpose of the operation, a riot would break out and the officers would be in imminent danger.

The Executive Committee was in session when I took Chkheidze a draft of an order to the garrison: "In these troubled days, no soldier should appear on the streets with arms. Each order to leave the barracks must come from the Executive Committee and must be in writing, on a form with the Soviet letterhead. It must carry the seal of the Executive Committee and be signed by at least two of the following five members of the Committee . . . Before executing any order, ask the Tauride Palace for its confirmation by telephone."

Chkheidze signed the order and five minutes later it was wired to all military units. At once we had General Kornilov on the telephone and informed him of the Committee's decision. The chairman of the Soldiers' Section said to him, "General, we do not wish to undermine your authority by ordering the regiment back to the barracks. Please give the order yourself." After a moment's hesitation he replied, "The order is under way."

A few days later Kornilov resigned his post. This humiliation left a deep scar on his political views: he became obsessed with an hysterical hatred of the Soviets.

The Committee's order had shown how strong the Soviet's authority was at that time. The tension in the streets began to subside. On the afternoon of May 5 the Provisional Government issued a declaration clarifying Miliukov's ill-fated memorandum. Although intentionally weak and vague, this was a concession to the Soviet and the Executive Committee decided to accept it.

That evening the Soviet convened again in the Naval School. Both worker and soldier deputies were elated by the outcome of the conflict and proud of themselves for the restraint they had shown in the crisis. Tseretelli, who reported for the Executive Committee, was the hero of the day. During his speech I drove with Dan to the plant of *Izvestia*. Fewer people were in the streets than in the afternoon, but comparatively small groups—a couple of hundred here, a thousand there—were excited and aggressive. The supporters of the government occupied the sidewalks, the workers and soldiers kept to the middle of the streets. When hostile groups passed one another, they exchanged threats and jeers. Some people on both sides carried arms. When we were close to the corner of Nevsky and Sadovaya, our chauffeur remarked in a matter-of-fact way, "Now they will start shooting."

I took the front seat beside him for a better view of what was going on. Shooting began before he touched the accelerator. Both sides fired. A few persons were hurt. We stopped the car and rushed toward a group on the sidewalk. Both sides recognized the Soviet car and the shooting around us ceased, but shots rang out farther down the street. We were surrounded by anti-Soviet demonstrators—college students, high school boys and girls, intellectuals. They shouted accusations against the Soviet, then some of them recognized us and called our names loudly. The mood of the crowd changed—we had the reputation of moderates. Somebody complained bitterly, "You saw this yourselves. Unprovoked aggression!"

While Dan, a physician by profession, was administering first aid to the wounded, I spoke to the crowd. "It is not important which side fired first. Both sides carry arms, both have used them, and both are to blame. Didn't you realize that armed demonstrations at night are bound to lead to bloodshed?"

Some insisted they carried arms only in defense, others agreed with me. We drove back to the Naval School. Chkheidze interrupted the discussion to hear the report about shooting on Nevsky Prospect. Then a resolution forbidding any street demonstration in Petrograd for the next two days was passed unanimously.

On May 6 the streets of the capital were calm.

THE GOVERNMENT CRISIS

What was the political meaning of the riots? The Cadet newspapers accused German agents of having fomented the trouble, and the Soviet of having used armed force to exert pressure on the government. According to them, patriotic demonstrations on May 4 had overshadowed the demonstrations against Miliukov on the preceding day, and this was the main reason why the Soviet had forbidden all street demonstrations.[2]

---

[2] Miliukov remarks in his *History:* "The clash of May 3-4 ended with an indisputable victory of the Provisional Government." But he recognizes that during this clash the Petrograd garrison obeyed only the orders of the Soviet. He likewise

The Communists declined any responsibility for the unrest and ridiculed the demand for Miliukov's resignation when the entire Cabinet was, anyhow, a bunch of imperialists and reactionaries. They explained the riots as a spontaneous outburst of indignation of the workers and soldiers against the opportunistic majority of the Executive Committee.

Izvestia described the incident as a victory of the moderate wing in the Soviet. Whether it was a victory of the government or the Soviet, the events, and especially the failure of the artillery demonstration staged by General Kornilov in front of the Marinsky Palace, had revealed that the government had no armed force at its disposal. The reaction of the provinces and the army confirmed the weakness of the Cabinet, although it also showed that it enjoyed considerable prestige among the middle classes, officers, and professional people.

The position of the government and especially of Miliukov had become untenable. The solution of the crisis seemed to lie in broadening the base of the Provisional Government by including representation of the Soviet. Prince Lvov was among the first to recognize the need for this step, but his initiative met with strong resistance in the Cabinet. Miliukov's group had no desire to work with men from the Tauride Palace, least of all after the experience of the May days.

On the other hand, the leaders of the Soviet were not eager to join the government. When the question first came before the Executive Committee, only a small minority—including me—voted to participate in a coalition. The Communists opposed the idea, fearing that a strong coalition government would frustrate their plans for seizing power. The leaders of the Mensheviks were against a coalition for the reason that had determined their decision in March to stay out of the Provisional Government. Tseretelli and Chkheidze tried to postpone the decision because they were not sure their party would support its representatives in the Cabinet.

On May 9 the Provisional Government reported to the people on the first two months of its work. It mentioned the political amnesty, repeal of discrimination against national and religious minorities, first steps toward the reorganization of local administration, preparation of the first draft of the electoral law for the Constituent Assembly. This was not much, but it suggested that the government was fulfilling its agreement with the Petrograd Soviet. The report ended with a promise to continue efforts to broaden the base of the government by including representatives from groups that had not yet participated directly in national administration. The

---

recognizes that the Soviet had kept most of the troops in the barracks and took measures to put down the workers' demonstrations. It is puzzling to see how such facts add up to a "moral victory of the government."

next day Prince Lvov sent a letter to Chkheidze inviting the Executive Committee to open negotiations on its participation in the Cabinet. The Committee declined the offer by a small majority.

On May 12, Guchkov, the Minister of War, resigned. Apparently the immediate cause of this step was the clash between General Kornilov and the Petrograd Soviet. In the Tauride Palace Guchkov's resignation was taken as a sign of the government's disintegration. Without reopening the debate, the Executive Committee decided to enter a coalition government, this time by an overwhelming majority.

THE FIRST COALITION

Discussion of conditions for entering the coalition continued all night. It was decided not to ask for a majority or for key positions in the Cabinet but to submit a definite program to the new government as the basis of the coalition. This decision was wrong in my opinion: in turbulent times the composition of a government is more important than its announced program. Each point of the program provoked a heated debate in the Committee. The Bolsheviks tried to make the draft unacceptable to non-Socialist parties; the moderates sought to conciliate without yielding essential points.

Negotiations between the Committee and the government began on May 15. The Cadets insisted on keeping foreign affairs in Miliukov's hands and objected to the appointment of Chernov, the leader of the S-R party, as the Minister of Agriculture. Prince Lvov was particularly eager to have Tseretelli in the Cabinet, but the latter refused, preferring to continue his work in the Tauride Palace. Then Lvov suggested a compromise: Tseretelli was to join the government without administrative responsibilities, formally as Minister of Post and Telegraph but practically as a minister without portfolio.

Our draft of the platform was accepted without essential changes, despite the opposition of the right wing of the Cadets. The new platform went much further than the agreement between the first Cabinet and the Soviet.

It began with the declaration that the aim of the government was a just negotiated peace based on the right of all peoples to self-determination and that the new Coalition Government would take necessary steps to gain the Allies' support for this policy. Further, it outlined the government's policy for the army: to strengthen its fighting ability in defense and attack, on the basis of its new spirit and consolidation of its democratic organizations. The economic part of the program promised a relentless struggle against the crises in agricultural production, coal mining, the iron and steel industry, and railroad transport; strengthening of public controls in all these economic sectors; measures against speculation and black marketing; measures compelling landowners and industrialists to utilize available means of production as fully as possible; distribution of regulative functions between the central and local authorities. A program to protect labor was only briefly outlined in the platform, with the understanding that the Department of Labor in the new Cabinet would be in the hands of a man close to the Executive Committee, who would implement the recommendations of the All-Russian Convention of the Soviets.

Perhaps the most important clause was on land policy. While leaving to the Constituent Assembly the final decision of the agrarian problem—the legal transfer of land to the tillers of the soil—the platform committed the government to two immediate steps: to increase crop production by seizing, if necessary, the idle lands of big estates; and to transfer immediately to the peasants the lands of which they could make better use than the existing owners.

The financial section of the platform was not very realistic under the existing conditions. It stressed the need to reshape the fiscal system, with greater emphasis on direct taxes on the rich (inheritance tax, income tax, surtax on war profits, and so forth). The section on local government restated the efforts of the government to establish, as soon as possible, the net of democratically elected provincial, municipal, and other local councils, with broad administrative and economic responsibilities. The concluding section contained a pledge to expedite the convocation of the Constituent Assembly in Petrograd.

This platform was prepared hurriedly, in a few days of feverish consultations between experts and leaders of the Executive Committee. My task was to bring together the points accepted by the Executive Committee in literary form and elaborate them later in a series of articles in *Izvestia*. I have the reprint of these articles in my files. Rereading them now, in the light of past events, I can see how utopian was our hope that our platform would be implemented by a government with a strong majority hostile to the Soviets and the revolution. However, apart from this, the platform was fine as an outline of what the new Cabinet should have done immediately, even as a caretaker government, while at the same time expediting elections to the Constituent Assembly.

The reorganized government, again headed by Lvov, included fifteen members: three representatives of the Soviet (Chernov, Skobelev, and Tsereteli); three Socialists without direct ties with the Soviet (among them Kerensky for the army and navy); and nine representatives of non-Socialist parties, all close to the Cadets. Miliukov was dropped from the list.

On May 18 the Coalition Government published its program. The same day the Soviet convened to hear the report of the Executive Committee. The new Socialist Cabinet members were greeted enthusiastically. By an overwhelming majority the Soviet passed a resolution of *unconditional* confidence and active support of the new government. This vote was accompanied by a resolution whereby the Soviet confirmed its control over its own representatives in the government, on the principle used by political parties under a parliamentary system in Europe to exercise control over their representatives in the Cabinet.

The Tauride Palace was flooded with telegrams expressing the devotion of workers and soldiers to the Petrograd Soviet and the new government. On May 22 the All-Russian conference of Menshevist organizations opened in Petrograd and voted approval of Socialist participation in the coalition.

These were days of cautious optimism in the Tauride Palace. Things seemed to be moving in the direction of consolidation of the new order and greater unity of liberal forces.

The Communists were surprised by the people's response to the formation of the new Cabinet, but Lenin soon discovered the weak point in our new position: The masses expected too much of the Coalition and were bound to be disillusioned. On May 24, a week after the new Cabinet had taken office, Lenin wrote in *Pravda*: "The Coalition has been in power for eight days. What has it brought to the people? The war goes on. The landowners still hold their land, the capitalists continue to exploit the workers, prices are high, there is a shortage of bread and sugar in the cities. The Coalition Government has done nothing. The Coalition has proved to be a fraud. . . ." This was clever propaganda. The new government had not promised miracles, but the people expected them.

As time went on the popular mood began to change. By the end of May little remained of the enthusiasm with which the people had greeted the Coalition Government.

Now the stage was set for further events. The Bolsheviks would lie low, awaiting signs of rising restlessness in the masses and meanwhile fomenting trouble, undermining morale in the army, inciting workers against their representatives in the Soviet. The rightist groups in the government would do their best to paralyze the promised reforms and postpone elections to the Constituent Assembly, hoping that sooner or later the masses of the people would turn toward them as the party of order. The majority in the Soviet and their representatives in the government, absorbed in everyday troubles, would have no time to think of a long-range program of action to stop the incipient erosion of their popularity.

Perhaps our greatest error was in timing. It was later than we thought. Only a rapid convocation of the Constituent Assembly could have saved democracy in Russia. The leaders of the majority in the Soviet had insisted on accelerating elections and even obtained the promise of the government that the Constituent Assembly would convene in September, but this was a side-show in the great game of politics, and the Cadets, for whom postponement of the election was the main issue, could easily maneuver the government into breaking this promise.

WAR AND PEACE

New faces appeared in the Tauride Palace—delegates from foreign Socialist parties representing also the Allied and neutral governments. Officially, they came to bring good wishes to Russian workers and to learn more about conditions in Russia, but the most influential among them, such as Arthur Henderson of Great Britain and Albert Thomas of France, came to persuade the Soviet leaders to support the war effort of the Allies more effectively. They recognized the Soviet's principle of a just peace but insisted that such a peace must provide for the return of Alsace-Lorraine to France and the dissolution of the Austro-Hungarian and Ottoman empires. They described the damage inflicted by German aggression on the peoples of Belgium and France and pleaded that reparations were necessary to a just war settlement. Addressing the full session of the Soviet, they expressed their admiration of the Russian revolution but, in speaking before the Executive Committee, they made no secret of the fact that their thinking on war aims differed from the Soviet's.

Some delegates wished to get in touch with Russian workers and soldiers. I took them to meetings in factories and barracks. Once I took a French deputy to the night meeting of a rioting regiment. He found the situation similar to some phase of the French Revolution and kept saying on the way back, "Now I understand, I understand everything." Personally, I doubted whether he had understood anything of our problems.

Neither the workers nor the soldiers manifested much enthusiasm for the foreign delegates. On the other hand, the delegates were only moderately interested in our plan for an international Socialist conference and politely rejected our suggestion that *all* Socialist parties should be invited and that the majority Socialist parties should break with their governments. They also refused to pledge in advance to comply with the decisions of the conference. They pointed out that the differences between the right and left wings in the European Socialist parties were too deep, and the majority parties too heavily committed to the national policies of their respective governments, to accept in advance decisions taken by so unpredictable a forum as an international Socialist conference. They agreed to commit themselves only if the decisions of the conference were outlined in advance, in accordance with their concept of a just peace, and if only details were left to further negotiations. With this reservation, it was agreed that the conference would meet in Stockholm.

Since there was little interest in this idea abroad, the Soviet decided to send a delegation to tour the Allied countries to try to get support for the Soviet plan among the workers. The delegation seemed to be rather successful at the beginning. Though it did not kindle the imagination of the masses, it organized a few meetings, held conferences with national leaders, and published half a dozen articles in the labor press. In Russia, however, the campaign for the Stockholm conference made little progress. People close to the Executive Committee manifested little interest in it and the general press ignored it.

Indeed, the Soviet was much less absorbed in Socialist diplomacy than in such matters as fraternization on the front lines. The last problem overshadowed all other issues in the peace-and-war campaign in the spring of 1917.

CONDITIONS IN THE ARMY

The German High Command kept from one third to half of all its divisions on the Russian front, but these were largely incomplete and tired divisions in need of rest and reorganization. Interested in maintaining a lull on this front, the Germans did not harass our troops. As in all wars everywhere in the world, the lull was welcomed by the troops in our trenches, thoroughly tired after the long series of defeats that preceded the revolution. But in accepting the *de facto* truce offered to her by the enemy, Russia would actually be supporting Germany against the Allies. The policy of our High Command, therefore, was to exercise sufficient pressure on the enemy lines and to keep the army sufficiently strong to represent a threat to the enemy. The Petrograd Soviet and the army organizations decided to support this policy.

This was a difficult decision. At the outbreak of the revolution, the men at the front distrusted their officers, and the officers distrusted their men. But the revolution had called into being the new factor in the army—the soldiers' committees. They were an institution completely strange to the old-regime army, and the officers, especially the High Command, looked on them with suspicion. Indeed, they did not realize that the soldiers had manned their committees with the best men in their ranks, the best educated, most mature politically, most patriotic. Even in rear garrisons, as in Petrograd, the first regimental committees were made up almost wholly of responsible persons. In the active army, the moral level of soldiers' representatives was still higher. Indeed, the elected committees were the backbone of the revolutionary army. They kept the army from disintegrating and could have done much more to restore its military spirit if they had been supported by the commanding personnel. Unfortunately, few officers and only very few representatives of top brass grasped the situation. The men at the top of the military hierarchy were convinced that if they could get rid of the committees, and if the government could restore their disciplinary power, all problems of the army would be solved readily.

The situation in the Petrograd garrison was getting worse each week. The soldiers naturally disliked the idea of going to the front and preferred to stay in the capital and guard the conquests of the revolution. It was easy to understand this attitude, but I felt that my sympathy with the men in the Petrograd garrison was waning. After the May days, I became increasingly tired of my job as a troubleshooter in the barracks. I wanted to learn more about the men in the trenches and their problems. The first practical problem of revolutionary life in the trenches that presented itself to me was fraternization.

FRATERNIZATION

I do not know when and where the term "fraternization" was coined. It was used occasionally in left-wing Socialist literature before the revolution to describe friendly meetings of soldiers of two belligerent countries in the zone between the trenches. Such meetings have occurred at all times. Tolstoy described them in his stories of the defense of Sebastopol. During the Russian revolution they took a particular slant when the Communists attempted to use them on a large scale in their drive to power through world revolution.

Fraternization with the enemy was first reported at the conference of soldiers' deputies of the Central Front, in Minsk, at the end of April. Russian and German soldiers, it was said, met in crowds in a neutral zone. The Russians shouted to the Germans, "Go home, we'll not hurt you!" The Germans shouted, "Don't fire! We'll do you no harm!" Small gifts were exchanged: Russian bread and tobacco for German cigarette lighters.

The problem of fraternization with the enemy confronted the Executive Committee when it was discussing the celebration of May 1. A delegation from the front entered the Tauride Palace—two score men in dirty uniforms, unshaven, weary, carrying their rifles and cartridge belts. They had come directly from the trenches to ask us what to do about it. "We do not know whether this is good or bad. But if things go this way, very soon no front will be left. Tell us what to do."

We asked the soldiers to stay in Petrograd for two or three days while we studied the question. When they left the Executive Committee a passionate dispute broke out. Some Committee members suggested using the appeal for fraternization as the central theme of the May Day demonstration, but this proposal was rejected. The next day, however, Lenin published a signed article in *Pravda* in which he glorified fraternization as the best way to end the war.

Very soon it became evident that the Germans were sending specially trained "fraternization platoons" of staff officers, disguised as privates, into the neutral zone. One after another the army committees took a stand against fraternization, even committees dominated by the Bolsheviks. The fraternization meetings continued nevertheless. Then the Chief Commander of the Central Front issued an order to field commanders to stop fraternization by artillery fire if necessary. This gave Lenin a new argument: The High Command is against fraternization because it is afraid the soldiers will put an end to the war.

A delegation came from the northern front, headed by Kuchin, chairman of the Committee of the Twelfth Army, and Vilenkin, chairman of the Fifth Army. To my surprise I recognized Vilenkin— my companion in the Students' Council of 1905-6. There was still something of the dude in his brisk manner and dashing uniform of a hussar officer, but he talked about military affairs with authority and confidence and the three crosses for valor on his breast showed he had learned the hard way.

I asked him about his decorations, and he replied with his usual irony, "I entered the army at the beginning of the war. Just a whim, to show the 'true Russians' that Jews could be good soldiers. The hussars have seen some action since then. They could not make a Jew an officer, so they gave me these toys. Then the revolution came, they commissioned me, and the soldiers elected me chairman of the army committee. Thus I now have both the toys and the commission and, in addition, represent the army."

Kuchin was less martial in appearance—a young lieutenant with a gentle, pink face, nearsighted eyes, and blond whiskers. He was a Menshevist journalist, had volunteered as a private for patriotic reasons, and had remained in the trenches until the outbreak of the revolution. He was the first in the Twelfth Army to understand what was happening and to call for election of regimental committees to maintain order in the army. Now these two men represented two armies, and their word carried more weight than that of the commanders of those armies. They bitterly accused the Executive Committee of weakness and demanded that it give them clear instructions on fraternization. I tried to explain that what they described as weakness in our attitude was due to our unfamiliarity with the problems of the army. Of course we were opposed to fraternization, I said, but what should we do about it?

"First of all, say what you think clearly and firmly," replied Kuchin.

The Committee decided to address an appeal to the front, restating the Soviet's attitude on national defense. I asked Kuchin and Vilenkin to help me. Our draft denounced as treason the attempts to undermine discipline or incite soldiers to disobedience and, in particular, to fraternization with the enemy. After the appeal was approved by the Executive Committee, I wrote an editorial for *Izvestia* elaborating our policy, showed the copy to Dan and two or three other members of our editorial staff, and sent it to the printing plant.

When I reached the plant in the evening my editorial had not been set. The foreman explained that the manager of the printing plant had objected to the article. I returned the copy to the foreman and told him to set it at once. A few minutes later the manager rushed in and handed it back to me, declaring that he would not permit the printing of counterrevolutionary insinuations against Communist comrades and that his men would stop the presses rather than set it. Without replying, I dialed the nearest military barracks, called the chairman of the regimental committee to the telephone, and asked him to hold the line, telling him I might have an urgent message for him. Then I said to the manager, "If you try to sabotage the orders of the Executive Committee, I will call in a service company, occupy the building, and eject you and your men bodily from the premises."

"You don't dare do that," the manager shouted, but then he realized I was not bluffing. The editorial appeared the next morning on the front page.

By the middle of May no doubt remained that the Bolshevist slogan of fraternization amounted to a call for a separate truce as a step toward a separate peace with Germany. In fact, fraternization was limited to the Russian front, where the German Command openly supported it; there was practically none on the Western Front. Willingly or not, the Bolsheviks worked hand in hand with German militarists. They denied, however, that they worked for a separate peace, and the All-Russian conference of Communist Organizations declared it slanderous to accuse them of doing so.

The argument the soldiers understood best was that fraternization could lead to a lull in a sector of a front but could by no means bring a general, just, and durable peace. Once I tried to elaborate this argument in the full session of the Soviet. During a debate on war and peace policy in the plenary session I raised the question of the political implications of the fraternization campaign and said, addressing myself to the Communist leaders, "Your fraternization campaign serves only to weaken our army so that Russia would stand defenseless before Germany and be compelled to sign a separate peace."

I was interrupted by violent protests, Zinoviev leading the demonstration. Each time I tried to resume the speech the Bolsheviks drowned my voice in cries of "Liar!" and "Slanderer!" Such men as Zinoviev knew, of course, that I was interpreting their policy correctly, but the indignation of some of the Bolshevist soldiers may have been sincere.

UNREST IN KRONSTADT

In his strategy for seizing power, Lenin did not think of a showdown with the Provisional Government. He had the deepest contempt for the men in the Marinsky Palace and was confident they would disappear from political life the moment the Petrograd Soviet ceased to support them. His aim was to get control over the Soviets—first in Petrograd; next, in all other cities. If occasionally he condescended to attack and abuse the government, he did it only to discredit and vilify the Executive Committee of the Petrograd Soviet for its association with this "headquarters of counterrevolution." He picked Kronstadt for the first experiment in seizing power locally through a Soviet and for a showdown of force with the Executive Committee of Petrograd.

Kronstadt, the base of the Baltic fleet, is located on an island, Kotlin, in the mouth of the Neva. Together with coastal forts, Red Hill to the south and Ino (in Finland) to the east, it formed the defense of the capital from the sea. Its population consisted mainly of sailors, who had been completely isolated from civilians under the Tsarist regime. Most of them were inarticulate, embittered men, held to obedience by ruthless discipline. The worst bloodshed in the March revolution had occurred in Kronstadt. Taking vengeance against their oppressors, the sailors killed the commander of the Baltic fleet and many officers and threw others into the dungeons in which before the revolution enlisted men had been kept for insubordination and misconduct.

The Commissar of the first Provisional Government sent to Kronstadt reported deplorable conditions in the fortress prisons but could do nothing to improve them. In fact, he took at face value the assertion of the local Soviet that the arrested officers were in pre-trial custody. This theory, however, was unacceptable to the government. The local Soviets had no legal right to take people into custody, investigate their crimes, or try them. Thus the Kronstadt Soviet was violating the law of the land. The press loudly lamented the fate of the prisoners in Kronstadt. However, the first Provisional Government lacked strength to curb the reign of lawlessness at the gate of the capital. The Coalition Government appointed a new Commissar for Kronstadt and instructed him to straighten out the situation of the prisoners. Soon after his appointment, he asked me to go to the fortress with him and talk to the people assembled in the main meeting place, the Yakor Plaza. The leaders of the local Soviet, he said, would also speak at the meeting and a frank discussion would contribute to the political education of the sailors.

Yakor Plaza was packed when I got there on May 29. I estimated the crowd at ten or fifteen thousand—two thirds of them sailors; the rest, soldiers and workers. The elevated platform was surrounded by a Bolshevist clique headed by Raskolnikov and Roshal, the leaders of the local Soviet, and Trotsky, whom they had invited as the spokesman of the left opposition in the Executive Committee. I began my address with the usual greeting from the Executive Committee and went on to describe our foreign and domestic policy.

My speech was interrupted repeatedly by cries of "Warmonger! Imperialist!" The crowd would keep quiet for a few minutes and then angry shouts would resume. Raskolnikov, a young navy officer with the expression of undaunted energy on his handsome face, conducted the chorus. His lieutenant, Roshal, was a youth of hardly more than seventeen, with ecstatic eyes, shrieking voice, and gesticulating arms —a perfect leader of a teen-age gang, although nattily dressed.

After my speech, a man in a ragged and dirty soldier's uniform climbed on the platform, a written note in his hand. "Here is the truth!" he screamed: "The new government has ordered the peasants to pay four hundred rubles for each acre of land. Is this a fair price? We never heard of such prices under the Tsar. How can a simple peasant like me get four hundred rubles?"

I asked the man who had told him that nonsense. He replied, "You would never tell the truth. But others, whom the poor people can trust, told me this."

A slick sailor came next. "The rich people and the officers profit from the war. Why should they make peace? We, the sailors, know how to end the war! Guns and officers overboard!"

He was followed by another sailor, a bearded man with a slow, deliberate way of talking. "Take, for example, Tseretelli. He is in charge of the post offices. Ask him how it happens that the officers get letters every day, and we, the simple people, get none? He knows the answer. Did he not tell the mailmen to deliver mail only to the educated people? He must think we can wait. Is this fair, comrades?"

Then Raskolnikov and Roshal spoke in the name of the local Soviet, describing it as the true stronghold of the revolution. Trotsky had the last word. I had heard and seen him many times in Petrograd, but never as close as on Yakor Plaza. He was of middle height but seemed tall when he spoke. There was something commanding and at the same time something evil, diabolic, in his angular features. His voice was strong and clear, an ideal voice for an open-air harangue. I listened to him and tried to figure out whether he was sincerely obsessed with the ideas he was preaching and really was a visionary of the revolution, like Lenin, or a shameless demagogue.

Greeted with an ovation, he spoke of blood and violence as a necessary expression of the will of the people in a revolution. "The fine gentlemen in the Tauride Palace think they can make a revolution by negotiating and compromising with the enemies of the people. I tell you, heads must roll, blood must flow, there must be no mercy if we want to win! The strength of the French Revolution was in the machine that made the enemies of the people shorter by a head. This is a fine device. We must have it in every city, and, first of all, here in Kronstadt!"

This was cold-blooded, deliberate instigation to murder. Trotsky realized, of course, that the sailors of Kronstadt would not erect the guillotine on Yakor Plaza. His reference to the French Revolution was an oratorical embellishment, and its essential objective was to wake the slumbering beast in the listeners while leaving to them the choice of victims and lethal techniques. While driving the crowd to frenzy, Trotsky himself remained completely cool, visibly enjoying the effect of his rhetoric. By the end of his peroration, all my doubts were dispelled. I was listening to a brilliant faker for whom the revolution was a stage for the display of his talents and acquisition of power and fame.

I returned to Petrograd sick and disgusted. On the same day the Kronstadt Soviet passed a resolution breaking relations with the Provisional Government. "From now on," it stated, "the Soviet of Workers and Soldiers is the sole authority in Kronstadt. On questions of national importance, it will deal directly with the Petrograd Soviet."

The Executive Committee summoned the leaders of the Kronstadt Soviet to Petrograd to explain their resolution. Headed by Raskolnikov and Roshal, the delegates arrived on June 2. They explained that the resolution was an expression of the views of the Kronstadt Soviet but did not change the political status of the city.

They denounced as slander the suspicion that Kronstadt was preparing to secede from Russia. The Executive Committee spent a whole day talking with them. They left promising that the Kronstadt Soviet would issue a clarification of its resolution.

Indeed, such a clarification appeared the next day in Kronstadt newspapers. Although not entirely satisfactory, it left the door open to the settlement of the conflict. Tseretelli volunteered to go to Kronstadt with another Socialist minister for further negotiations with the local Soviet. They obtained a declaration of obedience to the government from the Kronstadt Bolsheviks and a promise to transfer all their prisoners to an investigation commission appointed by the government. The Kronstadt Soviet was called to an emergency meeting. It ratified the declaration and the crisis seemed to have been liquidated. But the next day a crowd of sailors assembled on Yakor Plaza and passed a resolution demanding that the local Soviet reaffirm it was the sole authority in the fortress. From the Plaza the crowd marched to the Soviet's offices, and the latter nullified, by a new resolution, the decision of the preceding day.

Indignation against the Communists for plunging the fortress into anarchy was mounting in the country. A group of soldiers and officers came to the Tauride Palace from Fort Ino. I was delegated to talk with them. Their spokesman, a non-commissioned artillery officer, said, "We, the garrison of Fort Ino, are a part of the defense of the capital. We disapprove of the anarchistic actions of Kronstadt and are ready to support you."

"What kind of support do you offer us?" I asked.

"If it comes to a showdown," he replied, "you cannot send troops to Kronstadt. But our fort, together with Red Hill, can force Kronstadt to submit." He explained that the heavy artillery of the mainland forts dominated the approaches to the Neva, including Kotlin Island and the surrounding fortifications. "The fellows in Kronstadt know this," he said. "They talk big, but we can call their bluff."

The delegates impressed me as resolute men, and I asked them to call a meeting of the troops at Fort Ino the next day and invite the representatives of the Kronstadt Soviet to discuss their stand. The meeting began at noon in an unusual setting, A flat sandy beach, a grove of pines in the background. Barracks and tents behind the trees, a platform under an old pine, ranges of small hills along the shore, big gun emplacements. The garrison consisted of artillery and engineering units. The infantry division that covered the fort from the land did not attend the meeting; it was stationed several miles away and had its own committee.

Roshal and a few other Kronstadt leaders came in a speedboat. The artilleryman opened the meeting. "We of Fort Ino, with Kronstadt and Red Hill, guard the naval gate to the capital. Now we must know where we stand in the clash between Kronstadt and Petrograd. The representative of the Executive Committee will tell us what the issues are. Next, the delegates from Kronstadt will present their case."

In this setting my task was easy. The artillerymen of the fort were suspicious of the sailors and considered them stupid ruffians. Moreover, they had no sympathy for the Bolsheviks in general.

Roshal, who followed me, began in a trembling voice, "Comrades, do you trust me?" Someone answered loudly, "Why should we? We have never seen you. You may be just an s.o.b."

Roshal's complaints that the Petrograd Soviet had treated Kronstadt unfairly found no response. In my concluding remarks I asked the Ino garrison for a clear yes or no decision and introduced a sharp resolution condemning the Kronstadt Soviet and pledging support of the Executive Committee and the government. The resolution was passed almost unanimously, with only six dissenting votes.

In the evening the Petrograd Soviet convened in an emergency meeting. Tseretelli pressed for a resolution condemning the Kronstadt Soviet and demanding its obedience to the orders of the government. Despite protests from the left, led by Trotsky, this resolution was passed by a two-thirds majority. The next day the All-Russian Congress of Peasants opened in Petrograd. This huge and somewhat loose organization, dominated by the right wing S-R, invited Tseretelli to report on the Kronstadt crisis. At the request of the left, the chair also invited Trotsky to defend Kronstadt, but the Congress refused to listen to him and some delegates threatened to eject him from the hall.

After two days of negotiation, Kronstadt surrendered and delivered its prisoners to the government's investigating commission. The Kronstadt Soviet recognized that there was no charge against about half of them, and these were freed at once. The others were transferred to Petrograd and released after the commission had checked the charges against each.

The unrest in Kronstadt was liquidated, we had gained the skirmish. Our victory was due partly to the authority of the Petrograd Soviet and the personal prestige of Tseretelli as the main negotiator for the government. There was a troublesome undertone in these negotiations, however. The effrontery of the Kronstadt Bolsheviks stemmed largely from the feeling of the local mob that, holding arms in their hands, they could challenge both the government and the Petrograd Soviet. They changed their tune when they realized that the heavy artillery of the mainland forts was not on their side. Things were rapidly approaching the point where disputes between the two wings of the Soviet would be decided not by arguments but by force of arms.

UNREST IN PETROGRAD

After the failure in Kronstadt, the Communists concentrated their efforts on the Petrograd garrison. Through agitation against orders to alert companies for the front they had aroused the soldiers' suspicions of their representatives in the Tauride Palace, who had voted to strengthen the army. By kindling these suspicions, the Communists persuaded the soldiers to elect, in addition to their deputies to the Soviet, a special conference of regimental representatives to discuss questions directly concerning the enlisted men. Since the greatest concern of the men in reserve regiments was how to dodge service in the trenches, the new conference rapidly developed into a shield to protect the dodgers against the hardships of the front. In no time the conference became strong enough to challenge the Soldiers' Section of the Petrograd Soviet. On June 24 it unanimously rejected the plan that had been prepared by the government and accepted by the Soldiers' Section to amalgamate the reserve regiments with corresponding units in the active army. The conference substituted its own demands: to supply the Petrograd regiments with no fewer than twenty-four machine guns per battalion, let enlisted men elect officers and demote those they disliked, and leave the reserve regiments in Petrograd to defend the revolution.

A conference of Petrograd factory councils was called in the Tauride Palace to discuss workers' grievances. Bolsheviks predominated in the conference, and their resolution demanding the transfer of all power to the Soviets was passed by an overwhelming majority. We still had a majority in both sections of the Soviet, but this majority was now offset by the conference of regimental representatives and the factory councils controlled by the Bolsheviks.

This situation meant a new wave of unrest in factories and barracks, and for me, personally, more sleepless nights with speeches before sullen, hostile crowds. But we were far from acknowledging defeat. The innumerable delegations that came to the Tauride Palace from all corners of Russian and all points of the front sustained our conviction that the great majority of the people supported our policy. The split was not between the majority in the Executive Committee and the masses of the Russian people, but between a part of the Petrograd workers and the bulk of the workers and peasants in the nation; between the demoralized elements of the garrison in the capital and the army at the front.

On June 16 the first All-Russian Congress of the Soviets of Workers and Soldiers opened with great solemnity in the Naval School. Its sessions lasted three weeks. The Congress of Peasant Deputies was meeting in Petrograd at the same time. Thus, the main democratic forces of the nation were represented in the capital. The Congress of Workers and Soldiers had some nine hundred voting members, with a majority of about six hundred and fifty to seven hundred supporting the policy of the Executive Committee. In the Peasants' Congress, our supporters outnumbered the left-wing opposition ten to one. But the minority was bracing itself for a showdown. The provincial delegates were unable to grasp the situation. Most of them had had some trouble with their Bolsheviks at home and managed them fairly well; what was going on in Petrograd seemed to them a squabble among local leaders. Both Congresses were still in session when the Communists called their forces into the streets, using the Anarchists as their shock troops.

ANARCHISTS

The Anarchists had appeared in the Viborg district of the capital in the early days of the revolution. Some of them, as political offenders, had been liberated from imprisonment and had installed themselves in an old vacant house on Viborg Prospect. The house was surrounded by a park and belonged to the former Tsarist minister, Durnovo. The local police did not object to having homeless people use it, and an apparently harmless Anarchist community developed on the Durnovo *dacha*.

Free-for-all meetings were held in the park but attracted little attention until the Anarchists decided to publish a newspaper. In search of printing facilities, they organized themselves into an armed commando and invaded the printing plant of a conservative newspaper. The printers fled from the premises, leaving the presses in the hands of the raiders. A crowd assembled around the plant, ready to break in and lynch the intruders. Somebody telephoned to our Congress. Representatives of the Congress rushed to the scene, forced their way into the besieged building, disarmed the Anarchists, and took them to the Naval School. The gang consisted mainly of young boys, bewildered and frightened by the unexpected outcome of their adventure. Since there was no evidence that any of them had actually threatened anybody with weapons, they were permitted to return to their *dacha* after a reprimand and warning.

Next day the Petrograd newspapers headlined the beginning of anarchy in the capital. The government decided to restore order and, with consent of our Executive Committee, the Minister of Justice served a warrant on the inhabitants of the Durnovo *dacha* to vacate the premises in twenty-four hours. This was meat for Bolshevist propaganda—the capitalist government evicting homeless people, former victims of Tsarism, from the *dacha* of the former Tsar's minister! By noon, all the factories in the Viborg district went on strike and workers were called to the park. A huge crowd assembled to defend freedom and the people's rights against the assault of the capitalists. Armed men milled about in the streets. Reinforcements were arriving from other districts.

The Congress of Workers and Soldiers turned its attention from national policy to Petrograd affairs. Trotsky defended the rights of the common man, glorifying the heroism of the workers of the Viborg district and calling on all other districts and the garrison to join them. Other Communist orators called on the sailors of Kronstadt and the Baltic fleet to rescue the revolution. The Congress voted a resolution condemning the Anarchist raid, the strike in the Viborg district, and the armed demonstration as acts of sabotage against the revolution. This did not help, however.

The next day unrest spread throughout the city. The *dacha* became the headquarters of a new revolutionary committee that allegedly represented ninety factories. Regiments sent their representatives to the *dacha*. As in the May days, the Executive Committee tried to keep the fire from spreading. Again we sat before telephones in the Tauride Palace, answering calls, sending out men to trouble spots. In some places we were successful; in others we met morose opposition.

The Bolsheviks decided the time had come for a decisive assault. Late on the night of June 22, the Congress was in session when a group of workers from Bolshevist *Pravda's* printing plant brought us proofs of the morning issue of the paper. The front page called workers and soldiers to mass protest demonstrations on June 23, with the usual Communist slogans. Contrary to common practices, however, the routes of the procession were not indicated: the Bolsheviks were keeping their plans secret not only from the Petrograd Soviet and the Congress, but also from the marchers. The obvious purpose was to get the crowds out, to excite them to the highest pitch, and then to throw them against strategic points selected in advance.

Chkheidze called an emergency session of the Soldiers' Section of the Soviet. It convened at 2:00 A.M. in the Tauride Palace. I gave our information about the Bolshevist plot. Members of the Soldiers' Section reported that there was unusual excitement in the barracks and that soldiers had been told to be on the alert, awaiting orders. The

Bolsheviks denied everything and, when I produced the proof sheet of *Pravda*, they declared it a counterfeit. The Section passed a resolution condemning demonstrations organized behind the back of the Soviet and the All-Russian Congress. I rushed to the Naval School with this resolution. The Congress was still in session. I showed the resolution to Chkheidze and he asked me to write an appeal to the soldiers and workers. The appeal was approved by a majority of the Congress, and a resolution forbidding street demonstrations during the next three days was voted unanimously. The Communists voted with the rest of the Congress; from the moment their plan for a surprise attack failed, they were no longer interested in the affair.

Members of the Congress spent the rest of the night in the barracks. I drew one of the most demoralized reserve regiments. When I got there, before dawn, the soldiers were milling about in the courtyard, some with arms and cartridge belts. I asked one group why they were out in the court at that hour. They said there was an order to be ready to cut the throats of the enemies of the revolution but they did not know who these enemies were or who had given the order. I called the men to a meeting. The crowd was grim. I began my speech by greeting the men in the name of the All-Russian Congress but was interrupted by outcries, "Yours is a congress of police officers and gendarmes!"

Then I read the resolution of the Soldiers' Section and the appeal of the Congress and asked those who opposed the order forbidding street demonstrations to come forward. Nobody responded, but several soldiers came out with the usual Bolshevist line: "The soldiers got nothing out of the revolution." "The government has been sold out to the capitalists." "Tseretelli got a bribe of ten million rubles." "What difference does it make to us whether Russia is ruled by Kerensky or the Kaiser?"

On June 23 the Congress met in the Tauride Palace. Provincial delegates who had spent the night in the barracks were mortified by what they had seen and heard. The session was spiritless; the Communists abstained from the discussion. The next day the Executive Committee met with the presiding board and the leaders of all political parties of the Congress. Tseretelli demanded drastic measures, first of all, to disarm workers' commandos. Martov, the leader of the left-wing Mensheviks, objected. A clash broke out between the two Menshevist groups. A weak resolution was passed. Seeing that the majority did not press the charge against them, the Bolsheviks demanded that the Congress condemn those who had raised the accusation against them. When their demand was rejected, they left the hall.

I was glad to see them go, but some members of the Executive Committee felt uncomfortable at having restricted the sacred right of the people to express their wishes by street demonstrations and suggested organizing a workers' demonstration under the auspices of the Soviet. The demonstration was planned as a farewell party by the Petrograd workers for the Socialist delegation about to go abroad to prepare for the international peace conference. Chkheidze was skeptical about this plan and I violently opposed it, arguing that the masses of workers in the capital either knew nothing about our delegation or believed what the Communists had told them. Besides, the Bolsheviks had made all their preparations for a demonstration, while the majority of the Executive Committee had not had time even to get flags and placards ready.

My objections were overruled. The demonstration took place on July 1. It was a complete fiasco. The Bolshevist banners outnumbered ours by about a hundred to one. The crowds marching in front of the Congress either ignored the Socialist delegation that was to go abroad or jeered at it.

The Communists felt this was their day—compensation for their defeat on June 23. The Anarchists decided this was their day, too. They marched from the Durnovo *dacha* in a column under a black banner. A huge crowd joined them, perhaps out of curiosity. From the Parade Plaza, they proceeded to the Crosses. A group of two or three hundred men broke into the prison, overpowered the guards, and freed a score of inmates—common criminals and a few persons held in custody on charges of espionage. The crowd took them triumphantly to the stronghold of anarchy on the Viborg Prospect.

THE OFFENSIVE ON THE FRONT

Unrest in Petrograd distracted public attention from developments at the front.

On March 21, soon after the outbreak of the revolution in Russia, the British and French armies had launched a general offensive, but they were unable to break through the German field fortifications. German submarines were gnawing at the lifelines of the British Empire. The tide had turned against the Allies, and in their distress they asked Russia to support them by an offensive, as the Russian High Command had promised under the Tsar.

The first Provisional Government was too weak to consider active military operations, but the reorganized Cabinet considered the possibility of breaking the lull on the front. The question was put to the High Command in Mogilev. The consensus of the military experts was that the army was in poor shape morally but was better provided with munitions than at any time since the beginning of the war. It seemed defensible to take a chance. The Coalition Government therefore decided to activate the front and published a declaration of its "firm conviction that the Russian revolutionary army will not permit the German troops to crush the Allies in the West and then turn all the fury of their arms against ourselves."

The High Command developed a plan that could either be expanded or limited in the course of the operations: to strike against the Austrian troops on the Southern Front and extend the offensive gradually northward, bringing fresh divisions into action. The military experts believed that Austrian troops were not in much better shape than ours and expected that our initial success would improve the morale of our soldiers.

The army committees were primarily responsible for the political and psychological conditioning of the troops for the operation, but the prominent role in this campaign fell to Kerensky, appointed to the post of Minister of War in the new Cabinet. This was an unfortunate appointment—for the army as well as for Kerensky—but he started the difficult job with great zeal, visiting the regiments designed for the assault, holding meetings, making speeches. Later he was ridiculed for an attempt to coax the troops instead of ordering them into action, but this accusation was unfair. Even if some of his harangues were in bad taste, there was nothing humorous in the idea of a direct appeal to the soldiers on the eve of a major operation, a method that has been used by commanders at all times.

While Kerensky was touring the front, the Communists opened a frantic campaign against the offensive, calling on the soldiers to disobey the order to attack. They could not break the hold of the moderate Socialists over the army at once, but they won salients here and there. To the Baltic fleet and Kronstadt they added the First Grenadier Corps on the Southwestern Front and single regiments on other fronts. Many other units were vacillating: they voted Communist resolutions, refused to execute orders, deposed their officers, and then, under the influence of the army committee and threat of reprisals, reversed themselves and pledged obedience and allegiance to the Petrograd Soviet and its Executive Committee.

Cases of open rebellion were rare, but we in the Tauride Palace felt that the Bolsheviks were testing their power and were getting ready for large-scale revolt at the front and in the rear. Their new strategy was clear: first, to sabotage the offensive and persuade the masses of soldiers that their party—and that party alone—was against the war and for an immediate peace; next, when the offensive started, to bring it to defeat; and then, as the third step, to use the military setback for a general onslaught against the Executive Committee and the moderates in the Soviets.

The offensive started on July 1, the day of the ill-fated street demonstration in Petrograd. The next day, opening the Congress session, Chkheidze read a telegram from Kerensky to the Provisional Government. It gave a glittering picture of the initial success of the Russian troops and demanded that the regiments taking part in the offensive be given red banners and the honorary title of "Regiments of July 1." The Congress responded with a long ovation. That day jubilant crowds marched along the Nevsky Prospect with red flags decorated with patriotic slogans. Kerensky was their hero.

The success at the front changed the political climate in Petrograd. Many leftists joined the patriotic bandwagon. The stronghold of the Anarchists was liquidated without bloodshed by an impressive task force organized by the Executive Committee. The Communist papers were filled with vituperation against the new crime of the moderates when the Petrograd Soviet met to take a stand on the offensive. Tseretelli's report was interrupted by both applause and jeers. I moved an appeal to the peasants, workers, and soldiers in the rear garrisons to support the front troops. Its concluding paragraph, condemning sabotage of the war effort, provoked tumultuous protest. The resolution was finally accepted, but the majority was small. We were fighting an uphill battle in Petrograd. Lenin's propaganda had begun to bear fruit.

REAR REGIMENTS PROTEST AGAINST THE OFFENSIVE

That same day the students of a military school in Peterhof, twenty miles from the capital, decided to celebrate the offensive by a church service and a parade on the school grounds. Soldiers of a reserve regiment located nearby opened fire on the students. According to the first report, many young boys had been killed. The Congress sent Vilenkin and me to investigate.

We reached Peterhof late in the evening, called the regimental committee together, and asked it to summon witnesses of the event. The witnesses testified that the regiment opposed the imperialistic war and was therefore provoked by the students' celebration. They claimed that the soldiers had no arms, that those who had guns did not fire, and that those who fired aimed in the air. If any students were wounded, they probably had hurt themselves in the melee. We told the committee we would question the students and announce our decision before dawn.

"Keep the men on the alert!" Vilenkin ordered. "All companies will be assembled to hear our decision."

Then we proceeded to the school. The first report proved to have been exaggerated. Nobody had been killed, but scores of boys had been wounded. The representatives of the students and the commander of the school asked us not to press charges against the soldiers: a trial of the culprits would only aggravate the relations between the school and the regiment. We agreed to leave this question to the judicial authorities.

We returned to the barracks after 3:00 A.M. A crowd of soldiers was assembled on the floodlighted exercise grounds. Vilenkin was shocked by their appearance and whispered to me, "You call this 'a regiment' in Petrograd? I would think it a bunch of tramps." I announced our decision. The acts of violence committed by the soldiers were inexcusable; the culprits had disgraced the regiment; we would confine ourselves to moral condemnation of the assault only because its victims had asked us not to initiate prosecution.

At first the crowd listened in sullen silence. Most of the soldiers disapproved of the attack against the students. But after I finished, angry cries burst out. Vilenkin stepped forward on the platform. His smart uniform and four crosses impressed the crowd. He began to speak somewhat nonchalantly, almost derisively. "I am chairman of the Fifth Army Committee, and when I return to the front, my comrades will ask me about what I saw in Petrograd. I want you to hear what I will tell them. A front soldier has only to look at you to know what kind of creatures you are. I am sorry I was not here with my hussars when you attacked the school. With a single squadron we would have taught you a lesson you would never have forgotten. This is what I shall report to my comrades."

He returned to his seat and I declared the meeting adjourned. The crowd was silent. I did not suspect then that only two weeks later Vilenkin would bring his men to Petrograd to beat back the Bolsheviks' onslaught against the Executive Committee.

REVERSE ON THE FRONT

A few days later the Russian offensive ended in a rout. As planned, it had been directed originally against the southern tip of the Austrian front, manned by tired and thoroughly demoralized troops. The Russian High Command expected the Austrians to shift reinforcements southward, thus weakening other parts of the line and permitting the Russians to broaden the offensive while advancing the left wing of their attacking troops. Events took another course, and very soon the whole operation became utterly chaotic.

The attack began according to plan. What Kerensky described in his telegram to the government was a wishful vision of a victory rather than the actual operation. "On July 1," he wrote, "the Russian revolutionary army, with tremendous enthusiasm, launched the offensive. Disregarding the small groups of cowards in some regiments and leaving them with contempt in the rear, the free warriors of Russia have affirmed by their offensive the new discipline based on the sense of civic duty. This day has put an end to vicious insinuations against the democratic organizations of the Russian army. . . ."

From the very beginning, however, there had been much confusion. Whole regiments disobeyed the order to charge or obeyed only after long hesitation. On the third day, a grenadier regiment, ordered to advance, decided to take no part in the imperialistic war, left its positions, and marched to the rear, opening a wide gap in the front lines. The High Command and the army organizations had to send reserve units to encircle and disarm the rebels.

Some regiments suffered heavy losses, especially among committeemen who went at the head of attacking forces. Other units advanced only until they met opposition. Some few returned to their initial positions after an irresolute push forward. Fortunately, the morale of the Austrian troops in this sector was no better than ours. Some Austrian divisions began to retreat before the Russians approached their positions, and the Austrian Command was compelled to regroup its forces by withdrawing units that had not been attacked. Thus the Eighth Army, under the command of General Kornilov, crossed the Austro-Russian border, and, almost unopposed, continued to advance, taking one city after another.

Then the German High Command shifted some of its crack troops to the Eastern Front. On July 19 they launched a general counteroffensive—not against the advanced units of the Eighth Army, but further south, against the famous "Regiments of July 1," which had not advanced since the initial attack. The front of the Eleventh Army was pierced at several points and our command began to pull back divisions that the Germans had not yet attacked. The retreat of the Eleventh Army exposed the left flank of the Seventh Army, which likewise fell back. Confusion on the front increased from hour to hour. By July 23 the retreat became a disorderly rout. Entire divisions left the line, abandoning their equipment and opening the way for the enemy's advance.

In this desperate situation, the Russian High Command in Mogilev ordered the Fifth Army, on the Northern Front, to advance. The commander of the army had advised against this operation, considering it hopeless, but the command at Mogilev overruled his objections. The Fifth Army started the operation but was beaten back. Then the High Command ordered the Eighth Army to fall back, and it returned to its initial position. After less than four weeks the whole operation ended in failure. From the purely military point of view, however, it was not a major disaster: the Austrians were unable to advance beyond the old front lines. Moreover, the ultimate objective of the operation —to relieve the pressure on the Western Front—had been attained, at least in part.

The political implications of the defeat were much more important. Patriotic *élan* was succeeded by bitter disillusionment. The High Command blamed the revolutionary organizations for the defeat. The committees accused the officers. The Cadets resumed the political offensive against the Soviet. Even before the final collapse of the operation, the Communists launched an offensive of their own.

THE JULY RIOTS

Lenin's plans were laid in advance: First, to induce or compel the Executive Committee to overthrow the Provisional Government; next, to purge the Committee, with the aid of the Petrograd regiments; then, using the authority of the Tauride Palace, to extend the grip over the front army; and finally, having all armed forces in hand, to take over the country. Before Lenin decided to strike with all his forces, however, a single regiment, the First Machine Gunners, opened the onslaught. This regiment had particular reason to be impatient: the front was urgently demanding more machine guns, and it was slated to send most of its men to the trenches soon. On the other hand, if the Bolsheviks were in power, the machine gunners would stay in Petrograd. This was the only issue that counted with the men, but political events gave them a chance to cover up their motives with nobler catchwords.

Four ministers, representing the right wing of the Cadet party, resigned on July 15 in protest against the agreement other members of the Cabinet had concluded with the Ukrainian National Congress, promising autonomy to that province. Their resignation neither surprised nor alarmed the leaders of the All-Russian Executive Committee which, after the All-Russian Congress of the Soviets, had succeeded the Petrograd Executive Committee as the mouthpiece of the democratic forces in the nation. This new body consisted of three hundred members. Half of them were elected by the Congress on the basis of proportional representation of all political groups. To these were added a hundred representatives of local Soviets (including the army committees), and the remaining fifty seats were allocated to the old Executive Committee in recognition of its leading role in the revolution. The representatives of the provincial Soviets had returned to their homes but were ready to come to Petrograd whenever the need arose. Together with the Executive Committee of the Peasants' Congress, this body was better qualified to speak in the name of the masses of the Russian people than any other organization—including the rump government.

The resignation of the Cadets' ministers made little change in the situation. They had been sitting on the edge of their Cabinet seats ever since the formation of the Coalition and had been a liability rather than an asset for the government. On the morning of July 16, the leaders of the Executive Committee met as usual for an informal discussion of current affairs. Tseretelli gave a brief report of the crisis. The Soviet representative had advised other members of the Cabinet to accept the Cadets' resignation. The government would continue in the present form until the plenary session of the All-Russian Executive Committee convened and determined the composition of the new Cabinet.

When we reached the Tauride Palace after this conference, we learned that the capital was in turmoil. Mass meetings were under way in the barracks and factories. Communist speakers and flags everywhere proclaimed "Resignation of Minister-Capitalists! All Power to the Soviets!" At noon soldiers in different parts of the city opened regimental arsenals and took rifles and munitions. Groups of enlisted men and workers went from barracks to barracks, from factory to factory; the First Machine Gunners were particularly active. In the Tauride Palace telephones rang incessantly. Men in the barracks asked for instructions: "Should our regiment go out? Who gave the call to arms?" We repeated the instruction of the Executive Committee: "No armed demonstrations in the streets."

Our men reported that agitation in the barracks was focused on the reprisals ordered by the government against the grenadier regiment that had fled from the battlefield. The All-Russian Executive Committee of Workers and Soldiers and that of Peasants convened for a joint session in the Tauride Palace and issued an appeal to the Petrograd garrison, explaining that, at the request of the army committee, the treasonous regiment had been disarmed. The appeal was sent to all regiments, read in the barracks, posted everywhere, and distributed in the form of handbills. It produced an effect. The mass of soldiers seemed to forget the disbanded regiment. But new slogans emerged. Now the Bolsheviks talked about the Declaration of Soldiers' Slavery.

Late in the afternoon regiments began to walk out of their barracks, fully armed, some with field kitchens and ambulances. The alarmed Commandant of the Petrograd Military District—without consulting the Tauride Palace—called up the High Command of the army in Mogilev and asked that reliable troops be sent to the capital. The reply came at once: Mogilev had other troubles; the whole front was crumbling. Meanwhile a call came to the Tauride Palace from the Fifth Army by direct wire. I answered it. Vilenkin was calling on behalf of the army committee: "If you need reinforcements, the Fifth Army can put a task force at your disposal." I rushed to Chkheidze's office. A few of the Committee's leaders were there. I told them about the offer of the Fifth Army. Chkheidze asked Tseretelli to discuss the matter with Vilenkin and urge the Fifth Army to send troops as promptly as possible.

At 10:00 P.M. the First Machine Gunners' regiment appeared in front of the Tauride Palace in marching formation. A non-commissioned officer, Jilin, a notorious Communist, was at the head of the column. He posted the regiment before the colonnade of the palace and sent a messenger to the Executive Committee to ask its representatives to appear before the soldiers. Chkheidze and I went to the entrance of the palace. Chkheidze had lost his voice and asked me to speak. I reminded Jilin that armed demonstrations were contrary to the orders of the Committee: "Your appearance in the streets with arms seems to indicate that your regiment refuses to recognize the authority of the All-Russian Executive Committee. If you do not recognize our authority, why are you here?"

Jilin replied that the Machine Gunners recognized our authority. Indeed, they recognized no other authority but ours. But they were disturbed by the rumors that the Executive Committee intended to enter into a new coalition with reactionary capitalists. The Machine Gunners would not stand for such a policy. They had suffered enough. The soldiers roared their approval: "All power to the Soviets!"

Jilin's profession of respect for the Executive Committee called for a conciliatory reply. I explained to him that the All-Russian Executive Committee would meet the next day to make decisions in conformity with the desires of the majority of the Russian people and concluded, "There are many hundreds of regiments like yours in Russia. We cannot give particular weight to your opinion just because you are nearer the Tauride Palace and are the first to express your views. Whatever our decision, you will have to comply with it."

The soldiers neither cheered nor jeered. Then the regiment marched past the entrance of the palace so that each battalion could salute our chairman and I could repeat what I had said to the head of the column. The soldiers marked time in silence.

Next came a grenadiers' regiment and a procession of workers with Bolshevist banners. Chkheidze and I again stood between the white columns of the palace. Chkheidze greeted each demonstration by waving his hands, and I spoke to the crowds. A group of Communists took their stand next to us. In the name of their party they urged the marchers not to be lulled by empty promises but to carry out their struggle for world revolution. Regiment after regiment marched past the palace. Some soldiers left the ranks, climbed the wide stairs, and entered the building. Gradually Katherine Hall was filled with armed men.

Our All-Russian Executive Committee and that of the Peasants met in a joint session that lasted until long after midnight. Violence and looting in the capital were reported. The chairman of the Workers' Section of the Petrograd Soviet read the resolution of the Section demanding that the All-Russian Executive Committee take over power. Provincial delegates accused the Petrograd workers and soldiers of trying to usurp power. "Petrograd isn't all Russia!" they screamed.

They were followed by angry representatives of the peasants: "You, rioters, Anarchists, traitors! The villages will put an end to your lawlessness!"

The Communists lost their aplomb. Trotsky denied that his party was trying to intimidate the Executive Committee. "What happened today," he explained, "was a peaceful demonstration of citizens." He also denied the reports of violence by Bolshevik-led crowds, arguing that all incidents were the work of the Cadets and *provocateurs.* Tseretelli announced that the presiding board of the All-Russian Executive Committee proposed to hold the plenary session of the Committee in Moscow, where it could work free from mob pressure.

I was not in the hall when he introduced this proposal, but friends told me later that its effect was as if a bomb had exploded under the cupola. If the All-Russian Executive Committee could not meet in Petrograd, neither could the government remain there nor could the Constituent Assembly convene in that city. Tseretelli's suggestion therefore amounted to transferring the political capital to Moscow. It was easy to visualize the implications of this measure: The Communists would then take over Petrograd with all its arsenals and military installations, including the Baltic fleet and munitions factories.

The peasant delegates applauded Tseretelli's proposal. Martov and his followers violently opposed it. No vote was taken, and the session adjourned before dawn.

THE SIEGE OF THE TAURIDE PALACE

I remained in the palace. With two members of the Soldiers' Section, I was now in charge of the defense of the building. We could keep a token guard around the palace, using service companies from military schools and some squadrons from cavalry or Cossack regiments. But this would indicate our distrust of the infantry regiments that represented the bulk of the garrison and might provoke a violent clash between our guard and the outfits coming to the palace to demonstrate against us. We therefore decided to call infantry soldiers first. If we had three or four infantry companies as a façade, we could use other units to reinforce them.

We began a roll call of the barracks, asking each regiment whether it supported the rioters or the All-Russian Executive Committee and whether it was ready to help defend the Tauride Palace. Some regimental committees replied that the regiment was neutral. Others told us they were taking orders from the Communist party as the sole true defender of the revolution. None would actively defend us. Only a few promised to send a service platoon to guard the palace . . . if other regiments also sent such platoons. By morning the forces at the disposal of the palace commandant had dwindled to an incomplete service company of the Pavlovsky Regiment and a few men from other units. Still, we tried to keep guards at the entrance of Katherine Hall and at large French windows along the façade, to make it appear as if the palace were defended by armed forces.

All the news from other parts of the city was bad. During the night meetings had been held in factories; arms had been brought in by the carload; shock commandos had been formed. In the morning armed demonstrations were resumed in the streets. Crowds roamed the city, firing and looting shops. The Communists brought reinforcements from outside. Battleships were called from Kronstadt. The First Riflemen's reserve regiment was marching from Oranienbaum; the Second was taking up arms in Peterhof.

We expected an onslaught on the Tauride Palace at any moment but continued to negotiate with the barracks by telephone. A few regiments that had sided with the Bolsheviks now announced they would remain neutral after all. Apparently they had changed their minds because of the looting and murder during Communist parades. A few Cossack regiments called the Tauride Palace to tell us they would help the Executive Committee to restore order in the streets if they were supported by infantry. Unfortunately, we had no infantry. A decade later Miliukov remarked pointedly in his *History:* "It seemed that the Provisional Government was forgotten. . . . the real center of the struggle was the Tauride Palace." This was true, with one reservation: There was no real struggle around the Tauride Palace either, only a war of nerves with overwhelming forces on the one side and, on the other, a handful of practically defenseless men who refused to yield.

Then the Commander of the Military District ordered the Cossacks to defend the Tauride Palace. I do not know how large a force he intended to use, but only a platoon, some twenty horsemen with a horse-drawn piece of light artillery, obeyed his order. Had we known of this expedition, we would have countermanded the order at once. There was not the slightest chance that a small horse detachment could pierce the ring of rioting regiments and crowds of armed workers around the Tauride Palace. Indeed, as soon as the Cossacks reached the central avenues overflowing with excited armed crowds, they met with deadly fire. Several men were wounded, a few were killed, and the rest of the detachment fled, abandoning the cannon. The commanding officer of the expedition, a lad of eighteen or nineteen, reached the palace without his side arms and the insignia on his uniform. He was hysterical, crying like a child, and blamed the Executive Committee for the death of his men. I felt very sorry for the youngster, but all I could do for him was to use shock treatment.

"Did we ask you to lead your platoon to our rescue?" I shouted.

"I got the order from my superiors. You had asked them."

"Then listen to what I am going to say. Only an idiot could have sent a platoon on horseback through streets full of foot soldiers with rifles and machine guns. We would not hesitate to use troops that could really fight, but we would rather let the mob ransack the palace than disgrace ourselves by luring a handful of practically unarmed men into a trap."

The palace was surrounded by a disorderly and openly hostile crowd of workers and soldiers when a delegation from the First Armored Division appeared. Its spokesman said to me, "You called on us this morning. Do you need us for a demonstration or for fighting?"

I replied, "If all you can offer is a demonstration, we don't need you."

"Then count on our tanks," he said. "Count on us!" the other members of the delegation echoed.

We drove to the division's barracks. The men, an unexpectedly small group, were assembled in the garage among their tanks, which looked like elephants in stalls. I told the soldiers that the All-Russian Executive Committee was encircled by a rioting mob and other crowds were moving toward the palace, but that we would not yield to threats. An attack was possible at any moment, and I asked, "Will you defend the Executive Committee?"

They replied as one, "We will."

The commander of the division stepped forward and barked orders, "Drivers and gunners, man your cars! Follow me with lids closed! Close formation! Ready for action!"

I took a seat in the narrow compartment in his tank. It carried a red flag and its lid was open; other tanks followed without flags and with guns protruding from their turrets. We cut our way through the crowds and heards whistles and boos about us—the people did not know what to think of our line of tanks. In front of the Tauride Palace we were met with shouts: "Long live the revolution!" A wide passage opened in front of the column and the tanks disappeared one after the other into the courtyard of the palace; only two stopped before the entrance, with guns turned to the street. With a roar of insults and threats the mob receded, clearing a space of about twenty yards before the colonnade.

It was 4:00 P.M. when Chkheidze received a new wire from the Fifth Army: "Preparations completed. The task force is boarding the trains. The first echelon is leaving. Vilenkin." We decided to keep the message secret. Premature disclosure might precipitate the attack. Furthermore, we were not sure our troops would not be stopped by rioting regiments or saboteurs.

The joint session of Executive Committees was resumed. The Communists seemed uncertain of themselves. They had reached the point at which the only further step was open violence—invasion of the Tauride Palace, arrest or murder of the most hated leaders of the Executive Committee. The momentum of the movement was pushing the mob in that direction, but the leaders feared the reaction at the front, in provincial Soviets, and among the peasants. Certainly they would have had no inhibition against throwing the mob against the Marinsky Palace and the "Minister-Capitalists," but the latter were not a party to the clash. The contest for power was between the Communists and the moderate Socialists.

During the session of the Executive Committee I was called to the telephone time and again. Something new was in the air. The spokesman of a regiment asked me nonchalantly about the situation around the Tauride Palace. I replied that he knew the answer without asking me. "That is not what I meant," he said. "Is it true you are bringing front troops to Petrograd?"

"This is true," I answered. "Our echelons are on their way."

He replied casually, "That's okay with us. Our regiment is neutral. All arms have been returned to the arsenal."

About 5:00 P.M. the Kronstadt sailors approached the Tauride Palace. Chernov, Trotsky, and I went to meet them. I recognized the Yakor Plaza mob, with drunks in the front row. The sailors were in a frenzy after a triumphant march through the city, punctuated by looting and shots at windows. Trotsky addressed them: "You are the flower and glory of the revolution!" During his speech a group of men surrounded Chernov and tried to push him into a car, shouting, "Take power, you s.o.b., when you are offered it!" Separated from Chernov, I rushed to the commander of the tanks and told him to deploy the division in front of the palace. Before he could do so, however, Trotsky succeeded in persuading the sailors to release their prisoner.

On the heels of the Kronstadt mob came crowds of armed workers. Brandishing rifles, they demanded that the Executive Committee take over power. There was no point in trying to talk to them. Nobody from the Committee went out. The crowds just marched in front of the palace, roaring demands, threats, and jeers.

The commandant of the palace came to see me. Only eighteen men of the service company of the Pavlovsky Regiment were on duty. In reserve were fourteen men from the crews of tanks. There were not enough for even the posts at the main entrance. Now the whole palace was full of armed workers, soldiers, and sailors. From the hall they made their way into the corridors and offices.

At seven o'clock, when a particularly aggressive crowd filled the plaza in front of the palace, a shot resounded. There had been so much shooting that day that one more shot made no difference, but somebody yelled that the shot had come from the palace. A panic broke out in the crowd. Those who were near the entrance rushed inside, dragging our guards with them. I remained outside the entrance, trying to figure out what to do next. Our citadel was in the hands of the enemy. The Communist leaders had retired, apparently leaving it to "the flower and glory of the revolution" to finish the job.

Suddenly martial music came from the far end of the street. It became louder and louder. I went to the edge of the colonnade to see what was going on. A regiment in march formation was approaching the palace with a band at its head, the regimental banner flanked by two red flags, officers in the front line of each company. . . . The regiment took up a position in front of the palace. An officer and half a dozen enlisted men climbed the steps and asked to see somebody from the Executive Committee. I went to them.

It was the 176th Regiment, stationed at Tsarskoye Selo, some ten miles from Petrograd. In the morning the regiment had received an order to march to Petrograd to defend the revolution. It left as ordered, without asking where the order came from. While crossing the capital, the soldiers were disgusted by the signs of pogroms, but they continued their march toward the headquarters of the Executive Committee. They were shocked again when they discovered that the Tauride Palace was surrounded by a rioting crowd. Now their representatives asked me what they were to do. I said, "Take over guard duty. The commandant will show you the posts. Your first assignment will be to clear the building of intruders."

Dan and I went along the lines of the regiment, greeting each company in the name of the Executive Committee. Company after company entered Katherine Hall, making its way through the bewildered crowd. A quarter of an hour later guards had been posted at all doors and windows on the ground floor, and squads of soldiers of the 176th Regiment were clearing the building.

Calls began to come in from the barracks. The soldiers were returning their arms. The regimental committees assured us that their regiments had not participated in the pogroms and regretted having taken part in the demonstrations. From almost every regiment came the question: "Is it true you have called troops from the front?" We confirmed the news. "Yes, we have."

The tide turned so suddenly that the Communists did not realize at once that they were beaten. The joint session of the Executive Committees was listening to delegates of the Petrograd garrison, elected on the night of July 15. Some of them came to the platform with loaded guns in their hands. Threatening the "compromisers" and "traitors," they demanded that the Executive Committee depose the government and assume all power. A messenger came running with the report that the Ismailovsky Regiment—one of the largest in Petrograd—was deployed in front of the palace. As in the first days of the revolution, the regiment wanted to present itself to the Executive Committee and asked Chkheidze to come out to receive it. I invited the regiment to enter Katherine Hall and parade there before the Executive Committees of Workers and Peasants.

The regiment marched in to the tune of the *Marseillaise*. The Committee members came out, the Bolshevist leaders and the garrison delegations disappeared. We had won the day.

The commission in charge of the palace's defense met for the last time and wired an order to all regiments of the garrison—to send one platoon for guard service to the Tauride Palace to reinforce the Pavlovsky and 176th Regiments. Shortly before dawn our commission dissolved itself. I stepped out into the garden of the palace. Dizzy after two sleepless nights, I sat down on the flagstone steps and fell asleep.

THE TIDE TURNS

When the task force of the Fifth Army reached the outskirts of Petrograd, all was over. Factories were working as usual and the workers were cursing the Communists for having cheated them. The Bolshevist agitators did not dare appear in the barracks. Men like Jilin maintained their prestige only by stressing their loyalty to the All-Russian Executive Committee. What was wrong, they asked, in reporting the wishes of the people to the comrades in the Tauride Palace?

The pendulum swung to the right. Reactionary forces that had taken no part in quelling the riots now tried to capitalize on the failure of the revolt. "Vigilantes" roamed the city, breaking into private apartments in search of suspects. Public opinion demanded drastic measures. There were rumors that four hundred had been killed during the riots.[3] The wrath of the citizens against the Bolsheviks as instigators of the riots was understandable. Lenin and some of his lieutenants disappeared behind the Finnish border. Trotsky was arrested.

On July 18 rumors circulated among the soldiers that officers planned to arrest the committeemen in regiments that had participated in the rioting. Soldiers were threatening to "get" the officers. I spent that night at the telephone in the Tauride Palace, talking with the representatives of the garrison. About 3:00 A.M. a young officer came in, straight from a secret meeting. "I betray no one . . . but they will provoke a massacre," he mumbled. He asked me to go with him to the meeting of the officers and try to reason with the ringleaders.

We drove to the barracks of the former Imperial Guard. The hall of the officers' mess was packed. There were uniforms of all the services. Senior officers sat behind a long table on a dais. A colonel was bitterly accusing the government of weakness and the Executive Committee of cajoling the Communists. I approached the chairman and asked for permission to attend the meeting as the representative of the All-Russian Executive Committee. The chairman looked at me as if I were a ghost and asked, "Who told you of this private conference?"

"That doesn't matter. What counts is that a representative of the Executive Committee asks admission to this meeting."

The chairman hesitated a moment, then rose, interrupted the colonel, and announced, "Gentlemen! There will be a change in our agenda. The chair recognizes the representative of the Executive Committee of the Soviets." Violent protests from part of the meeting were drowned out by applause. It looked as if many people in the hall were not unhappy about the "change in the agenda." Instead of giving a speech, I offered to answer questions.

The officers complained about the lack of discipline and accused the Soviets of undermining their authority. I reminded them of the March revolution. "There were no Soviets in those days," I said, "but where was your authority? Were you strong enough to stop the massacres?" Then came charges that the Executive Committee was weak: "Why haven't you taken any measures against mob violence?" "Why haven't you called on the Cossacks and military schools?" "Why don't you crush the Bolsheviks in the Kshessinskaya Palace?" I

[3] This figure seems exaggerated. As far as I know, the exact number of victims has never been established.

replied by describing the events of the past days and ended by saying, "We won the day without ducking personal danger and we spared the lives of those who were ready to defend us. Is this weakness?"

Then I tried to explain our policy toward the palace of Kshessinskaya, the Communist stronghold. At noon the Soldiers' Section had sent its representatives to the Commander of the Military District, asking him to attack it at once. Since the building was guarded by armed workers' commandos and strong detachments of sailors and machine gunners, it was decided to oppose them with forces that would make any resistance futile. "This is all I can tell you," I said.

That, indeed, was all I knew about the plans of our Soldiers' Section and District Military Command. There was a noise in the street. Officers rushed to the windows. Files of soldiers were advancing along the sidewalks, rifles in hand, followed by a column of armored cars. Next came a cavalry squadron and several Cossack hundreds.[4] A dozen infantry companies brought up the rear. I turned to the officers. "This answers your question about the palace of Kshessinskaya. Its liquidation is a question of hours."

The chairman announced firmly, "There will be no more questions. Our thanks to the Executive Committee. Do you agree, gentlemen?" The answer was a unanimous "Long live the Executive Committee!"

An officer jumped to the dais, shouting, "It will be hell to explain tonight's meeting to the enlisted men. What should we say?" "You came here to discuss the situation with a representative of the Executive Committee," I replied. "If your regimental committee wishes to know more, it may call me at the Tauride Palace." The chairman, shaking my hand, said to the audience, "Gentlemen, I move a resolution of loyalty to the Executive Committee. No objections? Accepted unanimously."

END OF THE COALITION GOVERNMENT

On July 19 the commanding officers and soldiers' representatives of the task force of the Fifth Army came to the Tauride Palace to greet the Executive Committee. The next day the force paraded through the streets of Petrograd. It was not very large compared with the crowds of July 16-18—ten to fifteen thousand in all—but it was perfectly disciplined and well equipped. The troops then drew up before the Tauride Palace.

The Communist assault had been beaten back, but the political situation had become more confused than ever. The Coalition Govern-

[4] "Hundreds" in Cossack regiments were equivalent to squadrons in regular cavalry.

ment had distintegrated. Even before the rioting, Prince Lvov had decided to resign in view of his clash with the Minister of Agriculture, Chernov, who was encouraging rural communities to take over lands abandoned by big landowners. Kerensky had disappeared during the riots. He returned after order was restored, explaining that he had spent those hectic days at the front in search of reliable troops, but could find none. The four Cadet ministers had resigned before the outbreak of the riots; Tseretelli, Skobelev, and Chernov were busy in the Tauride Palace; other members of the Cabinet were simply forgotten in the turmoil.[5]

Our most urgent task was obviously to establish a new government that could inspire confidence in the masses of the people, and it seemed such a government could be established only on the basis of agreement among the leading political groups.

For practical purposes, three groups counted: the Communists, who were discredited by the failure of their attempted coup but who preserved their grip over a part of the Petrograd garrison, the Baltic fleet, and a considerable part of workers; the majority of the Soviets, which had emerged victorious from the clash, controlled the armed forces at the front and in the rear, and were supported by the peasants; and the Cadets, the only organized political party of the right, which had followers among intellectuals, government officials, officers, and employers and could speak in the name of property-minded, non-Socialist elements.[6]

The decision was in the hands of the central group, the working majority of the All-Russian Executive Committee of Workers and Soldiers. Its choice was between a government of the Soviets, which would amount to a coalition with the Bolsheviks; a government of the moderates, without the extreme left and right; and a government based on a coalition with the rightist groups. We knew that a government of the Soviets would be only a transition to Communist rule.

[5] Only the Minister of Justice had attempted to counter Lenin's propaganda by declaring that Lenin was a German agent. The accusation was based on flimsy evidence, however, and Chkheidze declined to publish it in *Izvestia*. Miliukov's *History* represents this announcement as the main cause of the Petrograd garrison's change in mood. It is, of course, impossible to ascertain how many soldiers believed this accusation. Personally, I was in constant touch with the garrison during this time. Not a single soldier so much as mentioned that charge to me when trying to explain the change in his regiment's or company's attitude. All spoke about the movement of troops from the front to the capital: That was the factor that had turned the tide. When the soldiers of Petrograd realized that the Bolsheviks had led them to a conflict with the front army, they turned to us.
[6] The Cadets claimed to represent the whole nation but were unable to substantiate this claim by the popular vote. They showed themselves very weak in democratic elections to rural and municipal councils in 1917, and the subsequent elections to the Constituent Assembly gave them less than 2.5 per cent of the seats.

Since this policy appeared completely out of the question after the July days, we had to choose between a government of the moderate Socialists and a coalition with the right. Most of the moderates in the Soviet felt, however, that their group alone would be unable to form a stable government. They realized that the July assault was not Lenin's last bid for power. His plan had failed this time only because his lieutenants had lacked courage at the decisive moment, before the tide turned in our favor. Lenin would let his men study the lessons of that defeat. When he hurled his armed followers against us again, they would not give us time to strike back. Lenin had disappeared from Petrograd but was getting ready for a new onslaught while in hiding somewhere in Finland. The rightist elements outside the government would soon provide him with slogans to rally his forces.

Moreover, we were in a shaky position with the Soviets. A government of moderate Socialists would be possible if it could count on the unanimous support of both Socialist parties through thick and thin. But there was a deep split within the majority parties. Not all leaders and rank-and-file members of the Menshevist and Socialist Revolutionary parties liked Tseretelli's firm policy against the Bolsheviks. To some of them, the Communists were not enemies but "misinformed comrades." They were unhappy about such measures as the appeal to the troops at the front or the use of armored cars to defend the Tauride Palace. Would they support a middle-of-the-way government in all measures it deemed necessary?

Thus there remained only one solution—a new coalition.

Since the Soviet leaders believed such a coalition the only way they had left, their prospective partners were able, despite their political weakness, to dictate their conditions. The non-Socialist groups declared, from the start, that they would not participate in a coalition without representation of the Cadets; the latter declared they would not join a government dependent on the Soviets. New difficulties developed after the President of the Provisional Government, Prince Lvov, resigned, and the rump Cabinet appointed Kerensky its head. This was a shrewd move on the part of the right elements remaining in the government. As an appointee of the rightist group, Kerensky was bound to become its puppet.

THE IMPASSE

On July 21 the rump Cabinet published a declaration of its policy, conforming in essential points with the demands of the moderate Socialists. Although the composition of the Cabinet was wholly unsatisfactory, the Executive Committee made an attempt to strengthen it by investing it with almost dictatorial power. On July 24 it resolved:

"The nation and the revolution are in peril.

"The Provisional Government is proclaimed the Government of Salvation of the Revolution.

"It is invested with unlimited authority to restore order and discipline in the army, to struggle against counterrevolution and anarchy, and to execute measures outlined in the declaration of July 21.

"The Minister-Socialists will report to the Executive Committee on their activities at least twice a week."

The idea of this resolution came from Tseretelli; the wording was mine. The resolution was passed by 262 affirmative votes and no negative ones, with forty-seven Bolsheviks abstaining. Superficially it sounded fine. The trouble, however, was that there was no government at that time but only a group of persons representing nobody and preoccupied with the distribution of portfolios among themselves. Two days later even this shadow Cabinet disappeared from the scene. On July 26 all the ministers resigned, leaving negotiations on the formation of government to Kerensky, who in the meantime had moved his residence to the Winter Palace.

Since the non-Socialist groups refused to participate in a government dependent on the Soviets, he undertook to organize a cabinet of individuals of his own choice. After unsuccessful negotiations with the Cadets and representatives of industry and commerce, Kerensky also resigned and left the Winter Palace on August 3. A new attempt was made to form a government on the basis of an agreement between the leading parties, the Executive Committee, and the Duma Committee. After this attempt failed, the right-wing Cadets came out with an ultimatum: Kerensky must organize the new Cabinet. The Cadets made no secret of their contempt for Kerensky, yet they picked him as their man, confident that if they brought him to power he would work with them against the Executive Committee.

Facing the alternatives—a Kerensky Cabinet or no coalition—the moderate Socialists yielded. On August 4 Kerensky returned to the Winter Palace and on August 7 the new government was formed. It was a poor shadow of the first Coalition Government. It included some excellent people (Chernov for Agriculture, Peshechonov for Food Supply, Avksentiev for Interior, and Zarudny for Justice), but most of its members represented only themselves, and the new head was no replacement for Prince Lvov. From its very first day, it was doomed to fail. The Bolsheviks had avenged their defeat in July.

THE QUESTION OF THE CONSTITUENT
ASSEMBLY

The political confusion of this period is illustrated by the controversy over convocation of a Constituent Assembly—the ultimate aim of the liberation movement in Russia since the 1870's. The idea was revived in 1905 and accepted by the first Provisional Government, which had pledged itself to make every effort in its power for prompt convocation of a democratically elected Assembly that would assume full power over the nation. Very soon, however, the conservative elements, represented by the Cadets, discovered that under prevailing conditions they were not likely to get enough votes to win even a few seats in the Assembly. Believing the nation would elect a "better" Assembly if elections were postponed until the storm of the revolution blew over, they made such postponement the main objective of their policy. Their strongest argument was that national elections should not be held until local administration was firmly established and had had time to prepare the lists of voters and until each citizen had had an opportunity to see that his name was included in these lists.

In the beginning, the leaders of the Soviet were not seriously interested in this issue, believing it not very important whether the Constituent Assembly convened three months sooner or later. Thus the Cadets succeeded in persuading the eighty-member Special Committee appointed by the government to proceed slowly and cautiously in formulating the electoral law. When, during the negotiations about the first coalition in June, the Soviet demanded the convocation of the Constituent Assembly at an earlier date, Prince Lvov remarked pointedly that no less than two months had been lost through the fault of the Soviet, which had failed to reply to the questions raised by the Special Committee and to send its representatives to it.

By that time, however, the Soviet had realized the danger of a further delay. After a serious clash with the chairman of the Special Committee, the spokesman of the Soviet obtained a pledge from the Coalition Government that elections would be completed by September 30 and the Constituent Assembly convened on October 3. The Cadets, however, resumed their campaign for postponement. The local administration, they argued, needed more time to draw up voters' lists; there was not enough paper for the sealed envelopes required for secret balloting. At the same time they maintained there need be no hurry since the Assembly would not make much change in the situation.

In this psychological climate, the Cabinet quietly postponed the elections until December. Two months were added to the interregnum. The Cadets considered this delay a major victory. Actually, it gave the Communists time to recover from the July defeat, regroup their forces, and prepare a new coup.

FAREWELL TO THE TAURIDE PALACE

In the Tauride Palace a persistent feeling of approaching catastrophe was mixed with apathy. The Executive Committee met every day. Heroic resolutions were passed. I was busy writing passionate appeals to workers, soldiers, peasants, citizens, anyone. I wrote with an increasing feeling of frustration, hating the clichés I had to use. "The nation is going down!" "The revolution is in peril!" "Let the new government be a government of salvation!" Once I facetiously suggested that the Executive Committee use a telegraphic code in its resolutions and appeals: "Nagodown" for "Nation goes down," "Repril" for "Revolution is in Peril," and so on. The formation of the Government of National Salvation (Gonsal, in my code) had degenerated into mysterious behind-the-scene deals and resulted in transferring power to a group of persons whose names and words meant nothing to the nation.

I did not witness the final stage of the formation of the new government. I was so disgusted with the new course of affairs in Petrograd that I began to think of quitting the Tauride Palace. Five months of work as trouble-shooter and pen-pusher for the Executive Committee had been perhaps the most frustrating phase of my political life. Even now I remember this time as a long nightmare, full of unbearable tension, helplessness, and boredom. Sleepless nights, endless speeches, an ocean of strange faces, suspicious eyes, unanswered questions, decisions that decided nothing, resolutions that left all problems unsolved. My rare moments of light, satisfaction, and enthusiasm were like sparks of a bonfire in a pitch-dark night: they did not disperse the darkness but made it thicker.

My deep depression was due partly to overwork and nervous exhaustion. We had no organized timetable of work—no office hours, no Sundays, no holidays, no regular hours for meals, no time for reading the newspapers or talking with one another. In those five months I hardly had five meals at home or in a restaurant with Emma. There were nights when the telephone would awaken me for some meeting that seemed very important at the moment but actually was as irrelevant as most of the things we were doing. In all that time I had not a single evening when I could go to a theater with Emma or spend a few hours with her or my mother and sister. Back in Petrograd after ten years' absence, I yearned to visit the Hermitage, to see again the public works I had managed as president of the Council of the Unemployed, get a glimpse of the University, take a walk along the quays of the Neva, but there never was time for anything like that.

I still looked strong, but inside me something was caving in under the self-imposed pressure of work. These months were even harder on Emma. She worked in the information department of *Izvestia*, covering the activities of different bureaus in the Tauride Palace. We had an apartment not very far from the palace but saw little of each other. We spent only one Sunday together when, for some reason, my commitments for that day were canceled. I suggested that we go by train to visit my parents. I hoped the memories of my childhood and early youth attached to that place would revive, come back to life. The place, however, was dead for both of us, but at least we were together, far from the turmoil of politics. We compared our impressions of what was going on around us. Our life in the new, democratic Russia, at the hub of historical events, seemed empty in comparison with Irkutsk.

Emma was as tired of the Tauride Palace as I. We felt that our group was engaged in a desperate defense of a lost cause, that whatever it was doing did not matter. It did have two major victories to its credit—the first over the defeatism of Miliukov, the second over the demagoguery of Lenin. But what was left to us to defend in Petrograd? An *opéra-bouffe* government that we ourselves had invested with the title of Government of National Salvation but that had no strength, no vision, no courage, and no prestige.

We had no personal plans for the future and felt we were drifting with the tempestuous stream of the revolution. We returned to Petrograd with a feeling of resignation, but Emma did not suggest that I quit my political activity nor did I give any thought to such a possibility. I thought only of moving from the Tauride Palace to some other field of work.

In this mood I talked a few days later with Stankevich, with whom I had worked in Petrazhitsky's seminar in 1904-5. Since then he had become professor of law, had joined the army, and had been elected to the Petrograd Soviet by the officers of his battalion. He was the only officer in the Soviet and one of the leaders of the moderate group in the Executive Committee. On political questions he was right of center, his main interest being the army. Then he quietly disappeared from the Tauride Palace. When I met him again he was serving as the Commissar of the government and of the Executive Committee on the Northern Front.

When he heard that I was tired of my work in the Tauride Palace, he asked me whether I would like to go with him to the front. I accepted on condition that Emma could go with me if she wanted to. There was a rule forbidding the wives of military personnel to follow their husbands to the front, but a few exceptions had been made for the members of the High Command. Stankevich persuaded the War Ministry to make a similar exception for us, appointing Emma as my personal secretary. The Ministry did not expect her to perform any definite service, but Emma actually shared my work at the front and remained at the post under most taxing conditions, after all the male members of my staff had left. That story, however, comes later.

When I told Chkheidze I was leaving the Tauride Palace and asked him to sign my credentials for the front, he said gloomily, "I do not blame you. I wish I could leave too!" Stankevich and I left Petrograd on July 28. Emma joined me in Riga a week later.

ON THE NORTHERN FRONT

The army and front commissars were direct representatives of the government (actually the War Ministry) and the Executive Committee. As such, they acted as a link between the High Command of the army and the soldiers' organization. Their main task was to strengthen the morale of the troops. Each commissar had his own program of action. Stankevich's pet idea was to improve the morale of the soldiers by better technical training, substituting sports for the traditional drill. Army committees were not enthusiastic about this idea, and he had difficulty in finding a language in common with them. Generally, he was more successful in dealing with officers than in contacts with enlisted men. I think the main reason he was so eager to have me with him was that I could talk with the soldiers.

The Northern Front had headquarters in Pskov and originally consisted of two armies, the Twelfth on the right, with headquarters in Riga, and the Fifth on the left, with headquarters in Dvinsk. Later the First Army also became part of it.

My first conference with the front commander, General Klembovsky, and his staff was disappointing. The generals looked bored when Stankevich outlined his program and merely waited for him to stop so they could unload their grievances. I felt that their trivial frictions with the army committees interested them more than the war with Germany. The front commander was a man with obvious symptoms of advanced senility. In his youth he probably had measured some six-feet-six, but his frame was bent by arthritis. He had a huge purple nose, a trembling head, shaking hands, and bloodshot eyes that could not focus on a point for more than a couple of seconds. His speech was incoherent, as if he were drunk. When Stankevich asked him to specify his grudges, Klembovsky admitted that the situation in the Fifth Army was well under control, and he recognized reluctantly that Vilenkin, the chairman of the Fifth Army's committee, was not a German spy. But the Twelfth Army, he declared, was in hopeless confusion.

Very different were the two army commanders whom we met at the front headquarters. General Danilov of the Fifth Army was a true leader of his men. He knew his army and identified himself with its officers and enlisted men. His remarks were brief, but one felt that his thoughts ranged far beyond the technical questions we were discussing. General Parsky of the Twelfth Army was less sophisticated —an elderly man with short-cropped gray hair and a tanned, deeply creased face. With no decorations on his uniform, he looked like a sergeant with a general's insignia on his shoulders. He was newly appointed to the Twelfth Army and during the conference he listened and seemed to memorize every word but said little himself.

THE TWELFTH ARMY AND ITS COMMANDER

From Pskov, Stankevich and I went to the headquarters of the Twelfth Army in Riga. The city was located fairly near the front line and had a mixed population. Landowners of German origin formed its upper crust; the middle classes were Russian, and most of the workers, Lettish. Long before the revolution the military command had formed Lettish *tirailleur* battalions—a half-volunteer organization that comprised some thirty thousand men. They were reputed to be good soldiers but refused to recognize the authority of the committee of the Twelfth Army, the Iskosol, and were suspected of leftist leanings.

Several regiments of the Twelfth Army were apparently dominated by the Communist party. One of them, the Novo Ladoga Riflers, had joined the party openly and was publishing a Bolshevist daily newspaper under the title *Pravda Okopov* (*Pravda of the Trenches*). The commander of the army, on the insistence of the Iskosol, had shut down the paper after the July riots in Petrograd, but the regiment remained highly unreliable. There was also a Ukrainian division that insisted on being transferred to the south to defend the Ukraine and threatened to leave its positions if its demand was not granted. Stankevich proposed that I assume responsibility for the Twelfth Army and stay in Riga while he returned to Pskov and concentrated on front affairs and the Fifth Army.

My first task was to establish relations with the Iskosol. I had often asked myself: Why didn't an army whose indoctrination rested on the idea of service to the Tsar disintegrate at once when the Tsarist regime collapsed? The answer lay partly in the patriotic feelings of the soldiers and partly—as in the Twelfth Army—in the work of a throng of men who had emerged from the ranks to become leaders of the enlisted men in the early days of the revolution. The chairman of the Iskosol, Kuchin, had been made a lieutenant just before the revolution, and he wore the officer's tunic with a private's cross for valor. He was not a powerful speaker but he had won the unstinted devotion of his comrades. The vice-chairman, Kharash, was a young man, tall and athletically built, with the round face of a teen-ager, an easy smile, and bold eyes. A student at law school, he was one of the Jewish intellectuals who joined the army early in the war to prove that Jews would defend Russia and, if necessary, die for it. He was a born fighter—strong, cold-blooded, fearless, resourceful, a leader of men under fire. With two crosses on his tunic, he was an ideal soldier. Among other members of the leading group in the Iskosol were an attorney and a mining engineer, both from wealthy Jewish families of Moscow, both members of the S-R party, both volunteers (for the same reasons as Kharash), and both decorated for valor. The men around them were less colorful but equally devoted to the cause of freedom and democracy. Themselves soldiers, they sympathized with the enlisted men and understood the sacrifices they demanded of them. The whole group was tightly knit together and worked like a team—a handful of men of strong will and courage who had replaced the old authorities wiped out by the deluge of the revolution.

The Soldiers' Executive received me rather coolly. The board assembled to meet me, and Kuchin, after introducing me to his comrades, asked me to present my program. "The Twelfth Army," I said, "is the key to the nation's defense. If the enemy strikes, he will strike here. Yet this part of the front is one of the weakest. Fraternization has reached dangerous proportions; some battalions are in almost open mutiny; treasonable propaganda has been spreading from the Bolshevist regiments of this army to other fronts. Am I right?"

"Of course you are," Kuchin replied. "You learned all this from our reports. But what about the reactionary officers who undermine our work? We have asked the War Ministry repeatedly to relieve the army of them. Will you help us in this matter?"

"I will do all I can to help you about the reactionary officers," I said, "and ask in exchange the privilege of working with you on the revival of the army's morale."

Kuchin's face became gentle and friendly. He stretched out his hand. "That is a deal. Now, your plans, please!"

I told them about the July days in the capital and the change in the mood of the garrison after the failure of the Bolshevist conspiracy. "Extremist demagoguery is not dead," I said, "but the Communists have been licked. Their prestige has been shaken. We can try to use this moment to weed out their influence in the army and restore unity among the troops on a platform of national defense and democratic discipline." Kuchin and his comrades agreed that this plan was timely, and we started to outline our campaign. My task was to bring to our side the troops that refused to recognize the authority of the Iskosol —the Lettish battalions and notorious Communist regiments.

That same evening I called on General Parsky and told him about our plans. He listened quietly, chewing his lips, and then remarked, as if thinking aloud, "Surely it will take time to make first-rate crack troops out of confused and embittered men. But you are on the right track in trying to start with restoring unity and self-confidence among them. Disicipline and military valor will come afterward."

I looked at the old man in surprise. He went on, "I don't understand anything about politics, parties, or programs. But I have spent all my life in service, and I know the Russian soldier. He is good. At times he is the best soldier in the world. At other times he is not much to look at. He is superb in an offensive—cheerful and fearless. But when he takes to his heels, the cavalry cannot catch up with him. A remarkable soldier! If you distrust him, he will make a fool of you and himself. If you trust him, he will go to his death just to show you how good he is."

I asked the general what he thought of the demands of the Supreme Command that capital punishment be restored for certain military crimes.

"That is politics," he replied. "This is not my field. You cannot run an army without compulsion. The heaviest crimes must draw the heaviest punishment. But the threat of punishment alone will not change the spirit of the army. Can you make a desperate man or a drunk or a fool behave by threatening him with court-martial?"

After a moment of silence he continued, "Psychology is part of our trade. When I was commanding a division, I noticed that our artillery gave little support to the infantry. Then I thought I found the reason. The artillerymen and infantrymen did not know one another. I began to arrange joint parties and urged all our units to do the same. Whenever infantry officers came together to play cards or drink, they must include artillery officers. I encouraged the soldiers to go to the batteries when there was some celebration. Some of the officers thought, 'Parsky is crazy,' but we got results. All the divisions around us had the usual troubles between the two services, but on my sector everything clicked . . . more or less. . . ."

I asked the general whether he intended to make a tour of inspection. Smiling, he put his wrinkled hand on my shoulder and said, "Yes, I shall make the tour, but after you, and in a different way. You are lucky—there are no rules of procedure for commissars. With a commander of an army, this is different. I am bound to hurt somebody if I break the conventional rules. You can start your tour with the worst units and tell your men directly why you have come to see them first. But can a commander of the army say to a division commander, 'I am here because your division is behaving like hell'?"

A PLEDGE OF DISCIPLINE

The Lettish battalions were not united in regiments but served as reinforcement to regular infantry divisions. They had their own political organization, the Executive Committee of Lettish Tirailleurs, independent of the Iskosol. I called a meeting of this Committee and asked about the relations between the Lettish Tirailleurs and the Twelfth Army. "Rightly or wrongly, the rest of the army distrusts you. What can we do to improve the situation?"

The leaders of the battalions complained about false rumors. What could they do against lies and slander? I suggested that the misunderstanding could be dispelled by a joint campaign for unity of the Russian and Lettish troops. With the chairman of the Committee, I made a tour of the battalions. Meetings of soldiers and officers were called. I asked the men whether they considered themselves soldiers of the Russian army or had other ideas about their role at the front. The answer was that the Letts had no other desire than to get along with the rest of the army. They were offended that their loyalty was suspect. Then I asked, "Is it true that you have passed a resolution to end the war by fraternization? Wasn't this the reason for your clash with the Iskosol?"

The Letts explained that they had never taken the resolution seriously. There was some fraternization in their battalions but not more than in the Russian regiments. The Germans, they said, knew too well that the Letts were their archenemies. If the army decided against fraternization, the Letts would be the last to run counter to that decision.

I could not judge the military quality of the Lettish troops, but they showed themselves in orderly formation, their barracks were clean, their trenches well maintained, and both men and officers had an appearance of military fitness. After the tour I proposed to the Lettish leaders that they reaffirm their loyalty to the government and All-Russian Executive Committee, accept the platform established by all army organizations, and recognize the authority of the Iskosol. Then the Iskosol would clear them of all suspicion. For my part, I would defend before the commander of the army their claims for consolidation of battalions into larger units and promotion of their officers to higher grades.

The most influential person among the Letts was Colonel Vazetis, a shrewd, level-headed man with considerable military experience. I learned that he was a career soldier, fond of his job but embittered. He complained about favoritism in the old army, and it was clear that his main criticism of the old regime was its failure to make him a general. I asked what the reaction of his Tirailleurs would be to the promotion of one of their senior officers to the rank of general. He blushed and answered with conviction, "That would show them the new regime is fair toward the Letts and would strengthen their ties with the rest of the army."

When I suggested to General Parsky that Vazetis be promoted, he asked at once for his files and, after having leafed through them, said, "His record is good. The promotion is overdue at least six years. Surely he must be embittered."

General Vazetis became the most valuable link between the Lettish battalions and the army. Thanks largely to him, we had no more trouble with the Tirailleurs—until Kornilov's mutiny stirred up the army and triggered its disintegration.

Next on my tour came the lion's den, the Novo-Ladoga Regiment. The Iskosol was not on speaking terms with it, and my visit was arranged by the division commander, who volunteered to accompany me. The regiment was stationed in an advanced position. As we drove toward them, the general confessed that he had not visited this outfit in the last two months, since it had declared its allegiance to the Communist party.

The regiment's reserves were housed in tents in a clearing. The regimental committee awaited us in front of a tent; the officers were assembled in front of another tent on the opposite side of the clearing. Soldiers were milling about in between or lay on the ground. I went with the committeemen into their tent. They asked me whether I had any special desire concerning the agenda for the meeting. I replied that I intended to talk with the regiment about military affairs. In a short time, I said, the nation will elect the Constituent Assembly, and at that election everybody will be free to express his opinions by ballot. What the Assembly decides will be the law of the land. I therefore have no intention of talking politics with the men. But I would like to clarify some questions about the attitude of the regiment as part of the Russian revolutionary army—about such things as fraternization, discipline, execution of service, and battle orders. And I asked the committeemen whether they agreed with me on the need to discuss these topics frankly.

The chairman of the committee asked me whether I regarded the regiment's decision to join the Communist party collectively a breach of military discipline. I answered that the resolution was absurd. A regiment as such cannot join a party and I had no time to talk about nonsense. The only trouble was that the regiment, by its resolution, had alienated itself from the army and placed itself in the position of a leper colony. I had come to see if there was any truth in the widely held opinion in the army that the Novo-Ladoga Regiment was a bunch of cowards, capable of betraying other troops by refusing to obey battle orders. If this opinion were true, something had to be done to protect the rest of the army against the danger of treason. If the suspicion were false, something should be done to restore the good name of the regiment.

The chairman explained that the men knew very well that the by-laws of the Communist party did not provide for collective membership. The decision "to join the party" was just a way of expressing the political views of the majority of soldiers on that particular day.

"Why didn't you make this clear to the army long ago?" I asked.

He replied that the regiment had been insulted by the charges hurled at it. "Moreover," he added, "many people who sympathized with the left in June have changed their views since the July days."

"I am happy to hear this," I said. "I know how rumors spread in the army. Perhaps your comrades have misunderstood you. I was told that the Novo-Ladoga Regiment declared it would take no part in the imperialist war and would obey only the Communist party. As soldiers, you must agree that we would have a strange army if each regiment were to decide from what party it takes its orders."

The committeemen, red in the face, confessed that the resolution had some foolish words but insisted they were just a slip. Then I said, "I must trust you. A few weeks ago I saw a radical change in the mood of the Petrograd garrison. Many enlisted men had passed resolutions endorsing the Bolshevist slogans, and then they all joined the majority in the Executive Committee in condemning the same slogans. Such things happen sometimes."

The committeemen liked my approach. "Perhaps we are not the best regiment in the army," the chairman said modestly, "but we are honest and say what we think. And when we see that we were wrong, we say so."

"It would be fine if all soldiers were this way," I replied diplomatically. The conference ended in a friendly spirit.

The regiment assembled before the tents. The soldiers stood in rigid formation but looked grim and suspicious. Introducing me, the chairman stressed that the committee was in agreement with me on military matters. I began by saying I had a dual task—to learn what the situation in the regiment was and to find out what could be done to improve its relations with the rest of the army. I had heard ugly rumors about the Novo-Ladoga Regiment as a bunch of Communists, cowards, and traitors. But, after a frank talk with the regimental committee, I was satisfied these rumors were based on misinterpretation of the regiment's resolution about joining the Bolshevist party. Obviously this was an error. The men had voted with their hands, rather than with hearts and brains. They did not realize that by this resolution they seemed to be betraying their country, renouncing allegiance to the army, and becoming moral lepers in the eyes of other soldiers.

There was some movement of protest among the soldiers. The chairman whispered to me, "Tell them about the Petrograd garrison." I told the story and moved the resolution: "The regiment declares that it is a part of the Russian army, ready to defend the country and revolution in conformity with the orders of the government and the All-Russian Executive Committee and the platform accepted by all revolutionary organizations of the army."

The chairman asked permission to introduce an amendment: "The regiment protests against rumors about its treasonable intentions." With this addition, the resolution was accepted unanimously. When the chairman announced the result of the vote, the men shouted "Hurrah!"

After the meeting the division commander and I went to the car surrounded by a cheerful crowd of soldiers. Some shouted, "Good luck, Comrade Commissar!" The division commander was flabbergasted. "I cannot grasp the trick," he said. "You called them traitors, cowards, and I don't know what else. They would have killed me if I had spoken that way, but they took it from you. How did you manage it?"

"I didn't tell them that they *were* bad," I replied. "I only said that that was how they *looked* to other enlisted men. Then I showed them how they could improve their reputation without losing face. Thus they felt I had come to help them. Weren't they right?"

"I'll be damned," said the commander. "Probably this is another piece of the psychology our new commander of the army talks about. It isn't the way we were taught to run our outfit."

On August 12 a conference of all revolutionary organizations of the Twelfth Army and local workers convened in the city theater. After a proper introduction, I moved the resolution:

"1. Fraternization with the enemy is an act of treason. The culprits will be dealt with as traitors to the country and the revolution.

"2. Disobedience to orders has ruined the southern armies. From this day on, all battle and service orders will be executed at once, without discussion.

"3. In the interest of survival, all units of the Twelfth Army must eject and deliver for trial any individual who disgraces the revolutionary soldiers by acts against the security of the army."

A representative of the Communists asked me about the exact meaning of the words ". . . will be dealt with as traitors." I replied, "This means that the culprits will be court-martialed. It will depend on you whether this measure will be applied in this army."

The Communists demanded some changes in the resolution's wording. I answered, "Introduce your amendment, and it will be put to a vote. Whatever the conference decides will be carried out."

After a brief recess, the Bolsheviks declared that in the interest of unity they would abstain from presenting amendments and would obey the decisions of the conference. The resolution was carried unanimously, signed solemnly by all members of the conference, and sent at once to the printing plant and telegraph offices.

The next day thousands of copies were distributed in the trenches. The impact on the soldiers was overwhelming. Fraternization and discussion of orders stopped. Now we could proceed with our efforts to bring more order into the army and tighten its discipline.

By this time the new government was established in Petrograd. The Cabinet began with an hysterical appeal to the nation, written in stilted language, a poor imitation of the quasi old-Russian style of the Tsar's manifestoes. We in the Iskosol felt that the Government of Salvation of the Revolution was becoming a Government of Panic and Confusion.

A SICK ARMY

The army was sick. We were wholly ignorant then of such matters as mass neurosis and its therapy, but in retrospect I realize that the trouble lay largely in the neurotic state of the masses of the enlisted men.

The real foundation of an army is necessarily an indoctrination that leads men to a definite pattern of thinking and feeling and insures their reactions under battle conditions; summed up, this amounts to discipline and military valor. The indoctrination absorbed in the Tsarist army had been wiped out when the Tsar was deposed and imprisoned as a criminal. In addition, the soldiers were tired and embittered after three years of war. They had long since lost respect for their officers and they wondered why they should stay at the front and eventually expose themselves to danger. Most of them had a vague feeling of duty and responsibility, however; otherwise they would have abandoned the front at the beginning of the revolution. But this feeling was fading and could not replace discipline. The task was to develop a new morale, a new *esprit de corps*.

Resentment, bewilderment, self-pity, and other contradictory emotions often led the soldiers to irrational outbursts. A regiment would declare that it would no longer clean the barracks: Let the officers do the job if they thought it necessary. Another regiment would decide that the men needed no further drilling or training: "We have had enough of this!" Either decision led to mass disobedience to service orders. By insisting on the execution of his order, an officer would bring revolt into the open. In some cases it therefore seemed wiser to seek a compromise: for example, to limit training to more or less tractable companies and reduce it to exercises in shooting. It was more difficult to handle a regiment in the line when it refused to maintain fortifications, declaring to the officers, "Why should we kill ourselves working? The Fritzies won't come!"

When the men had special grudges against officers, shots were fired at officers' tents at night, hand grenades were thrown. Fatalities were not numerous, but in some cases all the officers had left the regiment. The military value of an outfit in such a state was, of course, nil.

In their efforts to stir up unrest, the Communists found unexpected allies in the most reactionary elements of the army—former gendarmes, old-regime sergeants, the junior officers most hated by the soldiers, persons with criminal records—all of whom tried to ingratiate themselves with the troops as defenders of soldiers' rights. These were the authors of the most arrogant resolutions and extravagant demands.

There was a strange rhythm of unrest in the army. After two or three weeks of "foolishness," a regiment would quietly resume training, clean barracks, and maintain fortifications. A regiment located in a reserve line would announce that it would not go to advanced positions, but when the order came it would march forward. The Novo-Ladoga Regiment was an example. After it had decided to go along with the rest of the army, it became a regiment like any other, recognized the authority of officers and obeyed their orders.

Together with the Iskosol, I tried to strengthen self-confidence in the better elements of the army, to increase cohesion among the soldiers, and to raise the prestige of regimental committees among the rank and file. Home-backed resolutions carried more weight with the men than orders of the High Command and appeals of the government.

An incident tested the soundness of our approach to the problem of military discipline. The commander of a regiment stationed in a front-line position wired to the Iskosol: "The regiment demands that new shoes be distributed to all enlisted men. The regiment declares itself unfit for battle. Unless fifteen hundred pairs of shoes are delivered in three days, the men will abandon the position."

I told the Iskosol I would go to the regiment at once. Kharash went with me—he seldom let me go alone to particularly dangerous points. We did not talk as we drove; both of us were angry. The regiment's tents were in a shallow valley flanked by grass-covered hills. The soldiers, silent and grim, sat on the hillside, rifles in their hands. The place for the speakers was at the foot of the hill. I walked over to it with Kharash, the colonel, and the chairman of the regimental committee and said, "I represent the All-Russian Executive Committee and the government. I am here to listen to your demand and answer it."

"Fine," soldiers shouted. "We want a prompt answer. If the shoes are not delivered . . ."

I turned to the chairman of the committee: "Please read the resolution."

"But you know it, Comrade Commissar!" he replied. "The colonel wired it to the Iskosol."

"Before I give any answer, I must have all the facts. I want to hear the resolution and be sure it is truly the decision of these men."

The chairman read the resolution, stumbling and obviously realizing for the first time how stupidly arrogant it was. But the soldiers enjoyed themselves and interrupted him with signs of approval. When he finished, I said, "Give me the paper. I want to have it in my hands before I give you the answer." Then I tore the paper to pieces and threw them away.

Hell broke loose. The colonel stood at my side with a livid face; the chairman looked down; Kharash stepped closer to me, smiling his approval of my gesture. The soldiers shouted, brandishing their guns. When the noise subsided enough so that I could speak, I said, "Your resolution is a disgrace to you and the army. I have destroyed it to clear you of that disgrace. A pair of shoes to each one of you, and you will defend your country and die for it, if necessary! No shoes, and you become a bunch of deserters and traitors? You cannot have meant this! But this is what your resolution says. This is why I tore up that damned paper."

The soldiers sat silent. The chairman of the committee said awkwardly, "But surely, Comrade Commissar, nobody here meant it that way. All we wanted to say was that we need shoes. Come on, boys, show your shoes to the Commissar!"

I asked the chairman to put to a vote a resolution repealing the previous decision. A recess of the meeting was announced and the regimental committee went into a huddle to prepare the new text. Kharash and I remained where we were to show the men we had no part in the committee's deliberations. The men surrounded us, showing their shoes, complaining of the rain, insisting I had misunderstood them. They were friendly, some even sentimental.

Then the committee appeared with a new resolution. "The regiment has firmly decided to defend the motherland and the revolution to its last drop of blood, but feels that without shoes it would be unfit for battle. It therefore asks the commander of the army, the commissar, and the Iskosol to take necessary steps to procure fifteen hundred pairs of shoes for the outfit." I took the resolution to show the commander of the army; Kharash got a copy for the Iskosol.

As we returned to our car, the colonel whispered to me, "Mr. Commissar, I take the liberty of reporting . . . They might have torn you to pieces, and that would have been the end of us all. . . ." Kharash replied for me. "There was no danger. Comrade Commissar showed the men that he was angry, that he lost his temper. But even so he treated them as human beings. The men felt they were wrong and became ashamed of themselves."

There was one aspect of the situation that Kharash, himself an enlisted man, did not see. It was easy for us to be firm with a sick regiment: our prestige protected us like an invisible coat of mail. But the officers had no such armor, and they had to live with their men through days and nights. Their task was immeasurably more difficult than ours.

The campaign to strengthen discipline among the troops went along without serious clashes. The other part of our program—purging the army of criminal elements—proved more difficult. I had invited the prosecuting attorney of the army to the Iskosol and asked him to help us enforce the law. The attorney, a middle-aged, important-looking man in a well-fitting uniform, replied icily, "What 'law' do you expect us to enforce? A resolution of the Soviets is no law. The legality of the orders of the Provisional Government is questionable."

I reminded him, "After the revolution you took an oath to serve the new government. Its decrees are laws to you as well as to me. If you denounce your oath, you cannot be a law-enforcement officer." His hands trembling, he shouted, "In the law I enforced for more than thirty years the worst crime of all was an attempt against the sacred person of His Majesty, the Emperor. There is no law in the books that could be used against the Bolsheviks which does not apply also against Mr. Kerensky or you, Mr. Commissar!"

On my insistence, the man was fired and ordered to leave Riga, but this did not solve the problem. The reactionaries in the judicial service of the army regarded our struggle against the Communists as a clash within the ranks of criminals, enemies of the Tsar. General Parsky, with whom I discussed the situation, said quietly, "Since we have no time to reorganize the judicial branch, we must go ahead without it. It is more important to weed out the traitors than to have them convicted. We can initiate prosecution, despite the sabotage of the courts."

ENFORCEMENT OF A WARRANT

Serious troubles developed in a regiment. Soldiers had disobeyed a routine service order of the colonel. The regimental committee told them to comply with the order. Then a sergeant named Wirt called a meeting of the regiment and, on his suggestion, the soldiers elected a new committee. The latter arrested the colonel and other officers and appointed Wirt regimental commander.

At the request of the Iskosol, I went to the regiment. Wirt reported to me as the commanding officer. To my questions of when and by whom he had been promoted, he replied he had been elected by his men. "In our army," I said, "enlisted men do not elect officers. To me you are still a sergeant."

We were surrounded by an excited crowd of soldiers. I asked Wirt to call the regiment to an orderly meeting. He refused. Pointing to the crowd around us, he shouted, "These people are the meeting."

I scrutinized the man. Middle-sized, lean, not very young, perhaps in his thirties, he had an insignificant face, a thin mustache, arrogant eyes, and an hysterical high-pitched voice. A half-educated man, probably made sergeant by mistake, suspicious of his superiors, intoxicated by his new power. When I asked him where the regiment's officers were, he answered, "Under arrest, on my order."

Then I said to him, "Sergeant Wirt, you now have confessed actions amounting to treason. If you think you can get away with this, you will learn better. I hold you personally responsible for all that has happened or may happen in this regiment."

The crowd shouted, "Hurrah for Wirt, our Red commander!"

The next day the division commander sent Wirt a warrant summoning him to divisional headquarters. Wirt replied by sending a resolution of his men to the Iskosol: "The regiment will defend its elected commander with arms and asks other troops to support it in the struggle for soldiers' rights."

The Iskosol decided that Wirt must be arrested. Parsky concurred. "This is open revolt," he said. "It must be broken. But I think you should go ahead without officers." The same evening the Iskosol organized a task force of units in the army reserve—two infantry regiments, several squadrons of cavalry, several batteries, a division of tanks. The Iskosol men explained the situation to each unit. Before dawn, Wirt's regiment was surrounded by the Iskosol's troops.

With Kuchin, who directed the operation, I arrived on the scene at 2:00 A.M. and waited in the car. Kuchin was ready to send a trumpeter to deliver an ultimatum to the rebellious regiment when I proposed another tactic. "The men are hysterical," I said. "Somebody may fire. Our troops will answer in kind. Won't it be better if I arrest Wirt in his tent?" Kuchin accepted my plan. He deployed the tanks in a long file on the road beside the camp, and we agreed that, as soon as the lookouts on the road noticed movement or heard noise in the camp, the lights of the tanks would be turned on and the troops would be alerted for action.

The camp was separated from the road by broad exercise grounds. Contrary to regulations, no sentries were in sight. I crossed the grounds unchallenged. Wirt's tent was the first on the right, in the front row. I went in and called loudly, "Sergeant Wirt, get dressed! I am Commissar Woytinsky. You are under arrest."

Men jumped from the bunks. Someone lit a candle. Wirt stood before me in his underwear, repeating, "You will hang me?"

"You know very well," I replied, "that we do not hang people. But you will go to jail."

The camp woke up, and the tent filled with excited men. The place was flooded with light. I saw the line of our tanks over the heads of men at the entrance. Trumpets on the road sounded the attack. Other trumpets repeated the signal from the forest. I said to Wirt, "You will not compel us to use force. Be quick about it and follow me."

Then I stepped out of the tent so as to face the crowd in the open air and to be seen from the road. Lights now were seen all around the camp. I shouted, using all the strength of my lungs, "Attention! One regiment cannot defy the army. Here are our tanks. . . . There are our batteries. We don't want to use them, but we mean business. Wirt, are you ready?"

Wirt, fully dressed, said in a choked voice, "You cannot do this to me!"

I replied: "You are a soldier and subject to the same law as anybody here. . . ."

Somebody shouted, "Wirt, do as you are told. There has been enough trouble."

I walked toward the line of tanks. Wirt followed me. The operation that threatened to become a tragedy ended peacefully. Wirt was confined to division headquarters. Order was restored in the regiment, and the commander and officers returned to their posts, accepting the soldiers' apology. A new regimental committee was elected and the men went back to routine service. It was again a regiment like any other—neither very good nor exceptionally bad.

Wirt remained under arrest in the division headquarters. Three weeks later I received a long letter from him. After apologizing for the trouble he had caused, the sergeant volunteered his advice on the best ways to run an army. Simple men, he wrote, like to be treated with firmness. If they notice they can get away with any kind of foolishness, they will try to. He therefore advised introducing corporal punishment into the army.

This was the only case in which we had to display force to break a revolt. In all, we arrested some ten or twelve troublemakers, but we did not bring a single case to trial. We did not want to expose ourselves to the danger of sabotage by the judicial branch and acquittal of the defendant by a soldiers' jury.

A CORPS COMMANDER

The Iskosol asked me to persuade the commander of the army to remove his aide, General Baltisky, and also General Boldyrev, commander of the 43rd Corps. I told General Parsky about this demand.

"I know both men well," he said. "Baltisky talks too much politics. This is not good in his position. Write me an official letter, and I shall find some arrangement satisfactory to all parties. But Boldyrev . . . have you met him? No? Then I ask you to meet him before we discuss his case. I'll call him up and tell him that, at my request, you will visit his corps tomorrow."

And he added with a sly smile, "Boldyrev does not like the new order in the army, but I fancy you will like him and he will like you."

The next morning I drove to the headquarters of the 43rd Corps, in a farmhouse in a small hamlet, Stript, close to the front. Boldyrev was a man in his late forties, not tall but very broad-shouldered, with a broad pock-marked face, bushy eyebrows, and a short and broad beard—a typical Russian muzhik. His manner betrayed a man accustomed to being obeyed. He took me into the map room and pointed out the layout of his troops, reserves, and road networks.

I asked him about the special task of his corps. He showed a point on the map. "This is where the enemy will strike. Next, he will fan out in these two directions. I must absorb the first blow."

"Do your men know this?"

He looked at me incredulously. "You mean I should tell them they are in the most dangerous spot on the front? That is the last thing I would do. Should I encourage desertion?"

I asked in turn, "Would you object if I tell your men what task has been assigned to them?"

He scratched his beard with both hands, then said, "If you believe it will not scare them away . . . that is your business. I'll tell them how to maintain the trenches, and you will talk politics."

After a short drive through a forest torn by shells, we reached the first line of trenches. The commander of the regiment, a handful of officers, and members of the regimental committee were assembled in a blockhouse, a rather flimsy but well-disguised structure at the entrance to the trench. The commander reported to the General on conditions and recent events in the area. Boldyrev introduced me and asked the committee members what progress had been made in improving the trenches since his last visit. The chairman replied, "Comrade General, we have cleaned up debris and repaired breast-works. But we are shorthanded, you know. . . ."

Boldyrev said coldly, "The order was 'six feet,' was it not? Now let the Commissar admire your masterpiece of field fortifications."

We went along winding trenches, too narrow to let men pass in double file. The trenches were apparently kept in order. Sentries were at their posts, machine guns were properly manned. But Boldyrev was grim. At the crossing of two corridors a group of soldiers surrounded us. Boldyrev stopped and turned to the committeemen. "The order was 'six feet.' Your trenches are five feet or less in many places. This is a mousetrap. Now I will show you what the difference of a foot in depth and six inches in width can do for you. Suppose the Fritzies open the barrage. You [he pointed to one soldier] are killed. Drop to the ground, here! I am wounded." He threw himself flat on the soil. "Now, carry me to the first-aid post."

Two soldiers tried to lift the heavy General, and a third came to help them, but they could not pass over the supposedly dead comrade.

"Hurry, hurry, boys!" shouted the General. "Any of you might be in my place, bleeding to death."

Then he pushed aside the would-be stretcher-bearers, got up, and said severely, "I know what you think, boys, when I order you to make the trenches six feet deep and three feet wide at all places. You think, those are old-regime regulations. I was a private, then a sergeant, before any of you could say 'Mama.' And when I give an order I expect it to be carried out. I don't want to lose half my men in the first hour of a barrage. I need every one of you to throw the enemy back. And my order stands: All trenches must be brought up to the prescribed standard within eight days. For the reason why, ask the Commissar. My business is to tell you *what* to do."

The regiment was called together. I read the Riga resolution, explained it, and talked about the special job of the corps. The men nodded assent. Boldyrev stood at my side, keeping both hands on his beard in the muzhik fashion. He had the last word. "Now, boys, my order: Six feet by three! All dismissed."

Driving back to the headquarters, the General grumbled, "That is our army now. Committees, meetings, speeches. . . . Okay. We shall see what we can do with this mess."

I said to him, "I would be happy if I were as close to these men as you are. They seem to like you. And the orders you give are for their good. Why are they reluctant to do what you tell them and why do you think they will do it after I have explained to them the situation on this section of the front?"

"I would like to know the trick," the General replied.

"I think they like to have someone speak to them man to man, not always giving orders like a general to enlisted men but explaining the reasons, just as you did today in the trenches. That was also a 'why' demonstration."

Boldyrev exploded in a loud merry laugh. "That is an old trick. I am too old to learn the new ones, but I will try."

Back at Riga, I told Kuchin, "Boldyrev is just the man for the new army, but he does not know it. When you get to know him, you will agree." There was no further question of removing the commander of the 43rd Corps. I remained in close touch with him until the end of his service with the 43rd Corps when, at my insistence, he was appointed Commander of the Fifth Army to succeed General Danilov.

I PASS THE TEST

The Twelfth Army was recovering. Cases of insubordination were becoming less frequent. But things do not run smoothly in an army of half a million men in the midst of a storm of revolution. Again I was in my old role of trouble-shooter, but now, working with the Iskosol, I felt we were doing the necessary thing and doing it successfully. Dealing with rioting regiments was not as difficult as it had seemed from the outside. I was well protected by my coat of mail—

the prestige of my office, as a representative not of the government but of the All-Russian Executive Committee.

My new work continued to be harder for Emma than for me. I was on call day and night. Emma worked in the educational service of the army, lecturing at the Soldiers' Club, and also handled my appointments and kept in touch with the Iskosol during my trips to the regiments. The members of the Iskosol were surprised to discover that she was second to none of them in facing a difficult and dangerous situation, and she gained not only the respect but also the warm affection of these gallant soldiers. Out of regard for her, they were inclined to spare me some trips to the trenches. I found the new work to my liking, but at the same time I felt a little awkward at being the only civilian among military people. To bridge the gap, I devoured textbooks on tactics, logistics, and military history whenever time permitted, but reading could not compensate completely for my lack of basic military training.

Once this lack put me in an embarrassing position. Unrest broke out in a regiment in a remote section of the front. Kharash and I drove to division headquarters. There we learned that all the bridges on the road to the regiment had been bombed out. The division commander and his staff were ready to go further on horseback and horses were brought for us. Since I could not bring myself to confess I had never been on a horse, I carefully watched the officers mount. Start standing at the left of the horse, left hand on the pommel . . . then put left foot in the stirrup . . . a jerk, a jump. . . . As simple as that!

I approached my horse, held by an orderly, tried the trick, and, to my surprise, found myself in the saddle. Then I concentrated on watching how Kharash held the reins and managed the horse. The road was bad. We galloped across open places, trotted on forest roads, moved slowly across swamps. I rode my horse alongside Kharash's and asked, "How is my riding?"

"Nothing special," he replied. "Routine."

"I am glad it is no worse. This is my first trip on horseback."

He thought I was joking (we often joked in the Iskosol). After an hour I began to feel an excruciating pain in my back. But I had to go on for another hour. Then came the worst ordeal—dismounting—and after that, limping and exhausted, I had to face the officers and men!

The trouble in the regiment was easily settled. There was friction in the outfit and some trench Bolsheviks had threatened to get even with the officers, but there had been no open disobedience or violence. After a thorough investigation of the officers' complaints, a meeting of the regiment was called in which the officers reassured the soldiers of their loyalty to the revolution and the soldiers pledged to obey battle and service orders. We left after dusk. In the darkness nobody noticed that I had to try three times before I was on the horse, but Kharash saw that I did not feel well. "Are you tired?" he asked.

"No. Tell me again, how is my riding?"

"Nothing special," he laughed.

There was too much special in the way I felt the next day.

ANARCHY AT THE TOP

All the political news from Petrograd was disheartening. The new government was a complete failure. Trying to show the right that he was independent of the Soviets, Kerensky was losing the last crumbs of prestige among workers and soldiers. He took over the personal quarters of Nicholas in the Winter Palace; appeared in public accompanied by two adjutants, one in naval and the other in army uniform; opened his speeches with the words: "I and my government," and as a result was covering himself with ridicule and heaping ridicule on his Cabinet.

The central theme of high politics at the moment was the feud between Kerensky and the Supreme Commander, General Kornilov, who had emerged from obscurity after the outbreak of the revolution. The first thing heard about him was that he had been imprisoned by the Austrians and had escaped back to Russian lines. I do not recall how a legend happened to grow up around this trivial incident, but Kornilov was the type of military man who fitted into a legend well. Everyone who had met him recognized his magnetic personality, courage, strong will, and integrity.

In the turmoil of the first days of the revolution the Tsar had sent Kornilov to suppress the revolt in the capital. He reached Petrograd too late to do anything for the crumbling throne, but the last Mohicans of the monarchy succeeded in planting him in the post of Commander of the Petrograd Military District. There he remained until the May days, when he had his first opportunity to display his strategic talents by dispatching artillery to the Marinsky Palace. Forced to yield to the order of the Soldiers' Section of the Executive Committee, he resigned, a mortified and embittered man.

During the July offensive, Kornilov's name reappeared in the newspapers as Commander of the Seventh Army. How successful he was in that position I do not know. True, his army took a dozen Austrian cities. But resistance was weak and there is no evidence that he would have been better than other generals if his army had been facing crack German divisions. He was catapulted to national fame, however, during the rout on the Southern Front.

I talked with many officers and soldiers who participated in that operation but I could not get a clear picture of what happened. The sight of panic-stricken, fleeing troops is always ugly and humiliating. Divisions, regiments, even single companies, lose contact with one another and with the central command. Each unit feels abandoned and surrounded by the enemy. Officers and soldiers alike become victims of rumors and often of hallucinations. When a unit sees or hears that another unit is withdrawing, it likewise seeks safety in retreat. But not all the men who roll back without an order from the central command can be branded as cowards and deserters. More often than not, retreats are ordered by local commanders who realize—or believe—that their men are on the verge of a breakdown. Such orders may be issued prematurely, but military people make a distinction between such ordered retreat and flight from the battlefield. Not every case of confusion in a retreating army is an act of treason.

General Kornilov, however, unable to stop the retreating troops, opened a barrage of reports to the nation, picturing events at the front in the darkest colors, accusing soldiers of treason and cowardice, denouncing the revolution and the new order in the army as the causes of the disaster, and demanding drastic measures to restore order and discipline. And so he emerged as a hero on a white horse.

In this new campaign Kornilov was supported by the high brass in Mogilev and by Savinkov, then Commissar of the Seventh Army—a man destined to play an important role in later events. Savinkov was a strange person. A former S-R, a member of a terrorist organization, he had begun his revolutionary apprenticeship under the famous police provocateur, Azev, leader of a terrorist group of the party. To maintain his prestige in both the party and the police, Azev used to carry through some terrorist plans and frustrate others by reporting them to the police. To play this two-faced game he needed people who were blindly devoted to him and at the same time were respected by their companions. He picked Savinkov for this role and used him for the terrorist plans that were to be carried out.

Thus Savinkov became a successful political gunman. After Azev was exposed, Savinkov abandoned politics, became a fiction writer, and enriched Russian literature with a couple of sensational novels—a mixture of pulp-magazine technique with revolutionary yarns and a cheap imitation of Dostoevsky generously spiced with eroticism imported from France. I cannot say how it happened that a man with such a background could have been appointed a commissar of the army. But there he was, emerging from nowhere as a former revolutionary, holding the stirrup of the general on the white horse.

General Kornilov's telegrams attracted national attention that his military talents had not earned. On July 20, Kerensky, as Minister of

War, appointed him Commander of the Southwestern Front. Immediately Kornilov sent an ultimatum to the Provisional Government (actually non-existent) demanding that it stop the offensive and reorganize the army on the basis of strict discipline. Both demands were sensible in appearance. Our offensive had already been stopped by the Germans, and tighter army discipline was overdue. What was new in his demands was the arrogant style and the prominent place they gave to restoration of the death penalty in the army.

When the new government was formed, it did not try to curb the roaring General. On July 25 it passed its first decree, reintroducing the death penalty for acts of treason at the front. This provoked passionate dispute, widened the split between the right and left wings in the All-Russian Executive Committee, and gave new fuel for Communist propaganda; but it had little, if any, effect on the army.[7] In our drive to revive the Twelfth Army, we occasionally warned the left-wing political leaders in Riga that they would force us to introduce martial courts, but we never used this threat with rioting soldiers. Although opposed to capital punishment in principle, I recognized that in war a situation may develop in which death becomes the inevitable punishment for most heinous crimes. But this question did not interest me then. I was thinking of ways to restore psychological equilibrium to the sick troops, and I knew the threat of court-martial and the death penalty could not serve this purpose. Moreover, in prison I had seen too many people who expected the death sentence or had been condemned and were awaiting execution to believe that a law imposing the death penalty intimidates.

Meanwhile, the High Command in Mogilev demanded that the government repeal the Declaration of Soldiers' Rights, dissolve the elected committees, and extend the death penalty generally. This was an outburst of madness rather than a political program. There was not the slightest chance of carrying out such measures against the unanimous opposition of the masses of soldiers. A revival of the army on the basis of strict discipline could be achieved only through co-operation of the commanding personnel with soldiers' organizations. But, having broken with the Soviets, Kerensky was too weak to resist the pressure of the strong, single-purposed men in Mogilev. On August 6 he made Kornilov Supreme Commander and appointed Savinkov Deputy Minister of War. Now Russia had two governments: the

---

[7] This decree was never enforced. In fact, it could not be enforced. It required the formation of a martial court (three officers and three soldiers), and it was very doubtful whether the soldier-judges would ever return a verdict of "guilty" in cases in which the defendant faced the death penalty. A case of obvious, arrogant mutiny and treason was submitted to a court-martial on the Southern Front, and the defendant was acquitted by a split vote of the court.

civilian government in Petrograd under Kerensky, and the military, in Mogilev.

Savinkov was supposed to represent Petrograd in dealing with Kornilov, but actually he represented the General in dealing with Kerensky. Relations between the two men became more and more hostile. They no longer fought for the program—Kerensky had none —but for power. All the odds would have been on the side of the Petrograd government if it had wished to use the support of the Executive Committee and, therefore, the support of the army. But it did not want to owe anything to the Soviets and tried instead to appease and outmaneuver the enraged General. This policy had a disastrous effect on the nation and particularly on the army. As on the eve of the fall of Tsarism, confusion and anarchy were spreading throughout the country, not from the depths of dark emotions of the people but from the top.

The Supreme Commander was beginning to lose control over his nerves and sent out orders that occasionally were so stupid that the army commanders could not even reveal them to their subordinates. General Parsky showed me one such order and asked, "What should I do? Shall I explain the situation to the Supreme Commander? If I do, my answer and his telegram will become known to at least half a dozen persons. I would hate to embarrass the Supreme Commander."

The telegram of the Supreme Commander had been provoked by a minor incident in the Twelfth Army—an outburst of panic in a regiment during the night. The incident had been settled by regimental representatives, and order was restored so promptly that local command had had no time to inform the Iskosol or me of the event. Some twelve hours later came Kornilov's telegram instructing Parsky to destroy the "fleeing" regiment immediately by artillery fire. There was no "fleeing" regiment by this time and all was quiet on the front, but this was an operational order to be executed at once. I said to Parsky, "Publication of this telegram would be a terrible blow to the authority of the officers. File it and forget about it." He followed my advice and did not even answer Mogilev.

Yet General Kornilov remained under the impression that his order had saved the situation in the Twelfth Army. A week later, addressing the National Conference in Moscow, he described this incident as evidence of the salutary effect of severe measures: "A few days ago, during the German offensive against Riga, the 56th Siberian Regiment, which had covered itself with glory in battles, left its positions, threw away its arms, and fled. Only the pressure of force of arms, after I had telegraphed an order to annihilate the fleeing regiment, made it return to its position."

This was a complete distortion of the truth. Even the number of the regiment was wrong.

With progressing anarchy at the top, it was becoming increasingly difficult for us in the Twelfth Army to maintain discipline among the troops. Conditions in other armies were no better.

THE NATIONAL CONFERENCE IN MOSCOW

About this time the government tried to restore its prestige by calling a National Conference in Moscow, a huge gathering of representatives of existing and non-existent organizations, including 300 members of the four Tsarist Dumas; 400 representatives of the newly elected Municipal Councils; 300 delegates of consumer unions; 100 delegates of the Executive Committee of the Soviet of Workers and Soldiers; 100, of the Executive Committee of the Soviet of Peasants; 100, of the army committees; 100, of labor unions; 120, of associations of manufacturers; 100, of the union of landowners; 100, of universities; 75, of professional groups; 80, of national minorities. In addition, individual invitations were to be extended.

The obvious purpose of this list was to stress the importance of small reactionary groups in comparison with those representing peasants, workers, and soldiers.

True, the government declared in advance that no votes would be taken and that the only objective of the conference was to allow the various groups to air their views. This statement, however, did not explain why it was necessary to invite a hundred landowners who had only one thing to say—that the land reform demanded by the peasants was sheer robbery.

The whole plan impressed me and my Iskosol friends as absurd. But this was a matter of high policy to be handled by the All-Russian Executive Committee. The Twelfth Army had five seats in the conference, and Iskosol appointed Kuchin and four other committee-men to go to Moscow. Kuchin accepted reluctantly. "What shall I do in that circus?" he asked his companions.

He returned from Moscow disgusted and furious. All the reactionary forces—the landowners, manufacturers, the majority of the four Dumas, and the military high brass led by Kornilov—had rallied for an attack against the Soviets and the army committees. Their common watchword was: Russia needs a strong government independent of the people to put an end to the revolution. This was most effective propaganda . . . for the Communists!

Despite the insistent request of Kerensky that he keep away from the conference, Kornilov joined it and became its principal star. He accused the government of a vacillating policy and demanded it introduce iron discipline in the army and at the rear. Though he did not threaten the government directly, his speech sounded like a threat. The list of speakers was made up in advance, and the delegates of the army committees were not permitted to reply to the Supreme Commander. Kornilov was seconded by a Cossack general, Kaledin, who bluntly demanded the abolition of the Soviets and the committees in the army and at the rear and the resignation of Chernov, the Minister of Agriculture, as a defeatist. Kerensky replied by threatening both the left and the right. The conference was treated to a verbal duel between two budding Napoleons—one in uniform, the other in civilian clothes.

In the absence of Communists, the left wing of the conference was represented by the majority of the Executive Committee. Tseretelli defended the policy of the Soviets in the revolution; Chkheidze presented a cautiously worded platform of the Executive Committee demanding tighter economic controls, a democratic tax policy, antiinflationary measures, development of democratic local government, and reorganization of the army on the basis of strict discipline without prejudice to the civil rights of soldiers and with preservation of the role of soldiers' committees. These speeches, however, were overshadowed by the clash between Kornilov and Kerensky. Soldiers' representatives who had attended the conference came back deeply worried about the future of democracy in the army.

The most important single political event of that period was the collapse of the campaign for a negotiated peace. The British government, acting in accord with the Russian government, denied visas to British Socialists who wished to attend the International Socialist Conference in Stockholm. The campaign was abandoned after this rebuke. Although there had been little interest in this campaign among the workers and soldiers in Russia and abroad, the news that there would be no peace conference, because the British and Russian governments were against it, produced a deep impression. Step by step, the Communists were regaining what they had lost in the July days.

THE GERMAN OFFENSIVE

Early in the morning of August 30, Parsky telephoned to me and asked me to come to his office. I found him in front of the wall map. He showed me a point on the Western Dvina and said:

"We have important intelligence. The Germans will try to cross the river here."

It was exactly the place Boldyrev had indicated to me some ten days before. It was held on our side by General Dorfman's 186th Division, which belonged to the 43rd Corps. The division was one of the best in the army. During preceding weeks, considerable reserves had been concentrated at its rear. Parsky explained our plan of defense:

"The Germans, with their superiority in guns, can silence our front batteries and pulverize the first line of field fortifications. We have no way to keep them from crossing the river, but on this bank they will be surrounded by our forces. Their advance will reduce their advantage in artillery. The first task of our troops is to oppose the crossing, so as to gain time for us to gather strength for the second phase of the operation. Then we must annihilate the enemy or throw him back before he moves his batteries forward." He asked me to go straight to the 186th Division to help its commander and the regimental committees prepare the troops for the impending battle.

In the division, everything seemed to be in good shape. Positions had been reinforced and blockhouses covered with fresh sod. The men were exhilarated, as on the eve of an important event. On the way back I stopped at the headquarters of the 43rd Corps. Boldyrev was bristling with confidence in his troops but less sure of his fresh reserves, especially the Lettish battalions. I drove to the Tirailleurs and phoned from there to the General that he had nothing to fear from that side.

In the afternoon an Alsatian who had crawled over to our lookouts reported the attack was to start at dawn. An order was sent to the 186th Division to keep the men in the blockhouses and get the masks ready for a gas attack. I wanted to drive back to the trenches, but Posochov, the army's Chief of Staff, advised me not to risk night driving without lights. Moreover, the Iskosol called me to a meeting about last-minute instructions to the regiments.

Early the next morning a call came from army headquarters: The Germans have started the attack; communication has been broken; no news from the 186th. Parsky came to the phone. He did not ask me to go to the front but said calmly, "Communication is always our weak point. If you go to the troops, please keep in touch with me. Each time communication is restored, even for a short spell, call me up. And may the Lord protect you!"

I am ashamed to recall that I had left Emma with a vague explanation that I had been called to the front for some routine matter.

The headquarters chauffeur knew all the roads and drove like mad.

The thunder of artillery became louder every moment. Suddenly the road left the forest and entered a broad open meadow. Shells were falling right and left and the road was pitted in many places. The chauffeur turned to me and asked, "What do you order, Comrade Commissar? Turn back, stop, or step on the gas?"

"Step on it!" I shouted.

Soon we reached Stript. Not a living soul in the hamlet. A few houses were ablaze. The house in which the 43rd Corps had had its quarters had been abandoned in a hurry, its floor littered with papers, a broken field telephone on the porch. I heard the tune of the *Marseillaise:* a Lettish battalion was marching to the front. Its commander showed me the written order: "To proceed to the village Walden; to occupy the hills next to the village, right of the road, and attack the enemy when he approaches." Half an hour later I found the 43rd Corps—General Boldyrev, his chief of staff General Simonov, a handful of staff officers, communications service men, and messengers with saddled horses. All was in good order, but the corps had no word from the 186th Division. All efforts to restore communication with it had failed. It looked as if the entire division had vanished into thin air. The regiments on each side of its position reported that the Germans had established a pontoon bridge and had begun to cross the river. About noon they had moved a few pieces of light artillery to the right bank, but our scouts had not yet located them.

Boldyrev remained confident. "A river," he explained, "is not a serious obstacle to a party with superior firepower. The pocket is not large. Now we will counterattack." He sent stern orders to local commanders. The latter reported that the morale of their troops was good and that the officers had perfect co-operation from the soldiers' committees. But there was no report on the progress of the counterattack.

General Simonov said to me, "This happens. Communication never works when you need it most."

Then the reports began to arrive. Some units ordered to advance had occupied assigned positions but met no enemy; others had to change positions because their flanks were not protected; still others had been forced to retreat under German pressure or were ready to retreat because of lack of artillery support. Some reports were very dramatic: hurricane fire, tremendous losses, heroic valor of the troops. Boldyrev doggedly sent orders to outfits in reserve. Simonov was absorbed with the maps. Then he reported, "The pocket is no larger than five miles by three, but we have no continuous line of defense. The Germans could be here at any moment."

Headquarters was moved some five miles east. By dusk it became clear that the counteroffensive had failed. All orders had been obeyed, but the troops lacked the cohesion and initiative needed to stop the enemy. Units sent to reinforce the front lines felt encircled and lost, and the commanders ordered their men to dig in or fall back, reporting to the corps that they had given these orders in view of the enemy's overwhelming superiority in firepower. Meanwhile our batteries got lost somewhere in the forests and marshes or fell back because of lack of infantry protection.

There was no rout like that in the south in July. The troops retreated in order, carrying their wounded and munitions, blowing up the bridges. But the enemy advanced steadily. I was bewildered and could not piece the reports together. Boldyrev and Simonov were grim but not discouraged. "Such things have happened before," Simonov repeated. "It is too early to judge the situation. The enemy seems to be overextending his lines. The tide may turn."

New reports poured in. The tide had not turned, the Germans were widening their pocket, our troops were falling back. Boldyrev said to me, "Now they will brand our soldiers as cowards and traitors. . . . An army can stand a reverse so long as it keeps its self-confidence, but if we let the enemy kill its spirit, all is lost. . . ."

As soon as communication with Riga was restored, I wired to General Parsky, the President of the government, the War Department, and Chkheidze: "On September 1, after hurricane artillery fire, the enemy crossed the Dvina. Most of our batteries covering the river were put out of action or destroyed. . . . Our troops were pushed back four miles on a stretch some six miles wide. Reinforcements are being sent to restore the situation. I testify before the nation: There was no disgrace in our reverse. The troops executed all orders loyally, attacking the enemy with bayonets and braving death. No instances of flight or treason have been reported by field commanders."

Before sending the telegram I showed it to Boldyrev. He hugged and kissed me, saying, "Every word is true. Thank you."

During the night of September 1, we waited for the report from General Scalon. His division occupied the position left of the 186th, and Boldyrev had ordered it to attack the enemy forces that had crossed the river on its flank. The order was duly acknowledged, but nothing was heard from the general. None of the messengers sent to him had returned. I told Boldyrev I would try to reach the division by a detour. The difficulty was in driving without lights over roads that had been under fire throughout the entire day, but I relied on my chauffeur and he did not fail me. I do not know how he found his way in almost complete darkness but, after two hours of breakneck driving, we found the division, still in its old position. It had been reinforced by a few companies from the 186th Division, but its right wing hung in the air; beyond was a dark, silent forest, with no sign of German troops or of ours.

I asked General Scalon about the operation. He reported that the German artillery barrage was the strongest he had ever experienced. He was proud of his men. But with both wings and the rear unprotected, without communication with the corps, and in view of the enemy's superiority in number and artillery fire, he was forced to call off the attack and return to his old positions. I talked with the soldiers' representatives. They confirmed their commander's story. The number of casualties was unknown. Many men were missing, but they might have lost their way and were expected to return by breakfast-time.

I also learned that the maneuver demanded of the division was extremely difficult; the troops deployed along the banks of the river facing the enemy in the west had to attack in northern and northeastern directions through a screen of dense forest. The division had successfully executed this operation. Then it lost contact with the enemy in the thicket and fell back to its old positions.

Back with the corps, I told Boldyrev all I had seen and heard during the night. He reproached Scalon bitterly. "If you could reach him and come back," he said to me, "one of his officers could have reached me. As to the men, what more could they do than they did?" He gave me a batch of fresh reports. I was concerned primarily with the spirit and behavior of the troops, but Boldyrev wished me to have a complete picture of what was going on. Again I wired to Riga and Petrograd: ". . . The situation remains very serious. A further setback is possible. . . . However, the reverse should not cause despair. I confirm the testimony of the commanding personnel. The army has done its duty loyally and has yielded only to the fury of the enemy's superior forces."

The Germans continued their offensive on September 2. They proceeded slowly, consolidating their positions, moving more and more artillery to the right bank of the Dvina. We had ten or twelve divisions against their five or six, but on our side confusion increased from hour to hour. As usual, the communication system had broken down. Each division was left to itself, and none knew exactly what was happening to the left and right of it. The units engaging the Germans or attacked by them felt outnumbered and outgunned, and the engagement ended with our troops in retreat. Moreover, division by division and battalion by battalion, our outfits were no match for the Germans. The enemy knew the terrain better than our commanders. Without contact among themselves, our regiments wandered aimlessly in the woods. Some reached the German lines and attacked but were beaten back by hidden German batteries. The bulge was growing. Back roads were crowded with soldiers who had lost their outfits. They were not deserters—all carried their arms and cartridge belts, all knew the name and number of their regiment and company. When an officer told them where their outfit was, they trudged obediently in that direction.

Reinforcements shifted toward the perimeter held by the 43rd Corps did not change the situation. Time and again the Germans found the weak points in our fluid lines. We were engaged in a large-scale maneuver that required co-ordination and precise timing of movements, flexibility of troops, and bold initiative of commanders. We lacked these qualities.

THE FALL OF RIGA

Boldyrev, Simonov, and I sat around a table covered with maps and half a dozen field telephones. Simonov kept track of operations, Boldyrev sent out orders, I answered the calls of soldiers' representatives, explaining the operation to them. Our aim was to stop or at least slow down the advance of the Germans until heavy guns from other sections of the front could take up positions. Late in the evening the wires went dead again. I fell asleep over a map. Boldyrev covered me with his overcoat.

Before dawn the general awakened me and showed me the new map of the location of the troops. "This is how things look now," he said grimly. "The Germans are making no effort to fan out. They do not intend to attack us from the rear and are not trying to broaden the bulge. But they are building a corridor across our positions, cementing the gap in our lines. Their objective is the highway between Riga and Pskov. If they reach it, they will cut off the right wing of the army." He asked me to drive to Riga and report the situation to the army commander. I replied that military questions were beyond my competence. He waved his big hand. "The operation is in a phase that requires difficult decisions from the army commander. More than purely military decisions, perhaps. Five minutes ago Parsky was on the line. He said he would like to talk with you. Then communication was cut off."

A few minutes later I was in a car speeding toward Riga in the predawn twilight. Confusion on the rear roads was worse than at the front—crowds of soldiers without arms . . . empty vehicles rushing in opposite directions. On the main highway an endless line of heavily loaded trucks moved slowly southward from Riga. Thousands of soldiers were plodding in the same direction. Some were marching in columns, eight men abreast, with officers in the front line; others, in disorderly groups in the fields flanking the road. Technically speaking, this was not a "rout" but a "readjustment" of the front line, yet the picture was disheartening. I stopped two motorcyclists with M.P. armbands, showed them my credentials, and ordered them to clear the way for me. With them in front, my car made good speed. Several times I saw outbursts of panic. A shell would fall in the crowd or in a nearby field, and men would scatter in all directions.

In contrast, all was quiet in Riga. The sidewalks were crowded with people who seemed in festive mood—the German uppercrust of local society. At headquarters, Parsky, his chief of staff Posochov, and a few senior officers were assembled around a long table. Posochov was sorting papers and handing them, one after another, to Parsky. The latter signed them and pushed them on to the officers, who sealed the envelopes. On my arrival Parsky said quietly to his chief of staff, "Wait a minute, Andrei Andreievich. We may be able to find some other solution."

He began to question me on the state of operations. He had received reports from Boldyrev and other field commanders and had made up his mind, but he still had a faint hope that his decision could be changed. Alas, my story corroborated other reports. Listening to me, Parsky nodded his gray head. Then he turned to Posochov and said, "Go ahead, Andrei Andreievich. All we can do is to extricate the troops and save some matériel. Go ahead."

He explained to me, "We are going to abandon Riga." Noticing how this news struck me, Parsky poured me a glass of water, then laid his arm on my shoulder and led me to a window, trying to comfort me. "The first reverse in your battle experience? . . . I see, I see. . . . We have lived through worse reverses, Wladimir Savelievich. . . . A reverse is not the end of the war. . . ."

He returned to the table. The army now had to perform the difficult operation of regrouping, by withdrawing its right wing eastward and pulling back all the units north of the former positions of the 43rd Corps. The new line of defense encircling Riga on the east and south —Venden positions—had been prepared and fortified as early as 1916. The question now was whether Boldyrev's badly mauled and inefficient troops could oppose the enemy's advance long enough to permit the rest of the army to occupy the new positions and evacuate the munitions dumps in front of and around Riga.

At Parsky's request, I returned to the 43rd Corps. On the way I stopped at the Iskosol and learned that some members of the organization were with their units and others had gone to Venden, new army headquarters. Before they left Riga, they took care to evacuate Emma. Thus, I knew that she was safe, but I could not send her word that I was alive.

Before dusk I was with General Boldyrev again. The situation had worsened in the past twelve hours. The Germans now held a pocket some twenty miles long and twelve miles wide, had thrown half a dozen pontoon bridges across the river, and installed more heavy artillery on the right bank. An area some ten miles deep around the pocket was under continuous enemy fire. Our troops were rolling back slowly. All attempts to provide them with artillery support failed; the enemy knew all the spots we could use for artillery positions and bombed them relentlessly, while our batteries, rushed from the rear to the front, got hopelessly mixed up. Some lost their way, others had no ammunition or had the wrong caliber.

Because of the poor maneuverability of our troops, the Germans could advance through the gaps in our lines. A German regiment did not mind being surrounded, while our troops withdrew as soon as they noticed that the enemy was on their flanks and at their rear. It seemed as though the enemy would overrun our flimsy defense lines, but somehow fresh troops appeared in the gap and the German advance units were temporarily stopped or pushed back. Meanwhile, however, the enemy had gained ground at some other point. In three days the Germans advanced ten to twelve miles in this way.

There would have been no sense in appealing to the soldiers. Well or not very well, they did what they were ordered to do. All Boldyrev asked of me was to talk with officers and soldiers' representatives, trying to explain to them the significance of our rear-guard delaying operation. I drove back and forth as a liaison man between the corps and its allegedly cut-off units, thus demonstrating to the men and officers that the roads were passable and they were not surrounded. At dawn on September 4, I wired the government, the War Department, and the Executive Committee: "Developing his initial success, the enemy is continuing to advance, and our troops are retreating. There has been no flight from the battlefield, no disobedience of orders. The source of our weakness is lack of self-confidence of the troops, their insufficient training for maneuvering, and the enemy's superiority in firepower. We have suffered heavy losses but many units are fighting as bravely as in the first days. In others, fatigue is noticeable."

Headquarters of the 43rd Corps was located some two miles from the battle lines, not more than ten miles from the nearest point on the Riga-Pskov highway. Unexpectedly, the Germans began to turn northward in an enveloping movement around Riga, bringing reinforcement to their left wing but diminishing the pressure on our lines. Our troops launched an attack against the enemy's exposed right flank. This operation gave the Army Command two more days to complete the evacuation of Riga. Not until September 7 did the Germans enter the city. The Twelfth Army had been evacuated to its last unit, with hospitals, artillery, and munitions.

That same day I drove to Venden, where I found Emma, who had been without news from me all these days. When shells began to fall on Riga, she went to the Iskosol and learned that I was in the front lines. In the hope of getting in touch with me, she remained with the Iskosol although the building was the main target of German long-distance guns. She left Riga for Venden on one of the last trucks the army provided for the evacuation of nurses. Those days had been particularly hard on her. During one of her aimless strolls through Venden she suddenly saw me arriving in an army car.

My friends in the Iskosol told me about the events at the rear. The delaying action of the 43rd Corps had prevented the worst catastrophe. The army was safe in its new positions, and its losses in men and matériel were lighter than might have been anticipated.

Compared with the mass retreats and surrenders before the revolution, in 1914-16, the loss of Riga was not a major disaster. Yet Mogilev circles tried to use the reverse for political purposes. The Supreme Commander issued a press release about the "disorganized crowds of soldiers wandering aimlessly along the Riga-Pskov highway." This was a strange way to report on a major battle still under way and grossly contradicted the official reports from the Twelfth Army and my testimony. The leftist and moderate papers accused General Kornilov of slandering the army, while the rightists blamed the Commander of the Twelfth Army and the Commissar for undermining the authority of the Supreme Commander. Kornilov, in an outburst of anger, announced that he would court-martial Parsky and me for spreading false information.

On the night of September 10, the Iskosol met in Venden. I remember the long, narrow room, men in soiled uniforms around the table, the droning voices, and, above all, my irrepressible drowsiness. I had slept hardly more than eight hours during the preceding eight days and had to make superhuman efforts not to let my comrades see how exhausted I was. But most of them were equally tired.

Stankevich, who came from Pskov to attend this meeting, tried to get a straightforward story of the German offensive and our retreat. Why couldn't our troops stop the enemy? Defending the soldiers, the Iskosol men accused the commanding personnel of a poor system of communications, lack of road maps, poor selection of positions for artillery, lack of plans for defense in depth, and so forth. All this was true, in a general way. But the officers as individuals were no more to blame for the reverse than the soldiers. I therefore defended the commanding personnel. No particular officers were to blame—it was the fault of the military organization as a whole. The Iskosol people conceded that Parsky, Boldyrev, and a few others were okay. But what about General Scalon? Couldn't he have saved the situation by a more energetic counterattack? I believed he could not perform miracles under the circumstances and with the troops at his disposal, but the representatives of his division urged that he could have put more vigor into the operation and that the men would have followed his orders. Then Stankevich suggested that a military court investigate the case. I agreed on condition that I be called as a witness to testify in the General's defense.[8]

Before dawn Stankevich and I left for Petrograd, to which the War Department had summoned us urgently for consultation. On the way to the station Stankevich tried to brief me on the new friction between the government and the Supreme Commander, but I fell asleep and did not awaken until we reached the capital.

THE MUTINY OF THE SUPREME COMMANDER

From the station, Stankevich drove to the Winter Palace to see Kerensky, and I went to the new headquarters of the Executive Committee. It had been moved, together with the Petrograd Soviet, to the building formerly occupied by the Smolny Institute, a finishing school for girls of the nobility.[9] I asked the guard at the door whether any of the members of the Executive Committee were in the building. A sergeant took me to Chkheidze's office—a large room, white and strangely bare. Its furniture consisted of a dozen white chairs around a small white table. There sat the leaders of the Executive Committee —Chkheidze, Tseretelli, Chernov, Gotz, and others, grim and tired after a sleepness night.

Tseretelli asked me, "When did you leave the army? What is the situation there?"

"I have come directly from the session of the Iskosol at Venden. The regrouping of the army has been completed, the new line . . ."

A Menshevik member of the Committee interrupted me. "That is not what we are interested in. What are Kornilov's forces on the Northern Front?"

"Kornilov's forces? What do you mean?"

"I mean, what forces can Kornilov muster against us and the government?"

"No regiment and no company of the Northern Front will execute Kornilov's order unless it is confirmed by the army committee or by me."

[8] After my testimony the investigation commission cleared the General without presenting the case to the court.
[9] The Tauride Palace did not have sufficient office space for the numerous departments, commissions, and special services of the Executive Committee and the Petrograd Soviet.

The Menshevik jumped from his chair. "General Kornilov has already taken a corps from the Northern Front and sent it against Petrograd."

"That is sheer nonsense!" I shouted. "What corps is it?"

"The Third Cavalry!"

"There is no such corps on the Northern Front!"

Chkheidze said meditatively, "That is strange. Did not the Commander of the Northern Front, along with other front commanders, promise Kornilov full support?"

"If he did, I have heard nothing about it," I replied. "However, General Klembovsky is a notorious fool, and he might have promised Kornilov anything. But this I do know: No troops will obey him if he orders them to march against the Soviets or the government."

Chkheidze showed me a bundle of papers. "Read these. Then you will know what is going on here." The papers were copies of telegrams, appeals, communiqués. They told a fantastic story of mutiny by the Supreme Commander against the government.

Kerensky and Kornilov had hated and distrusted each other for the good reason that each regarded himself alone as the man predestined to save Russia. With two would-be Napoleons, one in Petrograd and the other in Mogilev, and both surrounded by unsavory characters, political intrigue filled the air. Counterrevolutionary circles in Mogilev plotted a coup to establish the military dictatorship of Kornilov, while Kerensky dreamed of getting rid of the Communists, the Soviets, and the intractable generals in Mogilev. Both candidates lacked the three features that had brought Napoleon to power—genius, the halo of victory, and devoted troops—but each had worked himself into a state of mind in which such trifles did not count.

Kerensky had persuaded himself he would save Russia if he had troops of his own, independent of the revolutionary Soviets and committees. He believed Kornilov could provide him with such troops. It became an obsession with him to coax the Supreme Commander to put at his disposal some wholly reliable regiments—as if the general had them and could manipulate them at his will. With this purpose in mind, he sent Savinkov to Mogilev to persuade Kornilov to dispatch his shock troops to Petrograd.

Later, Kerensky pretended that the Provisional Government had decided on September 3 to begin preparations to transfer the government to Moscow and to bring from the front a reliable task force to be placed at the government's disposal. No record of this decision has been found, and none of the ministers remembered discussion of such plans in the Cabinet. During the investigation of the so-called Kornilov affair, Kerensky explained that this was not a formal decision of the government but his own plan; however, one member of the Cabinet, whose name he could not recall, had asked him about the danger of possible rioting in the capital, and he answered that all necessary measures were being taken. Since no one objected, he interpreted the silence of the ministers as the confirmation of his plan and could consider it approved by the government.

By promising that the government would comply with Kornilov's program to reorganize the army, Savinkov persuaded the Supreme Commander to send the Third Cavalry Corps, reputedly one of the most dependable in his reserve, to Petrograd. It was agreed to keep the operation a secret. Officially the corps would be sent to reinforce the Northern Front for strategic reasons. Kornilov promised to inform Kerensky when the concentration of the corps around Petrograd had been completed. Kerensky would then proclaim martial law in the capital and begin energetic action. Probably he himself did not know what the action would be, but Kornilov's order to General Krymov, the commander of the Third Corps, was clear: Liquidate the Communists and the Soviets. In the language of both generals, that might have meant either shooting or hanging. The deal Kornilov and Savinkov thus concluded in Mogilev was, of course, a conspiracy against the Petrograd Soviet, which was then supporting the Provisional Government, but it is not clear whether or not Kerensky was informed of all the details of the plot.

Precautions were taken against attempts by railroad workers to stop the echelons as they had stopped the Tsar's train in March. A railroad engineering battalion with all necessary equipment was sent ahead of the corps. The expedition was organized carefully in every respect except that the generals had not asked the soldiers whether they would support them against the Soviets.

While the troops were en route from the Southern Front, a clash developed between Kornilov and Kerensky. The general summoned Kerensky and Savinkov to his headquarters as if he were already the ruler of the realm. Kerensky replied with an order to stop the movement of the Third Corps and removed Kornilov from his post. Kornilov refused to relinquish his command and repeated his order to the corps to proceed as instructed to the capital. Next, Kerensky issued an appeal to the people, telling his side of the story, and Kornilov did the same. If Kerensky's appeal was somewhat vague and puzzling, Kornilov's manifesto was absurd. "All in whose breasts beats a Russian heart, who trust in God, I call on you to rush to the altar and pray our Lord to show the miracle, greatest of all, by saving Russia!" In anticipation of the miracle, the general declared that he could no longer recognize the existing government. All the front commanders declared their solidarity with the Supreme Commander, thus offering their swords—if not their armies—to the service of the mutinous general.[10]

After reading the papers, I said to Chkheidze, "All this comes from a madhouse. The movement of the Third Corps is sheer nonsense. Kornilov's troops are phantoms. They will vanish into thin air before the first shot is fired."

THE DEFENSE OF PETROGRAD

Chkheidze asked me to join a Special Commission for the Defense of Petrograd, and once more I stepped onto the old treadmill—telephone calls, messengers, delegations. Some members of the Commission did not share my belief that Kornilov's operation was a "humbug," but we had no disagreement about our defense program: First, to explain to the troops of the rebellious general that they were to be used against the Soviets of Workers and Soldiers and the All-Russian Executive Committee; second, to throw a line of defense around the capital so that the approaching units, should any of them reach this line, would recognize that they must either fight the soldiers and workers of Petrograd or join them. I was convinced that the third phase of the defense—actual fighting on the outskirts of the capital—was improbable.[11] The companions who considered my view

[10] What impressed me most in this episode was the childish stupidity of the operation from a purely military point of view. Kerensky had planned to transform his ephemeral power into a dictatorship with the aid of a cavalry corps. A few days later, the Supreme Commander tried to establish his own dictatorship with the aid of the same corps. Neither of them had any other force for the operation. The firepower of a cavalry corps, however, does not exceed that of an infantry regiment. How could the course of the revolution be changed with such a force? In addition, how could Kerensky or Kornilov be sure that the men thus brought to Petrograd would serve their political schemes? Both, while copying our July strategy, had overlooked the fundamental difference in the situation. Each man in our task force knew what he was asked to do and why, and we had the great majority of the people behind us. In the Kerensky-Kornilov operation everything depended on the blind obedience of a handful of soldiers, against the wishes of the great majority of the people and especially of the army.
[11] Miliukov later described the panic in "the government and the best informed circles" at the news of approaching forces of the Supreme Commander. According to him, these circles considered Kornilov's success certain. Similarly, General Denikin later described the "deadly fear" in the ranks of revolutionary democracy of Petrograd and testified that some members of the government were ready to flee abroad. Most pathetic is Kerensky's testimony: "There was a night when I walked back and forth [in the Winter Palace] almost alone—alone not because I had not wanted to act with other people, but because the psychological climate was such that people thought it was best to keep away from a lost cause." Stankevich, who was close to Kerensky at that time, also reported that a feeling of despair and doom prevailed in the Winter Palace.
I am inclined to accept all this testimony at face value. Some persons in Petro-

of the situation too optimistic thought that the units of the Third Corps would attack our defense line but were sure this attack would be beaten back. Meanwhile we had to take precautions against sympathizers of the mutinous general in the capital.

In planning to defend Petrograd, we did not think of getting in touch with the government, partly because we knew it could not help much and partly because we were not sure whether it sided with us or with Kornilov. But Chernov, himself a member of the government, suggested we should check what the Military Command was doing.

With him and Gotz, I drove to the War Ministry to the office of Savinkov, now appointed Military Governor of Petrograd. His desk was in a luxurious room, with paintings of battles on its walls. We did not exchange greetings. Gotz asked about the defense plans of the Military Command. Savinkov replied through tightened lips, "Whatever I consider necessary has been done."

Gotz asked about precautions against riots instigated by Kornilov's partisans in the city and received the answer, "I do not consider such measures necessary."

I asked Savinkov whether he wished to keep in touch with the Smolny to co-ordinate action and exchange information. He replied, "I have no such desire."

He turned to his papers, making it clear that the audience had ended. We left his office convinced that he was working for Kornilov. Gotz stopped at the door and said loudly enough to be heard by the Military Governor, "We must watch this s.o.b. closely." I replied equally loudly, "He can't do much harm."

In the hall of the Ministry, General Bagratuni, Chief of Staff of the Military District, approached us. "You are interested in our preparations? That is my responsibility." He took us to his office and showed us a large wall map of the Petrograd area with blue circles on the roads leading to the capital from south and west. "Here are our positions," he said proudly.

I noticed lettering on the circles: ½ C; 1 C and ½ B; 1 B; and so forth. "Half a company; a company with a half battery; a battery," I read aloud and asked, "Are those your preparations? Where are your reserves? Do you intend to stop the advance of the adversary with a single line of lookouts on the edge of the city?"

The general replied with a smile, "Surely, this is only a façade. It will never come to shooting. Some compromise will be worked out."

---

grad were probably panicky and believed Kornilov would succeed; Denikin may have seen "deadly fear" among them. Such persons, however, were very remote from the "revolutionary democracy." Kerensky was alone because he was caught between two fires and expected reprisals from both sides—from the left, for having conspired with Kornilov; from the right, for having betrayed the general. But in the Smolny, the center of Petrograd's defense, the mood was very different.

"A political compromise," I interrupted him, "is no business of the military. But you are right, there will be no shooting on your positions. If the mutinous regiments push that far, they will meet our troops some twenty miles before they get to your line."

The general looked at me incredulously. "Then you will have a front of fifty miles to cover. How will you man the lines?"

"Do not expect us to inform you of our operations," I replied.

The general looked sheepishly at his map.

The Special Commission met for a brief session. Organization of the defense was progressing smoothly. The defense line we had planned outside the city was divided into sections, each assigned to a definite group of regiments and factories. Young officers loyal to the Soviets were sent to select and organize positions. Workers and soldiers were ordered to dig trenches. Before noon, more than a hundred thousand workers had enrolled for action.

There were rumors of secret meetings of counterrevolutionary elements. The Commission sent detachments of soldiers to arrest the suspects. Somebody proposed freeing Trotsky and other Communists taken into custody after the July days. I pointed out that their liberation might be interpreted by the public as evidence that we could not defend the capital without them. The proposal was withdrawn. The patrols brought the suspects to the Smolny. A group of lawyers (all servicemen) were assigned to interrogate them and set free those against whom no serious charges were presented. Stern orders were sent to the barracks to deliver all suspects to the Special Commission, the only body authorized to investigate the charges.

By the morning of September 11, all roads leading to the capital from the west and south were occupied by our troops and armed workers' commandos. By noon, activity in the Smolny began to subside. The offices of the Soldiers' Section were half empty. A few members of the Special Commission slept peacefully beside silent telephones. I began to think of returning to the front, but the transportation section of the Executive Committee warned me that both the railroad and highway between Petrograd and Pskov were in the hands of the rebels.

In the evening the Petrograd Soviet convened in the main hall of the Smolny. Fewer than half the delegates were present, for the others were busy in positions encircling the city. Since there was no quorum for a formal session, it was decided to hold an informal conference. Chkheidze asked me to report on the fall of Riga and the military situation on the Northern Front. The Soviet was dominated by left-wing Socialists, and I was not very popular with them. Yet the audience greeted me with a long ovation, probably as a tribute to the Twelfth Army and my telegrams from the front. My talk was focused on the question: What should the rear garrisons and the workers do to strengthen the army? The audience was responsive and friendly.

The next morning, September 12, Stankevich and I decided to ignore the warnings and to drive to Pskov. On the highway at the outskirts of the city we overtook crowds of workers with shovels rushing to the "front" to dig new, bigger, and better trenches. Then we passed our positions, with trenches stretching far away from the highway, with lookouts, nests for machine guns, and grounds for batteries.

Some ten miles farther we drove into a strong detachment of cavalry. Our car was stopped and a sergeant asked us to show our papers. He returned our credentials. "Lucky travel, Comrades Commissars!" Stankevich asked him what he and his men were doing here. "Reconnaissance patrol," the sergeant replied. We were not sure whether this was Kornilov's advance patrol or our men returning to the defense line. Twenty or thirty miles farther we noticed from the crest of a hill that the road ahead was barred by troops advancing in a wide column, not only on the highway but also over the fields along both sides of the road. A strange formation! Horsemen first, foot soldiers immediately behind them, horse-drawn field guns in the midst of infantry. . . . Were these the famous crack troops of the Supreme Commander? The formation seemed to violate all tactical rules and military regulations.

A young officer on horseback approached our car, and we recognized the chairman of the soldiers' Soviet in Luga. "Are you with General Kornilov?" Stankevich asked him.

"Not on your life! We are the advance outfit of the Luga garrison on the march to defend the revolution!"

"Then why are you going to Petrograd?" I inquired.

"To find favorable positions and join the Petrograd garrison," was the reply.

We drove on. Luga seemed deserted, but after we crossed the city we noticed a few peasants in fields near the highway. They told us that the scouts of the Third Corps had appeared near Luga on the tenth but had not entered the city. The garrison had left the city by several roads, falling back toward the capital. The staff of the Third Corps was located in a hamlet a few miles west of Luga, on a country road branching out from the highway. Stankevich was ready to go on to Pskov, but I suggested we get in touch with the headquarters of the corps. Probably it had been cut off from the troops. Perhaps the troops had already learned the purpose of the operation and were in open revolt. We could ask the staff to surrender.

Ten minutes later we were in the hamlet. A score of peasants were massed in front of a house.

"Where is headquarters?" I asked them.

"This is where it was last night," an old man replied. "But the nest is empty. They flew away, the blackbirds."

"Were there many of them?"

"A hundred or so Cossacks. They left at dawn, ahead of the generals. The officers said they expected to make forty miles before night."

We drove back to Luga and wired to Chkheidze: "The highway to Pskov is open. Kornilov's troops are retreating. We are proceeding to Pskov."

Farther on we overtook a motorcyclist with a Cossack hat and a black leather jacket. He was leisurely examining his cycle, which was turned upside down in the ditch. I stopped the car, went up to the Cossack, showed him my credentials and asked, "What is your unit and what are you doing here?"

He replied readily, "Sergeant of the Scout Detail, second regiment of the Ussury Cossack Division, Third Cavalry Corps. Carrying a message from the division chief, General Gubin, to the commander of the corps."

"Give me the message!" I ordered. The Cossack looked at me with a shrewd smile, pulled off his hat, took out an oblong yellow envelope, and handed it to me. "We Cossacks are always ready to oblige, Mr. Commissar," he remarked.

The division chief was reporting to the corps commander that his trains with men, horses, light batteries, and equipment had reached the station of Yamburg. There rumors spread among the Cossacks that they were being sent against the people of Petrograd. The Cossacks asked the officers what the purpose of the expedition was, but the officers themselves knew nothing. The division chief asked for instructions from the corps commander and concluded: "The state of the division is such that I am compelled to unload everything and billet the regiments in surrounding villages."

I returned the message to the Cossack after writing under the signature of General Gubin: "The envelope has been opened and the message read. Commissar Woytinsky." The messenger asked me with a sly smile, "Something urgent? Or some nonsense that can wait till I tune up the cycle?"

"Very urgent. Step on the gas, son." He disappeared in a cloud of dust.

The message was indeed urgent. The Ussury Division was the largest unit in the corps. Without it, the corps had ceased to exist. The appeals of the Executive Committee had reached the Cossacks.

Billeted around Yamburg, the men realized they had been sent against the Soviets. They arrested their officers, appointed commanders from their own ranks, and sent a delegation to the Smolny to explain that they had never faltered in their loyalty to the revolution. The campaign that began as a mutiny of the generals ended as a mutiny of enlisted men. Only one shot was fired, and only one life was lost in the operation. After receiving the note from General Gubin, General Krymov, the commander of the Third Corps, realized that General Kornilov's attempt had failed. He drove to Petrograd and went to the Winter Palace, formally surrendered his sword to Kerensky, and blew his brains out.

By the evening of September 13 all was over. In elation over the easy victory, we did not realize that the democratic revolution was approaching its end. The generals' mutiny had opened Lenin's way to power.

THE ARMY AFTER THE KORNILOV MUTINY

The Kornilov affair had a disastrous effect on the morale of the army. It opened the old wound—distrust between the enlisted men and officers. All our efforts to reconcile the two groups had been wiped out. We had to start again from scratch.

Stankevich was transferred to Mogilev as Commissar at the Headquarters of the Supreme Commander. I took over his office in Pskov as Commissar of the Northern Front. General Klembovsky, who had promised to support Kornilov, was permitted to resign. His place was given to Cheremissov, a comparatively young general who had acquired fame as a division commander during the offensive of the Eighth Army on the Southern Front, but was particularly successful in political intrigue. Ambitious and completely unscrupulous, dreaming of future advancement, he tried to gain popularity with the soldiers by taking a more radical stand than the army committees. His arrogance, however, was tempered by cowardice. He could stop in the middle of a tirade when he felt he had gone too far. Cheremissov and I understood each other. He was suspiciously reserved with me. I avoided him, preferring to work directly with the armies' commanders.

One of my first tasks was to restore the Third Cavalry Corps, which was now assigned to the general reserve on the Northern Front and was completely disorganized, its units dispersed over some five hundred square miles, and all its officers held in custody by their men. Since the charge against them was not without foundation, I could not simply order the Cossacks to release them. My task, rather, was to restore the men's confidence in them.

First of all, the corps had to have a new commander. When Kornilov sent the troops to Petrograd, he had instructed Krymov to deploy his corps into an army under his, Krymov's, command, putting the Third Cavalry Corps under the command of another Cossack general, Krasnov. The latter reached Pskov when the ill-fated operation was nearing its end and was taken into custody by the local Soldiers' Committee. Two days later he was brought to our office under escort. A tall man of impressive appearance, his gray head held high, he looked intelligent and self-confident. He did not deny his knowledge of Kornilov's plans and his readiness to execute them. Obviously he was guilty of intending to take part in the mutiny but could not be accused of participating in mutinous actions. Stankevich and I decided not to press charges. I called Stankevich into the next room and said to him, "The corps needs a new commander. My choice is this man." He agreed, and we returned to the office where the general awaited further interrogation.

"You may be called later as a witness in this affair," I said to him, "but since it has been established that you did not participate in the mutiny, your personal case is closed." The soldiers who had escorted the general were dismissed and Krasnov was ready to leave when I asked him, "Will you help us reconcile the Cossacks with their officers and restore order in the corps?"

"I would be happy to do so," he replied.

"Would you accept the post of commander of the corps?"

"I am a soldier and obey orders," the general answered.

A few day later Krasnov was officially appointed commander of the Third Cavalry Corps. I introduced him to the Cossack committeemen, and he gave them a talk about the Cossacks' traditions of freedom. He was an excellent speaker, with a flair for martial romanticism.

Then we began a tour of the units of the corps. I explained to the Cossacks that Kornilov had held the purpose of his operation secret from officers. Indeed, they had learned the whole story almost at the same time as the enlisted men, from rumors. This was evidenced by the message of General Gubin I had intercepted on the Luga-Pskov highway. On the other hand, I tried to explain to the officers that, in the tragic situation created by Kornilov's mutiny, the best thing that could have happened to them was to be arrested by their men. "Suppose you had taken your men to Petrograd and ordered them to charge," I said. "They would have refused to fire on their brothers, and you would have had an open revolt on your hands, under battle conditions. Even if they had charged—some ten thousand horsemen against twenty times as many foot soldiers supported by artillery—you and your troops would have been mowed down by men defending their freedom and yours. Would that have been better than a couple of weeks in custody?"

Step by step, peace and order were restored in the corps. In explaining the events to the Cossacks, I made it clear, without reservations, that the expedition had been the result of a conspiracy. "Let the Investigating Committee decide who is to blame. You, the Cossacks, have done your duty by stopping the operation. You, the officers, became victims of this mess, but you cannot blame your men for what happened to you."

With the aid of regimental committees, I gradually succeeded in restoring the authority of the command. Meanwhile, Krasnov was regrouping the echelons, consolidating them in regular formations. By the middle of October the work was completed. The Third Cavalry Corps was again a fighting unit.

DISINTEGRATION OF THE GOVERNMENT

It was more difficult to restore the soldiers' confidence in their officers in other units of the army. Soldiers made no distinction between Kerensky and Kornilov, between their immediate commanders and generals playing politics in Mogilev. To them, all officers were members of the same gang. Deadly poison had been injected into the troops. At first it worked slowly, but gradually the infection penetrated deeper and deeper, into the blood, brains, and heart of the army. And again, as in 1916, the disintegration of the state authority was coming from above, from the Winter Palace.

Kerensky, who had disappeared from the scene during the crisis, remained President of the Government and added to this title that of the Supreme Commander, convinced that his name would inspire confidence and devotion in both the officers and enlisted men. Actually, however, he was one of the most hated men in the army. The effect on the army of his self-appointment to the post of the Supreme Commander was perhaps worse than that of Kornilov's mutiny. With good reason or not, soldiers considered Kerensky a partner in Kornilov's conspiracy. Now that the conspiracy had been frustrated by the All-Russian Executive Committee, one of the conspirators had succeeded the other as Supreme Commander!

My office in Pskov occupied the ground floor of a large building, a former high school. At the back were a few rooms that could be used as living quarters. Emma and I took one room for ourselves, another was occupied by the chief of the office, the third was converted into a field-telegraph office, with direct wires to the armies, Petrograd, and Mogilev. I had inherited from Stankevich a staff designed mainly to record information on events at the front. My assistants were nice lads, but none of them could step into a crowd of rioting soldiers and none knew how to work with the army committees. Since I could not use them in field work, I left them to carry on the office routine while I continued my old role of itinerant trouble shooter.

The situation at the front grew worse from day to day. The Kerensky-Kornilov affair destroyed all the work of such men as Vilenkin and General Danilov in the Fifth Army, or Kuchin, Kharash, and Generals Boldyrev and Parsky in the Twelfth. One regiment after another deposed their old regimental committee and elected a new one packed with Communist sympathizers. The army committees were losing their hold over the masses of soldiers. The troops ignored service orders. Riots and acts of violence broke out every day. I had preserved some vestige of authority as the commissar whom Kornilov had threatened to court-martial for defending the soldiers. The story was told in the army with the usual exaggeration: there were rumors that Kornilov ordered me to be shot or hung or both and that I escaped by miracle. This legend gave some weight to my words when I addressed rioting men. As before, I could afford to speak forcefully to a trigger-happy mob, but I felt that the prestige of the All-Russian Executive Committee was dwindling because, by supporting the Provisional Government, it had put itself in the boat with Kerensky.

During the excitement of the Kornilov mutiny, the government had resigned, leaving all power in the hands of Kerensky, apparently to give him full freedom of action against the Supreme Commander. I do not know what he was expected to do after the Soviet had crushed the mutiny. I was not in Petrograd in those days and can neither explain nor understand how the All-Russian Executive Committee, with all material power in its hands, could allow the formation of the irresponsible "Five-Man Directory" with Kerensky as president. I learned later that the arrangement was accepted in a hurry, for a two or three days' interregnum. The crisis, however, lasted more than four weeks, and throughout this time Russia actually had no government.

The newspapers were filled with stories—not all equally true—about the Kornilov-Kerensky conspiracy. The only way to erase the disastrous effect of these rumors on the army would have been to let everyone involved in it stand public trial. Instead, Kornilov and a few generals were arrested while Kerensky, in his dual capacity as the head of government and Supreme Commander, commuted between Petrograd and Mogilev. Vicious rumors had it that he stayed in Mogilev to suppress the evidence of his role in the conspiracy. As if this were not enough, he was appointed—I do not know by whom—to form a new Cabinet, and he promised to fill the posts in the Cabinet with representatives of industry, trade, and the stock exchange, eliminating any dependence of the government on the All-Russian

Executive Committee—as if a moderate government could stay in power without the support of the forces that had beaten back the assault of the Bolsheviks in July and frustrated Kornilov's mutiny in August! The Bolshevist tide was again rising.

On the night of September 13, the plenary session of the Petrograd Soviet voted a resolution demanding that all power be given to the Soviets. Chkheidze put the question of confidence. A new session of the Soviet was called for September 22, and the left bloc obtained a majority of 513 against 474, with 67 abstentions. Trotsky was elected the new president of the Soviet. On September 20, the Bolsheviks gained the majority in the Soviet of Moscow.

The All-Russian Executive Committee remained the last stronghold of democratic forces in the nation, the last dam against the Bolshevist flood. The outcome of elections of municipal and rural councils held on the basis of universal suffrage in September gave it a new prestige. In rural elections, the S-R party was far ahead of all other groups. Among thousands of members of the rural councils, only a few Cadets and Bolsheviks were elected. The Cadets gained a few seats in urban councils while the Bolsheviks obtained the votes in rear garrisons and a majority in industrial precincts in Petrograd, Moscow, and other large cities. But the great majority of urban voters cast their ballots for the S-R, the Laborites, and the Mensheviks. Although these elections were not a substitute for the Constituent Assembly, they revealed the mood prevailing in the country.

The democratic leaders faced a dilemma. If they supported the new Provisional Government, headed by Kerensky but dominated by the Cadets, they would be acting against the wishes of the majority of the people; if they refused to support it, they would have to take power into their own hands or form a united front with the Bolsheviks. The solution could have been the prompt convocation of the Constituent Assembly, but this course was no longer possible. After the government had postponed the elections until December, preparations had been slowed down, and it was extremely difficult to make up the lost time.

THE DEMOCRATIC CONVENTION

In the midst of the political confusion, the Executive Committee decided to call a convention of representatives of all democratic organizations in the nation: the Soviet, army committees, rural and municipal councils, co-operative unions, and associations of national minorities. The Soviet of Petrograd, now under the control of the

Bolsheviks, passed a resolution opposing such a convention and reiterating the demand for an immediate transfer of all power to the Soviets. On the eve of the Convention that met in Petrograd on September 26, the plenary session of the Executive Committee assembled to discuss the problem of the government. I received a telegram calling me to attend. More than two hundred persons were present, but the discussion was lifeless and no decision was taken. The Executive Committee went to the Convention with no program, no definite policy.

The official meeting of the Convention in the Alexandrinsky Theater was preceded by caucuses of political groups. The S-D caucus opened with reports by the leaders of the three factions within the party, but the discussion revealed that each faction had two or three different points of view. A dozen resolutions were put to a vote. A small majority favored a coalition government, and about an equal majority was against a coalition with the Cadets. No binding decisions were taken. The caucus of the S-R party was equally sterile. The moderates who had directed the policy of the Soviets since April were hopelessly split.

The Convention was a cumbersome and motley gathering, with groups of unequal importance and some overlapping in organizations, but it represented fairly well the democratic forces of all parts of Russia. The largest representation was given to the new rural and municipal councils (500 seats) and central Soviets of workers, soldiers, and peasants (300 seats); next in number came the representatives of local soldiers' organizations (150), consumer unions (150), and trade unions (100). In addition, 225 seats were distributed among national minorities, professional organizations, and various other groups.

In the military section of the Convention, delegates from the front outnumbered those from rear garrisons. Politically, this section represented the center of the Convention. The Soviets of workers, dominated by the Communists, formed its left wing. On the right were peasant organizations, rural and municipal councils, and co-operative unions controlled by the right-wing S-R. Perhaps it would be possible to achieve a workable majority in the Convention by taking a vote by section, but such a vote would only emphasize the deep split in the democratic forces.

Chkheidze was in the chair. Kerensky, invited to address the Convention, delivered a speech in his usual style, too emotional and affected to impress a suspicious and, to a large extent, unfriendly audience. The new War Minister, General Verkhovsky, opened the discussion of military affairs. He was a young man in a dashing uniform, very lean and tall, with a pale face, horn-rimmed glasses, and a resounding voice. He professed his faith in the potentialities of an army that had emerged from a revolution. Such an army, he said, could repeat the pattern of the prerevolutionary military organization but must have a new spirit and seek new forms. His speech was the highlight of the day.

Discussion of the chief question—the formation of the government—began the next day. The left claimed all power for the Soviets. The center leaned increasingly toward a coalition with progressive, non-Socialist elements, excluding the counterrevolutionary groups, but the spokesmen of the right wing of the Convention declared they would not participate in a coalition that excluded the Cadets, whom they considered the only influential non-Socialist group in the nation.

The Bolsheviks began to interrupt the speeches, shouting, "Disgrace! Bread!" to imply that the moderates in the Executive Committee were to blame for the shortage of food in Petrograd.

Voting started on October 2, after a week of speeches. The resolution in favor of a coalition government passed by 766 votes to 688, with 38 abstentions. Next, an amendment excluding the Cadets from the coalition was passed by 593 votes to 483, with 72 abstentions. Then the amended resolution was voted down by 813 to 180, with 80 abstentions. The Convention had failed.

The Convention then decided to elect a permanent commission—the Democratic Council—representing all democratic organizations, to act as a substitute for a parliament until the Constituent Assembly convened. More than four hundred persons refused to vote. The decision was taken by a majority of 829 votes to 106, with 69 abstentions. Organization of the Democratic Council began the next day. A throng of little-known groups claimed seats in the new body. The presiding board, refusing to admit some doubtful organizations, distributed 308 seats among the groups represented in the Convention. Bargaining went on without the customary obstruction from the left: The Communists and their sympathizers were absent, attending the session of the Petrograd Soviet in the Smolny, where they denounced the Democratic Council of Counterrevolution.

The Convention ended on October 5. The concluding session was gloomy. Chkheidze sat at a long table on the stage, a picture of melancholy and despair. Many chairs at the table were empty. I wanted to leave also, but Chkheidze implored me to deliver the concluding speech. There was not much to say about the results of the Convention. Then Chkheidze got up and left the stage, forgetting to declare the meeting adjourned.

The Convention had not solved the government crisis, but the Council it elected was later expanded—or perhaps just watered down—by inclusion of property-owning groups and representatives of non-Socialist parties. In this way the Pre-Parliament, or Council of the Republic, was formed, an organization that might have had a chance to supplement a coalition government . . . if such a govern ment were to be organized.

Unfortunately, negotiations on the formation of a government ended in complete failure. The Cabinet that emerged out of these negotiations became known as the Third Coalition, or the Second Kerensky Government. Actually, it was neither a coalition nor a government. It consisted of men picked individually by Kerensky from business circles and intellectual professions. Some were able men with good reputations in their own fields, others were little known to the public, but together they were not much better than the Directory. I was at the front when the Council of the Republic recognized this Cabinet as the new government in Russia.[12] If I had been in Petrograd perhaps I too would have voted with the majority of the Council, but I recall my feeling of frustration in reading the declaration of the new Cabinet—timid, poorly written, and leaning backward toward reactionary demands.

AGONY IN THE ARMY

The Communists had discovered the Achilles' heel of the All-Russian Executive Committee and army organizations: Since they had not repudiated everyone involved in the Kornilov conspiracy, they could all be branded as Kornilov's gang. There was no defense against this charge. Troubles in the regiments became increasingly grave. Whole divisions announced they would withdraw from the front unless peace were concluded by November 1. This time they meant what they said. The Iskosol was actually a prisoner of the Lettish Tirailleurs. Several battalions had left their positions and installed themselves around the building occupied by the army committee in Venden, declaring that they were there to keep the Iskosol from committing treacherous or counterrevolutionary acts.

My own status with the soldiers remained a trifle better than the officers'. At least I could expect to find a few friends in each regiment. I no longer dealt with divisions and corps, but with single regiments and battalions. So I continued to tour the front. The autumn rains had turned long stretches of road into quagmire. I usually traveled at night so as to reach the trouble spot in the morning. The car crawled in fog. The roads were flanked by pitch-black walls of forests, inter-

---

[12] As far as I remember, this reluctant recognition was the new Cabinet's only formal title to authority.

rupted by campfires—sometimes lonely flashes of light, sometimes large clusters of fires in the distant gloom. These were the camps of deserters on their way home. Not infrequently a rifle was discharged in the direction of my car. More often the soldiers around the fire would merely raise their rifles and take aim, as an unfriendly but not necessarily threatening gesture. They knew that the only car traveling at night was that of the Commissar of the Front.

One night my car got stuck in knee-deep mud. The chain on one of the rear wheels broke. The chauffeur and his helper tried to replace it. I joined them. The mud was icy. Three fires were blinking among the trees not far from the road and illumined the figures of men moving in front of them. I said to the chauffeur, "We cannot spend the night here. I'll ask for help."

He replied, "I'd rather sleep in the mud."

I climbed the slope from the road to the forest and approached the nearest campfire. Stern, bearded faces turned toward me, but when I stepped closer nobody so much as looked at me or answered my greeting. I said to the soldiers, "I am the Commissar of the Front, Woytinsky. My car is stuck. Will you give me a hand?"

After a long silence, a middle-aged man, looking more like a muzhik than a soldier, replied, "We know who you are and why you drive at night. You don't think of us common men any longer. You don't help us. Why should we help you?"

I felt humiliated and said angrily, "I also know who you fellows are and why you are here. Yet I have asked you for help. You refuse. Now I'll ask you in another way. Who wants to earn ten rubles for vodka?"

In the uncertain light of the fire it seemed as if the muzhik looked at me with sad reproach. Then he got up. His voice was flat and cheerless when he asked his companions, "Should we help the Commissar? He wants to treat us to vodka." Nobody moved. Then the muzhik said with a sigh, "Let's see what his trouble is. And you, lads," he shouted to the men around the next fire, "come with us." A score of soldiers in ragged, soiled coats, some dragging their rifles, came down to the road, scowling at me.

All four wheels of the car were sunk deep in the mud. The soldiers surrounded the car and began to shake it, trying to pull it out of the hole. They worked in silence, without the usual jokes, knee-deep in water. I worked with them. When at last the car was on firm ground, I thanked the men and handed a ten-ruble note to the bearded muzhik. He pushed my hand back. "Keep your money, Comrade Commissar. Do you think we helped you for the tip? This is what you, an educated gentleman, think of us. And we, simple people as we are, think you have changed sides and are not with us any longer. Maybe you do wish good for the people . . . in your own way. Who knows? Go in peace, and God forgive you and us."

I looked at the faces of men around me, grim, covered with splashes of mud. Lost friends, all of them. . . . I shook hands with each one. Some smiled sadly. Then I got into the car, feeling intolerably lonely. How different this situation was from that in this same army only two months earlier! We had lost the confidence of these men and millions like them as a result of the conspiracy at the top of the government and our inability to disassociate ourselves from the culprits.

A GENERAL LOOKS FOR A CIVILIAN ON A WHITE HORSE

Some officers realized what the disintegration of the government meant for the country and especially the army, and believed that the trend could be reversed if power were given to somebody whom the soldiers at the front would trust.

I was called to a regiment of General Scalon's division to look into friction between the regiment commander and the enlisted men. The division was in comparatively good shape and the trouble was trivial. A dispute on some administrative matter had developed, and both sides had agreed to ask me to arbitrate it. Though I had to drive more than a hundred miles over fearful roads for actually nothing, I felt relaxed in talking with the soldiers and officers. Then General Scalon arrived unexpectedly on horseback with two staff officers. He was a big man. A deep scar across his face, from the right temple to the chin, had not disfigured him but gave him, rather, a martial look. He greeted me, asked the colonel whether the dispute was settled, and then invited me to see his other regiments. This was a rather unusual invitation, but I accepted it. The roads between positions were impassable for a car, and the colonel offered me a horse with a mounted orderly to take care of it. We visited two regiments. The soldiers were friendly, and the general seemed to be on good terms with the committees.

As we were returning, the general made a sign to his staff officers to fall back and moved his horse closer to mine, so that our stirrups were touching. "Mr. Commissar," he said, "would you consider it improper if I talk with you about political matters with complete frankness, as man to man?"

"Mr. General, I'll be equally frank with you."

Scalon continued, "For many a sleepless night I have thought of the affair of General Kornilov. He is a good man, a brave soldier, a Russian patriot, but the results of his attempt to save Russia have been bad. I asked myself, 'What was his mistake?' And I think I have found the answer. A military commander must not undertake such a thing. The initiative must come from a civilian. Am I right, Mr. Commissar?"

"The civilians in the government and the Executive Committee are doing their best to restore order in the nation and discipline in the army," I said, not very convincingly.

"They are not doing the proper thing," Scalon replied sadly. "All authority and all responsibility must be in the hands of a single man— a man whom the people will trust and the army will obey. A dictator must come from the army, but not from the ranks of commanding officers."

"You mean, from the ranks of enlisted men? From the army committees?" I asked.

"No. Just as soldiers would not accept a general as a ruler, so officers would resent having an enlisted man put over them. I am thinking of men who command respect of both sides . . . such as the front commissars. . . ."

"Remember that Savinkov, a commissar, was backing Kornilov," I said, "but that did not help him."

"I am not thinking of fakers who come to the front to play politics, but of those who joined the army to strengthen it and who understand both soldiers and officers. . . . I am thinking of you, Mr. Commissar."

"Thank you most sincerely, Mr. General," I replied, "but you are on the wrong track. If the people in the army trusted me, that was because I had no political ambition. Moreover, I have neither will to power nor skill in maneuvering among political groups and parties. In short, I have none of the attributes of a dictator. What I am doing is as much as I can contribute to the defense of Russia."

The general remarked, "I was afraid that would be your answer. But I was not sure and wished to try." After a moment of silence he added, a little stiffly, "I hope you will not consider this conversation improper. Please forget it."

"No!" I said. "I shall remember it with gratitude to you for your confidence. But this I promise you—nobody will learn of our conversation."

We returned to my car in silence, shook hands, and I drove back to my office. This was my last conversation with the general.[13]

---

[13] When I wrote an account of these days in the early 1920's, I omitted this incident. Now, after forty years, I no longer feel bound by my promise. General Scalon died soon after this conversation. After the seizure of power by Lenin in

TRANSFER OF TROOPS

The Council of the Republic had little more authority than the government. The Communists had withdrawn from the Council at its first meeting, on October 20, and their press had succeeded in creating an impression that the Council was a part of the government. But the government departments continued to function, largely by inertia, without relation to the policy of the Cabinet. Thus I remained in close touch with the War Ministry, which was facing a serious problem. During the Kornilov mutiny a division stationed in Finland had massacred most of its officers and arrested the others. It was now in a state of open rebellion, threatening to march on Viborg and Helsinki. Since there was no way to bring the division to heel, the War Ministry decided to transfer it to the front. That step could be justified by military considerations: There was no real danger of a German attack through Sweden and Finland, while the Northern Front needed reinforcements. Since the troops stationed in Finland belonged to the Northern Front, the Ministry asked General Cheremissov to take the Finnish division into his reserve, billet it where it would not do much harm, and send other troops to Finland.

The Commander of the Northern Front shoved the order at me, saying peevishly, "They have mixed up papers in Petrograd. I have no use for this damned division and am not interested in politics. This is a dish for you, Mr. Commissar." I read the memorandum and replied, "This is a service order. I will do my best to carry it out but I shall need the aid of your staff."

"That you can have," Cheremissov snapped. "All I want is to have nothing to do with the business."

I prepared an order to the Finnish division to be ready to move to the front in fifteen days. The order included an explanation of the strategic situation and stressed the need for equitable rotation of regiments between service in the rear garrisons and at the front. Cheremissov signed the order reluctantly and I countersigned it, attaching to it the resolutions of front regiments demanding rotation with military units at the rear.

The Communist papers in Petrograd published the reply of the Finnish division: "The division has dedicated itself to the defense of

---

1917, the new government sent him to Brest-Litovsk, to serve as military adviser to the Russian delegation in peace negotiations. He went to the conference hoping to be permitted to defend the honor of Russia. When he realized that Bolshevist delegates, headed by Trotsky, were ready to sell out the vital interests of the country and were interested only in the preservation of the power of their party, he blew his brains out.

freedom and peace and will not break its pledge by going to the front." My office made copies of *Pravda's* communication and sent these to the front regiments that expected to be transferred to Finland. In a covering note, I explained to the men that their transfer to the rear would have to be delayed.

Three days later my office was flooded with resolutions from the front demanding that the Finnish division be sent forward at once. Some regiments declared themselves ready to proceed to Finland to smoke out the traitors who had dug in there. Then I sent these resolutions to the Finnish division with a stern confirmation of the marching orders. The Bolsheviks were reluctant to stir up a quarrel between the rear garrisons and front regiments. The division boarded the train on schedule. True, the soldiers decorated the train with Communist banners, and the division proved to be so demoralized it could not be used for any service. But at least Finland was relieved of riotous gangs and the officers held as hostages by the men were freed. More important from the political point of view, the operation proved it was still possible to fight Communists in the rear garrisons with the aid of the front troops.

Elated by this success, the War Ministry asked Cheremissov to transfer some regiments of the Petrograd garrison to the front and replace them with units from front positions. The general again threw the operation into my lap. I prepared for his signature an order to the Commander of the Petrograd Military District, who was his subordinate in strategic matters, instructing him to designate four infantry regiments to exchange places with four regiments at the front. The Petrograd Soviet decided to send a delegation to discuss the matter with the soldiers in the trenches and offer them a substitute plan: To quit the front at once, without waiting for replacements. I immediately wired the Petrograd Soviet inviting its delegation to come to my office in Pskov to meet the representatives of the army. Cheremissov was reluctant to take part in this conference, but I told him that his absence would be interpreted as a snub to the Petrograd Soviet.

The delegation arrived in Pskov—some fifty soldiers from different outfits. Some of them knew me from my work in the Tauride Palace and some others had met me in their barracks. To my surprise, they greeted me as an old comrade. Opening the conference, I asked Cheremissov to brief our guests on the situation at the front. He spoke in a bored manner, showing that he was not interested in troop rotation. Then I began to cross-examine him. "Do you believe that the Northern Front may be attacked by the Germans in the near future?"

"Yes."

"Do you believe that the front troops are tired, deserve a rest, and should be rotated with units at the rear?"

The general's answer was evasive. "Yes, of course . . . but on the other hand . . . you cannot satisfy everybody. . . ."

Then I fired my last question. "Do you think that the Petrograd soldiers are such a gang of cowards, such 'revolutionary trash'—to use your words—that you do not want to have them under your command? Please answer directly, yes or no."

The conference was spellbound. The general, red in the face, turned to me to reply with his usual arrogance, but changed his mind and said casually, "I really do not know what you mean, Mr. Commissar. I would be happy to have the gallant Petrograd regiments here."

Then the Petrograd delegates were on their feet, yelling that "rotation" was nothing but a pretext for disarming the Petrograd garrison on the eve of its final victory over the people's enemies. "Rotation will not help the soldiers at the front," they shouted. "Peace is our common aim. Go home, join forces with the workers and soldiers fighting for peace!" The front soldiers were used to such speeches, but when they heard men from a rear garrison use these phrases as excuses for refusing to replace them in the trenches, they saw red and replied with vehement accusations and threats against the loafers in Petrograd.

In closing the conference, I invited the Petrograd delegation to appoint a committee of ten or twelve men to tour the front and talk with the men in the trenches. The committee was appointed and reported to the Petrograd Soviet a week later that the soldiers of the Northern Front supported the demand for troop rotation. We were close to winning the campaign, but our time was running short. The Communists, who had made good use of the postponement of the Constituent Assembly, were ready for the decisive attack.

THE BOLSHEVIKS STRIKE

The Council of the Republic was debating the problem of war and peace. Opinions ranged from those of the right-wing Cadets to the left-wing Socialists. The debate ended on October 31. A dozen resolutions had been put to a vote but none got a majority. The Council turned to foreign policy. Three lines of action were advocated: Miliukov's policy, confirming the war objectives of Tsarist diplomacy; the policy of the majority of the All-Russian Executive Committee, demanding a revision of war aims and seeking a negotiated democratic peace; and the policy of the left-wing Socialists, demanding a break with the Allies, repudiation of secret treaties and direct negotiation with Germany. Again none of these policies got a majority of the votes. The Council was at an impasse.

Meanwhile, the Smolny was bracing itself for the final assault. The Petrograd Soviet openly appointed a military revolutionary committee to make preparations to seize power. A conference of local Soviets of the Petrograd district met in Kronstadt and reiterated the demand for an immediate transfer of all power to the Soviets. A conference of Soviets of the northern region passed a similar resolution. On November 3 a conference of representatives of the Petrograd garrison proclaimed its allegiance to the Soviet as the sole authority recognized by the soldiers. Then the Soviet of Moscow proclaimed itself the sole local government.

In a dramatic appearance before the Council of the Republic, Verkhovsky demanded immediate withdrawal of Russia from the war. His appeal increased the confusion. The Council could not change the course of foreign policy except by overthrowing the government, but the War Minister did not think of this implication of his proposal. The government ordered him to resign, and the Communists used this order as evidence that any step toward hastening the end of the war was a crime in the eyes of the government.

Moreover, the War Minister's proposal came too late. Perhaps the end of hostilities and demobilization of the army would have given new strength and stability to the Provisional Government in July or August, when the moderate Socialists controlled almost all the military forces of the nation. But the dissolution of the coalition after the July days, the delay in elections to the Constituent Assembly, the conspiracy of the generals, the leniency of the moderates toward persons involved in this conspiracy, the weakness of the new government, and the disunity in the ranks of democracy had altered the political setting.

Perhaps, even then, a bold reshuffling of the Cabinet could have saved the situation. However, Kerensky decided that this was the time for him to save Russia single-handed. Without consulting the All-Russian Executive Committee or the Council of the Republic, without even informing these bodies of his intentions, he called troops from the front—as if there were troops that would follow his call!

Late in the afternoon of November 5, Cheremissov summoned me urgently to the front headquarters. There he handed me a decoded telegram from Kerensky ordering him to send reliable troops to Petrograd at once. "They are crazy in the Winter Palace," he said. "I have no reliable troops. If you have some, you may send them to Mr. Kerensky. I wash my hands of the matter."

For me, however, this was not a request of "Mr. Kerensky." How could I know he was acting without the knowledge of the Executive Committee, the Council of the Republic, or even other members of the Cabinet? I therefore replied that as the representative of the Executive Committee and the government on the Northern Front, I would do what I could to carry out the order.

Back in my office, I called General Parsky on a direct wire, told him of the call from Petrograd, and asked which units of the Twelfth Army could be moved to the capital. Parsky replied that the army High Command could do nothing and advised trying to act through the Iskosol. Kuchin and his companions promised to explore the situation and keep me informed. Then I telephoned Boldyrev. The situation in the Fifth Army was hopeless. The Communists controlled the army committee and would block any movement of troops toward Petrograd. The reaction of the Commander of the First Army and its committee was equally discouraging.

Then I concentrated on negotiations with individual members of the army committees. My idea was to send the government single battalions or even companies that would be consolidated as a task force somewhere on the outskirts of Petrograd. At dawn the situation became clear. There were still some reliable units, but none of them would move in response to a call from the Winter Palace. The order must come directly from the All-Russian Executive Committee.

On the morning of November 5, the War Ministry telegraphed me to ask about progress in building a task force. I answered by direct wire that none of the army commanders could move as much as a platoon toward the capital. The only hope lay in the authority of the army organizations and the willingness of men to take arms against the Communists, as in July. Nobody would listen to the appeals of the President of the Government, but conceivably a task force could be organized on the direct appeal of the All-Russian Executive Committee. After a further exchange of information and a long pause, the spokesman of the Ministry at the other end of the wire replied, "We will take all necessary steps to obtain a formal confirmation of the call for troops by the Council of the Republic."

This promise fell short of my request for a direct order from the Executive Committee, but it was as far as the government was ready to go. I wired at once to the Iskosol and some individual members of the committee of the Fifth Army, urging them to take preliminary steps so that the operations could be started as soon as we received an order from the Council of the Republic. They answered that such an order would not be sufficient. The soldiers would not march without a formal call from the Executive Committee. Yet they promised to start preparations in anticipation of such an appeal.

On that day, November 6, Pskov was full of rumors. The newspapers announced that the Bolsheviks had taken the Fortress of Peter and Paul. The War Ministry wired that Kerensky had appeared before the Council of the Republic and asked for unconditional support of measures taken by the government to check Communist riots. According to the Ministry, the Council responded with an enthusiastic ovation. A couple of hours later, however, we learned the particulars of that session. The Council had replied to Kerensky's plea with a resolution demanding revision of foreign policy, distribution of land to the peasants, and convocation of the Constituent Assembly at the earliest possible date. After Kerensky rejected these demands, the Council broke off all relations with the government. It was perfectly clear that what Kerensky called the "measures taken by the government" existed only in his imagination. The only hope of the crumbling regime lay in troops from the front. There was a hope that some would respond to the call of the All-Russian Executive Committee, but it was clear that no soldiers would march on Kerensky's personal order.

Late in the evening, the Commander of the Petrograd Military District wired me: "The Bolsheviks are taking over public buildings and railroad stations, one after another. The troops refuse to execute orders. The military schools are giving up their arms without resistance. The Cossacks refuse to leave their barracks. The Provisional Government is in danger of being overthrown."

Time was running out. The Northern Front could do nothing without an appeal by the All-Russian Executive Committee. My task now was to get such an appeal. I summoned a telegrapher to the teletype in my office and began to call the members of the Committee's presiding board in Petrograd one after another. The telegrapher at the other end of the line could not find any of them. After an hour or more of futile calls, Gotz, one of the leaders of the Committee, appeared at the teletype. I told him, "The government is calling for troops, but no soldier will respond to its call. There is hope that an appeal of the All-Russian Executive Committee would be more effective. I am awaiting your instructions."

After midnight I received the answer. "The board of the All-Russian Executive Committee approves the call of troops from the front and authorizes you to act in its name."

At that time I did not know that the Executive Committee, like the Council of the Republic, had broken off relations with the government.

AN ATTEMPT TO RESIST

I wired an appeal to all regiments at the front. That same night the All-Army Committee of Soldier Representatives convened at the headquarters of the Supreme Commander in Mogilev and passed a resolution protesting against the mutiny of the Petrograd garrison. It called on the army committees to support the government and the Council of the Republic. All fourteen army committees met the next day; twelve passed resolutions against the upheaval in Petrograd, while two declared that the army on the front should not interfere in political affairs. Unfortunately, the dissenting resolutions stemmed from the First and Fifth Armies, both on the Northern Front. We could count only on the Twelfth Army.

I tried to reach the Iskosol by direct wire, but the line was dead. By noon I received a message from Kharash: The Lettish Tirailleurs had tightened their siege of the Iskosol's quarters and cut its direct communications with the army and Pskov. The soldiers might arrest the members of the Iskosol at any time. Now the Twelfth Army was also out.

There remained only units in the general front reserve not allocated to any of the three armies. After negotiations with such regiments and companies, I found that actually only the Third Cavalry Corps would respond to our appeal. The corps consisted of fifty squadrons ("hundreds" in Cossack regiments), with machine gunners and light artillery attached to them, and included, in all, about ten thousand men. Many of these, however, were dispersed on guard service at munitions depots, railways, communication centers, and the like. Only eighteen squadrons were available for immediate action.

I called General Krasnov on the direct wire, told him about the situation, and asked whether his troops would respond to the appeal of the All-Russian Executive Committee. He replied that he was confident of his men. He had received a similar request from Petrograd signed by Kerensky two days earlier. The telegram was very confusing, however, and since it had not been confirmed by Cheremissov, his direct superior, he had decided to disregard it. Now he would start preparations at once. He remarked that not much could be done with the forces at his disposal, but he hoped other units would join the task force in the course of the operation. The essential thing was to start. "Orders are under way," he concluded.

I wired to the War Ministry and Mogilev: "Preparations are being made to move units of Third Cavalry Corps toward Petrograd." And I asked Mogilev to supply reinforcements. The Ministry inquired about the fate of a motorcycle battalion allegedly sent to Petrograd from the Northern Front, but I had heard nothing about it.

Meanwhile the wave of unrest reached Pskov. On the afternoon of November 7, a Military Revolutionary Committee was formed in the barracks. I called all the troops stationed in Pskov to a meeting in the court of the riding school. The soldiers, a crowd of some twenty thousand, were morose but orderly. I described the situation in Petrograd, stressing that the Constituent Assembly alone was authorized to decide matters concerning all Russia. By usurping its power, the Petrograd garrison was provoking civil war. To prevent this disaster and insure the convocation of the Constituent Assembly, the All-Russian Executive Committee had asked the army's support. In the Committee's name, I called on the front troops to join the task force that was ready to move to the capital.

"Those of you who do not join the task force," I concluded, "must continue the usual service without interfering with the movement of the echelons sent to the capital." What I hoped to obtain from the Pskov garrison was a pledge of neutrality that would give me time to organize the expedition. The response of the meeting showed that for most of the local soldiers neutrality seemed the easiest way out.

Then I received a new call from the War Ministry. Its building was still in the hands of the government, but the situation was desperate. Soldiers had dispersed the Council of the Republic. The Cabinet was in session in the Winter Palace, surrounded by mutineers. An onslaught on the palace was expected at any moment. The voice from the Ministry begged me to hurry the troops and asked, among other things, whether I knew where Kerensky was. He had left the Winter Palace as if to meet the motorcycle battalion and had disappeared.

At seven o'clock we received a telegram signed by the temporary President of the Government, Konovalov: "The Petrograd Soviet of Workers and Soldiers has declared the government deposed and has demanded that it relinquish power, threatening otherwise to shell the Winter Palace. The government will not yield and relies on the support of the people and the army." The Winter Palace was now in the plight of the Tauride Palace in the July days. Its guard had shrunk to a handful of military cadets and a company of women volunteers.

My office was crowded with delegates from the Cossack companies, asking for confirmation that they were being sent to Petrograd on the order of the All-Russian Executive Committee. Krasnov telephoned that some companies of his corps had boarded the railroad cars but the trains were not leaving. In some cases the locomotive was out of commission, in others the engineer had disappeared or the track was blocked by other trains.

Officers brought complaints that Cheremissov was sabotaging the expedition, advising them to keep hands off the "adventure." I telephoned the general and asked for an explanation. He replied that as a senior officer he had talked frankly with junior officers who came to consult him. If this interfered with my plans, he would withdraw completely until the political situation was cleared up. An hour later he called back and announced, "Mr. Commissar, for your information. Following the order of the Supreme Commander, I have stopped your echelons." I reminded him of Konovalov's appeal, but he replied, "The old government has been deposed. For the time being I must execute the orders of the Supreme Commander. Next, I shall probably assume the Supreme Command myself."

I understood that Cheremissov had been in touch with Kerensky and obtained the order from him to stop resistance to the Communists. Although I had acted in the name of the Executive Committee rather than the government's, I was still the government's Commissar of the Front and could not carry on the operation in opposition to the head of the government. Moreover, I did not know what the relations were now between the Executive Committee and the government and since the night conversation with Gotz, I had had no word from the Committee. I was ready to take responsibility in a political campaign, but I had no desire to start an individual guerrilla war. So I said to the general, "I will not take back my orders. I resign."

After midnight, a delegation of the local Military Revolutionary Committee came to my office. The Committee had learned of my resignation and asked me to remain at my post as the Committee's Commissar of the Front. I replied that I appreciated the confidence of the soldiers but could represent only the All-Russian Executive Committee. The delegates went away disappointed. The Winter Palace was calling. The chief of the political department of the War Ministry, now in the palace, told me the enemy was tightening the ring around the building. Defense forces had dwindled. When would the first echelons from the front reach the capital? I replied that Cheremissov, acting on Kerensky's order, had announced to the troops that the Provisional Government had been deposed and had stopped the operation.

"The government has not been deposed yet . . . ," said the voice from the Winter Palace. After a moment's pause it continued, "The cruiser *Aurora* has opened fire. The Bolsheviks have started an assault. If someone calls from here, check his identity. Send troops." The line went dead.

THE GOVERNMENT FALLS, RESISTANCE CONTINUES

Later I heard about the storming of the Winter Palace from many eyewitnesses. A huge crowd of soldiers, sailors, and armed workers assembled at the Palace Plaza. They crossed it, shouting, firing in the air, and brandishing arms, and flowed, like a human river, through the ground floor of the palace. Not a shot was fired in its defense. The women volunteers and military cadets were pushed aside and disarmed, and the mass of men continued to move from one suite to another. When they reached the room where the government was in session, they declared its members under arrest.

Telegrams were pouring in from the echelons Cheremissov had stopped, and I was trying to decide how to answer them when General Baranovsky, member of the staff of the front, telephoned to ask me to his private apartment for urgent business. There I found Kerensky and Cheremissov. Kerensky lay on a sofa in a state of complete prostration, Cheremissov was pacing the room with an air of authority. I asked Kerensky why he had stopped the expedition of echelons to the capital after having himself called for troops. He answered, "General Cheremissov is in command. I have appointed him Supreme Commander of all fronts. Ask him." Cheremissov interrupted him unceremoniously. "You *promised* to appoint me but you have not signed the order. I stopped the echelons on your order."

It was impossible to be angry with Kerensky—he was in a state of collapse. But there was no excuse for Cheremissov, who had used this situation for his own ambitious plans. Calling on General Baranovsky to support me, I tried to explain the situation as I saw it to Kerensky. I told him that all was not lost, that resistance to the assault of the Communists in Petrograd was possible, that many men were ready to risk their lives for the cause of democracy, and that surrender at this moment would be treason. Cheremissov only shrugged his shoulders and murmured, "That is not how I see things."

An hour later Kerensky withdrew his order to stop the movement of the echelons and signed a dozen new orders and appeals to army commanders, soldiers, railroad officials, and so forth. He also appointed General Krasnov commander of all forces operating against the rebels in Petrograd. Leaving Kerensky under the tutelage of General Baranovsky, I returned to my office to disentangle the chaos Cheremissov had created by stopping the echelons. General Krasnov was waiting for me. He was alarmed by Cheremissov's order and thought of treason. I told him what had happened and went to bed to get a few hours of sleep after sixty hours without a moment's rest.

While the crowd was invading the Winter Palace, a meeting opened at the Smolny. The Communists described it as the second All-Russian Congress of the Soviets, but actually it was a gathering of hand-picked delegates from different parts of Russia, without credentials. This meeting declared that the All-Russian Executive Committee was dissolved and that the Provisional Government was deposed. It appointed a new government, the Council of People's Commissars headed by Lenin, abolished the local democratically elected councils, and ordered transfer of local authorities to the respective Soviets. The old Executive Committee declared all these decisions illegal and proclaimed that until another Congress of the Soviets was properly elected, the old All-Russian Committee remained the only legal central organ of workers and soldiers.

Both the Communist convention and the old Executive Committee called on the army for support. The government was again out of the game, the constitutional crisis was again the clash between the moderate and extremist groups within the Soviets. I phoned to Krasnov to brief him on the changed political situation, stressing that my functions as Commissar of the Provisional Government had ended but that I remained at my post as the Commissar of the All-Russian Executive Committee. He assured me of his and his men's unshakable allegiance to any government fighting against the Communists. Then I advised him to get in personal touch with Kerensky. Reluctantly, the general agreed.

On November 8 the first echelons of the Cossacks left Ostrov, not far from Pskov. Kerensky had asked Krasnov to let him enter Petrograd with the head echelons. The general agreed to his presence in the task force on condition that he keep clear of military operations and make no speeches. I remained in Pskov in the hope that I would be able to persuade more soldiers—and at least a few companies of infantry—to join the task force. Telegrams were arriving about echelons sent toward Petrograd from other fronts, but they had to cover long distances and I was not sure they could get there in time.

We still had friends in the ranks. The politically alert and patriotic elements in the army realized that the seizure of power by the rioting Petrograd garrison was a disaster for Russia. Delegates from individual companies scattered along the front came to my office with offers to support the expedition. Unfortunately, each company would have had to cross an area held by other troops; none could be transferred to the railroad in regular formation, as a unit. The men had to travel inconspicuously, in small groups. This was a long procedure, and time was short.

On November 9 I received a telegram from General Krasnov. His head echelons had reached Gatchina in the morning, had occupied the station and telegraph office, and were in control of the city, with headquarters in the Imperial Palace. The news was of stupendous importance. Gatchina had a garrison of some twenty thousand men reputed to be in sympathy with the Communists. The fact that Krasnov could occupy this city with some three hundred Cossacks showed that the new government had no power outside the capital.

Krasnov urged me to send reinforcements at once; he could not advance with the forces at his disposal. I knew, of course, that the outcome of the expedition depended on speed. But several companies ready to join the task force were stopped by regiments favoring the coup in Petrograd. Others had reached the railroad but could not proceed because of sabotage by railroad workers. A delegation from the Military Revolutionary Committee again appeared in my office. They explained that politically they supported the Communists in Petrograd but were against the participation of the army in the squabble. They asked me to stop the movement of the troops to Petrograd, promising on their part to abstain from sending reinforcements to the revolutionary garrison.

Since we then had at least thirty trains loaded with soldiers and equipment and my purpose was to move them as quickly as possible, I insisted on my original formula of neutrality. The army as such would take no part in the conflict in Petrograd, but single outfits and individuals would be free to support either side on a voluntary basis. My main purpose in raising the question of the two forms of neutrality was to gain time. We talked at length, and the delegation left to discuss my proposal. I spent the day at the direct wire, receiving reports from the echelons and answering questions from the front. The echelons made slow progress; some had been stopped and wired asking for permission to unload. I tried to persuade them not to desert the cause of freedom. New units declared their willingness to join our operation. Communist agitators appeared in the barracks, assailing the policy of neutrality.

A telegram arrived from Petrograd: Lenin asked me to join the new Council of the People's Commissars as War Minister and Supreme Commander. I did not know whether this offer was a trap or what other motives had made Lenin think of me in these hectic days, but I considered the upheaval in Petrograd as a deadly blow to democracy and freedom in Russia, and I was absorbed with the task of mustering enough armed forces to keep the revolt from spreading. I therefore did not reply.

NARROW ESCAPE

In Pskov, the barracks were in turmoil. My office was in the midst of a hornets' nest. I was not sure whether the members of my staff approved of my activity, which was very different from the normal work in the office of a commissar of the front. I had neither the time nor the desire to argue with them and continued to carry the whole work load and responsibility, with Emma to help me with direct wires and the telephone.

In the evening the Military Revolutionary Committee called a joint meeting of the local Soviet and representatives of the troops stationed in and around Pskov. The meeting, held in the city theater, opened with reports on the storming of the Winter Palace by the people. Next came the announcement that the new government, the Council of the People's Commissars, had offered a truce to Germany and had given land to the peasants. There remained only one obstacle to peace, freedom, and socialism: the counterrevolutionary forces of General Krasnov moving against the capital.

Soldiers were sent to my office to take me to the meeting to be questioned about my role in the expedition. When the men arrived, Emma was with me in the telegraph room helping me in reading, sorting, and answering the telegrams. She had no illusions about the seriousness of the situation, but believed that we were right in trying to resist the Communist assault. Before leaving I told her I was going to the theater. She remained at the direct wire with our telegraph operator.

The theater was packed, and armed soldiers were milling around it. The front rows in the hall were occupied by the members of the local Soviet—the S-R and Mensheviks on the right, the Bolsheviks on the left. Representatives of the troops occupied all the other seats in the orchestra. The aisles, galleries, and the space behind the seats were jammed with armed men. I took a seat on the stage, at the chairman's table, and asked him what information the meeting wished from me.

A local Bolshevik, a civil engineer, jumped to the front of the stage, screaming that I was one of the warmongers who had dragged Russia into the imperialistic war and was growing fat and rich on the sweat and blood of the simple people. If it had not been for me, the war would have ended long since! After this introduction, he took up my role in calling on the troops against revolutionary Petrograd and read a transcript of my telephone calls and telegrams—my office wires had been tapped. The crowd responded with shouts of rage. Only the men in the front sat silent.

When I got up to reply, I was greeted with a furor of curses and threats. I began with a warning that unless the crowd kept quiet I would not speak at all, and they might miss some points they would like to hear. Then I declined to discuss politics with my accuser. "You soldiers know me well enough," I said. "I shall not waste time in answering this individual. The question that troubles you is who sent the troops to Petrograd. I sent them."

Then I described the situation in Petrograd, stressing that civil war threatened to engulf the nation. And I concluded, "I have called and am calling on all of you to rescue the All-Russian Executive Committee, the highest revolutionary authority in the nation. It has not relinquished its office. It has called on the army for support, and I will do my best to bring its appeal to the men on the Northern Front."

The Mensheviks and S-R in the front rows applauded enthusiastically, but the great majority of the audience kept a sullen silence. After a pause, I said to the chairman that I believed the meeting could now discuss its business without me. I stepped down from the stage and started down the central aisle toward the entrance door.

When I was at the middle of the hall, someone screamed, "Hold him! He is going to send more troops to Petrograd." The crowd in front of me stiffened. Other voices shouted, "Kill him!" A few men tried to come to my rescue but were held back by others.

Feeling I was less safe in the midst of the excited mob, I returned to the stage. Angry cries raged about me, but something restrained the mob from violence. Back on the stage, I faced the hall and stretched out my arm. The noise subsided. I said that I had intended to leave the theater because I believed there was no longer any need for my presence. If there were still questions the meeting wanted to discuss with me, I would stay for a while, but not too long.

I sat down close to the chairman's table, but my bluff had not deceived the crowd. Two soldiers with fixed bayonets appeared behind my chair. I was under arrest. The situation was not encouraging, although it did not seem as alarming to me as it did to Emma, who, I learned later, was watching from the rear of the theater. She had worried about my long absence and persuaded an officer from the Iskosol who came to my office to take her to the hall. He warned her of the danger to which she would expose herself as the only woman in an excited and hostile crowd, and made her promise she would keep still no matter what happened. "A movement, an outcry from you may provoke an outburst," he told her. "Then they may tear you and your husband to pieces." I could not see her in the rear of the hall, but she had seen my unsuccessful attempt to get through the seething crowd although she did not betray her presence.

My accuser, maddened by my remarks about him, resumed his vituperation, when two artillery soldiers stepped from behind the wings of the stage and approached the chairman. The face of one of them seemed strangely familiar to me and his eyes twinkled as we looked at each other. Somewhere I had seen this daredevil with smiling eyes and a firm, tight-lipped mouth. The chairman got up and interrupted the screaming engineer. "Comrades! The representatives of the First Reserve Artillery Division in Luga are here to greet us!"

The man with the familiar smiling eyes stepped forward. He received a thunderous ovation! The Luga division had a formidable reputation, and it meant a lot to the Pskov soldiers to have it on their side. He began to speak. His division, he said, had sent him and his companion to find out what was going on in Pskov. Now he had seen enough to report that the Pskov garrison was a mere mass of hooligans. He had seen the Pskov soldiers arrest the Commissar of the All-Russian Executive Committee, an old revolutionary who had spent many years in the penitentiary for having defended the common people.

"I was in the same cell with Comrade Woytinsky, in the tower of Ekaterinoslav," he shouted angrily. "I was chained there, awaiting a death sentence. I know who is a friend and who is an enemy of the people."

Then I recognized him: Nikolai Komarov, of whom I had heard nothing since I left Ekaterinoslav! The crowd was silent. The guards posted behind my chair had disappeared. I stood up and held out my hand, interrupting his speech. "I am glad to see you alive, Nikolai. But I believe you are mistaken. The men here may be somewhat rude but are not hooligans. Obviously they do not want me to leave the meeting because they still have questions to ask me. Am I right, Comrade Chairman?"

Komarov resumed his speech. The First Artillery Division and the Luga garrison disapproved of the seizure of power by the Communists in Petrograd. The division believed that all political disputes must be submitted to the Constituent Assembly. This sounded to the crowd like thunder from a clear sky. It was easy for Pskov soldiers to choose between Kerensky and Lenin, but the choice between Petrograd and Luga was more difficult. Leaving the stage, Komarov gave me a sign to follow him—it was natural that he wanted to have a talk with his old friend.

We left the theater through the back door. There were many things I wanted to tell Nikolai, but he stopped me. "This is the end of your services in Pskov," he said. "The boys do not know what to do, but the ringleaders will go on. First of all, they will arrest you. . . . Perhaps in an hour or two they will send a detail to get you!"

He urged me to go to Luga at once with him and the other artillerist, and I agreed. They had a car hidden in the outskirts of Pskov. As we approached Luga, however, I decided to go on directly to Gatchina, to Krasnov's task force. Nikolai offered to give me a lift. We parted in front of Gatchina Palace. That was the last I saw or heard of my gallant cellmate in Ekaterinoslav.

Emma, as I learned later, went back to my deserted office to take over my job. Braving imminent and steadily growing danger, she remained there as the last link between our task force and Pskov.

GATCHINA

The headquarters of the task force was on the ground floor of one of the wings of a fortress-like palace. The suite of rooms, transformed into offices, was deserted. I learned that Krasnov and his staff were with the troops advancing toward Tsarskoe Selo. I took a service car and drove in that direction. In a hamlet not far from Tsarskoe, a sentry stopped me. After looking at my papers he told me that General Krasnov was at the front. I went on. Soldiers with guns and cartridge belts barred the road at the outskirts of Tsarskoe. The crowd stretched some hundred or two hundred feet into the fields on both sides of the highway. A military truck surrounded by a handful of mounted Cossacks stood in front of the crowd. Krasnov was speaking from the truck: "Enough foolishness, boys. The people of Russia will not yield to the garrison of a single city. Lay down your arms and return in peace to your barracks. Do not compel me to use force. . . ."

The soldiers—about ten thousand of them—listened, undecided. Krasnov backed the truck a hundred yards or so and parked it on the roadside. The Cossacks moved to both sides of the road. Then a light artillery piece appeared on the highway, not more than two hundred yards away. The Cossacks installed it in full sight of the crowd and fired into the air twice. The crowd did not disperse, but somebody yelled, "Don't fire, you devils! We don't want trouble."

Krasnov drove into the middle of the crowd again. "I don't want trouble either," he said. "Put the guns and munitions on the truck! My men will take care of them." He came down from the truck and walked back. The soldiers pressed around the truck, throwing away their rifles and cartridge belts. Two empty trucks drove into the crowd to collect weapons.

Krasnov noticed me and came closer. I asked him what forces he had. He took a tiny notebook out of his pocket and opened it. I read: "October 27, 6:00 A.M.: 3 hundreds, 6 artillery pieces. October 27, 6:00 P.M.: 6 hundreds, 16 artillery pieces, 6 machine guns with crew." In turn, he asked me, "What do you have loaded, on wheels?"

"Perhaps thirty echelons in all. A third of them parts of your corps; the rest, single companies, batteries, munitions. A few echelons are under way from other fronts. An armored train. A division of tanks. I don't know exactly where they are. Not all will break through. The railroads are not in our hands."

Krasnov sighed. "What is going on here is contrary to all rules. A single cannon in plain sight of a foe with rifles and machine guns! They could have shot us all like partridges. We may bluff them this way once or twice, but no longer. Everything depends on reinforcements."

Back at the palace, I put through a call to my office in Pskov. The line was dead, but I got front headquarters and asked the telegrapher to call Emma to the teletype. This was my first call to her since I had left the office to go to the garrison meeting in the theater. I did not intend to tell her about the circumstances in which I had left Pskov, but she told me she had been in the theater and knew everything. Now she was in the Commissariat, alone in the huge deserted building. None of my staff had reported for duty. Armed soldiers had come in several times to look for me, but they were not aggressive and did not ransack the office. She had returned the codes, maps, and secret documents to front headquarters.

I was chiefly concerned with Cheremissov's ambiguous attitude and feared that after I left Pskov he would do all he could to stop our echelons. It was necessary to replace him with some other general. I had, of course, no authority for effecting such a change, but I believed that Cheremissov would not violate the rules of the puppet play and would yield to the word of the puppet Supreme Commander. So I asked Emma to get in touch with General Baranovsky and find out whether he would accept the appointment to succeed Cheremissov as the Commander of the Northern Front if Kerensky offered it to him. With Emma's aid, using the wires of headquarters in Pskov, I also tried to re-establish contacts with the railroad stations, echelons, and the military units around Pskov that had agreed to join the expedition. The news was not encouraging. The echelons were advancing very slowly, and some units on which I had relied had fallen back.

By evening, Tsarskoe Selo was occupied by our forces. On November 11 Krasnov had twelve hundreds and squadrons of cavalry, an armored train of four cars, a tank, and a company of infantry. But swarms of Communist agitators had descended on Gatchina and infiltrated into the ranks of the task force. They were asking the Cossacks, "Will you fight your brothers, the soldiers and workers of Petrograd, to bring Kerensky back to the Winter Palace?"

Krasnov asked me to talk with the corps committees. The latter decided, at my suggestion, to publish a declaration outlining the political aims of the task force. It stated that the troops were marching to Petrograd on the order of the All-Russian Executive Committee of Workers and Soldiers. Their aim was to insure the convocation of a democratically elected Constituent Assembly, from which Russia expected the realization of its old dreams: peace, land for the tillers of the soil, a better life for the workers, freedom and human rights for all. The declaration was duplicated and sent to all armies, given to the press, and wired along rail lines. The immediate result was that the Soviets of Gatchina and Tsarskoe Selo proclaimed neutrality and declared that the garrisons would not interfere with the movement of the task force.

Meanwhile, new faces appeared in Gatchina Palace—political adventurers of all kinds, offering their advice to Kerensky and Krasnov. Conspicuous among them was Savinkov, who proposed to Krasnov that he arrest Kerensky and appoint him, Savinkov, to head the government to be installed in Petrograd.

"This is politics," replied the general. "Discuss your plans with Mr. Woytinsky."

Savinkov came to me, but in the meantime he had changed his plan. Kerensky could stay on as a private person, but he, Savinkov, should be the leader of the crusade and the spokesman of the task force. I answered, "I am not familiar with your qualifications as a leader. Moreover, the task force needs no spokesman. It can speak for itself through its committee." And I gave him a copy of our declaration. All committees were anathema to Savinkov. He collapsed like a punctured balloon.

On November 12, Krasnov's advance units were stationed in Tsarskoe while the headquarters remained in Gatchina. We waited for reinforcements. Three Cossack hundreds arrived with two pieces of artillery, but the officers complained that their men had been affected by leftist propaganda and were not wholly reliable.

In the evening, alarming news came from Petrograd. Students of the military schools had made a desperate attempt to overthrow the new government. Although partly disarmed by the soldiers a few days before, the schools still had several thousand rifles and a hundred or more machine guns. They also counted on the Cossack regiments. Their plan was to seize the central depot of armored tanks, occupy the central telegraph and telephone stations, and strike against the main stronghold of the People's Commissars, the Smolny. The assault on the telegraph and telephone stations turned out well. Then soldiers rushed from their barracks, surrounded the stations and the military schools, and presented the students with an ultimatum to surrender. Only one school tried to resist. The soldiers opened point-blank artillery fire against it. The building was taken by storm,

Several hundred boys were killed and thousands were taken prisoner, mistreated, and jailed. The Cossacks refused to support the students—some, because they considered the whole adventure as hopeless; others, because the Communists had persuaded them that the purpose of the revolt was to restore Kerensky to power.

Moscow had offered more resistance to the coup, but here also the forces opposed to the new government were crushed by the garrison.

Meanwhile an anti-Bolshevist Committee for the Salvation of the Revolution, politically close to the Council of the Republic, had been organized in Petrograd. Its delegates came to Gatchina in the evening. They described the conditions in the capital. All public services were paralyzed; all employees of government departments and banks had gone on strike against the new regime. The railroad workers were split —some recognized the new government, others refused to execute its orders. The Communists felt themselves insecure. The delegates implored Krasnov to strike at once, with all his forces, and assured him that the resistance of the Petrograd garrison would be very weak.

Krasnov called Kerensky and me to his office and briefed us on the military situation. A straight offensive against Petrograd with the available forces was out of the question, he told us. After posting guards at strategic points to safeguard communications, he would have no man left for further operations. On the other hand, without an offensive the task force would begin to disintegrate. Krasnov therefore decided to undertake a limited offensive for a local objective, using all his forces but keeping open a means of retreat to initial positions. The offensive would be directed against Pulkovo.

The operation started at dawn. The Cossacks reached the outskirts of Pulkovo without opposition. Further advance was barred by a line of flimsy field fortifications, similar to those we had used against Kornilov's troops in August. Such fortifications would not have withstood heavy artillery fire but were effective enough against cavalry supported by a few light field pieces. The Cossacks had to dismount.

The Petrograd troops had no artillery, and their fire was not very effective, but they greatly outnumbered the Cossacks. They did not try to counterattack but maintained a continuous fire from their trenches. By evening, Krasnov ordered a retreat. But rear action continued, and the Petrograd detachments also left their positions. We learned later that several hundred defenders of Pulkovo had been killed. Casualties on our side were nine or ten men killed and a score wounded. For a small task force, without reserves, these were sizable losses. Krasnov decided to abandon Tsarskoe and withdraw to Gatchina.

During this engagement I remained in our Gatchina headquarters.

Here I got a telephone call from the local Soviet. An excited woman's voice urged me to come at once. The Soviet was located a few blocks from the palace. I found the building surrounded by Cossacks and officers, most of them not from our task force. A piece of artillery—the only one left in Gatchina—was posted in front of the building. A young Cossack officer was directing an assault. I asked what he was doing there and on whose order.

"Assignment: to liquidate the Bolshevist nest. . . . Whose order? I don't know. . . . Somebody told me."

I shouted, "You do not know the rules of service. Under battle conditions you have taken a cannon and men for an operation that was not ordered by your direct superiors! If you molest the Soviet, you will raise the whole garrison against us. Perhaps a *provocateur* put this idea into your head."

The officer grasped the situation. "Exactly so, Mr. Commissar," he said. "I ought to be court-martialed."

"Get your men together. Put guards on both corners of the block, not at the building itself." Before I had finished, the young officer was barking, "Cossacks! Listen to the order! Fall in! Attention!"

TRIP TO LUGA

I returned to the palace. Krasnov again called me to his office. "The enemy had at least fifty thousand men, perhaps more, in the field," he told me. "They could have crushed us but their tactics were miserable. Next time they will have regular officers with them. Without reinforcements, we can neither advance nor repulse the enemy if he decides to attack." He asked me to go to Luga and if possible to Pskov, to check conditions along the railroad and take the necessary steps to speed up the movement of our echelons. My first task was to learn the whereabouts of a train with munitions that, according to reports, had passed Luga and was stopped somewhere not far from Gatchina.

Before leaving, I put a call through to my office in Pskov. Emma was alone in the Commissariat. None of the staff had reported for duty, but people from Petrograd were swarming into the office, seeking information and aid. General Baranovsky was ready to accept appointment to the post of Commander of the Northern Front and thought that Cheremissov would relinquish his command without much fuss. Then I wired Emma Kerensky's order releasing Cheremissov and appointing Baranovsky to succeed him. Kerensky had signed this order on a page of my notebook—it was, I think, the last order he signed in his public career. Removal of Cheremissov was also Emma's last act in Pskov. There was no point in her staying longer in the abandoned Commissariat. I would try to reach her again through the front headquarters.

Driving along the railroad, I found the munitions train. It had been delayed by the sabotage of the engineers, who pretended the locomotive had broken down. When I showed them the declaration of our task force, they admitted the locomotive could be repaired in two hours. After further discussion of the political situation, they conceded the repair might be completed in half an hour. Twenty minutes later the locomotive whistled and the train started toward Gatchina.

In Luga, things went smoothly enough at the beginning. I went to the local Soviet and complained to the chairman that several trains with our volunteers and munitions were detained in or around Luga. The chairman replied that if some regiments had stopped them, the Luga Soviet could do nothing—it was neutral. This led to a discussion about the meaning of neutrality. "The Luga Soviet," I insisted, "has committed the whole area under its control to neutrality. This means that volunteers of both parties must be permitted to pass through this area."

"Does it mean," the chairman asked, "that you, in Gatchina, will also let the Communists cross your lines on their way to Petrograd?"

"Of course not! We do not pretend to be neutral."

Finally the chairman agreed to send telegrams to all railroad stations and barracks around Luga, admonishing all whom it might concern to observe strict neutrality and abstain from interfering with the movement—in either direction—of volunteers and munitions trains. The chairman warned me, however, that he could not enforce the order since the Military Revolutionary Committee disputed the Luga Soviet's authority in military matters.

On the highway between Luga and Pskov a patrol stopped my car, explaining that they were ordered to deliver suspects to the Military Revolutionary Committee. I objected that their order could not refer to me. "I am not a 'suspect,' but Commissar of the All-Russian Executive Committee." The soldiers apologized. "Maybe you are okay, Comrade Commissar, but we are ordered to suspect everybody." I insisted, "You are mixed up, brothers. I have just come from your Soviet, where the chairman told me Luga was neutral." One of the soldiers remarked, "Maybe we are mixed up. Maybe we are neutral. Who knows? But we must deliver you to the Revolutionary Committee." He confessed, however, that he did not know where the committee's quarters was. "Don't worry, comrade," he comforted me. "We will find out."

It took time to find the committee. When we found it, its chairman declared that he was new in politics and did not know what neutrality was and what to do with me. Finally he decided to turn the affair over to the Soviet. An emergency session of the Soviet opened an hour later in the waiting room of the railroad station. The chairman asked me to present my point of view. After a long discussion the Soviet decided that, since Luga was neutral, everybody was free to join either side in the civil war and that my detention had been illegal.

I intended to drive to Pskov at once, but my chauffeurs refused to start before dawn. They were short of gas, the road was bad, the lights were out of order, one of the tires needed to be replaced. In brief, they had their own ideas of neutrality. I had to spend the night in Luga, at the station. During the night three echelons passed eastward unmolested, and I phoned Krasnov of their movement. In the morning I got a wire from General Baranovsky or someone on his staff: The situation in Pskov was extremely tense. The echelons could be handled, but my arrival and attempt to expedite the operation might provoke violence. I had no choice but to return to Gatchina. Then I discovered that my car and chauffeur had disappeared during the night. A locomotive whistled, an eastbound train was ready to leave. I squeezed myself into a crowded coach.

TRUCE AGREEMENT

In front of the Gatchina station I met a group of officers carrying guns and cartridge belts. One of them shouted to me, "The Bolsheviks are in the palace. Kerensky has fled!" Another broke in angrily, "They are looking for you in the palace, Mr. Commissar. When it comes to an accounting, no politician is there!"

The officers were on their way to the armored train. I went to the palace. Apparently nothing had changed there. The same confusion, the same crowd. I found Krasnov alone in his room. He was sitting at his desk, making notes on a small pad—his account of the last operation. He told me what had happened in Gatchina during my brief absence. At dawn, two sailors with white flags approached the Cossack sentries at the Tsarskoe-Gatchina highway and offered a truce: The Cossacks were to withdraw from the civil war; in return, the Soviets would assure them free conduct to their homes, with their officers, arms, and horses.[14] The sentries told the sailors that they could not negotiate with them but agreed to take them to their committee. At once the rumor spread in the task force that the campaign was over.

Krasnov went to Kerensky and advised him to drive to the Smolny with a white flag. Kerensky refused and, in the general confusion,

[14] In Cossack regiments, horses and small arms were the private property of the men.

escaped from the palace.[15] The committee of the task force was in session with the sailors, discussing the conditions of a truce, and Krasnov thought the Cossacks would welcome my presence. I went to the committee.

Ten Cossack representatives sat on one side of a long table facing the sailors. One of the latter was a big, strikingly handsome man with broad shoulders, a tanned face, pitch-black beard, and bright, arrogant eyes. This was the notorious Dybenko, the ringleader of the Baltic fleet. The other, Tushin, was small, with an insignificant pale face. He seemed to be the brains of the pair. When I entered the room, the question of safe-conduct for the Cossacks had been settled. Now the Cossacks were demanding the release from prison of officers and students of military schools. Dybenko was furious. "These dogs are not Cossacks and are none of your business," he yelled.

"They are our business," replied the Cossack chairman. "We stood for the same thing."

"To hell with what you stood for. Think of your own hides!"

"We did not ask you for a cease-fire," exploded the Cossack. "You asked. If you wish a truce, make it fair."

Dybenko turned to his companion. "What do you think, Tushin? I would not mind turning those blackguards over to them. Why should we feed them?"

The small sailor nodded. The chairman read the clause of the agreement: "All officers and students of military schools arrested after November 5 in Petrograd will be set free."

"Now about Lenin and Trotsky," said the chairman. "They must go!"

"None of your business!" shouted Dybenko.

"Make it fair," insisted the Cossacks. "You told us that Kerensky must not be in the government until he has cleared himself of having conspired with Kornilov. We agreed. Well, weren't Lenin and Trotsky charged with being German spies? Until they clear themselves, they must not be in the government. . . ."

"Did you catch them spying?" Tushin asked angrily. "Or are you repeating the dirty slander of capitalist newspapers? Now we see what kind of birds you are."

"All we say is that they must stand public trial. If they are not spies they have nothing to fear."

The discussion went on. Finally Dybenko shouted, "These damned

15 Krasnov pretended that he had helped Kerensky to escape. Later Kerensky accused Krasnov of intending to deliver him to the enemy. I think both versions are false. If Krasnov had intended to arrest the former Supreme Commander, he could easily have done so. On the other hand, he hardly would have thought of arranging the escape of a man for whom he had no friendly feelings.

Cossacks are as stubborn as devils. We are just wasting time with them. What do you think, Tushin?"

"Let them have their way," the small sailor remarked casually. "I rather like their guts."

The chairman wrote: "Lenin and Trotsky will withdraw from the government and abstain from any public activity until they have cleared themselves of the charge of having worked for the enemy." I offered an amendment: "Lenin and Trotsky will abstain from any public activity until the accusations against them of having worked for the enemy and *against democracy* are investigated by the Constituent Assembly."

Dybenko turned toward me like a furious bull. "You are no Cossack, mister! What are you doing here?"

"I am the Commissar of the Northern Front and of this task force," I replied.

The chairman backed me up: "The Citizen Commissar is our man."

"He may be your man, but we are here to negotiate directly with the Cossacks, without middlemen," shouted Dybenko, pounding the table with his fists. "No amendments or no truce!"

The chairman did not insist on my amendment. He read the whole agreement aloud. It began with the declaration that the Cossacks and other military units belonging to the task force assembled under the command of General Krasnov at Gatchina would stop fighting against the Petrograd garrison. Then came the clause assuring safe-conduct for all participants in the campaign, other men and officers of the Third Cavalry Corps with members of their families, and all Cossack regiments stationed in and around Petrograd. This was followed by clauses about the arrested officers and students of military schools and about Kerensky, Lenin, and Trotsky. In view of the relative forces of the two parties, the truce agreement was amazingly favorable to the Cossacks.[16]

The chairman of the committee took the signed document to Krasnov. The general ordered all the sentries around the palace to retire and all troops to assemble in the courtyard. It took time to get the men together. Petrograd soldiers, sailors, and workers with rifles and cartridge belts filled the palace and the courtyard, leaving only a place in the center where the Cossacks stood in a rigid square, each

[16] It was signed by Dybenko and Tushin in the name of the Soviet of the People's Commissars, but the latter declined to ratify it, pointing out that the delegates had exceeded their authority. They had been authorized to arrange a cease-fire and not to negotiate a peace agreement with the Cossacks. The People's Commissars honored only the clauses relating to the Third Corps and other Cossack regiments.

hundred one step from the next. How small our task force looked! Hardly more than two thousand men, a drop in a raging sea. Krasnov asked me to accompany him when he took a place before his troops. He read the agreement and added, "Now my job is to take you home. We have done all we could. Not ours is the shame for what is going to happen in Russia."

We returned to the palace.

TAKEN PRISONER

The rooms formerly occupied by the headquarters of the task force were now in the hands of the Communists, some tense and bewildered, others intoxicated by victory or plain drunk. No officers were in sight. I was sitting in a comparatively quiet corner in a remote room, dead tired, almost asleep, when three men approached me—a student of the Mining Institute of Petrograd and two workers.

"I am the chairman of the Gatchina Soviet," the student said to me. "Some sailors are threatening to get you. If you do not object, we would rather take you into custody and whisk you out of here to a safe place as our prisoner." And he added in a whisper, "These comrades and I are S-R. You can trust us."

I looked at them. There could be no doubt of their sincerity. The two workers rushed to the adjacent room and returned with a score of soldiers with guns and fixed bayonets. People around us had noticed that something unusual was going on. The room was full of Petrograd soldiers. The chairman of the Gatchina Soviet posted his men around me and said sternly, "Citizen Commissar! The Gatchina Soviet has ordered us to take you into custody. Guards, march!"

The Gatchina soldiers escorted me to the entrance of the palace. They were hand-picked, tall, husky fellows, and I was well hidden among them. But as we were descending the steps in front of the palace, Petrograd sailors recognized me. Someone yelled, "Look, there goes the bloodsucker!" Excited men pressed around. The student shouted, "Attention! This man is the prisoner of the Gatchina Soviet. All power to the Soviet!"

My escort made its way slowly through the crowd. I noticed several Cossacks, without arms, among the Petrograd soldiers. They pressed forward as from curiosity. Then they formed a ring around our small group, and a young Cossack whispered to me, "Don't worry, Comrade Commissar! You are one of ours, nothing will happen to you."

He smiled at me, I smiled at him. We emerged from the crowd into the quietness of a dark street. The Gatchina soldiers broke formation and we walked together—the soldiers, the student, a handful of workers, and I.

The student asked me what they should do next. I said, "Take me to the Soviet. In the morning call the presiding board and pass a formal resolution that, after having checked the charges against me, you have found them insufficient for my detention." The escort was dismissed. I shook hands with the soldiers and thanked them for having rescued me. After a long detour we returned to the Soviet building. Although it was not far from the palace, it seemed the safest place for me. I installed myself in the reading room on a heap of newspapers and fell asleep.

When I awoke, the room was full of men in uniform and I saw Trotsky in front of me, in a quasi-military overcoat. An officer who accompanied him introduced himself. "I am Muralov, in command of the Petrograd garrison. Comrade Trotsky is in command of the People's Army, operating against the forces of the counterrevolution." I shook his hand but refused to shake Trotsky's. The latter said to me, "Citizen Woytinsky, you are prisoner of the revolutionary people, accused of counterrevolutionary conspiracy and mutiny."

I followed the two commanders to their car. The trip from Gatchina to Petrograd took several hours. The highway was barred by roadblocks at many points. It was like driving through an endless military camp. All the forces of the Petrograd garrison, Kronstadt, and the Baltic fleet and scores of thousands of armed workers were concentrated in the area between Gatchina and the capital—an array of some two hundred thousand or more armed men.

I was taken to the Smolny and locked in one of the rooms converted into a temporary detention depot.

BEHIND BARS AGAIN

The detention depot in the Smolny was as good an observation point as any. Soldiers and sailors brought in suspects. Other soldiers and sailors sifted them. Some few were released, others were sent to regular jails.

The coup in Petrograd aroused sullen disapproval among the peasants and misgivings among a large part of the workers in the province. Government officials and employees, from top to bottom, refused to recognize the new government and struck against it. The Council of the People's Commissars remained essentially a military junta. The country was plunged into anarchy, and armed gangs were formed in Petrograd to quell and conquer it.

A dictatorship began to emerge from the chaos. Printing plants were taken over by the government. Political clubs were closed. All meetings except those called by the government parties were prohibited. Jails emptied by the March revolution were packed again. After the announcement of peace negotiations with Germany, the front army was no longer a threat to the Communists. It had simply ceased to exist. Regiment after regiment deserted positions and moved to the rear, by train and on foot, carrying with them loot seized in military warehouses.

Our Iskosol friends, on learning of my arrest, helped Emma to reach Petrograd, sacrificing one of the last cars at their disposal. She had travel papers as a delegate from the front to the Petrograd Commission on Elections to the Constituent Assembly. Reaching Petrograd after midnight, she obtained permission to see me before dawn. We were permitted to see each other again for a short time in the following days. Indeed, as a prisoner I had more opportunity to talk with her than I had had in the preceding eight or nine months.

After a week I was called before the investigating judge. To my surprise, he was nobody less than Anton. His assignment was to obtain assurance that I recognized the Council of the People's Commissars. I refused to discuss politics with him and demanded that I be released at once: first, because I had followed the call of duty by defending the All-Russian Executive Committee; second, because, according to the Gatchina truce agreement, no member of the task force was to be arrested. Anton replied that the legal aspect of the affair was above his head.

A few days later I was transferred to a solitary cell in the Fortress of Peter and Paul. Before the revolution, its dungeons had been used for exceptionally dangerous political prisoners, but there was nothing particularly sinister about them except that the complete silence on the corridor was oppressive. The day after my delivery to the fortress, the prison physician paid me a call. He was an unusually tall, lean man with a pale face and sad eyes. "Have you any complaints?" he asked.

"None," I answered without particular friendliness.

He entered the cell, ordered the guard to close the door, and introduced himself. "My name is Manukhin. I was appointed fortress physician after the revolution, when the Tsarist ministers were brought here. Now the members of the Provisional Government are in my care. I found your name on the list of new arrivals. Welcome! If you wish to write to your family, you may give me your letters." Noticing my suspicious look, he added, "It is pure accident that we have not met at the house of Gorky or some other friends we have in common."

After that day, all my letters to Emma went through the doctor. During one of his routine visits he said, "I am worried about some of my patients. They are terribly depressed. None of them hopes to live to see his family again. I would like them to have their daily walk with you. You have had prison experience and could cheer them up. I shall tell them that my prescription is a walk with Woytinsky."

The prisoners were allowed a half-hour walk in a small pentagonal court in the heart of the old bastion. The court was so arranged that one could see nothing but the five white walls, the small doors in each corner, and the sky. But the sky was deep blue at that season and the air was fresh and crisp. There I met the members of the Provisional Government. Most of them were no weaklings and had plenty of personal courage, but all were haunted by fear for their lives and were unable to accept danger as soldiers do in the trenches. The Communist newspapers were carrying on a slanderous campaign against them as the deadliest enemies of the people, and this campaign bore fruit in the attitude of the troops stationed in the fortress. A company of guards had passed a resolution threatening to massacre the prisoners if the enemies of the people continued their criminal activities. I remember a peculiar expression in the resolution; referring to the example of the French Revolution, it threatened to "repeat the November massacres." The style of the resolution made me think of Trotsky's oratory at Yakor Plaza.

The families of the former ministers implored the People's Commissars to transfer them from the fortress to a safer place. Finally the government permitted the transfer of two members of the deposed Cabinet, Shingarev and Kokoshkin, to a private hospital. That day, during the usual walk in the court, I met Konovalov, a man for whom I had developed sincere sympathy and respect. For the first time he spoke not of death, but of snow and sky. Next morning I saw him again. His face was ashen and he was propped up against a wall, unable to walk. He said to me, "They murdered them in their beds. . . ."

The evening after Shingarev and Kokoshkin were transferred to the hospital, a band of soldiers and sailors entered their room, tore them from their beds, and beat them to death. The murderers were not prosecuted and the affair was interpreted in Bolshevist newspapers as a spontaneous manifestation of the people's wrath against their oppressors. Mob lynching was becoming routine.

On her next visit to the fortress, Emma pressed into my hand a tiny package of cyanide—to spare me humiliation and torture in the ultimate emergency.

THE CONSTITUENT ASSEMBLY

Elections to the Constituent Assembly were scheduled for December. Extensive preparations had been made, all parties had nominated their candidates, and the electoral campaign was in full swing when the Communists seized power in Petrograd. In the hectic propaganda barrage that preceded the coup, the Bolsheviks accused the Provisional Government of sabotaging the elections and promised to carry them out at once. After they seized power, they did their best to get a majority in the Assembly so that the elections would amount to a popular endorsement of their coup. Sweeping decrees promising everything to everybody followed one another. At the same time the Communists had monopolized all channels of propaganda, harassing and closing the opposition newspapers, prohibiting public meetings of the opposition parties, and jailing the opposition candidates.

Elections took place late in December. A cell in the Peter and Paul Fortress was transformed into an election booth. Together with the members of the deposed government, I cast my ballot. We had no illusion about the outcome of the contest of ballots against bullets.

We underestimated, however, the political maturity of the Russian people. The voters sternly disowned the usurpers of power. The Bolsheviks prevented tabulation of the votes, but the result was revealed by the composition of the Constituent Assembly. On the day it convened, 707 deputies registered at the Tauride Palace. Among them, 175 were Communists and non-partisan fellow travelers and 40 were left-wing S-R, ready to side with the Communists. The right-wing S-R had won 370 seats. Of the remaining 122 seats, 86 had gone to national minorities, all anti-Bolshevist, 17 to the Cadets, and 16 to the Mensheviks, while the party affiliation of 3 deputies was not ascertained. Many of the 101 absent deputies were in jail. In all, the Communists, the left S-R, and their sympathizers captured only about 25 to 26 per cent of the seats. Only 2 per cent of the people voted for the Cadets. More than 70 per cent voted for the moderate Socialists.

The official history of the Communist party, published two decades later, makes no mention of the Constituent Assembly as a slogan used in the November coup and refers to it only in enumerating the tasks the Bolsheviks faced after the seizure of power. Their job of dissolving the "capitalist" Constituent Assembly is mentioned along with the liquidation of all kinds of counterrevolutionary organizations.

In December, 1917, things did not look as simple as that. After having promised to expedite the convocation of the Assembly, the People's Commissars could not tell the people bluntly that they wanted to dissolve it. When the results of the election became known, they launched a campaign to discredit the Assembly. It was molded, they told the people, after the pattern of parliamentary institutions of capitalist countries. Its convocation was a proper aim of a bourgeois revolution, but Russia had reached a higher stage of revolutionary development and there was no place for a Constituent Assembly in that exalted society! Furthermore, they argued, the elections had been held too early, before people had had time to get acquainted with the new regime and realize all its advantages.

The next step of the Council of People's Commissars was to raid the offices of the Union for Defense of the Assembly. Some thirty men, all moderate Socialists, were arrested and taken to the Fortress of Peter and Paul.

The day of the Assembly's opening arrived. The S-D and S-R had planned demonstrations in the streets and in front of the Tauride Palace. The government announced that drastic measures would be taken against such demonstrations. The Assembly convened in the Tauride Palace on January 18, 1918, at four o'clock. Doors and windows of the palace bristled with machine guns. Katherine Hall was packed with soldiers, sailors, and armed workers. The galleries were full of armed men. The aisles and the space behind the deputies' seats were occupied by Kronstadt sailors, hand-picked as guards of the Assembly. Many seats of deputies were empty, mute reminders of people's representatives held behind bars.

The Communists announced to the Assembly that its only task was to dissolve itself, with a declaration that it recognized the new government and all its decisions. But the majority of the Assembly was not inclined to act as a rubber stamp. Chernov was elected chairman of the Assembly by a two-thirds majority, amid stormy protests of the mob representing the public. Noisy demonstrations, threats, clicking of guns in the galleries and the aisles continued during discussion of the question of whether the representatives of the people should yield to the government or the government should yield to the will of the people. This was a continuation of the dispute between the Second Duma and Stolypin in Tsarist days. Again, as a decade earlier, Tseretelli spoke for the democratic sector of the Assembly. He was met with a furious barrage of taunts and threats, and his speech was interrupted at every sentence. He spoke facing rifles pointed at him. Then the frenzy began to subside and the armed mob listened to the last part of his speech in tense silence.

Addressing himself to the left wing of the Assembly, Tseretelli called on the new government to yield power to the Constituent Assembly. "Not only the experiments you describe as socialistic but the very fate of the Russian revolution are at stake. For eight months, you say, we held all the power. But the curse of those eight months was the absence of a national, universally recognized Assembly closely tied to the people and expressing their will. We were trying to call such an Assembly to life. . . . If you suspect us of delaying the elections, why did you carry out your coup on the eve of the convocation of the Assembly? Even if you were right in accusing us, here is the Constituent Assembly, here is the body expressing the will of the great majority of the people, a body that unites all national groups in Russia and can lead all of them to the common goal. If this body is destroyed, if you cross this last line, the protracted anarchy of civil war will weaken and bleed our democracy, and thus, following this only way open to it, counterrevolution will conquer what was once called the Russian revolution. . . ." [17]

The Communists were unable to dispel the impression of this speech on the audience. But they had no intention of yielding. Processions of civilians converging toward the Tauride Palace from different parts of the city were stopped by machine guns and many demonstrators were killed or wounded. Emma was in one of these processions and told me of these scenes of horror and despair.

At midnight the Assembly began to discuss the war and land problems. The left withdrew from the hall, leaving the rump Assembly at the mercy of the mob. The guards demanded that the chairman close the session, their sergeant explaining, "We are tired and want to go to bed." The meeting continued, however, and three declarations were voted—on the republican form of government, transfer of land to the peasants, and peace negotiations in the name of the Assembly.

The next day the Tauride Palace was guarded by troops and the deputies were not permitted to enter. A day later, on January 20, the Council of People's Commissars announced that the Constituent Assembly had been dissolved because its counterrevolutionary majority had refused to recognize the conquests of the revolution. This was the end of the democratic revolution in Russia. The country entered a long period of civil war from which a new form of absolutism, the totalitarian state, was to emerge.

IN RETROSPECT

The defeat of the democratic revolution in Russia was a turning point in world history. It was also a turning point in the lives of millions of Russian intellectuals, mine among others. It therefore seems appro-

---

[17] Tseretelli meant the counterrevolution of the right. Actually, all values for which the liberation movement had stood and fought were destroyed by the Bolsheviks themselves.

priate to add a few marginal comments to my recollections of the terrible year 1917.

How will history evaluate the meaning of the successive phases of the revolution in Russia? I have described the coup in November, 1917, as the *fall* of Russian democracy in contrast to its *rise* in the preceding March. On the other hand, many foreign observers held the seizure of power by the Petrograd garrison to have been a step forward in Russia's struggle for freedom, like the victory of the Jacobins over the Girondists in the French Revolution. There must be some objective criterion for solving this controversy.

I believe that the criterion should be sought not in the procedure of transfer of power but in the response of the people to such transfer. Every revolution is a break in legality and an act of mutiny from the point of view of the deposed government. There is no legitimistic halo around a government that emerges out of a revolution, but, sooner or later, the people pass judgment on the change in regime. They may accept the new order as liberation or merely submit to the new rule. If they accept it, the new regime does not fear opposition and will ultimately bring freedom to the people. If they merely submit, the new government is condemned to maintain itself by force and terror.

This was the fundamental difference between the March and November revolutions in Russia. The nation accepted the overthrow of Tsarism unanimously and jubilantly. But the majority of the people, through their votes in the elections to the Constituent Assembly, condemned the seizure of power by the Bolsheviks. Two circumstances make the results of these elections particularly significant: first, the government overthrown by the Communists was extremely weak; second, the elections were held under strong pressure by the new government. The fact that in such circumstances the great majority of the people preserved their faith in democracy and elected representatives of the democratic, anti-Communist parties determines the historical meaning of the November coup as a defiance of the will of the people, an uprising against the democratic revolution.

This is also the difference between the events in Russia in 1917 and those of the French Revolution. The moderates in the Soviets were not Girondists. They had the masses of the people behind them and proved their capacity for resolute action by quelling riots in May, crushing the Communist revolt in July, frustrating Kornilov's mutiny in September. Yet they must carry full responsibility for the defeat in November. It cannot be denied that Lenin came to power by capitalizing on their mistakes.

I have asked myself many times the cause of Lenin's victory—or, more exactly, of the collapse of democratic forces in Russia in 1917. The simplest explanation is that democracy proved unable to solve the problems it faced. In a very general way, this is true. But this statement does not answer specifically the question as to what the mistakes were that brought the democratic revolution in Russia to collapse. Observers and historians of the Russian revolution have mentioned four errors of the democratic regime: weak policy concerning war and peace; delay in land reform; delay in electing the Constituent Assembly; failure to organize a government.

The war, of course, was a heavy liability for democracy. But a democratic government could have overcome this difficulty if the people had felt its sincere desire to end the war with a just negotiated peace. The mistake of the democratic forces was that they had left foreign policy in the hands of men who were opposed to their aspirations, hostile to the idea of a negotiated peace, and inclined to use the issues of war and peace as a weapon against the new revolutionary order.

The delay in land reform was not a major cause of the collapse of the democratic regime. Reform was on the way under Chernov's rural committees at the time of the first Coalition. Moreover, the peasants, who were directly concerned, resisted the Communists longer than did any other group of people.

The delay in elections to the Constituent Assembly was a major mistake that changed the course of events. Responsibility for this mistake is divided among many groups. The right, headed by the Cadets, fought tooth and nail to postpone the election in line with its policy of impeding consolidation of the new order. The Communists were interested in postponing the election as a means of prolonging the period of instability and gaining time to prepare to seize power. The democratic forces pressed for an earlier election, but not strongly enough. They yielded too easily and finally left the matter in the hands of a government that was a puppet of the right.

The delay in the national election was, however, only one aspect of a more serious failure of democracy, its failure to organize a stable and strong government. This can be proved, I think, by the sequence of events. In the early phase of the revolution, the democratic forces were gaining ground and the new order was being consolidated gradually. In July, the moderates in the Petrograd Soviet frustrated the Bolsheviks' bid for power. Three or four months later they had lost their grip over the army, and the political system supported by them in the Soviets began to disintegrate.

This course of events suggests that our main mistakes and the causes of our defeat must be sought in the period after the July days. The outstanding events of that period were the dissolution of the first Coalition, the formation of the new Cabinet independent of the Soviets, postponement of elections to the Constituent Assembly, and

Kornilov's mutiny. The four events were closely connected with one another and represented consecutive phases of the same process.

The Cabinet formed after the July days, with the consent of the moderates in the All-Russian Executive Committee, represented a set-back for the cause of democracy. Yielding to the pressure from the right, we saddled ourselves with an intolerable burden—a government that represented nobody and could not command the respect of the people. The Cabinet's decision to postpone elections to the Constituent Assembly was a new victory for the right. It further weakened the prestige of the moderates with the masses and brought the Communists closer to victory. There would have been no "ten days that shook the world" in November if the Constituent Assembly had been elected in September, as the first Coalition Government had promised in May!

The most terrible blow to the democratic regime was Kornilov's mutiny—not its final phase, after the break between Kornilov and Kerensky, but its initial phase, the Mogilev plot to use troops against their will to liquidate the Soviets. The democratic parties finally lost the army by tolerating in the government persons who had been involved in this conspiracy.

These mistakes of the moderates in the Soviets stemmed from a common source. In each case, the democratic leaders made concessions to the right because they were not sure of their own strength and were reluctant to shoulder entire responsibility for the government. Each time, yielding to the right, they sacrificed their own real power in a futile hope of gaining support from quarters that actually had nothing to offer because they lacked the support of the masses of the Russian people.

Ultimately our weak policy sprang from lack of unity within the ranks of democracy and lack of will to power among its leaders.

Years of Wandering
1918-1935

I REMEMBER the years 1918-35 as years of wandering—not in the sense of continuous movement from country to country but in a deeper sense. Wherever we lived during those years, the land under our feet was not our land, the language spoken around us was not our language, and, no matter how hospitable and friendly the people were with whom we worked, we were foreigners among them.

The Russian revolution had left a deep impact on the lives of the peoples in the countries to which our wandering took us. We saw the mailed fist of the Communists crush budding democracy in Georgia, in Transcaucasia. We witnessed the rise to power of Mussolini, Lenin's faithful pupil in the art of building and running a police state. And we saw the Communists bring down the Weimar Republic and raise to power another graduate of the same school—Adolf Hitler. Except for the modest help we were able to give our friends in Georgia and Germany in defending their freedom, we were spectators, rather than actors, in the historical drama of that period.

PETROGRAD UNDER THE REDS

The Communists' case against me—conspiracy and armed mutiny against the People's Government—was originally in the hands of a Special Investigating Commission consisting of Anton and another shabby character. Then the Commission was dissolved for some irregularities—whether accepting bribes or straight stealing, I cannot recall—and its unfinished business was turned over to the Commissariat of Justice, then headed by a leftist S-R. Emma, who handled my affairs better than any attorney could have, went to him and challenged him to take my case to the People's Court.

The new courts were modeled after the mob trials of the French Revolution. A jury of soldiers and workers was called up to try persons charged with counterrevolution, sabotage, and treason. The jurors were instructed to follow their "revolutionary conscience" without regard for judicial procedure and law. In insisting that I appear before such a court, Emma had an encouraging precedent in mind. The Commissariat of Justice had brought the former treasurer of our Executive Committee, L. M. Bramson, before a People's Court for his refusal to transfer the Committee's funds—more than three million rubles—to the new government. Bramson courageously insisted that he had used the money for the purpose for which it was intended—to defend freedom and democracy—when he had turned over the funds to the union of public officials striking against the Communist usurpers of power. A score of workers from various Petrograd factories rose in court to defend Bramson. The mood of the crowd in the courtroom was such that the jury could not send the defendant back to jail and was forced to release him. Emma was confident that if I had a public trial, mass deputations of factory workers and soldiers would come to my defense.

The Commissar of Justice also realized that to try me in public would humiliate the government. Sidetracking the matter of a trial, he tried to persuade Emma that the wrath of the people against me was so strong that the soldiers in the fortress would tear me to pieces if they saw me go free. Emma replied, "Nothing will happen to my husband unless you incite the mob to violence as you did against Shingarev and Kokoshkin. Hand me the order for his release, and I shall not have the slightest worry about the fortress garrison." The Commissar felt insulted and refused to talk with her any longer, but finally decided to add my name to the list of prisoners to be released from the fortress. Emma met me at the gate of the dungeon. The court was full of soldiers. They looked at us—some with curiosity, others with indifference. None showed any inclination to tear us to pieces.

I found Petrograd in a state of panic and chaos. All government offices were on strike. Economic conditions were deteriorating day by day. The city was flooded with paper money, prices were soaring, unrest was mounting in workers' quarters. If elections to a new Soviet had been held at that time, the moderate Socialists would have obtained a majority. Only the soldiers and sailors were supporting the new regime. Thousands of enlisted men from Kronstadt and the Baltic fleet had settled in the capital, and one saw sailors' uniforms everywhere. The city was also crowded with deserters from all parts of the front, in ragged uniforms, without insignia.

The People's Commissars showered the country with decrees. Some of these reiterated the decrees of the Provisional Government—abolishing class discrimination, repealing restrictions on religious and national minorities, and so on; others held out promises for the future— nationalization of heavy industry, mining, banking, and foreign trade; repudiation of foreign debts of the Tsarist government. People did not seem to expect much from these promises. The new foreign policy was a bitter disappointment. The German High Command treated Russia as a defeated enemy after unconditional surrender. It bluntly announced that Russia was to be dismembered; Poland and the Baltic provinces were to become "independent" states under the control of Germany—actually, German colonies. Turkey was to receive a slice of the Caucasus. Germany was to control the foreign trade and foreign policy of truncated Russia.

All this was a heavy blow to the prestige of the government, which had promised immediate peace without territorial concessions to the enemy. The Communists could not call on the army to brace itself against Germany—the army was fading away, and the units still at the front—for lack of transportation facilities—would not offer even token resistance to the Germans. On the other hand, the Communists could not tell the Russian people that they relied on the eventual victory of the Allies. All their propaganda had been directed against the French, British, and American imperialists and warmongers and based on the contention that German and Austrian comrades were ready to stretch out their hands to their Russian brothers! Thus, the new government did not try to stop the advancing German troops. It frantically mobilized the workers' Red Guard; sailors and soldiers, armed detachments, marched in the streets of Petrograd, but none of them was dispatched to the front. All were sent against the Ukraine, which had declared itself independent, against the Cossacks, and against villages that refused to sell their produce to the cities. Petrograd looked like a city occupied by hordes of barbarians.

To celebrate my liberation, Emma bought tickets for *Faust*, with Chaliapin as Mephistopheles, in the Marinsky Opera House. I had never heard the great singer and did not hear much of him that night. We had seats in the orchestra. It turned out that all the orchestra seats except two rows had been reserved for the "flower and glory of the revolution," Kronstadt sailors. Some of them recognized me. Faces turned in our direction and we heard whispering. "Look, Woytinsky is here!" "Isn't he in jail?" "Call Smolny!" A sailor rushed to the entrance. There was no point in waiting for his return. Emma seized my arm and whispered firmly, "We must go at once." When the curtain rose and all eyes were turned toward the glittering stage, we got up quietly and left the theater.

The next day soldiers in a streetcar recognized me and we learned that some people in the Smolny had protested against my release from the fortress. Petrograd was becoming too dangerous for me. I had to go into hiding.

A friend brought us a message from Tseretelli. A military hospital train was ready to leave for the Caucasus with Georgian soldiers and officers, and Tseretelli asked us to go with him to Georgia, which was under the control of the Mensheviks. We accepted the plan.

Our friends provided us with the necessary travel documents: Emma as a military nurse returning home, and I as an artillery private who had left his battery for personal reasons, that is, a "comrade deserter." I also obtained an oversized military cloak, torn and soiled with tar, dingy trousers, and a cap to match. A barber near the place in which I was in hiding cropped my hair and shaved off my mustache. In this disguise I went to our apartment, where Emma was finishing preparations for the trip. When she opened the door I asked hoarsely, "Is Comrade Woytinsky at home?" "No, he left three days ago," she replied. I stepped in and said, "All right, I shall wait." Only then did she recognize me. She was shocked to tears by the change in my appearance, voice, and manners.

I vaguely remember the parting from my family. My father and brothers were away from Petrograd, but my mother and sister came to say good-by to us. I did not see my mother again until years later, in Paris. This was the last time I saw Nadya.

CROSSING RUSSIA

The trip from Petrograd to the Black Sea by train normally took two days. Our military hospital train covered the distance in about three weeks. Again, as a year earlier, we were crossing the expanses of Russia, but the contrast with March, 1917, was striking. This time the country was in a paroxysm of fear, suspicion, and hatred.

Georgian soldiers and officers were predominant among the passengers, but other people also found their way into our train—deserters, peasants with heavy sacks of flour and potatoes, merchants with mysterious bundles and suitcases. Trains had no timetables in those days; each moved on its own when the track was clear. At each station the commander of our train went to the local committee to ask for a safe-conduct. If the road ahead was clear and the committee members were decent and sober, the permit could be obtained in an hour or two, but sometimes negotiations lasted for five or six hours. The permit of the Council of the People's Commissars was not enough. The local committee would wire along the line to check where our train came from. Then gangs of soldiers would descend and search the passengers for arms.

Stations and tracks were packed with trains loaded with soldiers—some in rags, looking like outlaws, others in new uniforms from a ransacked warehouse. Some trains carried cannon—to use against the landowners, as soldiers explained. Frequently a train had a "mobile position" at each end, with sandbags packed around the cannon for use if the train was ambushed.

We arrived in Kursk early in the morning and were kept at the station until dusk. Excited people, mostly civilians, crowded the station. In my dirty cloak I could go among the crowd and ask what was going on. The station was two miles from the city over snow-covered fields, and the civilians at the station were local factory workers who claimed they had fled from Kursk after it was captured by the S-R, who had obtained a majority in the Soviet election. They had fled to the station to get reinforcements—mainly artillery support—to liberate the city, and complained bitterly that the soldiers in passing trains were not interested in the revolution. Another train arrived. The refugees from Kursk rushed to the cars. After a heated discussion, a cannon was unloaded from the rear platform. The soldiers moved it along the track to an open place from which one could see church spires on the horizon. Then they started bombarding the city. A man in a railroad uniform came running. "You damned fools!" he shouted. "How dare you fire without reconnaissance? How do you know that these birds are not Cadets? Let them show their documents!" The refugees from Kursk had no documents. So the cannon was put back on the train.

As we proceeded further south, travel became increasingly difficult and the search parties more and more arrogant. A train committee was elected to deal with the station authorities and pay ransom "for cultural purposes." Our committee also tried to get in touch with the searchers' superiors, but more often than not they had none. Frequently soldiers from a train waiting for clearance sent a searching party into our cars. Our train was cleaner and less crowded, most of its passengers wore neat uniforms, and they carried no arms; thus they seemed different and therefore dangerous. Emma and I were fairly safe. Our papers were in order and I looked like any other soldier returning home. But Tseretelli's life was in danger, since his presence in the train was no secret—all Georgians knew him.

There was a supply of liquor and wine in the ambulance car, and our committee decided to use it to expedite our progress. Instead of filling in the forms at the commissar's office at a station, the committee would invite him and his aides to the ambulance car. After sampling choice Caucasian wine and vodka, they would agree that our train was okay. Then they would be led through the cars and invited to search the luggage. At this stage, however, they had no desire to look under the benches. This public-relations policy proved highly successful, but once it backfired. At Tichaya, south of Kharkov, three men boarded our train: the commissar of the station, the commissar of its garrison, and the commissar of the traffic service. They enjoyed the refreshments and one of them ordered the switchman to let the train pass, forgetting that he and his companions were on it. When the people at the station discovered their commissars had disappeared on a suspicious train, telegrams flashed along the line: "The Cadets have kidnaped the revolutionary authorities of Tichaya. Stop the train!"

When we approached the next station we found the semaphore open and the switchman's signal to the train to go ahead. Then the train was switched to a siding surrounded by machine guns, and all the passengers were ordered to alight. Armed soldiers boarded the train. Three men jumped out of our ambulance car. One of them, in a military overcoat with a red armband, shouted, "All power to the Soviets! What in hell is going on here?"

An angry voice replied, "You blackguards have kidnaped the commissars from Tichaya."

"You are a liar," yelled the man with the red armband. "I am the commissar of Tichaya, and here are my comrades."

Then we were permitted to continue our journey.

At the Kavkazskaya station we found two committees, one countermanding the orders of the other. We were told that Cossacks had cut off the road southward. The troops assembled around the station did not know what to do—to attack the foe, await his attack, or retreat. We were ordered to surrender all arms, but we had none. Then the commander of the local troops offered to provide our men with arms if they would join his outfit and march against the Cossacks. The Georgians agreed to form a commando of some hundred and fifty men, provided that the station authorities would guarantee the security of our train with the women, children, and sick. They were confident there were no Cossacks in front and, if there were, they would make a deal with them and regain the train. At the last moment, however, the station committee decided it would be safer to get rid of the Georgians and we were ordered to proceed.

After that we zigzagged, trying to avoid the principal cities, often retracing our route. South of Rostov, not far from the Black Sea, we lost our train, for soldiers at a small station, after inspecting the cars, declared, "We can use a medical train in the civil war. Get out quickly!" They generously offered us five passenger cars and safe-conduct to the nearest port on the Black Sea, Tuapse.

The broad avenue leading from the railroad station of Tuapse to the harbor was packed with soldiers. But, despite the display of rifles, machine guns, and cannon, it looked like a country fair, peaceful and gay. Merchandise of all kinds was piled on the green lawns and under the trees lining the avenue. Local people, men in white shirts and women in bright dresses, mingled with soldiers.

A regiment from Trabzon, on the southern shore of the Black Sea, had landed the day before, bringing with it a portion of supplies that had been stored at the front. Each regiment had had a choice of selling its share to the Turks in Trabzon or taking it away. The goods brought to Tuapse had been divided evenly among the twelve companies, and each of these distributed its share among the men. Now everybody was selling his merchandise to the civilians. Prices were reasonable: a machine gun for two hundred paper rubles, a field cannon for two thousand rubles. With the paper ruble worth five kopeks, this was a bargain. The soldiers boasted they were selling fairly. I saw a substantial citizen bargaining for a couple of tons of sugar. The soldiers refused to sell him more than the fifty pounds the other customers got. "You want to make money on our sweat and blood?" one said reproachfully. "We would charge you ten kopeks a pound and you would resell our sugar at a ruble a pound? You must be one of Kornilov's gang!"

From Tuapse we could reach Georgia only by sea, via Batum. A military transport, the *Saratov*, was leaving the next morning. The ship had been taken over by her crew, merchant sailors who were operating her as a private enterprise carrying freight and passengers, tramping the Black Sea and picking up business wherever profit beckoned. They had brought the Trabzon regiment, which had paid its way in flour. Now the ship's military revolutionary committee, which consisted of merchant and navy men, intended to exchange the flour for petroleum in Batum.

The sailors were the terror of the Black Sea region. They lived on merchant and military ships like medieval barons in their castles, raiding the shores. A battleship or destroyer would approach a coastal city, fire a dozen shells into it, and send a speedboat with a detail to warn the citizens that the city would be destroyed unless it paid a tribute—so much in foodstuffs and petroleum, so much in cash. The tribute would be paid at once. Often a warship took possession of a city. Supported by ship's guns, sailors would descend on it, arrest or kill the members of the city council, install a "people's government," take hostages, arrest suspects. Prisoners would be brought to the ship to be tried and shot, hung, or drowned.

We hesitated to trust our lives to the Communist crew, but reliable persons in Tuapse reassured us: The Black Sea pirates had a rogue's code of honor and would not mistreat their paying passengers. We went on board the *Saratov* at twilight and left Tuapse in the morning. The sailors looked at our group with unconcealed suspicion —in this region Georgians were known to be Mensheviks. The ship stopped for several hours off Sukhum, a lovely little town on a hillside covered with luxurious tropical vegetation. With other passengers, Emma and I went ashore. The town was deserted, all the shops were closed, all doors locked. Finally, on the outskirts, we found an old man working his orchard. He explained in broken Russian and by eloquent gestures that in the morning the Communists—some twenty men, mainly fishermen and boatmen—had occupied the hall of the municipal council. By noon the council officials threw them out. In the afternoon a cruiser appeared in the harbor and opened fire. Most of the shells exploded in gardens and orchards and little harm was done to the houses, but people expected that after the artillery barrage the sailors would land and ransack the town. Hence they fled to the mountains, the waterfront Communists along with the others. The warship, however, left without sending a party ashore.

We were on the slope high above Sukhum when a gun salvo came from the sea. We rushed toward the harbor to get aboard our ship. Then another salvo followed. When we reached the bay, speedboats from the *Saratov* were waiting for her passengers. Here we learned that our ship had fired at the town because somebody told the crew that counterrevolutionaries were attacking it from the mountains, but since the situation was not very clear the sailors decided to abstain from further operations.

The *Saratov* cast anchor at the entrance to the harbor of Batum. Several tugboats surrounded her, and port authorities boarded her to check the passengers' papers. But inspection was perfunctory. Our companions let Tseretelli, Emma, and me disembark by the first boat leaving for the shore. When we were a few yards from the ship, one of the oarsmen recognized Tseretelli. He asked him something in Georgian and shouted to his companions, "Khaki is here!" Khaki was Tseretelli's nickname of endearment in Georgia. Batum was in the hands of Georgian Mensheviks. A telegram was sent at once to Tiflis, whence came an order to reserve a special train to take Tseretelli to the capital. But local political leaders whisked him away for a conference.

Waiting for the train, Emma and I strolled along the waterfront and nearby streets. They were full of armed men in homespun garb, men with gray beards, and teen-agers. They did not look at all like soldiers and differed strikingly from the Red guards we had seen in Petrograd. I was still wearing my disreputable artillery cloak, and an old man asked me to which division my regiment belonged—a polite way of inquiring from what outfit I had deserted—and what my business was in Batum. I told him my uniform did not mean anything—I had just arrived from Petrograd with Tseretelli. The old man shed tears of joy when he heard Khaki was back. I asked him about the armed men in the streets. He pointed to the mountains around Batum. "There we live," he said. "Many people. They told us that the Turks were coming to take Batum. They asked who would defend it. So we came down."

The strains of the *Marseillaise* sounded from around the corner. In a tiny square some thirty men were standing in a circle, leaning on their rifles and singing. I could not understand the words in Georgian, and they sang in an unusual way with an undertone of sadness that was almost like a prayer before death. Unmistakably, however, this was the anthem of the French Revolution.

THE TRANSCAUCASIAN MAZE

In Tiflis I plunged into Caucasian politics. Through the centuries the Caucasus had been the arena of clashes between different civilizations, feuding empires, and local kingdoms and tribes. Russia did not establish herself firmly in Transcaucasia until the second half of the nineteenth century. She built highways, the ports of Baku on the Caspian Sea and Batum on the Black Sea, and a railroad and a pipeline between them. She introduced civil administration and courts and developed a network of schools designed to Russify the population. But the bulk of the people—small farmers, artisans, and merchants—preserved their old languages, religions,[1] customs, and garb. Except for a dozen Moslem tribes in the mountains, the region south of the Caucasian range was divided into three parts—not unlike Gaul in the time of Julius Caesar. The Georgians (some two million) lived in the western part along the range; the Tartars (about three million) east of them, closer to the Caspian Sea; and the Armenians (two million) further south, along the Turkish border.

At the elections to the Constituent Assembly, the Tartars voted for the national Moslem party, which was controlled by the big landowners and clergy, while the Armenians and Georgians cast votes for moderate Socialists—the Armenians for the Dashnak party (close to the Russian S-R), the Georgians for the S-D Mensheviks. All three groups had declined to recognize the November coup in Petrograd and formed a government of their own—the Transcaucasian Commissariat, based on representation of all national groups and parties in the region. Originally, this was to be a temporary arrangement, but the split between Transcaucasia and Russia became deeper after the Communists dissolved the Constituent Assembly. Political conditions in Transcaucasia were aggravated by frictions among the three national groups, especially between the Armenians and Tartars. When we reached Tiflis, Transcaucasia, split and defenseless, lay at the mercy of Turkey.

At the outbreak of the March revolution Russia had an army of two hundred thousand men on the Turkish front. At the beginning of the war, this army had penetrated deeply into Asia Minor and occupied the northwestern corner of Turkey, including Trebizond (now Trabzon). The positions of the Russian and Turkish armies did not change until the November coup in Petrograd, when the Russian

[1] Christianity spread among the Georgians and Armenians a thousand years earlier than in Russia. Both peoples belonged to the Eastern group of Christian churches, but formed separate denominations, different from the Russian Orthodox Church in ritual, organization, and tradition.

army began to fade away. As on other fronts, regiment after regiment left its positions. The Army Command tried to replace the fleeing troops with Armenian and Georgian volunteers, but the Communists launched a violent campaign against the native Caucasians, calling on Russian soldiers to blow up the munitions dumps or hand them over to their brothers, the Turkish soldiers—to help them fight their own ruling classes—rather than leave arms to the Armenian and Georgian imperialists.

When the Caucasian front had been reduced to a flimsy screen of poorly equipped and untrained men, the Turks opened an offensive, under pretext of protecting local Moslems from the Armenians. The front line was pushed back to the prewar Russian frontier. The Moslems burned down Armenian villages, and the Armenians retaliated where they could by massacring the Tartars.

After the Communists had signed the separate peace treaty at Brest-Litovsk, ceding two Armenian districts and Batum to the enemy, the Turkish Military High Command ordered the Transcaucasian Commissariat to evacuate their areas. Turkey was then only beginning to transform itself from an oriental despotism to a modern nation and was still the land of bloody sultans to its neighbors, the non-Moslem peoples of Transcaucasia. For the Armenians, resistance to the Turks was a fight for life. For the Georgians, the situation was less desperate, but they were facing the imminent loss of their only commercial port and realized they had only a slim chance against the Ottoman army. That is why the volunteers in Batum sang the *Marseillaise* as though it were their last prayer.

Despite the difficult political situation in Transcaucasia, Tiflis looked like any other southern city, full of sun and flowers. It was the main cultural and political center of the region. The palace of the former Viceroy, the Tsar's uncle, Grand Duke Nicholas, was now the seat of the Transcaucasian government. The government's pillars were the Georgian S-D party and the Soviet of Tiflis. The head of the party, Noy Jordania, was also chairman of the Soviet.

My recollections of Tiflis are inseparable from the memory of this man. I had met him occasionally in Petrograd and Finland after the first revolution, but he had not impressed me. In Georgia he looked taller, his voice was stronger, and a slight stammer added weight to his words. There seemed to be the halo of the tribal prophet around his majestic head with its thin gray hair and full beard. Indeed, he was more than the head of a political party. He was the uncontested leader of his small nation, surrounded by love and devotion, and the remarkable unity of the Georgian people stemmed largely from his influence.

IN TIFLIS

The day after our arrival in Tiflis, Jordania asked me to join the party's daily, *Bor'ba* (*Struggle*). The party had two newspapers, one in Georgian and the other in Russian. The first was designed primarily for rank-and-file party members; the second, *Bor'ba*, for the intellectuals and general public that could not read Georgian. Its chief editor was a Russian provincial journalist who had served in the Russian Caucasian army, had been stranded in Tiflis during the demobilization, and had more interest in Georgian wines than in Caucasian politics. We worked together for a week or two. Then he left Tiflis, and Jordania asked me to take over the newspaper. My heritage from my predecessor was a huge filing cabinet packed from top to bottom with empty bottles of all sizes, colors, and shapes.

Emma became the executive secretary of *Bor'ba*, I its chief editor. Commercial and financial matters were handled by the party treasurer. Our office was in a government building, and Jordania's apartment was on the same floor, with a door into our office. Very often he would drop in to chat for a moment about politics. Sometimes he would suggest the topic for the editorial. He had a rare flair for journalism; his idea of good political writing was very simple: "Each article must have an idea, at least a small one, and the reader must be able to grasp it."

The newspaper was no larger than a twelve-page tabloid, but, since it had no syndicated articles and few outside contributors, our editorial staff of four or five had to fill the entire paper, day after day. *Bor'ba* soon became popular with its readers. Rereading clippings, I find that it was indeed a good newspaper and served a worthy purpose by defending the freedom of a small nation.

Bor'ba's best friends were the Georgian workers and farmers. For them, this was a *Russian* newspaper and the only Russian paper that understood them and supported their aspirations. Emma and I once stopped at a poor farmhouse in a tiny hamlet. I do not recall what took us there—perhaps we were asking our way or wanted a glass of water. Rules of oriental hospitality did not allow the farmer to ask who we were, but he looked at us with undisguised curiosity. So I told him that we worked for *Bor'ba* and gave him my name. His Russian was very poor, but when he heard my name he said proudly, "I have a whole book of yours." And he produced a homemade scrapbook in which he had pasted a dozen articles of mine, though he could read only their titles.

Although *Bor'ba*, as the official organ of the party, was also the mouthpiece of the government, we had complete freedom in running the paper. Jordania, an old journalist himself, would sometimes give advice on handling this or that issue, but no official communications were submitted to us for publication and there was no censorship of what we printed. We defended the cause of freedom in Transcaucasia —and later in Georgia—with the arguments we considered proper and just. The newspaper was strongly anti-Communist but never anti-Russian.

Transcaucasia was engaged in peace negotiations with Turkey that had begun soon after the dissolution of the Russian Constituent Assembly. The Transcaucasian government had hoped to settle the dispute with the Turks on the basis of *status quo ante bellum*, but after the Brest-Litovsk treaty and the Turkish ultimatum claiming Batum and two Armenian districts, negotiations were broken off and the Transcaucasian delegation returned to Tiflis. The government and Seym—the parliament formed after the dissolution of the Constituent Assembly—were split. The Tartars openly welcomed the advance of the Turks in areas with a mixed Moslem and Armenian population. On April 13, Seym addressed an appeal to the peoples of Transcaucasia, calling all men to arms. The Tartars abstained from voting.

The war started with heavy odds against the Georgians and Armenians. The Russian army, which had shielded the Caucasus against the Turks, was gone and had carried away or destroyed almost all munitions except what it had sold to the Turks. The military forces of Transcaucasia consisted of half a dozen Armenian battalions and a handful of Georgian volunteers. The forts of Batum fell after two days, and the main Armenian fortress, Kars, capitulated two weeks later.

Peace negotiations were resumed in Batum, now a Turkish city. The Transcaucasian delegation was ready to accept the Brest-Litovsk peace treaty and insisted only that negotiations be conducted with all the Central Powers, rather than with the Turks alone. But the Turkish delegates declared that the latest victories of their army had made the Brest-Litovsk agreement obsolete and demanded further "adjustments" of frontiers and control over Transcaucasian railroads. When a deadlock in negotiations developed, Germany offered to mediate. The Transcaucasian delegation accepted the offer, the Turks rejected it. Then the People's Commissars in Petrograd entered the arena, warning Germany against dealing with Transcaucasia and denouncing the Tiflis government.

Turkish troops were advancing along the Armenian railroad. In Batum, Transcaucasian Tartars sided openly with the Ottoman delegation. North Caucasus was in a state of open civil war. Moslems on the southern fringe of Georgia decided to join the Ottoman Empire. Influential groups among the Armenians were thinking of restoring ties with Russia. Under these conditions, Seym proclaimed the dissolution of the Transcaucasian Republic. The same day three independent republics were formed: Georgia, Armenia, and Azerbeidjan.

Georgia began its life as an independent state with a population and area about as large as West Virginia's, completely encircled by unfriendly neighbors. There was no jubilation in Tiflis. The Georgian leaders realized that national independence had been imposed on them by a chain of calamities beyond their control. Their first task was to stop the Turkish offensive. On June 4, the Georgian government signed on the dotted line the Treaty of Peace and Friendship submitted by Turkey, but at the same time it asked the Germans to assume control over Georgian railroads. Three days later German pickets appeared on Georgia's border and along her railroads to insure regular traffic.

The threat of Turkish invasion faded. The Germans, perfectly drilled automatons in gray uniforms, entered Tiflis quietly. They were not many, hardly more than a battalion, and were under strict orders not to mingle with the local population. The government quartered them in a large apartment house in the center of the city, half a block from *Bor'ba's* office, with armed sentries posted at its entrance. Uniformed men were seen at the windows, and from time to time a German platoon would march through the streets, always in silence, without songs or military music. At first the local population looked at the Germans with sullen hostility, but as time went on relations improved. There was no fraternization, the German soldiers and officers remained strangers in Georgia, but the Georgians recognized that Germany was protecting them against the Turks and, for the time being, also against the Communists.

CIVIL WAR IN RUSSIA

In contrast to her precarious international position—open hostility on the part of the Communists in Russia, and friction with neighbors— Georgia enjoyed internal peace. The people were united around their leaders. The government was neither very efficient nor particularly bold in planning long-range reforms, but it was honest and progressive and close to the people.

North Caucasus was ablaze at that time, and sparks of the civil war reached Transcaucasia. In the spring of 1918, the Communists had a firm hold on only a part of central and northern Russia; the rest of the nation was split among local anti-Bolshevist governments and war lords. Soon after the Communist coup, a group of generals, most of whom had been involved in the Kornilov mutiny, decided to organize a Volunteer Army that would become the nucleus of the military forces of the restored Russian Empire. They started from the haven of monarchist elements of the Don region, but their call for volunteers brought only a feeble response; out of more than three hundred thousand former officers, fewer than three thousand enrolled. The "army" counted a dozen regiments, battalions, squadrons, and special units, but these were merely skeleton organizations; actually, it had no more firepower than one regular battalion. The minimum age for enrollment was sixteen years, but many younger teen-agers were lured into the adventure. Volunteers were required to sign up for four months of service, but some left before this term was up. At times, the "army's" actual strength sank to a thousand men.

Despite this modest beginning, the Volunteer Army played an important—and tragic—role in the civil war in south Russia. Wherever it went, it forced the people to choose between Tsarist and Red despotism, and the final result of its operations was to restore to the Bolsheviks the moral prestige they had lost after the dispersion of the Constituent Assembly and the Brest-Litovsk treaty. The strength of the Volunteer Army lay in its superb military organization, the fighting spirit of its original cadres, and the people's hatred of the Communists. Its weakness was the political blindness of its leaders, their stubborn attempt to wipe out the revolution and bring back the old regime.

At the beginning of 1918, Russia also had other anti-Communist armed forces: the Polish legion in the north, the Czech legion in the south, the Ukrainian divisions and the Cossack regiments on the Don and the Kuban, in the Urals and in Siberia. Together they might have crushed the armies of the People's Commissars, but they never joined forces.

In January, 1919, the Communists launched an offensive against the Don. Many Cossacks declared themselves neutral, a few joined the Communists, a handful enrolled in the Volunteer Army. Village after village and town after town fell into the hands of the Reds. The Communists used ruthless terror to suppress resistance. Thousands of prisoners, including the wounded in hospitals, were tortured and killed. The Volunteers retaliated by public mass executions. In February, Communists occupied the Don region. The Volunteer Army—then four thousand men under the command of Kornilov and the political leadership of Alexeev—began to retreat south, toward the North Caucasus. Kornilov's long career was ended by a shell, and General Denikin, his successor, led what was left of his troops into the steppes at the foot of the Caucasian ridge. Meanwhile Cossack villages that had declared themselves neutral took up arms against the Reds. The anti-Communist movement spread from the North Caucasus north-

ward to the Don. The Communists, in their turn, received heavy reinforcements. The region became the main theater of the civil war and
the scene of unbelievable atrocities.

Tiflis was full of refugees. We did not know which of their gruesome
stories to believe. Then we met one eyewitness whom we had to trust.
One evening someone knocked at our door. The visitor was a very
tall, broad-shouldered man in a Caucasian Cossack uniform, with a
colonel's shoulder straps and a high gray fur cap. Standing on the
threshold, he saluted smartly. "May I enter, Mr. Commissar?" I
could not remember having seen him before. "Colonel Artifaxov," he
introduced himself. "The 54th Armored Division, the Twelfth Army,
now liaison officer of the Volunteer Army, reports on the special assignment received in Gatchina."

Now I recognized him. My first day in Gatchina, the trains with
the armored division had been stopped by the Reds some twenty
miles from Gatchina and the echelon forced to unload. Major Artifaxov, sent to Gatchina for reconnaissance, came to Krasnov's headquarters. He believed he could bring the division to Gatchina by detour roads. I provided him with a road map and necessary papers.
When Artifaxov returned to his outfit, however, the officers had been
arrested and the tanks put out of commission. He was seized by the
Reds but escaped, thanks to his exceptional physical strength. Later
he joined the Volunteer Army. Because of his command of Caucasian
languages—his wife was a Georgian—he was picked for a special mission to Tiflis. He chanced to hear I was there, and he came to report.

We sat at the table and had tea together; a soldier proud of his
army and its chiefs, he told us about the Volunteers' marches and
battles. Then his face became grim and he said with visible effort, "I
know you do not see many things as we in the army do. That is why I
want to ask you something, with your permission." I listened silently.
"We took a village. The Reds fled. I came to the church. Its door
stood wide open. I went in. In front of the altar lay dead men, their
skulls shattered by butts, their brains blown out. Among them was the
priest, an old man in a black cassock. The door of the altar was broken
to bits. The altar itself was filthy and stinking; it had been used as a
privy. Is this not a sacrilege?"

I nodded. He went on looking past me, as if speaking to himself. "A
sacrilege! But across the green, in front of the church, was the house of
the village council. A man had been nailed to the boards of the fence.
Naked, dead, his hands and feet pierced by nails, as if crucified. His
toes charred. The remains of a fire on the ground beneath him. And
over his head a board with a single word scribbled in large letters:
'Commie.' Our men had done that. Russian, Christian men! Is that
not also a sacrilege? What hope is left to us? . . ."

I had no answer.

By the beginning of May, the Communists had been thrown out of a large part of the Ukraine, the Don, Kuban, and North Caucasus, but political conditions in the area remained chaotic. Each local government acted for itself. Their armed forces were poorly organized, little more than gangs of guerrilla fighters. The Volunteer Army had not increased much. It continued to be hated by the local population, as deeply hated as the Reds. Even the local anti-Communist governments did not trust it. They gave it lukewarm support as a military ally in the fight against the Communists but firmly refused its command the right to speak in the name of the Russian people.

Internal conflicts and tensions in Georgia, however, seemed mild in comparison with the tragic developments in Russia.

ABBAS TUMANI

Tiflis was wonderful in spring but lay prostrate in suffocating heat in summer. Jordania advised Emma and me to go with him for a week or two to Abbas Tumani, a tiny resort in the highlands, in the western corner of Georgia. A tuberculous Grand Duke had established his residence there, and for a decade or more only his personal guests were admitted to the place. After the revolution, the Transcaucasian government decided to convert the abandoned ducal mansion into a resthouse. The place, however, was too close to the settlement of the Adzhars, a warlike Moslem tribe that did not recognize the Georgian Republic, and our Georgian friends warned Jordania and us to keep away from this hornets' nest. But Jordania thought differently.

"The Adzhars never strike without reason," he said. "If we should arrive with guards and baggage, they would have reason to attack us. But if we have neither weapons nor valuables, why would they?" This sounded plausible, and we decided to go.

The road from the railroad station ran in long zigzags along a heavily forested slope. Not a single house for more than a hundred miles. Tall pines and firs replaced the magnolias of the lowlands, but the forest remained so thick that one could not see either the valley on one side of the road or the peaks on the other. Here and there the forest wall was cut by narrow clearings that looked like gates into another world, but trees blocked the far view.

Abbas Tumani, perched on a level green alp, had a fascinating view over a borderless ocean of virgin forest. The air was fragrant and fresh. The old caretaker showed us the estate. It had two substantial two-story frame buildings, each encircled by balconies. One had been designed for the Grand Duke and his guests; the other, for the staff, servants, and guards. The main houses were surrounded by outbuildings—barns, stables, a kitchen, greenhouse, and the like. The Adzhars had looted the main houses at the beginning of the revolution and carried away furniture, pictures, curtains, rugs, linen, silver and china, even windowframes and doors, but left the library, kitchen, and greenhouse untouched. The windows and doors of the mansion had been boarded up for protection against winter snow, while the other house had been refurnished with military cots and unpainted tables and chairs.

I discovered a tiny clearing surrounded by firs not far from the mansion and spent my days there, lying on the grass and trying to keep my thoughts from the revolution of 1917.[2]

One day a horseman emerged from the dense forest. He carried a rifle, a dagger, and a saber, and a band of cartridges encircled his body twice. He dismounted and asked to see the chief. Brought to Jordania, he respectfully told him that the Adzhar princes wished to pay him a visit. Jordania replied he would be glad to see them the next morning.

The princes came at the agreed time—four majestic, gray-bearded men in long robes glittering with silver, with elaborately ornate daggers at their belts and sparkling cartridge pockets on their breasts. Jordania received them at a table set for the occasion in the shade of a walnut tree, in front of the looted mansion. Wine was served. After a long and very quiet conversation, Jordania led his guests to the mansion and took them around the estate. Then conversation was resumed under the tree. An hour later the guests left, bowing respectfully before the President of the Georgian Republic.

Jordania was beaming. I asked him about the discussion.

"First, they told me that this place belonged to the Adzhars and offered their protection," said Jordania. "I thanked them and said we felt safe here and needed no protection. Then they asked if I had enough guards and arms, and I explained that I had no guard in Tiflis, where all people are decent, and needed none at this place, because the Adzhars are known the world over for their honesty, love of peace, valor, and respect for strangers. Then I offered to show them the estate. When they saw my room, they became ashamed of its shabby furniture and offered to return some armchairs taken from the mansion. I said I did not need any. They replied that neither did they need those things; they had taken them only for safekeeping. You see, the Adzhars will never rob you unless you have valuables or weapons."

[2] The booklet I wrote was later published, and I went back to it in writing Part V of these memoirs.

THE ELDERS OF TWO NATIONS MEET

The mountains on both sides of the central part of the Caucasian range were inhabited by Ossets, descendants of a Samaritan tribe— some eighty or a hundred thousand on the southern slope and twice as many on the northern. Their villages, like fortresses, dominated the passes along both the highways that linked Georgia with North Caucasus. In the summer of 1918 the passes were closed to traffic because of frequent holdups on the highways.

At the beginning of the revolution the Ossets had elected a National Council that became their government. Its emissaries appeared in Tiflis to offer the services of their men to patrol the highway crossing their land, asking for flour, sugar, and gunpowder as security pay. The Georgian government held endless conferences with them, trying to persuade the Ossets on the southern slope to join the Georgian Republic as an autonomous, self-governing province. If their chieftains declined this arrangement, the Georgians would like to see Ossetia as a formally independent republic bound to Georgia by a treaty of peace and friendship. The Ossets dragged the negotiations along. They were reluctant to commit themselves until the status of North Caucasus became clearer.

At last an Ossetian delegation told the Georgians that their elders wanted to meet with the elders of Georgia. It was agreed that Tseretelli and two members of the government would conduct the negotiations, but it was difficult to decide where to hold the convention. Some sixty chieftains were supposed to attend, and Ossetia had no house, no school, and no church large enough to accommodate such a crowd. The Georgians suggested any one of their towns near Ossetia's border. The offer was politely declined. Some of the chieftains suspected of highway robbery refused to come. Finally it was decided to meet under the open sky, beside an old church on the Tiflis-Vladikavkaz highway. Tseretelli invited Emma and me to cover the meeting for *Bor'ba*.

The Georgian delegation went to the convention in two cars with a convoy of fifty horsemen. The officer in command of the convoy explained to me that we had to have a guard of a proper size. If the guard were too small, the Ossets might consider that the delegates were not very important people. On the other hand, if our guard were too large, they might become suspicious. Considering that some chieftains were venerable old men and would not participate in a brawl if one developed, the convoy must be less numerous than that of the Ossetian delegation. The modest size of our guard would show the Ossets that the Georgians were not afraid of them. Yet, to be on the safe side, the officer intended to deploy his force in such a way as to keep the chieftains guessing how strong we were: he would put two horsemen at the scene of the meeting; two, half a mile away, on the edge of the meadow; and the rest along the highway, at intervals of a half mile between the posts. I told him that even Napoleon could not have thought up a better disposition of troops.

The old church, built of rough stone, was on a knoll half a mile from the road, under a solitary old oak. The meadow sloped smoothly from rugged rocks at the north down to a thick forest. We arrived a little ahead of time. Two or three men were sunning themselves in front of the locked door of the church, their horses tied to the rings in its walls. They did not look in our direction. Then horsemen began to arrive, singly or in small groups, from all points of the horizon, all in native garb, heavily armed, on beautiful horses. They dismounted before the church, greeted us with dignity, tied their horses to the tree or the rings, and sat down cross-legged on the ground not far from us. More and more horsemen appeared on the meadow. Some of the old men came with a youth or two who took care of their horses and stood behind them when they sat down on the ground. The Georgian delegation, a dozen civilians, looked humble in comparison with the elders of the Ossetian nation.

When all were assembled, one of the old men made a sign and the assembly came to order. The elders formed a broad circle, sitting cross-legged, each holding his gun in his lap; the younger men stood around, leaning on their rifles. About one fourth of the circle was left open for the Georgian delegation. The old church and the lonely oak with the horses tied to its hanging branches formed an impressive background.

Then the same old man opened the discussion. He spoke slowly, without expression on the deeply tanned face almost hidden behind a full beard that began just below his eyes and descended to the hilt of his dagger. His speech sounded like the bubbling of a stream. A Georgian who sat at my side whispered a translation.

"They welcome us. . . . This is the land of their forefathers . . . since creation of the earth. . . . Georgians and Russians came later . . . took their land . . . built cities and roads. . . . They wish no part in the new things. . . . We have closed the highway. . . . The Russians have desecrated the mosques. . . . They rely on God and the valor of their sons. . . . They love us . . . wish to listen to us. . . ."

Tseretelli followed this speech through an interpreter, then replied in Georgian. Unaccustomed to speaking cross-legged, he stood up but talked in the same monotonous vein as the old man. His speech was translated, sentence after sentence, into Ossetian. It was impossible to determine whether the elders were impressed or not. Their faces seemed to be carved out of stone.

Others spoke in the same noncommittal way as the first old man, repeating that they wished their neighbors to trust them and be their friends. But, above all, they needed flour, sugar, and gunpowder. As long as there was plenty of traffic on the highway, they had everything in abundance. Why then did the Georgians and Russians close the road?

One of the Georgian delegates pointed out that traffic had stopped because of frequent holdups. The Ossetian delegates disagreed. "When there is enough traffic, there is enough money in our land," they said. "Everybody is happy. No robbery. When traffic stops, there is no money. People starve. Then they take what the Almighty sends them."

The convention was futile. The Ossets had no intention of reaching an agreement with Georgia. They only wished to show the Georgians how sensible they were. They aired their grievances but pressed no particular point.

In comparison with Ossetia, the Georgian Republic was the big brother. Yet the Georgians played the game with patience, as the Homeric setting demanded.

Before dusk the convention broke up. A Georgian spokesman had finished his speech. The Ossets sat silent. Then the elders began to stand up, bowed to the Georgian delegation, and went to their horses.

We walked to our cars. As the cars proceeded southward, our convoy fell in gradually behind us, two horsemen at a time.

RUSSIA'S LAST HOPE OF DEMOCRACY
IS CRUSHED

In August, 1918, the Volunteers appeared at Tuapse and, moving along the Black Sea, reached the Georgian border where they met troops of that republic. There were about three thousand men on each side. A dispute about the border district, an area with a population of some two hundred thousand, where the native population had decided to join Georgia against the protest of Russian landowners, supplied the Volunteers a pretext for attacking the Georgian troops. The main force of the Volunteers, however, was tied up in the north. The Volunteers and the Georgians continued to face each other until the end of the year. In January, 1919, the Volunteer Army launched an offensive. In April, the Georgians counterattacked. The struggle went on, with vacillating success. Thus Georgia found herself in open war against the Volunteer Army while at the same time irreconcilably opposed to the Communist government of Russia.

In the summer of 1918, it seemed for a brief period that a free and democratic Russia might emerge out of the chaos of civil war. This hope had been kindled in democratic circles by the movement of the Czech legion, a military outfit organized before the March revolution by the Tsarist government through enrollment of volunteers among Austrian war prisoners. The organization was planned as a liberation army to support the Czechs in a revolt against Austrian rule. Politically, it was under the control of the Czech National Council headed by Masaryk, with headquarters in Paris. Before the November coup, the legion was transformed into an army corps and billeted in the Ukraine. After the Brest-Litovsk treaty, the Czech National Council decided to evacuate it from Russia to France by sea, via Vladivostok. The corps had some forty thousand men when it started its march eastward but increased to perhaps sixty thousand by enrollment of volunteers, mainly also Czech war prisoners. It proceeded with its munitions and other equipment in about a hundred trains, fanning out over the railroads in eastern Russia.

In May, the German Military Command demanded that the People's Commissars stop the Czechs, and Trotsky, People's Commissar for Military Affairs, ordered them to surrender their arms. The Czechs agreed on condition that each train would keep 150 rifles and a few machine guns for self-defense and that the echelons would be permitted to proceed to the Pacific coast. Then Trotsky ordered Russian troops to stop the Czech trains and shoot every armed Czech on sight. The legion had no choice but to fight its way. By that time, a few Czech echelons had reached Vladivostok; others were still on the Volga, while the bulk of the corps was scattered between the Urals and the Pacific coast—nearly twice the distance from New York to San Francisco.

In clashes between the Czechs and the Reds, the Czechs invariably had the upper hand. And as soon as they disarmed a Red garrison, the local population would overthrow the Communist-dominated Soviet and elect a new government. On June 21, the Czechs took Samara on the Volga after a fierce fight with the Communist garrison, and the civilian power in the city was taken over by the Committee of the Constituent Assembly, dominated by the S-R. In a few weeks the Samara government raised an army of thirty thousand men.

The Allied governments were impressed by the success of the anti-Communist popular movement. It seemed to open new perspectives: could the Allies restore the former Russian front, with the Volga as its base?

Like the eastbound march of the Czechs, the new project was not an attempt to liberate the Russian people, but a purely strategic move, subordinated to the plans for the French-German front. In preparation for the Second Front, the Allied High Command ordered the Czech corps to stop its eastward movement and redeploy along the Volga.

In September, a conference of members of the Constituent Assembly, the Samara government, the Siberian government (Omsk), Cossack regional governments, and various political organizations met in Ufa to lay the foundation of an All-Russian government. Politically, the members of the conference ranged from the S-R to stout reactionary Cossack atamans. It was not easy for such a motley gathering to reach agreement, but finally a solution was found. Executive power would be held by a Directorate of five members responsible to the Constituent Assembly, purged of the Communists and their sympathizers. The Assembly was to convene on January 1, 1919.[3]

The Directorate included two S-R, two Cadets, and General Boldyrev, serving as a military man without party affiliation. This group seemed to have a chance to unite anti-Communist forces all over Russia. Many Russian officers stranded in Tiflis left for North Caucasus in the hope of finding their way to Siberia. But Ufa also became the rallying point for reactionary adventurers. The city was crowded with groups hostile to the Directorate. Cossack atamans brought their gangsters nearer the seat of the government. Monarchists infiltrated the military units. The anti-democratic forces around the Directorate found their leader in the person of Admiral Kolchak, former commander of the Black Sea fleet. By appointing him War Minister, the Directorate had signed its own death sentence.

On November 10, Cossack officers kidnaped the S-R members of the Directorate and left-wing members of the government. The right-wing ministers then declared the Directorate deposed and proclaimed Kolchak the Supreme Ruler of Russia. Two weeks later, members of the Constituent Assembly and ranking civilian officials of the Directorate loyal to the Assembly were arrested. A revolt of workers broke out in Omsk, and Kolchak used the occasion for a summary execution of all political prisoners in his hands. Some were shot, others run through by sabers. Several friends with whom I had shared exile in Siberia and worked in the Tauride Palace were among the victims.

The democratic forces of Ufa were no more. Now the Tsarist extremists alone opposed the Communists: the ill-fated Volunteer Army in the south, Kolchak in Siberia, Cossack war lords in the Urals and the Far East. Without the support of local populations, all these troops were bound to degenerate into armed gangsters. In the sum-

---

[3] A quorum of 260 members was to be necessary to validate decisions of the Assembly. If such a quorum was not at hand, the convocation of the Assembly would be postponed until February, when a quorum of 170 would suffice.

mer of 1919, Kolchak was forced to retreat behind the Urals. Amid revolts of workers, peasants, and his own regiments, he fell back along the Trans-Siberian Railroad. In November, the Czechs refused to support him, and early in 1920 they turned him in to the military revolutionary—non-Communist—committee of Irkutsk workers, who shot him after a trial.

There was a tragic similarity between the fates of Kolchak and Kornilov. While both believed they were fighting Communism, Kornilov actually paved Lenin's way to power and Kolchak broke the people's revolt against the Communist yoke.

GEORGIA AFTER THE END OF WORLD WAR I

News of the Allied victory reached us suddenly in Tiflis. We knew of the failure of Ludendorff's offensive in the summer of 1918 and the success of the French counteroffensive on the Marne. We also knew that fresh troops from the United States had reached France, but the general situation on the European front was not clear. The capitulation of Bulgaria in September, 1918, was the first sign of the doom of the Central Powers. Then came the big news: the Germans had given up.

German headquarters in Tiflis seemed deserted. Not a man appeared at the windows. When Ebert, the leader of the German S-D party, succeeded Prince Max as Chancellor, the Germans in Tiflis did not try to ingratiate themselves with the Georgian Socialists. They left Tiflis quietly, following an order from Berlin, and surrendered their arms to the British naval units in Batum.

Before Christmas the British took their place in Tiflis—a military mission with the escort of a Scottish company. The colonel, head of the mission, was a big man with a reddish face and blond mustache. Immediately after his arrival, he sent an orderly across the street to the Government Palace to announce that he wanted to see the head of the local government. The orderly brought back the answer that the President of the Republic would receive him the next morning. The colonel arrived with his aide and a Russian interpreter. He told Jordania that he had been sent to Georgia to maintain order, assure regular operation of the railroad, and supervise the evacuation of the German and Turkish forces. If his orders were not executed or his men were molested, he would hold the local government responsible.

Jordania quietly replied, "Colonel, I must brief you about our country. This is an independent land. We were not at war with your country and you are here not as a conqueror, but as a guest. I had expected you would show some sign of appreciation of the honor of being received by the head of state. I would have offered you hospitality and friendship and have asked you what I could do for you. This would have given you an opportunity to talk about the railroad and whatever else you had in mind. Would not this have been a proper procedure between civilized people?" The colonel wheeled and left the room. The Georgians were proud of their President but they felt a little uneasy. Was this the right way to talk to the representative of a great power?

Two hours later a British officer appeared at the palace with a letter. The colonel, as the commanding officer of the British detail to be stationed in Tiflis, informed the President of the Republic of his arrival and requested the honor of a personal audience. This time the colonel was exquisitely polite. He talked with Jordania and members of the government about his mission and the political and military situation in Europe and asked them about their country. After the audience, shaking hands with Jordania, he remarked casually that he would appreciate it if the President forgot his first appearance at the palace. Jordania slapped him on the shoulder and assured him it was forgotten.

The British established friendly relations with the government, but the common people in Tiflis could not reconcile themselves to the Scottish uniform. I heard some old Georgians express their deep disapproval. No self-respecting man would wear woman's garb, and what could one say of soldiers who ran around without trousers, in girls' skirts?

The end of the war did not bring peace and security to Georgia. The threat of Russia was becoming more and more real. The future of Georgia as an independent nation seemed to depend on her recognition by the Peace Conference in Paris, which proposed to redraw the map of Europe and the Middle East. Georgia was a minor pawn in the global game, but she counted on the Allies' announced stand on self-determination of peoples and on her own record of self-government. Most of all, Georgia counted on the support of public opinion among European liberals and moderate Socialists.

Through the British mission, the Georgians obtained permission to present their case to the Allied Supreme Council, the Big Four. Chkheidze and Tseretelli were named to head the delegation, which also included representatives of other political parties in Georgia. Anticipating that Communist sympathizers and Russian reactionaries would oppose Georgia's demand for recognition of her independence and assail her for her pact with Germany, the Georgian government decided to present the Conference with a well-documented record of its foreign policy. Chkheidze asked me whether such a memorandum could be prepared in two weeks. I thought that Emma and I could do it if we had access to all the files of the Department of Foreign Affairs and sufficient clerical help and no delay in the printing.

I worked on the files, reading, sorting, and grouping the documents. Emma supervised the processing of the material and the printing. We went over several thousand documents and selected 261. Not a single item of importance was withheld because of its secret character, and not a single word was changed or deleted in the records. Arranged in fourteen chapters, the documents gave a graphic picture of the road Georgia had traveled since the November coup in Petrograd. The book, of more than five hundred printed pages, was in Chkheidze's hands ten days after the project was launched. An expert eye would discern the difference in the types used by the three printing houses that set the text, but, apart from this and a few typographical errors, our *Documents and Materials on the Foreign Policy of Transcaucasia and Georgia* was a respectable job. It was a major influence on Jordania's decision that we should go abroad with the delegation.

Chkheidze and Tseretelli left for Paris early in February, 1919. The rest of the delegation was delayed a few days by visa formalities and got only as far as Constantinople (Istanbul), where the Inter-Allied Police decided that we would not be welcome at the Peace Conference. Days grew into weeks, weeks into months. Emma and I were ready to return to Tiflis, but Chkheidze asked us to wait while he tried to get visas for us directly from the French government.

We spent our time studying economic conditions in postwar Europe and preparing a book on Georgia, which was later published in Italian and French. Our observations of new economic trends resulted in a series of articles in *Bor'ba* and a practical suggestion to our friends in the Tiflis government—to cultivate economic relations with Italy in preference to Great Britain and France. We thought that Italy, because of her scarcity of raw materials and lack of colonies, would deal with Georgia as a partner rather than treat her as a vassal.

After four months of red tape, the Ministry of Foreign Affairs in Paris informed the Constantinople authorities that we could not enter France. We returned to Batum in July, 1919, aboard a British destroyer. Jordania and other Georgian friends thought that our trip abroad had not been futile; it had produced the "Italian project."

In our absence the situation in Georgia had worsened. The republic's finances were in poor shape. Taxes were not collected, the government relying mainly on the printing press. Georgian bonds were losing value. In addition, Georgia was practically blockaded. It had no fleet to export its manganese, and Batum, now restored to Georgia, was a dead city. There was no mass unemployment among Georgian workers, but Tiflis was full of refugees from Russia with no means of existence. Black markets developed in all important goods: leather, fabrics, metal, flour, sugar. Moreover, relations among the Armenians, Georgians, and Moslems deteriorated. Armed clashes occurred along the borders of the three republics.

In January, 1920, the Supreme Council of the Allies recognized the independence *de facto* of the three Transcaucasian republics. This was only a partial success, however, and would not keep the Volunteer Army and the Communists from overrunning Transcaucasia. Yet, despite their domestic and international difficulties, the Georgians remained cheerful and devoted to their government, seeking comfort in comparing conditions in their country with those in other parts of the former Russian Empire—civil war, pogroms, famine, terror.

Soon after our return to Georgia, an Italian mission arrived in Tiflis. It consisted of a tall, well-groomed major and a short, stocky lieutenant. The major presented the compliments of his government to Jordania, expressed Italy's desire to establish diplomatic and commercial relations with Georgia, and offered his services in accompanying a Georgian mission to Rome. The government decided to send a mission that was a combination of a diplomatic delegation and an exploratory economic expedition. An amiable young man, a graduate of the Sorbonne, was named Georgia's diplomatic representative and head of the mission. The economic work was entrusted to a Georgian oilman and myself; Emma was charged with information and press relations. We left Tiflis at the end of August, followed by the good wishes of our friends and companions.

ALLAH VERDI

The people, customs, and scenery of Georgia have remained deeply etched in my memory, not only as the last impressions of Russia I took with me on my further wanderings, but also because of their particular charm. Before turning this page of my life, I want to record a glimpse into the wilderness of this hospitable land.

. . . The mayor of Telav invited us to visit his place. "Telav is not much of a city," he said modestly, "but you must see it if you want to know Georgia. And then we would go to Allah Verdi together."

"What is Allah Verdi?" I asked him.

"An old church, a shrine, a fortress. Far away in the mountains. Its annual festival is wonderful."

We agreed we would go to Telav by train two days before the festival, and he would arrange for a conveyance to take us to the mountains.

Only the central part of Telav looked like a town. Dusty cobbled streets ended a few blocks from the railroad station. Beyond them were vineyards and orchards, with cottages of rough stone hidden among the trees and bushes, a maze of winding country roads and footpaths, tiny patches of land, tiny fields studded with flowers, flooded with sun, slumbering in luxurious laziness.

The mayor showed us his bachelor's house, then took us to see some of his friends. Each treated us to homemade wine and showed us his vineyard and garden. Everyone talked of local affairs and world politics. The World War would end in a universal peace; all peoples would disarm, recognizing the futility of wars; Communism in Russia would disappear. I felt the optimism of these people came from the blue sky and balmy air. Drowsy from endless talk, wine, and sun, we went to bed in the mayor's house. Next morning we got up early, but our host told us that the horses were not ready and that some more people wanted to meet us. Why should we start before lunch? After lunch, he suggested a rest. Life was leisurely indeed in that land!

The road by which we traveled crossed a broad valley, climbed hills, plunged into another valley, and rose again, crossing fields and stretches of woods. We stopped overnight at the house of a distant cousin of the mayor. The house, built in the seventeenth century, was a cube-shaped structure of rough stone. It had two stories and an open porch —a modern addition. The windows on the ground floor looked like loopholes for rifles. The only door was narrow and flanked by buttresses designed for its defense. This had once been a feudal castle, but little remained of its ancient splendor. Its owner claimed the title of prince but tilled his vineyards and fields with his own hands. He was a husky man, slow-moving and taciturn. A bachelor, he lived with his mother, a small frail lady with manners appropriate to an imaginary court. Inside, the house was bare and shabby, but the family had preserved its coat of arms and a beautiful dagger in a silver scabbard. At table we talked politics. Our host did not care for a republican government in Georgia: "Why a republic when the people could have chosen a worthy ruler among a dozen old royal families?"

We left the mansion early in the morning. The road wound upward among the hills. We passed people walking in the same direction in small groups, two or three families together. Some were dragging a sheep or a goat. We passed carts drawn by nondescript mares. Horsemen overtook us, some of them poorly clothed but mounted on beautiful chargers.

It was after dusk when we neared our destination. The road passed through a thick forest. From afar came tunes of plaintive songs and oriental string music. Then campfires appeared among the trees. The music became louder—the whole forest seemed to be singing with a thousand voices. Perhaps these sounds would have impressed a more musical ear as sheer cacophony, but to me they harmonized marvelously with the star-studded sky and the pitch-dark forest spangled with sparks of fires.

We crossed an immense camp. People were sitting around the fires, roasting meat over glowing charcoal, drinking wine, and singing. They drank from wineskins as in the time of Homer. As long as the bag was full, it produced a red or amber jet at a slight pressure, but we also saw a man press the wineskin under his knees to extract its last drop of liquid. And we saw an old man showing some youths how their forefathers used to drink. He was tall and stout, with snow-white hair and a full beard, and wore a long Caucasian robe with a silver belt and two strings of cartridges on his breast. He lifted the wineskin, containing perhaps two gallons of wine, high above his head and pressed it expertly so that the red jet ran directly into his open mouth, without loss of a single drop. To judge from the rapturous expression on the spectators' faces, this must have been a difficult trick.

Finally we reached the monastery. The church, more than five hundred years old, was built like the keep of a medieval castle—a square tower with loopholes for archers. Its spire was crowned by a cross. The building was all white or looked so in the light of the hundreds of campfires around it. The wall encircling it, also white, was more than fifteen feet high. Roofs of buildings inside the enclosure could be seen above the wall. A towerlike structure guarded the entrance.

We were knocking at the gate of an enchanted castle in an enchanted forest. Georgian kings of olden times, warlike and pious, had erected it as a stronghold of Christianity for the missionaries who preached the Gospel among the Moslem mountaineers and for the troops guarding the frontier. Here lay the boundary between the Christian kingdom in the lowlands and the tribes settled further to the north in inaccessible canyons. And it became the custom for both highlanders and lowlanders to assemble once a year around the cloister for a feast of peace and brotherhood. The Christian monastery had received a Moslem name and preserved it through the centuries, outliving the old kingdoms. The mayor did not know to what Christian saint the church had been dedicated or what the religious name of the monastery was; since childhood he had known this place only as Allah Verdi.

A bearded monk greeted us at the entrance. The mayor asked him for a room in the monastery guesthouse for us, his friends from Tiflis.

"All the rooms are gone, brother," answered the monk. "We have twenty persons to a room. Not an inch left." But he rushed to report our arrival to the Father Superior. We waited at the gate in the circle of fires, deafened by thousands of voices and the clangor of unknown musical instruments. Strange shadows moved through firelight, slender men with glittering daggers, women wrapped in black shawls, knights and maidens from an oriental fairytale. Then the Father Superior came to the gate. We were welcomed to the monastery. The guests spread on the floor of a large bare room were squeezed together a bit, and we received an armful of fragrant hay as sleeping accommodation.

In the morning the monks gave us tea with black bread and honey. Everything looked different in the daylight, not as mysterious as at night, more cheerful and friendly—the majestic old Byzantine church, the crowded fair in the immense enclosure, the thick forest around and the rugged peaks above. . . .

A stream of men and women, young and old, was moving into the church, entering through the main arch and leaving through a side door. Nobody stopped inside to pray or listen to the service; their purpose was only to leave a gift for the monastery and light a candle before an icon. The mayor explained that this was an old custom faithfully observed by both the Christians and Moslems of the region. Cash donations were few. The faithful were carrying produce —a sack of potatoes, a bundle of carrots, a chunk of cheese, or a quarter of a sheep. We joined the line. A counter was set under the vault of the dark, cool anteroom at the entrance. Two monks were accepting the gifts, sorting them and throwing them over their shoulders onto the heaps behind them—vegetables, cheese, meat.

For most people the festival and the fair were chiefly an occasion for meeting friends, but some business was transacted. Men from the highlands brought sheep, colts, homespun woolen fabrics; a few had brought valuable daggers and silver belts, heirlooms from their fore-fathers. Those from the lowlands had cows tied to their carts, flour, wine in wineskins, sugar, gunpowder. They did not know much about the rates of exchange between Tsarist rubles and the paper money of the Provisional Government, or between the Transcaucasian and Georgian bonds. To barter a dagger for a cow seemed simpler. Another obvious advantage of barter was that a single transaction could be stretched over a whole day, with some twenty men bargaining on each side.

At noon the space around the monastery walls was cleared of carts and campfires for a contest of horsemen. Mounted youths whirled around with shrill whoops. They looked skillful and spirited to us, but the old-timers were disappointed: the performance was not as good as before the war. Next dancing began, but without a contest of skill—there were too many tribes, each with its own tunes and customs. People preferred to sing and dance among themselves, in small groups.

Before dusk the noise began to subside. The crowd became thinner; people were quietly fading away, to return home by footpaths and trails in the forest. Campfires still glowed around the monastery, people were still drinking, singing, and dancing, and groups of youths strolled from one fire to another. But the old monastery and the eternal forest were falling back into a slumber that would last another year, until the next annual feast of Allah Verdi.

The mayor, Emma, and I stood on the balcony of the monastery guesthouse, looking into the night, listening to the distant voices and tunes, fascinated by what we had seen and heard—an outburst of timeless happiness and friendliness of the people.

A STOP AT CONSTANTINOPLE

On the way from Tiflis to Batum we thought of our first trip from Batum to Tiflis, in the spring of 1918. How eventful the intervening two and a half years had been! We cherished the new friendships and experiences, the trust of our new Georgian friends, and hoped we would come up to their expectations. Personally, we were in better shape than after the ordeal of 1917—rested, relaxed, and closer to each other.

An Italian ship waited for us in Batum. From its deck we looked at the city, half hidden behind blossoming trees and surrounded by verdant mountains. We had no premonition that this was to be our last glimpse of Georgian—and Russian—soil.

The ship stopped at Constantinople and anchored in the middle of the Straits. Passengers were permitted to go ashore for three or four hours. We took a walk in the city and returned to the ship an hour before the time set for departure. A young man in Turkish uniform, a fez on his head, stopped me at the gangway and asked in French, "Are you Mr. Woytinsky?"

"Yes. Who are you?"

He showed me his badge and a card identifying him as an officer of the Inter-Allied Police. "I have an order to search your luggage."

The Italian major, whom I called in as a witness, protested, but the police officer showed a second warrant, to detain me. In our stateroom the sleuth opened one suitcase after another but did not touch anything until he saw a batch of issues of *Bor'ba*.

"You know this newspaper?" he asked me.

"Of course. I am its chief editor."

He took the bundle and asked us to go with him to the Inter-Allied Police station. The Italian major accompanied us. The station was a few blocks from the waterfront. A French officer led us to the private office of the police chief. Emma and I waited in the hall while the major disappeared behind an opaque glass partition. We heard him shouting, "This is an outrage! Do you think you can prevent His Majesty's government from dealing with other countries as it pleases?"

Then another unmistakably French voice: "But, monsieur, be reasonable! This newspaper . . ."

And the major shouting again, "Nonsense! This is the official organ of the Georgian government."

And then again the French officer: "This is a Communist paper. And the government of Georgia is a gang of Communists."

"Stop this nonsense!" roared the major. "This is going too far. I am appointed by my government to escort Mr. and Mrs. Woytinsky and their party to Rome as guests of my government. If you try to interfere with my instructions, I will immediately telephone to our ambassador and you will have diplomatic complications."

After further negotiations, the major came out with the officer who had searched our luggage. He returned the copies of *Bor'ba*, saying in purest Russian, "Keep your chattels." He was a Volunteeer Army spy.

We rushed back to the waterfront. Our steamer was not there. The major ran to the next pier and learned that the ship had changed its anchorage and was lying at the mouth of the Straits for final passenger inspection. We tried to get a boat, but the sea was rough and the boatmen refused to go out. The major asked us to wait, ran to another pier, and returned beaming. He had obtained a speedboat from the Italian navy to take us to the steamer.

We boarded the ship as the last passport formalities were nearing their end. The passengers, assembled in the main saloon, were showing their papers to three officers at the table—British, French, and Italian. Emma and I were at the very end of the line. The French officer looked at my passport and said, "You will have to go to the Inter-Allied Police station."

"I have just come back from there."

"What did they tell you?"

Before I could reply, the Italian major stepped forward and announced sternly, "They apologized. Mr. and Mrs. Woytinsky are going to Rome as members of a diplomatic mission, on the personal invitation of my government."

The Italian control officer asked for the major's credentials and returned them with a bow. He said, "The case is clear," to which the British officer added, "I concur."

The Frenchman was still not satisfied and asked me, "What will be your address in Italy?"

The major replied for me, "The Ministry of Foreign Affairs, Rome."

Being cleared by the Inter-Allied Police was not enough, however. The first-class passengers remained suspicious of us.

At Taranto, a swarm of customs and police officers appeared on the deck. Passengers were again lined up for inspection of papers. We stood at the railing and were watching the crowd on the pier when two limousines with Italian flags appeared at the shore. Our major turned to the head of our mission: "Those are for you and your party, Your Excellency."

As guests of the Italian government, we were not subject to inspection, and as we descended the gangway we were followed by the respectful glances of the first-class passengers. Our reputation had been restored.

THE EUROPEAN SCENE

After a year in Italy, our work for Georgia took us to France, Great Britain, Switzerland, and Germany. We helped the Georgian missions in these countries in establishing contacts with the press, organizing information services, preparing memoranda, and so forth. Essentially, this was journalistic work that had to be kept on a high professional level to offset the fundamental difficulties—we represented a small country actually unknown in Europe and had to defend it against formidable Soviet propaganda.

Often our work was frustrating, but it provided us with an insight into local political life and brought us into contact with many persons who played prominent roles on the political stage of postwar Europe. I do not know whether it was pure chance, but the statesmen who impressed me most belonged to the older generation, already at the decline of their political careers.

Our work for Georgia ended in 1922 after the little republic was overrun and conquered by the U.S.S.R. Then we settled in Germany. There, under the Weimar Republic, we took an active part in local politics. This was another desperate fight for a lost cause. Once again I had to learn that the worst enemy of democracy is democracy itself, with its lack of unity, nearsightedness, and inability to act at the decisive moment.

Apart from this spell of political activity, we were spectators of the historical drama of Europe rather than actors and, in contrast to the hectic days and nights in the Tauride Palace, we had plenty of time to meditate on the meaning of unfolding events.

Europe was emerging from the nightmare of the war that had ended her political and economic hegemony in the world. Three empires—German, Austro-Hungarian, and Ottoman—had been wiped off the map. The Russian Empire had raised the banner of world revolution. The foundations of the British Empire were cracking. The League of

Nations seemed a poor substitute for old-time equilibrium maintained by the balance of the strengths of the Great Powers. The new haphazard boundaries crisscrossing what had been Austria-Hungary and Turkey were so many scars on these parts of Europe and the Middle East, but the psychological wounds were deeper than new political boundaries and economic injuries. The air was full of hysterical nationalism, hatred, suspicion, and fear. New ideologies—Fascism and Communism—thrived in this poisoned air, and their struggle for the heritage of old Europe was the main theme of the historical drama.

The events that unfolded before my eyes in those years remain engraved in my memory, as a continuation and aftermath of the Russian revolution.

ITALY AFTER A FUTILE VICTORY

The immediate task of our mission in Rome was to gain the interest of the Italian government and business circles in developing Georgia's resources, especially her coal, manganese, and forests. Jordania and his friends believed that if Italy were to be the first of the European nations to start business with Georgia, she would support the claim of Georgian independence. We were racing against time to obtain an international guarantee of Georgia's independence before Russia overran Transcaucasia.

Rome revealed itself to us in all its splendor under the dazzling sun of early autumn. The crowds in the streets were cheerful and lively. Smart military uniforms with lots of decorations—battle and campaign medals, service ribbons, and insignia of all kinds—added bright colors to the crowd, but the uniformed men did not look very martial. Both the officers and men cursed the government and the parliament and accused them of cowardice, weakness, and venality. Their most hated enemies were the Socialists, but they suspected that the Liberals were not much better. The dragon's teeth planted by the war were beginning to sprout.

On the day on which the Minister of Foreign Affairs, Tittoni, had invited our mission to a reception, the newspapers carried sensational headlines. D'Annunzio, the famous bard of Italian nationalism, had led some soldiers and a crowd of armed volunteers into Fiume (Rjecka), a Croatian port across the Italian border then occupied jointly by the Allies. Italian troops and sailors in the port joined d'Annunzio's forces, proclaiming the city's annexation to Italy.

At the Ministry we were received by the Undersecretary, Count Sforza. The reception room was furnished with old tapestries, a carved mahogany table, and gilded leather armchairs—exquisite museum pieces of the sixteenth century. The handsome and distinguished Undersecretary, with his charming manner, fitted this setting. He apologized for the absence of the Minister. "We have had a busy day, you know," he explained with a smile. "This Fiume affair has upset our timetable. A trivial border incident, of course, nothing serious. Instructions have been sent to everyone concerned. Indeed, the incident has been settled already. But there are formalities, papers to sign. The Minister is unhappy that he cannot see you." And so dismissing the Fiume affair, Count Sforza turned the conversation to questions of common interest to Italy and Georgia.

The next day the President of the government, Francesco Nitti, denounced in parliament the anarchistic acts of d'Annunzio and his followers and threatened to counter them with force, but the nationalistic newspapers enthusiastically supported the coup. The most fanatic among them was the Milanese *Popolo d'Italia*, published by a former left-wing Socialist, Benito Mussolini, who combined ardent nationalism with revolutionary catchwords such as "Revolution is an idea that has bayonets," "Who has steel, has bread." His paper had not been taken seriously in political and literary circles in Rome, but in the turmoil created by the Fiume coup it rose to national prominence. Volunteers thronged to join d'Annunzio, who established himself as the head of the Italian administration in the disputed city. Under the pressure of public opinion and the military, the government recognized d'Annunzio's coup as a patriotic act.

Italy was a member of the Triple Alliance of the Central Powers when the war broke out in 1914, but the people opposed participation in the war on the side of Austria-Hungary and the Italian government declared the country neutral. Very soon, however, a strong movement developed in favor of joining the anti-German coalition. Its victory would give Italy the southern province of Austria, with its predominantly Italian population. After France and Great Britain had promised adjustments of her northern frontier, Italy declared war on Austria, but the war brought her a chain of humiliating defeats. Three times her armies started an offensive, and each time they were thrown back with heavy losses. In the fall of 1918, after Bulgaria and Turkey had asked for an armistice and the Austrian army had begun to disintegrate, the Italians attacked for the fourth time and, meeting no serious resistance, pierced the enemy's front line. After the surrender of Austria, the Italians easily persuaded themselves that they had won the war. Their national pride was deeply wounded when they discovered that the French and British did not share this notion.

Ultimately Italy obtained all that the Allies had promised and more. Indeed, in comparison with her contribution to the common victory, she got probably more than any other member of the Entente. Nevertheless, the people believed that someone had cheated them. They had joined the war on their own volition, won it at the price of two thirds of a million killed and a million wounded, had suffered many wartime privations; yet they were as poor after the war as before it. Who had robbed them of the fruits of victory? The answer was: the Allies! Opposition to the Versailles Treaty developed in Italy even before the treaty was signed. The masses of the people, disappointed by the lack of spoils of victory, turned against the government. Nitti's cabinet began to lose ground in the badly split parliament.

MUSSOLINI RIDES THE TIDE OF ANARCHY

The general elections in November, 1919, failed to clarify the political situation in Italy. The pendulum swung to the left, and the Socialists emerged as the strongest single party in parliament, followed by the Catholic People's party (*Populari*). After all the drumbeating in Milan, Mussolini got only 5,000 votes out of 350,000 cast in that city. Soon after the election, I met the Socialist leaders Turatti and Modigliani. Both were in low spirits. They complained of dissension in the party and labor unions, economic difficulties, weakness of the government.

I also met Bissolatti, the leader of the right wing of the Socialist movement. Old, with a mild, almost shy, manner and a soft voice, he impressed me as a man of great wisdom. He was deeply concerned about the political situation—no solid majority in the parliament, no unity among the people. "The parliamentary system," he said, "depends on the assumption that people are rational and that most of them will draw the same conclusions from objective facts. It cannot work when people are dominated by emotions. Since our party and the Catholics cannot agree on common action, they are bound to paralyze each other. This must lead to the collapse of the parliamentary system."

Nitti, the head of the government, was more optimistic. He believed Italy would gradually return to peacetime normalcy, and he managed somehow to keep the reins in his hands. There was no evidence of improvement, however; rather, the tide of anarchy was mounting.

Italian trains left and arrived several hours late and the stations were jammed with waiting passengers. A person planning to leave Rome for Milan on a two o'clock train would begin to inquire about the whereabouts of his train at three or four o'clock and would get a casual answer: "Five hours late." Some three hours later the answer would be "Seven hours late." Finally, the train would leave after midnight. Only once did I catch a train on time. When I asked when it would leave, the official shouted, "Hurry! There it is." It was yesterday's train, just twenty-four hours late! Other public services—postal, telegraph, and telephone—were in a similar state.

Prices were soaring; the purchasing power of the lira shrank to less than one fourth. The Socialists in parliament bitterly denounced the greed of the ruling classes. The workers demanded higher wages. A wave of strikes rolled through the country, most of them spontaneous, unauthorized by the unions. Many walkouts were accompanied by street demonstrations, inflammatory speeches, occasional violence. More often than not the strikers went back to work under the previous conditions, cursing their leaders. After each unsuccessful walkout, the newspapers reported that union cards were thrown into the gutters. One governmental crisis followed another, and each new government was weaker than the preceding. In the summer of 1920, Giolitti, the great elder statesman, succeeded Nitti, but the political situation remained as precarious as before.

As the strikes became more and more violent, bands of Mussolini's Black Shirts appeared on the scene as volunteer strikebreakers and vigilantes. I saw them at work during a streetcar strike in Rome. This wildcat walkout had caused considerable discomfort to the public, and the latter had no sympathy with the workers. The Fascist papers called on patriotic Italians to put an end to the strike. The government called on loyal citizens to maintain order. The streets were full of excited crowds. Impromptu meetings were held at corners, before governmental and Fascist posters. Along the main street I saw a procession led by two police officers in glittering uniforms, with red feathers on their hats. The procession consisted of some eighty or a hundred men, mostly captive uniformed streetcar motormen, surrounded by a cordon of youths in Fascist black shirts and flanked by small groups of other black-shirted youngsters, shouting, "Long live Italy! Long live Mussolini!" Some of them carried sticks.

People on the sidewalks greeted the procession by raising their arms in a Fascist salute. Then two men who stood next to me jumped to the middle of the street, broke through the black-shirted convoy, and slapped the prisoners' faces. A few others from the opposite sidewalk followed their example. The procession halted. The prisoners did not defend themselves but only screamed and cursed. The crowd shouted, "Long live the King! Death to the traitors!" The next day the strikers had returned to work.

Late in the summer, the metalworkers walked out in Milan. The management responded with a lockout in all the iron and steel mills in that area. The strikers occupied the mills to keep the strikebreakers away. Then the manufacturers closed all the metal mills in Italy. The workers seized more plants. The Socialist leaders were disturbed by the outbreak and neither supported nor opposed it. In several places the movement fell into the hands of the Anarchists. In some occupied mills the workers resumed operations and marketed their output, with the understanding the proceeds would be distributed among the strikers. In many places armed Red guards were organized to defend the mills against the police or a Fascist assault. There was plenty of fist-swinging, but casualties were few. The newspapers demanded that the government take drastic measures. Mussolini offered the services of his Black Shirts to restore order. The Ministry of Labor urged the workers entrenched in the mills to vacate them.

After the attempt to operate the mills failed, the movement began to subside. The plants were restored to their owners. The government prided itself on having settled the crisis without bloodshed, but this incident became the turning point in Italian politics. Mussolini had emerged as the last hope of the conservative, property-minded elements, the strong man who would restore order to the country. Money flowed into his treasury. His publications still carried revolutionary slogans and used anarcho-syndicalist language, but now he was the champion of order, strong government, national traditions, respect for property—all this in the interest of the common people, the victims of capitalist exploitation.

I listened with amusement to the talk about the sources of Mussolini's philosophy: Machiavelli, Sorel, Blanqui, Nietzsche. To me, he was a disciple of Lenin. For him the essential was not the program but the movement itself, and in this he followed Lenin's formula: strict centralization, a pyramid of obedient agents, a single will at the top, substantial leeway for local units within the framework of general directives issued by the center. The Fascist organization was kept in a state of continuous frenzy by inflammatory propaganda. It had no positive program nor did it claim to have one. It had only negative objectives: against the Socialists, against the Liberals, against the rule by ballot. All this was undiluted Leninism, with only incidental similarity to Machiavelli (the cult of authority and ruthlessness), Sorel (anti-parliamentarism), Blanqui (action by small groups directed from the top), Nietzsche (glorification of brute force).

By the end of 1920, Mussolini openly claimed all power for himself and his Black Shirts. This claim seemed preposterous to political observers accustomed to measure the pulse of a nation by ballots. It did not seem so to me. The November coup in Petrograd had shown that a handful of resolute men, supported by the garrison of the capital, can seize power in a nation in a period of internal dissensions and strains.

Mussolini cut a strange figure on the scene of Italian politics: an ignoramus in comparison with Nitti; a street urchin in comparison with Giolitti, Tittoni, or Sforza; a nonentity in comparison with Turatti, Traves, or Bissolati. But he was a man of tremendous energy, an egotist with insatiable ambition. His proclamations were good enough to incite the simple people. When read in the newspapers, his speeches were cheap trash, but people who heard him at mass meetings told me he could electrify an audience. But his main strength was the fact that he was the first among the Western politicians who had studied the November coup in Petrograd and learned from it how to prepare for and carry out such an affair.

Mussolini understood that anarchy was paving his way to power. Beginning in the autumn of 1920, he directed all his efforts toward increasing tension and disorder in the country. His Black Shirts pretended that they were fighting the radicals and Socialists in labor unions and municipal councils, but they did not attempt to oust them by winning elections. Their weapons were pistols and knives. In a particular skirmish it was not always possible to determine which side had fired first, but the Fascists held the upper hand because of their better organization and ruthlessness. Moreover, the essential for Mussolini was not to win each clash but to keep the country in a state of creeping civil war.

Like Hitler in Germany a decade later, Mussolini found allies in the left wing of the labor movement, among the Communists and their sympathizers. They believed that the rising tide of anarchy would carry them to power and concentrated all their efforts on fighting the moderate Socialists and liberal non-Socialist groups. We left Italy before Mussolini's victory, but the march on Rome was not the decisive battle in his rise to power. Rather it was a dramatic finale, similar to the storming of the Winter Palace in Petrograd and the burning of the Reichstag in Berlin—a spectacular celebration of the end of a long campaign to undermine and destroy the democratic institutions of a nation paralyzed by confusion, divided against itself, and unable to defend its freedom against the resolute and purposefully organized minority.

Our work with the Georgian mission in Rome proceeded fairly sucessfully. Among other tasks, it included negotiations with a group of Italian banks on a coal concession in Georgia, a rather complicated and ambitious project. But at that time the political campaign was more important for the Georgian Republic than economic projects, and Jordania asked us to go to Paris, where this campaign was centered.

OUR DARK YEAR

Our year in Italy was the darkest year in our lives. Soon after our arrival in Rome, Emma felt pain while visiting the Vatican galleries. The next morning she could not get up. The physician diagnosed an acute form of peritonitis and urged an immediate operation. One of the best surgeons in Italy performed the operation, which lasted three hours but was not wholly successful. Emma had to undergo several more operations before the infection was stopped.

For six months she hovered between life and death, but not once did she complain to the doctors and nurses or to me. I spent the whole day from ten to six at the hospital, leaving only for conferences at the legation. Each morning Emma greeted me cheerfully saying, "I feel fine today," even when she lay motionless, unable to turn her head on the pillow. The chief surgeon told me that in all his long practice he had never had a patient with such strength of will. He believed that medical science would have been helpless in Emma's case except for her courage and unyielding will to live.

The personnel of the clinic consisted largely of nuns. The elderly, important-looking Mother Superior was the directress of the hospital. The nuns did their jobs diligently, but they were reserved and cool in their attitudes toward the patients, always maintaining a certain distance. Their indifference ended, however, at the door of Emma's room. She was surrounded by exceptional attention.

Most devoted to her was a nurse named Giuseppina. When she was preparing Emma for the first operation, Emma noticed a small bandage on her finger. Afterward, when Emma opened her eyes, still under the effects of ether, she saw Giuseppina caring for her and asked softly, "How is your finger? Does it hurt?"

The girl continued to work, but her hands trembled and another nurse took her place. A moment later I saw her standing at a window in the hall. She turned toward me, in tears, and whispered:

"If this lady does not recover, there is no God!"

The nuns used Emma as an example to patients who went to pieces from self-pity and fear, and many came to her bedside to talk about their personal affairs. Some were simple country girls, others came from middle-class surroundings and were more sophisticated; only a few could speak a little French. Talking with them, Emma picked up enough Italian for everyday conversation. Gradually she learned to read and speak Italian fluently, and this turned out to be of substantial help to both of us later in our work in the field of world economics.

Before the last operation, the Mother Superior came to Emma

and said, "Signora, from the way you carry your cross, you must have a strong faith. Why don't you join our Church?"

Noticing Emma's surprise, she explained, "That might help. . . . And if the Lord takes you to Him, our Church might canonize you sometime. . . ."

Emma thanked the Mother Superior warmly but could not oblige her.

A month after the last operation, Emma was out of danger but still very weak. I took her to Frascati, a little town in the mountains not far from Rome. After two weeks, she walked for the first time from her bed to the balcony. This was a memorable hour for both of us as we stood looking at the skyline of Rome, dominated by the dome of St. Peter's against the setting sun.

Emma was regaining strength when we received Jordania's letter asking us to go to Paris. The surgeon did not object to the trip but warned Emma that complete recovery might require several years. He underestimated her strength—a year later she was climbing mountains, carrying a heavy knapsack, and she has never again been ill.

FRANCE, LAUREL-CROWNED AND BLED WHITE

In Paris, we joined the Georgian legation. Tseretelli had succeeded in establishing close ties with the anti-Communist elements in the European Socialist parties. On his initiative, an international Socialist commission had gone to Georgia. It included such prominent labor leaders as Ramsay MacDonald (Great Britain), Pierre Renaudel and A. Marquet (France), Emile Vandervelde and Louis de-Brouckère (Belgium), and Karl Kautsky (Germany). They returned deeply impressed by what they had seen, and their reports gained many friends for Georgia. But the big newspapers showed little interest in Georgia's fate, and our assignment was to organize a press campaign to gain the support of the general public.

France was deeply confused. Had she emerged from the war victorious or defeated? The tricolor had become the symbol of war; the red flag, often with the hammer and sickle, the symbol of peace. At one extreme, there was drumbeating and a demand for unyielding vengeance against Germany; at the other, battle fatigue and a passionate desire to relax, to forget, to be let alone.

France had won the war at the price of four and a half years of superhuman effort and suffering. We saw black veils and armbands everywhere. Almost every woman was in mourning for someone—a son, husband, brother, sweetheart. With one and a half million men killed and two and a half million wounded, France had been bled nearly to death. The people yearned for some tangible fruits of the victory but wanted to have them without further effort and new sacrifice. Perhaps the weakness and instability of the French governments were rooted less in the squabble between political factions than in the fact that the man on the street was confused, deeply dissatisfied but unable to formulate his aspirations.

Economic conditions in France were not quite as bad as in Italy but followed the same pattern. Prices were more than treble those before the war. Wages had risen in some industries but remained unchanged in others. Strikes were going on in many places—thousands of small local walkouts, scores of disputes of national importance. Some strikes ended in a compromise, but more frequently work was resumed under the old conditions.

Communism had not yet appeared on the French scene as an independent political force: Soviet agents were hard at work but did not reveal their real purpose; they infiltrated the labor unions, the Socialist party, the war veterans' associations, and the press. Communist straws were in the wind—inflammatory speeches during the strikes, anti-militaristic declarations of combatants, glorification of the Soviets. Soldiers in the streets, in old unbuttoned capotes without insignia, reminded us of the comrade deserters in Russia in 1917.

My main contacts were with the press—a new world for me. My plan for a press campaign was very simple. I did not try to squeeze into the newspapers articles pleading for recognition of the Georgian Republic but put out brief items about Georgia that read like news and might interest the average reader. The idea was to select the news in such a way as to show the role of Georgia as an outpost of democracy in a remote corner of the world. For a while, this plan worked satisfactorily enough. Not all the newspapers printed our releases, but some did. The most respectable, *Le Temps*, published a dozen such notes, then suddenly lost interest in Georgia.

A couple of weeks afterward, the head of the foreign affairs department of the newspaper called our legation to ask the press relations officer to come in for a talk. I was received by a rotund gentleman, very vivacious, voluble, and sympathetic. He explained with admirable candor that neither his nor any other big newspapers would print my notes merely because of interest in them or through sympathy for the small country somewhere thousands of miles away. Going over the foreign news in the last issue of the paper, column by column, he said to me, "As good friends we should have no secrets from each other. All this stuff is paid for. This is not politics—it is business. We are doing all we can for our friends and all we expect from them is to manifest their friendship for us by sharing our expenses. Your little

stories are journalistic gems. . . . Listen, if you swear to keep this
secret from other legations I will make you a special price. . . . For
only one hundred thousand francs a month I'll give you five Paris
newspapers of your choice. You will have no worries. Just put each
note with four carbons into the mailbox—with my name—and tomorrow you get them all printed."

I finally convinced the rotund gentleman that the Georgian legation had no funds for the press. He expressed his sympathy for my
predicament, and his friendly manner did not change. "I shall see
what I can do for you," he said. "Keep on sending your releases to
me. Perhaps I shall be able to use them from time to time, but give
me your word of honor you won't tell anybody your notes have been
printed free. That would demoralize the market."

THE FALL OF GEORGIA

The efforts of the Communists to infiltrate Georgia and incite trouble
among the workers and peasants had failed. The prestige of the
government remained as high as ever. But the international difficulties
confronting Georgia were increasing. After the withdrawal of the
British from Tiflis, the Communists launched an offensive. In November, 1920, the Soviet troops occupied Baku. The Tartar government
was overthrown, and a Soviet republic was established in Azerbeidjan.
The Kremlin sent assurances of goodwill and friendship to the
capitals of the two remaining Transcaucasian republics, Erivan and
Tiflis, but six weeks later the Russian armies invaded Armenia. This
time military operations were combined with fifth-column work and
diligently prepared riots. The conquest was disguised as a revolt of the
masses of the people against their government.

Georgia was now encircled on all sides by Communist forces.
Its only hope lay in the Great Powers. The latter were only moderately
interested in this issue but, since Georgia was a modest pawn on the
chessboard of European politics, the Supreme Allied Council decided
to make a noble gesture by recognizing her as an independent nation
de jure.

Tiflis was jubilant. At the official celebration on February 4, the
representatives of the Soviet government were among the guests of
the President of the Republic. A few days later, however, Russian
troops crossed Georgia's borders from Armenia and Azerbeidjan,
through the passes of the Caucasian range and along the Black Sea
coast. On February 23, the Turks appeared around Batum. By the
end of February the Russian forces were in sight of Tiflis. The capital
was evacuated and the Georgian army retreated toward the Black

Sea. Skirmishes lasted three more weeks. On March 17, when the remaining Georgian forces had been pushed back almost to the outskirts of Batum, the Georgian government recognized that further resistance was futile and disbanded the troops. Members of the Cabinet and the Parliament escaped abroad by sea.

It became our task in Paris to mobilize public opinion in support of Georgia's cause. There was still hope that, in the course of final settlement of frontier disputes, the Great Powers would force Communist Russia to relinquish Georgia.

The moderate Socialist parties used Georgia's case to challenge European Communist sympathizers to take a stand on this flagrant violation of the rights of small nations.[4] But all efforts were futile to mobilize moral forces in defense of a small nation raped by the Red Giant. The free nations of Europe were passing through a difficult crisis. The Entente that had crushed Germany was crumbling. Civil war was flaring behind the Rhine. France and Great Britain were drifting further and further apart. Great Britain was becoming increasingly interested in the economic recovery and stabilization of political conditions in Germany, while France preferred to see Germany economically weak and politically divided. The Great Powers, ready to make a deal with the Soviets, would not lift a finger or even raise their voices to help Georgia.

Jordania, members of his government, and a few other political leaders came to Paris. The Georgian legations in Paris, Rome, and Berlin had to pool their funds to support the refugees. Salaries of the personnel retained by the Paris legation were cut to bare subsistence. We moved from our expensive apartment to very modest quarters, but, as long as the legation needed our services, we continued to work with it.

About this time my mother came to Paris. She told us of my father's death. The Communist coup in November, 1917, had found him in Terioki, Finland. After the withdrawal of Russian authorities, a local council was established in the township. All groups of the population elected their representatives to the council, and my father was nominated by the landowners. In 1919, Finland was invaded by the corps of General Mannerheim, a counterrevolutionary gang similar to Denikin's Volunteers. My father was arrested. Threatened with death, he suffered a stroke in prison. After they brought him home, a second and fatal stroke followed.

As soon as the Finnish frontier was opened, my mother went to Terioki to care for my father's grave and liquidate the estate. Then

[4] The Georgian legation in Paris published a symposium of articles and resolutions on Georgia and its annexation by Russia (*L'Internationale Socialiste et la Georgia*, 296 pp. & viii, Paris, 1921), which Emma and I had prepared.

the frontier was closed again, and she was stranded in Finland. Finally she was able to reach Paris, but she planned to return to Petrograd. Nadya's letters were cheerless. Life was hard, but she liked her work—teaching art courses at the University—and had no plans to go abroad. My mother had no worries about Emma and me; we were safe. All her thoughts were with Nadya, and her only desire was to rejoin her as soon as possible. Emma did her best to make her life with us comfortable, but we could not persuade her to remain.

GERMANY DEFEATED AND DEFIANT

I went to Berlin for a couple of days to help the Georgian legation draft a memorandum. Berlin bore no apparent scars of the war. The streets were clean, the people adequately clothed. But the war had left deep scars in the social fabric of the nation.

In Berlin I found many refugees from Russia, a motley crowd of professors, lawyers, journalists, officials of the Tsarist regime and the Provisional Government, officers, landowners, and businessmen.

Old acquaintances advised me to move to Germany, where I could get literary work or a teaching position in a university. A Russian publisher, Grzhebin, who had settled in Berlin, offered me such work. Trained as an artist, he was a close friend of Gorky, and book publishing was his passion. His main business in Germany was printing textbooks for Russian schools, but he thought that Berlin, with freedom from censorship, was also the proper place to collect material about the Russian revolution. He offered me a contract for three volumes of memoirs for his series of *Annals of the Russian Revolution*.

When I returned to Paris, Emma and I discussed this proposal. Our work with the Georgian legation was nearing its end; life in Berlin was less expensive than in Paris, and I would have a better chance there to return to scientific work. The language made no difference —our German was as good as our French. So we decided to go to Germany.

We left Paris in the summer of 1922 and spent some weeks on the Rhine—one of the most charming spots in old Europe, a land of hills covered with vineyards, quaint villages in the valleys, and romantic castles towering above them. From Bonn we hiked upstream along the river with knapsacks, going from village to village, crossing the Rhine by steamboat wherever the ruins and spires on the opposite bank attracted our attention. There were no visible traces of fighting along the river, but evidence of defeat was conspicuous: Senegalese riflers and British and Belgian soldiers at railroad stations; flags of the Allies on official buildings; orders of the occupation command posted in prominent places.

Defeat had come to the Germans unexpectedly. Long after the German High Command realized that the war had been lost, it kept the people ignorant of the approaching catastrophe. As early as September 29, 1918, Field Marshal Hindenburg and his chief of staff, Ludendorff, wired the Kaiser that they could not hold the front any longer and asked that negotiations for an armistice be started at once. Then came the revolution. Early in November a mutiny broke out among the sailors in Kiel. Riots spread out among reserve troops and the civilian population. Crowds in the streets demanded the abdication of the Kaiser. He fled to Holland, Germany was proclaimed a republic, and the S-D, as the strongest party on the left, came into power.

Councils of workers and soldiers were established in all the cities. Two weeks later a conference of representatives of local governments convened in Berlin and decided that a National Constituent Assembly should be elected at once, on the basis of universal suffrage. A handful of left-wing Socialists (Spartakists—members of the Spartacus party) opposed the idea of a parliamentary regime in Germany, demanding that all power be given to the councils of workers and soldiers. In order to prevent the convocation of the Constituent Assembly, they made a desperate attempt to seize power in Berlin four days before the elections. The attempt was suppressed by the government. Two leaders of the Spartakists, Karl Liebknecht and Rosa Luxemburg, were seized by a group of officers and murdered on the way to prison.

The Spartakist riots, planned as a repetition of the November coup in Russia, became the counterpart of the July riots. In Russia, however, the rightists had used the riots to postpone elections to the Constituent Assembly, while in Germany they did not repeat this tragic mistake. The elections were held as planned. The National Assembly convened in Weimar on February 6, 1919. A republican constitution was promulgated, and the S-D leader, Ebert, was elected President. The Weimar Republic, however, left intact the bridges leading back to the past: the military forces, reduced by the peace treaty, remained in the hands of the old Prussian generals; the courts, in the hands of the judges appointed by the Kaiser; the schools, in the hands of reactionary superintendents.

The abortive *Putsch* in Berlin in March, 1920, was a fairly close counterpart of Kornilov's mutiny in Russia. A commander stationed in the capital encircled and occupied public buildings with his troops and made an official of the old regime, Kapp, head of a new government. Labor unions declared a general strike and called the workers to arms. The local governments announced their loyalty to the Republic. In three days all was over; Kapp capitulated. This incident, however, revealed the weak point in the armor of the Republic—the deep split in the ranks of the workers. In some provinces, the Spartakists and some left-wing Socialists used the confusion to seize power under Lenin's slogan: "All power to the Soviets." Long after order was restored in Berlin, civil war was smoldering in the Ruhr.

A new Reichstag was elected in June, 1922. The election showed a shift to the right in the nation. A parliamentary government could not be organized except through a coalition in which non-Socialist elements predominated.

The major task of the coalition government was to liquidate the aftermath of the war. Germany had been disarmed and humiliated. It had lost a sizable part of its territory, all its colonies, and its merchant marine. It was blockaded, partly occupied by foreign troops, compelled to deliver coal, lumber, cattle, and railroad rolling stock to its enemies. Above all, it was saddled with reparations of undetermined size.

The great majority of the German people could not understand that these calamities were the results of military defeat. Their army had not been beaten! Wasn't it standing on foreign soil when the armistice was signed? The German cities had greeted the returning troops with triumphal arches: "To our victorious soldiers!" "To our invincible troops!" Why had this army been ordered to surrender? Who was to blame for the national disgrace? Either the people had never heard or had forgotten that Hindenburg and Ludendorff had asked for an immediate armistice. They were made to believe that Germany had fallen a victim to treason. Wilson had lured her into peace negotiations; the mutineers in Kiel had destroyed her glorious fleet; the Socialists in Berlin had forced the good Kaiser to abdicate. Germany's political leaders realized that their country had to bear the consequences of defeat, but the prevailing spirit of the people when we went to Berlin in the spring of 1922 was a mixture of bewilderment and self-pity, suspicion against everybody and doubt of everything, humiliation and suppressed arrogance, blind hatred of the Versailles Treaty, and hope of revenge.

The political pendulum swung from left to right during the eleven years we spent in Germany. Time and again people went to the polls and voted one way or another, but their general psychology remained the same. As a nation, the Germans did not regain peace of mind, and there was neither national unity nor stability in the Weimar Republic.

A REPUBLIC WITHOUT REPUBLICANS

Our work in Germany took us into academic and political circles, especially to leading circles in the labor movement. We were aliens but no longer outsiders. We watched the death struggle of the Weimar Republic from inside and took an active part in that losing fight. As in Russia in 1917, this was, basically, the struggle between moderates on one side and the united forces of red and reactionary extremists on the other. Practically, in terms of parties, moderate Socialists and the Catholic Center were defending the Republic against the onslaught of the Communists and Monarchists (Nazis, in the later phase of the struggle), who occasionally fought each other but usually acted in unison against the forces of the Republic.

Perhaps the moderates were doomed in advance. Under the Weimar Constitution, Germany had all the attributes of a republic: an elected President, an elected Reichstag, elected provincial legislatures, a parliamentary government. It also had universal suffrage and all civil liberties. It failed in only one attribute of a republic—the republican spirit.

Born of defeat, the Weimar Republic had no appeal to the masses of the people. Its flag—black, red, and gold—meant little to the man in the street, was despised by the military, hated by the right, ridiculed by the extreme left. Reactionary farmers described the colors of the Republic as black-red-yellow dung. The government sued the men who had used these words in a public address. The defense attorneys displayed the flag of the Republic in the courtroom and pointed out that the stripe officially called gold was not of gold color, but rather yellow, like dung. The court sided with the defense, using the case to humiliate the Republic. School children were taught to revere the glorious past of the Empire and to despise republican institutions. Pictures of Hindenburg and the Kaiser were on the walls in all middle-class apartments. Good bourgeois who disliked the last Kaiser and were critical of the provincial princes had even less enthusiasm for the Weimar Constitution. Socialist youths sang cheerfully, "The Republic is not all, socialism is our goal!" For the left-wing Socialists, the Weimar Republic was associated with the murder of Karl Liebknecht and Rosa Luxemburg.

During our summer vacation in 1923, we went to a tiny city perched in the hills of Thuringia. The station was decorated with imperial flags. The city was illuminated, and jubilant crowds led by bands were parading the streets. We took a room in a tourist house and asked the elderly landlady about the cheerful demonstrations. "Oh, we are so happy!" she replied. "Our beloved princes have got their palace back."

This was the seat of one of the small dukedoms. Many of its inhabitants had been close to the court, if not as officials or purveyors to the ducal household, at least as relatives, neighbors, or acquaintances of court purveyors or officials. After the revolution, the duke fled abroad. The republican government confiscated his estate, turned part of the palace into a school, and opened its magnificent park for public use. The duke's attorneys went to court and finally won the case. The people were not sure whether the duke would come back, but it was enough for them to know that his park would be closed again and the school thrown out of his palace. They were celebrating the duke's victory!

Feudal institutions had left a deep imprint on the German national character and it could not change in a few years, especially under the circumstances in which the Republic came to life. Society remained stratified, everyone clinging to his old position. In the scale of values of the people, order and discipline ranked higher than freedom and equality.

German workers who had reached the upper rungs of the political ladder preserved almost servile respect for their former masters and diligently imitated their ways of life. Acceptance of social inequality was bred in German bones. The first President of the Republic, Ebert, had been a leather worker and his humble origin remained a wound to his self-respect, a blemish on his name. Right-wing newspapers alluded to him as a former cobbler's apprentice. His chancellery sent letters to the newspapers to correct the statement: "Mr. President has never been a cobbler. He was a saddlemaker in his youth." The newspaper refused to recognize this subtle distinction, and the President sued it. After a court had thrown out his case, he appealed without success. He was sure that, in protesting against the accusation of having been a cobbler's apprentice, he was defending the dignity of his office.

The Germans we met—mainly intellectuals with progressive leanings—impressed us as a strong breed of men, intelligent, decent, with highly developed feelings of duty and unusual stamina. Perhaps their sense of humor was somewhat different from ours, and they took themselves too seriously. Certainly most of them were infected by extreme nationalism combined with self-pity. This form of political neurosis, widespread in postwar Europe, was particularly acute in Germany.

THE WORLD IN FIGURES

After I had completed my memoirs for Grzhebin's *Annals,* we still had some savings but no plans for the future. I thought of returning to scientific work in economics and statistics but, after so many stormy years, it was difficult to pick up the lost threads.

Christmas, 1924, was approaching, but there was no snow in Berlin. Emma and I longed for real winter, as we had known it in Siberia, and decided to spend Christmas week in Marienbad, Czechoslovakia.

On the train I tried to take stock of what I remembered of economics. I thought primarily of descriptive economics rather than abstract theory. . . . I had not followed the literature since 1905. . . . All had changed since then. . . . I would have to learn from scratch, proceeding systematically: population, the labor force, agriculture, industry, trade. . . . Then it dawned on me that many people were in a similar position. War and revolution had swept through the world and broken the continuity of its development. All students had to catch up with events. The best way to bridge the gulf between the past and present was to try to measure the changes. I could do it by reading, studying, and writing, all at the same time. I said to Emma, "I think I know what I want to do. This will be a book on the changes that have occurred in the world in the last two decades—a statistical book covering everything that can be measured." I could not sleep that night. By dawn I had a general plan ready.

Marienbad was buried under snow. We had a room on the second floor of a boardinghouse, with an entrance from an open balcony and a view of snow-covered hills. We spent most of our time outdoors, coasting or hiking and having a wonderful time. Back in our room in the evening, I scribbled a detailed outline of the project, a seven-volume study entitled *Die Welt in Zahlen* (*The World in Figures*).

I intended to write in Russian and offered the project to Grzhebin, but his business wasn't prospering. The Soviet government had barred the import of his books to Russia. Thus we started without a publisher in sight. We worked in the library of the Prussian Statistical Board. By the time the first volume—some three hundred pages in pencil draft—was completed, the Russian department of the publishing house of Rudolf Mosse had become interested in the project.

The main business of Mosse was the newspaper *Berliner Tageblatt,* the largest daily newspaper in Germany, but the firm also published books as a sideline. The Russian department was a small branch of a big business, and we did not take its interest in our project too seriously. But its manager, a Russian refugee lawyer, believed he could sell the idea to the German director and asked me to let him see the manuscript. In a week or so he telephoned to say that the German director had authorized him to go ahead, provided that Professor Bortkiewicz approved the project. Accordingly, he had sent the manuscript to the professor.

The draft was almost unreadable in parts, with only rough pencil sketches for the charts. How could anyone approve such a messy manuscript for publication? Emma and I wrote off the affair with Mosse. About a month later, however, Mosse's office sent me Bortkiewicz' comments—some ten pages of notes in longhand, full of captious remarks about the selection of sources, the spelling of Swedish and Norwegian names, arrangement of some tables, generalizations that required reservations. And at the end a peevish question: "Why should these books be published only in Russian? They may be equally useful for German readers."

This last remark did not dispel our impression that Bortkiewicz had rejected the project, but when I went to Mosse to pick up the manuscript the German director greeted me with a broad smile. "Your project has passed the most difficult test. Do you know that the publishers have stopped asking Bortkiewicz to review their books? All his comments have been murderous! And here he is, asking why we don't consider publishing your books in German! Most certainly we will publish them in both languages—German and Russian." He offered me a contract for both editions, with substantial royalties from the Russian edition and a more modest rate for the German translation. Thus I found my way back to economics and statistics, the interests of my youth.

Emma and I worked together. It was hard work—all day in the library, without taking time out for lunch, munching sandwiches at a desk covered with books and papers. We had no secretary, no draftsman, no typist, not even a calculating machine. We shared the work of assembling the material; Emma made most of the computations and also did our housekeeping. I wrote the text and drew the charts. We worked sixty to sixty-six hours a week for five years, but the work was fascinating. I was making up the time spent on politics, in prisons, and in exile, and I particularly appreciated the opportunity to work with Bortkiewicz.

When I learned that he was to pass judgment on my manuscript, I wanted to explain the idea of the project to him. Mosse's office called him to make an appointment, but Bortkiewicz replied, "I shall be glad to meet the author, but if I do, I will return the manuscript to you without reading it. I do not review the work of persons I know and I don't care to meet authors whose work I have to appraise."

Before signing the contract with me, the publisher asked Bortkiewicz to endorse the series as its editor. He rejected the offer. "I do not put my name in books I have not written. Moreover, a publisher must not impose his editor upon the author."

I went to see Bortkievicz. He lived in a modest apartment, crowded with books. He was tall and handsome, with penetrating eyes and cropped gray hair—very formal and very cold. His Russian was perfect; he had been born in Russia and was a graduate of St. Petersburg University. When I asked him to take editorial responsibility for my series, he replied with some irritation, "What is the idea? Should I take credit for books I have not written, or give my name to such books?" I replied that, because of the long interruption in my scientific work, I felt insecure in the new literature. I would be grateful if he would check the manuscript for completeness of documentation, methods, and conclusions. He finally agreed, and thus began our joint work.

Bortkiewicz was probably the best statistician in Europe, and I had much to learn from him. We discussed the outline of each chapter. When the chapter was completed, he read the Russian draft and commented on it, usually in writing. Then he read the German text, occasionally correcting the style and watching the terminology. He returned some chapters without comment, but even for these his oral suggestions during the preliminary discussions were most valuable.

Bortkiewicz had a photographic memory and knew the literature on practically any topic of economics and statistics. He had the rare ability to visualize a statistical series as an expression of a continuous economic or historical process. And he had a philosophy of statistics that he had never developed in his writings. For him statistics was not a body of mathematical formulas and techniques but the art of quantitative thinking. An outstanding mathematical statistician, he liked to play with formulas and had published many articles full of algebra, but this was more or less a game; very often the purpose of his mathematical essay was to prove the futility of mathematics. To him the essence was to use measurement to obtain a better understanding of facts of life. Strangely enough, however, he could not express himself simply so that laymen could understand. *The World in Figures* represented the kind of statistics he liked. He did not have the slightest resentment at seeing such statistics produced by a younger man who lacked his erudition and experience. As time went on, our relations became less formal. Emma and I frequently met him and his sister socially, and we became good friends.

Bortkiewicz' outstanding characteristic was his scientific integrity, a high standard for precision in the written word. His reviews of books, even when devastating, were never personal or biased. In Germany he was called the Pope of Statistics and had more admirers than friends. The success of our *World in Figures* was due to some extent to his endorsement. I was a newcomer in Germany. An attempt of an individual author to cover a great variety of subjects in a single study was contrary to German scientific tradition, perhaps even more so than in the United States. The name of Bortkiewicz as the editor of the series was a guaranty that such an attempt might be made and that the author was qualified to undertake the experiment.

The Russian edition was discontinued after the second volume. The Soviet government forbade importation of the series into Russia. Our royalties shrank accordingly to about one fourth of what we would have received from both editions. But the German royalties and the fees for articles we both wrote for scientific magazines enabled us to live comfortably. Working intensively ten months of the year, we could afford long vacations. We spent them in the high mountains, usually the Alps.

IN THE MOUNTAINS

We discovered the high mountains by accident. After our first hike along the Rhine, we went to the Black Forest. There we saw patches of snow on the slopes of the Feldberg. Our trip took us to the Bavarian Alps and the Tyrol, where we fell under the spell of valleys rising from the verdant plain to evergreen forests, rocky gorges, glittering glaciers. Our first ascent was of the Wildspitze, the highest peak in the region. We made it with a guide, with ropes, cutting steps in the glacier wall. The climb was too strenuous for novices, but we were exhilarated by the experience and decided to come back to the Tyrol.

I was approaching forty, and Emma was in her early thirties. We were a little late in starting apprenticeships in mountain-climbing, but we learned the art quickly and the high mountains became our passion. Even now I think that mountaineering is the perfect sport for those who can master it. It demands considerable strain of muscles and nerves, but the rewards for one's effort are lavish.

The mountainous part of the Tyrol, useless for farming, was the domain of the German-Austrian Alpine Society. The shelters and tourist hotels that chapters of the society had built were open to anyone who could reach them. The entire region was organized as a playground for lovers of nature, with shelters separated by six- or eight-hour walks; trails were cut in the rocks, dangerous stretches secured with ropes or cables. One could wander for two weeks or more from shelter to shelter without ever descending to the lowlands.

We would start from a railroad station at the mouth of a valley after shipping our luggage to another station in another valley. We carried only essentials, about fifteen to twenty pounds each, in knapsacks, and went from shelter to shelter, often crossing and recrossing the range, spending each night on another pass or peak. Then we descended to the station where our luggage was waiting. Usually we made three or four such excursions each summer. We learned the basic rules of mountaineering: to keep an even pace, neither too fast nor too slow; to watch the trail; to stop for rest at the proper time and at a convenient place. After five or six years of mountaineering, we were no longer amateurs. We ascended many lofty peaks of the Tyrol and could handle without a guide any route accessible to experienced climbers.

In all our trips in the Tyrol, the Bavarian Alps, the Pyrenees, Norway, and Switzerland, we had only one accident—on the Gross Glockner, one of the most popular peaks in Austria. The ascent of this mountain is not difficult and takes four or four and a half hours from the Alpine hostel at the foot of the mountain to a shelter close to the summit, the Eagle's Nest. We spent the night in the lower hostel and discovered, about four o'clock in the morning, that all the guided parties had left shortly after midnight. Only two hospital nurses and two railroad employees, all of them from Vienna, were still in the hostel. We decided to go up together. We traveled light, with almost empty knapsacks, leaving most of our equipment in the valley—woolen socks and mittens, sweaters, shawls, and the medicine kit with the obligatory little bottle of rum. We thought we would not need these things for a one-day hike, since it should not take more than eight hours to get to the summit and back.

From the terrace in front of the hostel I could see our path clearly through field glasses—a steep rocky trail, a level stretch across the glacier, then a climb up the face of an almost vertical rock. The guidebook said that the last section of the trail was secured by a steel cable.

The first part of the route proved easy, and the passage across the glacier was delightful. We walked as on a bridge of ice. As we were approaching the rock wall on the far side of the glacier, the weather suddenly changed. Black clouds appeared in the sky, and the air became heavy and motionless. Something strange was going on, and we began to run toward the rock wall. The moment we reached it, a blizzard broke. In the whirling snow one could not see one's own hands. The howl of the wind was deafening. The temperature fell below freezing, perhaps below zero.

All six of us stood pressed against the rock. We tried to give the Alpine signals of distress, but they were lost in the wind. We huddled together and considered waiting until the storm subsided. It was becoming bitterly cold, and one of the Austrians shouted, "We shall freeze to death here. Let's climb! Here's the cable." He was a tall, robust man and had an extra pair of woolen socks on his hands. Grasping the cable, he placed himself at the head of the column. I fell in behind him, but the icy cable burned my bare hands like a red-hot iron and I could not hold it except with my elbows. Emma, who followed me, dropped the cable and crawled on all fours, clinging to the stones on the trail. The two nurses crawled behind her holding the cable; the second railroad man brought up the rear.

In ordinary weather, the last lap would have taken no more than an hour, but in the storm, icy cold, and pitch darkness we made slow progress. At some places the path hewn in the rock, now packed with snow, was no more than six inches wide. Fortunately, the wind was blowing from the glacier, pressing us against the rock.

At last the three of us reached the top of the mountain. The shelter was packed. Several husky guides rushed to the rescue of our companions. Other guides surrounded us, examining our fingers and toes. The man with the woolen socks on his hands had no complaints. My hands were dark blue, but Emma's were not affected; she had done the proper thing in dropping the cable. Meanwhile, the other three members of our party were helped to the shelter. The hands of the nurses were in horrible shape—almost black, the skin ruptured, covered with blood. From their clinical experience they knew what this meant—imminent danger of gangrene. The end man had frozen only the tips of his fingers.

My hands could be saved by rubbing with snow—Alpinist fashion—but I was so chilled and exhausted that I did not care what happened. Emma took charge. She poured brandy and several cups of strong tea with rum into my mouth while two guides held my hands in a bucket of snow and rubbed them mercilessly. With restoration of circulation came acute pain in my frostbitten fingers, but drowsiness eased the pain somewhat and I fell asleep under six blankets.

The next morning the sky was cloudless, the weather perfect. We descended to the valley. My hands were bandaged, but otherwise I felt fine. The only unpleasant thing was that the guide's bandaging was Tyrol style: strips of cloth soaked in kerosene. The poor nurses had a much worse time. They were taken to a hospital, and not until six months later did we get a letter from them saying they hoped to avoid amputation of their hands.

On the trail and in shelters we often met young boys on crutches or with artificial limbs—war veterans returning to their beloved mountains. In the museum of the German-Austrian Alpine Society in Munich we saw a vast collection of pictures of the war amputees on different peaks: men with bared stumps of legs and arms, their artificial limbs and crutches alongside in the snow. The Germans cherished such gruesome pictures as evidence of their stamina and endurance. Not until much later did I discover another type of heroism, when I saw pictures taken in USO clubs: smiling, laughing girls and boys whirling in a dance, all the lads wih service ribbons, their artificial limbs hidden under smart military attire.

ECONOMIC JOURNALISM

The success of *World in Figures* brought me requests for contributions to scientific magazines in Germany and the Scandinavian countries. In some articles I dealt with theoretical and methodological questions, but very soon I began to specialize in articles on the international, European, and German economies in which I could use statistical data and charts. I was particularly interested in the unification of Europe, and my book *The United States of Europe* appeared in German in 1926 and in French in 1927. Later I returned to the same idea in a volume, *Europe, Fact and Figures*, published by the Pan-European Union. In retrospect, I feel that the weak point of both books was overemphasis on the economic aspects of the problem. The difficulty of pacifying and unifying Europe—then as now—lay in the psychology of the people rather than in their conflicting economic interests.

For two or three years I contributed regularly to the monthly theoretical magazine of the Social Democratic party, *Die Gesellschaft*, edited by Rudolph Hilferding. Hilferding was considered the greatest theoretician of the Marxian school in Germany, but we never discussed theoretical questions with him. I was moderately interested in Marxian doctrine and did not think his theory of financial capitalism had essentially improved or enriched that doctrine. He was full of praise for the economic articles I gave him, printed them without changing a single word, and wanted to have them in every issue, but he had no use for my theoretical ideas. Politically, we did not see eye to eye. He was the best spokesman of the S-D faction in the Reichstag, very subtle, always keeping himself on a high scientific level, but I did not like his readiness to compromise with the left and right and ascribed it to opportunism and personal vanity.

Despite our personal aloofness, we collaborated rather smoothly until we differed on the question of whether it was permissible to check Marx's formulas of surplus value statistically. I insisted that any economic theory could and should be checked by empirical observation and offered, as an example, a study of ratio of payroll amounts to value added by the United States manufacturing industries. Hilferding declared that my article was contrary to the spirit of Marxism and could not appear in *Die Gesellschaft*. Even now I do not know whether or not my approach was compatible with Marxian doctrine, but I recognize that, as editor of the magazine, Hilferding was entitled to reject my article, the more so as it was too long and too technical for general readers. At the time, however, I thought the magazine should have published it, at least as a matter for discussion. Since Hilferding insisted that the fundamental principles of Marxism were not subject to discussion in his magazine, I broke with *Die Gesellschaft*.

By that time, however, my books and articles had attracted the attention of the labor unions representing the economic arm of the S-D party. In general, the unions had little respect for the intellectuals in the ranks of the labor movement, but since I had received recognition outside the movement, they decided I might be useful to them. Thus the Board of the General Federation of Labor Unions (ADGB) invited me to join its staff as chief of the statistical department and consultant on questions of economic policy. I faced a serious problem, for, in joining the staff of the ADGB, I would again have to leave my ivory tower of economic study and free-lancing for the turmoil of politics.

GERMANY A DECADE AFTER
WORLD WAR I

Germany was then completing her economic recovery. Her economic comeback was spectacular. Less than a decade after the war, she was again the greatest economic power in Europe, outstripping both Great Britain and France. But politically she was a colossus of brass with feet of clay, unable to produce a strong and stable government. Her political structure—the Weimar Republic—hung in mid-air, having neither historical roots nor the support of the masses of the people. This precarious situation had been aggravated by the 1922-23 inflation, which had ruined Germany's middle class. German industry was expanding, its products were reappearing on world markets, its wages rising, but the middle class, including farmers and professional people, had no part in this prosperity and blamed the Republic for their predicament. The very existence of the Weimar Republic depended essentially on the support of manual and white-collar workers. Unfortunately, labor was deeply split. The existence of socialistic and Catholic labor unions was only a minor handicap—the two worked fairly well together. But Communist propaganda was injecting a deadly poison into the German labor movement. Working from inside the labor organizations, the Communists were making frantic efforts to undermine the Weimar Republic. In the 1920's, Germany was the target of Moscow's global strategy. The Weimar Republic was the keystone of the political system established by the Versailles Treaty. To destroy it would open up new revolutionary possibilities in Europe, and Moscow believed that the German Republic could be destroyed by crushing the S-D party.

The Kremlin gained its first success in the elections to the Reichstag in May, 1924, when the Communists got 3.7 million votes and 62 seats as compared with 6.3 million votes and 100 seats for the S-D. The Communists' success was due largely to their promise to free Germany from reparations and wipe out the Versailles Treaty—the formula that brought Hitler to power a few years later. The Dawes Plan of August, 1924, relieved much of the pressure of reparations, and nationalist passions seemed to subside. At the new elections in December, 1924, the Communists lost a million votes and seventeen seats. The extreme nationalists likewise suffered a setback. But the Communist threat remained. The danger was in the silent alliance between the extreme left and the extreme right. The Military High Command and the leaders of German heavy industry contemplated building munitions and aircraft factories on the Volga for the future rearmament of Germany. There was a nationalist undertone in the sympathy of German intellectuals for the Soviets. They brushed aside the danger of a Communist coup in Germany: "It can't happen here. Germany is not Russia."

The combined forces of the rightists and the Communists clashed openly with the forces of the Republic after the death of Ebert, when Germany had to elect a new President. In the first contest in March, 1925, the right bloc won 10.4 million votes; the S-D candidate, 7.8 million; the Catholic Center, 3.9 million; and the Communists came fourth, with 1.9 million. In the absence of an absolute majority, a second election was held. The rightist forces backed General von Hindenburg. Only a united front of the republican elements could have blocked his election. The S-D decided to join forces with the Center. The Communists stuck to their candidate, Thaelmann, the "transport worker," and directed all their vituperation against the S-D. Hindenburg was elected by a plurality, 14.7 million votes to 13.8 million for Marx, the republican candidate, with 1.9 million for Thaelmann. This was the turning point in German history, the beginning of the end of the Weimar Republic.

The socialistic unions, with six million members, were the stronghold of democracy in the nation. I had more faith in them than in either the S-D party or the Center and reproached them only for their lack of initiative, their hesitancy in facing difficult problems, and their readiness to let the S-D party make decisions for them. Now they were asking my advice on economic questions. I had no desire to go back to political struggle, but to advise the unions on economic policy might be different. My advice might be useful to them and the whole labor movement in Germany. It was worth trying.

I decided to accept the offer of the ADGB.

AT THE HEADQUARTERS OF THE GERMAN LABOR UNIONS

The ADGB directly represented about eighty per cent of German organized labor, and its influence was increased by the German system of plant councils and compulsory arbitration of industrial disputes. The board of the ADGB consisted of two dozen presidents of the largest national unions. Leipart, former head of the Lumber Workers' Union, presided. All the board members had risen from the ranks of manual labor. None of them had the quality of a great leader, but they were all able men, devoted to their unions, unimaginative, honest, and, above all, good German patriots.

The senior professional staff of the federation consisted mainly of self-educated union men, hard-working and competent in their fields. There were only two intellectuals in key positions: Lothar Erdman, the chief of the publications department and editor of the monthly periodical, *Die Arbeit*, and I. Erdman had a broad philosophical education, and his aim was to inspire the labor unions to an active role in defending the nation's cultural values and, above all, its cultural freedom. He was a self-effacing man who never spoke in public and seldom signed his articles, but his ideas found expression in resolutions and declarations of the ADGB and in speeches he wrote for Leipart. He opposed pacifism and was as nationalist a German as other labor leaders, but his nationalism was of a special kind. He was convinced that a new war was unavoidable. After her defeat Germany must seek revenge.

Once, when we were discussing the role of Germany in the League of Nations, Erdman turned to the wall map of Germany above his desk and said mildly, "Suppose you found this map in an old parchment, knowing nothing of the country except how it looked after a defeat." Then, pointing to the corridor separating East Prussia from the rest of Germany, he continued, "Wouldn't you conclude that this country either went to war again to rectify its frontiers or perished because of lack of faith in itself?" But Erdman abhorred anti-Semitism even more than pacifism. "Germany has been humiliated enough by her powerful enemies," he once said at a board meeting, "but if it takes revenge on the weak, especially its religious minorities, it will be disgraced forever." Perhaps this was too subtle for the board, but its members were proud of Lothar. He was one of the best men in the German labor movement, and his end in a Hitler prison, after unspeakable torture, grieved but did not surprise me.

My own position on the board was somewhat unusual. As an alien, a Russian and, above all, an intellectual, I could not mix well with this group of old comrades. I was offered the highest salary, just below that of the president, and the board listened to my advice, but nobody would call me by my first name as they called one another; I remained to them "Herr Doktor."

Politically, the union leaders were all members of the S-D party, and the ADGB supported the party at elections. They often used the threat of a walkout in their negotiations with employers but preferred to settle disputes by bargaining or arbitration. The system of compulsory arbitration at the demand of either party often led to collusion.

A dispute, for example, developed in the iron and steel industry. The union demanded a raise, temporarily withholding the bill of particulars; the employers seemed adamant in refusing any concession. More than a million workers were involved. The Ministry of Labor summoned the representatives of both sides. The union delegates came with a voluminous memorandum I had helped to prepare. The head of the employers' delegation took the president of the union aside and asked him about the union's specific demands. I do not recall what they were; perhaps we asked for a raise of ten pfennigs per hour and were ready to settle for five. When the employers' delegate heard that the union would not settle for less than ten pfennigs, he said, "If we reject your demand you will ask for arbitration and get five pfennigs. Better begin asking for twenty-five pfennigs. We shall struggle, you will go down to twenty and then fifteen pfennigs, and, in the end, we shall settle on ten. You will get everything for your men and we shall have saved fifteen pfennigs per hour for our clients." The union president accepted the deal and asked for adjournment of the conference to prepare the case.

My work with the ADGB originally focused on labor statistics. I reorganized union statistics of unemployment and collective agreements and developed the statistical section in the annual reports. In addition, I lectured and wrote articles for labor magazines. Contrary to my expectations, there was not much politics and very little fighting in that work. Emma was busy with articles on women's labor conditions and municipal policy. She had also translated the first two volumes of my memoirs, published in 1931-33, from Russian into German.

Suddenly the economic scene in Germany began to change. After a decade of economic expansion, a crisis arose, and at once I again found myself in the middle of political controversy.

THE GREAT DEPRESSION IN GERMANY

Germany's great depression began as a part of the world-wide economic setback in 1929, but it was aggravated by the disastrous economic policy of the government.

At first people were not very much concerned about falling prices and inching-up unemployment. Official unemployment statistics in Germany were based on the reports of the labor unions on the percentage of unemployment among their members. The rate averaged 8 to 9 per cent in 1927-28 and rose to 13 per cent in 1929—the same level as in the United States a year later. I rearranged the federation's unemployment statistics to segregate the industries with seasonal fluctuations in employment from those in which unemployment reflected changing business conditions, and in this way obtained seasonally adjusted unemployment figures. Early in 1930, we in the ADGB became alarmed by the continuous rise of the unemployment rate in the non-seasonal group, but observers outside the labor unions did not take the situation seriously.

The government was wholly absorbed in the problem of reparations. This was a purely political, rather than economic, question. Germany actually was paying less in reparations than she was receiving in credits and loans from the Allies. Now, however, contraction of foreign trade made it hard for Germany to make even trivial reparation payments, as required by the Dawes Plan, to the creditor nations. Chancellor Brüning demanded and obtained a revision of the Plan. Many German politicians, elated by this success, concluded that the depression was helping their country to free itself of the shame of the Versailles Treaty. I considered the situation increasingly serious, however, and prepared for the board a series of charts and tables showing the trend of unemployment in the nation. One fifth of the union members were out of work and no improvement was in sight. I explained that the German economy was caught in a deflationary spiral of wages and prices, production and employment. A heated discussion followed. Union presidents agreed that the situation was alarming, but Otto Wells, the president of the S-D party, was highly displeased with my paper. He was a stout, tall man with enormous hands, an enormous neck, a double chin, and small eyes under a very low forehead. Although not very bright, he was a man of goodwill, respected in the party. "All this is sheer nonsense," he grumbled. "The situation is not bad. Unemployment has even helped us with reparations."

Leipart closed the meeting after asking me to report to the board if anything new developed. A month later I reported that the rates of unemployment in non-seasonal industries had continued to rise and further deterioration in business conditions could be anticipated. Leipart asked me if I had any practical proposals. When I replied that I had none, he asked me to give thought to the question.

In September, elections to the Reichstag took place. Hitler's pictures and his coat of arms, the swastika, were everywhere. The Communist and Nazi commandos, in similar brown uniforms and with similar red banners, paraded in the streets. The crowds in the mass meetings of the S-D party were sullen and unresponsive. The election brought victory to the extreme wings. The Nazis got 6.4 million votes, as against 800,000 in 1928; the Communists increased their vote from 3.3 million to 4.6 million. The S-D, still the strongest party in the Reichstag, went down from 9.2 to 8.6 million.

The Reichstag did not have a working majority. All the parties of the right were now behind Hitler's banner; together they had 260 seats as compared with 231 deputies of the combined forces of the S-D, the Center and the Democrats. The Communists held the balance. I became obsessed with the idea that these disastrous political trends could be reversed by breaking the deflationary spiral and giving jobs and hope to the people. Perhaps because I recalled the St. Petersburg Council of the Unemployed, I began to think of public works—on a large scale, of course—not as a welfare measure but as a means of changing the economic trend. But how to finance the project? The more I thought, the clearer it became to me that unemployment, the main problem of our organization and labor in general, was actually only a dramatic manifestation of a more general economic problem Germany was facing—deflation. This question was new and little explored, but I felt that, to defend itself against the tide of mass unemployment, labor must attack this broader national problem— a deflation due largely to the wrong orientation of the whole economic policy of the Republic.

An accidental observation confirmed this feeling. The newspapers wrote about the "strike of consumers" who postponed purchases in expectation of the further fall of prices. Not far from the ADGB the windows of a large store displayed furniture at marked-down prices. One morning I noticed that the old price signs had been replaced by a big poster: "These are our final prices. There will be no more cuts. We will burn our entire stock or let it rot rather than cut a single mark from today's prices." Wasn't this a way to break the consumer's strike?

That day I decided to present to the board a program of economic policy based on the combination of two ideas: to establish public works, and to fight deflation by injecting purchasing power into the economy through bank credits. My report was ready two weeks later. It provoked sharp controversy. The union presidents were all for public works but could not grasp the idea of financing public works through credit, as an antideflationary measure. One of them shouted angrily, "Now, I don't understand a damned thing. I paid sixty marks for this suit. Do you wish me to pay eighty marks for it?"

I replied, "If you were out of work, you could not buy a new vest for five marks. I wish you to pay a hundred marks for the suit and twenty marks for the vest, and still have enough money to buy a pair of trousers worth fifty marks."

This argument stuck. He got the point, and later used the argument in his speeches. Leipart said meditatively, "At least we have a practical proposal, the first practical suggestion since unemployment began to rise. Maybe there is something in it. . . . Doctor, turn your statistical department over to somebody else or let it go to hell altogether. From now on, work only on your economic program."

A PROGRAM TO END DEPRESSION

After the meeting, Erdman suggested that I start a public campaign for my program at once, without waiting for the board's formal decision. He offered to carry my articles in *Die Arbeit*. His magazine became the advocate of what became known as "the active economic policy," built around two ideas—public works and support of prices through bank credits to finance these works. The second proposal implied public spending and unbalancing the budget not only as a means of financing public works but also as a vehicle for injecting purchasing power into the anemic economic system and reversing the deflationary spiral.

I was not then familiar with the early works of Keynes, which would have helped me in developing my arguments. But in the reports of the Financial Section of the League of Nations on gold policy I found the answer to the problem. A moderate increase of purchasing power or money in circulation would raise the price level or stop its decline and would encourage expansion of production without danger of a runaway depreciation of the currency. Partly under the influence of these reports, I decided to present my plan in terms of an international policy in the struggle against the world crisis.[5]

[5] I developed these ideas in a book *Internationale Hebung der Preise als Ausweg aus der Weltkrise* and in a series of articles in *Labor, the International Labor Re-*

Even in this form, the contention that the fight against unemployment must be combined with a rise in the price level was a direct challenge to Chancellor Brüning, who believed the crisis could be solved by a further cut of prices. This was also a challenge to the S-D party, which silently supported Brüning's economic policy, opposing it only insofar as it threatened to affect real wage rates. I was so absorbed in developing the technical details of my project that I did not realize its political implications. Lothar warned me, "You are stepping on the toes of many important people."

The reaction of the S-D party to my first article in *Die Arbeit* showed that he was right. The principal organ of the party, *Vorwärts*, published two articles accusing me of luring the labor unions into a new inflation. I considered this accusation an appeal to the prejudice and ignorance of the readers. In the mind of the economically illiterate public, the word "inflation" was associated with the runaway inflation of 1922-23 that had ruined many honest people and enriched a handful of speculators. "Inflation" was a bad word, while "deflation" was just one of those terms the man on the street could not understand. I immediately sent a rebuttal to *Vorwärts*, but the chief editor of the newspaper refused to publish it, under the pretext that this was a complicated technical question and the paper had already printed two articles on the issue. Other S-D papers followed the example of *Vorwärts*.

Meanwhile economic conditions took a turn for the worse. After the elections in September, 1930, Brüning was looking for some dramatic step to strengthen his government, and decided that an economic union of Germany with Austria would be the right move. This idea backfired. The government's announcement of its intention to promote such a union was interpreted abroad as evidence of Germany's intention to bring about a political merger with Austria, which would be a violation of the Versailles Treaty. In retaliation, the foreign banks began to cancel short-term credits to German and Austrian firms. Considerable payment difficulties developed. Several Austrian banks collapsed. A panic broke out in Berlin. People rushed to the banks demanding their deposits. In July, all the banks were compelled to close. This was a crisis within a crisis, similar to the bank holiday in the United States in 1933.

In the absence of a working majority in the Reichstag, the government was running the country by legislative decrees. Alarmed by the bank crisis, the Chancellor came out with a new bunch of decrees

---

view of the International Labour Office and other magazines. My book, published by the Society for Business Research (*Gesellschaft für Konjunkturforschung*) in Frankfort, did not attract much attention. In recent years, however, it has gained some recognition in Germany.

designed to cut production costs, wage rates, and prices. The S-D party approved this policy but opposed certain features of Brüning's decrees, and Hilferding came to the ADGB to clarify the party's position. After his report I asked him, "Do you criticize the decrees because you believe prices will not fall enough to offset the cut in wages? Would you support the decrees if you were sure prices would drop more than money wages?"

"Decidedly so," he replied.

"I, too, am against the new decrees," I said, "but for a different reason. They will slash prices without cutting real wage rates, but the final effect will be a further increase in unemployment."

A sharp exchange between Hilferding and me did not clarify the problem to the board. Union presidents listened to our dispute in sullen silence. They liked my idea of public works but were accustomed to look upon Hilferding as the greatest authority on economic theory since Karl Marx.

After the board meeting I discussed the situation with Lothar in his office. "You are continuing to step on the toes of important people," he told me. "Are these decrees so significant for your program?"

"They touch the core of the problem," I replied. "The question of 'public works' or 'no public works' is incidental. What counts is whether to fight depression by deflationary or anti-deflationary measures—that is, inflationary measures. This is where my program clashes with that of Hilferding and Brüning. I am deeply convinced that these two, with all their good intentions, are leading Germany to a terrible catastrophe. Do not look at me as if I were crazy."

"There are so few people who are deeply convinced of anything that they must seem crazy," remarked Lothar, "but without such crazy people we would be lost."

Active economic policy, with large-scale public works as its cornerstone, remained my obsession. It seemed to me that I saw—physically, with my eyes—how Brüning was leading Germany to a tragic end. At a time when evaporation of purchasing power and decline in prices were the main evils, he treated the country to ever more deflation, and with each step he took unemployment increased, the Nazi-Communist tide mounted, and the country came closer to the abyss. Yet Brüning was a man of high intelligence and irreproachable integrity. His suicidal policy stemmed from his general philosophy. He feared the phantom of a runaway inflation; he did not like the idea of pampering the unemployed by creating jobs; and he thought that a public works program was a luxury Germany could not afford.

Brüning, however, must not be blamed too severely for his errors.

He shared his false ideas with many of his advisers in his own and the S-D party. Had the latter not supported his policy, he might have abandoned it. Unfortunately, the economic policy of the S-D parliamentary group was directed by Hilferding, who had committed himself and his party to a definite program and loathed the idea of reversing it under pressure by the unions.

Such was the state of affairs in Germany in July, 1931, when Emma and I went on a summer vacation. This time we were hiking in the southern Tyrol and the Italian Alps. From this wonderland of rocks and canyons we went to Venice and finally landed on Capri. There we spent ten days far from politics, without newspapers. While we enjoyed the blissful leisure, important events were taking place of which we learned when we returned to the mainland.

After checking our luggage at the railroad station, we went to the nearest bank to exchange our German marks for lire. A crowd was gathered in front of the bank. People were talking, shouting, gesticulating. The hall of the bank was packed. The bank officials were sitting at their desks but were not transacting business. I asked one of them what was going on. "Oh, signore," he replied, "the sky fell on the earth!"

"This is bad news," I agreed, "but I would like to buy some lire."

"Oh, signore, there is no exchange today. The Bank of England has collapsed. The British have slashed their pound!"

I was elated rather than alarmed. I believed that the British had done the proper thing by launching an anti-deflationary policy, and that their move would have a salutary effect on the world economy.

In this mood I returned to Berlin. That afternoon the ADGB board met to hear Hilferding on the British devaluation. He characterized the decision of the Bank of England as insanity. London had abdicated its role as the economic center of the world. It would need half a century to recover. Other countries should disengage themselves from the British mess and build up the world economy without Great Britain. Germany's main task continued to be to protect its currency.

I asked Hilferding, "How will the devaluation of the pound affect unemployment in England?"

"Unemployment will increase," he replied without hesitation.

"How soon will the increase begin?"

"In a few days . . . or perhaps a month. Certainly very soon."

Then I said to Leipart, "For a year the board has been torn between two lines of economic thinking—that of Brüning and Hilferding and the one I have presented to you. Now you can test them. Hilferding has made his prediction. I shall venture mine: Great Britain has turned the corner. Her credit will be strengthened, other countries will follow her example and devaluate their currencies, British exports will grow, her production will expand and her unemployment decline. Great Britain is on the way out of the crisis!"

"Nonsense!" Hilferding shouted.

"Either my projection or yours is nonsense," I replied. "Three months from now we shall know which of them is sound."

Leipart said grimly, "We do not know whether Dr. Hilferding or Dr. Woytinsky is right. We shall wait and see."

The British economy recovered by leaps and bounds. But the winter of 1931-32 brought more misery to the German people. More than eight million workers—over 40 per cent of the total labor force —were idle; nearly half of those who had jobs were working part time. The unemployment rate was about double that in the United States, and there was no hope of improvement. Brüning stuck to his policy doggedly. Even if his party felt its failure, it did not dare change horses in the middle of the stream. The S-D party followed Hilferding, who supported the government's policy of defending a sound currency.

One morning Leipart called my office. "We have a board meeting this afternoon. Are you ready to report your program?"

I was ready. I had dropped the international part of my original plan. The world economy was slowly recovering, and Germany was now the heart of the depression. The situation demanded that she act at once by launching large-scale public works at the price of a controlled inflation. I had discussed the matter with many experts. A prominent bank executive had approached the former president of the German Central Bank, Schacht, who expressed his opinion that credits for two billion marks for public works could be opened at once. To accelerate the start of the program, I set a very modest immediate goal—jobs for one million workers. This would be the first step.

CONFLICT WITH THE S-D PARTY

Leipart opened the board's meeting. "Four months ago," he said, "we discussed the events in Great Britain. Hilferding predicted the ruin of the British economy, Woytinsky predicted recovery. The British have proved to be wiser than the Germans. Now our unions must take full responsibility for the economic policy of German labor." The board accepted my program unanimously. Wells was silent during the discussion but remarked after the vote, "You, the unions, have voted a program for legislation. This has never been done before. In the past the party developed the program and cleared it with you. Do you intend to clear your program with us?"

"We are confident that the party will support us," Leipart replied. "Am I right, Otto?" Wells did not answer. He was not interested in an issue that he did not understand. All that counted with him was the jurisdictional aspect of the controversy—who should determine the policy of the party.

In the following weeks the board continued to discuss the details of my plan. I suggested inviting a government official, an expert on public works, to the board meeting. He explained the mechanism of bank credits for financing a project and tried to show that advancing money cannot produce a runaway inflation. The members were visibly interested, but Otto Wells asked sarcastically:

"What will you build? We have enough roads, enough houses. Do you intend to let us build pyramids as they did in Egypt?"

Our expert answered, "This is an excellent idea, Mr. Reichstag's Deputy. A country that cannot think of anything better must build pyramids as an eternal monument to its stupidity. I do hope, however, that with some effort Germany will find better projects."

The idea of public works was becoming increasingly popular with the unions most severely affected by the depression—the building trades and iron and steel workers. The argument that this program would cause inflation seemed to be wearing out, partly because it became widely known that the banks did not oppose the project. It looked as if we had gained the first round of the campaign. Then one morning Leipart called an emergency session of the board and announced that the S-D party had refused to support the ADGB. The Central Committee of the party considered our program an act of mutiny. Moreover, the Central Committee had decided it had to consider, above all, the employed workers, the bulk of the voters. The unemployed were voting for the Communists or the Nazis, so let those parties think of what to do for them.

I do not remember in which form this decision of the Central Committee was published and whether it was ever officially announced, but that was what Leipart told us. It was a heavy blow to our hopes. The party would now mobilize all its forces against us; mutiny must be crushed. To stop the ADGB, the party hurriedly prepared a platform of its own, with all kinds of socially desirable plans but without specific measures against the depression and without public works. The union leaders scornfully rejected the bait.

In May, Brüning resigned after a clash with Hindenburg, who had vetoed his plan for a mild agrarian reform. Von Papen, a representative of the reactionary landowning aristocracy, became Chancellor. He had good economic advisers, and his first step was to reverse Brüning's deflationary policy. But the only way he knew to pour money into circulation was to cut the taxes of the rich. This did not help the unemployed. Crowds of jobless workers milled about in front of the employment offices. Most of them had long since exhausted their benefit rights. Many spent nights on benches in public squares and subway tunnels. But the Communist commandos and Nazi shock troops offered jobs to husky young men. Those who enrolled received shelter, food, a smart uniform, sufficient pocket money, and hope for the future.

Through all these events we continued our campaign. The idea of public works began to attract more attention in the press—except, alas, in the S-D press. Many economists were ready to recognize that public works would be the proper vehicle to bring more money into circulation. It was time to broaden the ADGB plan, and I asked Fritz Baade, member of the Reichstag, and Fritz Tarnow, president of the Lumber Workers' Union, to work out a practical plan with me. Baade was one of the ablest economists in the S-D party, a man with a strong will, a keen sense of reality, and imagination. His main interest was agriculture, but he recognized that the distress of German farmers was due to deflation. More than once he had expressed himself in favor of an active economic policy along the lines recommended by the labor unions. He could contribute not only new arguments but also new ideas to the program. Tarnow was the heir apparent of Leipart in the ADGB, an intelligent self-educated union leader, independent in judgment and an excellent speaker. He did not contribute much more than his name to our work, however. We signed the document jointly—Woytinsky-Tarnow-Baade—and it became known as the WTB Plan—an amusing anagram, since the German official news agency, Wolff Telegraphen Bureau, signed its communications with the same three letters.

The Plan gained more and more popularity in the nation, but the S-D party remained adamant and refused to use the slogan of public works in the Reichstag election campaign in July, 1932. It preferred to stick to Brüning's guns—defense of the currency. The results of the election were catastrophic for the Republic. The Nazis gained more than one third of all the votes and 230 seats out of the Reichstag's 568. The new Reichstag had a clear anti-republican majority of Nazis and Communists and was unable to form a republican government. All parties began to brace themselves for a new appeal to the voters.

Leipart called me to his office. "The party," he told me, "has agreed to meet with us to discuss the plan of public works. There will be forty party representatives and as many from the labor unions. Will you prepare our case for the conference?"

I asked Gerhard Colm, a scholar of national reputation, not

connected with the labor movement, to be our reporter. The party named Hilferding as its spokesman. I was slated to open the panel discussion with a rebuttal of Hilferding's arguments.

The conference was held in a large room in the Reichstag building. Everyone sat around a horseshoe-shaped table covered with green cloth. Wells occupied the chair, with the union people at his right and the Reichstag members at his left. Red in the face, he opened the discussion grimly. "It is time to end this silly dispute. Inflation-deflation, public works . . . I do not know what. . . . This nonsense must be stopped."

Colm spoke in an academic way, developing a theory that since has become commonplace. The price level and volume of economic activities can be regulated by monetary and credit measures. Public works is the best, and politically the most expedient, approach to the problem.

Hilferding was the next speaker. "Colm and Woytinsky," he said, "are questioning the very foundations of our program, Marx's theory of labor value. Our program rests on the conviction that labor, and labor alone, creates value. Prices deviate from labor values under the impact of the interplay of supply and demand. Depressions result from the anarchy of the capitalist system. Either they come to an end or they must lead to the collapse of this system. If Colm and Woytinsky think they can mitigate a depression by public works, they are merely showing that they are not Marxists."

My first thought was that Hilferding could not have taken that nonsense seriously. Obviously, he had a limitless contempt for his listeners and did not condescend to argue before them but appealed to the clichés in their brains. A score of deputies listened to him as to an oracle. Wells sat motionless in his armchair, his eyes closed and his head sunk on his breast. Hilferding ended with an appeal to the party to rise united to the defense of a sound currency and Marxism.

I began my rebuttal. "The flood of unemployment is rising, the people are at the end of their patience. The workers, holding us responsible for their misery, are deserting the party to join the Communists and Nazis. We are losing ground. There is no time to waste. Something must be done before it is too late. Our plan has nothing to do with any particular value theory. Any party can execute it. And it will be executed. The only question is whether we take the initiative or leave it to our enemies. It is not true—"

I felt that I was gaining the audience, but suddenly a deafening noise came from the head of the table. Wells was pounding the desk with both fists and shouting, "Shut up! I will not permit—"

"You will not permit what?" I asked in consternation.

"You said '*It is not true.*' If what Hilferding said is not true he must be a liar! I will not permit—"

Hell broke out, a dozen people shouting. Wells fell back into his chair, with closed eyes and his head sunk on his breast, sound asleep. Leipart asked me to continue, but the effect of my speech was completely lost. I elaborated the technical and financial aspects of the Plan. Nobody listened—for the union people this was old stuff and the Reichstag deputies did not care. After a few remarks from both sides, Leipart put the ADGB plan to a vote. All the representatives of the unions raised their hands in favor of it, all the representatives of the party except Baade voted "nay."

The break between the party and the unions was complete.[6]

THE END OF THE WEIMAR REPUBLIC

The Weimar Republic was crumbling. The Nazis and the Communists, who together had an absolute majority in the Prussian Landtag, by a joint vote overthrew the Prussian government headed by Otto Braun, the strong man of the S-D party. Since the Landtag did not have the working majority requisite to appoint a new cabinet, Von Papen took over the administration of Prussia, thus adding the Prussian police to the other strongholds controlled by the monarchists—the army, the judiciary, the schools, and the presidency. Next, Von Papen offered Hitler the Vice-Chancellorship, but Hitler rejected the offer. He would take nothing less than the post of the head of the government. At the new elections held early in November, the Nazis again got one third of the votes; though their forces in the Reichstag went down slightly, their losses were more than offset by the gains of the Communists. The combined strength of these two parties increased from 289 to 296 seats.

In Berlin and other German cities the streets were now in the hands of private quasi-military organizations—the brown-shirted shock troops of Hitler; the armed groups of the Steel Helmets, controlled by the old-regime military brass; Communist commandos. Hitler's troops were the most arrogant. They paraded with drums and bugles, the head squad of the column often armed with rifles and machine guns. The tune of their marching song was that of the Communist *Internationale*, but the words were different:

[6] I realize now that my impression of Hilferding's speech at our conference was false. He sincerely believed all he said about the labor-value theory: Let the world perish but save the dogma! There was tragedy in his folly, as in his end. Delivered by the Vichy police to Hitler's hangmen after the fall of France, he took his life.

> *When the blood of Jews spurts from your knife,*
> *Germany enters a new happy life.*

The S-D and other democratic organizations tried to create a republican mass organization that could oppose the Nazis and Communists in open-air demonstrations and, eventually, in street fighting. This organization, the Reichsbanner, claimed to have several million members but consisted mainly of substantial middle-aged bourgeois who abhorred marching and other military exercises.

Von Papen resigned after a clash with von Hindenburg on the question that had led to the resignation of Brüning—the division of large estates in East Prussia. Then von Hindenburg appointed General Schleicher as Chancellor.

There were rumors that the new head of the government was inclined to follow a middle-of-the-road policy. In addressing the press, he made some remarks designed to gain the sympathy of the workers. Then he invited Leipart to the Chancellery. An emergency session of the board was called to receive Leipart's report on his interview with the general. "He sat across the desk from me, but he did not look at me and he seemed to be talking to himself," Leipart reported. "He said that as a military man he would prefer to serve his Emperor on the battlefield but he was ready to defend the Republic against the Communists and the Nazis. He could keep them off if he had forces on which to rely. He asked me whether the unions would support him if he committed himself to execute their economic program. I asked him what kind of support he expected from us. He replied that he had thought of direct action, striking, street fighting. I told him he should have addressed himself to the Reichsbanner and the party. He said that he distrusted the politicians but would be ready to act with us because he considered us good, honest German men. He seemed sincere and he took a serious risk in talking to me that way. But I do not trust him. He is not a cold-blooded schemer, but he may be a daydreamer. . . ."

The board decided to wait and see. Berlin was full of rumors. Schleicher was gaining the support of the army . . . Schleicher was planning to arrest Hitler and von Papen . . . Schleicher intended to call a committee of psychiatrists to examine the health of the senile President and confine him in a mansion with padded walls. Then, on January 30, von Hindenburg issued an order removing General Schleicher from the Chancellorship and appointing Hitler in his place. That evening a torchlight parade was held in front of the President's palace. Hitler's Brown Shirts and the Steel Helmets had joined forces. Von Hindenburg and the new Chancellor together accepted the allegiance of the good people of the capital. The crowd sang, "When the blood of Jews spurts from your knife. . . ."

New elections were announced for March 5. Hitler's cabinet was based originally on the coalition of the Nazis with other right-wing parties. Very soon, however, the moderates were removed or had resigned, and the Nazis remained the sole masters of the central and Prussian governments. The fourteen years of the Republic were officially declared the Era of Treason. Newspapers were forbidden to publish information or articles contrary to the designs of the new government and were forced to carry everything submitted by the authorities. These regulations were officially described as the "co-ordination" (*Gleichschaltung*) of the press.

The Republic had ceased to exist.

THE BEGINNING OF THE THIRD REICH

Our board met every other day, mainly to exchange information. The reports were brief, matter-of-fact. Hitler was touring the country, cursing the Republic, the Socialists, and, above all, the Jews, promising everything to all Germans. Göring was directing the Brown Shirts. The police, purged of republican officers, were ordered to support local patriotic organizations, shoot first, and investigate thereafter. A wave of terror rolled through the country—assaults on Socialists, Jewish pogroms. Mobs raided the offices of the S-D newspapers and the Reichsbanner. On February 25, Göring issued an order making the Brown Shirts an auxiliary police force.

Late in the evening of February 27, the Reichstag building was set on fire. This was one of most dramatic and least mysterious events of the Nazi revolution.[7] The over-ornate gilded structure, built with money France had been forced to pay to Prussia after the war of 1871 and originally conceived as a monument to Prussian militarism, had become the symbol of parliamentarism in Germany. Its burning symbolized the end of the Republic. While the Reichstag was still smoldering, the government issued a declaration accusing the Communists of arson and suspending all Communist and Socialist newspapers. Göring's police and the Brown Shirts raided the apartments of Communists, their sympathizers, S-D leaders, and intellectuals

---

[7] Either the Nazis or the Communists could have committed the crime. If the Communists had beaten Hitler, they would probably have burned the building and then accused the Nazis of arson. As things stood in February, 1933, the Communists were interested in preserving the Reichstag as a legal cover for their further work, and Hitler's gang was interested in destroying it as a hateful symbol. The fact that the arsonists entered the closed and tightly guarded building through a tunnel connecting it with the residence of Göring across the street left no doubt about the origin of the crime.

with republican leanings. Thousands were jailed and mistreated. Many Jewish shops were looted.

The situation was vividly reminiscent of Petrograd after the Communist seizure of power. Hitler and Göring were getting ready for elections the way Lenin had staged the elections to the Constituent Assembly some fifteen years earlier.

The people were called to the polls on March 5. The leftist parties were deprived of many means of propaganda but were permitted to distribute handbills with the names of their candidates, to keep posters with their names in front of the polling places, and to have representatives on the commissions supervising the balloting. The S-D found it hard to get volunteers for electoral work in those troubled days, and the local organization asked Emma to join the campaign. She took party handbills to distribute and also went to the electoral commission. The party workers were instructed to climb to the top floor of an apartment house, push the handbills through the door slots on that floor, and run down to the next landing before the tenants above had opened their doors; then run to the next lower landing, and so on. At the meeting of the electoral commission, Emma did not say a single word, for fear of giving herself and the party away by her foreign accent.

Despite the orgy of terror, the Nazis failed to win the majority in the new Reichstag. They got about 270 seats out of 600. Other right-wing parties won some fifty seats. With their support, Hitler had a meager majority of 320 to 280. The S-D was the strongest opposition party, with some hundred deputies. About an equal number of seats were divided between the Center and other middle-of-the-road groups. The Communists had some eighty seats. By expelling them from the Reichstag, Hitler increased his majority to 320 against 200. With this majority, the Reichstag abrogated the Weimar Constitution, invested the government with dictatorial power, and dissolved itself.

The Nazi "revolution" was going on. No gas and torture chambers yet, no concentration camps—all these came later. But there was a reign of lawlessness and mob violence, a rising tide of bestiality, political murder, beating and flogging of prisoners. Then came organized manifestations of the new era—book burning and officially endorsed large-scale Jewish pogroms.

The burning of books was more of a demonstration of the new spirit of the Third Reich than an attempt at systematic destruction of undesirable literature. Trucks with brown-shirted young men roamed Berlin, stopping in front of bookstores, newspaper offices, publishing houses. They seized books they considered suspicious—books about Russia, pacifist literature, S-D publications, books of authors with Jewish names, and so on. Hundreds of truckloads were dumped at a designated place; a giant pyre was built, soaked with gasoline, and set on fire. Two of my books were burned among others—the German edition of my memoirs.

In the ADGB we continued our routine work, waiting for the blow to strike. In the early days of the Third Reich, the labor unions were not subject to special persecution. Their members and officials were assailed mainly in connection with their activities in the S-D party and the Reichsbanner. The tension of uncertainty and vague expectations became unbearable. I went to Leipart and asked him what he thought organized labor should do. He said, "I wish I knew. Maybe you know the answer."

"Perhaps a general strike?" I suggested.

"We have missed the time," he replied. "We should have struck on February 28, after they burned the Reichstag."

But he considered the possibility of a local strike in the event of a direct attack on local unions. He raised this question at a meeting of the board, and in a general way everyone agreed that the unions must be ready to meet the challenge. But how, when, and where? All the union presidents had the same feeling: "We have missed the time." In April, Brown Shirts occupied the headquarters of several unions. This step did not seem to warrant a general strike. Perhaps a local walkout? But who was to order and lead it?

May Day, the traditional Labor Day in Europe, was approaching when the board received a letter from the new Ministry of Labor. The government had decided to make May 1 the day of unity of the German people. The Führer himself would head the festivities. Workers would have an opportunity to manifest their patriotism and devotion to the new regime. Our federation was invited to participate in the parade, with all other German men and women. The members of free unions would march in separate columns under their banners. Their participation in the national parade would testify to their "co-ordination" with the new regime.

Leipart read the letter at the board's meeting. He was a broken old man. His voice trembled when he said, "Here we are. We have no choice."

All sat in silence. Leipart turned to me. "Or do we have a choice? You advised us two years ago, Woytinsky. What would you say now?"

"Your choice," I replied, "is between handing over your unions to the Nazis or letting them come and take them. This does not make much difference now, but the day will come when it will make a big difference."

"Your advice?" Leipart insisted.

"Not to surrender."

Leipart called the roll of the union presidents. Their response was unanimous: "We have no choice."

Leipart concluded, "I shall reply to the Ministry that the federation will take part in the parade."

I felt no bitterness toward my colleagues, but their decision had drawn a line between them and me. I asked to speak on a personal matter. "The co-ordination of the unions," I said, "implies that they have become a part of the Nazi state, but I cannot take an oath of allegiance to this state. So I must resign. This is by no means a protest against your decision. I will always remember with pride the years I have worked with you."

Leipart said gently, "We are deeply indebted to you. If you remained with us, we would do all in our power to shield you. But what good would that do? An additional liability to us and no help to you. You have made the right decision. But we have no choice."

I shook hands with him and other members of the board and left the conference room.

On May 1, the board of the ADGB marched in the Nazi parade like a group of captives dragged behind the chariot of the conqueror, exposed to insults and derision from the crowds on the sidewalks. When this ordeal was over, Göring sprang the trap. A commando of Brown Shirts broke into the ADGB building and arrested all the board members and senior officers of the organization. Until the van came to take them to jail, they were forced to run up and down the stairs of the six-story building and kneel before Nazi banners.

Later one of my colleagues in the ADGB wrote me: "You were right in advising us that the surrender would not save the unions. We had the choice. . . ."

ON THE ROAD

After the burning of the Reichstag we felt we were no longer safe in Germany. Of course, no person with democratic convictions could feel safe amidst this orgy of violence, but my position was worse than that of my German colleagues. I was a foreigner, a Russian Jew active in the German labor movement. However, I could not desert the ADGB so long as the organization contained a spark of resistance to the Nazis. Its decision to participate in the May Day parade changed the situation. When I returned home after resigning, Emma insisted that I leave Berlin at once. She had gotten visas for Switzerland in advance and had packed my suitcase. She herself would stay in Berlin for a few weeks, have our furniture and books stored and later moved, settle accounts with the publishers, withdraw money from the bank, and so on. I objected to her plan, pointing out that she would be in imminent danger if the Nazis raided our apartment and found me gone. Finally I yielded to her arguments, a step I do not recall with pride. She went to the station with me. I crossed the frontier without trouble and wired to her in code as we had agreed.

Emma had a hard time in Berlin. The police were looking for me; the Brown Shirts came to the door for contributions to their party, which she refused to give on the pretext that the Führer himself had forbidden foreigners to intervene in Germany's domestic affairs. The publishers dodged their obligations, the banks limited withdrawals to small amounts. She had a narrow escape at the Swiss border before she joined me in Zurich.

We had chosen Zurich as the largest and most industrialized city in Switzerland, in the hope that I would find some professional work there. Very soon, however, we discovered that the only contacts we could establish were with the leaders of labor unions and a few intellectuals close to them. The unions were engaged in an electoral campaign. Their leaders were interested in measures against mass unemployment. They knew the WTB Plan and the Plan for Work in Belgium, promoted by deMan and partly copied from the ADGB program. They asked my advice in drafting a program adjusted to local conditions. The central idea of the plan I drew up for them was to establish public works projects for each canton so that work could be started as soon as unemployment exceeded a definite limit, the cost to be met jointly by the federal and cantonal governments.

Although the chances of finding regular work in Zurich seemed slim, we tried to settle in Switzerland for good. But the Swiss immigration authorities asked us for evidence that our lives were in immediate danger in Germany and that we had no other place to go. When we answered that, under the regime of violence and lawlessness in Germany, we were in the same situation as thousands of other people and that we could find asylum in half a dozen other countries, beginning with France, the Swiss denied us permanent visas. We went to France, where the government had offered asylum to refugees from Nazi Germany.

Paris had changed little since we had left it in 1922. As before, the French Socialists were divided on all issues of domestic and foreign policy. The Communists had capitalized on the collapse of the democratic regime in Germany. They had succeeded in persuading the public that only they had opposed Hitler under the Weimar Republic, and that the Republic fell because of its betrayal by the moderate Socialists.

Léon Jouhaux, the president of the French Confederation of Labor (CGT, for Confédération Générale du Travail) invited me to serve on a committee of experts charged with the development of an economic program of the unions. Jouhaux then was full of vigor, at the peak of his career. His committee was studded with big names, including half a dozen Academy members. How they could talk! Jouhaux himself was a fine speaker, too, but he paid tribute to the French passion for eloquence only at the beginning and conclusion of his addresses, taking enough time in between for a sober discussion of the problem. Soon the celebrities disappeared from the committee, and only five or six men remained to work out the program. I suggested building it around two planks: social security and a guarantee of employment for all workers. Jouhaux liked the idea. He and I wrote the final text of the program. Its title was the same as in Belgium— the Plan for Work (*Le Plan du Travail*). I do not remember how many of my pet ideas remained in the final draft, but I felt that the WTB Plan, killed by doctrinairism of the S-D leaders in Germany, had returned to life in France.

My French was not good enough for a teaching position at a French university, but the Statistical Institute of the University of Paris asked me to make a survey of the world economy, and the French-Russian Scientific Institute offered me a professorship in statistics. Emma took graduate courses in the École des Hautes Études Sociales at the Sorbonne and prepared two papers on economic conditions in the United States before and during the depression.

All this kept us busy but provided very little income. I began to think of regular work for the French press. An acquaintance introduced me to the chief editor of a large evening paper, who offered me a weekly column of some two hundred lines on world economics. As a beginning, I was to write a dozen articles for very small pay and large publicity.

My selection of topics was not very good, but the articles passed the test. Several weeks after the first had been published, I met a well-established French journalist. "Congratulations, *cher ami*," he greeted me. "Now you are settled financially." I told him that my honorarium was just enough to pay for the typing of the articles. He looked at me as if I were saying something very stupid. "Honorarium? Who speaks of honorarium? They give you a name, now you go and cash in."

We sat down at a sidewalk table of a café, and he explained the trade to me. "You read business gossip in the morning paper. There is always something. Today, for example . . . the Bank of South France . . . investments in Algeria smell. . . . You call on the director of the bank and ask for information. He is happy to oblige you, all his files are at your disposal. But he, in turn, will ask you for a favor. . . . You see, he has been thinking for a long time of asking you to prepare a memorandum on the railroads in Argentina for his bank. There is no hurry, take your time. . . . The honorarium will be paid in advance. . . . Say ten thousand francs. . . . You are not expected to live on your printed articles, but on those which nobody reads. . . ."

"A little blackmail?" I asked.

His face got red. "Not in the least, Monsieur. You did not threaten him and should never threaten anybody. Why would you? Perhaps there is nothing wrong with Algerian investments! The director simply wants to make friends with the press. If you are very particular, you may even prepare the memorandum!"

I decided to forget about a journalistic career in Paris.

Unexpectedly, I received a telegram from the International Labor Office in Geneva, inviting me to attend a two-day conference on causes of unemployment. I went with a carefully prepared ten-page statement. The conference was poorly organized. The staff of the ILO had not assembled material that could serve as the basis for the discussion. The foreign experts came empty-handed. Mine was the only paper submitted at the opening session, and the chairman suggested starting the discussion with it. My paper was essentially methodological. In it I tried to dispel the myth of hard-core technological unemployment and had outlined statistical criteria for determining the source of unemployment in any industry or geographic area at a given time. My proposals would not have sounded very original in the United States in the late 1940's, but they made an impression in Geneva in 1934.

After the conference, the vice-director of the ILO, F. Maurette, asked me to develop my ideas in book form. I wrote the book in three or four months and sent the manuscript to Maurette with an outline of another study on the social consequences of the economic depression in various countries. Maurette was delighted with both my manuscript and the new project, and suggested that the facilities of the ILO would be available to me in my work on the second book.

We gave up our Paris apartment and went to Geneva with the understanding that we would either settle there or go to the United States.

At that time the ILO was celebrating a happy event: the representative of the U.S.S.R. had appeared on the scene! When he learned that my report was in production, he demanded the galleys and, following the usual procedure, was given the paragraphs dealing with his country. Two days later Maurette told me that the Russian representative had objected to the description of the U.S.S.R. as a primarily agricultural country since the Soviet Union was a highly developed industrial nation. I refused to change the statement but agreed to delete any reference to Russia from my book.

The air in Geneva was thoroughly poisoned by the presence of the Soviet observer when Jouhaux raised the question of my appointment to a key position in the ILO. His suggestion was that I serve as a permanent spokesman for the labor group (Jouhaux himself was its president in the conferences and the governing body of the organization). Maurette supported my candidacy, but the director, Harold Butler, refused to appoint me—perhaps fearing this appointment might hurt the feelings of the Russians. In retrospect, I feel greatly obliged to him. Without his intervention, Emma and I would have had two decades of a comfortable but rather dull existence but would have remained political refugees, strangers among strangers, to the end of our lives.

WE GO TO THE UNITED STATES

Even before the collapse of democratic Germany, when we were successful and financially well off in that country, Emma had tried to persuade me to go to the United States. Somehow she felt this would be the proper place for me to work in my special field. After our flight from Germany, she fell back on this idea. "See what is going on in the United States," she repeated insistently. "The country is full of dynamism. The people are rebuilding their economy. They could use your experience, abilities, imagination." I was not convinced; I no longer felt young and I was tired. This was not the physical pressure of age, for, while I was approaching my fiftieth year, in the high mountains I could do everything strong lads in their twenties were doing, except canyon climbing. Nor was I tired of intensive work in my own strenuous tempo. But I was tired of wandering from country to country, a stranger everywhere, despite the recognition and success that came so unexpectedly after our *Welt in Zahlen*. Without particular linguistic aptitude, I had written and lectured in Russian, German, and French. Must I now start from scratch in the United States, writing and lecturing in English?

I had yielded to Emma's insistence reluctantly and had promised her that work with the ILO would be our last attempt to settle in Europe. Now that attempt had failed. My course in statistics in the French-Russian Scientific Institute made us eligible for a non-quota professorial visa. We had enough money for the trip and a few months' living expenses. So we applied for the visa.

A few Russian friends came to the station in Paris to say farewell.

Some of them had tears in their eyes. Not out of pity for Emma and me—we were strong people, more successful than others in that small group. But to them our decision to leave Europe was an admission of defeat. If we were conceding failure, how poor were the chances of other members of our circle?

The crossing of the Atlantic was rough, and I did my best not to think of the future. But Emma was confident that we were heading toward a new and permanent home.

We Discover America
1935-1960

O UR personal life in the United States has lacked dramatic high lights. After our long wandering, we at last became a part of a great country and shared its hopes and anguish at the time of its "rendezvous with destiny." Our only noteworthy adventure in these years has been the discovery of America.

I know from books that this discovery is usually credited to Columbus, but the Admiral did not see much of the New World— nothing but islands in the Caribbean and a stretch of the mainland that he believed to be some offshore island of China. America has been discovered step by step by the generations of pioneers who helped to build it. But have they discovered all the New World? Will its discovery ever be completed?

When we left Europe we were not wholly ignorant about the United States, but many of our notions proved wrong. Moreover, looking at the United States through Russian-European eyes, we have seen many things in a different light from that in which they appear to people born and reared in this country. We have been impressed by things that native Americans take for granted and unmoved by other things that seem very important to them. Our America, the America we see and love, is tinged with our experience. Talking, lecturing, and writing about America abroad, I have often felt that the America we have discovered is different in many respects from its widely distributed portraits.

THE GATEWAY TO THE NEW WORLD

The towering skyscrapers of Manhattan that greeted us that sunny October morning in 1934 impressed me only moderately; I had often seen this skyline pictured in books. My overwhelming impression of New York was of bigness and confusion. The rush of the motley crowd in the streets, the stampede at the subway entrances, the roar of the Elevated, the striking contrast between the display of luxury in the shop windows of Fifth Avenue and the untidiness of the streets a few blocks away—all this was more or less in harmony with what we had expected to find in the New World. But this new world held far more for us than this conventional picture.

We met many Russians in New York—the older generation of refugees from Jewish pogroms, people who had left Russia after the revolution of 1905, the new refugees who had fled from the Communist regime. Some made their living the hard way, others had settled down and found security, a few seemed to be wholly successful. They were all a part of the old Russia, but they were also a part of their new country. They spoke of the United States with warmth and pride and kept telling us what a wonderful land America was. Some called it by an endearing Russian word: "Americhka"—little America. They told us how friendly the people were in this country, free from prejudice, ever ready to help their neighbors. This was new. We never heard immigrants to France or Germany speak this way of the country to which they had come.

We entered an attractive little bakery on Broadway. The owner, an old man, asked us with an unmistakable Jewish accent, "You are Russians? New here?" And then came his story, told in atrocious Russian mixed with English. He had left Russia during the Russo-Japanese War to escape military service and pogroms, settled in New York, and had spent some thirty years here. Though he had seen almost nothing but New York, to him there was no land in the world like America. He had two sons, both doctors, and a daughter who had married a lawyer. What would have become of them if he and his wife had remained in Russia? He was proud of his children, of his own success in life, and, above all, of America.

We talked to many people, humble, lower-middle-class men and women. Most of them were immigrants—Jews, Italians, Greeks. As soon as they learned that we were newcomers, they became talkative. Some complained that business was slow, but all had the same warm attachment to America.

Such was our first impression of New York . . . an overgrown, overcrowded city, but, behind its rush and noise, so much human warmth. This first impression remained vivid in our memories despite other, divergent images superimposed on it. We have seldom found this sentimental attachment to their country among native Americans. Their attitude is more complex. Their emotional attachment is to their state or the town in which they were born, rather than to their country as a whole; they take the United States for granted. The immigrants are richer in experience with which to compare their new country, and they do not hesitate to express their feelings.

We have found less flag-waving in the United States than in European countries. For the intellectuals, this brand of nationalism is in bad taste, tolerated only in political campaigns. We have observed the feeling of national superiority in the American people, but it has usually been expressed in naïve notions about the Old World and tempered by a sense of humor and a widespread inclination to criticize their own country and government. This last tendency has struck us particularly in meeting American tourists abroad. Many of them never tire of complaining about the high taxes in the United

States, the weak government, creeping inflation and so on. Occasionally they will defend their country against attacks by local Communists, but their defense is seldom as strong as their criticism.

It is easier for a foreigner to learn to love or dislike America than to understand it. The emotional slant usually develops on the basis of first impressions combined with the personal predisposition of the immigrant. Some fall in love with this country, despite the hardships they meet at the beginning, because it is different from what they left behind them; others reject it, because it is different. . . . In either case, the immigrant's emotional attitude toward the past determines his appreciation of contrasting features in the American scene.

Before telling about our life in the United States, I will try to describe what we have found here, in the New World—the land, the people, patterns of feeling and thinking, political ideas.

THE LAND

The American scene captivated us. The open horizons, borderless expanses, and endless variety have a particular charm for us who have known the spell of the Russian steppes, the Siberian rivers and forests, and the wild ranges of the Caucasus.

We had an insatiable desire to see the new country, from coast to coast and from the Canadian border to Mexico. To our passion for travel was added a more serious purpose. As an economist, I had to deal with the economic problems in various parts of the country and, at the beginning, felt lost among the geographical subdivisions of the United States. Such terms as New England, Deep South, Tennessee Valley, the Midwest or the Great Plains were empty words to me, without visual associations. They inspired a desire to see these areas with my own eyes. Emma was no less eager to explore the United States, which was becoming increasingly our country. During our first fifteen years here we spent all our vacations traveling by car, and we have crossed the country fourteen times from coast to coast and eight times from the Canadian border to the Gulf and the Rio Grande.

There is an indescribable magic in the variety of the American scene, from the green hills and tiny towns of New England to the tropical swamps of Georgia and Florida; from the metropolitan areas of New York and Chicago to the plains of Kansas; from the lofty peaks of the Rockies and the High Sierras to the deserts of Arizona; from the bare canyons of Utah to the luxuriant orchards of California. Almost every aspect of this panorama has its counterpart in Russia, the only other country in the world that has a similar variety of climate and topography. This endless diversity of patterns is, to us, the key to understanding the American scene. In whatever direction you look, you know that things are different beyond the horizon. This is what keeps the frontier of the country open.

The national parks were among our major discoveries. There are few spots in the world equal in harmonious beauty to Mount Rainier, Crater Lake, Zion National Park, or the Grand Teton. We visited the Grand Canyon several times, and each time, each hour of the day, it looked different. It was fascinating to look from the rim into the depths of the earth and discover its weird beauty. Nor is the charm of the national parks limited to their natural beauty. We were impressed by the preservation of wild life—the tame bears in Yellowstone Park, the elk and buffalo herds—and we liked the campfire talks of the Parks' rangers about their trees, flowers, wild animals, and rock formations.

We have also been impressed by the thoughtfulness, skill, and good taste that has been used in developing these lovely spots. No big hotels, no coffee shops at outlook points. Modest accommodations inconspicuous from a distance, beautiful access roads, inviting trails running into wilderness. The national parks have become a portion of our picture of the United States, not only as a part of its natural scenery but as an evidence of the people's love and understanding of nature. It remains a puzzle to us why so little attention is given to this aspect of the United States in the popular descriptions of this country. Indeed, the guidebooks give more space to the Empire State Building or Rockefeller Center in New York, to the luxurious hotels in Miami and famous eating places in New Orleans, than to the Grand Canyon and other national parks.

THE PEOPLE

One of the things we had heard about the United States before we came here was its conformity, the lack of individuality of its people. This myth is widespread throughout the world and can be found, in a new form, in modern books on mass psychology in this country. We have not found more standardization in the United States than in other countries. Standardization here is limited to the techniques of living. People wear the same kinds of clothes, enjoy the same movies, use the same clichés in speech. They have undergone the impact of the same public schools. They have the same drugstores and cafeterias from coast to coast. Yet they are deeply individualistic. Perhaps there is a strong pressure toward conformity in small communities, which we have not had occasion to observe, but diversity of patterns rather than standardization characterizes the nation as a whole.

We have seen forty-eight state capitols. There is, of course, a great similarity in their domes and columns, but nearly every capitol houses its own historical museum and Hall of Fame, with statues of local great men unknown beyond the state's borders. Each state has civil and penal laws of its own, its own tax system, labor legislation, social security programs and political tradition. Each state pretends to be a republic (or a commonwealth) with a legislature, president (governor), cabinet of ministers, often complete with a minister of state. This system goes much further than decentralization of government in most European countries. Even in Congressional elections, local issues are often of decisive significance. Comparing political life in the United States with that of Europe, we were surprised to notice how little control the national parties have over local primaries.

Political decentralization tends to diminish conformity in thinking and feeling in this country. If there is a general tendency to be like the Joneses, an individual tries to imitate the Joneses of his own parish rather than some rigid pattern equally venerated throughout the nation.

Particularism also prevails in the religious life of the country—innumerable denominations, tiny houses of prayer everywhere, few large churches, very few cathedrals dominating the skyline of a city, as in Europe, Latin America, or Canada.

I do not know whence came the concept of the United States as a melting pot of races and nationalities, but this term fails to describe properly what America has done to the peoples from old countries. The function of a melting pot is to destroy the identity of the raw materials and obtain a new stuff that meets certain specifications. This may be the Nazi idea of absorbing immigrants, but such an amalgamation has never been demanded of the immigrants to this country. Here we have met the Irish and Dutch, French and Italians, Poles and Lithuanians, Norwegians, Scots, Germans, and Russians. All of them have brought their language, religion, and national customs with them. Those who settled in compact groups have preserved national characteristics through many generations, but do not feel themselves to be the less American. American society is a product of integration rather than melting. It reminds me of a multicolored mosaic. National groups and denominations are the stones in the mosaic, each with its own color; combined, they form a picture. The design would have lost its brilliance if the stones had been subject to melting and reduced to uniformity.

The contrast between the United States and the countries of Europe is largely that of age. Here people look about them with wide-open eyes, enjoying life, grasping avidly for new toys—chrome-covered cars, electrical gadgets, TV sets. And thus the Joneses come into the picture. Whatever new toy the Joneses have, their neighbors want the same—but bigger and better.

It would be an exaggeration to say that the people of the United States are free from prejudices. We met manifestations of anti-Semitism, distrust of Roman Catholics, antipathy toward the Mexicans, the Italians, Poles, and foreigners in general. There is the bleeding wound of discrimination against the Negroes. But here the manifestations of nationalistic, racial, or religious intolerance are characteristic of definite groups of the population rather than of the whole people. The Irish brought with them the grudge against the British. Southerners have been poisoned by hatred of Negroes and contempt for them—contempt because the Negroes' great-grandfathers were slaves of the whites; hatred because some Negroes were masters of the whites during the short period of Reconstruction after the Civil War or have proved themselves more successful today. These ugly prejudices are in striking contrast to the general spirit of tolerance that characterizes American civilization.

In our lecture tours in Latin America and Asia, we have often been asked about the treatment of the Negroes in the United States. We have tried to dispel the false notions planted by anti-American propaganda—for example, that Negroes are not admitted to high schools or colleges and are corralled in their homes after dusk—but we have neither denied nor minimized the seriousness of the Negro problem. Explaining the roots of the deplorable situation, we have stressed the complexity of the American agglomeration of conflicting cultural currents. The great majority of the people in this country, we have said, have definite ideals of decency and justice in human relations and do not feel that these ideals have been realized in our institutions and everyday life. Democracy is a continuous struggle for a better life and greater justice. The defense of rights of minorities is one aspect of this struggle, and what has been achieved in this field in the past two decades shows that the country is moving in the right direction.

EQUALITY

The feature that impressed us most in the American character was the feeling of social equality, a feature that native-born Americans fail to notice because they take it for granted. The inferiority complex that haunted the first President of the German Republic would have been impossible in America, where an important political person is inclined to boast of having been born in a log cabin even though he was born in a mansion with a silver spoon in his mouth. The interest of some middle-class Americans in European titles, dubious royal arms, German barons, French counts, British lords, or Russian and Georgian princes does not belie the democratic spirit of American society. Those are bright rattles, harmless exotic toys. Even silly people in America do not take them as seriously as in Europe, and those who do take them earnestly belong to the exclusive circle of irremediable fools whose opinions do not count.

When, after many years in the United States, we revisited Europe and were asked about the American national character, we could only repeat what de Tocqueville had told his countrymen after his visit to the United States. We stressed the feeling of social equality as the main difference between the New World and the Old and pointed out the contrast between the stratified society in Europe and the classless society in the United States.

RESPECT FOR WORK

The most striking manifestation of the deeply rooted feeling of social equality in this country is respect for work—work of any kind, including manual labor. The European concept of democracy, born in ancient Greece, has been rather limited in this respect. Originally, it excluded from citizenry those who performed any kind of manual work or were engaged in any economic activity other than usury or exploitation of work of others, and it bestowed political rights only on those who were rich enough to devote all their time to politics, the military arts, and "virtue." The nineteenth century broadened the concept of democracy, but the old distinction between the working masses and higher classes of the society has outlived all reforms and revolutions in Europe. Even now one finds there a scale of occupations, and a man customarily engaged in a certain pursuit feels humiliated if he takes, even temporarily, a job with a lower rating. We motored in a private rented car in Greece. Our chauffeur, proud of his profession, was eager to have the car washed every other day but never did the washing himself—that would be degrading. Instead, he hired somebody else for the job.

The European refugees came to the American shores ready to accept clerical jobs but unprepared psychologically for manual work. Some quickly acquired another scale of values; others defended their prejudice to the bitter end. I remember a tragic case of the clash between these two attitudes in the 1930's, when jobs were scarce. A young refugee from Hitler's Germany, graduated in law from a Midwestern university, was hunting desperately for a job. Finally he was offered one in a gas station. This humiliation was the last blow—he went home and took his life.

Yet we have met many American boys, some with a better educational and social background, working unconcernedly during their vacations at filling stations or on construction of roads and buildings, proud of their ability to keep pace with strong Negro youths. In that work they were testing not only their muscles and physical endurance but also their moral strength, the discipline and suppleness of their minds. This was the school, though perhaps not the best conceivable, for absorbing the most valuable heritage of American civilization— respect for work and one's fellow man—and learning at the same time how to get along with people and make friends. Another aspect of American life that has impressed me is that of having young boys work on newspaper routes—especially sons of comparatively well-to-do parents who care little about the money the boys earn but value their experience, as a means of developing their sense of responsibility, discipline, independence in handling money, and, above all, respect for work.

The passion of adults to work with their hands—to wash their cars, make necessary repairs and occasional alterations in their homes, and so on—stems from a deeper source. But practice of "do-it-yourself" would not have taken root and spread so widely if it had not been supported by the traditional respect for labor. People born in this carefree land take it for granted that a man's natural pastime during the weekend is to work, stripped to the waist, under his car, on the lawn, in the basement workshop, or on the roof of his house. The picture of a suburban American residential section on summer weekends is striking to a European. The U. S. Information Service is remiss in not having shown this aspect of the American scene: a banker, a professor, a high official, and, on the other hand, a grocer, a factory worker, a milkman, a mailman, a taxi driver—all at work in their spare time, all in the same attire—and let the reader guess who is who among them!

SOCIAL PHILOSOPHY

What is the prevailing social and political philosophy in this country among people of different origin and with different cultural roots? So many voluminous treatises have been produced on this topic here and abroad that I do not dare join in the chorus. Least of all do I pretend to have discovered the sources of the characteristic features of the American social and economic system, and its political habits and institutions, as an expression of a definite scale of values or principles substantially different from those prevailing in Latin America, Europe, and other parts of the world. I do not believe that the difference in the attitudes of the Catholic and Protestant theology toward property, acquisition of material goods, and economic activity in general explains the divergence in economic and social trends in the United States and South America—a theory popular in Latin-American countries. Particular features in socio-political institutions and ideas in the United States can be explained, of course, by historical factors. But such an explanation simply traces back the origins of certain phenomena; it offers a rationale of what has happened, instead of showing why things have happened this way.

My impression has been that the prevailing pattern of thinking in the United States is pragmatic rather than deductive; it moves from observation, experience, and emotion to action, rather than from general premises to conclusions. This approach to reality is plebeian rather than aristocratic, searching and active rather than contemplative. An American seldom starts from general concepts and principles, but looks ahead for a conclusion. If the conclusion is in harmony with his own experience, emotional inclination, or prejudice, he readily accepts the theory supporting this conclusion. He is ready to change his views in the light of a new experience—new facts or what he considers new facts. But he is not likely to change his attitude toward practical problems because of a change in his general views on human society, history, or ethics.

It seems to me that the social philosophy of the great majority of the American people does not go deeper than a very general yearning for fair play, justice, decency—without further definition of what is fair, just, and decent. Perhaps that is an asset of this country. Its political thinking may be volatile and superficial, but the country is immune to the attacks of mass insanity induced by fanatical faith in some abstract dogma, such as Fascism, Nazism, or Marxism, a dogma that pretends to enunciate absolute truth and demands from the people blind submission to the logic prescribing the path from this truth to inescapable conclusions.

MATERIALISTIC AMERICA

Many Europeans believe that the United States is the land of the golden calf. This notion was firmly established long before World War I, when poor farmers and workers prevailed in the flow of European immigrants to the New World and rich Americans came to Paris, London, and Rome in search of ways to spend their dollars.

Europe had few contacts with American intellectuals and knew little of American universities, science, literature, and art. Times have changed, but the old clichés remain. During our trip to Europe in 1950 we heard a lot of talk about American materialism, and more recently, touring India in 1955-56, we listened to Indian intellectuals who contrasted their spiritualistic approach to life with American materialism. We have also observed with amazement that many Americans felt themselves on thin ice in discussing the comparative ranking of spiritual and material values in Asia and America. But we believe that, whatever the definition of materialism, there is no evidence that modern America is more materialistic than Europe or Asia.

Good food and wine constitute an essential part of the French concept of the aesthetics of life. American gastronomy does not satisfy the palate of French connoisseurs. To some of them, the quick lunch in a cafeteria or at a drugstore counter is evidence of a lack of civilization in the United States. We were treated to a fine dinner in Paris. My neighbor at table, a young professor of history, remarked with a polite smile, "Don't you agree that a nation is not civilized unless it has learned to appreciate fine food?"

"Your yardstick of civilization is new to me," I replied. "The ancient Greeks despised the barbarians for their elaborate meals and preferred their own simple fare."

I have heard German philistines discuss "American civilization." From the height of their own achievement—of course not during World War II—they looked down on materialistic America: insufficient understanding of serious music, little interest in philosophy, lack of higher spiritual values. But was it not superlatively civilized Germany that aligned itself behind a half-illiterate thug with the moral instincts of a gorilla? Perhaps materialism is characteristic of all modern civilization. Except for totalitarian countries where human behavior is governed by fear, and areas where only a primitive subsistence economy exists, money is the mainspring of human economic activity in all modern societies. The United States is no exception to this rule. Its businessmen are in business not for the fun of it but for profit, and are accustomed to measure success and failure in terms of money. But money does not mean more in the United States than in the older countries. Here, as there, some people kill themselves in an effort to build up bank accounts, while others take life easy. It is characteristic of this country, however, that brains and skill often yield more income than does hereditary wealth. It is also fairly certain that the creative element in the operation of big business and the spirit of competition are more important for the big captains of industry in America than in the old countries.

During our European trip, we met a man who had spent the war years in this country, an intelligent, dynamic, self-made fellow who must have fitted perfectly into the American scene. Strangely, he returned home convinced that nothing counted in the United States but money. I suggested that he compare similar situations in everyday life in this country and his own. "Take two boys on a university campus," I said, "a rich boy of indifferent scholastic achievement and one who works to pay his way but leads in the classroom and sports. Who would have a better chance with the girls?" My opponent conceded that in his country the wealthy boy would have a better chance with most of the coeds. I assured him that the opposite is likely to be true in American universities.

Then I asked him, "Suppose you discuss her suitors with a grown-up daughter. Would you take into account, among other things, the wealth of their families?" "That is not very important," he replied, "but we do pay some attention to such things." I assured him that decent people in the United States would not be likely to discuss such a matter with their children.

It was in India, however, that I grasped the real meaning of the problem of spiritual and material values in different civilizations. The concept of spiritual values is used in the Indian press as loosely and indiscriminately as the concept of free competition in the United States, but no Indian intellectual whom we met was able to define the spiritual values of India specifically. Then I tried to offer my own definition. Do not *spiritual* values mean the same thing as *moral* values, that is, a pattern of human relations that meets certain ethical standards? I found that Indian intellectuals were inclined to accept this definition. My next question was: What is the yardstick for measuring the ethical value of human relations and social institutions in different countries? This was not an abstract metaphysical question to me. As I said in telling the story of my youth, at the University I sat at the feet of Professor Petrazhitsky, and I have remained true to his psychological theory of law and state. The foundation of any political system is the common concept of the people of what is just and decent.

My question amounted to a challenge: Let us compare what we, in both countries, consider to be social justice; what are the inalienable rights of an individual in the United States and India; what each community provides for each of its members; which system implies greater respect for human dignity and work. On all these counts, the United States does not have to apologize for its moral code. The application of this code is not perfect in either country or, for that matter, anywhere in the world, but to reduce the problem to its essence—the dignity of the common man—this country is far ahead of the democracies of Europe and the dreamy East.

VIOLENCE

There are some hard facts that do not fit into my picture of America.

The daily chronicle of events in the newspapers of the United States is full of crimes of passion, murder, rape, juvenile delinquency, and other violence. Even taking account of the size of the country and the demand of the reading public for a complete coverage of these macabre events, this gruesome chronicle does not accord with my picture of America as a land of kind, friendly, easygoing people who are more inclined to smile than to scowl. I do not know how to reconcile this contradiction. Perhaps the explanation lies in the coincidence of many factors: lack of uniformity in communal life, lack of tradition, excessive mobility of the population, volatility of the American character, defects in the school system, lack of discipline in family life and, of course, the usual social evils—poor housing, weakness of the social welfare system, and so on.

The wave of violence epitomizes a number of important unsolved problems. I do not believe, however, that these problems are a distinctive feature of current American civilization. Similar phenomena exist in other countries, and there is no reliable common yardstick for international comparison of their frequency. There may be some consistent bias in recording acts of violence in the United States in comparison with the countries that have a less efficient press and less developed means of communication.

Moreover, along with manifestations of moral anarchy, the daily chronicle of this country records acts of goodwill, kindness, and often heroism that could fill many columns in the newspapers were they reported in the same detail and with the same gusto as are the sordid stories. There has to be something extraordinary—a touch of tragedy or sentimentality or humor—to convert the better side of human nature and national character into a good newspaper story.

The average American is too civilized to find pleasure in bullfighting, but he must have a properly assorted supply of horror stories with his breakfast, and the newspapers do their best to meet his demand.

A NATION ON THE MOVE

Driving across this continent, we often had the impression that the people of the United States have not yet settled down in the expanse between the two oceans. The center of population is still moving westward, several miles each year, according to our decennial censuses. The movements of people are like currents in the ocean. There is a continuous long-range movement and there are migrations related to changing business conditions, the season, and the new patterns of enjoying life after retirement.

New cities emerge, if not overnight, then over a decade. A fascinating picture for Europeans, who are accustomed to trace the origins of their cities through centuries, often back to the time of ancient Rome or earlier! People change professions, sell their houses and buy new ones, try their hand at one occupation or industry after another. A lawyer takes a job in a fire department, a schoolteacher becomes a house painter or a taxi driver, an insurance agent takes a place on the assembly line in an automobile factory. People are mildly surprised when a champion boxer becomes a university professor or a professor doubles as a night-club entertainer or trades his academic career for that of a professional wrestler. These are extreme cases, of course, but, apart from them, the mobility of labor characteristic of the United States is unknown in Europe, where long years of apprenticeship—a heritage from the Middle Ages—discourage occupational changes. In London, five years is the normal apprenticeship for a waiter in a restaurant; in Paris, four years is the apprenticeship for making buttonholes in men's vests.

Once I went to the office of a notary public in Paris. It was in an old and delapidated building. Visitors had to walk across two tiny back yards and climb three flights of stairs not much broader than fire escapes in modern cities. An opaque glass partition separated the notary's cubicle from the reception space. Waiting in the latter, I examined the engravings on the wall. All were of the same size, in similar frames. All were licenses to perform notary duties at the court. The first two had been issued by the French kings, the third by the revolutionary government, the fourth by the Emperor, and so on. All bearers of the licenses had the same surname and address. Seven generations of notaries public had officiated in that cubicle over nearly two centuries! I am sure that the eighth of the same name still has his office there.

I remember another picture. At the Statistical Board in Berlin, I saw an old official. His desk was in the corner of a large room beside the window. He had an array of tiny flower pots with minuscule plants on the windowsill and a cage with a canary above them; an embroidered seat cover was on his swivel chair and a box of cigars and an alcohol stove for boiling water on his desk. He had spent twenty-eight years in his swivel chair at that window.

These cases are typical af the manner of life in old European countries—continuity, tradition, stability.

How strikingly different in this respect are the patterns of social relations between the United States, where mobility is so usual that it is taken for granted, and, say, Japan! Young Japanese graduates get their first jobs just before they leave school. Lists of available jobs are shown to them, graded more by opportunity for promotion and social prestige than by initial pay, which is very low in all pursuits. Priority of choice depends on academic achievement—the best students in nationally prominent schools get the best jobs, while only manual labor may be open to mediocre students. This allocation of jobs among beginning workers is a crucial event. Most of them will stay with these employers throughout their working lives or until the dissolution of the enterprise.

Explaining the structure of the American economy to the students in one of the largest Japanese universities, I mentioned that we in the United States consider it normal for a young man to change jobs in order to acquire experience and test his abilities—not only his technical skills but also his ability to get along with people and find his way in a new environment. The audience, both students and faculty members, seemed interested but somewhat incredulous. When the question period came, a professor remarked, "In our country, if a man has changed employers two or three times, he is regarded as an unreliable, quarrelsome individual." At this point Emma entered the discussion. "In the United States the fact that a young man has worked in various cities in all four corners of the country rather speaks in his favor by showing that he has initiative and courage. In contrast, a man who spends all his life on the same job is likely to be thought a failure." This remark met with applause and polite laughter. In closing the meeting, the dean summarized the problem. "The American professor," he said, "explained to us why people in the United States are not afraid to change their occupation. You also should have more courage and should not hesitate to change your position, but not before you have secured another job." There was again applause and polite laughter. It looked as though mobility of labor in the United States and immobility in Japan had suddenly epitomized for our listeners the contrast between the American and Japanese ways of life.

In the United States mobility affects all aspects of our lives. People come and go, and today's neighbors may be hundreds of miles away tomorrow; people promptly become friends and promptly forget one another; human relations become less formal than in more settled communities but also more superficial. Mobility prevents stagnation but also makes it more difficult to crystallize opinions and tastes; it favors the development of social and moral instability. It has advantages and disadvantages, but how assess them so as to establish an exact balance? Studying this question in connection with the structure of the population and internal migrations in this country, I was perhaps inclined to stress the bright side of the picture. My opinion may be biased, but I feel that the United States would be wholly different if its population were as firmly settled as it is in the Old World.

F. D. R.

We came to the United States at a turning point in its history, when it was emerging from the great depression and bracing itself for the impending cruel test by fire and blood. This era was dominated by the personality of the President, Franklin Delano Roosevelt.

Not all the economic and financial reforms invoked by F.D.R. were equally wise. Occasionally they collided with one another. Some were directed against monopolies and concentration of economic power, while others (for example, industrial codes) favored such concentration. Some fought deflation; others (for example, accumulation of reserves by the Social Security program) were deflationary in nature. However, despite my doubts about some measures of the administration, I admired their general spirit. I felt nobody could be lukewarm toward the policy of F.D.R.—one must either love it or hate it. Roosevelt had no blueprint for prosperity and did not believe that anybody knew a correct solution of the problem. But he felt a solution must be found and was seeking a way out of the depression. His approach was pragmatic, experimental. His economic philosophy seemed to be: "We cannot wait doing nothing. We must try, and ultimately we will find the solution." And he succeeded beyond the most daring expectations!

I realize that my first impression of America was influenced largely by the personality of F.D.R.—his warmth, his courage, his freedom from prejudice, his informality, his lack of pomposity. I heard the recording of Roosevelt's first inaugural address and forever remembered its concluding words: ". . . The only thing we have to fear is fear itself—nameless, unreasoning, unjustified terror which paralyzes needed effort to convert retreat into advance." Nor shall I forget the voice of the speaker: no bravado, rather an expression of sadness at the pervasive strength of fear that overwhelms the strong and subdues the brave. Our own lives have taught us that a man has nothing to fear but fear itself, but never had I heard that thought expressed with such strength and in such beautiful words.

It appeared for some time that Roosevelt was approaching difficult economic issues as more or less occasional chores. To him the essential was to keep high the people's faith in themselves, to sustain their hope for the future, rally them in a common effort. Was it an accident that in the speech he was preparing on the day of his death he returned to the theme of his first inaugural address: "We must go on to do all in our power to conquer the doubt and the fears. . . . The only limit to our realization of tomorrow will be our doubts of today."

Roosevelt had another characteristic that endeared him to us as Europeans. Before the advent of radio, the heads of state in Europe had relatively few occasions to address the masses of the people directly. Mussolini may have been the first to use the new medium. His screams from the balcony in Rome opened a new era in political rhetoric. Then came Hitler, who added the roaring of a beast to the political concert. I can still hear his opening: *"Deutsche Männer und deutsche Frauen"* (German men and German women). These words reared a wall of hatred, suspicion, contempt between the Germans to whom the Führer addressed himself and other people who might hear him. The speaker was working himself into a tantrum, and the response of the crowd revealed the wild beast slumbering in the hearts of his listeners despite the varnish of civilization.

Those who had never been exposed to such oratory will hardly understand our reaction to Roosevelt's fireside chats. His was a wholly new concept of a political speech. He addressed not a crowd but the nation, not from a rostrum but from his home, seated at the fireplace, just as many of his listeners might be seated. When he started his chats, his simple, warm words, "My friends," embraced everyone who was listening. An invisible aura of goodwill and faith emanated from the White House, enveloping this country and spreading far beyond its borders.

I did not agree with every word of the President. I heard an undertone of social demagoguery in some of his fighting speeches. Perhaps he occasionally overemphasized the rights of citizens without sufficiently stressing their duties; his diatribes about the responsibility of the government for the well-being of individuals sometimes seemed to minimize the responsibility of the individual. These were details, however. Above all, Roosevelt was a master politician; he knew his aim and how to reach it. His aim was magnificent. He enjoyed a good fight, made few mistakes, and suffered few defeats in his political career. One shudders to think where the United States and the world would be without his superb skill in political maneuvering.

Even in the 1930's and 1940's, Washington was full of people who were more or less critical of the New Deal. Many critics were concerned about the growth of the national debt and the expenditure of money on public works, which they condemned as boondoggling. During our trips across the country, we observed many post office buildings with columns emulating the façade of a Greek temple. Perhaps some of these architectural creations could have been trimmed down a bit but, seeing them, I thought of Germany. The government of the Weimar Republic had a chance to stop the tide of the bitter reaction. It could have reversed the deflationary spiral, given work to the unemployed, restored the self-confidence of the people and their faith in the Republic. Instead, it chose to keep the budget balanced and defend the currency, and it defended the currency until the Republic collapsed. It saved the currency and thus Hitler could plunge Germany and the world into the abyss of destruction.

In the national parks we visited temporary barracks of the Civilian Conservation Corps. In the inspiring environment of some of the most beautiful spots on the continent, young boys from the slums of the big cities were at work—building roads, dams, and bridges, clearing forests, fighting tree diseases. For most of them this was the first job they could love; for many, the first job in their life. We talked with the boys and their squad leaders. In a national park in Colorado we met a youngster, a former barber's apprentice. Reared in Jewish slums, he had never seen a forest until he enrolled in the CCC and was brought to this enchanting place. Here he had learned to work in the open air and studied books on forestry in his spare hours. The rangers had promised him a permanent job with the forestry service. His term of work with the CCC was nearing its end, he told us, but he would never return to the city. He would stay here as a forester and he revealed to us his dream. "Later, if I am good enough, I may become a ranger."

In another park, a supervisor told us about a problem he faced with new recruits. The regulations provided that only boys in good health could be accepted. Minimum weight was fixed. But many boys were undernourished on arrival and could not pass the test. "We keep them as guests of the other boys for a week or two and try to feed them up. A skinny boy can gain ten pounds in two weeks."

We saw the roads, culverts, and shelters the boys had built and the stretches of forests they had cleared—a marvelous combination of conservation of natural resources and human beings. And again I could not help comparing the situation in the United States and Germany. These healthy, cheerful, friendly boys will never forget what their country has done for them. They returned to their homes better men and better citizens. . . . Was not F.D.R. building his nation as effectively as Brüning had been destroying the Weimar Republic? Simple people whom we met in all parts of the country considered Roosevelt *their* President.

Many of our Washington friends were slightly ironical about what they considered our uncritical admiration of Roosevelt. To some of them he was too radical; to others, not radical enough. Some reproached him with having concentrated too much power in his hands, encroaching on the rights of states. The source of the difference between the critics of the President and ourselves lay in our political background. Comparing the situation at the depths of the depression in Germany and the United States, we felt that Roosevelt, with his big heart, bold vision, undaunted courage, and political skill, had saved his country from catastrophe such as had engulfed Germany.

The first Roosevelt speech we heard on the radio was his famous address to the Philadelphia Convention in June, 1936: "To some generations much is given. Of other generations much is expected. This generation of America has a rendezvous with destiny. . . ." He could not have known then that history was approaching a turning point at which the destiny of the United States would be to save the democratic form of government throughout the world.

ISOLATIONISM

The predominant orientation in the United States in the middle 1930's, when we came here, was isolationist. The people knew little about international affairs, cared even less, and did not realize that developments in Russia, Germany, or Japan could affect their vital interests. Rather, there was a strong feeling that the United States was so richly endowed with natural resources and was so big and so strong it could follow its own road, leaving the European nations to solve their problems. This attitude was not necessarily an ideological neutrality between the forces of freedom and Nazism clashing in the Old World. Some isolationists had better arguments in support of their views. The European powers, they said, have always fought one another, and the United States has never taken sides in their internal strife. If we should wish to support any definite party, how could we do it? Would not the attempt of our government to intervene in European affairs result in dividing this nation against itself? Thus was born the idea of the fortress America protected by two oceans, like formidable moats, against attack or encroachment by overseas powers. The task of the government, according to this conception, was to fortify these defenses and be ready to repulse any assault of the enemy. Isolationism, in different forms, was predominant in the United States in 1937-38, although some people realized even then that, in the event of a major war, this country would be compelled to take a stand and probably to take up arms.

Roosevelt was one of the first statesmen in this hemisphere who realized that the world was in revolutionary convulsions, that a total war was impending, and that the United States could not remain a passive spectator. Yet even he was unable to alert the people to the imminent danger. His "quarantine the aggressor" speech in Chicago in October, 1937, found no response even in his own party.

Crisscrossing the country during our vacations, we realized that isolationism was a natural product of the nation's geographic and economic conditions and its history. It had never been attacked since the War of 1812, and had so much wealth within its borders that only experts could see its economic limitations in the event of a war or a blockade. An average American had pacifism and anti-militarism in his bones; military preparations and alliances were incompatible with his passionate desire for peace; his isolationism was deeply emotional. Moreover, political thinking beyond debates in Congress and state legislatures or national and local elections was contrary to American custom. People had not been taught to discuss politics in terms of national aims in coming decades and even less to visualize them against the background of world history. American isolationism, nurtured during more than a century of sheltered living, could be dissipated, in Toynbee's language, only by a violent shock as a response to a challange, or, in Roosevelt's words, at the time of the nation's rendezvous with destiny.

AMERICA AT WAR

The President's quarantine speech in Chicago met with public disapproval. Was not F.D.R. luring the nation into a military alliance and, eventually, a war far from American shores—a direct violation of the century-old tradition of American foreign policy?

With Munich, the war came nearer. More people began to think something had to be done to stop Hitler. After the Hitler-Stalin pact, the war became unavoidable. People in the United States began to realize that Hitler was a threat to the entire world, including America. Great Britain seemed to be the next victim.

When the British King and Queen came to Washington and Hyde Park, the President displayed his showmanship at its best, trying to kindle friendly feelings for the Commonwealth. He received the royal couple like young friends—not quite in distress, but in a rather difficult situation—with sympathy and respect for their courage in the face of adverse fortune. Perhaps there was a shade of patronizing informality in his attitude. The newspapers reported that the President said to the King, "Call me Franklin, I shall call you George." "Yes, Mr. President." It seemed to me that the people in the streets of Washington began to love the royal guests just because of the dignity and courtesy with which the President entertained them.

Then came the war. The Communists denounced British, French, and American imperialists and warmongers. The liberals in Washington were bewildered. Confusion increased after the invasion of Poland by the joint forces of Hitler and Stalin. Some of the "friends of Russia" began to realize that the rulers of the U.S.S.R. were stooges of Hitler in his war against democracy and Western civilization; others closed their eyes and continued to follow the party line. After the surrender of Poland and a short spell of "phony war," Hitler threw his forces against the Netherlands, France, Belgium, and Norway. Then the anguish of the summer of 1940: Dunkirk, the capitulation of France, the beginning of the Battle of Britain.

The forces of isolationism did not yield without a struggle. Those on the extreme right glorified Hitler's invincible legions; those on the left denounced the British and prophesied their imminent defeat. But the United States had a gallant captain who led the country firmly to the rescue of Great Britain. In December, 1940, the President appealed to the technical genius of the nation to transform the country into the arsenal of democracy. Remembering the interwar years in Europe, where political life was poisoned for many years by the dispute over the interallied and reparations debts, I could readily appreciate the significance of the Lend-Lease act passed by Congress in March, 1941.

Communist pickets paraded in front of the White House, denouncing the President as a warmonger. Wild strikes in munitions factories spread through the country. Stalin was doing everything in his power in support of the Nazis. By this time the liberals had broken with isolationism, but many defended the neutralist policy of the U.S.S.R. as an oriental variety of isolationism. After the shabby treatment the Russians had received at Munich, they argued, the Kremlin could not trust the Allies! When I told my American colleagues in Washington that Stalin was not an impartial onlooker but had an active part in the conflict on Hitler's behalf, they considered my interpretation of Russian policy unfair. In their minds, there was no connection between the Kremlin and the anti-war activity of local Communists.

Suddenly the war took a new turn. One evening late in June, 1941, we turned on the radio. And there was that voice we would never forget, the roaring voice from dark jungles. "*Deutsche Männer und deutsche Frauen!*" Hitler was announcing to the Germans that his troops had invaded Russia and were moving toward Moscow.

Windows in all the houses around our place were open. All our neighbors were listening to Hitler's speech in English translation. We went into the garden. The neighbors came to ask us what effect Hitler's new aggression would have. I said, "Tomorrow all the strikes in munitions factories will be called off and the pickets will disappear from the sidewalk in front of the White House." Indeed, the American Communists promptly reversed their pro-Hitler policy. The attitude of the public toward Russia changed as rapidly as the attitude of the American fellow travelers toward the war. Now people considered the U.S.S.R. an innocent victim of Hitler's aggression. Stalin became a hero.

We realized, of course, that Hitler's attack on Russia was a blessing for Great Britain and its Allies from a purely military point of view. The political implications of the new development were another matter. The ideological meaning of the war was blurred. Before June, 1941, a bloc of democratic nations opposed the three totalitarian countries—Germany and Italy in the front line, with the U.S.S.R. in the rear. Now the ideological unity of the anti-Nazi bloc was destroyed. Many American liberals held that the Hitler-Stalin clash was not a split in the camp of enemies of democracy but the beginning of a new Holy War of the forces of freedom led by Stalin against the legions of evil headed by Hitler. They argued that the best thing the United States could do now was to follow the Red generalissimo.

December 7, 1941: Pearl Harbor! The bombs brought to light new features in the American character. The country, utterly unprepared for a major war, took up arms, confident it would master the situation. I do not remember having met anybody who expressed doubt of our final victory. Industrial mobilization went on with unexpected success: "What is difficult we do at once. The impossible will take a little longer."

The war became a test of all the material and moral forces of American civilization. This was the decisive hour predicted by F.D.R. The country passed the test with flying colors.

A chain of reverses marked the beginning of the war. The United States had only a few fully equipped divisions and practically no air force. It had insufficient cadres of trained officers and no military traditions. The bulk of its navy was destroyed by the Japanese in the first attack. Political and military leaders realized the seriousness of the situation. Foreign observers in Washington doubted whether there would be time enough for the United States to train and arm troops and take them to the battlefields before Hitler's final triumph over the free world. But the man in the street simply did not believe the United States could be licked.

The other striking feature was the nation's genius at improvisation. Long-range systematic planning is obviously not in the national character of the United States. Either people do not have enough patience to plan in advance or they do not believe that detailed plans can be of great help in case of emergency; they prefer, rather, to reduce advance thinking to a minimum, relying heavily on last-minute decisions.

The most recent developments in military technology and strategy may have changed this attitude, but in 1942-43 the industrial and military mobilization was a chain of amazing improvisations rather than the execution of deliberate plans. I do not know whether this was true also of the military operations in the four corners of the world, on the land, in the air, and on the sea.

A bottleneck developed in the production of mines for the navy and air force because of a shortage of skilled workers to make the intricate wiring system that represents an important part of each mine. The factories hired all the watchmakers available in the nearby area, but the men—most of them elderly craftsmen—though accustomed to handle fine watch mechanisms, were unprepared for this job-task. Somebody suggested trying lacemakers. Lacemaking was an old, almost obsolete industry in the area, and there were many women who had once engaged in it. They were called to munition factories. What was demanded of them seemed like a new pattern in lacemaking. The bottleneck in mine production was solved.

I saw how new methods were developed in shipbuilding, how a new design of a landing craft was born, how a new technique was introduced in building roads and airfields on swampy ground. . . . These were ingenious solutions of problems arising in emergency situations.

The results of the systematic work of countless committees and sub-committees were less impressive. They moved in a pedestrian way and were the less effective the higher the level of their members in the bureaucratic hiearchy.

IN A SEPARATION CENTER

My few glimpses of life in the United States Army during the war left me with the impression that the military were, after all, civilians in uniform. It was amazing how promptly a tenderfoot youngster became a perfect soldier, how easily an insurance agent or a lawyer became a naval officer and leader of men in battle. Perhaps these transformations had something to do with the mobility of the people, the fluidity of American society, the American genius at improvisation. I had no opportunity to see American soldiers in action, but I liked their looks —not overdrilled, free in their movements, very youthful, in smart uniforms.

Shortly before the war's end I was invited to lecture to the groups of occupational counselors the army was training for the separation centers. The counselors were to talk with each boy discharged from the armed forces, familiarize him with his rights and privileges as a veteran, and help him in his first steps back to civilian life. Training courses for these counselors were arranged at several separation centers. Usually half the students were officers and half enlisted men. I was a guest lecturer and gave only one two-hour talk to each graduating group. My topic was the economic outlook after the war. The gist of my talk was that there would be enough jobs for everyone, that the GI's would hardly need to use their special re-employment rights, and that the best thing for them would be to act like other boys of their age and skills.

After one lecture I told the commander of the school, who was also the C.O. of the separation center, that it would help me if I could see the operation of the center. He took me to the barracks where separations were processed, introduced me to the counselors, and invited me to sit in at the interviews in any of their private offices. One of the counselors was, to my surprise, a woman, a professor of psychology. She handled the most difficult cases. Since I was interested in simple, typical situations, I chose a counselor in the uniform of a non-commissioned officer.

In his cubicle, the counselor handed me a bunch of personnel folders. I chose one at random. He opened it, read the first page, and said, "This is a sad case." He called in the boy, who was waiting in the hall. The small, skinny soldier sat down at the counselor's desk, visibly frightened.

I had his personal story before me. Jack ———, born in 1919. State orphanage. Sent to reform school for larceny in 1934. Released in 1937. No further trouble until induction into the armed forces. No record during basic training. Assigned to a post in the Pacific. No record. Three months in the hospital (malaria). Returned to the post of previous service. No record. Two months in a hospital (malaria). Transferred to the mainland in view of health conditions. Arrested for disorderly conduct in the barracks. Arrested again for disobedience. A.W.O.L. Resisted MP. Escaped from the stockade by means of forgery. Stole the car of the C.O. A.W.O.L. Arrested again. Court-martialed. The sentence of the court: "Dishonorable discharge and three years' imprisonment." Resolution of the division commander: "Confirmation refused. The court has failed to investigate to what extent the behavior of the defendant, after his return to the States, might have been due to his sickness." A new trial. The new sentence: "Not guilty. Honorable discharge on health conditions." Sentence confirmed.

The counselor asked the boy casually, "What are your plans, Jack?"

The soldier replied defiantly, "Must I answer this one? Am I not discharged?"

"Sure you are. But how can I write out the railroad ticket for you if I don't know where you plan to go?"

The boy thought a minute and then named a city.

"That isn't your home town, Jack," said the counselor. "But if you prefer to pay the additional fare out of your own pocket, that is your business."

The boy named another railroad station. "That's better, Jack," said the counselor. "Here are your discharge papers."

The boy's hands trembled as he asked, "What kind of a paper is this?"

"An honorable discharge, of course, as ordered by the court."

The soldier took the paper, read and reread it, checked the corners for secret marks. The counselor said gravely, "Now listen, Jack. The army has only one kind of honorable discharge. Your papers are as good as mine. You go out of this door, and for the rest of your life you will be an honorably discharged veteran. The army has recognized your services overseas. Everything that happened afterwards has been wiped out. You were a sick man. You are in good health now."

The boy was shaking all over. He was still sick. The counselor explained the GI rights to him. "Whatever happens, the army will back you. You are our boy. . . ."

The strain seemed unbearable for the soldier. He asked, "May I go now?"

"Not yet. There is still another formality. Your severance pay."

"Severance pay? For me?"

"Here is your check. Three hundred dollars."

The soldier turned the check over in his trembling hands. He had neither expected nor understood this "formality." The counselor rose from his chair, came nearer to him, and put his arm on his shoulder. "Remember this, Jack. Your papers are as clean as discharge papers can be. The army has been fair to you. The rest is up to you."

The boy left the cubicle without showing his feelings. I watched the separation procedure in half a dozen other cases and returned home with the realization that the United States Army could be thoughtful and humane.

"THANK YOU, SIR!"

Later, talking with people in France, Germany, Italy, and Japan, I asked about their impressions of our men in the armed forces, especially the GI's. They were impressed by the equipment of our men, mostly by the quality of their uniforms and shoes and the abundance of trucks and jeeps. They noticed that the GI's were not as well drilled as the German soldiers and that there was less rigid stratification among our troops. In many respects, the GI's off duty seemed to be fairly independent of their officers. But what surprised people abroad most was that, off duty, the GI's were just boys released from an unpleasant task and did not pretend to be anything else. Foreign observers invariably described them as noisy and exuberant but friendly, kind, generous with money and rations, ready to help, and very fond of children. Our officers abroad were also in most cases warm and sympathetic. There were complaints and individual instances of abuses—usually black marketing—but as human beings our men in the armed forces, both privates and officers, impressed the local people as humane and kind.

Our Japanese interpreter, who became our friend and accompanied us on our lecture tour through his country, told us of his first contact with the American troops. A journalist by profession, he was covering Manchuria during the war and acquired some knowledge of English and Russian. During the war he was made an interpreter at the military headquarters in Tokyo. Then came the surrender of the Japanese army; the Americans appeared in Tokyo and ordered the Japanese command to supply them with interpreters. Our friend was assigned to U.S. headquarters. His first order was to accompany an American colonel to what was left of the business district of Tokyo. The colonel stopped at the first bootblack and, when his shoes had been polished, asked the interpreter what he had to pay. Giving the money to the bootblack, he said casually, "Thank you, sir!" "This struck me," said our friend. "Shoeshining is one of the lowliest occupations in Japan. We never thank the shiner, and nobody had ever said 'sir' to that man before. And now he heard this word from an officer of the most powerful army in the world! At this moment I understood that the United States was bringing a new civilization, and what this civilization meant for us in Japan!"

This colonel represented the same breed of military man as the division commander who refused to confirm the harsh sentence against Jack ——.

MY WORK WITH THE U.S. GOVERNMENT

Our discovery of America would not have been complete without our work with the federal government. There was nothing dramatic in this experience. It included work with agencies of high standard, run by competent and devoted people. I keep a pleasant memory of them, and they seemed to attribute some value to my contribution, though actually I did not fit into the bureaucratic machinery very well and was not overenthusiastic about the way in which things were done around me. I worked for the Central Statistical Board and later for the Social Security Administration; between these two jobs I was with the Social Science Research Council, engaged in research in the same general field.

Emma worked for the Social Science Research Council, the Board of Economic Warfare (later the Foreign Economic Administration), and the Department of State. In addition, my interest in general economic problems has kept me in touch with a half-dozen departments and agencies, and more recently we both have worked in contact with services of the Department of State in Washington and abroad.

CENTRAL STATISTICAL BOARD

I received my first government job the third day after we came to Washington. We arrived on Tuesday night, and next morning I went to see Isadore Lubin, Commissioner of Labor Statistics. Lubin was engaged in a long-distance call when I came to his office. A Negro messenger sat at a small desk in the waiting room reading a newspaper, one foot on the desk and the other in an open drawer, a posture unknown in Europe but popular with U.S. government officials, mighty and humble. (Later I learned that this posture is supposed to improve the circulation.) When Lubin appeared in the doorway, the boy looked at him over the newspaper and continued to read, without changing his comfortable position. This was my introduction to the informality that characterizes U.S. government services.

Lubin was familiar with my German publications and thought the Central Statistical Board might be interested in my work. He called the chairman of the Board, Stuart Rice, and the latter asked me to come to see him in the Commerce Building across the street. The following morning I took the oath of office and entered employment with the government.

The Central Statistical Board was one of the youngest agencies in Washington, still in an experimental state, and I was more impressed by its spirit than its efficiency. Its chairman was a man of broad interests, a brilliant speaker, and a gentleman. Most of the staff members were competent and enthusiastic young men, but the program of the agency seemed to me somewhat vague, while to my colleagues my own ideas seemed far-fetched. My assignment was to explore the scope of statistics that the census would have to supply for the Social Security Administration. I produced a report showing that the Social Security Board itself would collect information required for its current operations.

On the other hand, I suggested, the Social Security program was only one of the New Deal reforms that entailed a reappraisal of the

whole system of official labor statistics, including the program of decennial censuses. I recommended making a clear distinction between
employees and self-employed persons in the labor force and classifying
workers by industry rather than by occupation, as had been done before; this last idea I developed in several papers. To my surprise, the
old guard in the Bureau of the Census strongly opposed my proposal.
Very soon, however, our labor force and employment statistics were reorganized in this direction. I do not believe that my papers played any
role in this change: the change had to come.

SOCIAL SCIENCE RESEARCH COUNCIL

My work with the Board ended as briskly as it began. My assignment
brought me in touch with the Committee on Social Security of the
Social Science Research Council, and its director invited me to join its
staff. I thought that the Committee would want me to write about
social security in Europe, but he explained, "We shall look at European experience through American eyes. What we expect from you is
to explore our economic and social conditions as seen through European eyes." This was a challenging assignment, and I readily accepted
it.

My work with the Committee gave me an opportunity to examine
many aspects of U.S. labor economics—the structure of the labor
force, labor turnover, fluctuations in employment and unemployment,
wage rates, trends in wage differentials, and so on. The Committee
published some six of my books on these related problems, but it is
difficult for me to judge how much these publications contributed to
a better understanding of social security problems in this country.

Some of my methodological suggestions, such as the construction of
a "calendar of employment," found practical application in this country and Canada. Some ideas, for instance, the observation that "additional workers" appear on the labor market during depressions, provoked criticism and have remained controversial. Some notions, for
example, on the mobility of labor, have been confirmed by other re-
searchers and universally accepted. Perhaps some of my observations
on the trends in earnings have been useful in discussions of the revision of the Social Security program. All in all, the five years of work
with the Committee on Social Security were uneventful but well
used. I learned much about the economic and social system of the
United States and felt that I was participating in a collective work
centered around the implementation of the Social Security Act and
the further development of the Social Security system.

SOCIAL SECURITY ADMINISTRATION

My second government job was with the Social Security Board, with a somewhat loose attachment to its various divisions and rather vague responsibilities. There was an informal agreement that I myself would carve my proper niche in the organization and thus I had considerable freedom in selecting topics for study.

The Board had the well-deserved reputation of being a perfectly clean agency—not very imaginative, but liberal and broad-minded in interpreting its programs and planning for their further expansion.

The Social Security Act of 1935 was an outstanding piece of New Deal legislation and brought several programs under a single administrative roof. Unfortunately, its program for old-age and survivors' insurance was patterned after private old-age pension insurance, as a system of compulsory individual policies, with obligatory accumulation of reserves for the remote future. With certain reservations, it could be described as a program of compulsory thrift, each individual being obliged to pay for his own insurance and participate during several decades in the accumulation of reserve funds that would reach astronomical proportions by the time the program matured.

After a careful analysis of this program, I concluded that its plan of financing was unsound and that the system should be financed on a pay-as-you-go basis with only small contigency reserves. In this way, each generation of working age would support the old people who had been economically active in the preceding generation; in their turn, people currently of working age would be supported by younger people when their time came. In other words, I thought that, instead of a system built on the principle of individual thrift, a nationwide old-age insurance program should be based on the idea of solidarity of successive generations. It must be recognized, however, that there were serious considerations for writing the original plan for old-age insurance into the law. It was a means of appeasing the right-wing opposition in Congress and forestalling the charge that the program would ultimately affect the distribution of incomes in the nation, which would have made the Act unconstitutional.

As the principal economist of the Board, I was not bound by such political considerations, and about the first thing I did was to develop projections showing how the program would operate under continuously changing conditions—rising wages and probably rising prices. These projections indicated that the program was incompatible with a sound economic and social policy. Naturally, my findings provoked objections from the actuaries of the Board. We had a heated exchange of memoranda, but, whatever the merits of my arguments, I was invading the hunting grounds of the actuaries and had no chance against them. The Board continued to defend the original program. As time went on, however, the whole plan was revised and amended by Congress. The theory of individually purchased policies and huge reserves was abandoned in favor of a sound plan to finance benefits on a pay-as-you-go basis, with modest reserves for a transition period and a rough adjustment of benefits to the wage level of the beneficiaries before their retirement.

I was no longer with the Social Security Administration when the program took its present shape, but, observing its evolution, I found a new confirmation of my theory on the ways of progress in this country. Everything begins with confusion (as in the discovery of the New World by Columbus); at that stage no logical argument can clear up the problem; but step by step things become clearer until a point is reached when no argument can make the original absurd situation appear sensible. Then comes change.

My work on problems of manpower, employment, and unemployment was more successful than my desperate attempt to change the old-age insurance program. Here I worked with Ewan Clague, later Commissioner of the Bureau of Labor Statistics. In the field of research, he was guided wholly by the desire to get the facts and find out what they meant, without any concern as to whether the findings would please or displease labor, management, or politicians. He was an excellent public relations man and inspired confidence and goodwill in everyone with whom he came in contact. Using materials developed in his organization, he was scrupulous in giving credit to his associates, sometimes even crediting them with his own ideas. Association with him is one of the most pleasant memories of my work with the government.

I saw eye to eye with Clague in appraising the existing unemployment insurance system, which leaves almost complete freedom to the states in planning and running their programs. Since its inception this system had been severely criticized as illogical and impractical. Though I considered that unemployment was a national problem and could be handled most efficiently on a national scale, nevertheless I felt that the system established in the original Social Security Act could operate smoothly enough and had certain advantages over a streamlined, nationwide program. Under a uniform national program, I thought, the size and duration of benefits would necessarily be determined by conditions prevailing in low-wage, socially backward states—not necessarily the most backward but those below the national average. In contrast, the present system favors improvement of the standards in the industrially developed states with strong labor unions and comparatively high wage rates.

A study of unemployment compensation programs in different states led me to conclude that most of them demanded higher contributions than were necessary to pay the established benefits, or provided benefits too low in relation to contributions. The unemployment insurance agencies in the states had, of course, noticed this discrepancy, evidenced by a rapid accumulation of reserves, and, along with the improvement of the benefit formula, were cutting down the contribution rates by following the principle of experience rating for individual industries and sometimes individual concerns. I tried to facilitate such adjustments by developing actuarial formulas for long-range estimates of the cost of unemployment benefits under alternative assumptions concerning business conditions, pattern of labor turnover, benefit rates, maximum duration of benefits, and so on. It seemed to me that these formulas, translated into a series of tables, could be used for unemployment insurance estimates in the way mortality and survival tables are used in life and pension insurance. Later my method was adopted by almost all the states. Perhaps this was my only significant contribution to the development of social security.

ECONOMIC FORECASTS

The problem of economic mobilization was solved in a truly American way—without elaborate blueprints, as an upsurge of improvisation amidst apparent confusion. The government allocated orders for munitions to enterprises that were eager to get them although they had neither experience in the field nor the necessary equipment and labor force. Contractors sent out scouts to get workers wherever they could find them. Unskilled workers were upgraded after a brief in-job training. Women were called upon to replace men at the lathes and benches. Old people formerly considered unemployable went back to work. Recruiting agents invaded universities and high schools. They stopped workers at the gates of textile factories in New England and in front of garment shops in New York and offered them free tickets to jobs in California at wages two or three times those they were earning.

As a result, the labor force gravitated to the points where it was most needed. The problem of mobilizing civilian labor was practically solved before interdepartmental conferences had agreed upon a plan of action. A bill for national service was introduced in Congress when the war was approaching its end and industry had started demobilization.

I also participated in several interdepartmental commissions that tried to estimate and classify the reserves of the labor force, establish principles concerning convertibility of occupations, and so on. And I was impressed by the fact that this country could find a practical solution of a problem with greater ease than it could agree on theoretical principles for its solution. I remember a conference in which a score of labor economists and statisticians exchanged views on the reserves of potential metalworkers in the country—that is, the number of men familiar with the use of simple metal-processing tools. Some of the experts offered fairly precise estimates running between a million and a half and two million. I volunteered my guess—about twenty million —explaining that, with a little preliminary training, every boy who can repair his car with tools borrowed from the next filling station is a potential metalworker.

As the war went on I became increasingly aware of the unbelievable flexibility of our economy. The United States was turning out arms for its army of more than ten million men, rebuilding its navy on an undreamed-of scale, and providing food and munitions of all kinds to its allies. And it was accomplishing all this without apparent strain. Its war economy was not an economy of a desperate effort and austerity. Apart from the ban on the production and use of passenger cars and of certain electrical appliances and the rationing of sugar, gas, fuel, and a few other products, it imposed few privations on the citizens. I called it a "war economy de luxe." My feeling was that life was grim for the men on the battlefield but soft, perhaps too soft, for those in the rear.

There was no unemployment; jobs went begging. Unfilled orders piled up in almost every factory. Earnings were unusually high, but, all in all, the manner of life remained sober. People were not in the mood for spending and were putting earnings aside, not for a rainy day but for sunny days after the war.

Meanwhile, the government became concerned over the situation it would face during the demobilization and later, when the apparent mirage of prosperity faded away. The Social Security Board asked me to work out projections of probable developments in postwar economics.

I began with an attempt to visualize, month by month, what was likely to happen after the end of the war. Munitions orders will be canceled, millions of workers laid off. . . . But consumer-goods industries will need more workers to cope with the buying rush of consumers and to make up for the shorter hours of work. Some ten million men will be released from the armed forces. . . . But not all of them will look for jobs at once, and millions of women will withdraw from the labor force. Government spending will decline . . . but not at once. And there will be a spree of spending by civilians. Munitions factories and shipyards will be abandoned . . . but expansion of private consumption will require large investment in consumer-goods industries.

Some economic dislocations in the period of readjustment of the whole economic system seemed unavoidable. But it also was evident that they would be cushioned by the thawing of the savings frozen during the war and capital reserves accumulated during that period.

In order to assess the danger of postwar depression, I went back to the conditions prevailing on the eve of the great depression in 1929. It had been preceded by an orgy of stock speculation; imaginary values flooded the country with billions of dollars of stage money; agriculture was disorganized and impoverished. Since that time many things had changed as a result of the New Deal reforms—support of agricultural prices, public control over the security markets; insurance of small bank deposits, the Social Security system, a new pattern of industrial relations, powerful and well-established labor unions. . . . These differences made a depression of the 1929 style or even the 1919 style utterly improbable. The nation was entering a period of postwar expansion similar to that in the early 1920's, but this time it was better balanced and well protected against a sudden breakdown. All signs pointed to a bright future. Ultimately, I came out with a reassuring memorandum:

Economic demobilization will begin long before the end of the war and will be completed before the final repatriation of the armed forces from overseas. The cancellation of munitions orders and the release of men from the armed forces will be paralleled by the return of women to their homes and increased enrollment in colleges. Inflationary forces will prevail after the war, but there will be no runaway inflation and very little unemployment.

I also presented numerical estimates of national income, maximum unemployment during the reconversion, and so on. Although I was sure of the soundness of my general forecast, I did not take my illustrative figures too seriously and was surprised when they hit the bull's eye. This accuracy was largely accidental. I can claim credit only for my contention that a major depression after the war was out of the question.

My forecast of postwar prosperity was a challenge to the theory then predominant on the bureaucratic Olympus and in the liberal press. The Social Security Board declined to accept my views as the basis for its planning, but decided that I was entitled to express and defend my theory and ordered my report to be processed and circulated, confidentially, among other government agencies. The report became widely known in Washington and had a devastating effect—on my reputation. The chief of a very important war agency ordered my memorandum to be filed with his notation on the cover: "The piece is so absurd that it is not worth reading." A liberal magazine in New York, which expected postwar unemployment of many millions, reproached the callous government statisticians who predicted less unemployment and remarked scornfully: "There is even a man in Washington who believes that there will be no mass unemployment after the war." I was that bad man. My friends in the Social Security Board told me that some very influential government economists thought that my forecast stemmed largely from my nonco-operative and opinionated disposition, which I have never denied having and do not deny now.

Despite this unenviable reputation, I was invited to defend my views before staff conferences in various agencies. This was an exciting campaign. I was defending not only my economic analysis but also my faith in the United States, in the strength of its economic system.

The developments after the war vindicated my forecasts. The transition from war to the peacetime economy was effected even more smoothly than I had anticipated. My reputation as an economist was more or less restored. As time went on, I even discovered that I was credited with having correctly predicted the postwar economic outlook for the United States when it seemed to be unpredictable. In retrospect, I cannot accept this credit. The situation was so obvious that one did not need much skill in economic analysis or great perspicacity to foresee the general trend in our postwar economy. The mysterious aspect of the episode is that many competent economists had failed to foresee it and guessed so badly. Indeed, I know of no other case in the history of economic thought when so many scholars piled up so many false arguments to prove the unavoidability of events that, by the very nature of things, could not happen.

I believe that the explanation of this mystery lies in certain characteristics of public opinion in this country. From time to time, definite ideas become a fashion and people accept a notion as if it were firmly established, although it has never been proved and may turn out on closer examination to be absurd. In the early 1940's, a batch of false notions, such as the maturity of the United States economic system and its propensity to oversaving and deflation, blurred the sight of the economists. In addition, the theoretical question—what was likely to happen to our economy after the war—was mixed up with the political question as to what the government and Congress must do to avoid suffering among the masses of the people. Prediction of a depression became an argument for measures designed to prevent hardships it would bring to the people. Well-intentioned people tried to spur Congress to drastic action by scaring it with the prospect of mass unemployment, and ended by scaring themselves to such an extent that they began to take their own arguments seriously.

My economic forecasting was again put to a test in 1949, 1953, and 1957. In all three cases, the problem was to determine, in the early phase of the economic setback, how long it would last and how far the contraction in production and national income would go. There is no scientifically irrefutable answer to such questions. Rather, the answer depends on a number of assumptions, the most important among them being the predominant rhythm in the economic system. I was convinced that the stabilizers developed by the New Deal had made a major depression impossible but had left our economy unprotected against minor setbacks. I anticipated, therefore, in all three cases, a brief and relatively mild recession and defended this forecast in numerous articles and conferences.

In the spring of 1958 I found myself once more on the side of the optimists in predicting an early upturn in business. About this time, however, I revised my appraisal of the cumulative effect of jolts in our economy. These apparently harmless shocks, following one another at brief intervals, might have a very harmful cumulative effect on the economic progress of the nation.

STUDY OF THE CHANGING WORLD

Soon after the end of the war, Emma and I left government service for pure research work. The Twentieth Century Fund—a non-profit research organization in New York—had commissioned me to direct a study on labor economics in the United States. At the same time, Emma and I began a study of world economic and political trends.

This project was somewhat similar to our seven-volume *Die Welt in Zahlen*, but with more emphasis on interpretation than presentation of facts and statistical data. Ever since our arrival in the United States, we had thought of a study that would give a panoramic picture of the world, stressing the new trends—acceleration of technological progress, shifts in economic and political power, liquidation of colonialism, formation of new independent states, friction between East and West. My work on the economic structure and social security programs in the United States had temporarily diverted my attention from international problems. But the war brought these topics to the foreground. A new system of world economy and new patterns of world politics were emerging from the ruins and ashes. The slow processes of interwar years had developed explosive speed; the task of reviewing the new world trends and outlooks was becoming increasingly challenging. After my attempt to find a private publisher for a study similar to *Die Welt in Zahlen* had failed, Professor Joseph H. Willits, then Director of the Social Science Department of the Rockefeller Foundation, suggested that the project might be carried out under the auspices of his Foundation. Later the project was expanded, financed jointly by the Foundation and the Twentieth Century Fund, and administered by Johns Hopkins University.

This project was the first major literary venture Emma and I had undertaken on the basis of complete equality. In Germany, she had helped me in my statistical and economic work but did not try her hand at doing part of it on her own. Now she took all responsibility for entire sections of the study, mainly those requiring extensive work in libraries (agriculture, mining, individual industries, transportation), while I worked on sociological and political sections (population, migration, government) and general world surveys. This division of labor was in line with our personal inclinations. We had no assistants and did all technical work ourselves. Emma prepared computations and supervised typing, I took care of charts and maps. The project took almost seven years of extremely strenuous work, and our report was published by the Twentieth Century Fund in two huge volumes under the titles *World Population and Production* (1,300 pages) and *World Commerce and Governments* (about 1,000 pages).

Critics in the United States and abroad have been generous in appraising these books, although some reviewers have pointed out their weaknesses: because of the broad scope of the subject matter, we could not handle all subjects in depth and keep to a strict plan in allocating space to each one. Indeed, our allocation of space was determined partly by the abundance or scarcity of available information and sometimes by our particular interest in certain problems. The reviews most gratifying to us have been those that stressed the general ideas of our books and our interpretation of the trends in individual countries, including the United States, as manifestations of general changes characteristic of our times.

In the following years we came across our books in all the countries of Latin America and many countries of Asia. Each time we had a feeling of great satisfaction in seeing them in the hands of local economists and students or on the shelves of university libraries. This is the moral dividend that authors get from their writings: particles of their thoughts are floating in the air, and occasionally the orbits may cross the path of those who originated them. I am not ashamed to confess that I greatly enjoy the privilege of meeting again with my ideas and opinions reproduced in a language I cannot understand, in strange characters I cannot read.

Another moral dividend awarded to the author is in the work itself.

All research has a fascination as a continuous chain of challenging problems, but to me the most fascinating is research on broad, vaguely defined problems that open ever new vistas into unexplored fields.

Our study of the changing world gave us an opportunity to appraise the place of the United States in the world of today and its contribution to current civilization. We felt the unprecedented concentration of wealth and the productive capacity of this country were not the real contributions of America to the modern world, such as the Declaration of Independence had been in the eighteenth century, or the open door for immigration and the example of a steadily expanding republican form of government in the nineteenth century. We were not impressed by the display of glittering hardware around us, reflected in our statistical tables and charts, and we knew too well that many of the material achievements of this country were rooted in the science, inventions, genius, and skills brought to America from the other side of the Atlantic.

More important to us was the country's psychological climate. Is not the new scale of values the true message of the United States to mankind? More and more we have gone back to our first impressions of the American way of life—equality, opportunity for all, respect for human dignity, respect for labor.

There were, however, too many things we wished to say in our books, and I fear they have not expressed these ideas clearly enough. But we have had ample opportunity to elaborate on this subject in more recent years.

EUROPE REVISITED

In the final phase of our work on *World Population and Production*, we undertook, in 1950, an extensive tour of Europe to get first-hand information on the impact of the war and the progress of reconstruction in Great Britain, France, Germany, Italy, and other West European countries.

Once more we saw Europe after a destructive war: scars of air bombardment in London; ruins in Rotterdam, Hamburg, and Cologne; ruins marking the roads of liberation in France and Italy; bitter resentment in Norway, with promises never to forget, never to forgive the enemy. . . . This was a sad picture. But Europe was beginning to recover from the terrible shock. Both the anguish and the hopes of Europe were close to us. We looked with nostalgic delight at the old cathedrals and walled towns, witnesses of the long history we missed in the United States. But we saw Europe also through American eyes, just as, fifteen years before, I had looked at the United States through

European eyes. And I felt pride in the United States. Its star shone over Europe as the star of hope. The European nations were facing a disastrous economic and political crisis when the Marshall Plan gave them new strength. The United States had come to the rescue of Great Britain in her darkest hour, and now aid was coming from America to all suffering nations, all peoples ruined by the war, without distinction between victors and vanquished, allies and former enemies.

The details of Washington's policy were not very clear to the Europeans. They could not understand the zeal with which Americans preached free enterprise, free trade, and free competition—at the same time demanding strict planning; or American objections to what the Europeans considered necessary measures of social policy—at the same time helping to organize militant labor unions. They were a little amused by the American campaign for productivity, epitomized by washing machines and electrical household appliances. But they were full of admiration for the kindness of the American GI's and the generosity of the U.S. military command toward the civilian population —distribution of food and medicine in liberated areas, rebuilding of roads and bridges, dispatch of fuel and raw materials for the resumption of operations of local factories. Europe had not expected such attention to her needs.

Then had come the 1947 crisis in Europe, produced by poor harvests but rooted largely in the scarcity of goods for exports needed to maintain imports of vitally needed foodstuffs, fuel, and raw materials. The setback threatened to develop into a major economic and political catastrophe. The Communists were mobilizing their forces to exploit the approaching troubles and instigate street riots and upheavals. The Marshall Plan turned the tide. Its psychological and political impacts were even more important than its immediate economic effects.

There was much improvisation under the general heading of "Marshall Plan." Its implementation in different countries, under different heads of mission, was not without contradictions. But the general idea was perfectly clear: The United States was offering Europe economic aid to the extent of more than four billion dollars a year, essentially in merchandise and raw materials needed by the respective countries, without either payment or obligation of any kind and on only one condition—that the European countries themselves make full use of this help to improve their economy.

When we visited Europe, the Plan was in full swing. It was violently attacked by the Communists, but the prevailing opinion among European economists and statesmen as well as simple people was that it had saved Europe.

We met innumerable manifestations of the deep impact American aid has left on the feeling and thinking of people in Europe. I will never forget the beautiful Exhibition of Reconstruction in Rome.

In the entrance hall we saw a single symbolic sculpture: light emerging from human work. On the white wall was a single brief inscription in golden letters: "The free people of America have contributed three billion dollars to the reconstruction of Italy." In the endless succession of rooms, all phases of reconstruction were shown in pictures, sculptures, maps, dioramas, charts, and statistical tables. Large cities and humble villages, hospitals and schools, bridges and harbors, factories and power stations—all were represented as they were before the war, as they were lying in ruins, and as they were reconstructed. The rebuilding of human beings was illustrated by their improved nutrition and health. Every hall gave statistical records of the sources from which each project had been financed.

We reached the last hall, where the walls were formed by unequal blocks of marble, each one with a huge headline from some Italian newspaper, telling the history of the last fifty years. The headlines on the first wall covered the period 1900-25—the general uneasiness after the turn of the century, World War I, growing unrest all over the world, the Communist revolution in Russia and the Fascist revolution in Italy. The second wall told the story of the two decades 1925-45—the Nazi upheaval in Germany, Hitler's conquests in the West and East, the collapse of democracies, "*Italy attacks France*," "*Italy declares war on the United States.*" And then the end—defeat and annihilation of the forces of Nazism and Fascism, Italy prostrate in ruins. . . . The third wall, 1945-50: "*The United States renounces all claims for reparation from Italy.*" "*America sends food to the Italian people.*" "*Wheat from overseas reaches Italian ports.*" "*American ships bring medicine, coal, gasoline, and machinery to Italy.*" "*The Italian people can live, breathe, and work in peace.*" Finally, "*The Marshall Plan unites all free nations of the world.*" The fourth wall carried a message: "*Such were the events of the last fifty years. The future is in your hand, Italian citizen. If you maintain in Italy the spirit of humanity and international unity manifested to us in recent years, our future is bright.*"

This exhibition expressed feelings that were then widespread in western Europe.

The Germans were more reserved, even sullen, bewildered by the sudden fall from their position as the Masters of Europe to unconditional surrender. The United States puzzled them; they did not completely trust it, but they believed that America would help them in economic reconstruction. And many times we heard German intellectuals say, "They have dismantled and dynamited our industrial plants that survived the air bombardment. This was to be expected.

But now they are going to restore them. This has never happened before. . . ."

The attitude of the French was more difficult to define. The nation was in a state of deep neurosis, divided against itself, lost in a delirium of glory and humiliation, unable to separate dreams from reality. New personages appeared on the political scene, in the press, in leading positions in government agencies—men from the Resistance movement, young, dynamic, aggressive. They brought a new spirit into the old rusty bureaucratic machinery and were openly contemptuous of the old bureaucrats and politicians.

We met Jean Monnet and his younger associates. Monnet, probably the best economist and the most influential man in France at that time, was directing a peaceful industrial revolution—the systematic modernization and re-equipment of leading industries. This was a daring venture requiring imagination, determination, detailed knowledge of the national economy, and exceptional administrative skill. Monnet possessed all these qualities plus the rare ability of inspiring his associates. "After the war," he said to us, "France faced the choice of becoming a second Spain or rebuilding her economy. She has made her choice."

He outlined his plans; his associates brought a handful of volumes with detailed plans for each industry. I felt they must succeed but realized that the results of their work would not become apparent immediately. Moreover, Monnet, his group, and the men from the Resistance did not represent the mood then dominant in France, a mood reminiscent of the first years after World War I—self-pity, suspicion, hostility toward foreigners, especially the British and Americans.

We visited our old friend Léon Jouhaux, then a high dignitary, seated in palatial quarters at an overornate glittering desk almost as large as his entire office in the Confédération Générale du Travail had been in the old days. He was extremely friendly, even sentimental, and talked and talked, mainly complaining of the Americans. We left him with a feeling of deep disappointment—nothing remained of his brilliant mind as a champion of labor and human rights; his thoughts were wandering in dark corridors of a distorted imagination and suppressed emotions. He seemed to personify a sick nation.

Paris was full of American tourists and officials, and for most of them the city was the center and mirror of Europe. This was the source of the impression they brought back with them—the completely false impression that anti-American feelings prevailed in Europe.

During our tour in 1950, we had no opportunity to stop in Greece and we did not visit there until five years later when it was recovering from the long civil war instigated by Communists from abroad. With peace came American aid. In this small, densely populated country, everybody felt the friendly hand of Uncle Sam. Malaria, the ancient scourge of the people, was disappearing; orchards had been freed of pests; water had been conducted to arid fields; new crops had been introduced. The countryside looked poor—rocks, eroded overgrazed slopes, humble hamlets—but, here and there, one noticed signs of recovery and progress. Our driver pointed out verdant patches: "They found water here . . . improved seeds . . . they started a co-operative there . . . cotton from the United States. . . ."

A farmhouse, no larger than a hut, probably with a single room, attracted our attention. It was very poor but submerged in flowers. We stopped the car and alighted to take pictures—Emma with a movie camera, and I with a Leica. An old woman came out of the house, with a deeply tanned face, poorly dressed in black. Our chauffeur told her we were from the United States. She greeted us and began to speak softly, telling her story: Her husband died long ago; the children are far away; it is difficult for a woman alone. She still has some land. . . . The chauffeur translated. Her voice expressed gentle resignation, her eyes were sad and tired; her hands, brown like the earth. We were ready to leave but she made a gesture to stop us and said something to the chauffeur. He translated, "She wants to give you a present." She went into the house and reappeared carrying a plate filled with grape leaves, a few nuts, a handful of figs, and some apples. Emma asked the driver whether we could leave her some money, but he felt she would be offended. We took the present and shook hands with her. She was smiling. If I had not been so moved I would not have missed taking a close-up of her.

IN JAPAN

In 1955 we went to Japan at the invitation of the publisher of the Japanese translation of our *World Population and Production*. Originally, we were expected to hold a series of conferences before the Chambers of Commerce and manufacturers' associations in various parts of the country, but the Department of State asked us to get in touch with our embassy in Tokyo, which offered to arrange to have us lecture in universities as well.

Japan was completing its recovery from the war. We faced a great nation with a long cultural tradition, poorly endowed by nature but unsurpassed in courage and ability to respond to grim challenges. Its comeback after almost complete obliteration of its cities, factories, power stations, railroads, highways, bridges, and harbors was marvelous.

Later, during our tour in Latin America, lecturing on the factors of economic growth, I referred time and again to this miracle. "Persons who have not visited Japan," I said, "can hardly imagine the destruction that country suffered from bombing. Practically all its industry, all the wealth accumulated in four score years of strenuous labor and thrift, was reduced to heaps of ashes and rubble. All that was left to Japan was her people, with their hands and brains, skills, patience, and discipline. They started to rebuild their country with their bare hands. A decade later Japan had a bigger and better industrial plant than she had before the war, a better developed network of railroads, better bridges and harbors, power stations with greater capacity."

And I contrasted this observation with a different imaginary situation.

"This miracle of postwar recovery makes one think of the possible aftermath of another war, a war fought with a new weapon—a hypothetical death ray that passes through the thickest stone and cement walls and steel plates as the sun's rays pass through windowpanes without affecting plants or lower animals. But it does weaken human brains and make people forget everything they have learned since childhood—reading and writing, professional and occupational skills, ability to work together. A country defeated in such a war would keep all its industrial plant, its means of transportation, department stores and banks, but it would not know what to do with these riches. Such a country would sink to abysmal poverty in a shorter time than it took Japan to rebuild her economy."

The conclusion was obvious. The decisive factor in a country's economic progress is its people rather than its natural resources or the accumulated capital and technology built up through the efforts of the preceding generations or imported from outside. Many examples from history support this generalization, but the resurrection of Japan is the most eloquent among them.

The scenery of Japan—especially the Japanese countryside—is in striking contrast to that of the United States—no open horizons, no feeling of endless expanses, everything carefully measured, each square inch of good soil put to work with amazing skill and patience. Yet almost all Americans who spend some time in Japan fall under its spell. Perhaps the goodwill toward Japan among the Americans living there is even stronger than the goodwill of the Japanese toward America.

American troops were still on Japanese soil when we were there. They were there to shield Japan from aggression and, at the same time, guard the outer line of our national defenses, but their presence was creating some awkward situations. The local Communists blew up any trivial incident into a national issue, playing on nationalist feelings in concert with the extreme chauvinists—the old game they had played in Germany in attacking the Versailles Treaty and the Weimar Republic.

We were not surprised by the complaints of some intellectuals about the bad manners of our High Command, vacillation in Washington's foreign policy, U.S. tariff policy, discrimination against Japanese immigration, limitation of trade with China, and so on. Nor were we surprised by the resentment of the proud nation against the enemy that had forced it to unconditional surrender. But despite all complaints, we found a great interest in, and even fondness for, the United States. The Japanese recognized that the United States was interested in maintaining their independence and had shown moderation and generosity toward them after the war. They remembered the days after the surrender when the American troops landed on their shores. The people were prepared to meet vengeful White Devils who would murder, rape their women, loot and burn the houses spared by air bombardment. Great was their surprise when the Americans turned out to be smiling big boys who gave chocolate bars and chewing gum to the children and canned food to the adults.

One of our Japanese friends told us of the arrival of an American regiment at a large industrial city. Men and equipment were moving in trucks. The concentration of troops on the city's outskirts was completed late in the afternoon, and the commanding officer decided to enter the city early the next morning. The panic-stricken municipal council decided to take measures to mollify the conquerors. The mayor drove to the camps with several truckloads of girls and offered them to the regiment, imploring the commander to spare the lives and honor of the rest of the female population. The gesture was in the best tradition of medieval Japan, and the mayor could not understand why the colonel rejected the offering and sent him back with his caravan, explaining that the Americans neither conduct war nor make love this way.

We left by a small steamer from Fukuoka to Osaka across the Japanese Inland Sea. The temperature dropped after sunset, and I was the only passenger on the open deck. A sailor approached me and, bowing, invited me to follow him to the sheltered pilothouse. Here were three men, apparently the helmsman and his mates. They smiled and let me understand that I would be more comfortable there than on deck. Then they showed me their modest equipment and navigation maps. A map in a special case with two movable rulers marked the course and position of the steamer. I noticed that the rulers had not been adjusted to the movement of the ship in the last hour or two. When I showed how I would adjust them, all three men were delighted, laughed, slapped me on the shoulder, and talked in unison. I could not understand a single word. One of them disappeared and returned with a small, dark-faced man in a warm sweater. He greeted me in reasonably good English and told me that his comrades were sorry not to be able to talk with me. He was the radio operator. Soon we were standing at the broad window of the cabin and talking about the war.

"When the war ended, I was in the merchant marine because we no longer had a navy," he explained somewhat apologetically. "Before that I was on a battleship, but your airmen sank her. We had little time to abandon her and were in the water some forty hours. Many of us drowned. When we reached the Australian beach only fifty of us were left. We had to wait for a ship to pick us up. But Japan had few ships left by that time, and we waited many months before one came and brought us back. The navy needed no more men, all the ships were sunk, and there were no shipyards left to build new ones. Then they made me a radioman for the merchant marine in the Inland Sea.

"My younger brother ended up better. He was the best of all of us in the family, so strong, so brave. They took him into the air force, and he was very happy. But he had received only one mission—to attack your cruiser and explode his plane on her deck. They chose the very best for this task. But he miscalculated, missed the target, and dropped into the ocean alongside the ship. I do not know where he is now, but he must be happy—he was always such a good boy. Perhaps he is living at the bottom of the ocean with other brave boys, hunting and fishing. Who knows? He liked so much to fish from his boat. . . ."

The radioman had a mild, high-pitched voice like a child's, and it seemed as though, gazing through the window, he saw his brother roaming in darkness at the bottom of the sea. After a brief silence he said smilingly, as if apologizing for a sad story:

"I am also a very happy man. Tomorrow, in Osaka, I will get my pay and go with my two boys to buy Christmas tree decorations."

"Are you a Christian?" I asked him.

"No, I am a Buddhist. But my boys go to a Catholic school, the best school in the city. I was uneasy at first about what they would learn there. But one day my older boy came home from school and said, 'Do you know, Daddy, what the teacher told us? He told us that God is love.' This is what I wanted them to learn. . . . God is Love and Love is God. I am very happy."

He went to the map, exchanged a few words with the helmsman, and returned to me.

"Hiroshima is just north of here, only thirty miles away. I was on the ship at this point when the bomb went off. I thought of an earthquake and volcano eruption. . . . That light was so bright and the clouds so white. But then we learned this was the bomb. . . . Some of my people say you should not have used it against us. I asked myself: Would we have used the bomb against the Americans if he had had it? I know we would. Bad is war and those who cause it. . . ."

I do not know how typical of the sailors of the Inland Sea that little radioman was, but he looked and sounded just like the others in the pilothouse. When I think of Japan, I remember him.

Culturally, Japan was gravitating toward Germany after the turn of the century and in the interwar years. Now she is gravitating toward the United States. We could observe this shift in orientation among members of university faculties in sociology and economics. The teachers were tremendously interested in the American economy and economic thinking, but few could speak and read English. On the other hand, almost all the elderly professors could read German, and many of them were familiar with our *Welt in Zahlen*.

Like many other American and European observers, I was inclined at first to regard Japan as the bridge between East and West. The Japanese intellectuals we met did not think of their country in that way. We talked with an outstanding Japanese scholar and educator, Mr. Koizumi, former president of a leading university and chief tutor of the Emperor's eldest son. He was a tall man with penetrating eyes and deep scars on his face; his house had been burned over his head during a bombardment of Tokyo. After a series of operations, his face carried traces of suffering and disaster, but by some miracle his eyes and voice were saved, and his mind was as clear and precise as ever. He was considered a champion of the pro-Western and pro-American movement in Japan. I asked him what he thought of the role of Japan as a link between the East and West.

"The idea of a cultural bridge does not apply to Japan," he replied. "The roots of our civilization—language, religion, arts, customs—are, of course, in the East. Historically and geographically, Japan is a part of Asia. But our ties with Asia's mainland have been broken. We are no longer interested in developments in Asia unless they affect us directly. In contrast, we are interested in American and European science, literature, arts, and politics. We read your books and newspapers, adopt your customs. We are a Western nation."

Japan publishes more books each year than any other country in the world except the U.S.S.R. And in no other country are books published with such care, artistic skill, and good taste. Actually, the Japanese public has all the modern literature of the West at its disposal in translations and excellent editions. Because of the language barrier, Japan cannot act as a transmitter of Western civilization to the East, but she avidly absorbs Western ideas, digesting them in her own way, and is inclined to take these ideas from the United States rather than from Europe.

Our lecture tour in Japan provoked considerable interest in academic circles and attracted the attention of the local press, not so much for the content of the conferences as because this represented an attempt to exchange ideas, a search for mutual understanding.

IN SOUTHEAST ASIA

In connection with the trip to Japan, we also visited India, Pakistan, Ceylon, Burma, Thailand, and Hong Kong. This was a lecture and study tour, fascinating in its abundance of new, often conflicting impressions. We wandered through the oriental fairy-tale lands of Thailand and Burma and in the gardens of mysterious dreams and legends of Ceylon, observed with puzzlement the seemingly impossible yet prosperous Hong Kong. It was India, however, that made the strongest impression on us—a great nation at the turning point in her history, struggling desperately against her own grim past and toward a brighter future. We saw India walking a tightrope between the Western democracy she was trying to imitate and her traditional suspicion and resentment toward the West; between yearning for economic progress and veneration of old customs incompatible with such progress. India's neutralism stems partly from her split personality, partly from the tortuous ways of Asian policy.

We were surprised to discover how deeply the United States was involved in the internal clash of ideas in India. To the local intellectuals, it seemed to be our country that epitomized all the negative features characteristic of capitalism and Western civilization. Even when they were assailing colonialism and imperialism, they seldom thought of the British; the British, whom they had learned to know in their happy college years in England, were nice fellows after all, and had proved so by leaving India graciously. So the tag of imperialism and colonialism has been pinned on Americans without regard for historical evidence —merely because the United States is a powerful and prosperous Western nation.

We lectured at a dozen universities and held several public conferences under the auspices of the Congress for Cultural Freedom, finding everywhere considerable interest in the United States mixed with suspicion. Political debates are a favorite pastime in India, and the question periods after a lecture easily developed into disputes with sharp verbal exchanges but no real animosity. We liked these debates, answered all questions that indicated a sincere desire for additional information, and usually had a great majority of the listeners on our side.

In view of her great differences in geographic and climatic conditions, in her history and cultural and religious traditions, the new socio-economic system India is building in search of a brighter future can hardly be expected to duplicate Anglo-Saxon or American democracy. But she has adopted a constitution that combines fundamental features of the British and American constitutions and is organizing her economy in a similar way. In this respect, India is not neutral between ideas of democracy and dictatorship, but wholly and wholeheartedly on the side of the West.

We visited India when she was putting final touches to her second Five-Year Plan. Though I disagreed with some details of the Plan, it impressed me as the most remarkable piece of economic planning that has been developed within the framework of democracy in peacetime. Moreover, most impressive from my standpoint is the Plan's least ostentatious part: the Community Development program, designed to raise the standard of living of the peasants in backward villages by teaching them how to work together to solve their common problems —how to get more water for their fields, improve their seed and cattle, build better homes and better roads, and so on.

Apart from the ruins of her fabulous temples, which attract tourists from all corners of the world, India has many things that command respect and admiration. Outstanding among them is her drive for economic revival, her struggle against hunger and misery—an uphill fight against terrible odds. The problem of poverty in this part of the world cannot be solved by two or three five-year campaigns. India faces a long hard road. If she succeeds, as I earnestly hope she will, her march toward victory will probably be like the wandering of the children of Israel in the wilderness. Few of those who led the nation at the beginning will be permitted to live to see the people reach their goal—freedom from want for all.

I will not go into the details of our tour in other countries of southeast Asia. My general impression was that all those countries could gain from a closer association with the United States. America would have more friends and could exercise a greater influence in this part of the world if the local peoples, and particularly their intellectuals, knew better what the United States really is.

IN LATIN AMERICA

Our last trip abroad was to Latin America, under the educational exchange program of the Department of State. This was a carefully planned study-and-lecture goodwill tour. In fifteen countries we had in all 176 lectures, conferences, round-table discussions, meetings with the press, and television and radio talks. In each country we met with leading economists, journalists, government officials, and labor leaders.

With the aid of the International Co-operation Administration (Point Four) missions, we visited remote rural areas. We saw many ambitious industrial projects—some completed, others in an initial phase or abandoned—and tried to mingle as much as possible with local people, workers and peasants as well as businessmen and hacienda owners. We visited many rural schools, saw the best housing projects and the worst slums. Our conferences covered a broad range of economic and social problems, but, whatever the topic, our ultimate purpose was to help the listeners understand the United States, not only its economic and social system but its spirit, the patterns of its thinking, its attitude toward other peoples.

Usually I spoke in English and Emma translated my words into Spanish. She had learned this language in three months especially for this trip, and at the beginning she was not very sure of herself. But her Spanish proved to be excellent—*puro castillano*, the local newspapers called it. In comparison with professional interpreters, her advantage was in being wholly familiar with the subject and my way of presenting it. Thus, what we offered was actually a bilingual lecture, without a moment of interruption between the English and the Spanish texts. The listeners appreciated our effort to reach them in their own language, and the press emphasized that *Doctora Emma* had learned Spanish especially for the visit.

We avoided anything that could sound like political propaganda and tried to expose the Communist lies about the United States in a positive way by describing the American socio-economic scene. This approach proved effective; our reception was invariably friendly, even in the universities with leftist reputations. After each lecture young people surrounded us, asking for a copy of our talk to be used in seminars, for an interview for the students' magazine, or simply for autographs. Since the psychological climate was unfavorable for the leftists, they usually limited themselves to polite questions designed to embarrass us; actually their questions gave us an opportunity to elaborate on our point of view.

Our talks before workers covered about the same range of subjects and were on the same "academic" level, though more popular in form. We tried to show that labor unions are a constructive force in a modern democracy and that their historical task has been to improve the living conditions of workers within the existing society.

Our travel in Latin America showed us the fallacy of the concept of Latin America as a potential geopolitical unit—a happy family of twenty-odd sister republics. Indeed, these sisters have little in common except their common heritage of colonial days, a heritage cherished by some and hated by others as the memory of the destruction of the native civilization by cruel and greedy conquerors.

On our first visit to Mexico, before the war, we had seen two giant statues at the entrance to the capital—a Spanish warrior in armor and helmet and an Indian—symbolizing reconciliation between the two civilizations that had clashed centuries ago at this place, with tragic results for one of them. This time we saw a change. The conqueror's statue had been removed and two Indian braves guarded the entrance to the city. The shift away from the Spanish colonial heritage is one aspect of the revival of Latin America. The trend is away from the rigid social stratification of Old Spain and certainly away from the Spain of today; Latin America bitterly resents the friendship of the United States with Franco. Under these conditions, the common memory of Spanish domination cannot be a very strong link between Latin American countries that have waged numerous wars against one another since they gained their independence from Spain.

We found a dynamic concern for reconstruction in Mexico, Puerto Rico, and some parts of Brazil. We met government officials, business-men, and politicians with vision and courage in Colombia and Peru, and talked with many charming, well-educated, and well-intentioned people all over the region, but nowhere did we find an economic drive comparable to that in India. Concentrated energy in prosecuting economic aims and executing vast plans is not a widespread virtue in this part of the world. These people express themselves better in the creative arts, in their enjoyment of life, in dreaming and playing. North and South complement each other in the Western Hemisphere in this respect, and their closer co-operation would be most profitable for both sides.

In general, Latin American intellectuals are inclined to a more radical political ideology and phraseology than prevails in the United States. They are closer to the liberals than to the conservatives in this country. Therefore, the editorials about Little Rock or the preferential treatment accorded—or allegedly accorded—to dictators by our Department of State do not necessarily express an anti-American attitude or indicate Communist leanings on the part of Brazilian, Chilean, or Mexican newspapers.

Driving through a Latin American city, one sees signs including the word *Servicio* on public buildings. These are reminders that the respective agencies have been established by co-operative efforts of the national government and the Inter-American Institute or the Point Four mission. In every Latin American capital one crosses Franklin Roosevelt or Lincoln Plaza, passes a Roosevelt Boulevard or Park, sees a Roosevelt Hospital, a Roosevelt High School, or a Roosevelt Youth Association. The Latin Americans have accepted Franklin Roosevelt and Lincoln in their pantheon along with heroes of their own like Bolívar and San Martín. The names of Roosevelt and Lincoln are not necessarily associated with their parties but symbolize aspects of United States civilization dear to the heart of Latin America.

The Tennessee Valley development has left a deep impact on economic thinking and planning in Latin America. We observed its influence in the Cauca Valley project, which the Colombians refer to as the "Little Lilienthal Plan" because the former chief of the TVA, David E. Lilienthal, greatly contributed to the formulation of the project. The United States has also inspired the program of development in Chillan, Chile, the regional development programs in Brazil, and the Papaloapam project in Mexico, which promises to become the local TVA.

The interest of Latin American youth in the United States is evidenced by the success of the binational Institutes, in many of which we lectured. Some counted their enrollment in thousands and had more students than the local university. Among the students they counted not only teen-agers but many professional and business people. The primary task of the Institute is to teach English and English and American literature; actually, they introduce their students to North American civilization. At the same time, the number of Latin American young people enrolled in our universities is steadily increasing.

This interest marks an important shift in the cultural orientation of the countries of Latin America. Only two decades ago, families that could afford to educate their youngsters abroad sent them to Europe, mainly to France. Now the United States is the magnet. The new generation of intellectuals returning from this country brings back new customs, ideas, and attitudes.

All in all, time is working for stronger economic, political, and cultural ties between the United States and Latin America. Unity of the Western Hemisphere—Anglo-Saxon nations in the north and Latino-Indian countries in the south—is geopolitically more real than the sisterhood of Argentina and Peru, Chile and Mexico, or Uruguay and Haiti. In brief, the idea of geopolitical togetherness of the Western Hemisphere has a good chance to become the cornerstone of our policy in Latin America, while the idea of unity of *Latin* America alone can hardly be translated into a policy that is consistent and effective.

The weakness of the United States policy in this area is the lack of a clearly recognized long-range objective. Too much attention is paid to temporary considerations, pressures of vested interests, and extrinsic motives. Our position would be strengthened by recognition of the basic fact that geography and history have determined the destiny of North America and South America—to live and grow in a common living space—and that this situation is largely independent of the vicissitudes of the global cold war.

However, this field is beyond my story, which is the story of the life of an individual in relation to the events that unrolled before the eyes of his generation. In concluding that story, I would like to return to the problem that has haunted me during our recent travels abroad, the problem of "America's message to the world."

Without using that pompous phrase, we tried to give our listeners in foreign countries our interpretation of what the United States had contributed to human civilization, in terms not of technical gadgets but of human values. We realize, however, that our concept of the United States differs from the official picture of Uncle Sam. In our trips we met American economists and foreign service officers who were convinced that the United States' message to the world is private enterprise, free from government intervention. We met American businessmen who lauded their dream of America with all its achievements—cars, refrigerators, color TV, movies, electrical appliances, air conditioners—but deplored its "evils"—the "confiscatory" profits tax, progressive income tax, big labor unions, public utilities policies of the federal and state governments, and "creeping socialism" in the guise of social welfare. We also found that the literature distributed by the U.S. Information Agency contained too many boasts about our economic progress and not enough tribute to the human values of our civilization. Most of all, we missed in this literature the awareness that democracy is not a program but a dream, a search for improvement and higher standards of justice, a process that can never end.

Without quarreling with the official portrait of Uncle Sam, we tried to depict the United States as we see it: a hard-working people with a deep respect for their fellow men; opportunity for all; little admiration for hereditary wealth but a profound esteem for individual success and—to some degree—for individual effort even when it has not been crowned with conspicuous success. We spoke of the United States as a community of free people who have learned through experience to work together and trust one another. We stressed that the rich in our country do not live in greater luxury than the rich in poorer countries, but that the great difference is in the conditions of life for the masses. We explained that our mass production is based on mass consumption, on the availability of a broad domestic market that is an aspect of our democratic society.

Perhaps the American civilization we were describing, without concealing our affection for it, lacks the refinement of more stratified societies. Perhaps, also, ours is a slightly idealized vision of America. But the world people believe in is always a compound of reality and their dreams, and little would be left of reality if it were stripped of what man believes it to be.

A few words more on my own behalf. If this apperception of the

United States in its relation to other countries is biased, the bias stems from my background. My scale of values was molded in early youth by the storm that shook Russia in 1905 and was the fore-runner of the revolutionary convulsions that spread over the whole world twelve years later. My early participation in the Russian revolutionary movement, followed by long years of prison and exile, strengthened my concepts of what is important and what is not. Thus, I met the terrible year of 1917 with less youthful enthusiasm and fewer illusions than I had met the first Russian revolution, and by that time I was politically mature enough to resist temptations offered by the victorious upheaval—preserving my scale of values, fighting the tide of extremism in Russia, and later leaving the country of my birth. Through the ensuing years of wandering in many countries and witnessing many events, I continued to use the same yardstick in appraising peoples and their institutions. It is this yardstick I have used in appraising the promised land I discovered at the end of my stormy passage.

Index